ISBN-10   1523208538
ISBN-13   978-1523208531

The principal editor of this book was Linda Goudge.

Until the Twelfth of Never

by

Bella Stumbo

Betty Broderick smiles as she hears the jury convict her on two counts of second-degree murder after her retrial, December 10, 1991. Her lawyer, Jack Earley, looks down (© J.T. MacMillan / U-T San Diego / ZUMA Press)

When 'Until the Twelfth of Never' first appeared, it became a literary sensation, subsequently winning the Edgar Award for non-fiction.

This republication marks its twentieth anniversary and it is with great pleasure that we re-release this astounding book to a new generation of readers who may, for the first time, be learning about one of the most explosive American divorces ever to be captured in print, ending in the double-murder of Daniel T. Broderick III and Linda Kolkena Broderick in the early hours of the morning of November 5, 1989.

Bella Stumbo, legendary reporter of the *Los Angeles Times*, spent several years meticulously researching this book before she 'put pen to paper', largely dictating it over the phone to her sister, Linda Goudge, who was the first and principal editor of this towering work. Famously, Bella Stumbo rarely either ate or slept while she composed her newspaper articles; so what must she have gone through to produce the five hundred plus pages of this book?

By the time 'Until the Twelfth of Never' was published, Betty Broderick had begun serving two consecutive sentences for second degree murder; two *Lifetime* television movies had been made; and Oprah Winfrey had aired two of her highest-rated programs ever, discussing the case.

Additionally, several other books were published to explain what happened and hundreds of thousands of print inches were devoted to the question of how seemingly blessed lives could end in such wanton blood and violence.

However, 'Until the Twelfth of Never' has always been regarded as the definitive account, pleasing neither the Broderick and Kolkena families, nor Betty Broderick with whom Bella Stumbo was in regular contact right up until Ms. Stumbo's death, with its even-handed treatment of the breathtaking details.

The jury verdicts were controversial—it took two trials for a jury to convict Betty Broderick of second degree murder—and the American public was sharply divided over who was the Broderick monster—Dan, Linda or Betty—in the story of a 'perfect wife and mother' or a wife from hell, either way disintegrating from a once beautiful, wealthy and accomplished woman into a relentlessly outraged double murderess.

That the crime took place years after Dan Broderick had left home, and why, is explained in detail in 'Until the Twelfth of Never', and we will leave it to you, our readers, to form your own opinions on what led to the blood bath.

Since the publication of 'Until the Twelfth of Never', the author of this book has succumbed to cancer (in 2002) and Betty Broderick has remained in prison, still unable to persuade the legal system that she has the slightest remorse for what she did.

In 2010, Betty Broderick faced her first parole board since her conviction and sentencing. All four of her now-grown children attended the hearing, as did Larry, brother of Dan Broderick, and Roger, brother of Linda Kolkena Broderick. Two of the children argued that their mother should be released; the rest argued against.

The 2010 parole board refused to order her release on the grounds that there was no evidence that Betty had moved on, that she remained anything other than locked in a private cell of remorseless rage, still wishing to punish the two people who she feels destroyed her fairytale former life, and whom she has already killed.

But this much is beyond dispute: to this day, two trials later, Betty still frequently speaks of Dan Broderick, and sometimes Linda, as if they were still alive and well and tormenting her.

"He's such a shit!" she exploded one day, nearly fifteen months later, after reciting

some past example of his sins against her. "I'd like to kill him!"

"But, Betty," her listener replied, "you did."

Silence. Pause. Then a small, confused laugh. "Yeah, well … but I didn't get revenge … he didn't suffer enough."

Whatever Betty Broderick truly is—cold blooded killer or permanently damaged victim—she remains one of the most fascinating people alive and this is her story …

Kathleen Hewtson
Taylor Street Books

Part One

Betty

Chapter 1

Betty

At last, she had become too disgusting, too pathetic to bear, but only she could not see it. She grew fatter, messier, uglier each day, until finally she could wear nothing but sweat suits. Her hair was yellow straw, jerked back in a rubber band, a bristling ponytail, accentuating her pasty, multiple chins. She looked like a frowsy blimp, like some low-class Twinkies freak from a cheap trailer park; and her old friends, remembering how lovely, how willowy, how elegant she had once been, flinched and turned their own pretty, smooth faces away. How could she let herself go like that, they whispered among themselves, making mental notes to double their time at the gym next week.

And she was even worse to hear. So loud, so foul-mouthed. She was no longer the witty, poised, proper woman they had known for years, and it was all because her husband had left her for another woman. But she no longer even spoke of him as her former husband. Now he was "the cuntsucker," the new woman in his life was "the cunt," and together they had "fucked me". She raved, she called old friends constantly, she lumbered like some awful beast into all of La Jolla's quietest, most fashionable restaurants, slamming her heavy body down, uninvited, into their polite company. No luncheon was safe from her embarrassing intrusions, her nasty mouth, her rantings. Up and down the stylish streets of La Jolla she went, into all the perfect boutiques with their $300 cotton blouses and $10,000 gowns, into the stately calm of the La Valencia patio café, through the private gates of the La Jolla Beach and Tennis Club. She was everywhere, searching out the women she had once delighted with her intelligence and charm.

But now she was a woman gone mad. Over and over again, she told them the same story, the tale of a woman deceived and cheated. Over and over, she told them, showed them, what it might be like to be a divorcée in La Jolla.

And she was always crying. At school soccer games, when everyone else was basking in the sun, wrapped in well-being, she sat in the bleachers, crying. "My son," she would tell them through red eyes, tears shamelessly streaming, "can't play soccer because his father won't let him go to practice. He's a class joke." She cried at an Anne Klein trunk show at Saks, leaving halfway through, because "I can't wear my pretty clothes anymore, I'm so fat I don't know why I even came!"

Worse, she expected them to sympathize. Wasn't her ex a joke, she would demand, loudly, shrilly. Wasn't he a laughingstock in La Jolla? Weren't they all laughing at how the cuntsucker had hit forty and left his family for the office bimbo, a cheap slut? Wasn't it ludicrous how he had bought a red Corvette and run off with a woman young enough to be his daughter, how he had cheated her out of a fair settlement in the divorce, this hotshot, pretentious, millionaire lawyer everybody so admired? Wasn't it a scream what a hypocrite he was? For four years he had stalled before she even got a property settlement—and then she had been robbed blind. Look at her monthly support—only $16,000—a pittance of what he actually made, and hardly enough, she complained, to maintain her lovely La Jolla home in the hills overlooking the sea. Not enough to shop at Capriccio's, to travel to Europe, not enough even to buy her favorite praline chewy candies at Neiman-Marcus once a month anymore. The bastard had even refused to pay the country club fees. Worse, a judge had once ordered her to take vocational testing. The sonofabitch wanted to turn her into a clerk at I. Magnin's!

Now, she told them, after sixteen years of marriage, she was virtually broke, forced to budget, and still she couldn't make ends meet. She was having to sell her beautiful seaside house and move into a tacky condominium across from a shopping center on the edge of town. Her new view would be pizza parlors, cinemas, and junky drugstores. Just the other day, a pilot light had exploded in her face. See, she said, shoving her drooping jowls closer, how she had no eyelashes or eyebrows left?

Atop all else, he had taken her four children away, too, him and his legal buddies on the San Diego bench. They had given him sole custody and denied her even visitation rights for nearly three years—all behind closed doors in sealed proceedings. Even now, she only got them for two weekends a month.

Didn't it make them sick? Didn't they want to vomit along with her? Could they imagine a perfect mother like herself being treated this way? Could they? And now, she told them, the asshole was torturing the children, too. While he was vacationing in Greece with his simpering whore, their oldest daughter was practically starving in college, he had put her on such a tight budget. He had written their other daughter out of his will entirely because "she won't kiss his ass." And her two small sons were both suicidal, they missed her so much.

Could they imagine such a cruel, phony, cheap piece of shit? Weren't they shocked? Weren't they outraged, too?

They studied their flawless nails, they made excuses to go: The gardener was waiting for his check. The decorator was coming. They were late for a committee meeting for the Jewel Ball. Bye-bye, darling, wonderful to see you. Kisses all around. And she would be left, sitting alone, or pawing frantically through her phone directory for the next old friend to call, to tell her story all over again. To seek sympathy where there no longer was any. Everybody saw but her.

What they saw was a woman who had made all the wrong choices, a woman who had lost her man, a woman who was now alone, and so angry they couldn't relate. Crazy Betty, they called her behind her back. They didn't believe her lunatic tales of legal abuse behind closed doors. It was too much. All they knew was that this raving woman had been jailed twice, once for six days over her vulgar mouth. She had been committed by her ex-husband to a mental institution for three days after she ran a car into his front door. She was even rumored to be a child molester—and it made sense. How else in this day and age to explain a mother who had been denied even visitation rights? How else to explain the closed courtrooms for so many years, unless there was something truly horrible to hide?

They shivered, they averted their eyes. For, in the end, all they saw, even the divorcées among them, was a woman they did not want to ever, ever be. Crazy Betty. She had become a nightmare in their midst, a woman in ruins.

And, at last, she saw it, too.

She awoke around four A.M. and stared into the darkness, listening to the sounds of her ten-year-old son breathing softly beside her. Little Rhett. He wore her robe around the house, he insisted on sleeping with her. Danny, thirteen, was down the hall. It was her weekend with the kids, and today she had promised to take them to Tijuana. She hated Tijuana. So dirty, so noisy … Why couldn't she sleep?

She moved away from the boy. She had fallen asleep again in her clothes. A linen pants suit tonight. Too tight already. She shifted heavily, rising. The button was ready to snap. She was ready for the next size. So soon. What was it now, coming up? Size eighteen? Twenty? Her mind screamed. Why in hell couldn't God let her sleep through just one night, like everybody else? Everywhere in the La Jolla hills around her, normal people would wake at eight or nine, read the newspapers, eat buttered croissants, plan their perfect days.

But she was awake in the dark.

She got up and wandered into the kitchen. Maybe if she ate something …

But she couldn't eat. She was so tired of eating. She went outside for the newspapers. It was Sunday morning, November 5, 1989. She moved softly, careful not to awaken those who still slept. Her jaw hurt. The dentist said she was grinding her teeth to nubs. She thumbed through the papers, comprehending nothing. Her mind was wild. She reached over and picked up the latest two letters from Dan's attorney to hers. More threats. More insults.

One letter rejected her attorney's latest custody proposal and made reference to her "pathological obsession" with Dan and his new wife. She could spend "substantially" more time with her children—but only on "a trial basis," and only if she changed her ways. If she abided by Dan's rules. If she allowed him to be judge and juror, arbiter of her behavior. If she agreed that he could automatically terminate the new arrangement without court action, if he saw fit. If, if, *if*.

She put the letter down and picked up the second.

"I find [your client's] actions completely inconsistent with the contentions of her psychotherapists that her emotional disturbance and mental disease are improving. The contrary appears to be the case," wrote Dan's attorney, Kathleen Cuffaro. The letter also threatened to reinstate her suspended nineteen-day jail sentence if she didn't stop befouling Dan Broderick's answering machine, if she didn't cease her "odious behavior."

Enclosed were transcripts of three telephone messages she had recently left on his answering machine. She skimmed them:

"… Rhetty pooh … Where are you? Unless the cunt is playing with the machine again. We're all so thrilled the little fucker's back in town. You can't hear this, honey?"

And, "Hey Rhett ... Why can't you hear this? Has the cunt been playing with the phone again? This really amuses me that she has nothing to do after all this time but play with the stupid phone. Marriage must be great. Ha ..."

She stopped reading. Her language was the same as it had been for years. Her brain fought for focus. Jail. That's what he wanted. He wanted to punish her again for her tongue. It would never end, not until he took away the last puny, pathetic weapon she had left.

She picked up a pencil and wrote on the bottom of the Cuffaro letter: "I can't take this anymore ... the cunt interfering with what little contact I have left with my children ... constant threats of court, jail, contempt, fines, etc. ... them constantly insinuating I'm crazy."

Then she started a letter to Cuffaro.

"Dear Ms. Cuffaro. Your verbatim transcripts of calls to my sons are of no use to anyone but to me to show the courts the endless abuse I suffer at the hands of the mentally deranged Mr. Broderick ... [Two judges] ordered my ex-husband to keep his office cunt off the kids' telephone line. ... I am really sick of being his victim ..." She stopped, shoved the papers away. Seven years of her life spent this way. Wasted. In two days more, she would be forty-two. Old. Old and failed. Old and disgusting. And alone. She would never be like Rose Kennedy after all. Never the sheltered, aristocratic Catholic matriarch, presiding over generations of children in her compound. No role, no future. Alone.

And why? Why? What had she ever done to deserve this shame, this pain, this unbearable fear?

Nothing. Nothing, was what.

She went to her car and pulled away.

It was near sunrise. The ocean shimmered in the distance, the air was damp and cool, dew dripped from the thick hibiscus and bougainvillea in the streets outside. A few Mexican maids trudged down the sidewalks, en route to demanding, early-rising masters. A lone, middle-aged jogger sprinted past, barreling toward the sea. Her handbag was on the front seat. Inside it was her little gun. The gun she had bought last spring. A .38 Smith & Wesson. She loved that gun. "My teeny weeny ladies' gun," she often called it. Sometimes she carried it around the house in the pocket of her robe. It calmed her whenever she touched its cool metal. It fit her hand so nicely. She had never fired it, though, not since the day she bought it. But she knew how. She knew guns. In school, she had been a marksman. So many years ago ... before she had traded everything away. For him. For the cuntsucker.

She roared out of La Jolla's hills and thundered onto the freeway, heading south, toward downtown San Diego, fifteen minutes away. Past the Price Club, past Sea World, past the airport she went, deeper and deeper into the city. Into Dan's new neighborhood. To what she always called his "mansion in the slums."

She parked in front. It was a looming, two-story house, on a cul de sac, just north of Balboa Park, with a red brick façade and white columns flanking the front door. Like a southern plantation. So like his father's house in Pittsburgh, set back from the street, with its big, fancy lawn. Towering eucalyptus trees whispered above as she crept across the grass, gun in hand. No traffic, no dogs. Dan hated dogs. Silence. The house was dark.

She went around to the back door. She used her daughter's key to let herself in. It was quiet, only the two of them were here now.

She slipped through the formal, expensive rooms, this fat, disheveled, broken woman, and moved softly up the stairs, and entered the bedroom.

And there they lay. Two of the world's beautiful people. Her one-time husband, the father of her children, Dan. So handsome. More handsome, in fact now, at forty-four, than he had been in their youth. Thin, dark, with a smile to die for. "The bong," she had called it, in college when they were courting, to describe the delirious feeling of young love. "The Way You Look Tonight," the Lettermen's big hit of 1961, had been "their song." But now, there he was, in his boxer shorts, lying next to the new wife. Linda. So young, only twenty-eight, and so undeniably beautiful, too. Slender, perfect features, her long, blond hair flung across the pillow. Tanned legs, red nails. Youth at its best. In black-and-white polka-dot baby dolls. Once the receptionist, now his wife.

They were perfect, this pair. They had it all. He was rich, and only going to grow richer. Past president of the San Diego County Bar Association, respected by all, an income of who knows how much last year—$2 million, $3 million? And Linda had him. They had been married six months. In the bathroom was the "Big O" calendar. Ovulation time. They were going to have a new family. He was trying hard to impregnate her. She was trying even harder to get him to.

Bang bang bang bang bang.

Two bullets struck Linda, one in her chest and, as she spun over, another in the back of her head. One bullet hit Dan in the back as he tried to dive off the bed. One hit a nightstand, the other a wall. He did not die instantly, as his wife did. Instead, he lingered on, anywhere from a couple of minutes to half an hour, according to the coroner, later, before strangling in his own blood.

She walked around the bed, stepped over his body, yanked the phone out of the wall, and left.

She went to a nearby phone booth, where she called one of her old La Jolla girlfriends and, according to later testimony, said, "I finally did it. I shot Dan. I could hear him gurgling in his own blood … and, it's true, they do shit their pants." The friend hung up on her in disgusted disbelief. Crazy Betty.

She also called another, newer girlfriend, one who did not hang up, and said, "I need help." She then drove to her daughter's apartment. By sunset, she was in jail, surrendered.

No problem, she told the anxious jail matron on suicide watch that night: "The matter has been resolved."

And that night, for the first time in months, Elisabeth Anne Broderick slept until sunrise.

San Diego, with a population of 1.1 million, is the sixth largest U.S. city, but it retains a remarkably sane, small-town flavor, clean and pretty, with dozens of distinctive neighborhoods abutting each other, many divided by small parks and brilliant blue waterways, with views of rolling hillsides, canyons, and the sea. City planners have refused to surrender open spaces to sprawling shopping malls and high-rise development. In San Diego, old buildings are not automatically razed for the new, but restored. The hills sparkle with pastel Victorians, Spanish adobes, and art deco monuments from the twenties. The city is so arranged that it's still possible to get almost anywhere in town within twenty minutes. Downtown is compact enough to cover by foot. Whenever the annual lists of America's most livable cities appear, San Diego is invariably named—and La Jolla, the elite coastal colony in the northern corner of town, is among the most prized addresses in San Diego or anywhere else in the world.

The relatively unspoiled nature of San Diego is due in large part to geography. Located at the southernmost tip of California, it is an isolated urban pocket, buffered to the south by the Mexican border—Tijuana is only twenty-five miles away—and shielded to the north from the encroaching sprawl of Orange County by a twenty-mile stretch of the Camp Pendleton Marine Base. Some thirty percent of San Diego is occupied by U.S. military installations, mostly Navy. Although it is only a two-hour drive from Los Angeles, San Diego has never been seen as a part of the California fast track, but, instead, as a lazy, conservative backwater with a world-famous zoo, a nice place to live, to retire, to raise families. Despite its size, it had never produced even one California governor until 1990, when former mayor Pete Wilson, a Republican, was elected.

But within its own boundaries, San Diego is a thriving city-state, a place where the movers and shakers are easily identifiable. Here, everyone with pretensions to influence and wealth knows everyone else with the same ambitions, at least by reputation. A few names dominate, and the local press chronicles their every move, not only in traditional society pages, but also in quaint, immensely popular news columns devoted to civic gossip.

The death of Daniel T. Broderick III and his new wife ranked as one of the biggest community shocks of the decade. San Diego has had its share of flamboyant crimes over the years—including the mass killer who shot twenty-three people to death in a local McDonald's a few years ago, as well as Robert Alton Harris, the first condemned killer to be executed in California in twenty-five years (for shooting two teenagers and then eating their Jack-in-the-Box hamburgers). But, in the main, murder is limited to all the usual places on the wrong side of the tracks. And seldom has any city seen one of its best and brightest gunned down so summarily.

Dan Broderick was an immensely successful medical malpractice attorney who dazzled most people with his credentials alone: he had both a law degree from Harvard and a medical degree from Cornell. In 1987, he served as the county bar association president. He was so polished, smart, charming, and handsome—from his perfect hair to his trademark rose boutonnière—that his friends openly predicted he would one day move on to the U.S. Senate and maybe even the White House. He had his enemies, of course—many doctors and attorneys who had tangled with him hated him and his tactics. But, in general, Dan Broderick was widely regarded as a model attorney, a dynamic litigator with a reputation beyond reproach. His track record was so impressive that a mere call from his office, it is said, was usually enough to cause defendants—and their insurance companies—to call it quits and settle out of court. His settlements were often astronomically high because he was increasingly able to pick and choose, accepting only the most dramatic, winnable, and lucrative of cases involving major institutions, both public and private. Small-time targets rarely interested him.

Linda Kolkena, a onetime Delta Airlines stewardess, had advanced from a pool receptionist in his office building to his personal legal assistant before becoming his second wife.

When Dan fell to bended knee in 1988, in front of a crowd of cheering attorneys, secretaries, and paralegals in a fashionable downtown bar to propose in the most old-fashioned of ways, it made the gossip columns. "The earnest-looking fellow down on one knee on the floor at Dobson's the other night was attorney Dan Broderick, asking his paralegal, Linda Kolkena, to marry him," the *San Diego Union* reported. "Much too public a proposal to turn down. They'll marry in April."

Even in a larger, meaner city beset by daily examples of human folly, the Broderick case would probably have attracted attention, it was such a glaring example of all-American values gone awry. This splendid little saga had it all. It was steamy, it was sexy, it was replete with obscenities and violence, it contained every cliché ever heard about the nouveau riche fallen beneath the weight of their own venality. It was the tale of a woman scorned, a woman locked in battle over her man, her money, her children, and her rights as a long-term wife. It was a morality tale of Biblical proportions, involving adultery and covetousness, all of it wrapped in a great big flag emblazoned with the almighty U.S. dollar—and concluding in what, on the face of it, appeared to be a most blood-curdling case of stark, premeditated murder in the first degree. Shooting them in their sleep? No soap opera writer could have concocted better.

It was the timeless tale, too, of the Happy Hour mating game, the story of young dandies and aging heroes drifting through their misty hazes in the evenings at the town's most popular watering holes, singing their college fight songs and speaking of power and money and their own latest, clever professional coups—they were "Players," all—while yet another subculture of young ladies—call them Jennifers or bimbos or mere innocents—cruised among them, their perfumes and mousses wafting through the air like chum in shark-infested waters, all hunting for a husband, and too bad if he already happened to be nominally some other woman's man. The rationale is always the same: that Old Love was dead. The Player told her so. Love. That is the language young women speak, while they are still young and firm and unscarred, and it isn't even their fault. It was the language of Linda.

The Broderick homicides riveted the entire city. Newspaper headlines blared, television crews turned out in force, trying to get a glimpse of the crime scene, the killer, the Broderick children, even their dogs. Throughout San Diego, cynical jokes were being made about what the Broderick case might mean to cheating husbands.

Nor was it a comfortable time to be a high-profile Other Woman. Within a few weeks, bumper stickers were appearing: "Do You Know Where Your Ex-Wife Is Tonight?" wisecracked one. "Bimbos of the World, Unite," read another. "Free Betty Broderick So She Can Kill Another Lawyer," said another. And, from the unamused: "Burn, Betty, Burn."

The funeral was a large, heartbreaking affair attended by at least a thousand mourners, including many of the city's most prominent lawyers and judges. The huge downtown cathedral echoed with sobs as friends and family passed by the two caskets—his covered with hundreds of red roses, hers laden with white ones. Because Dan was a loyal member of such Irish-American societies as the Friendly Sons of St. Patrick, a huge floral shamrock stood to one side, and an Irish American trio, tears streaming down their cheeks, sang "Danny Boy" and other mournful ballads.

"Dan Broderick was all that we could hope for in a lawyer," said U.S. District Court Judge William Enright, one of many to eulogize the couple. "A brilliant mind, a magnificent and eloquent speaker, a man of unquestioned integrity—his word was his bond, his reputation his most prized possession ... He made us all proud of our profession of lawyering, he represents the best of what we are and what we ever hope to be ..."

"Linda offered a new life, a second chance," said paralegal Laurel Summers, a close friend of both. "She gave him the optimism to marry again and to hope for a second family. Together they were such a delight with their broad smiles, twinkling eyes, rich laughter, and sweet terms of endearment ... Their life among us has ended, but all of us here will be together on days and nights in the future to drink and sing and laugh. Without Danny and Linda, the wine will never be as wet, the songs will never be as pure, and the laughter will never again be as joyous."

Vince Bartolotta, later president of the San Diego Trial Lawyers Association, tearfully remembered the slain couple's pet names for each other. Dan called Linda "Little One," and "Liebchen"; she referred to him as "The Boy."

Mike Reidy, one of Dan's most devoted friends, sang "Teach Your Children Well," as mourners departed to the cemetery.

The four Broderick children were pitiful to behold. The two older daughters cried helplessly. Dan Broderick's two small sons looked bewildered, ashen little men who would need years yet to comprehend.

Linda's tombstone inscription, selected by her sister Maggie, is a line from the poet William Blake:

She who kisses the Joy as it flies
Lives in eternity's sunrise.

Dan's is a line from the song:

Oh Danny Boy, We love you so.

She never tried to hide or run. She surrendered later that day, accompanied by a lawyer, at the downtown San Diego police station. The gun was still in her purse at her daughter's house. From there, Betty Broderick was transferred to the county jail for women, charged with two counts of first-degree murder.

A routinely ugly, sprawling, one-story complex, the Las Colinas Women's Detention Facility sits on seven weedy acres on the far side of Santee, a scrubby little town thirty miles east of San Diego, heading into the desert. The jail houses around four hundred and fifty inmates, mostly young minority toughs serving short time for drugs, assault, prostitution, and similar short-term offenses.

Betty had been there once before, for a six-day stay in 1987 on a contempt of court conviction over her foul mouth. But this time, Colinas would be home for two years, through two murder trials, and she would serve the hardest kind of time, in protective isolation from the general prison population, because, although she was something of a house pet to some inmates—the big, bad, funny, blond mama who had offed the abusive old man and his chick—she was to other prisoners a target, an intrusion into their world, the La Jolla "rich bitch" who couldn't cut it on $16,000 a month. They pushed her around, they scared her to death. Thus, after a few days, she was moved from the general population, where inmates eat together and have far more freedom of movement, and housed instead in a small area of the jail reserved for high-risk prisoners.

For the next twenty-seven months, she lived in an eight-by-twelve foot cell for two with a communal toilet against the opposite wall, a foot from the bunk beds. She was awarded clean cotton underwear once a week; microwaved meals were placed outside her door on the floor in Styrofoam containers. Sometimes, depending on who her latest roommate was, the sign on her door warned deputies: "Do Not Enter Without Backup." She rose with the sun to the bark of her jailers; from one small, hermetically sealed window she could peer onto the concrete and steel of other barracks and catch a small slice of the sky if she stretched her neck. No more palm trees and bougainvillea and ocean views for the former Mrs. Daniel T. Broderick III. No more "real coffee," only watery decaffinated. But the coffee, and the absence of dental floss, would be the only things she ever really complained about during the next two years. Betty Broderick adjusted to jail with astonishing speed. "I was glad to be in that little room," she said later, "away from everything, where nobody could get at me. For the first time in years, I felt safe."

She spent her first night at Colinas stripped naked in the so-called rubber room, a padded cell, under suicide watch—routine for accused killers. Normally, prisoners emerge from this solitary, degrading ordeal in predictable fashion: drained, shamed, docile, and terrified over what they have done. Typically, they ask for tranquilizers, priests, or attorneys, or all three.

Not Betty. Instead, she burst forth the next morning, according to later testimony, wearing a smile so bright, a manner so blithe, that both jailers and fellow inmates were fascinated. She was, by all accounts, nervous, wired, and talking too fast—but

19

she was talking. Small talk. Nonstop. "Cheerful," is how a jail psychologist later described her in court. No tears, no trembling. Mainly, she seemed embarrassed at all the fuss over her.

But it was the purity of her remorseless rage that transfixed everyone in her path. If she was sorry for what she had done, she would never say so. If she was even mildly uncomfortable over having just killed two people, it didn't show.

Instead, she told anyone who asked that she had performed "a public service." Shooting Dan and Linda Broderick, she said, "was the most sincere, honest act of self-defense that there can be in the world. It was justifiable homicide against a weapon you can't see—and nobody can tell me Dan Broderick and his cheap little bitch sidekick didn't have a weapon. His weapon was the legal system. I was under constant attack. You show me a soldier or a policeman or anybody that acts in self-defense—is he going to be held accountable for murder? Wrong!"

That she was unusually intelligent was instantly obvious. And her verbal skills kept pace with her racing mind. She knew her own defense in advance of any attorney's promptings: she was an emotionally battered woman, and a victim of "litigious assault" perpetrated by the white male power structure. She had thought so for years. Her story, she declared, had nothing to do with jealousy or even money. Hers was the timeless tale of the imbalance of power between the sexes, at least in traditional marriages. She was typical of millions of wives who buy into the age-old bargain—he works, she housekeeps—only to discover in middle age that, when he walks out, "The wife doesn't even have the elemental rights of a business partner who got screwed. If Dan Broderick had defrauded a business associate the way he did me when he broke our contract, he would've been the one in jail today, not me."

Nor was she ever at a loss for the perfect, colorful anecdote to drive her point home: "I would've been treated better if I'd been a good horse or a dog that served my master well for twenty years. At least you give that animal respect and thanks ... I was a faithful dog for all those years, and he couldn't even afford me the respect of saying, 'Okay, she's too old and I want to get rid of her.' Oh no. He had to throw me out and say, 'She was a piece of shit for twenty years and always a problem, and I couldn't wait to get rid of her and she deserves nothing.' He was the coldest, meanest asshole on earth." There was never a whit of self-pity in her tone—only brutal, naked rage born of screaming indignation and disbelief.

Otherwise, she treated jail like a minor nuisance in her daily schedule. Among her first acts, she instructed her attorney to get a court order for special hair coloring, and she sent change of address forms to *Time*, *Esquire*, and half a dozen other magazines.

She sent her daughter Lee a brisk memo of instructions:

"Pay DMV registration and tickets (No more tickets!); remove brass candlesticks from house to condo; meet decorator at condo to install oak floor from front door into closet at top of stairs. It is all paid for. $800! The bitch decorator's name is Carolyn Oliver; get condo garage opened; move ironing board to condo; [and] in condo cupboards at top of stairs, hope you find a pink box of Clairess hair color—202 Palest Ash Blond. Get it and go to Sav-On Drug and get two more just like it."

As she would do for years to come, Betty also enclosed a shopping list of beauty items she wanted, all carefully identified by brand name, everything from Clinique moisturizers (non-oily) to Revlon blush (glazed brownberry) and Lauder's Pink Caribe lipstick.

To Brad Wright, a thirty-six-year-old fencing contractor who had become her boyfriend after Dan divorced her, she wrote girlish notes addressed to "Poopsie," "Popeye," or "Sweetheart," telling him at one minute how much she missed him; then, in the next, issuing strict orders that he immediately pay all her bills. San Diego's most notorious female killer, charged with two counts of first-degree murder, didn't want to be seen as a deadbeat. "And make SURE," she wrote Wright, "that you pay Saks—it's overdue." She dotted his letter, and Lee's, with little happy faces.

In another note to Wright on November 19, she wrote: "Poopsie, if you're ever sitting there wanting to talk to me and I'm unable to call, could you write to me? If I had a letter from you, I could read it over and over when I'm missing you and can't get to a phone—like now."

She might have been Zsa Zsa, in for slapping a cop. Betty Broderick was an original prisoner from the very first—even before she discovered that she had become an overnight celebrity, too.

Through no intent of her own, she had tapped a universal nerve. Sympathy mail poured in from unhappy wives and divorcées everywhere. The local media clamored for interviews. Soon, the national press discovered the Betty story, too. Television moguls, book publishers, screen writers, talk shows, magazines—all were interested in the woman scorned, in the world's messiest divorce, in the battered husband, in the battered wife. Everybody had a different angle, but everybody was fascinated with the "socialite" killer. Although she never really was one, Betty Broderick would forevermore be labeled by the press as the "La Jolla socialite."

Her first defense attorney was so swamped by mail and media that within two weeks he hired a public relations firm to handle the traffic.

She took to her new forum like a duck to water. Soon she discovered the pay telephone in the jailhouse yard. She seized upon it with gusto and began making collect calls to San Diego reporters, who, she quickly learned, were always transfixed enough to print her every word, not only because of the sensational nature of her crime but also because of the sheer force of her personality. She was not only smart, she was also a laugh-out-loud mistress of black humor and outrageously brazen commentary. She played the press with the instinctive ease of a natural performer. Her telephone voice was consistently perky, cheerful, and defiant. Betty never bored.

"It makes me furious when people say Dan and Linda were the victims," she told the *Los Angeles Times* in one of her debut interviews, "because my children and I were the victims. There were two dead people but five victims ... In my estimation, they never suffered for a minute, but he tortured me and my children for seven years." She also said that she had shot them "bang bang ... no hesitation at all."

That story appeared the next day under a banner headline that said: "Broderick Confesses."

"Confesses?" she said later, fascinated at the media mentality. "What did I confess to? I didn't say anything that I haven't already told the police, my family, my friends, and anybody else who asks. Why would I even be in here if I hadn't confessed? These assholes don't have shit on me, other than what I told them. If I'd been planning this thing, I would've done a lot better job of it. I would've thrown away the gun in a dumpster, blamed it on some doctor—about a million of them hated his guts—and gone home to bed."

Even so, she loved it. At last, Betty Broderick could command the audience she had so long been denied. To the disgust of the prosecution, she played her case in the press for months before she ever went to trial. To the hair-tearing dismay of her own defense team, she was seemingly incapable of shading her rage with remorse, of dulling her own razor-sharp edge for public consumption.

She was obsessed with the unfairness of her situation. "It was like putting Muhammad Ali in the ring with a housewife," she said repeatedly. And now the same good ole boy network that had taken away her children in the first place to please Dan Broderick was refusing even to let her write or phone her minor sons from jail. "Dan Broderick is dead, and he's still torturing me and my children," she raged. And why was she denied bail? "If Marlon Brando's son is out on bail," she demanded, "then why not me?"

She became more defiant by the day. Her remarks ranged from bitter to blasphemous. "What a fraud," she once snapped, thinking of the lavish burial services for Dan and Linda. "The sonofabitch hadn't stepped foot in a church in all the years he'd been in San Diego, and they bury him like he's the pope. Why is he being buried like a good Catholic father when he deserted his family? He should've been buried like the asshole he is." To this day, she still often speaks of Dan Broderick in the present tense.

Other times, she was simply incredible. "My children are glad I did it. They hated him. They're glad he's dead," she said repeatedly.

Once, six years earlier, upon first learning of her husband's affair, she had not only burned his clothes in a backyard bonfire, she then poured paint over the smoldering embers for good measure. Now she was doing the same thing again—going that one step further, adding insult to injury with a crazy glee.

As for the killings—which she persistently referred to as either "the incident" or "the accident"—little annoyed her more than the "woman scorned" scenario advanced by much of the media. If she had been motivated by mere jealousy and revenge, she told a *Los Angeles Times* reporter, "I'd tie them up where they couldn't move, and I'd torture them every single day and single night for six years. I'd leave them where no one could hear them screaming, come back and give them cigarette burns and kick them like torturers do, because that's what it felt like they were doing to me."

At times, she seemed cynically amused by her own anger. Jail psychologists in particular made her laugh. "They all keep saying to me that I'm still angry," she said sarcastically. "Like that's a fault? You bet, boys—my frustration and anger is off the graphs! Totally. How many times can you bend over and get fucked and not get mad? What man wouldn't have been angry? Angrier sooner. But women aren't allowed to get angry, because that's an unfeminine trait, you know … It's always, 'Oh, well, of course she's crazy, she uses naughty words, and she's in contempt of court, so we better arrest her.' But, see, that's because the men write the rules. And the rules are that you're allowed to defend yourself—if you're a man. You're allowed to defend your home and your family and your property from thievery or people—if you're a man. But if you're a woman, you're supposed to go in the corner and cry and get fat and take pills and kill yourself."

The woman beyond the fury was almost impossible to find. She recoiled from all questions about earlier, better days. Her mangled emotions had withdrawn behind a wall too strong to breach. Despite her intellectual agility, what she had once felt was no longer an available memory. "Yes, yes, of course, I loved him, I admired him," she would snap impatiently, remotely, rushing past the point. "But he let us down, me and my children, he broke our hearts …"

She held San Diego in thrall. During her first trial, a local TV station would even interrupt its soap operas to broadcast her testimony live. In an extraordinary scene not long after the "incident," she put on lipstick and eye-shadow and posed for a *Los Angeles Times Sunday Magazine* photographer. Then, came the national media, starting with the TV tabloid *Hard Copy*, followed by the *Ladies' Home Journal*. And that was only the beginning. Within the next two years, she became one of the most publicized killers in San Diego history. Her second trial was televised live by the national channel *Courtroom TV*; she was featured on *Oprah Winfrey* in the talk show's second-highest-rated program ever (next to Oprah's diet tell-all). Her story became a two-part TV movie of the week, starring Meredith Baxter ("Thank God," quipped Betty. "I was afraid they'd pick Roseanne Arnold"). She even got thirty minutes in an episode of ABC's news program *20/20*, hosted by Barbara Walters. By which time she was so spoiled that she could only complain, barely joking, "Where's Mike Wallace? I want *60 Minutes!*"

Her sympathy mail came first from the San Diego area but, as the press stepped up its pace, from all over the United States and the world. Most of it was from educated, white-collar wives, women who had also been married to successful professionals, especially attorneys. But the Betty Broderick story crossed all social and economic lines in its appeal to women. From shy, polite librarians writing in careful script on pink stationery, to militant feminists typing on corporate letterheads, hundreds of women wrote to extend their sympathy, understanding, and prayers. They related their own stories as wives and mothers, left in middle age by their husbands for younger women; they told of their unfair experiences in white, male-dominated divorce courts; some confided their own urges to kill; others hoped that, thanks to her example, something positive might result, that divorce court laws might be changed, justice finally done. It didn't matter that the details of Betty Broderick's case were then unknown to any of these women—they knew enough to believe that if a woman says she got a raw deal in divorce court, she probably did.

"Dear Mrs. Broderick ... you have my understanding and sympathy ... I can relate to the inability of finding proper representation if the spouse is prominent," wrote one typical woman, who said her wealthy former husband, a physician, was paying her $95 per week in support, after 20 years of marriage. "If your ex-husband had been more fair, you wouldn't have been pushed over the edge."

"I had totally supported my husband and children financially while he spent more than twelve years in universities," wrote a San Francisco divorcée who had given her savings to her husband to help him develop two law practices. But then, when he left her, "I could not get a lawyer to represent me ... [and] he of course had been advised to postpone a settlement because of a change in the divorce laws ... the infamous no fault or Casanova's Charter ... I was a sitting duck and did not know it." She felt that the 'good ole boy' network had cheated her, as it had Betty. "There but for the grace of God, go all of us who have been stripped, raped, and pillaged by the court system, of our very life as we knew it or thought it to be, just because of the very success of the husbands, which we contributed to, or accomplished for them ...

"Your case will bring to light the inequities and prejudices in our court system where it pertains to women ... There are many people who do not consider that you are 'crazy' but who understand the possibility of being driven temporarily off-balance, given the proper circumstances and degree of fear and stress and emotional abuse. Have faith."

Other letters came from the radical fringes:

"Betty—-We love you. We admire you. We are with you. We will not abandon you ... We will never let them defeat you," read one, signed by sixteen women in Washington, D.C. "We think you were somehow chosen to say that it is NOT OK ... to hurt a woman because she cries. It is not OK to hurt a women because she doesn't cry ... It is not OK to take a mother's children away ... It is not OK to steal from the earth and from the Goddess that is Motherkind, or to cook a lamb in its mother's milk ... One woman will say NO, and all Motherkind will echo, NO ... You are at this moment ONE WOMAN AGAINST ALL PATRIARCHY. But all Motherkind is at this same moment standing up behind you."

And then there was the mail from her old La Jolla friends. Having only a few days earlier regarded Betty Broderick as an unpleasantry to be avoided, many of the ladies of La Jolla now hauled out their most gracious stationery and wrote letters that registered, more than anything else, an almost complete inability to comprehend her ugly act as a factual reality.

Less than two weeks after the killings, for example, she received a handwritten note on fragile stationery (complete with the same happy faces Betty so favored), from the president of the Coast Charter Investment Club, a small group of La Jolla women who dabbled in stocks. Betty had once been the club president.

"Dear Betty, In behalf of all us in Coast Charter Investment Club, we missed you at the meeting Monday at Maureen Brown's home," wrote president Diane McNary. "We had an interesting meeting. We voted the purchase of Europ-Disney SCA found on the foreign market ... This stock is associated with the Disney World being built in France and is valued about $15 a share ... Lucy Smith paid your $30 on Monday and plans to do the same in December. The December meeting, as tradition holds, will be at Bev Fipp's house. Thought you would like to know the current state of our little investment club. Will keep you posted."

And, from her hairdresser at Salon La Jolla: "Dearest Betty, Just to let you know everyone here at the salon is thinking of you, and we all send our very best ... I wanted to offer to do your hair for your trial. If you would like that, I would come and make you look and feel a little better with color and a blow dry ... Naturally there would be no charge, it would be my pleasure. Let me know ... We're all rooting for you. Best wishes, Danielle."

Others wrote chitchat: "Dear Betty ... Life must not be fantastic for you now, and I hope you have chosen a good lawyer and that you have a good rapport with him or her. My life is just the same, days full of a few classes and a bit of working at the Nutmeg Tree ... I send my love and support Judy."

With the perfect, trained grace of the La Jolla matron she had been, Betty issued prompt thank-you notes, written on her yellow legal pads, studded with little penciled happy faces. In the beginning, she frequently apologized for the inelegant stationery.

"Diane, You dear, sweet thing!" she wrote one woman. "I, too, always wished we had shared more time. No one out there has any idea of the extent of what I was forced to endure. It was a very private grief. I don't know if I'll ever be able to return to the person I once was, or even close Thank you for your kindness and caring. I really appreciate it. Love, Betty P.S., If I'm ever out—it's tea at Harry's for sure."

And, to another: "Dear Vivian, Thank you for your sweet, loving note Seems I have lots of people out there who sympathize with me! This is more of a story than just the usual husband dumps wife for younger woman. This is a story of legal terrorism and corruption, of using 'the system' to batter, abuse, terrify, and ruin your wife AND four innocent lovely children over a prolonged and never-ending time. Please keep in touch. Send me things to read and pray that we survive this. Sincerely Betty Broderick."

And, to the hairdresser: "Dear Danielle, Thank you for your sweet, kind and generous offer. I do have a court order that I can get my hair professionally cut and colored once a month—which is a hell of a lot more often than I ever did at home! [happy face] Let me know which day of the week would be best for you and you will be paid WELL for your time. Too bad things had to come to this. Love, Betty."

As most high-profile killers usually do, she also began receiving warm letters from fascinated men. Most were full of hurt-me-again sexual innuendo; but a few came from earnest men touched by her story, wanting to apologize for the cruelties sometimes inflicted on women by the male sex. But Betty couldn't distinguish.

Flattered as an undiscerning fifteen-year-old, she answered them all. Among her favorite male correspondents was a prominent La Jolla architect with a high-profile socialite wife, who was open in his defense of, and fascination with, Betty Broderick. First he sent her cards of encouragement, then advanced to sending her pictures of his boat, and finally even visited her in jail. "He gave me a kiss through the glass," Betty reported, blushing. It was one of the most delicious luncheon morsels to hit the Valencia patio in months.

So, no more Crazy Betty. Now she was, at least in some circles, a heroine. The sympathy she had wanted, the understanding that had eluded her for so many years, was now hers at last. She flourished.

She even started to look better. She was still fat, with double chins crowding her features, but she began to lose weight. Her blue eyes lost their dull glaze and began to sparkle at visitors through the Plexiglas; her complexion lost its pasty flavor. She began grooming her hair and wearing makeup—navy blue mascara, dun-colored eyeshadow, and shell pink lipstick. In time, she even stopped biting her fingernails. She laughed easily and often. For the first time, it was easy for an outsider, who had never known her until the homicides, to catch glimpses of the strikingly beautiful woman Betty Broderick had once been.

But she did not mellow. As the weeks and months passed, as the mail arrived by the armsful and the media spotlight grew ever brighter, she became ever more the victim, ever more confident of the righteousness of her actions, ever more flamboyant. In time, Betty would refer to her story with the possessiveness of a star. She joked that she wanted Bette Midler to play her part in a feature film. Not that she had anything against Meredith Baxter—but she could never understand why the actress didn't come to visit her in jail before making two movies about her.

"Wish you'd have called me!" she wrote Baxter cheerfully, after the first TV movie, which was decidedly unsympathetic to her. "Movie would have been a LOT better if you'd had a better understanding of exactly what it was that I couldn't 'cope with," she wrote in part. "Come see me—call or write—even though it's now a little late. I AM interesting [happy face]."

On the *Oprah* show, taped live by remote control from Colinas, she presented herself as a symbol "for all women who need to be scared ... who have been debased by the system."

But she didn't mean it. Despite her public pronouncements, Betty never really saw herself as a symbol of any other woman's plight. "Nobody has been through what I've been through," she said repeatedly from Colinas. In her mind, her case was always unique, larger than life. More money, more power lined up against her. More abuse than any average woman could know—because nobody else had been up against Dan Broderick. Nobody else faced an enemy so ruthless, so brilliant.

"The whole legal system is based on who can lie faster, sooner, quicker, bigger ... on who's cheating who better," she once remarked. "Lawyers are professional fighters—it's the acceptable social arena to beat the living shit out of the other side— and nobody was better at it than Dan Broderick. He could convince a jury that black was white. I was up against a master, and once he left me, I was just another case to him, another opponent for him to destroy." At bottom, it was always there—Betty Broderick's undying personal pride in the legal genius of the man she had married and killed.

She was obsessed, past the point of being able to sort it out in any logical way. Over and over again, the same reels rolled, pictures of all the lies, infidelity, and betrayal. She could not escape them, not anymore. The full truth, whatever it was, was now locked in her head, a stormy, mangled place. Sometimes, intellectually at least, even she seemed to know it. "You know, the Betty Broderick you see today isn't the same one that I was in 1983 before all this began," she once said, in a moment of quiet. "That Betty was a beautiful person to be around. I was a nice, loving, happy, centered person, and I was fun. Everybody liked me. And I know that Dan Broderick was proud of me, too—even if the fucking asshole went to his grave denying it."

Betty Broderick was of course not always this way. Once upon a time, she was just another girl next door, a woman so sheltered, so traditional that she might have been raised in the sedate fifties, not the explosive sixties. A virgin when she married, she never used a dirty word, and, in fact, at one time, used to fine her children twenty-five cents if they even said "Shut up." By every conventional standard, she was, just as she insists, "a perfect mother, a perfect wife," a pretty, energetic La Jolla housewife who rushed about town in her big Suburban van filled with children, its license plates reading "LODEMUP." Betty Broderick, now so lost in the past, was once a perfect example of what one of America's most ideal communities was all about—and Dan Broderick was, too. He was the handsome, picture-book husband, the consummate provider. Together, they seemed ideal. Which is why the destruction these two created, the distance of their fall, is so awful to see, for in the end, theirs is a story without saints or sinners. The Brodericks were just two more flawed human beings— a modern-day parable for us all—who failed almost every step of the way to honor that most ancient, sanest of all social maxims: Do unto others as you would have them do unto you.

Part Two

Betty and Dan

Chapter 2

La Jolla

That Christmas, La Jolla parties sizzled with talk of Betty's revenge, spurned wives, philandering husbands, and bimbos. Men known to be having affairs were careful to keep their mouths shut; others gave away their secret by leaping too quickly to Dan Broderick's defense, or, conversely, to Betty's. Older wives were either uncharacteristically militant or adoring; younger, second wives were visibly self-conscious. For a few fleeting weeks, tension hung in the air, because to discuss the Broderick affair required everyone to look into the mirror at his or her own relationships. What Betty Broderick had done, in short, was disturb everybody's Christmas.

But the intensity soon faded. By springtime, about the hottest topic in La Jolla, one of the world's most affluent white communities, was not Betty Broderick, but how to eliminate the civic blight of the local McDonald's, which had somehow wormed its way not only into the heart of La Jolla Village, but smack dab into the center of Prospect Street, La Jolla's answer to Rodeo Drive in Beverly Hills. It wasn't a real McDonald's, only a McSnack, but it was inescapably there, dispensing its Big Macs and fries in the midst of some of the most exclusive shops in town. How the owner had ever gotten a permit to operate in the first place remained a source of burning contention. But now the owner had gone one step too far—he had actually placed benches on the palm-lined sidewalk for the comfort of his clientele.

"When the benches are full, people automatically get the impression that it's okay to sit anywhere on the street eating hamburgers," fumed an art gallery manager to reporters. "It's just the greediness of the powers that be in this town to allow such a place to exist here, catering to people who think they can spend $3 on a hamburger and be provided a place to sit with a view, like someone dining in a restaurant in a dignified way."

La Jollans were also toying that summer with the notion of banning beer on their beaches to stem the rising tide of riffraff descending from greater San Diego. Another group continued its perennial campaign to secede from San Diego altogether, on grounds that La Jolla, the city's cash cow, was paying too much in taxes to support the rest of the city. And a leading local socialite pressed ahead with her Doggie Diners crusade, aimed at winning American dogs the same rights to sit in restaurants with their owners as French dogs. She took her own dog, Chelsea, with her nearly everywhere she went—so why not into the restaurants of La Jolla, too? "Chelsea is the most photographed dog in town," remarked *Los Angeles Times* society writer Dave Nelson dryly. "Chelsea moves in all the right circles."

Curled around one of the most spectacular half-moon coves in California, La Jolla is the quintessential Southern California dream town, a compact little colony—

population about forty-five thousand—of pastel homes streaming down the hillsides to the sea. Property prices range from expensive to outrageous. Here, realtors cruise their clients about town in limousines, and they do not bother with zeros in their ads. If it says $3750, with $70 down, and you don't know what that means, you can't afford it.

The few short blocks of shopping in La Jolla Village, along Prospect and Girard streets, offer many of the world's most prestigious designer labels. Minor excursions out of the Village to the Neiman-Marcus, inconveniently located five miles away in a noisy shopping mall, are of course permissible; likewise, everybody shops at the Price Club, a discount house five minutes away, especially for wines, liquors, and cheese. Otherwise, trips into downtown San Diego to shop are déclassé, although most everybody does it on the sly. A swank dress shop in the heart of the Village once had a special on $200 T-shirts emblazoned with sequined motifs of Mickey Mouse, the American flag, and the Mercedes-Benz crest. In the same window display was a black satin tunic with brass studs in the design of a dollar sign. And it was no joke.

In La Jolla, there is no grafitti, no homelessness, and, beyond all else, no ugly. Here, if you're not naturally beautiful, you make the most of what you've got. Joggers are everywhere, smoking is virtually unseen, plastic surgery centers are beehives of activity. Mailboxes in La Jolla are crammed not with flyers from Sav-On Drug and Sears, but with ads from local gyms, hairdressers, suntan parlors, and dentists wanting to bond your teeth to a newer, brighter white.

Every other car is a Mercedes convertible, although Jaguars and BMWs are also fashionable. The Von's supermarket lot is commonly dotted with Rolls-Royces. If you don't own such a car, a local rental service will pick you up for a mildly outrageous daily rate, and drive you about town in a Mercedes so that you can appear to own one after all. There are no car washes in La Jolla. Instead, residents pay $80 for detail jobs, executed mostly, it appears, by Mexicans illegals.

In fairness, there is a more substantive side to La Jolla, although it is often hard to see. The town's beauty has always drawn writers, artists, and scientists. Raymond Chandler wrote his thrillers there; Dr. Seuss wrote his fanciful children's books from his home overlooking the Cove. And today some of the world's most respected research centers are located there, including the Salk Institute, the Scripps Institute for Oceanography, and the Scripps Medical Research Center. The University of California at San Diego is on the far edge of the town, as well as the highly regarded La Jolla Playhouse.

But this was not Betty Broderick's La Jolla. Hers was the pretty, placid, uncomplicated La Jolla of PTA meetings, charity luncheons, fashion shows, and heady, ever-advancing social ambition. Betty was always more interested in meeting *Times* society writer Dave Nelson or Burl Stiff of the competing *San Diego Union*, than Jonas Salk. In that active, aggressive La Jolla circle that calls itself "society," it matters whose names are printed in the next morning's papers.

But it's not hard to crack La Jolla society. It's not about old money. You only need to have money, period—whether you got it yesterday or three centuries ago—or at least appear to have it. The La Jolla social structure is less dependent on pedigree and taste than on personality, hustle, and flair. If you can pronounce *foie gras* and *au pair*, identify all makes of Mercedes by alphabetical and numerical order, and spot a fake Vuitton at twenty yards, you're on your way.

Even so, serious La Jolla socialites felt their little town had been unfairly saddled with Betty Broderick, thanks to the tacky, sensationalizing media. True, she had lived there, true she had a $16,000 monthly support settlement, and, yes, she had worked a few charities and shopped at all the right places. Still, she was not one of them. Not actually.

"I always cringe when they say 'La Jolla socialite,'" said Alyce Quakenbush, society editor of the *La Jolla Light*, 'because she was not a part of the upper group ... She was very active in things for children, but ... I wouldn't have considered her to be the crème de la crème."

In La Jolla, to be seriously crème de la crème requires membership in Las Patronas, the most elite sorority in town. Only fifty women at a time can belong, by invitation only, for seven-year terms. Requirements are unwritten, but it is a definite plus to be married to a successful man. Or at least married to some man.

Once in, the duties of a Patrona are clear: to do anything necessary, from September until the next August, to ensure the success of the premier social event of the season, the Jewel Ball, a seaside bash on the terraces of the La Jolla Beach and Tennis Club—yet another elite organization with a waiting list years long, and where, naturally, most Patronas already hold membership. Jewel Ball tickets range from $250 minimum to $5,000 a table, proceeds donated to various charities and the arts.

The closest competitor to the Jewel Ball is the Monte Carlo Ball, held a week later, which raises money strictly for the San Diego Museum of Contemporary Art, also located in La Jolla. Although a few Patronas also help out with the Monte Carlo, it is mainly a function of the second-stringers who couldn't make the grade into Las Patronas. As underdogs, the Monte Carlo ladies bill their party as less formal but "more fun." Most La Jollans with serious social ambitions attend both balls. If you don't have the money to attend in style, then you borrow to rent both the proper car and clothes, and many do. "It costs me about $5,000 a year to look like I belong," said one local realtor, "but it's worth every cent of it. I just write it off on my taxes as a business expense."

In the old days, Betty loved attending both balls with her handsome, ascending young husband. It was the time of year when she shed her sweat suits, donned her increasingly expensive evening gowns, and, as she later said proudly, "held in with the best of them, all those women who don't do anything else all year but work on themselves."

"To Betty, those balls were the end-all, be-all," said one friend. "She and Dan both just loved being seen in all the right places."

But Betty never made it into Las Patronas.

"I don't think her name ever came up ...," says Barbara Zobell, one of the high priestesses of the La Jolla social scene and of course a retired Patrona herself. A tall, stunning former fashion model with long, straight blond hair and bangs, given to four-inch earrings and other flash that the average La Jolla matron would never dare wear, Zobell is, at least for social aspirants, among the most sought-after luncheon dates in town. For that reason, she was also one of the few prominent ladies of La Jolla with the self-confidence to discuss Betty Broderick openly in the months following the killings. Others ran for cover, distancing themselves as far as possible from the scandal. ("Oh, I can't talk, I'm too busy working on the Ball," said one typical society maven who had once liked Betty Broderick well enough to hostess a fortieth birthday party for her. The *Jewel* Ball, she stressed pointedly, not the Monte Carlo.)

Zobell had known Betty Broderick ever since Betty's first days in La Jolla, when Dan went to work with the same large San Diego law firm where Zobell's husband, Karl, is still a senior attorney. But the two had never become close friends. Betty had babies, Barbara had parties. But, because La Jolla is a small place, "All of us, of course, had heard about the breakup," said Zobell, forty-something herself, curling her nose over lunch at one of La Jolla's most "in" patio cafés. "It's such an old story, these guys running off with the office chicky-poo. I sometimes think, 'Don't these guys have any imagination?'." Still, Zobell added, "I just can't understand her reaction. I mean, it wasn't as if she was the first one to go through the Big D ... and $16,000—my God!"

The Big D is a common La Jolla euphemism for divorce. Few words, beyond menopause and cancer, have a harsher, more final impact on a polite luncheon. La Jolla is, at heart, still an old-fashioned place, where traditional marital roles are at least superficially observed. Here the men still go downtown each day to their offices; the wives stay home, running the house, chauffeuring the children to their private schools and spending the rest of the day at gyms or shopping and "doing lunch," which is, as one local divorcée put it, La Jolla's answer to scream therapy. The luncheon site of choice is usually the patio of La Valencia Hotel, an elegant old Spanish colonial structure, built in 1926, looming in hot pink, wrought-iron splendor in the heart of the Village. It affords the best view in town of other La Jollans.

Lunch is where women provide one another with peer counseling if their children are raging coke freaks or their marriages are menaced with the Big D. Here is where the exact measure of the new girlfriend's potential threat is taken; here is where women coolly help one another plot the counterattack, which hopefully will involve no more than a bit of cosmetic surgery and a new wardrobe, and then simply waiting it out. In most cases, the husband won't go so far as to leave the wife, he will simply keep the girlfriend on the side. And that is a widely acceptable solution.

Betty Broderick's final solution was so stunning that it literally lacked meaning. Murder? Dan and Linda's friends suddenly understood—murder meant blood, bullets, and who knows what kind of last-minute fear for their friends in those moments before Betty fired her gun. But, to peripheral observers like Barbara Zobell, who knew Betty and Dan only casually, it was abstract, less real than the latest hush-hush case of shoplifting down at Saks by one of the city's leading socialites, an aging lady who simply can't seem to stop herself, but is wealthy and well-connected enough to keep herself out of both jail and the gossip columns.

"Did she reeeeeeealy walk up those stairs?" hissed Zobell, green eyes glinting, grinning slightly, lips moist. "Did she realllly pull that trigger?" She looked, just then, like Patty McCormick grown up, "The Bad Seed" peeping intently from beneath her bangs at the locked shed she was about to burn down, with people inside. Zobell laughed and shook the moment away. But it was a perfect example of the effect Betty Broderick has on married women everywhere, once they start seriously discussing her and what she did. They lose, however briefly, their veneer of civility.

"A socialite, my ass. Of course I wasn't a La Jolla socialite, I didn't have time," said Betty Broderick later from jail. "I was a Supermom, is what I was. That's who runs around with kids, everybody else's and her own, and wears jogging suits and sweat suits all day, and is always covered with snot and peanut butter and spit-up. Because that's what mommies do. I was never a socialite. I never got my nails done, my hair done. I didn't drive around in a Mercedes, I didn't wear tennis outfits, I didn't even play tennis. I didn't have lunch every day of the week. I never did any of that. I was a baby machine.

"Then, when I finally got my tubes tied, when the really big money started to roll in, after all the years we did without and worked day and night—just as I was starting to enjoy a little bit of freedom—Linda Kolkena knocks on my door and says, 'Excuse me, I want your life.' And I'm supposed to say, 'Go right ahead, I'll just walk away'?

"I never got to the point of luxury. By the time I was in a place to actually have the time to even think about Las Patronas, I was divorced—and they don't take divorcées. It was Linda Kolkena who was going to be the socialite, not me ... I never got to enjoy a minute of what I helped Dan Broderick build. I didn't get the mansion, the cunt did. I never even made it out of the goddamn *tracts*!"

The Brodericks moved to La Jolla in 1975, two years after their arrival in San Diego. She was twenty-eight, he was thirty, they had two little girls, and they began modestly. The house they bought—their first and last as a married couple—was on a street called Coral Reef, in a subdivision on the south side of the hills, far from the ocean views. "Baja La Jolla," residents fondly called it. The house cost $130,000 and was perfect for a young, growing family. It was big and comfortable, with five bedrooms and a pretty, oversized backyard that spilled into a woody hillside.

It was also the perfect atmosphere for Dan and Betty Broderick. Up and down the street were other young, ambitious couples like themselves. Here, it went without saying that Coral Reef was but a stop on the way across the hills toward Coast Road, or La Jolla Shores, or the hilltop Muirlands area of gated mansions.

Dan was then earning only about $30,000 a year at Gray, Cary, Ames and Frye, one of San Diego's oldest, largest, and most prestigious law firms. But even in a community of hard-driving, aggressive overachievers, his dual degrees in medicine and law were cause for instant pause at any cocktail party. From the outset, the Brodericks seemed destined to move over the hills even faster than their neighbors.

35

Later on, during her murder trials, several of the Brodericks' old friends and neighbors from their Coral Reef days would recall their early impressions of Dan and Betty.

What most remembered was a thin, reserved young man mowing his lawn on weekends, or waxing his car, then an MG sports coupe, or sitting in the backyard reading legal briefs. His eyes were oddly intense, even disconcerting, but when he smiled, he dazzled. He looked like a teenager, all bony with knobby knees and an adolescent's bobbing Adam's apple.

"He loved that lawn," recalls Helen Pickard, an early friend who later became a prosecution witness. 'I'll never forget watching him on weekends, how carefully he went down one row, then back up, and down again. He had such a look of concentration. He wasn't just trying to get it done, he was enjoying it. And then he would work in his rose garden. I thought it was great. My husband wouldn't do a damned thing around the house."

Except for weekends, however, Dan was never around much, and when he was, he said so little that most neighbors never really seemed to know whether they liked him or not. But they do remember how proud his young wife was of him. His credentials were their credentials.

She was taller than he, a slender, pretty, bubbly woman, with a decided overbite, which, from certain angles, gave her face a pouty, sexy look, of the sort you see in fashion magazines. And, in fact, she told them, she had once done some modeling in New York, back in her college days. She told them that she had a degree in child psychology from Mount Saint Vincent's. But, beyond that, she didn't say too much about herself. It was always Dan's career she talked about. And their children. She was pregnant most of the time. In 1976 she had a third child, another in 1979, with a miscarriage in between. Most memorable was her way with kids. She loved them and they loved her. To make a few extra dollars, she began baby-sitting during the day for other wives who wanted a few hours to themselves. She called her little backyard day-care center "Time Out" and charged $1 an hour. She was an instant hit. Word quickly spread all over La Jolla that Betty Broderick was not only the cheapest but the best baby-sitter in town. "Betty always had the latest in any toy that was educational," one mother, Ann Dick, remembers. Another recalls being hurt when her own child came home and demanded to know "why I wasn't more like Betty Broderick."

"I remember going over there to try to take her shopping or to a movie or something," says Candy Westbrook, widow of an attorney, "and there would be Betty, standing in her kitchen, saying, 'Oops, no, not today, we're doing cookies, or biscuits, or fudge.' She always had half a dozen kids around her, splashing dough everywhere. The place was a mess, but she loved it. Kids were her whole life. She was a complete Mother Earth type. Once I went over and she was dressed like Miss Piggy. Betty would do anything to make a little kid laugh."

"She was always just such a neat mom. I'd go over and find her popping popcorn in a roomful of two-year-olds, and then she'd take the lid off so it would spray all over the room," recalled Pickard, whose own children stayed with Betty frequently. "And they would just squeal with delight. I would've never done that, because I wouldn't want to clean up the mess. But Betty didn't care. She was always so impulsive. I always wished I could be more like her."

"She was famous for her children's parties," Barbara Zobell remembered. "Once when we needed some party sticks [lights] for some charity event, and we couldn't find them anywhere in town, we called Betty—and she had a full supply in what she called her 'Kids' Closet.' She had everything imaginable in there for kids' parties—streamers, lights, crepe flyers, Halloween costumes. You name it, Betty had it."

Like a Norman Rockwell painting, Betty Broderick's home was also filled with needlepoint and wall-plaque homilies to the family unit.

"*The most valuable thing to spend on your children is your time*," said one sampler.

Another read: "*The best thing a father can do for his children is love their mother.*"

And she herself was always a living storybook, ready to delight children with spontaneous tales of Freddy the Frog or Oscar the Chimney Sweep and a million others. Even today, her memory for these children's stories remains extraordinary.

One day, two years after she was jailed for murder, she suddenly began reciting a favorite ditty, called "Cobwebs and Dust," over the phone. Her voice, normally so high-pitched and rapid, slowed and softened:

Cobwebs and dust will be there tomorrow,
But babies grow up, we've learned to our sorrow.
So cobwebs be quiet! Dust go to sleep!
I'm rocking my baby, 'cause babies don't keep.

Chapter 3

An American Family Album

That Dan and Betty Broderick would wind up in La Jolla, once they had moved to the San Diego area, was practically inevitable. These two had been primed from the cradle to succeed in all the conventional ways.

Their backgrounds were parallel in many respects. Both were products of large, devoutly Catholic, East Coast families, each affluent enough to send their many children to the best parochial schools from kindergarten through college.

Dan grew up in Pittsburgh, the oldest of nine children, where his father, Daniel Broderick II, operated a successful lumber brokerage. His family was Irish American, with all the usual Irish traditions. St. Patrick's Day was nearly as venerable a holiday as Christmas and Easter; song-and-ale was a family recreation, at least for the males—and it was a given that Dan, as well as his four brothers, would attend Notre Dame in Great Bend, Indiana, as their father had before them. His sisters attended Catholic women's schools, including the Notre Dame affiliate, St. Mary's. Although Dan later drifted away from the church and never visited Ireland, being Irish Catholic was at the heart of his self-identity until the day he died.

Betty was the third of six children, raised in Eastchester, New York, a forty-five-minute train ride from Manhattan. She graduated from Mount Saint Vincent, a small, prestigious Catholic women's college in Riverdale, New York, within driving distance of home. Her family was Irish on her mother's side, Italian on her father's. Her mother was part of a sprawling family of aunts and uncles studded with nuns and priests, many of them recent enough immigrants to still speak with an Irish brogue. Her father, Frank Bisceglia, the youngest of thirteen children of Italian immigrants, was a partner with his brothers in a second-generation family plastering business, and they chattered among themselves in Italian.

In both families, the children were assiduously schooled in Roman Catholic gospel, from communions to confessions. Lent was observed as faithfully as Christmas, the Catechisms were as central to their upbringing as their ABCs. Every child owned a rosary and understood from infancy that among life's taboos were divorce, adultery, abortion, and contraception. Sex was for reproduction, not pleasure.

Both the Broderick and Bisceglia families also placed a premium on higher education, self-discipline, and success. Success, as defined by both families, meant conformity to traditional values in every respect. You went to school, excelled, married, raised children, worked hard, and attended Mass—and, if you were truly successful, you would eventually wind up enjoying even more material luxuries than your parents did. Sex roles were clearly identified in both households: women were, first and foremost, wives and childbearers; men were the bread earners. And nobody in either family had ever, ever been divorced.

There the similarities end.

Although Dan's family, by all accounts, was somewhat wealthier, it was also stricter, thriftier, less concerned with the social amenities than Betty's. A stern, unsentimental man, Daniel T. Broderick II did not pamper his children, according to three of Dan's sisters, all now wives and mothers. Theirs was a no-frills upbringing—no new cars at age sixteen, no casual handouts for trips to the movies or ice cream parlors, no new dresses for every occasion. "Ours was a hand-me-down family," says Dan's sister Patti. "Our father had a very strong work ethic. We weren't raised to take money for granted, to spend frivolously." Instead, the Broderick children were expected to work for every penny of their allowances, which were always small. "We always had charts posted in the house, designating which one of us was supposed to rake the leaves, or mow the grass, or do the dishes. The boys did the outdoor work, we did the indoor things," says Dan's oldest sister, Kathleen.

Nor were the Broderick children indulged with summer camps and travel, [even to nearby New York City]. Instead, their father bought a summer home in Madison, Ohio, on Lake Erie, which became the family's annual vacation retreat. Life in the summertime was simple and unaffected. The Broderick youngsters swam in the lake, played hide and seek in the yard, and devised their own fun. They also had horses. Dan loved horses. But when he was about fifteen, his favorite, Dancer, broke a leg. His sisters still remember how Dan held Dancer's head in his lap as the lethal injection was administered. That night, Kathleen recalls, "We all sat in the living room, listening to Danny cry upstairs. And we cried, too. It's the only time I can ever remember all of us sitting together, as a family, and crying ... except for when Danny died ..."

It was also a rigidly patriarchal family. The senior Broderick was undisputed master of his domain, in control of everything from finances to dinner table protocol. Among his various household rules, for example, dinner was to be served precisely at the same time each night, and once he sat down at the head of his table, "You did not get up, not until dinner was finished, not even to answer the telephone," says Dan's youngest sister, Christy. Their mother, Yolanda, who had left college early to marry, was by all accounts an exceedingly passive partner.

It was not a household, in short, into which a pampered, pretty blond princess from New York was apt to find herself instantly at home. Years later, Betty would remember how the boys teased their sisters by calling them "Yuks—too wet to step on, too low to kick." Dan's sisters still remember it, too, with visible annoyance, although, says Kathleen, "They didn't mean anything hurtful by it—they just thought it was funny."

Throughout his childhood, Dan was accorded all the benefits and burdens of being the oldest son and father's namesake. On the one hand, he was the golden boy who could do no wrong, adored by both parents. But at the same time, the pressure was heavy on him to succeed, to do his proud father even prouder—and Daniel T. Broderick II was, according to Christy, "tremendously success oriented, and he valued his real property immensely." He conditioned all his children from childhood "to become as successful as we could possibly be in life," says Patti. As the oldest son, Dan bore the brunt of that message. Likewise, he was also accustomed from an early age to taking a leadership role in the family. Dan Broderick's adult personality, in short, was forged by a conventional, predictable family dynamic—and the result was the usual double-edged sword: If he later became a workaholic overachiever in life, he was also imbued with the confidence from an early age that he could accomplish anything he chose simply because he was Daniel T. Broderick III. Unlike the woman he would marry, Dan Broderick never suffered any apparent personal insecurities about anything.

Listening to the melancholy memories of Dan's sisters after his death, it's clear that they certainly saw their big brother as virtually perfect in every way. Sitting in a San Diego bar one day during trial, they recalled his personal quirks with tender amusement: What a candy junkie he was, always stealing the family car to make penny-candy runs. And such a clotheshorse, even as a child, that it was a family joke. When he went off to college, everyone waited with fond interest to see what the latest fad would be when he came home on vacation—suspenders, bow ties, bell bottoms. "Danny was always a trendsetter," says Kathleen. "And he always had some new word for the season, too. Once it was 'knave.' Everybody was a 'knave' for a couple of months. Another time it was 'succulent.' Everything was 'succulent' for months, especially the girls."

His sisters also saw a lot of their father in Dan as he grew older. The senior Broderick, for example, was apparently just as proud of his possessions, including his lawn, as Dan later would be. Every week, the sisters say, the family lawn had to be mowed, clipped, and made perfect—and usually it was Dan who did it.

As Dan grew into adulthood, those same personality traits he shared with his father led to occasional clashes between the two strong-minded men. Once, for instance, during the summer after he left Betty, Dan took Rhett to visit with his parents for a couple of weeks. His father jokingly threatened to shave Rhett's hair off as soon as Dan left—just as he had once done to Dan and his brothers in their childhood. Dan ordered him not to do it, but as soon as Dan left town, the elder Broderick had his way—he gave Rhett a crew cut straight out of the fifties. Years later, in the divorce trial, Dan's anger still showed. "I told him if he ever touched one of my kids again, he would never see them again," he testified.

Betty's family was more preoccupied with social graces and civic participation. Her parents were active in numerous church and community organizations, from the Knights of Columbus and the Bronxville Women's Club to school boards. They also spent more freely on the trappings of the good life, everything from clothing and table wines to housekeepers—a basic difference in acculturation that would divide Betty and Dan until the end of their story. Whatever the family budget could afford, the Bisceglia children were allowed to explore—travel, summer camps, dance classes, tennis lessons, music teachers.

Hers was also a warmer, more family-oriented upbringing. Betty's mother's sister, Kay, with four cousins, lived just across the Street, and each Sunday, relatives from all over the New York area converged on the Bisceglia household for dinner. Sunday dinners were a tradition, the highlight of the week, with a crowd of aunts, uncles, and cousins gathered at a table heaping with food, where Betty's jolly father exhorted everyone in Italian to eat more and more—"*Mangia! Mangia!*"—and, given the slightest opening, regaled them with tales of the Allied liberation of Italy, too, where he had proudly served in World War II.

To this day, Betty's adoration of her father is powerfully clear—as is her equally strong resentment of her mother. "My dad was such a sentimentalist," she says. "He would cry over anything. He's just a complete sweetheart." But, she adds, "He's also a complete wimp, just like me—he would never do anything to upset my mother because she would take to her bed in her satin bed jacket with the vapors. I love my dad and my mom. They're both good people—but they've led such nice, peaceful lives that they simply can't face anything unpleasant. And so they don't face it. They go to Paris instead and sing tra-la-la-la, and just pretend nothing's happening."

Betty's attitude toward her mother is the classic love-hate relationship between mothers and daughters, the age-old tug-of-war between two women so much alike that they are in constant competition and therefore loathe each other. At the same time, they must still love what they must see in the mirror reflection of each other's eyes, which is themselves. And Betty is a reflection of Marita Bisceglia in so many respects, from her fixation with "social awareness" to physical size—only Betty among the three Bisceglia daughters grew to her mother's imposing height, 5'10".

"When I was in the middle of the divorce, the bitch wouldn't even listen to me, because it was too upsetting to her, and Mother can't bear anything upsetting," Betty said later with venomous sarcasm. Then, after the homicides, her mother was so devastated that she "took to her bed again ... She would've rather I killed myself because it would've gone down better at the women's club." Her parents didn't visit her until more than a year after she had been jailed.

At the same time, Betty openly admires her mother. To this day, nobody's opinion, nobody's approval, nobody's forgiveness matters to her more than Marita Bisceglia's. One of two daughters of a New York City policeman and a Phi Beta Kappa graduate from Hunter College, Mrs. Bisceglia was an elementary schoolteacher before she married. Thereafter, she worried over her children's training in everything from cooking and thank-you notes to the etiquette of addressing housekeepers and waiters.

"She taught us how to do things right," Betty says proudly. "She was socially aware. She knew the right stationery, the right china, the right everything, and she always saw to it that we got the best of everything they could afford. From the time we were children, for instance, my sisters and I always got a piece of silver on every holiday. By the time we were in college, we had a complete set of quality silver to last a lifetime." Hers was also a family in which the girls were encouraged toward sentimentality—collections of stuffed animals, dolls, and other delicate things. In later years, Betty would still be complaining that, in the divorce, she had lost track of her collection of fragile demitasse cups, begun for her thirty years ago by her mother.

Once, from jail, Betty summarized, in a single trenchant paragraph, the differences in parental role models she and Dan had grown up with. "Mr. Broderick had nothing to do with the kids. But my father probably did seventy percent of the kid stuff. Everything. My mother refused to even drive a car while we were all young. Therefore, there was never any discussion of whether Mrs. Bisceglia was going to be driving to the Boy Scouts, the Girl Scouts, the piano lessons, the dancing lessons. Daddy did it all. Daddy bought all the groceries, because Mother didn't drive. But, then, after we grew up, she drove. I have to hand it to her," Betty finished with a chuckle, "she wasn't stupid."

And so, just as Betty Broderick's view of the proper, loving father was based on her own, so was her notion of the woman's role in the home based on her mother's model: Mother was queen, the center of attention at all times. Mother ruled.

Betty was also a physical novelty in her family. Besides being the only tall, rail-thin daughter in a family prone to overweight, she was also the only Bisceglia child born towheaded. When her blond hair began to turn mouse brown in high school, she kept it blond from a bottle. In time, she bore little resemblance to the rest of her family, except for her blue eyes, which Frank Bisceglia, Italian or no, bequeathed to all his children. She also inherited her mother's overbite, which she didn't correct until she and Dan had moved to La Jolla.

Like Dan, she was always a top student. Unlike Dan, as the middle child in a big family, she was never as secure in herself. Years later, during the sentencing phase of her trial, her Aunt Kay wrote the judge, in a plea for leniency:

"I remember Betty as the pretty little girl in the middle of a high-talent family, behind a supersmart older brother and a beautiful older sister, and followed by a winsome younger sister and brother[s]," wrote Kay Fenzel. "Betty always had to 'run very fast just to stay in place' ... even with her own special good looks and intelligence ... When Betty grew tall and willowy, no one acknowledged this as her own beauty asset. Downgraded in her own eyes, she adopted a frolicking, devil-may-care manner, which did not entirely conceal the lurking self-doubt in her eyes.

"Yearning for love herself, Betty Anne BESTOWS love—on younger children, wounded birds, neighborhood cats and dogs, and her 'little cousins up the road.' Her creativity and intelligence found humor in life and she regularly led the fun. When I would stop by the Bisceglia home, Betty was the one I would see carrying the baby of the family on her hip while keeping up light patter and hijinks. Ever and again, nonetheless, there was that lonely, hangdog look, that eagerness to please. Insouciance covered up self-doubt ..."

Betty only shrugs Aunt Kay's analysis away. No, she insists—it was never her parents whose demands shaped her personality, nor did she feel inferior to her siblings. Instead, it was the nuns who scared the hell out of her, she says, starting on her very first day in school.

She can't recall exactly what it was that she did, that day in first grade, to bring the wrath of authority down upon her head—but she remembers vividly that it was Sister Claire Veronica who punished her. She was forced to sit under the piano for several hours. "And maybe I learned right then that I wasn't going to spend my life being humiliated and standing in corners and sitting under pianos—instead, I'm going to kiss this woman's ass."

And that's what she did. Throughout her school years, "I was the goody-two-shoes, and everybody loved me," she says, her voice laced with self-contempt. "I figured out how to get more rows of gold stars than anyone else. I was the one that the teacher called on to mind the class when she went out of the room. I liked that. I even used to dust the Principal's office. That was like the biggest thing you could do in the whole school, was be the Principal's goody-two-shoes. All these nuns wanted me to be a nun. I learned very early in life that if you look real cute and you're a goody-two-shoes, everybody likes you. And I've been doing it ever since."

Her flashy good looks attracted attention early on. Boys began to buzz around the Bisceglia household as never before. And, after a church fashion show during high school, Betty began modeling professionally, a part-time job she kept up throughout her college years, eventually doing occasional shows at some of the large New York department stores. But modeling was never a serious career consideration, "because my mother thought it was too tacky. I was supposed to be a schoolteacher until I got married, because that was proper."

She was programmed from birth to be a wife, not only by her parents and the girls' schools she attended, but by her peers, too. "You were what I've often wanted to be," a college classmate once wrote her, in 1966. "You present ... the image of the model woman and—more so—the perfect wife." The girlfriend added that she "almost envies the man who marries you." For Betty, it was a world without options.

She lived at home throughout college, right up until the day she was married, commuting to school in a sporty little green MG. Partly, it was cheaper—the Bisceglias were comfortable, but never, as some later accounts had it, rich. In addition, says Betty, putting the best face on every situation as usual, she didn't want to live on campus. "What for? The nuns wouldn't even let you wear lipstick. I had more freedom at home."

But, in the next breath, she also remembers her parents' strictness. Her older sister hadn't dated much, she says, so now, for the first time, Frank and Marita Bisceglia faced swarms of boys banging on their front door, ringing their phone, wanting to court their pretty daughter. "And I would go out and have ice cream with them or something, and my mother thought I was a slut. I mean, if you talk to a boy, you're a slut, and she was always accusing me of stuff." She remembers taking a nap one day after staying up studying all night for an exam. Since she never napped in the daytime, her mother was suspicious. "She comes in my room, pulls me off the bed, screaming and yelling that I'm on drugs."

Another time, in college, she had planned a weekend skiing trip with Dan and several friends. "I had my car and luggage packed up—but my father cut the wires on my car so I couldn't go anywhere, and my mother broke the locks off my luggage looking for contraceptives and drugs," she says, laughing in exasperation. "And, mind you, I had never even *seen* a contraceptive yet, and I'd sure as hell never seen a drug. They were just trying to be good parents, to keep their daughter from becoming a loose woman—but they drove me crazy." She didn't go on the trip.

"The theme of the whole thing," she said later, in a rare moment of self-analysis, "is that I tried to be perfect. The rule book that I was given since the day I was born was the Catholic rule book. This is how to live your life: You don't lie, you don't cheat, you don't steal, you're kind to your neighbors, you show love to everyone, even if you hate them ... You get married, you have children, you put the kids through the best school possible, and then you're a grandma."

But it only works if the husband follows the rule book, too. That's why she said, "I would never in my life have dreamed of marrying a man who wasn't Catholic, who didn't share my views on divorce. That was the number one requirement."

She met Dan at Notre Dame, during a USC-Notre Dame football weekend. He was a senior premed student, bound for Cornell Medical School in New York. The year was 1965. She was seventeen, a college freshman. It was the most exciting weekend of Betty Broderick's young life, the first time she had been allowed to travel out of town overnight—chaperoned, of course, but that didn't dilute the thrill. She went with a girlfriend, both of them invited by dates at Notre Dame.

The Vietnam War was building to a thunder, Betty Friedan was just beginning to stir the consciousness of a whole new generation of American women, drugs were about to explode on college campuses, and Bob Dylan was turning a song called 'Blowin' in the Wind' into the anthem of an entire era.

But not for Betty and Dan. It might not have been the sixties at all, looking at these two. Theirs was a sweetheart romance right out of a Pat Boone-Terry Moore movie. 'April Love,' in fact, was one of their favorite songs.

Betty's most enduring image of feminists from the sixties was a negative one: they were, in her mind, radical, bra-burning lesbians from People's Park in Berkeley, circa 1968. They were a threat, and a challenge to all that she stood for, all that she finally killed for. They were not mothers and wives. Had Betty been politically oriented at all, she would probably have become a disciple of Phyllis Schlafly.

"I thought Berkeley was Moscow," she said later. "I thought feminists were crazy people, I thought draft-card burners were Communists, and I didn't know what that meant, except that it was bad. I never had the slightest interest in magazines like *Ms*, I never read Betty Friedan's book, I thought Gloria Steinem was pretty, but weird. I just didn't want to be any part of all that. We just didn't get into the real world. Besides, the nuns wouldn't let us. In my world, all that mattered was that you had the pleated skirt, the right Peter Pan collar, the Papagallo ballerinas, and a circle pin. If you didn't have the right uniform, you were dead!"

She remembers her first impressions of Dan Broderick vividly. She and her date were at a college club where Jerry Lee Lewis was performing, when Dan sat down at the same table and, a few drinks later, asked her for a pen. "And I, of course, being the proper little Catholic schoolgirl, always had in my purse a handkerchief, a dime to get home, and my little gold Parker pen." He wrote his name on a napkin. Daniel T. Broderick, MDA. Medical Doctor Almost, he explained to her with his wonderful grin.

"He was skinny, with these big glasses, he looked like a nerd," she says. "But I liked his wit. I liked him."

For his part, Dan seemed instantly smitten with the tall, striking, vibrant New Yorker. "I later heard that he told a friend that very night that he was going to marry me," she says now, with some faint hint of pride still flickering dimly amid the rubble of her ruined emotions. Somewhere, stored among her possessions, she still has an Indiana Club beer mug she saved as a souvenir from the night they met. She also remembers exactly what Jerry Lee was singing that night: " 'Great Balls of Fire!' What else?" *"Oh, baby, you're drivin' me crazy. Goodness gracious—Great Balls of Fire!"*

In later years, they attended the annual Notre Dame-USC game without fail. She would never get over the sentimental pain of those memories. It apparently took Dan a while, too. After he left her, over twenty years after they had met, he once called, tipsy, from a Notre Dame weekend, his first without her, to tell her, she says, how much he had once loved her. "And he was there with Linda," she says. "I don't think I ever hated him more than I did at that one single moment."

It was an old-fashioned courtship that lasted for the next three years. He came to see her in New York, they made dates to meet under the Biltmore clock, they listened to the Lettermen, and were soon enough two college kids in love. She still remembers the walks in Central Park, the movies, the fun they had exploring Manhattan's cheapest restaurants and bars.

Dan took his new love home to meet his family, and they were dazzled "She was so worldly, so sophisticated, at least in our minds—a glamorous New York model," Dan's sister Kathleen remembers. "She told me she made $17,000 in one year! And we hadn't been anywhere. She had three swimming suits—I only had one. She was so witty and gracious. And she always brought us little gifts—things from Tiffany, Doss apples ..." The Broderick family would continue to be charmed by Betty Broderick for many years to come.

During those years, while Dan was attending medical school, Betty and Dan also discovered an Upper East Side pub called Henny's and, within few months, turned it into a fashionable watering hole for Cornell medical students, thanks to Dan's endorsement. "Pretty soon the owner, a guy named Jim, was so grateful at all the new business, he didn't even want to charge Dan," says Betty. Never much of a drinker, she now refers hatefully to Henny's as "one of those wino places, a cheap Irish piece of junk." But back then she loved the Saturday afternoons she spent sipping Irish coffee at Henny's, holding hands with Dan across the table.

It was during these youthful, halcyon days, too, that Dan created "the Turtle" and "the Alligator," silly little drinking skits that he would still be performing virtually until the day he died. "The Turtle," says Dan' youngest brother, Terry, amounted to Dan lying on the floor, on his stomach, and kicking his legs. "The Alligator" was the reverse—he lay on his back and kicked his legs. Betty remembers that "I thought it was sort of cute at the time. And everybody drank ..." She shrugs it away. Even today, mention of the Alligator and the Turtle embarrasses her. As she denounces Dan Broderick in one breath as a power-maddened drunk Betty still tries, in the next moment, to protect his memory from the smaller humiliations. She wants the world to hate him—but not to mock him. Only she is permitted to do that. Even during her first murder trial when her defense attorney once launched into a sarcastic review of the Turtle for the jury, she could not bear it. "Tell Jack to drop it!" she scribbled an angry note to his assistant. "This isn't relevant!"

She was equally embarrassed when she once let slip that, during her many pregnancies, Dan also liked sometimes to impose the Turtle on her. "He thought it was funny to push me down on the floor or a couch when I was so heavy I couldn't get up unless somebody helped me," she remarked. "I'd just be laying there, floundering, trying to get my balance, with everybody laughing."

But, pressed for details, she hid them away. "It was no big deal," she snapped irritably. "I didn't mind it at the time. I guess I thought it was funny, too! I don't know what I thought!"

She loved him. He loved her. They became engaged.

"He was smart, ambitious, and fun, and so was I ... But what's love when you're only seventeen? I have no idea what either of us really thought about each other," she once said from jail, in a fleeting moment of fairness not only to herself but Dan, too. "All either one of us knew was that we were exactly what the other was supposed to be looking for in a mate."

It was a pretty time in their lives. On Friday afternoons she often waited for Dan in his dormitory room, where she listened to their special love songs on his record player. Besides the Lettermen, Johnny Mathis was a favorite—especially "The Twelfth of Never."

"It was great make-out music," she later remarked from jail, typically flip, in her outdated hip speak. But, then, in the next breath, in one of her whipsaw moments, Betty Broderick was suddenly, softly singing the lyrics into the telephone, every one perfectly intact in her memory, even after all those years.

"You ask how long I'll love you, I'll tell you true ..."

Her little-girl voice trembled slightly as she searched for the bygone words. In the background, in the small courtyard where she stood at the pay phone, the usual yelling, howling prison yard racket continued. Her voice rose as she continued singing her lost song.

Anyone from that generation would remember that Johnny Mathis classic with all its beautiful images of undying love. Hold me close. Hearts melting like snow. Forever and ever. Until flowers stop blooming, until poets no longer rhyme. Love forever.

She sang on, through the very last line.

"Until the Twelfth of Never, I'll still be loving you ..."

She finished with an embarrassed little giggle; then, typical of Betty when her emotions threaten to overflow, she hung up. Another prisoner needed the phone.

Chapter 4

Until the Twelfth of Never

They were married on April 12, 1969.

It was only months after the My Lai massacre; Nixon's secret bombing of Cambodia would soon surface. But the Brodericks were a world away from Vietnam: He would not be called to serve—he was a student and claimed a minor stomach disorder, according to Betty. Soon he would also be a father. It was the year of Woodstock, only miles away, but these two were lost to the Grateful Dead, Judy Collins, Baez. It was also just a few months before California and other states would institute no-fault divorce laws, in what at the time was considered a feminist victory. But Betty Broderick didn't know or care. Her life was on schedule, her script intact. Because of her wedding plans, she entered an accelerated child psychology program at college, and graduated in December with a B.A. She then won a coveted teaching job at the respected Anne Hutchinson School in Eastchester, just across the street from her parents' house, and she loved it. Her small, sheltered world never expanded. Dan, meantime, was finishing his last year of medical school. They had life by the tail.

Their wedding was preceded by a proper announcement in the regional newspapers, complete with pictures of Elisabeth Anne Bisceglia, her hair in a lacquered bouffant, looking a lot like a pouty-lipped Sandra Dee.

It was also occasion for Betty Broderick's first gynecological exam because "It's what you were supposed to do when you were getting married." What she discovered, she says, was that she had a remarkably confused body: two cervixes, two vaginas, two uteruses. The doctor performed a simple office operation to correct the dual vaginas, but, to this day, she says, she has two sets of all the rest. If her freakish condition bothered her then, it doesn't show today. All she remembers clearly, she says, is that the doctors told her she was at high risk of becoming pregnant even if she used female contraceptives, but that "I would probably never be able to carry a child through to full term."

* * *

The wedding was strictly her mother's production, a lavish, traditional affair that, judging from photographs, more closely reflected Marita Bisceglia's era than Betty's. The bridesmaids wore pink satin with gauzy headdresses and sprayed, teased hair. Betty wore spit curls. Her prim, high-necked white wedding dress came from one of New York's most exclusive bridal shops; the china pattern, Pickard, was listed at all the major department stores. The wedding cake was a spectacular, flower-encrusted work of art. Marita Bisceglia herself wore a hat wreathed in silk blossoms, and half the women in attendance were wrapped in fur stoles. The dress code for men in the wedding party, as dictated by Mrs. Bisceglia, was morning coats.

But Dan refused to abide. Instead, he showed up in a pin-striped suit, a paisley tie, and loud brown shoes with big shiny buckles. "He said he didn't want to wear rented clothes," says Betty.

It was the beginning of a lifelong loathing between Dan and Betty's mother. "I should have known then, I should have warned Betty Anne, when he came in those awful shoes—Dan Broderick never had any respect for anyone or anything but himself," Marita Bisceglia lamented years later at her daughter's second trial.

But, on April 12, 1969, it was only a minor squall. Nothing could ruin the glory of the day. Dan and Betty even wrote part of their rites. "Our agreement was 'for better, for worse, for richer or poorer, for fifty years.' That was a condition Dan and I put in— an agreement to be married for at least fifty years," Betty remembered years later.

An orchestra played Johnny Mathis's 'The Twelfth of Never,' their wedding theme song, and Pat Boone's 'April Love.'

Their honeymoon was a Caribbean cruise, ending at a friend's house in St. Thomas.

She was a virgin and, Betty insists, so was he. "And he raped me!" she says now. "He could never show his feelings without drinking, so he got drunk that night. It was awful!"

What really happened is anybody's best guess because, in subsequent years, after their marriage fell apart, both Dan and Betty Broderick viewed their history together through eyes so blinded by angry events that they probably effectively erased some of the softest, most magical moments in both their lives.

Today, Betty can only resentfully recall that, as soon as they arrived on the lush, romantic isle of St. Thomas, "Dan dismissed the servants … He said it was so we could be alone—but the point was, I was now the Wife. I was supposed to serve him, make his meals. From day one, the minute I married him, everything changed. He wasn't courting me anymore. I was no longer his princess—I was his housekeeper. He was just like his dad—he had no respect for women." What's more, she says, he showed no interest in either her or the exotic new world around them. Instead, "He brought all these books along—he read the whole time!"

For his own part, after he met Linda, Dan told friends that he knew from the first hours of his marriage that he had made a horrible mistake because Betty was too much like her mother for it ever to work. He once told attorney friend Brian Monaghan that, on their honeymoon, he was sitting on a bus one day looking out a window "and wanting to cry because he knew he had done the wrong thing—but he was Catholic, and he was stuck."

Theirs was always a specifically Catholic story—at least when it came to marriage, divorce, and sex. Although, as adults, both Brodericks stopped observing church rituals and sent their children to secular schools, neither of them ever fully shed the Roman Catholic values instilled in them from childhood. The nuns and the fathers were never far from their bed. Contraception was not a consideration—at least not for Dan. "He simply would not even consider it," says Betty. "Once, years later, I got a diaphragm, but any kind of contraceptive was disgusting to him, so I threw it away." For both, sex seems to have been: a shadowy affair, done but not discussed. "I never once even saw Dan Broderick naked," she later said. "He would put his underwear back on before he got out of bed, and he always came out of the shower with a towel." And she was the same way. Sex was a thing done in the dark.

At the time of her honeymoon, Betty was also naive as a child about sex. She was never given any formal sex education at home or in school, she says. In her household, sex talk was strictly taboo, a dirty subject. She still recalls her shock when she had her first menstrual period. She was twelve, and her mother had never even mentioned such a thing to her, she says. She had been at the school rifle range that day, she remembers, wearing a pair of shorts. "But when I lay down on the ground, suddenly the Father wouldn't let me shoot, he made me get up and leave and I didn't understand why, until I got home. My shorts were all bloody ... and either my mother or my sister—I can't remember which one it was—just threw a Kotex and belt into the bathroom. And that was it."

She came back from the honeymoon pregnant.

She was stunned. She loved her new job at the Hutchinson School and didn't want to quit. But, given the doctor's warnings, it never occurred to her that she would carry her baby through to full term, she says. But, to her amazement, the baby only grew and grew, and she got sicker and sicker. "So much for doctors," she says sourly. "They said I would miscarry. Instead, every time Dan Broderick walked through the room, I was pregnant."

She continued teaching right up until the day before she gave birth, on January 24, 1970, to her daughter Kim. And, from that day forward, Betty Broderick was no longer a career woman, she was a full-time wife and mother. Dan was in charge, Betty was along for the ride. The trade was complete.

Ten months later she was pregnant again, with Lee, born July 27, 1971.

It was only the beginning. Altogether, she was pregnant nine times in ten years. All her deliveries would be by Cesarean section, preceded by terrible nausea and discomfort. She would not end it until 1979, when she finally had a tubal ligation. Before then, she bore four healthy babies, had two miscarriages and two abortions. Her third child, a boy, died four days after he was born in 1972.

Nothing better reflects the extraordinary ambitions of both Brodericks than the misery they endured by mutual consent during the early years of their marriage.

He drove a cab part-time during medical school in Manhattan and worked after classes in a blood laboratory. She sold nurses' uniforms part-time while still teaching and pregnant with Kim. Afterward, she worked between pregnancies as a hostess at a Bloomingdale's cafeteria and took in baby-sitting jobs. In her spare time, while she was pregnant with Kim in New York, she rode her bicycle across Central Park to attend gourmet French cooking classes at the Dakota, where she learned, among other recipes, Dan's favorite, *Poulet Normandie*, a chicken dish with apples and mushrooms.

49

Dan began his medical residency in Pittsburgh. The young couple, then parents of one child with a second on the way, lived for a few months with his parents. Betty spent her savings, her parents kicked in for baby clothes and other necessities. Thieves stole their car—her MG—and his grandparents gave them a new one, a Volkswagen bug.

But she regarded all of it as a minor, temporary hardship. Soon, Dr. and Mrs. Broderick would commence their ascent to prosperity.

Then Dan turned their lives upside down by deciding that he didn't want to be a practicing doctor after all. He wanted to be a medical malpractice attorney instead. He was accepted at Harvard and enrolled without completing his medical internship.

"He wanted to get rich. So did I, of course," says Betty, "but I figured it was good enough to be a doctor's wife. But Dan told me we could richer faster if he was a malpractice attorney. I thought it was a great idea. I didn't object at all. I'd vote for being richer any day, wouldn't you?"

So the Brodericks embarked on an even harsher course. His parents, frugal people in the first place, believed it was their responsibility to educate their offspring through one college degree, but they refused to subsidize a second education. Hers agreed. Dan, Betty, and babies were on their own.

Those next years were the hardest ones. They moved from one cheap, cramped apartment to the next even cheaper one, some in bad neighborhoods, one a place without reliable hot water or heat during a long, harsh Boston winter. But what she best remembers today "is hauling dirty diapers to the laundromat in the freezing snow on a bus while he was out at some student activities event, or home studying. At the time, though, I didn't complain. We were a partnership, and that was my part of the job."

During those years, she also continued to work at assorted odd jobs to help keep them afloat. She sold Avon and Tupperware door to door, taking Kim and Lee with her, and, again, she took in home baby-sitting. At one time, they even supplemented their income with food stamps. They also took out $20,000 in loans for Harvard, for which, in divorce court almost twenty years later, she would be charged half.

But the picture that emerges of these two during Dan's Harvard years, as they sat around their bare little apartments amid the diapers and law books, is hardly that of a struggling young couple sacrificing for the greater good. Dan and Betty Broderick were sacrificing for their own good, period. They were completely removed from their own turbulent generation. Instead, they both methodically plotted their course for years to come right down to declaring her small, cash baby-sitting fees on their student tax returns. "Dan said we should establish a record with the IRS of being meticulous about small amounts so that someday, when he was really making big money, they wouldn't ever audit us," she says.

Money was always the goal, as she tells it, without shame. "I always thought Dan would make a great U.S. Senator, or a President someday ... and I thought it would be great to be First Lady. But he always told me that no way would he ever get into politics, because they didn't make any real money. It was one thing if you were the Kennedys—they already had money. But we had to make ours."

In those years, too, both agreed that his image on campus should be a priority item. "Dan always told me, image was everything, and I agreed. Harvard is the kind of place where you make contacts for a lifetime." And so, she says, much of their money went into ensuring Dan enough free time to participate in student government. He even took pilot lessons. Nor did he ever outgrow his childhood fixation with clothes. Later on, he would be noted around San Diego for his expensive suits and flashy sports jackets, his flamboyant cape and top hat at formal events. But even during the sixties, when everybody else was wearing jeans and turtlenecks, he was always beautifully turned out in tailored clothes, says Betty, despite the fact that they really couldn't afford it. In medical school, he even had custom-made lab jackets. "We called him Dapper Dan," she says, laughing almost fondly.

He was equally meticulous about his surroundings. Sometimes, even now, Betty recalls Dan's old habits with amusement. Once, for instance, she remembers buying him a case of Windex for Christmas. "It was back in Boston, when we had no money at all, and two babies, and I was expecting the third ... We had a glass-topped cheap coffee table, and we had sliding glass windows; and two toddlers, who of course, hold onto things to walk. Dan would walk in the door, and before he'd say anything, he'd get the Windex and clean the table and clean the window. I'm not kidding," she says, laughing. "The man was such a fanatic. So I went to the supermarket and literally bought him a cardboard case of Windex that Christmas, and I wrapped it and put it under the tree. He loved it."

They had few friends in those days, she says, because neither of them wanted anybody to see the poor conditions in which they lived. "Besides, Dan was always gone, out doing things. I was home all day with two little kids. It was lonely." But one couple who did visit them during that period remembers that "It was a very, very traditional relationship, in terms of roles, and both of them seemed happy with it."

Then it was 1973, Dan's last year at Harvard. Betty was twenty-five. Kim was three, Lee was two, and Betty was pregnant again. But now women all over the United States suddenly had an alternative. This was the year of Roe v. Wade, legalizing abortion. And Betty Broderick decided she wanted one. The sirens of the sixties had finally filtered through her Catholic training. Other voices were at last louder in her ears than those of the nuns, the pope, her parents, her girlfriends—and Dan.

"I was just so tired, it was so much work, we couldn't afford the children we had. And Dan was always gone. He was working hard himself, always studying, or doing something on campus. And I just thought, 'Oh, no, not this again. I can't do this again!' I was a cow! I was a baby machine. I didn't want a third baby in three years with no money. I didn't think that was the proper way to raise children. And I was deathly ill the whole nine months, throwing up ... and the two babies. It was the worst, because not only am I crawling around and throwing up every two minutes for nine months, Lee Lee was a colicky, crying baby, and I bled through every pregnancy. I'd be walking down the street and I would just hemmorhage, in the

51

supermarket, in restaurants. It was down your legs and on the floor. And Dan never helped … Minding a third baby was entirely on me."

And so, the Church be damned, she decided to have an abortion.

Dan drove her to the clinic in New York. And sat in the car and cried. "He begged me not to do it, he promised to stay home more, to help me out more." So she didn't do it.

But when she went into premature labor at seven months, he was gone on a ski trip. She was alone in Boston, miles from any relatives, with no one to call. She called the police. They drove her to a hospital in a snow storm. It was false labor. Dan returned that night, in time to drive her to the hospital a few days later, when the child was finally born. Ironically or perhaps providentially, the baby Betty had wanted to abort died anyway, four days later. And, for reasons clear only to her, she still has not forgiven Dan for not being there when the fear struck, the night the police came. "The sonofabitch lied to me! He wasn't there when I needed him most!"

And so when she became pregnant again, only a few months later, she didn't even ask him. "I just drove to a clinic and got an abortion. It was the first time in my life I ever stood up for myself."

When he found out about it, Dan cried again.

Betty would always be in conflict with herself over her immediate, inescapable motherhood. Sometimes, she would insist that mothering has always been her first and only goal: "I loved children, I always thought I wanted to have at least ten, even if I had to adopt. When I was in high school, I would always rather baby-sit for the neighbors than go on a date."

But that was never more than the mixed view of a woman who, in those days, had no choices—because, at other times, she would speak with wistful pride of how she had been such a good teacher and had always missed "the stimulation of the real world, the sense of independence that a job can bring." In fact, from jail during the summer of 1991, the only social issue in the outside world with enough power to penetrate Betty Broderick's own tangle of self-absorption was the antiabortion drive. "I can't believe this country is going to go full circle, to put my daughters back to exactly where I was twenty years ago!"

In later years, in between pregnancies, she would try at least twice to return to teaching. Then, after her last child was born, she got a real estate license. And, after the divorce, she considered going to either photography or law school. But by then, she had neither the self-confidence nor the will to seriously pursue anything beyond winning her "fair share" in divorce court for all the years she had put into her failed marriage.

Chapter 5

"Dearest Bets, Darling Dan"

The Brodericks moved to San Diego after Dan completed a summer clerkship in Los Angeles, where he met David Monahan, an attorney at Gray, Cary in San Diego. Monahan and his then-wife, Patti, persuaded the Brodericks to consider San Diego. And so Betty and Dan loaded their babies into their Volkswagen and drove down to visit. They were both instantly charmed by the quiet, civilized beauty of the city. "And Dan figured we could be bigger fish faster in a smaller pond, too," says Betty, "which was fine with me."

Dan had no trouble getting a job offer. His double degrees dazzled senior partners at Gray, Cary. "They wooed us like royalty," Betty remembers. Even so, Dan didn't begin his San Diego legal career with a royal salary, at least not for a young man with a growing family. His starting pay was about $17,000, says Betty, so, for some time, life was only a few steps better than their struggling student years.

Their first home, near the inner city, was a cheap, vintage Southern California apartment complex called the Plum Tree, a typical transients' refuge with a narrow courtyard swimming pool and neon palms emblazoned across the building front. They had no furniture, beyond beds and cinderblock bookcases. She remembers that Dan's brother Larry once bought them some patio furniture that doubled as a kitchen set for more than a year.

In a few months they moved to a small rental house in Clairemont, a working-class neighborhood across the freeway from La Jolla, where they stayed for another year until an electrical fire burned them out. Most of their personal possessions were destroyed, including a stuffed-animal collection Betty had hauled across country with her. But the fire turned out to be a boon to their ambitions. The insurance company promptly paid their expenses to move. They used the money to make the down payment on the Coral Reef house in La Jolla. It had taken Dan and Betty Broderick only two years to arrive at the most celebrated address in town.

The next years were ordinary, at least for the Brodericks. The nation was in historic crisis. In 1974, an American President had been driven from office, and, in 1975, while they were moving into their new La Jolla home, thousands of Vietnamese refugees were camped only thirty miles north of their doorstep, in a sea of tents at Camp Pendleton Marine Base. But while the country stared at pictures of their tearful, frightened faces and wondered what it had wrought, in San Diego, Dan Broderick mowed his: lawn and networked, while his wife was getting her first thrills from seeing her name in Burl Stiff's society column for her charity work. "We didn't talk about politics—or anything else, really. We didn't have time," she says today. "We were both so ambitious, we each took our jobs very seriously. We were just spinning in circles, during those years—but we never bumped into each other. And I thought we were both doing it all for the common good."

Just as they missed the sixties, so, too, did Dan and Betty Broderick miss the seventies. Their decade was still ahead.

Both Brodericks hit the ground in San Diego running.

Dan was an immediate star at work. Whatever he did, he did it well, and he drove himself remorselessly. "He was a superstar," recalls fellow Gray, Cary attorney Lance Schaffer. "Dan was the kind of guy who made all the rest of us look like loafers ... In his last year [at the firm] he billed something like 2,500 hours when 1,800 is considered tops."

From his earliest days in San Diego, too, Dan took an active part in extracurricular legal activities. "He was always off teaching, or doing this and that," Betty says. "He told me he had to do it, because when the: judges ask you, if you say yes, they never forget, but if you say no, the they don't want to hear about you when you appear in front of them later in court." That made sense to Betty. Nor did she complain when Dan began to socialize seriously after hours with the boys for the same reason. Just as they had during his Harvard years, both Brodericks agreed that contacts and high visibility were politically critical to their future, mutual advancement.

Dan's favorite Friday-night haunt, his new Henny's, was Dobson's, a fashionable downtown San Diego bar where bright young attorneys, future judges, politicians, and San Diego millionaires congregated, mainly to discuss their own futures. Here, Dan formed lasting friendships with many of the city's next generation of leaders. Today, any popular national registry of San Diego's top attorneys includes many of Dan Broderick's best friends, most of them immortalized in life, as Dan was, by small metal name-plates attached to Dobson's long, mahogany bar.

For her part, Betty was ready to live up to her half of the bargain, too—to become the perfect complement to her accomplished husband.

She plunged into community affairs. She became president of a San Diego art museum support group, took a leading role in an annual charity auction sponsored by a local radio station, and promptly signed on with the bar auxiliary for attorney's wives, which organizes the Blackstone Ball, the legal community's annual gala, and conducts courthouse tours for school children. She also taught Bible Study and fifth-grade Sunday School class at the church. Already she had begun to worry, too, about which schools her children should attend, what school activities she should lead. At the same time, she was going to be a career woman. That thought had not yet left her head. Initially, in an attempt to pick up her teaching career, she took a job as a fifth-grade teacher at a suburban private school. She was going to be Supermom.

Besides that, they still needed the money. The payoff was not yet at hand. So she also took a part-time job at night in a jewelry store.

Dan's inner circle, in those early days, consisted primarily of other aggressive young attorneys like himself—many of them Irish Americans. They became like a post-college fraternity. They joined the Friendly Sons of St. Patrick, marched every year in

54

the St. Patrick's Day parade, and loved singing mournful Irish ballads into the wee weekend hours. They also belonged to the Tuesday Morning Marching and Chowder Society, a group Brian Monaghan formed to discuss matters of law, although members invariably met more often on Friday nights over ale than on Tuesday mornings over coffee.

What Dan Broderick's friends remember best about him today was his style. He had class, a certain reserve, combined with a dry humor that set him apart. "Dan was not an emotional guy. If you hugged him, he'd stiffen," recalls Brian Monaghan. And even in a circle of high-achievers, Dan's professional drive stood out. By day, he was all business, a no-nonsense, sometimes brusque personality who kept his eye relentlessly on the ball: for example, in the early days he invariably left his calling card under every lunch plate and cocktail glass in town in an effort to drum up new business. In later years, friends—and Betty—learned better than to make a personal call during work hours unless they expected an impatient, thirty-second yes-no conversation.

But, for all his cool daytime veneer, by night, Dan became one of the boys. He loved hanging out in the pubs, talking law, shooting the breeze. With a few drinks, he would loosen up and entertain them all with the Turtle and the Alligator. He also developed another favorite routine, based on Inspector Clouseau, the "Pink Panther" character, with his dog. "He would crawl under the table and bark and bite my pant legs," says Monaghan with a chuckle.

After his death, Dan Broderick's friends did their best to defend his reputation from Betty's accusations, to lend him the humanity she was stripping away daily in the press and in court. Only the setting changed—from Dobson's to a new Irish pub, Reidy O'Neil's, just across the downtown square. Dan had invested in Reidy's just before he died, and now it stands as something of a shrine to his memory. At the entrance is a large drawing of him and his three partners, drinking beer and singing. His boyish grin is captured perfectly. Elsewhere in the bar, on walls covered with photographs of famous Irishmen, are other pictures of Dan, one of him as a child talking to a nun, another of him laughing with Linda. On any given evening, half a dozen of Dan's friends can still be found at Reidy's, eager to remember the way he was:

He loved the Blues Brothers, John Wayne, and all old movies. "Dan just got a kick out of life," says developer Mike Reidy, one of the few non-lawyers in Dan's circle. "He could put on dark glasses and do a skit from the Blues Brothers that left us all in stitches. He could spout lines verbatim from *The Quiet Man, Robin Hood* ..." And, of course, *Gone with the Wind*—Dan's favorite movie of all time. He was so enchanted with that film that he had a huge Clark Gable poster in his den. According to Betty, that's where Dan acquired his lifelong penchant for capes and top hats—and it was also the source of their son Rhett's name, after the movie's hero, Rhett Butler. He later had a cat named Scarlett, too. (Dan also had a classic poster in his den of Jimmy Cagney rubbing a grapefruit in the face of Mae Davis, from another old film, Betty growls.)

Nor was it true, Dan's friends say, that he only went to law school for the money. "Dan loved the law," says Monaghan. "He told me that he became a lawyer because he decided that being a doctor was too much like being a mechanic—no creativity."

As for his drinking, Dan Broderick was always a moderate social drinker, friends say. "I never saw him topped out more than five times in fifteen years, and when he was [drunk], he would go hide in a bathroom or a bedroom and sleep it off. Dan was always a gentleman," says Reidy. "Dan was the kind of guy who always ordered these sweet drinks that take you hours to get a buzz on, Spumanti and ice cream, Pink Monkeys, stuff like that," says Kathy Cuffaro. "And when he got loaded, he was so lovable that you wanted to take him and his Pink Monkeys home with you."

And they all got a kick out of Dan's foppish sartorial ways. He made them laugh with his brilliant pink jackets, his dandy rosebuds, his blinding plaids. "Dan was certainly different," says Reidy, a conservative, button-down type himself, "but it wasn't vanity, or ego. Dan just had fun with clothes."

Despite the fact that Monaghan, Reidy, and several others in Dan Broderick's San Diego crowd were Vietnam veterans, they also say that they never discussed Dan's draft status with him, not even during their most ribald, macho nights of drinking. "I don't remember that the subject ever even came up—it was a personal choice," says attorney Mike Neil, a Marine reserve general and much-decorated Vietnam War hero who became temporary commander of Camp Pendleton during the Iraqi war.

In death, Dan's friends would erect shrines to him. They renamed a conference room at the San Diego County Bar Association building for him, and today the local bar association issues an annual award in his name to an attorney selected for special "professional integrity." Just before Betty's first trial, the American Ireland Fund dedicated its annual fund-raising dinner to his memory; and, a year after that, several of the San Diego Irish American crowd went to the Broderick family's small ancestral village in Ireland to dedicate a new library in his name, and, of course, tip a few in his memory.

"It's a last way to say good-bye to our buddy," said Dan's friend Vince Bartolotta, an "honorary Irishman" whose firm inherited many of Dan's pending cases. Bartolotta also later became notable around town for copying Dan's habit of floral boutonnières, though he seems to prefer carnations to rosebuds.

But, if his friends deify Dan Broderick in death, some seemed equally in awe of him in life. As his professional reputation grew, and his personal poise blossomed, friends used to tell him that he was bound for bigger things than San Diego had to offer, that he should get into politics. And Dan had been interested, says Monaghan. "He thought about running for the Senate or President someday ... until this trouble with Betty started. Then he would ask, 'How can I run for any office with her trying to ruin my reputation?'."

Betty, meanwhile, was not having nearly as much fun during those years.

After only one school season, she quit her teaching job because the baby-sitter was costing more than she was earning. So she became a nighttime hostess at a franchise steak house, when Dan would be home to watch the children. As a fringe benefit, she got free food, enough to bring a late dinner home to Dan every night. She kept that job for several months—"until I was so pregnant with Danny that I couldn't stand up." By then, too, she had developed such serious varicose veins that she later had surgery to remove them.

After Danny's birth in 1976, she worked for a few months at another chain restaurant in between pregnancies. Before the arrival of Rhett in 1979, she had another abortion and two miscarriages.

It was five years before Dan finally began to earn enough money that she could stay home and run her $l-per-hour La Jolla day-care service, more for pleasure than money. At her murder trials, the prosecutor would go to great lengths to establish Betty Broderick as a greedy shopaholic—and, she did, in fact, eventually attach a price tag to her prior labors. But what can never be taken away from her is the fact that, from the day they were married until the year Dan Broderick's income first hit $1 million, his wife was never too proud or too lazy to work twice as hard as most women could or would.

During those years, too, she got braces to fix her overbite. "I liked my overbite," Betty says. "If you look closely at the pictures, a lot of models have one." But Dan didn't like it. "I did it to please him. Besides, I decided I didn't want to be a fifty-year-old woman someday with lipstick on her teeth." The dentistry changed the entire shape of her face. "I never looked like me after that."

Meantime, Betty was always the same funny, lively, madcap, eager-to-please personality her Aunt Kay later described to the judge. She invariably made adults as well as children laugh with her zany antics: she carried fake bugs into fancy restaurants and planted them in her plate to watch the shock on the face of the maître d'. She would dress up elegantly and then stun strangers by suddenly grinning broadly, displaying a mouthful of gag fake teeth, stained with green gunk. Betty was, everybody agreed, always a hoot, so much fun.

And she was everybody's friend. If a birthday party was in order, she provided it. If a sympathetic ear was needed, she was there. Her energy and interests were seemingly boundless. In return, she asked for nothing. She never displayed a sad face, she seemed incapable of having a low mood, she never volunteered a personal problem. She was so consistently Happy Betty, old friends say, that she was a constant joy to be around.

But Betty wasn't happy. Privately, she was lonelier and more disillusioned than she had ever been—not because of money problems, not because of her heavy work load. But because of Dan. He never came home. He was drinking too much. He was working too much. She was a single parent. He took her for granted. He didn't love her.

Years later, the prosecutor would attempt to depict the Broderick union as a Marriage from Hell from the beginning—all due, in the D.A.'s scenario, to Betty's personality flaws. In reality, Dan and Betty Broderick were probably no different, at least not in those early days, from most other young couples caught in the pressures of premature parenthood and blindly trying to live out pre-assigned sex roles passed

57

on from an earlier generation. Certainly, they were no different from so many couples who, if they grow to wisdom, finally realize that the two sexes, by definition, are born to speak different emotional languages.

Theirs was in so many ways the oldest, weariest story ever told: Betty wanted intimacy, emotional bonding, sharing. Dan didn't know what the hell she was talking about, since he thought he was sharing just fine. At Christmas, he even dressed up like Santa Claus. Why was she nagging him after he worked his tail off all day? What did Bets want? He always called her by that pet name, even after he left her for Linda. Was he supposed to change diapers at night, too?

Why not? she thought. She was working harder than he was, without half the pleasure.

Her resentments festered, particularly when she brought his dinner home from the restaurant at night. "He never even said thanks ... he'd just be sitting there when I got home, reading a magazine or a brief, twirling his hair. He always twirled his hair, always on the right temple ..." Betty often mentioned that old habit of Dan's, pausing each time. Then she would rush on, angrier than ever. "And then he'd wait for me to heat it up and serve him. Never once did he offer to turn on the microwave himself. He just took it for granted that every woman should work all day and still have his meals ready, too."

But that was only the tip of the iceberg. His wardrobe was more elegant than ever—but she still didn't have a washer and dryer. "It was seven years after we were married before I ever got that goddamn washer and dryer! In his opinion, I was supposed to be happy to have a car to go to the laundromat, since I'd done it on a bus before."

She was tired. Now she had three children—Danny had been born only a few months earlier. But her pretty, happy-ever-after script was not in order. This was not the happy home, filled with two loving parents and happy, squealing babies that she had imagined.

"The guy was just a phantom. And I was a workhorse from five A.M., getting all the kids dressed and all the homework done and everybody off where they're supposed to go. Dan got up and tweezed his eyebrows and puffed his hair, and he never had anything to do with any of it. I was never allowed in the master bedroom while he was doing his toilette. He was like Louis XV, powdering his wigs. The guy primped himself like you wouldn't believe. There was never a wrinkle, a flake, a piece of dust. He always looked perfect."

She remembered all the cold Boston winters, the Tupperware routes, the ugly apartments, the welfare groceries, the nights she waited up alone with the babies, starved for adult company. Nothing had changed. Her list of IOUs was growing. And Dan wasn't delivering. If he had an excuse during their student days, he had none now.

Worse, he wouldn't even acknowledge his debt. He never touched her hand, or her hair. He never kissed her or brought her flowers. "For twenty years," she once remarked, sounding tired, "I tried to get that guy to say, 'Yes, I love you, and you look pretty, and I'm happy with you, and I'm proud of you, and you did a good job with the kids, or dinner, or the house, or anything.' But no matter what the hell I did, he always had the air of, 'Well, it could be better.' All I ever wanted from that damned man was five minutes of eye contact a day!"

She couldn't stand it. If she had felt out of place in her own family, she didn't fit into this one either, except as a housekeeper, nanny, an sometime consort.

And so they quarreled. More and more.

By the autumn of 1976, Betty was threatening to divorce him and go back to New York. But she really didn't want a divorce—for all her talk that was unthinkable. She wanted a cure. And finally she thought she had found it. One weekend in November, 1976, she persuaded Dan to participate in a church retreat for married couples. It was called a Marriage Encounter, the object was to solidify relationships, and part of the drill was for spouses to write letters to each other on assigned topics.

Dan's letters from that weekend provide a glimpse into the mind of young man of thirty-one who, by then, must have been exhausted himself with his own grueling efforts to live up to the expectations of everybody he had ever known, from his parents to the priests, from a demanding God to a demanding wife, not to mention the escalating needs of three small children.

What is most striking about his letters, more than his raw materialism, is Dan Broderick's chilling, near-prescient preoccupation with his own mortality. In response to an assigned question on death, he wrote:

"Dearest Bets, I want to go on living because I enjoy life ... I do not believe in any kind of extension of existence after death. Once I die the only thing that will be left of me anywhere will be the memories people still alive have of me. I want these memories to be warm, respectful, loving. I want people to miss me, to mourn my death, to wish I were still alive, to wonder what I would have said and done in a situation if I were still around ..." He went on to say that he was sometimes "disappointed in myself for [my] shortcomings ..." But this "disappointment isn't too intense because I firmly believe that, given time, I will become a good husband, father, etc.. I tell myself that I've got to earn a decent living, establish myself as a lawyer, acquire certain necessary possessions, before I can indulge the luxury of being an attentive, thoughtful person."

At the same time, he worried that he might be "engaging in self-delusion ... Experience suggests that unless I change my attitudes now, I never will have time to be and do the most important things. One worldly goal will unplan another until it's too late. You will either have left or have resigned yourself to living a separate life with me, and the kids will have gone on their own way, feeling bitter and frustrated at having never known their father (I went thru that myself several years ago and it's miserable)."

He then critiqued his own lifelong tendency to postpone personal relationships until another day. He remembered thinking, during his school years, that "my personal relationships would get the attention they deserved after graduation." And now that he was working, "I have always thought about next summer, next year, after

I make partner, after I am earning enough money to be able to afford trips, boats, etc.."

But he couldn't fault himself, any more than he could help himself. "Even now I believe that our lives together will be much happiness when money ceases being a problem," he wrote. "It will enable us to do a lot of things like travel to Europe that will be shared experiences we will, I hope, enjoy and never forget. I want to be able to take you and the kids to South Bend every fall for a game without thinking twice about it ... to buy a piano if Kim wants one, to buy you a ring, a motorbike, a microwave, a camera, whatever you want when you want it. I honestly believe that having this ability will make me happy and secure and will make me a more loving and more lovable person."

But the pressures of passing time were weighing increasingly on him. He worried that "I may not make it before it's too late. I feel lately that time is running out on me ..." He recalled how he used to joke around in school that "the worst thing that could happen to me would be for me to finish medical school, finish law school, pass the bar, and then be killed ... If I were told that I had a short time left to live ... I'd feel that I had wasted my whole life. Everything I've done so far has been in preparation for the good life I aspire to ... to be successful at getting ahead in this world ... I want to make it—for myself, for you, and for the kids ... I have made many sacrifices ... I have made you sacrifice as well, perhaps even more than me. I want time to pay you back, to make it up to you, to reward you for all the deprivations. I want you to be happy, content, secure. To feel like the sacrifices were worth it ..."

It was for all these reasons, he said, that he had been thinking so much lately about going into practice for himself. "I want the financial security now so that I can get on with the important things in life ... I always tell myself that what I'm doing now, the way we're living now, is just a temporary situation ... To die now would be a tragedy ... especially if I haven't at least reached my goal of material success."

In sum, he had a lot of unfinished business. "I want to be a responsive sensitive husband and father. I want to be the type of person who will be genuinely missed when he dies ... but," he wrote, "I need time."

From there, he turned his attention to the nature of the weekend Catholic retreat they were attending. He wanted his wife to understand "why I have to roll my eyes once in a while ... The personalities of some of the leaders are distracting the hell out of me. How can I listen to and pay attention to a guy who gets choked up talking about his relationship with the Catholic Church? As far as I'm concerned, the Catholic Church is an utter irrelevancy, a meaningless show perpetuated by a lot of simple-minded, unenlightened weaklings who can't cope with life as it really is and who feel compelled to construct an elaborate network of fantasies to deal with realities that any strong, self-respecting person can handle rationally. I just have no respect for these people. Furthermore, they are basically uncool, unfashionable. I think we're above the level that they're operating on ..." Even so, he concluded, he was glad they had attended and wrote "I do believe you deserve every bit as much love, consideration and sensitivity as all of these women get from their husbands combined! I'll try. Love, Dan."

And, in part of another letter, in answer to the question: How are we going to share our couple love?

"... You and I (especially I) are private persons ... As far as I am concerned, this has been a personal encounter between you and me Although I have enjoyed it very much, I won't be advertising it or even discussing it with anyone else. As for changing our social habits, we pretty much do everything together already, now that I have stopped playing football and going out with the boys on Fridays ... As for things like PTA meetings, school open houses, etc., I hope to start attending them with you ..."

Betty's letters, by contrast, reflect the frustrations of a thwarted romantic, a twenty-nine-year-old housewife whose priorities were dramatically different from those of her husband.

"Darling Dan," she wrote. "The opposite of love is indifference. We've never hated each other, but we have, or I feel you have, been guilty of the opposite of love, and it really hurts ... I love you and hope we can accommodate each other better. One of the big hurdles I'm up against is your refusal to need to share. I really think ALL people do, but you're saying you don't. This has got to be a mutual thing of fulfilling each other's needs, but you keep saying you don't have these needs—which I believe—but in a way feel sorry for you that you don't open yourself up to some wonderful happiness. I think your self-image is so guarded that you're not living life and enjoying it to the fullest. Love, Bets."

And, in another letter, addressing a topic sentence concerning the differences between wants and needs:

"... I've been pestering [you] for a long time that I NEED [underlined eight times] a vacation. What I meant was to get you away from TV and work and Bartolotta and boys, to get you back to ME. This [weekend] has sort of fulfilled that, but I still need to have a family time. It could happen in our own home, if we would turn off everything else and just be a loving family for two days or a week or two weeks, without any worldly obligations or duties for any of us. It would be so relaxing and worthwhile and we all NEED [underlined seven times] it.

"Maybe something you can relate to better is we NEED a sofa—nothing else for our house ... There's lots we want ... but for now we NEED a sofa so you and I can be physically close in the evenings and share the day's events and feelings so we go to bed in love. Not what we have now. By the time we go to bed, I'm full of RESENTMENT for the lack of closeness and communication during the evening—how can I make love to that?"

In another essay, critiquing herself, she wrote, "I'm pretty, people like me, I'm a good mother, I'm a good teacher, I'm funny, I'm active." On the negative side, "Too demanding of myself and everybody else, too high-pressure." And, she added, in an essay called "Who Am I?" that "Betty Broderick is ... always busy doing something but never really does anything perfectly. She loves kids but feels trapped by them all the time ... She was never taught or shown how to keep house and do the wash and feels incompetent at it ..." She also wrote that "I am an awful listener—you've told me a hundred times. I really want to work at being a better listener for you ... [but] I don't

61

feel you want to tell me anything ... I try to be open with you in all areas. But you don't seem to be willing to open yourself up. I always feel like you're weighing your words for one reason or another." She complained, too, that Dan didn't include her in his decisions: "Example: the way you pick out a new car first, then tell me you've gotten it. I like to share in the excitement of the decision to get it. You never discuss YOUR plans for OUR house ahead of time ..."

Then, back to Betty the sentimentalist: "Do you remember how touched and thrilled I was with the gold charm [which he gave her] that says, 'I love you more than yesterday, less than tomorrow'? I believe you were sincere with those sentiments then. That charm is probably my most treasured possession. I cling to it hoping that it's still true or will come again."

In answer to a question on "how will you share your couple love?" she wrote: "I hope we will share our couple love with our wonderful children first. They need to feel close to us and we will enjoy being closer to them ..." She also hoped that their own loving joy would serve as an example to others—particularly the crowd at Gray, Cary. "Patti Monahan speaks of the Gray, Cary 'sickness,' how contagious it is. Warmth, happiness, contentment, and love are just as contagious. I hope we become the carriers of this new strain of disease."

But, at the same time, it was clear she wasn't optimistic, that she was still at least toying with the idea of leaving him.

"... You ARE the most important person I have in the whole universe, bar absolutely none, and I'd be lost without you. Even if we do separate, you will never be replaced. We have shared too much ... [but] I feel like I'm ... speeding along, wasting time, not seeing what is ahead—anticipating a terrible thing to happen to us at any second. Losing touch with the world. Unable to cling to anything secure."

It was the way they were drifting apart emotionally that frightened her most, she wrote: "I feel concerned that you are falling prey to such trivial 'strokes,' as you call them, from people who mean nothing to you. You react to the smallest thing. [But] when people that mean everything to you try to give you 'strokes,' you slough them off and don't react ... Trivial strokes are fun, but I can't do without the REAL ones. You seem to think they're interchangeable ... We used to marvel that we thought the same thought at the same second ... [T]he first moment I saw you, I liked you. Spoke to you, it stayed. Wrote to you and it grew. Dated you, it only got better and better. No one else I'd ever met before or since was as right as you ..."

But she was too unhappy to continue this way:

"I love you and want to share all that I am with you, but I also need to be loved by you and feel that I know everything there is to know about you like no one else on earth ever had or ever will. Every day I live with you I want to get a little bit closer to that goal ... striving toward the Impossible Dream to give my life meaning and worth. I don't feel anything like that now ... The number one thing I loved about you [in the beginning] was how much you LOVED ME and showed it. You know [all the other reasons]. In fact, I love everything about you now as I did then, EXCEPT that you don't show your love for me anymore."

62

She ended on a note of optimism, laced with the same pervasive futility. "Wouldn't it be fun to redo our marriage, just the way WE WANT it, like it should have been the first time? Let's really think about it. The ceremony, the guest list, the celebration ... holding hands, looking into each other—appropriate verses that really say what we mean. Such sincerity that we shut out everything else in the world and really listen and honor ..." She also wanted them both to start devoting ten minutes a day to writing each other love letters again, just as they had done in their courtship. "Writing and receiving love letters was a tremendously important factor in the development of our love. I think we both enjoyed it. . . [and] I want to know that I'm at least worth ten minutes. Now I don't feel that you even think I'm worth that."

But, she added dismally, "I honestly can't believe you'll do it. You're too tough, too cool, too hard to write a love letter every day and let me know you care."

With that, Dan and Betty Broderick, both briefly buoyed by their weekend encounter with emotions, both filled with good intentions and new vows, returned to La Jolla for several more years of the same old pain.

Chapter 6

As Good as It Gets

By 1978, Dan was earning about $32,500 per year at Gray, Cary. "But he was doing the work of three lawyers," Betty says. "Finally, I said to him, 'Hey, fool, they are not paying you enough!'." He agreed, but was nervous about going into practice on his own. Even now, Betty is proud of her role in persuading her husband that he could succeed. "Dan was a real doofus when it came to personal relationships—he didn't know people at all, but, as an attorney, nobody was better. He never went near an opponent until he was holding all the cards. He always told me that the first rule of the game was 'Never negotiate until you're sitting on their chest.'"

But it wasn't only financial ambition that motivated her. She was also trying to save her marriage. 'I'm a smart woman, and I knew trouble when I saw it. I wanted to get him away from those drunken oafs at Gray, Cary. He would work fifteen hours a day and drink away the rest. He was drinking, drinking all weekend, all in the name of getting ahead. He didn't eat, he didn't sleep, and he was always hung over. And he wouldn't call home because of peer pressures. He once said [Dave] Monahan told younger attorneys that 'Anybody who calls home is a wimp'."

The next few months provided a glimpse into what the Broderick marriage might have been, had these two been consistently interested in building a partnership based on mutual involvement in each other's careers. For the first time, Betty was a welcome participant in Dan's world. She took charge of decorating his new office. At night, they sat in the living room together, studying fabric swatches and paint shades, calculating costs and enjoying the thrill of what was the most exciting adventure of their married lives. In the end, she created a showcase of expensive taste far beyond their means. Dan worried about it, "But I told him exactly what he had always told me, back at Harvard—'You have to look successful to be successful'." And he respected her judgment. In the end, she says wistfully, "He had the prettiest office in town." They charged it all on credit cards.

But that was the end of their togetherness. Afterward, they returned to their separate worlds—and hers held little interest for Dan since it meant only one thing: babies. By then, she was pregnant again, for the tenth time, sick as ever, varicose veins throbbing. She was too ill even to supervise the finishing touches on his office, much less attend the champagne opening.

She also decided that Rhett was enough, and her doctor agreed. After his delivery, she had her tubes tied and her varicose veins repaired. She was thirty-two.

She was exhilarated by her new freedom. For the first time in Betty Broderick's life, sex would no longer carry with it the automatic penalty of pregnancy and pain.

And, this time, Dan didn't cry. He didn't even object.

His new practice was soon thriving. Because of his medical background he was able quickly to determine which were the most promising malpractice cases, and, as his reputation grew, he increasingly accepted none other. Eventually, even settlements in the low six figures seldom interested him.

Those were heady days. At first, "We used to go to the La Valencia dinner to celebrate when he won a $1 million settlement," says Betty, laughing. "But finally we were there three times in one week, so we decided that it wasn't worth making a big deal over, that maybe we should move it up to $10 million."

The payoff was at last at hand. Their struggling days were done. During the next four years, "We had a million good times," she says. "I liked to go to all the parties and legal functions—it was absolutely fun for a long time."

They were the perfect couple. Although in later years their friends would wonder who Betty and Dan Broderick had really been, to end in such bloody fashion, the Brodericks were the envy of everyone who knew them at the time. She shone with energy and high voltage wit, he dazzled with his quiet, wry charm. Betty wanted to be liked, and she was, by sheer force of her will. Dan was liked, whether he wanted to be or not, attracting by the pure sheen of success. "They were everything we all wanted to be," said one attorney's wife from those days. "They looked about as good as it gets."

Sometimes they even wore matching clothes. At the 1984 Blackstone Ball, for instance, long after their lives had turned into a private battlefield, Betty wore a strapless dress (her first ever) of red satin and black velvet, to match Dan's long black cape with its scarlet lining. In her private photo collection is one particularly stunning picture of them together, she so tall and striking in her slinky, form-fitting gown, he so debonair with his cape casually flung back to display its lining. Behind them, on an ebony piano, sat a vase of red roses, which Betty had arranged just so, providing the final, perfect accent. No detail ever eluded her. Only the strain in both their faces could not be hidden.

Like most people unaccustomed to big money, the Brodericks spent tentatively at first. He bought her a lynx jacket and a diamond necklace—but only as holiday gifts. His first big treat for himself was a flashy kit sports car laden with chrome fenders and old-fashioned tailpipes, which he spotted in an airport lobby and bought on a credit card.

They advanced their part-time Mexican housekeeper, Maria, to five days a week. By 1980, Betty even acquired a summertime "au pair"—a young student from England who performed menial chores and baby-sat the children in exchange for room and board.

The Brodericks also began traveling. In 1981, they took their first trip to Europe with Kim, although, says Betty, "We still lived like students doing Europe on $5 a day, staying in hostels and cheap hotels—but we had a ball." They also fell into a routine of holiday ski trips, first to Park City, Utah, then later to Keystone, Colorado, where Dan bought a condominium in partnership with his brother Larry. One summer they also took a cruise to Cancun, Mexico.

And they began searching for a home more appropriate to their grand new station in life. No more tracts. Mr. and Mrs. Daniel T. Broderick III were at last about to move across the hills, to the sea.

But, behind closed doors, they still quarreled, and for all the same old reasons. Nothing had changed since their Marriage Encounter weekend except that, now, Dan and Betty Broderick were no longer typical of most other young couples under ordinary pressures. Instead, they were now even further distanced from each other by the impending scent of extraordinary success, of even more fabulous riches just around the corner—which made it all the easier for both of them to shelve the personal problems for just a little while longer. Only a few years more. Then they would deal with their private discontents. Tomorrow. It was just as Dan had written in his Marriage Encounter letters—except now, Bet was buying into the waiting game, too. She became more interested in the price of a Mercedes than in Dan's staggering annual income tax, more focused on the menu for her next dinner party than in trying to woo Dan into spending a Saturday at the beach with her and the kids.

But she still felt overworked and unappreciated, and so did he. She nagged, he withdrew; she sulked, he stayed out later. The only real difference was that their quarrels were now less constructive than ever.

Once when they took a weekend vacation to a nearby mountain resort for example, she flew into a rage because, as soon as they arrived, she says, "He headed straight for the bar for a drink, and then got his bathing suit on and went to sit by the pool. He was acting just like a bachelor, leaving it to me to unpack the boogie boards, the skis, the clothes. He was still treating me like the maid." She was so angry she drove back to San Diego by herself. Let him get himself and the kids home as best he could.

At the same time, Dan was hardening, too. According to the later trial testimony of his daughters, his temper was always as explosive as Betty's—he was just slower to erupt, while she was more spontaneous. In the midst of an argument, Betty might throw something at him—for instance, a ketchup bottle once. Another time, she locked him out of the house when he came home late after a night of drinking by barricading the garage door with one of his skis; he spent the night in the car. Dan, by contrast, was more inclined to take his temper out on inanimate objects, according to his daughters. Once he smashed a defective lawnmower to smithereens with a hammer; another time he flung his sons' empty aquarium off the balcony; on another occasion he ripped a sliding closet door off its track and pitched it over the balcony. But the only living creatures he apparently ever attacked were the family dogs. He kicked them when they got underfoot.

Neither of the Brodericks apparently ever deliberately hit each other. Although Betty's defense attorney would later insist that Dan had given her at least one black eye, Betty herself insisted that it was only an accident. Nor did the children ever witness physical violence between their parents. Physical battery was never a viable aspect of the Broderick case.

As the years wore on, their quarrels increasingly centered around Dan's drinking. Betty's plan to get him away from the Gray, Cary crowd when he went independent had proven a resounding failure. Finally, like most people who don't understand the allure of alcohol themselves, she lost all tolerance and came to see her husband as a clinically sick alcoholic who needed to be committed to some fashionable drying-out tank. Long after she was in jail for killing him, Betty would continue to speak of her failed marriage as a disaster that might have been avoided, had Daniel Broderick only discovered the Alcoholics Anonymous Big Book.

She also began to aggressively detest many of his best friends, blaming them for Dan's drinking. In her eyes, Brian Monaghan was the chief ringleader, and he was banned from her dinner parties, no matter how much Dan liked him. Nearly as revolting to her was Mike Neil, whose battlefield heroics didn't impress Betty in the least. Instead, all she remembers today is how repulsive he was when several couples once went to Tijuana in a van, in the late seventies, to celebrate Neil's birthday. "Everybody was disgustingly drunk, and he [Neil] stuck his skinny, spitty tongue in my ear. Yuk!!"

Neil remembers that trip differently. "She was such a bad sport. She just sat there, disapproving of everybody else having fun," he says. "I felt so sorry for Dan—he was trying to have a good time, but she was such a wet blanket. She wouldn't even pretend for the sake of the rest of us. The poor guy should've left the bitch years before he did."

Ironically, of all Dan's closest men friends, it was only Brian Monaghan who showed any real compassion for Betty after the killings. Although he believed, like the others, that Betty was driven by jealousy and that "She thought she was the center of the universe," Monaghan had sympathy for her, too. "I think she just never felt loved, either by her parents or by Dan." She was like a child, he thought. "And kids need a dependable link of love. But Betty didn't have that ... not with her family, or with Dan, either. She just had her social structure to support her ... and when that eroded, she just fell apart."

And, although Monaghan didn't think either Dan or Linda were being deliberately malicious, he also agreed that maybe Dan had been too tough on Betty. "He was determined to discipline her, control her, like you would an unruly child ... It's a masculine sort of deal," he said, sipping an ale at Reidy's. "But you gotta take a stand!" In hindsight, Dan had obviously miscalculated, but, Monaghan added, shrugging, melancholy, "That's the Irish Catholic male for you. That's just how we Catholics do it. How long has it been—two thousand years? And we're still saying women can't be priests because they don't have peckers?"

Not until years after Dan left her did Betty develop any sympathy for a man with a hangover, when she finally got drunk herself—for the first time in her life, she says. She did it on a night out with girlfriends, on five glasses of Kir.

"And I went home and fell down on the bedroom floor, and I remember laying there giggling, because I had finally figured out why Dan Broderick was always doing the goddamn Turtle. That's the natural state of a drunk—on your back, giggling. And I felt like such utter shit the next morning. I said to myself, 'Now I understand why Dan

Broderick was always laying out in the backyard on Saturday with his wine bottle snarling at all of us, giving us those 'Drop Dead Eat Shit' looks."

But, in those earlier years, money was always the central source of friction. No story better reflects the old saw that money can't buy happiness than the saga of Dan and Betty Broderick. Now that they finally had it in abundance, they bickered constantly over how best to spend it. Dan thought Betty was spending too much altogether. She thought he had one helluva nerve, bitching about her expenses, since she had worked just as hard for their success as he had. It was so insulting. How dare he treat her like a child on an allowance? Those nerves were still raw years later in their divorce trial, when Dan puckishly lectured her one final time:

"Until the late seventies or early eighties, you were responsible in the way you spent and managed money ... you would adhere to a budget," he told her. But after that, he testified, she had become "grossly irresponsible ... you just wouldn't live within what I thought any reasonable person would consider reasonable expenditures."

Betty, in turn, was increasingly annoyed at Dan's spending patterns. In 1979, she had gotten a real estate license because "I thought it could be my sort of new home job. And I had a talent for real estate, an eye—I was going to help make us even richer." But Dan consistently ignored her advice. Instead, he invested steadily with his brother Larry in Colorado properties—often without consulting her, as he later admitted in divorce court. He simply didn't value her opinions.

The Brodericks couldn't even agree on which new house to buy. He wanted "a big mansion with an acre of lawn around it," says Betty. She wanted to live in La Jolla. But Dan was more interested in other parts of San Diego, such as Point Loma, with its spectacular sea cliffs, or the island of Coronado, miles away. They never would resolve the dispute. For the next five years, despite his escalating income, they remained at Coral Reef, gridlocked, literally until the day he walked out, each one still blaming the other for the impasse.

One good glimpse of life in the Broderick household in 1980 comes from their au pair, a young English girl, who wrote a series of letters home to her parents that summer.

Betty was very nice and considerate, but, the girl complained, she was always off to some school or charity event. Little Rhett, the girl wrote, "cries whenever she leaves the room, because she is not there enough." She also complained that the family never had a sit-down meal together because Mr. Broderick was always working late. Too often, she told her parents, Mrs. Broderick would simply order in pizza or Chinese before departing to some social function.

The girl disliked Dan intensely. He was "so cold and unfriendly," she said—except for one night when he had found her alone in the Jacuzzi. Then, she said, he had been too friendly, suggesting they go horseback riding the next day, "and he would tell everyone he had left his old lady." Also, she wrote in youthful disapproval, he made Betty cry because he was "always out tippling with the lads."

In another letter, she remarked that Betty seemed intimidated and afraid around Dan. Hers was an observation that others would later echo. "At about three o'clock every afternoon," recalls a former neighbor, Wilma Engel, "Betty would just change completely. She would stop laughing and panic and run around the house, picking up all the children's stuff because she said Dan hated to have it underfoot. When he was around, she was completely a different person, so much more quiet and subdued. She seemed afraid of him."

The truth was, of course, always in the eye of the beholder. "Dan was a different person around Betty," said his friend Laurel Summers. "She was always so critical, nagging. He seemed to have a hard time even smiling when she was around. After he met Linda, he was so much looser, warmer. That's when I realized I just hadn't ever seen Dan happy before."

Betty continued to threaten him with divorce, although she says today that she never meant it. "Sure, I said stuff like that all the time," she said later, wearily. "Sometimes I even thought of actually doing it. But it was never more than a passing fantasy. Where was I going to go with four children?" By then, too, she had seen her first divorce up close. Dave Monahan had left Patti—and the sight of this lonely, aging woman cast adrift gave Betty Broderick the shivers. It would never happen to her. Never.

For his own part, Dan Broderick apparently took Betty's threats more seriously—or so he said years later, after he had left her. "There were periods of time she was [happy with me]," he once told a reporter. "But there were demands for divorce hundreds of times ... She tells our children that we had a happy, healthy, blissful marriage until I went crazy when I turned forty ... [T]hat's just pure fiction ... When we'd been married a year or so, told me she had gone to a lawyer. I was in my first year at Harvard Law School. It was 1970 ... It may have been an attention-getting device, and it may not have been. I honestly don't know to this day."

During the next years, Dan only became more prominent, more successful in his world, and so did Betty, in hers.

He grew ever more handsome as time passed. Gone was the nerd of their student years, the skinny young man with the bobbing Adam's apple. He took speech lessons, and had some minor surgery on his nose. Now with his blow-dried hair, his new contact lenses, his wonderful smile, his fuller face, Dan Broderick was a man any woman would look twice at—even if he hadn't been a respected millionaire.

Betty, meantime, was at home doing what affluent young wives of prominent men in charming little communities like La Jolla usually do—which is to say, virtually nothing to incorporate herself info the large world beyond La Jolla's sunny shores. Always a voracious reader, her den was a clutter of books, magazines, and journals, ranging from the *Reader's Digest* to *American Scholar*. But they served mainly to make her the most interesting dinner conversationalist at any gathering. Otherwise, she spent her days fussing over the children's music lessons and soccer games, planning menus and centerpieces for her "gorgeous" weekly dinner parties and her "fabulous" Christmas parties, and issuing daily orders to the gardeners and the maid, while she thumbed through fashion catalogs over coffee. An early riser, she sometimes began placing mail-order calls to the East Coast at six A.M. for everything from crystal trinkets to clothes and candy.

By now, both Brodericks had become serious shoppers. She developed a taste for designer clothes, and so did he. The main difference between them in those days was his affection for larger objects—houses, cars, real estate. He became a serious collector of sports cars and Colorado properties. She, meantime, enjoyed buying smaller items for her home, the children, or herself. For years Betty had been saving clippings of items she would one day buy. For instance, "Long before I ever had a house, I saved a clipping from *Architectural Digest* on Bill Blass's personal swimming pool. I thought it was so beautiful—navy blue tile with brass lions' heads. I always thought if I ever had a pool, I wanted one just like that."

Now, the Bill Blass clipping was on the top of her files, not the bottom. Dansk flatware was another thing she had coveted since college. Soon now.

But, as she had done since their college days, she continued to turn all money matters over to Dan. He paid the bills, balanced the family and corporate budgets. "I didn't do bills," she once remarked from jail with a lingering pride. "I didn't have any interest in money, beyond spending it. I never had any idea of what we even owned." At times, toward the end before he left her, after the hard times had ended and the good times began to roll, Betty felt positively royal.

And so there she sat, in those years, as so many wives of tenure do, blindly pursuing her own course toward disaster. While Dan was out in the world, wheeling and dealing, Betty was just one more smart woman whose library led with Neiman Marcus catalogues and hundreds of children's books.

But, according to the rules that these two had laid down, she was certainly holding her own. She looked great, she dressed exquisitely, she was a perfect hostess, and she was the most active mother anybody had ever seen—she had transferred her child psychology training, and her schoolteacher aspirations, not only to her own children but to all their classmates as well. Children were her career.

And, like her own parents, she was always absorbed in education. She dreamed of what fine colleges her children would one day attend. Meantime, she made sure they were enrolled at Francis Parker or Bishops, two of the most exclusive private schools in San Diego. There was no lesson, no opportunity, no experience they weren't offered. Violin classes, summer camps, dance lessons, karate. She was room mother at school; she spent hours working on class projects. She staged Christmas parties for children at her home that became almost legendary. Her decorations, games, and food were close to art. She had Santa Clauses, mimes, music troupes, puppet shows. She thought like children do at Christmastime. Her parties were magic.

Most of her adult dinner parties also included children. And she always took special care to make sure that the evening was as easy as possible for the mothers. She often served shish kebabs, which she would grill and then pull off the sticks to pile info large bowls. "That way, if the kids didn't like vegetables, they could pick around them, and the meat was already all cut up, so Mom didn't have to spend half the dinner cutting up the kids' meat. I had this down to a science." At the same time, she had begun extending her social skills to include elegant little omelette brunches just for the mothers. She hired chefs and sometimes string quartets, her backyard tables were graced with fresh flowers, she served the finest champagne, and her invitations were always dispatched on the most expensive engraved Tiffany stationery. Just like her mother taught her.

She also began to escalate her charity activities. Years later, amid the hundreds of clippings she had saved over the years, were pictures of Betty from the society pages, with and without Dan. At about the same time, she changed churches, switching from the tiny Catholic Church in La Jolla, Mary Star by the Sea, to the larger, popular La Jolla Presbyterian Church She did it, she said later, because the Presbyterians had more programs for children. But, too, she remarked, "It's amazing that in a community as cosmopolitan, as sophisticated, as La Jolla, at least half the people who attend the Catholic church are the Mexican maids!" One more time, Betty had done the socially correct thing. By then, Dan was so removed from the church that he didn't care one way or the other.

By late 1982, the Brodericks were united, if in little else, in their ongoing house hunt. By 1983, they were also bound by their tax returns, for, in that year, at least in the eyes of the IRS, Dan and Betty Broderick had become bona fide millionaires.

That was also the year her world began to fall apart, and her descent began. She was thirty-six.

Part Three

Betty, Dan and Linda

Chapter 7

Mirror, Mirror, on the Wall

In later years, she would remember exactly the first words she ever heard him utter about Linda Kolkena. She thinks it was sometime in early 1983. They were at a party, when Betty overheard Dan remark to a friend, "Isn't she beautiful?"

No big deal, maybe, coming from a different man. But "Dan Broderick never said things like that about women," says Betty. "He was never a womanizer, he had no sense of himself as sexual at all."

And so, her antennae went up. With those three words, Dan Broderick had innocently tapped that reservoir of instinct, of danger alert that all women understand. "It set off a bell in my head. It was like everyone else in the room got quiet, and Dan was booming. All I remember is it was so shocking to my brain."

That night she asked him "as casually as I could" whom he had been talking about. He blinked at her, at first uncomprehending, she recalls, then remembered. Oh, he said, just some new girl at the office. A receptionist. He went back to his reading, and she put it on the back burner of her mind.

But she didn't forget—because she also remembers vividly the first time she ever saw Linda Kolkena at a social function. "I was shocked that this was the girl he thought was so beautiful. She was just another skinny little bimbo with a gap between her front teeth. She had all this hair, all pouffed up like Bridgitte Bardot, bobby pins and the whole bit, not a streak of blond in it. I was, to say the least, underwhelmed." It never occurred to her to speak to Kolkena. "Why should I lower myself?" she asks. "She was obviously just another nineteen-year-old airhead looking for a rich husband. She couldn't hold a candle to me. I was prettier, I was smarter, I was classier. It never occurred to me that Dan would be stupid enough to throw his family away for his office girl. It was just too much of a cliché to believe."

But, inside, she was believing.

That summer she took the children on a five-week camping trip throughout the Northwest. Dan flew up to visit them one weekend—and, Betty says, he was colder and more detached than ever. They argued. Steaming, she drove him back to the airport and told him to get lost.

When she returned to La Jolla several weeks later, in time to attend a wedding in Newport Beach, it was to find an altogether different Dan Broderick awaiting her. This one was not silent, withdrawn, and unreadable. Instead, this new Dan was hostile, critical, and stunningly blunt.

"On the drive to Newport, he told me that he was bored with his life, bored with me, that he didn't love me anymore. He said I was old, fat, ugly, and boring," she says. That is probably an exaggeration, although she would later repeat it in court, and cry on the witness stand as she did. Either way, it was Betty Broderick's clear impression of where her marriage now stood. Her husband was either having an affair, or thinking about it, with the office bimbo. She says she asked him directly if another woman was involved. But he denied it. She didn't believe him, even then. But she was happy with the lie. Never mind, she told herself. It's just a midlife crisis. It would pass. Long after she had shot Linda Kolkena dead, Betty would still be referring to her as "a nineteen-year-old bimbo without even a high school education—but, I have to give her credit, she pulled off every sleaze girl's dream."

Linda Bernadette Kolkena was, in fact, a high school graduate, and when she first met Dan Broderick she was not nineteen years old but twenty-one. She was twenty-seven when he married her, and twenty-eight when she died six months later.

Unlike Betty or Dan, she did not come from a background of ease or high expectations. She was the youngest of four children born to Arnoldus Johanes and Everdina Bernadetta Kolkena, Dutch immigrants who came to the United States in the fifties and settled in Salt Lake City. Her father, now retired, worked for thirty years as a freight handler for a trucking company until one of his lungs collapsed. Throughout most of his working life, A.J. Kolkena was lucky to earn $16,000 in a year, says Linda's older sister, Margaret (Maggie) Seats, thirty-six, a personnel counselor, house-wife, and mother in Portland, Oregon.

Theirs was a small, clean home filled with love, says Seats, but no luxuries. The children got fifty-cent allowances a week. It was a big occasion when a freight box broke, yielding such goodies as rock candy which her father was then allowed to bring home to his family. That is a how they often got their Christmas trees, too—from the broken debris of whatever was left upon the loading docks. Family vacations were car camping trips to parks a few hours from Salt Lake. Family recreation after meals often centered around a globe her mother kept on the kitchen table. "We'd test each other on world capitals," says Maggie, who remembers her mother as a gentle, intelligent woman—and the only female in her patriarchal Dutch family who was allowed to complete high school.

Her parents, both devout Roman Catholics, were so determined to send their children to church schools that A.J. Kolkena worked for years as a part-time janitor at St. Vincent de Paul's parish school to help defray tuition. For a while, the Kolkena family even lived over the bishop's office, rent-free in exchange for her father's handyman labors. But, by the time Linda was in third grade, Kolkena could no longer afford even reduced fees, so all his children turned in their brown-and-white checkered school uniforms and switched to public schools. They cried at the dinner table that night, Maggie remembers, and so did her father.

Meantime, it remained a far more rigidly religious household than that of either the Brodericks or Bisceglia clans. Four prayers were recited at every meal, says Maggie, and Christmas was observed as a strictly religious holiday, not a festivity. The Kolkena youngsters were never taught to even believe in such fancies as Santa Claus. Instead, Christmas meant midnight Mass, followed by a traditional candlelight Dutch breakfast of cold cuts, cheese, and bread, where her father would sit at the head of the table and read aloud to his family from the Bible. Gifts were given, but they were always modest. A.J. Kolkena apparently also practiced what he preached

76

about Christian charity: His first remark, upon hearing that his youngest child had been shot to death, says Maggie Seats, was, "That poor woman [Betty] needs help."

After a two-year battle with breast cancer, Everdina Kolkena died at age thirty-six. Maggie was then sixteen, Linda eleven. After six months of mourning, Arnoldus Kolkena, in formal, courtly Old World fashion, went into Salt Lake's substantial Dutch community in search of a proper mother for his children. His new wife was an upright Dutch widow, a neighbor lady the family had known for years—and who, in another sad twist of fate, is now also struggling with the same form of breast cancer that killed Everdina Kolkena. Life has not been kind to the Kolkena women.

The Kolkena children took odd jobs, as soon as they were old enough. While Linda was still in high school, she worked as a waitress, a clerk at a sporting goods store, then as a telephone operator at a law firm.

The premium in the Kolkena family was never on higher education or careers, at least not after their mother died, says Maggie. "Our expectation was to grow up and have children ... You worked to work, not to have a career. We weren't cultured that way. The man would always be the breadwinner." Only Maggie went on to graduate from college. Both brothers enlisted in the military and built careers there. As soon as Linda had graduated from high school, with average grades, she applied to become a Delta Airlines flight attendant, based in Atlanta.

Maggie tried to talk Linda into college but failed. "All Linda ever really wanted to be was a wife and mother ... She was the kind of person who walked into restaurants and asked to hold other people's babies. She was very traditional." In fact, says Seats, Linda was everybody's favorite neighborhood baby-sitter during her adolescent years. Just like Betty.

There were so many parallels between the two women Dan Broderick married. In later years, old friends of Dan and Betty would remark on how much the two women even looked alike—right down to their teeth. Like Betty with her overbite, Linda's teeth were her only real physical imperfection—she had a slight gap in front, until, friends say, Dan persuaded her to have it fixed. He even sent her to Betty's dentist, according to Betty.

"It was heart-stopping," said one old friend who attended both of Dan's weddings. "The woman walking down that aisle was Betty, except fifteen years younger."

When Linda was accepted for the Delta training program, the note placed in her records said: "Attractive. Very mature for her age. Appears and acts much more intelligent than her academic background indicates ... Educational background is limited and may be a problem. However, she is a good candidate."

But Linda's career with Delta had barely begun before it ended. Hired in June, 1981, she was off her six-month probationary status for only two months before being fired in February, 1982, for "conduct unbecoming a Delta employee." The specifics were these, according to records later subpoenaed for Betty's trial by the defense:

Linda and three other flight attendants, all of them off duty, were flying from Atlanta to Salt Lake City for a ski weekend, when they became involved with two obviously drunken male passengers. All six were sitting in the back rows of the airplane. According to on-duty attendants who lodged the complaint against Linda, she sat on one man's lap while he caressed her thighs; she was also loud and used vulgar language; then she went into a toilet with the man for several minutes, causing other passengers to joke about how this couple was "joining the Mile High Club." When the supervising stewardess on duty told Linda to shape up or else, she apologized, but gave them a false name and, according to the complaint, returned to her seat—only to continue openly smooching the same passenger.

In her later appeal to Delta management, Linda admitted that she had used a false name and bad language. But she denied taking the man into the toilet. Instead, she said—and her three friends backed her up—she had been sick all day with a queasy stomach and diarrhea, and the man had only come into the toilet with her to see if she was okay. And the reason she had been sitting with her legs across his lap, she said, was because he refused to get out of her seat. She was trying "not to be rude to a paying Delta passenger."

"It was these gentleman's [sic] first flight on Delta so we felt a need to put on our P.R. hats," wrote one of her three friends in her defense.

Whatever the real truth of the incident, this much is clear: pretty young Linda Kolkena, then not even twenty-one, at last liberated from the stern vigilance of her Dutch Catholic household, was having a little too much fun that day. But Delta was unforgiving.

From there, Linda worked briefly for an Atlanta attorney. Since she had never learned to type, she was a Girl Friday, a receptionist who also performed some semi-paralegal chores. Understandably, she didn't advertise the reasons for her dismissal from Delta. It is unclear whether even Dan Broderick knew. In a eulogy for the *San Diego Daily Transcript* three days after her death, her former boss, Atlanta attorney Don C. Keenan, wrote that Linda "wanted to do more with her life than be a flight attendant—with all due respect to flight attendants ... She was just wonderful with people." Keenan encouraged her to attend law school, he said.

Instead, Linda followed a boyfriend on a job transfer to San Diego. That relationship ended shortly thereafter, but she remained in San Diego—working as a pool receptionist in the same commercial building where Dan Broderick had his offices.

If Dan thought Linda was beautiful at first sight, she was apparently equally dazzled by the dynamic, handsome young attorney with the killer smile and droll wit who passed her desk each day. "She thought he was a god," a friend later said.

She hadn't been at her job for more than a few months before Dan Broderick, then thirty-eight, hired her as his personal assistant. Although she had no formal training as a paralegal and no experience in medical malpractice, her previous law office experience qualified her for the job, her friends later insisted. Besides, they agreed, Linda was remarkably bright, a quick study, a hard worker, and, in general, an asset to any office.

Betty Broderick begged to differ.

* * *

Summer passed uneasily in the Broderick household. Dan was working late hours as usual, Betty was in a heightened state of suspicion. But she said nothing. Maybe she was imagining it all.

It was a warm September evening in 1983 when Dan came home, late again, and told her over dinner that he had hired someone to help him a the office, beginning the following week.

"I thought, 'Great! Now the guy will have some time to spend with his family'," Betty recalls. She asked who his new assistant was.

Linda Kolkena, he said.

"Her! It was her!" She pauses, even now, years later, staggered by her own memories, strangling again on the wave of realization that had swept over her at the dinner table that night: It was true! He *was* having an affair. The bimbo was real.

"I asked him how in hell he could be hiring Linda Kolkena to be his assistant—she wasn't a paralegal, she didn't have a college education, she didn't even know how to type!" Again, she asked him for the truth. Again he told her that she was wrong, that she was being childish. Linda Kolkena, he told her, was just a bright young woman whose assistance he needed. She would do client interviews and research. Typing was not a job requirement.

By most later accounts, Dan Broderick was lying, even then. In a tale consisting of a long list of "What Ifs?" on both sides, here stands the first: What If Dan Broderick had been capable of honesty that night, of conquering his own doubts and fears, to accord his wife the minimal degree of consideration required to keep any human being's self-respect afloat, instead of stringing her along for another two years?

Instead, he only told her again that she was being silly.

But Betty didn't think so—and, in those days, she still assumed she had some household clout. Her solution was swift, devoid of pussyfooting small talk:

"I told him to get rid of the little bitch by October 1, or get out."

October 1 came and went, and Linda stayed. "He told me," she recalls now, struggling to control her rage, "that it was his practice, his decision and his house. He said that if anybody was going to move out, it would be me."

So much for Betty Broderick's perceived view of her authority over Daniel T. Broderick III. The nerd had disappeared forevermore, along with Betty Broderick's confidence that the ground beneath her feet was sure.

She was furious, she was insulted, she was dizzy with indignation. But she also recognized the altogether new sensation of fear. Before she could even finish the righteous speech her mind was trying to form, the clutch of fear smashed her in the chest, leaving her breathless, confusing her thoughts. In years past, Dan had stayed out with the boys almost all night, and she had always wondered if he'd been with a woman, if maybe they'd gone to see prostitutes like in the cheap novels, in some rite of passage, in some haze of drunkenness. But she had never felt more than a passing twinge of suspicion.

And never before, not once in fourteen years, had she felt so afraid. She went to the bathroom mirror and stared at her face. She was, she knew, a pretty woman. Now she leaned closer, studied the fine lines under her eyes. She smiled at herself, she fluffed her hair. She posed alone in the bathroom, in front of the mirror. Anger welled up. She was still a young woman. She was not old, fat, ugly, and boring. Or was she?

She felt nauseous. All those years, all those children ... Rhett was only four, Danny just seven, the girls only twelve and thirteen. No. It was not possible. It was a cliché. He was a smart man. He wouldn't. He couldn't. What would people say? What would his parents say? Her parents? No. He would not dare to leave his family. He would be disowned by everyone. She had leverage. Yes.

How could he? How could he touch another woman?

Casual sex was beyond her comprehension. In Betty Broderick's mind, sex was the single most important, final display of faith in a man any woman could ever make, for it meant complete surrender of all control, of freedom, of choice. Until her tubal ligation, it meant probable pregnancy and guaranteed pain, nausea, physical misery. Nine times in ten years. Sex meant forever and ever and ever.

Years later, in jail, her inhibitions remained so strong that sex remained the one subject she could never discuss with her usual witty glibness. Instead, she would always try to fly past it, to shrug it off. Dan, she would say, could never make love unless he had a few drinks to shed his self-conscious reserve. But she could never discuss her own.

She sat in her bathroom, staring into space. Dan wouldn't. He couldn't.

But if he couldn't, then why wouldn't he get rid of the girl? The girl who couldn't even type ... Oh, goddamn him! Was he even using contraceptives now, too? She wanted to cry.

Instead, she went into the family room, flipped on the TV, hunting for a news channel, and slowly her mind cleared. All her life, Betty Broderick had known how to get her mind off her own problems. She was not a sufferer—" I never liked being the victim," she said years later, long after she had made the passage from pain to something entirely worse.

In the next months, her fury fought with her fear, ego battled with insecurity, but she never controlled any of it, not then, nor ever again. From that day forward, October 1,1983, Betty made all the wrong choices every step of the way. And so did Dan.

"I should have divorced him then, before all the rest happened, before I let him convince everybody I was crazy, that he was justified in what he was doing," she remarked years later. "Because at that point, I still had my reputation and my sanity and my children."

But Betty was Betty, and it was only 1983. And she was never getting a divorce. Never. For all her threats in earlier years, not once did it now cross her mind to divorce him. The time for that kind of talk was done.

Instead, she went into a fierce retreat. She swallowed her ultimatum and her anger, and tried to pretend that there was no Linda Kolkena at the office.

She called her friends, she summoned the neighborhood kids for cooking classes, she took her children to museums and zoos, she worked harder with her women's groups, she went shopping. And she read. She was always one of the best-read women in her La Jolla circle. She was also in the habit of clipping articles that fascinated her. Years later, a review of her old files would uncover detailed folders on everything from fashion to the care and nourishment of roses to divorce and lawyers. By the summer of 1989, she also had a full file on the increase in handguns in America

But now, in the autumn of 1983, she went to the bookstore and ordered everything she could find on midlife crisis. She would fight this thing.

This was a task rendered easier by the fact that their material ascent was now proceeding beyond both Brodericks' wildest expectations. The money rolled in. Both of them adjusted beautifully to these fabulous new figures. In 1983, they bought a boat; they joined one country club and got on the waiting list for another. That spring, in a grand gesture, Dan also treated attorney Jim Milliken (later a judge) and his wife to a trip to Europe in reward for a malpractice tip from Milliken that netted Dan a multimillion dollar settlement. In contrast to their 1981 trip, this one "was five-star all the way," Betty recalls. By then Dan had even begun jokingly referring to himself as "the Count DuMoney" (pronounced du-mon-ā), she says.

And their search for the dream house intensified. She combed the city constantly, presenting Dan with profiles of fabulous homes. But, by then the house hunt had become a symbol of their doomed future. For all their money, they could not agree on a house to buy. In divorce court years later, Dan said that they looked at about one hundred different houses between 1979 and 1985—sometimes as many as eight to ten in a single week. But he blamed Betty for showing him homes that were too expensive. She countered that nothing suited him: everything she found was either too shabby or too grand. "He drove every realtor in town crazy, and me, too," she remarked at one of her murder trials.

They bought more and more things.

For the first time, her wardrobe began to exceed his. "Louis Feraud is it for suits, Oscar de la Renta is it for dresses, Bob Mackie is it for evening gowns, and, for sportswear, Escada," she said later from jail. "I just love what I always called the Oscar Blues—I look terrific in blue, and most of his clothes, if you notice, are blue."

Dan's pleasure in their new wealth was never any less aggressive than Betty's. But he still wanted to spend big bucks on big items, not domestic fluff. The Brodericks argued increasingly over priorities. "He wanted the kids to wear clothes from K mart, even though he wouldn't," she accuses. Simmering resentments came to a boil when he decided one day, without consulting her, to buy two lots in Fairbanks Ranch, a new glamour development north of La Jolla. His idea was to build their own custom-designed mansion there. He had bought the property not only as an investment, he said in divorce court years later, but also to put an end to their interminable house hunt. Besides, he said, he had thought Betty liked it there.

She exploded. She hated Fairbanks Ranch. It was tacky. All flash and no class. Nouveau riche. And, how dare he spend their money that way, without even consulting her? But that was Dan for you, she seethed later from jail. Mr. Image. Count DuMoney. She had a million examples.

"Once at a [charity] auction, for example, he bought two or three things, just to look important, and he wanted me to bid on a full-length black mink coat," she said. "I look like shit in black, and I didn't want it, and he was really pissed. All he cared about was appearances."

The acrimony built, the squabbles continued.

Even so, she was oddly lulled.

At least he was coming home. At least he was talking houses. Maybe his infatuation with the bimbo had passed.

Her perspective was restored in spades when he drove home one evening in a brand-new candy-apple-red Corvette, happy as a boy. He had bought it that afternoon in Long Beach, at $7,000 above the $30,000 sticker price, he told her. She didn't have time even to think about sharing his pleasure—because the next thing Dan told Betty was that, since he hadn't wanted to disturb her, Linda had driven him up to get it.

"I thought, Jesus Christ! Is this a spoof on midlife crisis or not?" she recalls. The Corvette still galls her today. Later that week, she says, since they had only a three-car garage, which was already full, Dan also talked her into selling her Jaguar, with the promise that as soon as they bought a bigger house, she could have a new one. She of course never got it, since he left her first. Adding insult to injury, not long after their divorce, he bought a new blue Jaguar for himself.

During a trip they took to New York City a few weeks after Dan came home with his new Corvette, Betty caught him in the St. Regis Hotel lobby calling Linda. He told her it was only business. She remembers looking at him and thinking, "How can the bastard look me in the eye and lie to me this way? How can he treat me like such a fool?" The next day, establishing a pattern that would last until she went to jail, she went "revenge shopping." She walked down the street to the Elizabeth Arden salon where she bought her first Bob Mackie evening gown, a pink-and-lavender concoction of sequins and flounces, sale priced at $7,000. "And the sonofabitch damn near died," she recalls with satisfaction.

Her birthday was only weeks away. On November 7, 1983, she would be thirty-six years old. Dan's new assistant was twenty-two. Betty studied her complexion in the mirror. Light skin, but still good skin, she thought. But maybe it could be improved.

She went to see a cosmetic surgeon.

It would be only the first of her visits. In the next years, she would also have her forehead lifted, her eyes done, and the loose skin on her stomach from all the pregnancies surgically removed.

But, this time, she only had her face peeled. Studying herself afterward she could still see all the same fine lines—"They just looked pinker. It hurt like hell, and I didn't look a goddamn bit younger," she says. Along with millions of women everywhere, and in common with dozens of her La Jolla acquaintances, Betty Broderick had joined in the familiar, costly war on time in a bid to keep her man.

During these months, too, she began to sound the alarm to her friends. She was everywhere, at school functions, in the La Jolla boutiques, in the supermarkets, telling them all of her suspicions that Dan was having affair.

In the beginning, her married friends invariably reassured her that couldn't be true—just look at her, she was gorgeous, slender, smart, and young, still young. Besides, they counseled her, even if it was true, it would pass. In La Jolla, as elsewhere in the world where career wives are threatened, the common answer is to look the other way. Do not panic. The husband won't risk the cost, embarrassment, and inconvenience of leaving the home. Many of them had been through it themselves. One of Betty's friends, for example, another attorney's wife, had endured her own husband's semi-public affair with an office girl. But that story ended neatly, when one of the other wives in the partnership marched into the men's lavish legal suite and ordered the boys to clean up the mess at once—in other words, get rid of the girl. The wayward husband wasn't about to buck the pressure. He followed orders. The young woman was reportedly paid to disappear. Years later, from jail, Betty would still recall that as the ideal solution to a bad situation. Why couldn't Dan have been as sensible? The other long-suffering wife had even been rewarded by her philandering husband with a new Porsche. "Because he knew he owed her," says Betty.

But, in the fall of 1983, she was not yet so cynical. She was only terrified. She looked around her, at the divorcées she knew, such a sad, failed lot, attending their singles clubs, sitting at singles tables at the Jewel Ball, women without men. She looked at her old friend Patti Monahan, now limited to $2,700 per month support after twenty-two years of marriage—a pretty, aging woman with bleached hair, wearing miniskirts and too much makeup, now forced back into the dating game of her youth in pursuit of a new relationship to replace the one she had lost. Betty shuddered. It was cheap, it was degrading. No, this could not be her. This nightmare was not happening. How could it be? "I was the perfect wife and the perfect mother," she said over and over, years later, still bewildered. "I did everything right."

That autumn Dan's parents visited them in La Jolla. His mother wanted to see her son in action, so she and Betty went to court one day. Remarkably, it was the first time Betty had ever watched her husband argue a case. "Dan always said it was tacky when families were there— and I agreed," she says.

But now, finally, nearly fifteen years after their marriage, here sat the wife in court, watching the husband do his money-making thing—when who does she suddenly spot, sitting across the room, but Linda Bernadette Kolkena, watching her husband, too, with wide, admiring eyes. "She was wearing this shitty little navy chino suit from JC Penny's, and she had on these little spaghetti-strap heels. Clickety-clack, clickety-clack, whenever she walked."

She pointed Linda out to her mother-in-law. "See that girl, Yo?" she said to the older woman. "She's trouble."

"Oh, nonsense, Bets," Yo replied, surprised. "You know Dan would never cheat on you and your wonderful children." Years later, Betty Broderick would still be repeating her mother-in-law's reassuring remark verbatim, as if it might somehow still come true.

Later, too, Betty would rail not only at her own family for letting her down as her marriage was collapsing, for refusing to support her, but also at Dan's. They were always tacky, rowdy Irish drunks, she would say, without any regard for women. She would talk about how "they had no class—his mother would come to La Jolla and embarrass me by shopping for clothes in the aisles of Von's [a supermarket]!" She would especially denounce brother Larry as a "drunken, sexist pig."

She doesn't mean it, of course—or at least she didn't, once upon a time. In truth, one of Betty Broderick's deepest hurts is the way Dan's family abandoned her, the minute that he did. Larry knew about Dan's affair with Linda Kolkena long before Betty did, but he didn't tell her. And she had trusted him. She had trusted all of them. They were her "extended family." After 16 years, she had not thought of herself as a disposable. How could they just throw her away when they had once liked her so much? And they had *all* liked her. Years after she was in jail, she would still be grappling with the betrayal, still reciting anecdotes to prove that she had been loved by the Brodericks.

Larry, for example: she remembered how, so many years ago, he had been "the only person on planet earth who remembered my college graduation, who gave me a present—it was a little wooden music box with Hummels on the top ... I still have it." Another time he brought her a Steiff teddy bear from a trip to Europe for her collection.

And Dan's sister Patti, who had a child born with Down's syndrome. "Everybody acted like it was the end of the world," says Betty. "But I told her, 'It's no big deal, it's still your little person, who needs love,' and she was so grateful that somebody gave her support. I still have the letter she sent me, telling me how much she loved me."

But she also still has a second letter Patti wrote to her, after the divorce was under way. "She accused me of defaming her brother! She sounded like she hated me ... that it all was *my fault!*"

After that, she got no other mail at all from the Brodericks. "It was as if I had never even existed!" It was one of the few times in the wake of the killings that she sounded close to tears.

As autumn turned to winter, she began to forfeit still more pieces of her pride.

One afternoon, she called a secretary she knew in Dan's office to ask "What's going on?" And she started to cry. Embarrassed, the secretary had murmured whatever comforting remarks she could think of, until Betty finally hung up.

But the secretary knew full well what was going on. By late 1983, she later told defense investigators, the affair between Dan and Linda was common knowledge in downtown legal circles. The pair took long lunches together and sometimes didn't return to the office in the afternoons at all. They drank together after work at the downtown pubs, they attended legal functions together. Linda was especially indiscreet, talking openly to other women in the office about her latest plans with Dan, said the secretary.

Dan Broderick's notorious workaholic ways had also dramatically relaxed, she said. Formerly he had been so meticulous, she said, that he would insist a letter be retyped entirely if it contained a single error, or if the corner of the stationery had been creased in filing. But now he was a changed man. He was no longer "cranking out the work," and, some days, she would arrive to find his office a clutter of food wrappers and empty wine bottles.

Finally, the secretary decided to tell Dan what she thought about the openness of his affair with Linda Kolkena. She had worked with him long enough that she felt comfortable, she said, in voicing a friendly opinion. And so at lunch one day, she advised him either to tell his wife about Linda or cut it out. Dan had been pleasant, she recalled—but he had also been firm. It was none of her business. "I'm doing it the way I want to do it ... My wife has made my life miserable for years," he told her. He didn't elaborate, she recalled, saying only that he didn't want to "rag" about his wife.

The secretary tried to ignore the situation thereafter. But, just a month later, days before Christmas, Dan fired her without explanation—and without severance pay. The year before, she said, he had given her a $10,000 Christmas bonus—but this year, he only reached under the office Christmas tree and handed her a cheap bottle of champagne.

"It was the feeling of such helplessness," Betty said later. "I couldn't make him get rid of her, I couldn't make him tell me the truth, and I couldn't fix it!"

And so, she was finally reduced to an act that still shames her more than most of the extreme steps she later took in her frantic attempts to bring Dan Broderick back home. It was the night of November 7. Her birthday. She was home with the children. "He didn't come home, he didn't give me a gift, he didn't take me out to dinner. I was just so depressed. I just felt so old and tired and failed. I really didn't want to live."

And so, "I tried to commit suicide. I slashed my wrists and took every pill in the house," she says. Later, in her first trial, she even showed the jury the scars on her wrist, apologizing to them that the wounds were so faint that the defense had to call a cosmetic surgeon to testify that they were actually there.

In reality, of course, it is unlikely that Betty seriously intended suicide. She was only trying to get her husband's attention in a pathetically immature way. And she knows it. Even today, the subject embarrasses her. "Well, no ... I didn't have to go to the hospital ... we really didn't have many pills in the house, just a few. I don't know what they were ..." As for her wrist wounds, "They weren't deep ... but they did hurt like hell." When Dan, the doctor, came home, he bound up her wrists, she says. He also reassured her again that "I was imagining everything, that there was absolutely nothing going on with Linda. What he didn't offer was the only thing she really wanted to hear: that he would dismiss Linda Kolkena the next morning, since it seemed to upset her so much.

The next day, she was awash with shame. For the first time, too, she began to doubt her own sanity. Maybe Dan was right—maybe she was going nuts. And so, that week, Betty Broderick took a timid step toward curing herself of her gnawing fears. She went to see a psychologist she had met earlier at a church seminar on self-esteem. "I figured if I was gonna do that kind of stuff, then I'd better get to see somebody fast, that Dan was right—I needed help."

Notes from that session echo her Marriage Encounter letters, except now the lonely, needy young woman was seven years older, seven years unhappier, driven less by hope than fear. She told the counselor that her worst fear was of growing old alone and being poor, like all the sad old ladies she saw in the streets.

But after four sessions, Betty quit therapy. Although in later years the judge would order her to seek therapy if she wanted even visitation rights with her children, that was the first and last time Betty would voluntarily visit any therapist, free of the angry defiance of a woman obliged. As one doctor friendly to her later remarked during her divorce trial, Betty only "plays at therapy."

"Fucking right," says the Betty who sits in jail today, permanently altered. "Because I wasn't the crazy one. He was!"

But, back then, in 1983, her fury was hardly so crystallized. In lieu of professional counseling, she resorted to the commonsense advice supplied by her girlfriends.

November 22 was Dan's thirty-ninth birthday, and one of her most loyal friends, Vicki Currie, sat her down and talked to her hard. "Vicki told me to fight back," says Betty. "She told me to do what wives are supposed to do—be confident, romantic. She persuaded me to get all dressed up that day and go down to Dan's office with a bottle of champagne for a birthday surprise."

Her hair was long then, and her face was mostly healed from the acid peel. She put on one of her most festive Diane Fries dresses, a flowery Gypsy frock with ruffles and swirling skirt. She wore matching colored pumps. She looked good. She took a dozen roses and a bottle of Dom Perignon, along with "a gag gift"—a 24-karat-gold tire pressure gauge to go with Dan's red Corvette. She planned her visit so that she would be at her husband's office in time for them to watch the sunset together.

It was a new office. Dan had so prospered since he first went into private practice five years earlier that he had moved to larger quarters in a more prestigious high-rise building. It was just one more measure of the distance between their daily working worlds that Betty had never been there before.

Now, driving into the parking lot, approaching her husband's sanctum, the place he shared with Linda Kolkena, she felt nervous, uncertain.

Nonsense. He was *her* husband. This was half her business, for heaven's sake. She took the elevator up.

The secretary, a woman she had never seen before, eyed her quizzically.

"Hi, where's the birthday boy?" Betty chirped brightly. "It's a surprise!"

Mr. Broderick was not there, the woman told her. Nor was his assistant, Ms. Kolkena. They had been gone, said the new secretary, since lunch. Betty had to identify herself as the Wife. She would wait, she said.

She remembers still her sick stomach, the tears rushing to her eyes as she strolled around Dan's new office suite.

"LINDA KOLKENA" said a brass plaque on Linda's office door. She opened it. It was magnificent. A window office with one of the most gorgeous downtown views of the bay that San Diego affords. Her eyes roamed the room. Expensive imported furniture, damask coverings, designer wallpaper. Her eyes stopped. Over Linda's desk was "a picture of Dan on a white horse, taken before we were even married!"

She went into Dan's office. Crumbs of chocolate mousse cake covered his desk, still in cake papers. Empty wine bottles. Balloons. She sat down and cried. "It was the worst pain I've ever felt," she said later. "I didn't want to believe it. I believed it."

She waited in Dan's office for a while, she can't remember how long. He never returned. She drove home, marched to the closet, and began ripping out all his expensive, tailor-made clothes. This time, it wasn't herself she wanted to damage. It was him. Trip after trip she made to the backyard, her children watched, wide-eyed. By now, her friend Vicki had arrived and begged her to stop.

But Betty kept marching with armfuls of clothes, tears streaming. When the pile was high, she poured gasoline on it and lit the match.

As the smoke billowed, as thousands of dollars of Dan Broderick's expensive clothes went up in flames, her children cried and screamed

When the embers cooled, Betty poured brown paint on them.

"I wanted to finish the job," she explained years later from jail. "And it was fun. When I put the gas on—I used lawnmower gas—it went 'Poof. *Poof,* you sonofabitch'!"

Dan came home several hours later. She met him at the front door, she says, "and I handed him his checkbook and told him, 'You won't move out, so I've moved you out. You're out of here'."

He ignored her, came in, and went to their bedroom, where the Brodericks had most of their quarrels. But there was no fight in the Broderick household that night. Dan didn't react at all, his daughter Kim said later. "He didn't act mad. He was real quiet."

Behind closed doors, Betty says, Dan only repeated his past speech. "He told me I was imagining it, there was nothing going on with Linda. He said the party was innocent, that they had gone to lunch, then Linda had gone shopping, and he had been at a deposition."

She was so pathetically willing to be deceived, to believe. She was in fact so embarrassed about burning his clothes that, according to later trial testimony, she even lied about it the next day to Maria, her faithful maid, telling her that Dan came home at two A.M., "stinking drunk" and burned his own clothes.

It took her months more to ask herself the obvious questions: 1) If Dan had been as innocent as he claimed, then why hadn't he been infuriated that she had burned a blameless man's clothes? And 2) If he had any compassion for her agony, whether real or imagined, why hadn't he agreed to let Linda go, in the face of this latest piece of high theater?

The answer, of course, was that Dan Broderick was neither blameless nor compassionate nor, apparently, willing to take responsibility for his own actions. Instead, he let the transparent deception drag on for another two years. He watched while his wife cried, whined, and tried to win him back. He watched the uncertainty grow in her eyes while at the same time he permitted her to play all her coy, humiliating games aimed at seducing him; and when she periodically snapped in angry frustration, he only looked away, vindicated again. Dan Broderick was like a cat caught by highway headlights, frozen by indecision, or a dog in heat, unable to turn any suitor away. Either way, he hardly acted in his own best interests, much less Betty's.

Not surprisingly, by the time the full truth about his affair finally emerged, in 1985, it was not Dan whom Betty most loathed, but herself for her own gullibility. Her self-hatred only grew, her sense of self steadily eroded. "What a dumbshit I was! In retrospect, if he hadn't been guilty, he would've had me put in jail then for burning his precious clothes." Worse, she adds with withering self-disgust, "I was such a wimp that I didn't even burn all of them. I saved his favorite things—like his damned silk top hat and that cape that hung to the floor, like a magician's, and a ridiculous straw bowler that he loved."

In any case, that bonfire was Betty Broderick's first act of direct violence against her husband—a full six years before she finally shot him to death.

Chapter 8

Triangle Plus One

That Dan and Betty Broderick survived 1984 together is a measure of human capacity for self-inflicted pain and deception. He deceived, she endured.

Periodically, she saw pictures of Dan and his pretty "legal assistant" in local legal publications. But she ignored them. Her La Jolla friends began to sigh with relief. Maybe the thunderclouds had passed over yet another of them. Betty was even beginning to seem like her old self again. Not that she didn't talk about her suspicions. But she didn't talk so much. The obsession seemed to have lifted; the naked panic had vanished.

But, downtown, Dan and Linda's friends looked on with increasing concern. Dan seemed more strained each day, and Linda was now crying openly over his refusal to leave Betty.

According to her friends, Linda had begun to ask the obvious questions: If the marriage was over, as Dan had said, if he was in love with her as he said, then why wasn't this drama coming to a speedy, logical conclusion? Why wasn't he divorcing Betty and marrying her?

The answer was old as the hills: however discontented Dan Broderick may have been at home, and however thrilled he was by his afternoon and evening trysts with this beautiful young woman who so adored him, he was not yet anywhere close to committing the unthinkable act of walking out on his wife and children, of scandalizing his family, of sinning in the eyes of the Church, no matter how "uncool" he thought that church was. What's more, a divorce, he knew, would cost him a fortune.

But if Dan was happy enough to have it both ways, Linda wasn't. She was unwilling to be the office bimbo, the Other Woman. Beyond her overriding desire to become the next Mrs. Daniel T. Broderick III, friends say she was also haunted by the ghosts of her upbringing. Her father's square, sturdy face, his direct, honest eyes nagged at her daily. He would not approve of what she was doing and she knew it.

"She didn't even tell me that they were involved, not until way after," said her sister, Maggie. "And she was so ashamed. She asked me if I still loved her. Linda did not sleep around." Seats guesses that her sister had a total of three lovers in her life, period.

After her death, Linda's friends were equally disgusted at the endless innuendos that she was just another pretty gold digger who used sex to snare a rich husband. "It's a joke—Linda was the most old-fashioned woman I ever met. She was the type who wore panties under her panty hose—and not bikinis either," said attorney Kathy Cuffaro, an attractive, vibrant young woman in her own right. Nor was Dan apparently any red-hot stud, Cuffaro added with a bawdy grin. "Linda used to complain that she didn't get enough sex out of him, that he would sit in the bathroom at night with the lights on after she'd gone to bed, reading briefs."

"Sure, face it, Linda had it made, when she married Dan. He was major money," says her sister. "But there was a whole lot more to that relationship for Linda than money. She was head over heels in love with him. Dan made Linda laugh ... they had fun together." Besides, Seats added, "Dan was brilliant. If Linda was just a bimbo, he wouldn't have been interested in her for a minute." It was just one more poignant, ironic footnote to Linda Kolkena's brief life story that nearly everyone, even her sister, consistently measured her worth based on Dan Broderick's standards—despite their perception that Dan had, for some reason, spent sixteen years married to a madwoman.

And even that small concession—that Linda was more than an airhead—came only grudgingly from some of Dan's male pals, according to Seats. "When their affair came out, Linda had to work very hard to win their approval. They were suspicious of her, that she wasn't worthy," says Seats For a long time, Dave Monahan, in particular, treated her with such condescension because she had so little formal education, says one girlfriend, "That it would make Linda cry. She was very sensitive about her lack of educational credentials—and, face it, Dan Broderick, with all his Ivy League degrees, was a hard act for anybody to follow. I bet even Betty probably felt inferior."

Even before 1984, Linda's closest friends had begun to counsel her to leave Dan if he wouldn't leave Betty. "That whole situation would have just killed my self-esteem," said Stormy Wetther. "I always told her to leave it behind." So did her sister, Maggie—"I begged her to run like the wind."

And finally Linda tried. She gave Dan an ultimatum: fish or cut bait. If he didn't divorce Betty, she was going to begin dating other men.

Dan Broderick was probably torn. But not enough to bend. He couldn't walk out on his family. He wouldn't. Instead, he told Linda to go ahead, to get on with her life. "Dan could be coldhearted, once he had made a decision," says Laurel Summers, Dave Monahan's closest female companion after his divorce from Patti.

But Dan didn't tell Linda to find a new job, too. Nor did she volunteer to quit. What for? they both asked friends. He needed her services, she loved her job. They could handle it. Whether they were hypocrites or just fools will always be an open question, though all evidence points to the former.

Enter Steve Kelley, one more casualty of the Broderick affair.

Kelley is a handsome, thirty-something editorial cartoonist for the *San Diego Union* and an aspiring comedian who has appeared on the *Johnny Carson Show*. A look-alike for actor Richard Chamberlain in his younger days, Kelley met Linda Kolkena at a realtor's office in the spring of 1983, while they were both shopping for condominiums. For Kelley, it was love at first sight: "I thought she was the perfect blend of independence and femininity. Very bright, self-assured. And she was so beautiful ... my cup of tea."

Their relationship lasted more than a year. But Linda never told him that she had been—or was still—having an affair with her boss. Instead, Kelley began to suspect it on his own. "I started to notice how much she seemed to admire [Broderick]. She talked about him constantly." Then there were the odd items: whenever Dan left town, he would leave his Corvette for Linda to drive. When she bought her modest condominium in a San Diego suburb, Dan cosigned for the loan. Not least, says Kelley, in the summer of 1984, while Dan was touring Europe with Betty—"trying to reconcile their marriage, I thought"—he sent Linda several birthday presents: "a dozen red roses, a color TV, and a piece of emerald jewelry."

But, like Betty, Kelley didn't fully absorb the real truth until he went to visit Linda at her office one day. He was stunned at the elegance of her quarters. "I thought, 'Hey, she's bright, but she doesn't even have any college—and she was his legal assistant?'."

When he finally confronted Linda with his suspicions, Kelley says, she at first denied it. Don't be silly, she told him—Dan Broderick is a married man with four children. Then she broke down and cried and admitted all. For months, she told Kelley, she and Dan had spent their lunch hour in her little apartment in Ocean Beach. "She sobbed and trembled when she talked about it," says Kelley. "She couldn't accept her own actions and she was sick over what her father would think." Like Linda's sister, Kelley insists that it was the adultery that tormented Linda even more than the unsatisfying end to her love affair with Dan Broderick.

But she told Kelley the affair was over.

That was enough for him. By now, he was in love. He wanted to marry Linda, and, if she loved working in a law office so well, send her to law school, too. He begged her to quit her job, "to get out of the picture, to let that marriage sink or swim on its own."

But Linda couldn't. She wouldn't.

A patient man, Kelley swallowed his pride and went to see Dan, hoping for a man-to-man talk, for some reassurance that Dan had in fact let Linda go. He told Linda he was going. She didn't try to stop him, he said—maybe because she wanted an answer, too.

Kelley remembers his encounter with Dan Broderick well. "I had hoped it would be a heart-to-heart," he says. "I made an appointment. I asked him if the relationship was over. He said yes. But he wasn't warm or engaging—he was cold. He had absolutely no compassion for what I was going through. He basically dismissed me."

Kelley remained in his relationship with Linda for several more months, never knowing if she was his, or theirs. Finally, he issued his own ultimatum. It was near Christmas of 1984, he says. Linda was planning to spend the weekend at Palm Desert with Dan, helping him on a case. She had to go, she told Kelley. It was her job. He told her either to commute daily or forget him. She chose to forget him, though they remained friends until her death.

Today, Kelley is remarkably sanguine about it all. His voice still softens when he speaks of Linda, but he shows no emotion at all toward Betty and only minor contempt for Dan. "Dan just cared too much about Dan," he says mildly. "Linda asked him to get dogs or a security system, but he said no. Where was his basic instinct to protect his wife? But his attitude was no dogs, no alarms, because Bets Broderick was not going to control Dan Broderick. Nobody was."

In retrospect, Kelley likes to think that Linda "was essentially in love with two people at once. Rationally, she knew I fit better in terms of age and everything else. But, in the end, he was her knight in shining armor. So he won. It's that simple." Obviously, he adds with a shrug, "She made the wrong call."

Every cliché was in place. The wife knew but was the last to actually be told. So Betty continued to persuade herself that it wasn't true. And Dan gave her plenty of help that year. He acted more like a husband than he had before. He came home earlier, even though he was now busier than ever, not only with his practice but with bar association activities, too. He didn't talk much, but then he never had. On the other hand, he talked about the things that mattered to Betty. When their daughter Kim, then 14, wanted a piano, he agreed to buy one, an $8,000 Bosendofer. He didn't object when Betty wanted to buy a family vacation unit at Warner Springs Ranch, a nearby mountain resort.

That summer, they even took a week-long vacation to London together. It was their first trip to Europe alone. They stayed at one of the most elegant, romantic hotels in the city—and Betty tried to act like a bride on a second honeymoon. "I did everything I could think of to make him happy," she bitterly remembered later. "It was, 'Anything you want, honey.' ... I followed him around like a Japanese wife. I didn't ask to go anywhere or do anything. The guy never even wanted to visit a museum. So I just sat around the bars with him, smiling and trying to be pleasing."

It didn't work. "He was so cold the whole time. I remember walking down a street one morning at dawn by myself, crying and thinking, 'What am I doing here? What am I doing wrong? What can I do that's right?'."

Linda. Linda never left her mind. Linda would never leave Betty's mind, not as long as she was still working with Dan. Every time Dan frowned at Betty's jokes and pranks, which he had once so enjoyed, each time he turned away from her touch, images of Linda blinded her. And, in her heart, she knew she wasn't crazy at all.

Or was she? After all, Dan was there, in London, with her. Maybe she was being paranoid. Let it go. Don't push, don't be a shrew ... Even if he was still dallying with the office girl, it would blow over. And Betty was willing to settle for that. The infidelity no longer scorched her mind. That part of her pride had long since died. Now, all she wanted was to remain Mrs. Daniel T. Broderick III.

Dan, meantime, was sending Linda flowers and jewelry, while she drove his Corvette around town.

* * *

Back in San Diego, Betty was more active than ever with the children, their schools, soccer clubs, and charity work. Every day she rose early and worked on herself. She got facials, haircuts, manicures. She dressed like a dream. She was more beautiful than she had ever been. Everyone said. Everyone but Dan.

Why couldn't he even smile at her anymore? Every time he walked through the door, he looked ten years older, the frown lines were so frozen. He couldn't even talk to the kids without looking distracted. His eyes, always so intense, seemed to her to be perpetually burning with some inner anger.

Linda. But, my God, she thought to herself—if he seriously wanted Linda Kolkena, surely he would have made his choice by now? Would he? Why did he keep denying it? Was she crazy after all? The madness continued.

By now, too, either Betty had begun to hallucinate severely from suspicion and fear, or Dan Broderick had turned into a man capable of genuine mental cruelty. One morning, for example, as he lay in bed with his eyes shut, seemingly asleep, she says that he began murmuring "Linda, Linda." She stared at him, aghast. He wasn't asleep. She could tell. She knew it. He was deliberately trying to hurt her. She knew it. She still knows it, to this day. But why? *Why?*

Another night, he came home late and, she swears still, deliberately laid his hand on the pillow near her face— "and it smelled of vagina! I was so grossed out! I lay there on my back, looking into the dark, with tears running down my face, and I thought, how can he do this to me?"

Recalling the incident later from jail, she began to sob. It was the first time in the year since she had killed him that Betty Broderick broke down entirely while talking about Dan. "And the worst part," she said through her tears, "was that he made me think I was crazy—just like you are thinking now—because then he got on top of me, and he kissed me, and told me he'd never slept with anyone else but me!"

Not until years later would Betty finally decide that Dan had been purposely flaunting his affair with Linda, at the same time he denied it, in an effort to drive her to divorce him. "He was trying to make me hate him. He wanted out, he wanted a divorce—but he didn't want to be the guy. He wanted me to file." Later she concluded, too, that he had literally been trying to drive her crazy so that nobody could blame him for leaving her. "Instead, people would just say 'Oh, poor Dan. See what a raving lunatic he's been putting up with all this time.' Which of course is exactly what happened," she added with a manic little laugh.

* * *

By late 1984, Betty Broderick was so riddled with self-doubt, so battered by conflicting signals, that she could no longer keep a single thought alive for more than a few days. Again, Dan wasn't coming home until after midnight. He said he was working. She knew he wasn't. He told her she was crazy. She knew she wasn't. Why wouldn't he just tell her the truth? The cruel mind games continued. On and on and on. Her mind turned into a yo-yo, flying back and forth from angry suspicion to childlike hope. And nothing gave her more hope that everything would be fine than the day she finally approached her husband, in yet another desperate bid to please, and offered the last concession she had: she volunteered to have her body surgically restored, if possible, to its original child-bearing condition. Maybe they should have more children after all.

And Dan agreed. He even went to see a gynecologist with her to discuss the possibility of having her tubal ligation reversed.

"She was expansive, upbeat, inquisitive," the doctor later testified at her murder trial. And Mr. Broderick had seemed "quite interested." Until the doctor recommended artificial insemination as a more feasible solution than surgery. Then, says Betty, Dan lost all interest. He said it was unnatural. Why he went with her in the first place is just one more unanswered question that Dan Broderick took with him to the grave.

Even so, Betty was encouraged. Surely his fling had passed. Her confidence grew.

That November, she threw herself into the grandest party she had ever planned— a five-day celebration of Dan's fortieth birthday. For weeks she immersed herself in the details, marching around La Jolla with her clipboard, ordering meals, hotels, flowers, gifts, stationery. When the sprawling Broderick clan converged, all was in perfect order. Betty had arranged for everything from baby-sitters to hourly entertainment—picnics, trips to Sea World, Mexican lunches, French dinners, a bus trip to the USC-Notre Dame game in Los Angeles, all culminating in a grand dinner on the night of his birthday. She even handed out mimeographed activity schedules. Later, the Broderick family applauded the success of her efforts—and nothing ever soothed Betty Broderick more than the warm bath of family approval. She relaxed even more. Dan's family loved her. Nothing had changed in fifteen years. She belonged.

By December, Dan and Betty Broderick seemed to be a closer family unit than ever, thanks mainly to housing matters. First, they were obliged to move from their Coral Reef home into a temporary rental because Coral Reef had a crack in its foundation that would take months to repair. Together, they located and leased a lovely new home on La Jolla Shores—seven bedrooms and an ocean view. The whole family loved it so much that Betty escalated her search for their new house. Now that they were out of Coral Reef, why should they ever move back there? Dan agreed. That very month, in fact, they made a losing $750,000 bid on another ocean-view home on the island of Coronado. By now, Betty had given up her demand that they remain in La Jolla. Whatever Dan wanted was fine. They could always move back to La Jolla later, after he recovered from his midlife crisis.

By Christmas, she was so certain that the affair had run its course that she grew positively cocky. "I thought we had weathered the storm. I thought we would go on, with our scars—but we would go on ... until I got his shitty Christmas present."

By now, Betty had put up with two years of his infidelity and lies, and she attached a big price to her forgiveness. What she expected that Christmas, in recompense for her patience, was a lavish expression of apology—something on the order of the new Porsche her girlfriend had gotten from her own philandering husband the year before. What Dan gave her for Christmas instead was "a rinky-dinky little ring that wasn't even big enough for my daughter!" She "threw it back into his face," she wrote later in an essay to herself. "I told him it wasn't even worth the gas it would take to return it."

It was an ugly Christmas morning scene, with the children looking on. "He owed me big for the two years of hell he had put me through," she said later. "My life had been the worst shit! And so, I wanted this humongous ring, a tsavorite ... I didn't need a ring! I had a ring! I wanted *the* ring! And the ring I wanted was in the thousands—I can't remember how many. $10,000? $30,000? But it was a major ring. I was looking for my reward. But instead, he had the nerve to give me this little piece of shit in the low hundreds!"

Even today, Betty isn't ashamed of her own naked greed, her ugly priorities that Christmas. Just as Dan would never assume responsibility for his own failings, neither would she. Both would always shift the blame totally to the other.

Either way, it was the best Christmas present Betty Broderick could have possibly given Linda Kolkena.

Two months later, on the night of February 28, Dan came home and told her, "I'm leaving."

He then went to his closet and began packing. She asked him why he was leaving. He told her "he needed some space for a little while, to think things through," she says. She accused him again of having an affair, and, she says, again he denied it. "He said Linda had nothing to do with it ... he said he just needed some time by himself. And then he asked me, 'Do you want me to leave now or tomorrow?'."

If she hadn't been convinced before that Dan was determined to make her the culprit in their split, she was convinced then. In her mind, even at the eleventh hour, he was trying to force her into ordering him out of the family home. "I told him, 'I've been married to a lawyer too long to fall for that one. You leave whenever you want to.'"

So he undressed and went to bed with her, she says, and moved out the next morning.

Dan's version of the night's events differed dramatically. He had not spent the night with her, he said during their divorce trial years later, but had instead told her flatly: "I'm leaving you. I'm going away. We can't live together anymore. It's been bad too long between us. This is not going to work. I have got to go." At the same time, he admitted that he hadn't told Betty he wanted a divorce when he moved out because, he hadn't yet decided "to do that." When he left, he said, Betty flung a jar of Dep hair gel at his departing back. Although she denies it, he said she also brandished a butcher knife at him.

In any case, Dan left it to Betty to explain his departure to their children. That was a mother's work, not his.

Any woman who has ever been left by a man, particularly for another woman, knows how Betty Broderick felt the morning after. Her mind was a stupid, dysfunctional tangle of shock, indignation, and self-pity, fading to hazy introspection, blurring to furious self-defense, finally collapsing into the only single emotion that, for the moment, at least, mattered: disbelief.

He was fooling, this man who had been her constant companion for sixteen years, her roommate, the one who watched her put on her makeup, who saw her waterbags break, who had seen her tweeze her eyebrows, whose meals she had cooked. This man who had kissed her, passed out, bit his nails, and snored in front of her. They had schemed, quarreled, laughed, and watched TV together. They had held hands while priests baptized their babies, they had pooled their dirty underwear in the bathroom hamper, and they had been carried back in time, wherever they were, together or apart, every time in the last twenty years that they heard the Lettermen singing, "Going out of my head, can't take my eyes off of you ..."

Nope. He was not serious. It was just another stage of his midlife crisis. Even if he was still carrying on with the cheap bimbo, he would come to his senses sooner or later. He was forty. That was all.

It is one of the most extraordinary aspects of the Broderick story that neither of these two would ever accept the decisions of the other. Dan would go to his death, still trying to make Betty behave like a lady, and she would go to prison, still incredulous that the man she married could actually leave her and mean it.

It would become one of the ugliest, most prolonged divorces that San Diego had ever seen—a divorce sordid enough that, by 1988, the *Oprah Winfrey Show* tried to get Betty to participate in a program on "The Messiest Divorces in America"—which proposed to include, among other guests, a California woman whose gynecologist husband had sewed her vagina together. Betty refused. That was tacky, she said. Hers, she told the network hustlers, was a case of substance, involving legal abuse, divorce laws, emotional battery, and, in general, the entire cosmic imbalance between men and women.

She was right about that. The Broderick story was never primarily about the ordinary, sordid details of divorce, such as money and children Theirs instead was always a struggle for power, but one totally out of whack. Because he had it, she didn't. He took it for granted, she never could.

It took nearly five long, grinding years more, before these two would wind up that last night together in his bedroom, with Linda Kolkena lying in her polka-dotted baby dolls between them, their war finally done.

Chapter 9

Dan's Space

Betty and the children stayed in the rental house at La Jolla Shores. Dan moved back to the Coral Reef house. Construction was nearly done, but the place was a shambles, and it had no furniture. He couldn't stay there for long, she thought. He would be back.

During the next days, she listened for his car pulling into the driveway. The children played, she went about her clubs, her shopping, and her school activities. Everywhere she went, she was cheerful, laughing, upbeat. She told all her friends that, in the latest phase of Dan's midlife crisis, he had moved out. But she made a joke of it. Her manner was that of a parent tolerating a rebellious teenager. It was all just too ridiculous, she said, but, what the hell: let him get it and the bimbo out of his system. And she didn't expect it to take long. She guessed he would be home within a matter of weeks, if not days.

Her friends winced. Her forced nonchalance was painful to see. By now, everybody could see that this split was about a lot more than "space."

Privately, Betty knew better, too. The weeks passed. He never called her, so she called him. But even then, she says—and he later agreed at their divorce trial—he never mentioned divorce to her. Instead, he continued to stall, talking about his further need for more "space."

And she would hang up the telephone and think about that.

Space?

She stared at her children, racing around the house, oblivious to it all. Kim had turned fifteen the month before he left. Lee was almost fourteen, Danny was nine, only two days before Dan moved out. Rhett was six just a week earlier.

She sat at her kitchen counter, drinking coffee and trying to concentrate on the morning newspapers. She phoned friends, she made notes and lists of things to do that day. And she shopped, more and more. Whether she was buying groceries, clothing, or a new bed of impatiens, it relieved her depression.

She listened to the children. Laughing, yelling, fighting. Making a mess. Her babies. Her head hurt. Her babies. Not his. Hers. He had to be kidding. Where's my space? her mind inquired. What is a Mommy? Where is Daddy?

Something hard began to form in Betty Broderick's mind, for the first time since she had quit teaching to have Kim. Why? Why were these her children?

But the thought wouldn't hold, her mind was too crowded.

What could she do, if he left her? How could she be a mother without a father? The fear was paralyzing, the notion staggering. What would her family say? Her friends?

The kids didn't even know why their father had left. So far, she had never told them about Linda. They had no idea why Mom and Dad were always fighting. She had always told herself they were too young.

But why shouldn't they know about their father's slut? she now asked herself. The hardness in her head grew, until the pressure hurt. But it wasn't fear anymore. "No, no, nooooo," as she would say later from jail, with chilling concentration to each syllable. Nooooo. From here on, it would be anger. Fuck him. What was she supposed to do for money, anyway? Where was her monthly allowance? For years, he had given her a household allowance for groceries, entertainment, assorted expenses that she might not be able to charge. Now what? Call and say, "Pretty please?"

What in the hell does he expect me to do? Where is my share of the money? Where is my choice? In June, the lease on the La Jolla Shores house would expire. Just where did the sonofabitch expect her and the children go? What exactly would Dan Broderick's pleasure then be?

She called his office more and more during those next weeks. Most times, she was the epitome of sweet docility—don't nag, don't push, her mind told her. But sometimes her anger overflowed, and she would end up castigating him for his juvenile selfishness. He was acting like a college kid on summer break. His manner was placating. He would not discuss coming home, but whatever she needed, he reassured, he would provide. Just charge it. Send him the bills, he would pay. She was thinking of taking the kids to Warner Springs the first week of April, for Easter vacation—yes, he said, that would be nice. Have a good time. Their sixteenth wedding anniversary was coming up, too. Of course, he said, he would be there. They would go out to dinner.

The signals were always so mixed. Less than a month after he left her on St. Patrick's Day in March, he came back to the house to see her. He was loaded, she says now. He stayed overnight. They slept together. But it shames her to discuss it, to admit that she did what so many women do—confused sex with commitment: "I don't know what I thought," she says, "except that he was still my husband."

But he didn't come back. More weeks passed. She hated him.

The rental house was close enough to the beach that the kids could walk down. It was also near one of La Jolla's prettiest little shopping centers, a quaint enclave near the sea where suntanned people wearing Rolexes, faded Polo denims, and expressions of complete well-being sit at outdoor cafés on weekend mornings, drinking Kona coffee and eating chilled melon as they skim their Sunday newspapers.

Betty loved the Shores. As soon as Dan came back, they would buy a house there. After what he was putting her through, he was going to owe her the home of her choice, and plenty more. No more Coronado.

She and the children spent Easter weekend at Warner's Ranch, a comfortable, unpretentious place with sports fields, horseback riding, swimming pools, and hiking trials. Betty and the kids always enjoyed it more than Dan did. Their condo, one of hundreds, was small but nice. Four years later, only days before she killed, Betty

Broderick would go there alone to nurse her wounds during the weekend of the USC-Notre Dame game.

But in the spring of 1985, she was still full of intractable hope. She spent the weekend almost relaxed. She pictured Dan rattling around their big, empty, messy Coral Reef house alone. He was probably already sorry. Maybe he would be back home when she and the kids got back to La Jolla, ready to beg her forgiveness.

She returned instead to a house full of rats. Rats. Big, brown roof rats. They were everywhere. She opened the door to the sounds of their scurrying feet. The children screamed, and so did she. Stringy brown bodies were darting through the kitchen, into the bedrooms. Just like New York City cockroaches in a fifth-floor walkup when the light is suddenly turned on at night, they were awesome to see in their teeming flight.

She walked through the house, horrified at their droppings, cringing at the sounds of their claws on the floors, their frightened squeals. They had been eating things for the week she had been gone, including, as her attorneys would later show in court, the hems of all her floor-length evening gowns.

Oh, God. Where was her husband? Where was the father of her crying, terrified children?

She snatched up the phone and called him. She was semi-hysterical, and furious. How dare he leave his family in a rat-infested house? Was he mowing his lawn today or fucking the cunt or what? He had to get over there immediately to help. It was time for him to act like a goddamn parent, not a college kid. In short, Betty was not polite.

And Dan got even, without a pause. "Good luck," he told her. And hung up. It was her problem, not his. She listened to the dial tone in disbelief. Rats were running over his children's feet, and their father was telling her that it was her problem?

Later, in their divorce trial, Dan agreed that he had been so antagonized by Betty's "tone" that day—she was rude and demanding—that he had hung up without offering to help. Besides, he added, he didn't see the big deal—if it had been his problem, he would simply have taken the children to a hotel or motel until the exterminators came. "You had thirteen credit cards, and you had plenty of cash and plenty of resources to go and live in any hotel in this country," he told her in court.

Thus did Dan Broderick, in his anger at his wife, punish his children, too. In the years to come, both Brodericks would hurl charges of child abuse at the other, and, certainly, Betty's eventual behavior would become far more garish. But the reality is that Dan Broderick also consistently placed his children's needs second to his own. Not only that, he set the precedent, by doing it first.

Betty and the kids killed the rats.

They set out traps, they called the exterminators. "For the couple of days, we couldn't sleep, just listening to the sounds of the traps snapping at night," said Lee Broderick later, during her mother's trials. "It was super gross!" Once, she said, shuddering, they caught a small rat in the toilet and flushed him down. Another time, they captured a rat in the oven and roasted him alive.

Four days later was their sixteenth wedding anniversary. Dan had said he would take her to dinner. She spent the day primping, and hauling out her favorite clothes. Something blue. Dan always loved her in blue. But late in the afternoon he called to say he couldn't make it after all. He had to go to a business dinner instead with "a bank teller."

She fixed dinner for the children and herself.

She tried to think clearly.

She thought about her family. Her father would be seventy-five years old on May 1. The family was having a party in New York. She would go. That would make her feel better. She had never needed her family more.

She shopped. She went everywhere, she bought everything: shoes, lingerie, party dresses. She didn't even look at price tags.

He didn't call. Day after day, he didn't call, not even to ask about the rats. He didn't care, even about his own children.

She made her plane reservations.

The bastard. Who did he think he was? What was she supposed to do with the children when she went to New York for the birthday party? What was she supposed to do with the rest of her life? Raise four children by herself while he went on his merry way?

Uh-huh. Right, Dan.

Finally, the idea that had been forming in her mind, the hardness in her brain, identified itself. Lee and Kim were fighting again, the racket was nerve-grinding, as always.

Pack up your things, she said to Kim. You're going to see Daddy.

Kim cried, but Betty was firm. "You're going to live with your father, she told the girl. She bundled her daughter into the car, as the other children gaped. Through the quiet streets of La Jolla she went, moving reverse pattern, from her pretty, palatial rental home on the Shores, back over the hills, back into the tracts from whence they had come. The Coral Reef house was dark. Dan wasn't home. She didn't care. Kim was fifteen. A big girl. Dan would be home eventually. She put Kim out of the car and drove away.

"I came home later and found Kim there, in this empty house, crying, Dan said later. "I couldn't believe Bets had done that to her own child."

But Bets had only begun. Over the next few days, she took the other three children to him as well. It was perhaps the single worst strategic mistake she would make during the next four years.

Later, she would argue that all she had done was to take the children from a rat-infested rental house to stay with their father in their own home while she attended her father's birthday celebration. Which was partly true. But the main reality was that Betty was using the children in an attempt to bring back Dan. "I wanted to show the sonofabitch that there was more to fucking than having fun—let him see what it was like to try raising four children," she later told a court-order therapist.

Rarely has a woman so misread a man.

"But you know what the fucker did?" she told the therapist, still amazed. "He just kept them!"

It is not hard to imagine Dan Broderick's shock when he arrived home in his red Corvette late that night, after a long day at the office, to find his daughter crouched in a corner of his dark, empty, cold house, sobbing amid her little suitcases of clothes and teenage trinkets.

What kind of mother ... ???

Then came the other three. All crying, all confused, all deposited on his front lawn with their clothes and toys, all wanting to know what was happening. Why was Mom acting this way? When would they all go home again?

What kind of woman!!??

Certainly, this was not how Dan Broderick had intended the script to go. He had left his wife. Wives who are left are supposed to mourn, weep, make scenes, do whatever women do. But good wives always comply. They talk to their girlfriends, they consult their mothers, their priests, their lawyers. They take classes at the local university, they get a new haircut, they get a job, and, presto, they are soon married to another man, a hardworking Joe who becomes a good father to the last father's children. That's how it's supposed to go.

What the wife never does is resist. She does not fling her babies onto the front lawn of the departed husband, who has made his decision, who has obligations, who has to go to work tomorrow morning, for Chrissake.

But now, in the spring of 1985, here sat Dan Broderick, age forty, in charge of four needy, weepy young children—with a twenty-three-year-old girlfriend waiting for him downtown.

What's more, here's the kicker: Betty would not repent. Not that day, not the next week, not for the next four years—never. Her best friends begged her to get the children back, but she consistently refused even to discuss custody without "a fair financial settlement, so I know I can support them the way I had always intended. If he's going to destroy this family because he wants to fuck the cunt, that's his business. But I want what's mine. Until I get it, until I know that I can give them exactly the same life-style, every privilege I had planned, then let him and his girlfriend raise them." Not least, she wasn't emotionally capable of raising four kids anymore, she said. How could a woman who had stupidly swallowed lies for so long teach children anything about self-respect, personal integrity, and honesty?

Also, by now, although Dan was still months away from telling her the truth about Linda, Betty was no longer under any illusions: her children had told her that Linda was constantly at the Coral Reef house. Her house.

But still she hadn't given up. Not really. Now he would see that he couldn't do without her, the mother of his children. He would give up his bimbo and come home. He could never raise them without her.

One more time, Betty misread her man. By her own renegade actions she had only supplied her runaway Catholic husband with further justification for his own actions, from that day forward. Even if he had none before, Dan Broderick now had concrete reason, in his mind, to loathe her. Never once did it occur to him that he was just as responsible for his children as she was. That was woman's work. She had failed. She was fired. This was war.

And so, instead of even picking up the phone to call her, to see if perhaps, as parents, they might discuss this business of child-care, Dan simply matched Betty's own hotheaded game. To hell with you, he basically said. Anything you can do, I can do better.

And he hired a housekeeper.

Betty's shock was total. Even now, she hasn't recovered from the insult. The sonofabitch had simply replaced her.

Chapter 10

Crazy Days

Dan Broderick was not cut out to be a single father. But, as Kim said later during the trials, "Dad tried. But he just didn't know what to do with four kids. We ate a lot of steak and Idaho spuds for a while."

At the same time, he bought furniture, redecorated the interior of Coral Reef, and redid the landscaping. He later said he was only trying to make the house livable for Betty and the children. Even then, he said, he still expected Betty to come to her senses and move back into the family home with the children. It was only natural. He planned to move to a condo. He also insisted that he tried to consult Betty on the new decorations, but she wouldn't discuss them. Betty says he never made any effort whatsoever to contact her.

Either way, one day in June, she walked into the house to discover his new decor. "I couldn't believe it! He had *ruined* my house that I had worked so hard to make beautiful. He put in this yukky wallpaper and flooring, and he tore out mature landscaping and put in fifty-cent marigolds. He *destroyed* my house!"

She picked up a can of black Rust-Oleum paint and sprayed several walls. She walked from one room to the other, spraying. "I wanted to ruin it," she said. Later, in moments of wry humor, she would refer to the paint incident as "the beginning of 'my fits.'"

It would not be her last attack on the Coral Reef house, not by a long shot—but it would be the last one Dan Broderick tolerated.

Meantime, the Crazy Betty scenario was already taking seed at luncheon tables all over La Jolla. Her best friends thought she was nuts, still defying the truth. When she told them that Dan was coming back home, that divorce had never even been discussed, they could only raise their eyebrows and frown and feel pity. Poor Betty.

"Betty just went crazy from the day Dan left. All the things that happened later, the legal things, the money—it had nothing to do with her state of mind. It happened overnight. The minute he left her, she was a different person," says her old friend Candy Westbrook. "You literally couldn't ask Betty about the weather without her finding a way to bring the conversation back to Dan and Linda. It's all she would talk about. She just didn't want it to be."

Another of Betty's friends, Lynn McGuire, wife of an attorney friend of Dan's, was so concerned about Betty's mental health that she tried to persuade her to check into a mental health facility. Betty, who could never directly say no to anybody, humored her, but kept putting her off, while, inside, she wept and raged. Why did everyone think she was crazy? Because she was angry? Why didn't she have a right to be angry?

Dan's friends, meantime, had also shifted the focus from Dan and Linda's affair to

Betty Broderick's fragile state of mind. The reason Dan could not be honest with Betty, they said in chorus after his death, was because he was so worried about her mental health. He simply didn't know what was the most compassionate course of action. In a word, he was trying to protect his poor, crazed wife, who had, up to that point, done nothing more impetuous than burn his clothes for lying to her and spray-paint the walls of her own house. No one ever seemed to take her earlier suicide attempt very seriously.

By 1985, Linda Kolkena, especially, was telling everyone what a wild woman Betty Broderick was—how she had tormented Dan for all of their marriage, vandalized their house, and, most recently, even abandoned her own children. Linda may have been just another young woman in love—but she was evidently also one without compassion for an older woman she had never even met, whose life was going down the drain. All Linda knew about Betty Broderick was what Dan had told her—here was a harpy asking for all that she got—and she accepted that.

But Linda at least stood for honesty, even if Dan didn't. Just as she had wanted Dan to leave his wife at the beginning of their affair years earlier, now she also begged him, friends say, to tell Betty that he was never coming back home.

But Dan wouldn't. Instead, he now chose to keep two massive deceptions going at once: he would neither tell Betty flatly that he was involved with another woman, nor that the idea of divorce had crossed his mind. Maybe he was afraid, maybe he was just undecided. Maybe the ghosts of his Catholic upbringing crippled him. In any event, he treated his wife of sixteen years with less honesty than he might have accorded a stranger.

By the time the June lease at La Jolla Shores expired, Betty had found a $650,000 house in the same area, on Calle del Cielo, one of La Jolla's prettiest hillside streets. The house was large, and it needed major repairs, but it was worth the price because of the location. She and Dan had once looked at it together.

The down payment was $140,000. Dan advanced the money to her without hesitation. He would, of course, collect it back in full nearly four years later from her share of community property in the divorce settlement, but, at the time, Betty only took it as further evidence of his commitment to their future together. She told her friends that the house was a "tear-down," and that she and Dan would soon be building a fabulous new home upon the site.

A few weeks later, she moved into her new house alone. Instead of taking any furniture with her, she shipped nearly everything in the rental back to Coral Reef, where her husband and children were. Why did she need furniture, she asked her friends brightly, when the whole house would soon be razed? For the next many months, Betty Broderick lived in her new house with its wonderful view and splendid neighborhood without even a bed, sleeping on the floor instead.

According to Dan, there was no reason for this deprivation. Even if he hadn't told her about Linda, even if he hadn't mentioned divorce, he insisted later in divorce court that he had at least clearly told her by now that he was not moving into the del Cielo house with her.

"She asked me if I would live there, and I said, 'No, Bets. We are not going to live together anymore' ..." But, he said, she would act "as if I didn't open my mouth," and say to him instead, "We'll put a second story on it and we will do this and we will do that." He says he told her, "Bets, you are not listening to me. I am not going to move into this house."

Betty says he lied. "He *never* told me that he was leaving me for good. Why else would I have moved into a house as big as [del Cielo] by myself?" she asks, appealing to logic. "Dummy me, I still thought I was shopping for a family home, because that's what he told me!"

Somebody obviously was either lying or not listening. In any case, whatever Dan told Betty, he clearly didn't say it well enough for her to comprehend. If the Brodericks hadn't communicated well before, now they could barely hear each other at all, short of landmine explosions.

Within the next month, Dan began to treat Betty as if she had never existed, either as a wife or a mother. He made every decision relevant to them both, and their children, without consulting her.

That summer, for example, he did not inform her when he decided to send their two young sons to a therapist—and not just any therapist either. Child psychologist Dr. Steven Sparta was also one of the best-known expert witnesses in custody disputes in the San Diego court system.

The insult staggered her. "I was furious. Why were my children being subjected to a psychologist, being treated as if they needed help? Help for what? Adjusting to their father's whore? Adjusting to the loss of their mother?"

But even then Betty remained as trusting as a slow-witted child. She could not understand that she was about to be divorced, and worse. Not unless Dan told her so.

On Father's Day, in yet another show of hopeful blindness, she made reservations for Dan and the children at one of their favorite restaurants and sent a rented limousine to fetch them at Coral Reef. The children later told her they all had a nice evening. But Dan didn't even call to thank her.

Then, in July, in his harshest blow so far, he sent their four children to their usual summer camps—but with orders that they be kept for an extended period "because I wanted to get them out of the middle of this," he said in the divorce trial. Then, after camp, he sent them to visit his parents in Ohio—with instructions that they limit the children's telephone contact with Betty. Compounding her shock, Dan didn't even name her as the next of kin on her children's camp records. Instead, he listed his brother Larry.

Any mother can probably relate to Betty Broderick's amazed rage. How dare he? She and Dan were still married, not even legally separated. Her children were living with their father in a house in both their names. So how could he unilaterally block her contact with them? What crime had she committed, beyond spraying paint on the walls of her own house? What entitled Dan Broderick to arbitrarily deny her contact with her own children, even in emergencies? Several times that summer, she called for her children at the summer house of Daniel and Yolanda Broderick in Ohio, only to be often told coldly that her children weren't available.

It was around about then that Betty Broderick's anger and hurt began to turn to pure hate.

Years later, in the divorce trial, only months before he died, Dan agreed that, in his anger, he had once more ignored his children's wishes. They were, he conceded, "very unhappy" about his decision to cut off their contact with their mother that summer. But he decided to act unilaterally, in their own best interests. "I admit I did that consciously ... I made it difficult for you to have contact with the children," he told Betty in court, "because of the way you were handling this anger you felt toward me."

And just how was she handling her anger in those days? Betty asked him. Beyond once defacing her own house, she had not at that time committed a single punishable offense. What precisely had she done that so branded her as an unfit mother?

But the judge told her that she was haranguing the witness, so Dan never had to answer.

Despite her rising rage, Betty carried on with her life that summer. She was going to enjoy this brief period of freedom from mothering and housewifing, she told friends. Let Dan worry about the children for a while. Until he got over his fling, she was going to travel, she was going to have fun. And, in many ways, she did.

"Living alone, at the very beginning, before I got depressed, was the most luxurious thing I ever experienced," she once said. "I had never had a bathroom to myself in my life, ever. I had never slept in a bed alone in my entire adult life. I suddenly had a closet to myself—Dan Broderick had ninety-nine percent of our closet. I never could hang my clothes up. And I had peace and quiet. You know, living with four kids gets a little noisy. I listened to music and I cut my roses and I was me, me, me. Which is what they tell you to do—take care of yourself. So I treated myself to champagne and caviar and the most expensive chocolates and the most expensive coffee, and I served everything in the most gorgeous crystal, and I tried to pretend I was having fun, and for a little while, I did."

While the children were at summer camp, she also took a two-week vacation to British Columbia. Photographs from that trip show a beautiful, slender woman in skintight jeans, smiling confidently amid the brilliance of the famed Bouchard Gardens. A friend from that period remembers her as a woman who "seemed to be on top of everything ... she had all sorts of interests, she wanted to go salmon fishing, she wanted to tour the city. There was nothing gloomy about her."

By then, too, Betty had met a handsome young man in La Jolla, Bradley Wright, with whom she would eventually have a sexual relationship, although she still has trouble admitting it. "Well, the first time, he practically raped me," she once snapped, embarrassed. Just like Dan. Translated, it only meant that Wright had to apply major pressure to persuade Betty Broderick to have intercourse with a second man on this earth.

But in the summer of 1985 Betty wasn't doing anything more with Brad Wright than cooking him dinner and allowing him to help her with "the boy jobs" around the house. She was still very much a married lady, after all. During her trip to Canada, in fact, she bought her husband "a real pretty tie." He sent it back.

Throughout these months, although Dan was paying the bills—the mortgage, the insurance premiums, the credit cards—she had no income beyond what he saw fit to send her. Traditionally, the Broderick family financial system worked in the simplest way: Betty spent whatever she wanted, and Dan paid. In addition, he also wrote her a monthly household allowance check from his business account, usually in the range of $4,000, which she used to pay for whatever items she couldn't charge, from gardeners to café tips.

In the months after he left, she relied mainly on credit cards. Sometimes he sent her checks, but, since he wouldn't talk to her on the phone, she never knew when they would arrive, or for how much. For the first time in her life, Betty Broderick had come face-to-face with her own dependency. She hadn't felt so helpless since she was twelve and had to ask her father for a dime for bubble gum.

She didn't know what to do about any of it.

But sure she did. She charged more and more, until, finally, her mushrooming bills got Dan Broderick's attention.

He came to see her one night in late August, evidently livid over her charges, which, he later said, were "just astronomical … literally thousands and thousands of dollars." He wanted to put her on a budget. He wanted her to start paying her own bills.

She was ready for him. No more sharp-tongued Miss Bitch. Now it was Miss Goody-Two-Shoes who awaited him. She looked good, she smelled good, she purred at him. Even today, Betty Broderick is a master of that people-pleasing personality mode, learned so long ago, with her father and the priests—a grown woman, batting her eyelashes, playing the helpless little girl. Most women know the strategy, but few perform the routine as well as Betty does.

Alas for her, Dan's mind was strictly on bucks that evening. Nor had he arrived in a spirit of either honesty or generosity. He had not come to tell her that he was in love with another woman and wanted a divorce, or that he was prepared to make amends by giving her the children, plus at least half of all that they owned so that she might continue to live the life they had mutually dreamed of, absent only the presence of Daniel T. Broderick III.

Instead, he sat at her kitchen table with a legal tablet and a calculator and worked out her financial requirements down to the last dime: $9,036 is what he decided her permanent monthly allowance should be. About half of that would go to meet her monthly mortgage; the rest would accommodate her living expenses. Since he was raising the children, he thought that should suffice nicely.

Yes, hon, she murmured to all that he suggested. She wasn't even paying attention to the numbers he was laying out that evening. Where, for instance, did the odd $36 come from? Instead, all she wanted was to please him, to be a vision of sweet reason. She wasn't a demanding woman. She was his wife and the mother of his children. He would see that. This would pass. She didn't even mention Linda Kolkena that evening. She was still dreaming. And he let her.

Not until later would it dawn on her that, compared to her former spending habits, she had just been hobbled. No more shopping binges at Saks, Neiman's. No more trips whenever and wherever she wanted. She had not even had the foresight to point out that her grocery bills were fully as large as his, since all four children were spending nearly as much time at her house as his.

Before he left that night, according to his later testimony, Dan told her that she was now financially on her own. "All right, now look, I am going to pay down all of your charge accounts," he told her, "but from now on, you are going to have to be responsible for your own credit card charges."

And, true to his word, the very next day, he promptly wrote each credit card company and said: "... It is all over now. I am not on these accounts anymore. We are separated ... Now Elisabeth Anne Broderick is going to have to be responsible for paying these herself, not me."

Her September check arrived promptly, for $9,036.

Less than a month later, he filed for a divorce.

She still remembers her shock, the sick pit in her stomach the day the process server arrived with the papers. Never, she insists, had Dan Broderick even mentioned the word divorce to her. Now, she could only sit in her house, gazing at the sea, and wondering why he didn't have the courage, or the decency, after 16 years of marriage and nine shared pregnancies, at least to tell her to her face that it was over. Why did the sonofabitch have to hide behind pages of legalese? Why did he have to divorce her by ambush?

Atop the shock of the divorce filing, it was also Betty Broderick's first school season without her children. Outside her front window she could see the neighborhood children in their crisp autumn plaids and shiny new loafers running down the sidewalks, their little school book packs bouncing, their eyes alive with excitement. Rhett was starting first grade today. She wondered what clothes he was wearing.

But she knew little Rhett wasn't happy that day. Both her sons had always made it clear to everyone that they wanted to live with their mother, not Dan. They told that to their friends, to Dan, to her, to every judge involved in the custody battle, and to their therapists. "I want to run away and kill myself. My heart is broken," Rhett once told a therapist, according to records.

Betty herself had no real life without her children. She missed them, she wanted them—but she would never back down. No money, no kids. She was a woman who had walked the gangplank in bravado, only to turn and discover herself cornered by the bayonets of her own stubbornness, and Dan's.

Her reaction was predictable: falling, she flailed ever more wildly.

One day in October when she came to visit her children at Coral Reef, she spotted a Boston cream pie on the kitchen counter.

She stared at it for several seconds. She was transfixed by it. "It was the shittiest little pie I've ever seen ..." For years, ever since the first days of their marriage, she had been baking those pies for Dan. They were his favorite. Slowly, it dawned on her—this was not a housekeeper's pie. No housekeeper would think to make a Boston cream pie for Dan.

Quietly, she turned to the housekeeper and asked, "Whose pie was this?" And the woman told her. Linda's.

She picked it up and walked upstairs to his bedroom. There, with a satisfaction that the years have not dimmed in the telling, Betty ventilated two years of pent-up frustrations in an orgy of custard and chocolate frosting. She dug her fingers into Linda Kolkena's Boston cream pie and flung hunks of it onto the bedspread and the walls. Then she opened his closet doors and stared in. What an anal asshole, she thought to herself, as she peered at the tidy rows of jackets and shirts and slacks, all arranged by color. All those fucking gaudy colors. Pinks, oranges, scarlet. Prints, paisleys, madras, plaids. Dapper Dan. What a cheap asshole! What a piece-of-shit Boston cream pie! She flung it at the clothes, crying, wiped her hands on his bedspread, and left.

Later Betty would minimize the damage, but even her favorite daughter, Lee, would not. "Man, she made a real mess," marveled Lee, who was home at the time. Apparently one small cake can go a long way if the assailant is committed to maximum mileage.

"Why the hell not?" she asked years later. "Here it was, months after the bastard had walked out, and he's still telling me there is no girlfriend—but there it was, my first direct evidence that the little cunt was not only in his bed, she was even baking her shitty little pies in my house!"

Dan's response was swift. Two days later, he applied for a restraining order to keep his wife from setting foot on their Coral Reef property without his consent.

Betty only laughed. Now the sonofabitch was going to try keeping her out of her own home? Good luck, Dan.

Two days later, on a Saturday morning, she marched into the Coral Reef house and flung a wine bottle through a window. She did it, she said later, because Dan had refused that day to let her son Rhett play in a soccer game at Francis Parker—where she had signed on as a coach. The only reason she was even at the Coral Reef house that morning, in fact, was to pick up Rhett for the game. But he was gone. Dan later said that he had taken the boy for a haircut instead.

When he returned to find his shattered window, Dan didn't pause. He called the police. He would have this insufferable witch jailed that very day if he could.

Instead, two bored La Jolla cops arrived, surveyed the scene—another petty domestic war among the affluent—and advised Dan Broderick to stop wasting their time. As an attorney, he should know as well as they did that "It's the lady's house. She can do whatever she wants to it."

It was the first and last clean victory Betty would ever score over her husband in the legal wars that ensued. Days later, a judge granted Dan's restraining order. Henceforth, Betty Broderick was forbidden from setting foot in her house without

Dan's permission. No more traipsing in and out to see her children whenever she felt like it. Not unless Dan said so.

It was more than her mind could absorb. They weren't even divorced. The house was half hers. Her children lived there. How could he just order her off her own property, away from her own kids? This was justice? Just when she thought her rage had peaked, it peaked again.

Finally, it began to dawn on her that she needed an attorney. And not just any attorney. She needed the best one in town to take on Dan Broderick.

She first called Thomas Ashworth, a leading San Diego divorce attorney she had known socially for years—and one she had often heard Dan praise. But Ashworth turned her down on grounds, she says, that he was about to be appointed to a judgeship and was therefore unloading his case file. The next time she saw him, he was sitting across a courtroom from her, representing Dan. Ashworth served as Dan's lawyer for nearly a year, until he became not only a judge, but presiding judge of the San Diego family courts, where the Broderick war was unfolding.

But well before that, Betty Broderick began to understand that she had a serious problem. None of the other topnotch local attorneys she called wanted her case either. They either knew Dan too well, they told her, or they had impossibly crowded calendars. Finally, Betty says, a well-regarded woman attorney told her flatly, "Go to Los Angeles, because no good divorce lawyer in this town is going to take on Dan Broderick." She gave Betty the name of a friend in Beverly Hills. Daniel Jaffe. Betty jotted the name down.

But she didn't call him. Instead, her mind was now playing new tricks on itself: none of this nonsense was necessary. Divorces took months and months. 'There was still plenty of time for Dan to wise up. Their friends, his family, everyone would be aghast once they heard. He would never go through with it. Best of all, she had the children on her side. They would never let him destroy their family. All she had to do was sit tight. Don't panic. Don't go running to take them back—which was, of course, exactly what she knew Dan expected her to do. No. She would outlast him. She was the perfect mother, and he knew it.

He did, too. Later on, Dan testified in divorce court that never in his life did he expect to become a single father. "I thought she would be a much better parent than I could be," he said. "Bets was home full-time and for many, many years in our marriage a first-class, excellent mother. I mean just an outstanding mother ... She was a much better parent before our divorce, our separation, than I am now. She was everything that you could want in a mother, loving and supportive and encouraging ..."

But now he had changed his mind. Well before the divorce was final in 1986, he said, he decided that Betty was not only an unfit mother but mentally unbalanced, too—and he had told their children as much.

"In a nutshell," he told the judge, "Bets has taken upon herself to involve the children in an unbelievable way in this divorce. She does not leave them aside and out of this but brings them ... to the center of the disputes between us, and on

110

countless occasions has told them that they're to blame for this ... that it's their fault that I have gone with another woman now, that they should do something to prevent this ... She has just done the exact opposite of what I have always understood parents were supposed to do in divorces ... [her] hatred of me has consumed her to the point that she has lost it. She needs to get it back and structure her life ... [then] she would still be the better parent."

In the margin of the court transcript, next to those lines, Betty wrote: "Five years of HELL in court. Anyone would hate him or kill him."

Chapter 11

Merry Christmas, Bets

For nearly three long years Dan Broderick had worn the hair shirt of guilt. He had tried not to leave his wife. He had made Linda miserable with his indecision. But, he was finally finished with his suffering. He had done his Hail Marys, he had at last made his choice. He was no longer going to be the good Catholic boy in perpetual pain. He was going to be with the woman he loved, and that wasn't Betty.

Having made that decision, it was not in the nature of Daniel T. Broderick III to look back. Nor was it in his nature to be held back. He was, as all his friends agree, not a man given to much emotional sensitivity, not a man who bent to the will of others, once his own will had been defined. And now he was about to get on with his life. With Linda.

And so, at last, there came the night in October when Dan Broderick did the right thing: he finally told Betty the full truth about Linda.

What happened that evening isn't clear, because Betty still can't stand to talk about it; she evades and omits.

According to her, she had asked Dan to come over "so I could tell him, again, how stupid all this was ..." She tried, one more time, to talk him out of leaving her. "I told him he was a fool, that it wouldn't last, and that, when he got over it, she would turn around and sue him for sex discrimination. I said, 'Dan, what are you doing here? I love you, we have a wonderful family, we've accomplished everything we've been working so hard for. The only person who's going to win in this whole thing is Linda Kolkena. Everyone whose last name is Broderick—you, me, and the kids—are going to lose.'" It was the first and last time in this story that Betty Broderick would ever mention the word "love" in reference to her husband—and she did it now with the breezy speed of a woman who still did not want to admit it.

That same night, she says, she also urged Dan to see a therapist. Then "he would see that he was exactly ripe for having the predetermined midlife crisis that every guy has." But Dan didn't want to discuss any of it, she says.

Finally, when it was clear to her that he wasn't going to change his mind, "I demanded the truth about Linda. I wanted him to tell me what I already knew—that I wasn't crazy, that I hadn't been imagining it!"

And he did. He told her, she says, that she had been right all along—he had been having an affair with Linda Kolkena for years. Not only that, he was in love with Linda.

So. There it was. Finally. She had known, but refused to know. Now there was no more hiding from it. She screamed, cried, and, in general, fell to pieces.

Years later, during her first criminal trial, Betty cried again, throughout the testimony of Dr. David Lusterman, an expert on infidelity, who said victims of cheating are fully entitled to their feelings of rage and betrayal. Little is more emotionally devastating,

Lusterman said, than the loss of trust and self-esteem that comes when the truth finally emerges, when the "victim" finally realizes that he or she has been lied to, day in and day out, by the one they most trusted. And the longer the lie goes on, the worse the psychological damage; typically, victims of infidelity temporarily lose all confidence in their judgment about everything else, too, including their parenting skills. Not least, said Lusterman, no real healing can occur until the "infidel" not only admits to the truth but also helps restore the victim's topsy-turvy sense of sanity by apologizing for the lies, thereby validating the victim's precarious clutch on mental health.

* * *

But Dan Broderick wasn't apologizing, not that night or ever. Instead, as he later agreed in divorce court, having finally confessed to his affair, he then wanted to take Betty to a mental hospital that night because he told her in court, "I thought you were going to commit suicide ..." Betty still has trouble tracking that logic. Granted, she says, she was hysterical. But didn't she have a right to be angry and upset "when my husband has just announced to me that, yes, he's been looking me in the eye and lying for years and now planned to destroy our family?" Why was it that suddenly the blame had shifted again? Why was she now the sick one, the poor crazy person who needed help? Wouldn't any normal woman have reacted the same way? And where was Dan Broderick's responsibility in all of it? How was it that he always so smoothly turned the tables?

Instead of going to see Dan's doctor, Betty got into her car and drove one more time over to the Coral Reef house, marched into the bedroom, undressed, and got into bed. That is where she slept that night.

She still can't explain why she did that. "Because ... I don't know ..." She flounders, she flails. "I just wanted to sleep in my bed! It was my bed!"

Dan followed her home. And he slept with her that night. Maybe he thought it was therapeutic.

A few days later, a doctor prescribed a tranquilizer for the sobbing woman who complained, according to records, that she had just degraded herself by having sex one last time with her philandering husband. She never filled the prescription because, she said later from jail, "I was afraid, at that point, I would just eat them all." And she won't discuss the sex question at all.

But reality had finally hit. That week she pulled herself together, got dressed to the teeth, and drove to Beverly Hills to see Daniel Jaffe, the divorce attorney she had been told was a match for Daniel T. Broderick III.

She hired him, with the understanding that Dan would pay his $10,000 retainer. To celebrate her deal with Jaffe, Betty went revenge shopping again. This time, she bought herself a maroon Jaguar, which she spotted parked on a Beverly Hills street with a for-sale sign in the window. It cost $15,000.

113

She was as thrilled with her new car as a teenager. Later, she cruised by the house of her neighbors, Brian and Gail Forbes, to show it off. Gail was gone, but Brian was there. She invited him for a spin. More than any other La Jolla couple, the Forbeses had been caught in the center of the Broderick divorce for years. A career attorney at Gray, Cary, Brian had known Dan since his first week on the job. Gail was one of Betty's closest friends, so loyal that, after Dan left her, she refused for a long time to invite Dan Broderick and his girlfriend into her house.

But, in the end, they both became chillingly overeager witnesses for the prosecution at Betty's trials. Among other details, Brian Forbes vividly recalled a remark Betty had made about Dan on the day they went riding in her new Jaguar. "She said she'd like to shoot his balls off," Forbes testified primly. According to him, he had admonished Betty for such talk. Whereupon, she had only laughed and said, "Oh, well, they're too small to hit anyway." Even a couple of jurors hid their smiles. Later, compounding the hypocrisy, Gail Forbes would be obliged to admit on the witness stand that she had been the one who taught Betty the word cunt in the context of a dirty joke. Among its other lessons, the Broderick story was a glaring reminder that "friendship" is often just one more frivolous, fleeting term. Some of Betty's very closest "friends"—most of them wives of attorney friends of Dan's—wouldn't talk to either the defense or the prosecution, for fear of aggravating their husbands. Instead, they either ran for cover, or, like Gail Forbes and Helen Pickard, served the prosecution. In the end, it was only the second circle of Betty's friends who stepped forward to try to help her.

The week after Dan "confessed" to Betty, his conscience at last cleared, he took Linda to his brother Larry's annual Oktoberfest party in Denver, and then to the Notre Dame-USC game in South Bend. It was the first game Betty had missed since she met Dan. Of all the hurts, real and imagined, self-imposed or inflicted by others, that she would experience over the next four years, the melancholy pain of college football always colored Betty's autumns—right up to November 5, 1989.

Finishing off the month of October, she also wrote to her mother-in-law, the same woman who had told her a year before that she was being silly, that Dan would never leave her:

"Dear Yo,

"I feel a little better now—(but am still totally devastated by this)—because after all this time Dan FINALLY told me the truth. As I knew all along, he has been sleeping with his cheap office girl for over 2 YEARS. He has also made a concerted effort to make me out a worthless lunatic so he could feel better about destroying our family. Larry knew about the whole thing and helped cover it up and foster it along.

"I will never believe he could come to this.

"—He has now sued me for divorce

"—Put restraining orders on me to keep me away from my house

"—Had me found in contempt of court and subject to incarceration.

"What has happened to the wonderful man I married? He's gone absolutely mad.

"Is there anything you or Dad can do?

114

She never got an answer. And, she says, her own family simply wouldn't listen to her troubles. At her father's birthday party in May, "I was told not to discuss my marriage in front of their friends—to lie, to pretend everything was just fine."

Her life was falling apart, piece by piece. She was learning the hard way a truth that luckier people learn much earlier: her world was only as secure as she was. She was all by herself now—alone, independent of people, places, and things, inside her own head. And the interior of Betty Broderick's head was fast becoming a desperate place to be. She was a defeated woman even then, although she was a long way from realizing it. She had gambled and lost. She had thought that forcing the children on Dan would end his love affair, bring him to his senses, bring him home. It hadn't. She had asserted her rights to enter and vandalize her own house. What had resulted instead was a restraining order, now making her a criminal if she set foot on property still in her name. She had settled meekly for less in her monthly support payments while he made up his mind. She had tried to use the age-old weapon of sex to win him back; and she had resorted to the equally pathetic female tool of tears and helplessness in her dealings with family, friends, and even strangers—only to watch them shift the burden back to her. Wherever she turned, the message was always the same: it was up to her to move on, to let him go, to let him have it his way, everyone told her. He didn't want her anymore. Their contract was canceled, because he said so. She was young and intelligent and healthy. She could start over, the way millions of other women do. The way women must do.

Her head was bursting with her inability to assimilate these nonstop messages. The more she talked, the more she tried to make people understand, the harder the barrage was returned. Now, because he was the one who had taken the offensive, she was on the defensive. If you don't shape up, Betty, her best friends told her, people will think you're crazy. You must take the children home. They were shocked at her militant behavior, just as much as Dan was. Forget money, they told her. Get the children. That's what mothers do.

No no no.

Then he would have won. He would have had it all his way. Where were her rights? It wasn't fair. Whatever else can be said about Betty Broderick, somewhere along the way she developed a deeper, more deadly definition of "fair" than most of us. To her, "fair" always translated not so much to money, as the prosecutor would later insist, but to an equal say in what would happen next. She always likened her marriage to a business contract. If one partner wants to dissolve the company, doesn't he have to buy out the other partner's interest? "That was my job, and I was fired without cause. I hadn't done anything wrong. It wasn't fair."

Dan and Linda spent the first weekend in November in San Francisco, following their Notre Dame trip. So much fun. And now, so little guilt. Now they were an open couple. He had filed for divorce, he had confessed to his philandering, now he was going on with his life—and Betty was home in La Jolla, taking care of their children. That's what they were doing to her now—turning her into their baby-sitter whenever it suited their plans.

On this particular fall day, as the drumbeat continued in her head, she was standing, once again, inside her old home on Coral Reef, looking in Dan's refrigerator. At her house, the refrigerator always bulged with wonderful foodstuffs. To Betty, a full refrigerator was synonymous with good parenting. She took occupational pride, as a mother, in her refrigerator. Kids should be able to find healthy, fun snacks there at any hour of the day. Food was warmth, food was love. She had always believed that. She could still hear her father exhorting everyone to eat more at their Sunday family dinners.

But now ...

She stared into Dan's refrigerator. It was a disgrace. One more sign of his selfish disregard for their children. Nothing fun there to eat. Only the basics. Frozen meats, milk, a few vegetables. Not even a box of Wheat Thins. No frozen yogurt bars.

But there was a bottle of champagne.

Not Dan's drink, she knew. He liked to suck on a cheap bottle of Gallo wine all weekend.

Thus, it could only be the cunt's. Champagne for the cunt, but no tasty, lovely snacks for her children ...

Uh-huh. Right.

She picked the bottle up and hurled it through a plate-glass window and watched, fascinated. The glass seemed to pause in shock as the web of cracks flew out around the hole where the bottle had crashed through. Then, almost in slow motion, the whole panel slid down, like melting ice, and shattered onto the floor. Actually, it was pretty. "It was fun!" she said later. Not since she had burned his clothes two years earlier had she felt such satisfaction. What Betty Broderick had discovered, as many women have, is that when all else fails, smashing things can feel good. She had discovered her own extended form of scream therapy, without having to go to a psychologist to pay for it. She had permanently crossed the line from 'Perfect Mrs. Everything' to 'Madame Who Gives a Fuck?'

What's more, she discovered that, even if he wouldn't talk to her, even if he hung up the phone when she yelled, this sort of activity definitely got his attention. In hindsight, everyone involved in this story would debate whether the final outcome might have been different if Dan Broderick had only reacted to Betty's early outbursts of anger with greater tolerance, or simply ignored them altogether, as a parent might ignore the attention-getting tantrums of a child. But Dan would instead become an increasingly punishing parent.

Yet, at other times, he seemed to almost cruelly nurture her hopes that the marriage wasn't over—while steadily building his case that she was truly nuts.

A couple of weeks after he had finally told her about Linda, for example, he took the kindly approach and talked her into going with him to see a psychiatrist. The purpose of that trip remains in dispute to this day. In divorce court later, Dan said, he was only trying to lead Betty, like a horse to water, to professional help because her "rampages of destruction" so alarmed him. "I didn't know what to do," he told her in court. "I did not want to have you thrown in jail. What I really wanted was for you to get psychiatric counseling so you could cope with this rage that you felt." He had only gone along that day in order to get her there, he said.

Betty's version is very different. According to her, Dan had deliberately led her to believe that they were going to see a therapist together for purposes of marriage counseling. So she had gone gladly, thinking again that there was hope. But, she says, once in the doctor's office, it became instantly clear that only she was to be "treated," not them as a couple. Furious, she walked out. Later, she decided that the visit had been just another of Dan's sneaky legal ploys: he had only been trying to set her up to confide in a therapist of his choice, who would later appear during their divorce trial, as a witness for Dan to further indict his crazy wife.

And, even by then, three years before the Brodericks ever got to divorce court, Betty Broderick, her world in shreds, was definitely beginning to feel crazy.

No doubt, Dan Broderick himself was probably beginning to feel a little off-balance, too. Like Betty, he could only make do with the emotional tools he had—and they were evidently severely limited, at least when it came to reading the woman he was trying to leave. A man accustomed to being in control, to living by the book, all he could now see was that, however belatedly, he had done all the right things. He had, at long last, told his wife that he was in love with another woman. He had filed for a divorce. He had tried to get her to see a therapist to cope with the loss of him, to channel her anger. He had gone the extra mile.

And he wasn't going one step further. Patience was not Dan's strong suit. Nor was introspection or self-doubt. From beginning to end, everything wrong with their marriage, everything that occurred afterward was, in his mind, all her fault. It never occurred to him, any more than it did to Betty, that fault might be shared. Until the end of their tale, both Brodericks saw themselves as blameless.

And now, Dan was sick of her refusal to behave like an adult. His concern for her mental health evaporated faster than his memory of yesterday's malpractice client, whose tragic "pain and suffering" he argued so masterfully in court. Now, Dan Broderick decided, the only way to tame his wife was within the arena of the law. His arena.

His weapon of choice was a judicial procedure called an Order to Show Cause, or OSC, in legal shorthand. In the next year he used it repeatedly to haul Betty before a judge to explain why she should not be held in contempt for violating the restraining order Dan had obtained in October to keep her away from him and his property.

The barrage started in November, two days before her thirty-eighth birthday. The first OSC cited the Boston cream pie mess and the broken windows. In time, the list of OSCs would expand to include a tossed toaster, a smashed stereo switch, a broken bedroom mirror, more windows, and countless other similar offenses against his property. No incident was too small to escape him. In divorce court four years later, he was still able to itemize every single bit of damage from those autumn months so many years earlier: "You pounded a hole with a hammer into a wall," he accused. "You broke the answering machine with the hammer. On another occasion, you broke the sliding glass doors. You spray-painted the wallpaper in several rooms, including the fireplace. You broke the television. . . . You broke the Plexiglas cover of the stereo, on another occasion you broke the front window of the house ..." Etc..

Moreover, he told the judge, his wild wife had made it impossible for him even to drop the children off on her quiet, respectable La Jolla Shores street without risking an embarrassing sideshow. Once, he complained, she had "thrown a rock at my car." On another occasion, "She had torn the antennae off my car. . . . She tried to pull the door open too far, so it would come off the hinge. It didn't. [But] there was a dent that had to be painted ..."

Betty admits to some of it, but, almost amused, denies the rest. "Oh, what bullshit, he's such a liar," she said later from jail. "Where would I get a rock? Our yard was all grass and concrete. And let's be logical here: do you think I'm strong enough to try ripping off a car door?"

Either way, thinking to cheat him of his newest form of authority over her, she promptly ceased all her petty vandalisms. And, for the next several months, there were no more OSCs—not until she discovered his answering machine and began leaving messages on it, ranging from the merely nasty to some so creatively obscene that Sister Claire Veronica would've fainted to hear them.

It never occurred to her that she could be punished for words alone. She was of course wrong again. Her phone messages, in fact, turned out to be Dan's richest source of OSCs. For the next three years, Betty Broderick's kitchen calendar was a tangle of OSC notations—OSCs served, continued, dropped, and heard. She would be scolded, threatened, fined, jailed twice, and threatened again. But she could not, would not stop. He would not strip her of this last little weapon. Whatever happened to freedom of speech in this country? Let them cut out her tongue. Sometimes she refused to even show up in court.

The mind games these two played would get much sicker, but they were never more baffling than at the very beginning.

Once, for example—two days after serving her with an OSC—Dan sent her roses for her thirty-eighth birthday, along with this handwritten card:

"Dear Bets,

"I know the circumstances will make it impossible for you to have a happy birthday this year. But I wanted you to know that the kids and I are thinking of you and hope you start to feel better soon. Dan."

Maybe he meant well. Or maybe, as she would always insist, he was merely taunting her.

Even so, on Dan's birthday two weeks later, she sent him "a gorgeous plaid shirt." He returned it. She gave it to Brian Forbes.

Meantime, by late fall, while the vandalisms were still ongoing, her new attorney, Dan Jaffe, was ready to tear his hair out—although, judging from his correspondence, he had a far better understanding of Betty than her former husband ever would.

Following yet another contempt summons filed by Dan, this one over a window-breaking spree, Jaffe wrote Betty a frustrated letter, begging her to shape up: "The wanton-damage nonsense has to cease," he warned her. If it did, he would be able to get the pending contempts dropped and proceed with her divorce case. Otherwise he was going to dump her as a client. "I cannot spend what talents I might have and what little time I have to utilize them in trying to justify to a court the unjustifiable, and I will not do so ... Although I am not a psychiatrist, I believe I understand the source of your rage at Mr. Broderick ... but your anger simply has to be diverted through legitimate channels, one of which is to proceed with a divorce from him and get your rightful share of the assets and support to which you are entitled.

"... If you can live within the guidelines, I will continue to represent you ... but I want to spend my time on finding out what happened to the Broderick monies and getting you some of them, rather than spending my time keeping you out of jail." He finished by urging her to seek psychiatric assistance.

Dan had decided, in the meanwhile, to sell Coral Reef and move to a different house downtown—a house that would be his, not theirs. Betty at first lent the idea lip service and even suggested a La Jolla realtor, although, within the next weeks, she would change her mind. Betty could never just say yes or no, at the risk of displeasing anyone. Later on, she would refer to it sardonically as her "wimp" factor. It hobbled her throughout her life.

But, however childish she was growing, her husband, in his own way, was displaying an equally petty streak. The only difference was that, while she was still refusing to live with any of their furniture, instead inhabiting a nearly empty house, Dan was now busy cataloguing and evaluating every piece of it, right down to the last cheap coaster.

In a letter to Betty the day before Thanksgiving, he advised that he was moving into his new house on January 3. She had until then to let him know what pieces of furniture she wanted from Coral Reef. Anything she didn't claim, he wrote, "I intend to take with me or sell."

Nor would this be any casual transaction. He laid out his instructions in meticulous, tedious detail:

"I will arrange for [the furniture transfer] as soon as you provide me with a WRITTEN list of what you want. I am well aware that you want the desk, armoire, and love seats that have been stored in the garage, but I am not sure about the piano, the living room couch, the dining room set, the pewter flatware, the red easy chair and stool, the pink swivel chairs ... the end tables, the table lamps, the serving table/china cabinet that used to be in the dining room ..."

Then, in admonishment: "Since June, I have been asking you for a proposed budget IN WRITING of the improvements you would like to make in your house and the furniture you want for it. For reasons I can't begin to understand, you will not give this to me. As a result, you continue to live in a state of relative deprivation. Why you want to do this to yourself is beyond me, but when you're ready to stop it, send me the budget and we'll get started ... Sincerely Yours, Dan."

"Fuck you. I've had the budget for months and you won't look at it," she scribbled at the bottom of his letter. By now, these furious little notes, which he would never even see, were her main form of emotional release, since he would no longer talk to her on the telephone. Her anger annoyed him too much. At his insistence, all communication was now either by mail or by courier—i.e., the Broderick children. Because Dad wouldn't talk to Mom, they were now obliged to act as go-betweens in arranging their weekend visits to her house. Sometimes Dan would let them go, other times not, depending on how Betty had behaved that week. And, as his daughters later testified, he would never render his final decision until Thursday night.

Meantime, at Francis Parker School, teachers were beginning to complain about the deterioration in the condition of the Broderick boys since the separation.

Danny and Rhett would frequently arrive at school improperly dressed, without even jackets in cold weather, admissions director Beverly Dewart later testified in Betty's trials. And so the school would provide for them from "the lost and found," she said. Also, Rhett sometimes came to school with "dirt caked behind his ears, his hair would be dirty," and he would often wear the same clothes for several days in a row, she said. In addition, the boys sometimes came to school so visibly ill that they would be put to bed on couches in the nurse's room until one of the parents came to fetch them. Rhett, especially, always seemed to have a bad cold, Dewart testified. On those occasions, the school called Dan first, since he was the custodial parent, but he was often unavailable. They would then call Betty, who, Dewart said, always arrived promptly to fetch the ailing child.

Then it was Christmas season, Betty's favorite time of year, the month when, in times past, she traditionally held her grand children's party, when she was busy twelve hours a day, racing around La Jolla, buying the best of everything, from sequined bulbs for the tree to scarlet felt place mats and candied apples. December was Betty's month.

But now she sat in her house wondering what to do. There would be no Christmas party this year. Those were family events, and she had no family anymore.

But, she thought, she would still take the children skiing that year, if Dan would agree. That was another family tradition—in years past, after her Christmas party, the family had usually taken a ski week vacation either to Keystone, Colorado, or Park City, Utah.

Dan agreed immediately. In fact, in a December 2 letter, dictated to his secretary, he urged her to take the children that Christmas "at my expense." But, as always, his correspondence had a command tone to it. He had plans to go to Park City himself on December 21, he wrote, and had intended to take the children with him. However, "If you would prefer to take them somewhere (at my expense) or want them to stay with you for Christmas, that will be all right with me." But, he added, since the time for making travel arrangements was short, "please let me know what your plans are by five P.M. on December 6. Sincerely yours, Dan."

It was the opening for another ugly scene. Betty says she didn't even receive his letter until the afternoon of his December 6 deadline. Why couldn't the sonofabitch have just picked up the telephone?

Not that it mattered. What mattered more was money. Dan offered her an extra $2,000 for the trip. The rest she would have to pay herself.

Don't be ridiculous, she said. The airline tickets, condo rental, and meals for herself and four children would cost three times that much, and he knew it. Why was he nickel-and-diming her to death?

But he refused to offer more.

And Betty refused to bend. She was too enraged. It was their money. These were their children. What gave him the right to dictate the terms? Furthermore, if she couldn't take the children skiing, she wasn't about to entertain them at home that season either. "Why should they have to suffer, because he's being a cheap bastard?" she asked later. "If he was going to deprive them of their traditional ski holiday, I wanted them to know it!"

But Dan didn't deprive them of their Christmas ski trip. Instead, he took all four of them along on his own ski trip to Park City. With Linda. All six spent the week together in a cozy little three-bedroom condominium he had rented. It was the first time Dan had gone public with Linda, with the Broderick children in attendance.

Probably no other single incident in the entire Broderick divorce war devastated Betty more. Although it eventually became far more complex, the Broderick case was always a crime grounded, not in sexual jealousy, but in Betty Broderick's sexual inhibitions. She was staggered, and still is to this day, that Dan would sleep with Linda in front of their children. Fathers were at least supposed to be divorced from the mother before they exposed their youngsters to naked adult lust. Dan Broderick had finally crossed the line in her mind from philandering college boy to vile cuntsucker. She would never recover.

"He kidnapped my children," she says from jail, still practically screaming in pain. "He took them to a condo where he fucked the cunt in front of them, and we weren't even divorced! What do you think my baby [Rhett] thought of that?"

The shock of it so seared her that, even today, she doesn't accept February 28, 1985, the night he walked out, as the true date of their separation. Instead, in her mind, the real date was December 21, the first day of Dan's ski trip—"the first time he had tried openly to replace me with Linda the Cunt Kolkena with my kids as witnesses."

Betty's hysteria aside, it was in fact fairly remarkable that Dan Broderick had so quickly overcome the moral code of his upbringing to cohabit with another woman with his children long before he was even divorced. Likewise, Linda Kolkena, for all her prior crying about the agonies of adultery, had also apparently overcome all guilt about consorting with a married man in the presence of his children, then aged six to fifteen.

Compounding Betty's sense of sick disbelief, Dan even sent her a bouquet of Christmas flowers from his trip, along with a perfunctory little card that read: "Bets, I hope you have a Merry Christmas. Love, Dan."

During the first murder trial, Betty's sister-in-law and former college classmate, Maggie Bisceglia, summed up her view of the case in a single, tight-lipped line: "She

121

killed him for the infidelity, period."

She passed that Christmas season alone, wild as an animal with its foot in a trap. She went over to the Coral Reef house, thinking for the first time that she might take a few pieces of furniture home to her empty house. Her mind was trying to make the leap, although it never would, to some new life. She would go on. She had to. She was smart, she was still not so old, she was still pretty. Other men would want her. Yes.

She stared at Dan's Christmas tree, with its bright packages beneath. She leaned over. "To Linda," said one. It was a big box, the kind department stores provide. Some item of clothing. A sweater? Or a nightgown? Her eyes went blind as she ripped it apart. She tore several other packages to shreds, too, then stood up and threw something, she can't remember what, through a wall mirror. And then she left, sobbing, and drove back to her empty home, where she sat for several hours alone in front of her Christmas tree before she fell asleep. She didn't even have the dogs for company anymore. They were at Dan's house, too.

Surveying the damage upon his return home, Dan filed his third OSC.

* * *

That was Christmas 1985. The finale came in a skirmish over a bunch of pine boughs worth $28.51. At issue was who owed a bill from Adelaide's Florist in La Jolla. It had been sent to Dan, but he promptly forwarded it to Betty. She barely glanced at it before concluding that the sonofabitch had billed her for the flowers he sent her for Christmas. She instantly mailed it back to him. "I do not want to pay for these ugly flowers you sent me before you went off with your cunt," she scrawled at the bottom.

With typical, cold determination, he sent it right back to her with a short, typed note: "Dear Bets: I am returning the statement you sent me from Adelaide's. ... I checked with Adelaide's bookkeeper and she has informed me that the December 14 charge was actually for two pine cone/evergreen arrangements with horns attached and that they were delivered to your address. No doubt these are the arrangements you bought to hang on either side of your front gate. In light of this clarification, I assume you will want to pay the bill. Sincerely yours, Dan."

She paid the bill.

In about the only note of warmth in her 1985 holiday season, Betty received a card from the young fencing contractor she had met. It was touching in its innocent simplicity.

"Dear Bets ... Have ever so enjoyed you and all your gooniness ... I'm very happy we've been able to do all we've done and look forward to much more in 'eighty-six. Please don't hesitate to ask me to help you whenever I can. Keep your cute little imagination going ... you can be so good with so little effort. Best wishes for the happiest new year you've ever had. Love, Brad."

Chapter 12

Good Day Lady Bets

The house Dan bought for himself was about as far from the vanilla serenity of La Jolla as he could get. A large red-brick colonial with green shutters and regal white columns flanking the front door, it sat back from the street, framed by two great eucalyptus trees, with a circular driveway in front, ringed by tidy beds of flowers. It was in a racially mixed downtown neighborhood on the edge of Balboa Park, bordering a thriving homosexual district. Although his house was one of four large, aging mansions in a cul de sac, the neighborhood itself was mainly small, unpretentious Spanish and frame bungalows with old cars parked in front, untrimmed lawns, and occasional graffiti. In Dan's new community, perfection was the last thing on anybody's mind. From his backyard, he had a view of the lovely wildness of the arroyo fronting the park.

Betty was horrified, both by the house and the neighborhood. Ironically, in better days Dan had once tried to interest her in the same house, but "I refused to even go inside. It was not a house for children ... It had no family room, it didn't even have a swimming pool, and it was miles from the kids' schools."

And so, now, at the eleventh hour, she balked at selling Coral Reef. She waffled, she evaded, she said the price ($325,000) wasn't right. She complained that Dan's new decor had undermined the house's real value. She gave every reason under the sun but the real one: to sell Coral Reef was to concede that her marriage was over. Coral Reef, the family home, was the last tie she had left to earlier, saner times when she knew who she was. Without Dan, without her family, Betty had no identity at all. She was literally incapable of severing that bond. But neither could she just say no.

Dan's interest in selling Coral Reef as soon as possible was of course both obvious and reasonable: he was now paying the monthly mortgage on three houses—hers, his, and theirs, which was sitting empty. Plus, as Kim later said in trial, "Dad thought that if he moved into his own house, maybe Mom wouldn't keep coming back and destroying things, because she wouldn't have such an emotional interest."

What followed was part comedy, part tragedy.

Once, when they had their first buyer lined up, she simply refused to sign the papers properly. The buyer walked out in impatience. Not until the end of January did a second buyer surface—and the same run-around began again.

The man caught in the middle of all this was attorney Dan Jaffe, who was representing Betty in the negotiations—or trying to. In a final, absurd episode, after the second buyer had been found, Jaffe flew to San Diego and drove Betty to the office of Dan's attorney, Thomas Ashworth, to finalize the paperwork. By now, Jaffe had extracted an agreement that Dan would not only pay Betty half of the selling price, but $18,000 extra—an amount she demanded to make repairs on her own new home. Jaffe's fee was also supposed to come out of the proceeds.

But upon arriving at Ashworth's office, Jaffe later testified, Betty refused to get out of the car. Instead, Jaffe was obliged to conduct what he called "shuttle diplomacy." He went upstairs, talked to Dan and Ashworth, finalized the papers, then brought them back down to the car for his client to sign. And, finally cornered, Betty refused: she had to "think about it," she said. Jaffe flew back to Los Angeles, undoubtedly as exasperated as he had ever been.

On the following Monday, Dan Broderick got a court order to sell the house without Betty's consent. He used what is called a four-hour notice, which means that he was able to make his case to the judge whether she was present or not—and she was not. Once the judge was persuaded that Betty was being unreasonable, a court-appointed official (or elisor) was assigned to serve in her stead, signing the required house sale documents.

Dan Jaffe would later testify that he had warned Betty such a tactic was not only standard but probable in cases where one spouse in a divorce was holding up a house sale. She denies to this day that Jaffe ever told her any such thing. "What is an elisor? I still don't know." Again, Betty apparently hadn't been able to hear.

She was in her kitchen cooking "a gorgeous pot roast and mashed potatoes dinner" when Jaffe called from Beverly Hills to tell her that Coral Reef had been sold that day. The boys were there and her parents were visiting from New York; she also had a summer houseguest from Canada, Brian Burchell (strictly platonic, she stresses).

She hung up the telephone and didn't even pause. This time, she knew in advance that she was going to make a major, major scene. She felt almost sick, she was so enraged.

Carefully, habitually, she turned the heat down on her roast, and brushed past her parents, sitting in the living room. "Be right back," she told them cheerfully. As she got into her car, she was trembling with anger. This couldn't have happened. Yet it had happened. Her husband, her hotshot, legal beagle husband, this arrogant asshole, had sold her house without her consent!

She wove in and out of traffic and squealed to a stop in front of his house. She almost ran to the front door, banged on it, waited, banged again, rang the doorbell.

He wasn't home, but her two daughters were. They took one look at Mom and knew that, whatever it was, it was going to be bad.

By now, Betty was afraid to walk into his house without permission, so she sat down on the front steps and waited.

All she wanted in the world, at that blind moment, was for him to tell her, How did he dare? It was her house, too. It was her life, her investment. How did these people just do these things? How could judges and courts and lawyers simply ignore her? How could they just sell her house without even her signature?

In less than an hour, Dan pulled into the driveway. He approached, tight-lipped. Where, she demanded, almost panting, was her house? Where was her half of the money? And how dare he sell her house?

Dan Broderick eyed her carefully. She was, he could see, in no mood for calm discussion. And he was in no mood to conciliate. He was sick of her temper fits. So

124

he did what he always did: he ordered her off his property. She was in violation of court orders. And he slammed the door in her face. Dan Broderick's coldness sometimes verged on the breathtaking. Years later, even Betty's defense attorney would privately marvel, in all sincerity, at the way Dan had treated his ex-wife: "He was either extremely stupid or cruel, or he had a real death wish."

In a delirium of anger, she left, and drove over to Coral Reef, where she rummaged through the garage and found a can of gas. She poured it around the house and started a fire. But before it did more than singe a small spot on the rug, she came to her senses. Why was she burning down her own house?

She stopped, mashed out the coughing matches, and drove back to his house. But this time, she did not park at the curb. Instead, she pulled into the circular driveway, then veered sharply to the left and onto the lawn. She backed up the van and pulled forward, until it was aimed directly at his front door, flanked by its white columns.

She gunned the engine, calculating her attack exactly. As she later said, "I didn't want to hit the place hard enough to knock it down, and I didn't want to hurt my car—because I knew the fucker wouldn't pay for the repairs."

Besides that, she didn't have enough distance to gain any real speed. But her heart was in it. Slowly, deliberately, and with enough rage to raze the Brooklyn Bridge, Betty Broderick roared across the manicured grass, across the driveway, onto the porch, and with a vicious crunch, smashed her two-ton Suburban into his pretty white door.

Inside the house, Dan Broderick, who was in the kitchen preparing for dinner with his daughters, froze. "Wow, it sounded like an explosion or something," said daughter Lee later. Kim thought it sounded like "a chainsaw."

Dan ran to the front of his house and stared at his living room door. Contrary to later gossip, it was not lying in splinters on his floor—it was only dangling awry from its hinges. He stepped through it and onto his porch and stared in amazement at his wife, behind the wheel of her Suburban. For once, his rage was fully equal to hers, and just as spontaneous.

He reached in, jerked her out of the van, and slammed her in the chest with his fist, knocking her to the ground. Lee tried to fling herself between her two grappling parents, "but they squished me." According to Betty, that was the only time Dan ever deliberately hit her.

Later, much would be made of the fact that Betty also had a butcher knife on the front seat of her car. According to her, it was pure coincidence—she had bought it just that afternoon, she said, along with a new trash can, also in the car. Not that it really mattered. At that point, butcher knife or none, it's unlikely that Betty Broderick intended to kill her husband, since she had not yet even accepted the end of their marriage. She was simply making an angry statement.

And now, Dan would make his.

He called the police—who arrived, took one look at the hysterical, weeping woman on the premises, put her in a strait-jacket, and drove her directly, not to jail, but to a local mental hospital for observation. They made that decision based on Dan's recommendation, as well as their own view that Betty was a threat to herself and others. As the police drove Betty away, Kim said, "Mom stuck her tongue out at me."

According to the defense later, Dan also identified himself on hospital admissions records that night, not as an attorney, but as Dr. Daniel T. Broderick III. "It was much easier for Dan Broderick to have his wife committed if he identified himself as a doctor, than as a lawyer who prosecuted doctors," Betty's attorney told the jury. The deputy district attorney countered, somewhat lamely, that maybe it had been Betty, not Dan, who had misidentified him. But it was unlikely that Betty Broderick had been coherent enough at that point to remember much more than her own name. She was slipping over the edge so fast now. And no one was there anymore to lend her a helping hand, to catch her fall.

Her parents left town the next morning without even visiting her at the hospital. They were angry, they were shamed, and her mother immediately felt ill. "All they said was, 'How could she do this to us?'" recalled Betty's houseguest, Brian Burchell. "It was real cold."

Betty remained incarcerated at the hospital under mental observation for seventy-two hours, during which time she was mostly uncooperative with hospital personnel. She told doctors the same thing she had been saying to everyone else for more than a year: "I'm not crazy—he is."

While she was there, Dan called, not to sympathize, but to ask her exactly what it was that she wanted? What would stop her maniac attacks on his property? By then, she was clear-headed enough to reply: she wanted $40,000 extra on the house sale to compensate for the bastard's damage to her house, her head, and her life. He promptly agreed, knowing of course that he would later collect back every cent of his cash advances in the community property division.

In a hospital report later introduced in her murder trial, Betty was described thusly: "... habitual maladaptive problems ... exploitation, glib social style, shallow, indifferent to the feelings of others ... histrionic and immature demands for attention." She denied being suicidal, the report said, but admitted to homicidal thoughts about Dan and Linda. The doctor's final diagnosis was that she was a "borderline personality ... histrionic and narcissistic."

When she was released, it was Burchell who came to drive her home, to comfort her as best he could. But nobody could touch the depths of her new humiliation. Whatever reputation she had left was now in shreds. The word was now out all over La Jolla—Betty Broderick truly was Crazy Betty.

Adding insult to injury, Dan even sent her the hospital bills. He would teach her responsibility for her actions, by God, or die trying.

But her resilience was always awesome to behold. In the next weeks, she ignored the whispers, the blushes, the awkward pauses whenever she ran into old friends on Prospect. Throughout the spring of 1986, she dashed about La Jolla, livelier, brighter,

126

more defiant than ever. She told everyone precisely why she had rammed her car into his front door: the bastard had sold her house out from under her—and the courts had let him. A woman being divorced had no rights whatsoever, she raged. Compounding their discomfort, she also lectured her friends: if it could happen to her, then it could happen to them, too.

She "wanted to kill him," she would say, or "wring his neck." And the judges', too. But Betty said these things so often, so spontaneously, that nobody paid any attention—they were just figures of speech, Betty's way of talking. But why couldn't she be quiet? Why couldn't she hide out at home and mourn her losses in private? Instead, she was shameless. She wanted the world to know that Dan Broderick had thrown the mother of his children into a looney bin. Nobody took her seriously anymore. She was fast becoming only pitiful.

Evidently, even Dan temporarily thought so, too, because only a week after her release from the mental hospital, he turned his children over to their mother for a week-long ski trip to Keystone. What's more, he agreed to pay for it in full. The same man who had only weeks earlier refused to pay his wife's $28.51 Christmas floral bill now promised, without a murmur of complaint, that whatever the cost, he would pay it. She would not be billed for it later.

Maybe he was feeling guilty, or maybe he was hoping to reverse a bad situation—his friends say even Dan was shocked by her parents' abrupt departure while she was still in the mental hospital. Either way, although she accepted, his gesture only further enraged and insulted her. One more time, the Count DuMoney was demonstrating his largesse—at his own pleasure. Where was her fair share? Where was her parity in this divorce?

While she was in Keystone with the children, Dan dictated a will, notarized by Linda Kolkena, leaving all his worldly goods to his four children. Later on, his friends would insist that he had always known Betty was homicidal. It is an assertion that hardly bears inspection, given his approach to the Betty Problem over the next four years. Frightened people don't poke sticks into a tiger's cage.

In making his decisions on which trips he would pay for, Dan later testified, he had been guided by Betty's "tone" during the spring of 1986. He agreed to pay for the Keystone week, for example, because her tone then had been suitable. But, six weeks later, he refused to pay a lesser amount for her to take the children on Easter week to Warner's ranch because, then, he said, her tone had been unsuitable: "She called me at the last minute and asked if I was going to pay for it ... and believe me," he told the judge, "if she had asked me, 'Dan, look I need the money,' or 'I wish you would pay for it,' or anything in that tone, I would have. Staying at Warner's is very inexpensive ... it wasn't the money. It was the tone. The names that were used at me. So, I said, 'There is no way I am going to pay for it.'"

So the Broderick children spent their Easter vacation confused and upset, again shuffling between his house and hers, because Dad was mad at Mom.

Dan Broderick was also apparently exceedingly touchy about community criticism after he left his wife. That spring, for example, he wrote a sharp letter to Wilma Engel, a friend of Betty's from her Coral Reef baby-sitting days. Engel, a striking, dynamic stockbroker—and a woman whose personality was just as strong as Dan Broderick's—was never shy about publicly saying what she thought of Dan's squalid treatment of his wife—and word soon got back to him.

"Dear Wilma, I understand that you sat next to an acquaintance of mine a few weeks ago on an airplane to Tucson," he wrote. He accused Engel of presenting a "warped perception" of the details of his life to his friends. Furthermore, he added, "I also understand you called him on several occasions at his hotel room in Tucson after the flight and later in Atlanta. For John's sake [Engel's husband], I'll keep that to myself.

"If you spent a little more time trying to cope with the obvious shortcomings in your own life and less time endeavoring to titillate people with stories about mine, you would probably be a lot better off. Sincerely yours, Daniel T. Broderick III."

"I took it as a blackmail letter," Engel said. "He was threatening to tell my husband I was having an affair if I didn't stop criticizing him. Dan Broderick was evil." Engel—who was not having an affair—immediately showed the letter to her husband, also an attorney, who was equally shocked at its petty, unprofessional nature. Four years later, both Engels volunteered to testify in Betty's murder trial about Dan's bullying tactics, but the judge ruled all character testimony concerning the deceased irrelevant.

Besides the money she got that spring from the sale of Coral Reef, Betty also received another $16,000 from Dan, who had sold their Fairbanks Country Club membership—again without consulting her. She was furious. On the other hand, she was again cheered by this money from Dan. Although she would eventually learn otherwise, she apparently still thought at the time that it was some sort of gift, a display of largesse on the part of a wayward husband, recompense for his sins.

Witlessly, she continued digging her own financial grave. Ever since Dan walked out on February 28, 1985, the clock had been steadily ticking away her share of their community property. But not until she finally got to divorce court years later would she fully comprehend what the financial liabilities of the ex-wife really are. Her lesson would come in the form of a subtle little sandtrap which, in California, is called an Epstein credit. Although the name varies, most community property states now have some equivalent of the Epstein—which, simply put, is the means by which the supporting spouse can, when finally divorced, charge the dependent spouse for one half of all community debts accumulated, not from the date of divorce, but from the date of separation. Epstein credits would later cost Betty Broderick nearly half a million dollars in her share of the wealth she had helped her husband accumulate. Epstein credits are just one more reason she killed him.

But, at the time, she "just assumed that the courts would automatically see that I got half of whatever we owned—I thought that's what community property laws meant."

* * *

Meantime, Dan refused to pay Jaffe's $10,000 retainer, despite the fact that he knew he would be reimbursed during the eventual property settlement for every cent he paid Betty in cash advances. Instead, as he later admitted in the divorce trial, he told Betty, "Pay him yourself." Why he took such a hard-nosed stand, given his persistent claim that he only wanted a speedy resolution to the divorce, is anybody's best guess. But the theory that makes the most sense is Betty's own: Dan Broderick, being a smart lawyer himself, recognized a heavyweight when he saw one. He didn't want Dan Jaffe fiddling in his finances. Jaffe, unlike Betty's next lawyer, was apt to take him to the cleaners, and he knew it.

But, at the time, Betty didn't care. She was, in fact, glad. If Dan wanted a divorce, he should pay for it. And if he didn't pay for it, maybe he didn't really want it? It was a confused point of principle and hope that she would never abandon. Besides, how could she be divorced if she wasn't participating in the process?

And so, instead of mailing Dan Jaffe a check herself to keep him on her case, she bopped around La Jolla all summer, complaining to everyone that Dan wouldn't even pay her attorney fees. And she wasn't about to pay Jaffe herself since she didn't even want a divorce.

Jaffe, meantime, who hadn't been keen to take on a San Diego divorce case in the first place, was not getting any happier.

"I admit I have been foot-dragging on this case in the hope that some competent San Diego family lawyer would rush forward and represent Mrs. Broderick in this matter," he wrote Dan's attorney, Ashworth, in January, 1986. "... [But] since it appears that, if Mrs. Broderick is ever going to obtain competent counsel it is going to be my office, I am prepared to go forward and represent [her] upon receipt of a $10,000 retainer payable by Mr. Broderick ..."

By April, Dan Jaffe, still unpaid, finally tired of all the games. By then, he was also as annoyed at Betty as Dan.

"Tom Ashworth has not returned a number of my calls wherein I tried to find out what was happening with you," Jaffe wrote Betty. "... It is clear that you still do not want a lawyer to represent you and there is simply no way I can help you in this matter." She didn't respond, and, days later, he officially quit in a second letter.

"I am not appearing as your attorney of record at this point, since I have not received a retainer," he wrote. But, in parting, Jaffe still tried to warn Betty that she was embarked on a course of disaster: Dan Broderick and his attorney were proceeding with the divorce. If she didn't move in her own behalf, he told her, the divorce would be accomplished by default—just like the house sale, it would be done with or without her participation.

But Betty couldn't hear. In time, three other attorneys would run into the same frustrating, self-defeating brick wall of Betty Broderick's blind stubbornness. One by one, she hired them, and then fired them, finding every reason under the sun to refuse their advice.

Meantime, Dan was busy in April, attempting to get her to agree to his proposed divorce settlement. In a friendly "Dear Bets" letter, he outlined a plan that, in its essentials, awarded joint legal custody of the children "with primary physical custody to me and reasonable visitation to you." He would provide no child support, but would continue to pay her $9,036 in monthly spousal support until "further order of court." As for the property issues, he asked her to accept his evaluations of their communal wealth, including his assessment of his law practice.

By his numbers, she would get half of their property, or $334,000; in addition, he would assume their community debts, estimated by him at $345,000; but in exchange, she would make no claim on his multimillion-dollar law practice. However, he added, in a note of sweet reason, "I think you should be entitled to share to some degree in the fees I later collect from my work while we were married and living together." But he intended to subtract forty percent from those fees for overhead, then prorate the rest, based on the time he had been living with her while he worked on the case. Admittedly, he conceded, the 40 percent overhead deduction was arbitrary, based on his own calculations.

He then provided a practical example of just how his formula would work: "Assume that I received a fee of $600,000, and that two-thirds or $400,000 of that sum was community property. This $400,000 figure would first be reduced by the overhead percentage, leaving $240,000. Your one-half share would be $120,000, and from that $120,000 I would be entitled to deduct what had been paid to you up to that point in time as spousal support. In other words, if you had received six months of support that had not already been taken into account in earlier distributions, then this hypothetical $120,000 would be reduced by six times $9,025, or $54,150." In short, she would get about $65,000 from his $600,000 case.

He urged her to let him know soon if his proposal was suitable and signed off with "Best regards, Dan."

"I didn't know what the hell it meant," she said later, "but I did know it sounded like I was getting royally screwed."

As it turned out, it was the most generous offer she would ever hear from Dan Broderick.

She ignored it. She also ignored an earlier letter from him in March, advising her that he intended to seek a bifurcated divorce. "This will authorize the court to separate the issue of our marital status from the property disposition," he explained to her. "This is fairly common in cases involving complex property issues." In other words, he wanted a divorce now, with the property settlement worked out later—years later, as it would so happen. She ignored that letter, too. He couldn't divorce her if she had no attorney and didn't participate.

Betty Broderick did not do women proud. Instead of acting like a rational female adult responsible for her own lot in this life, she opted instead to behave like the cute, helpless, wining little girl she had been trained from birth to be. Old habits die hard.

Unfortunately for her, she was now playing hardball with a master. Dan Broderick had been busy protecting his own interest ever since the day he walked out. But she would not figure that out—if she ever did—until nearly three years later when the Broderick divorce finally went to trial. At which time, in one of the most breathtaking examples of stupidity, blind faith, and arrogance that any woman ever displayed, she walked into court without a lawyer and represented herself in what amounted to her own financial beheading. She came out of it with a cash award of $28,000, while he walked off with his multimillion-dollar legal practice. Betty's modus operandi throughout this story was enough to cause even the most tepid of feminists to weep.

Everywhere she looked, during those early months of 1986, there were new lessons for a discarded wife to learn. According to her friends, she was supposed to "get out and meet new guys." She was supposed to get a job, get the kids back, go to school, jog, pay her bills, budget, hire a cheaper gardener. Loosen up, let him go, ignore them. Grow up, be classy, rise above it all. Be cool. Have fun. Be a new person. Don't be Betty Broderick anymore.

But she did take a few baby steps.

She got a part-time job at the Simic Art Gallery in La Jolla Village. And she liked it. "It was 7-Eleven art, so I didn't have to know anything about real art," she later said from jail, laughing. "But I had fun. I got to wear all my pretty clothes and see people every day, and the hours were flexible enough so I could still spend time with my kids after school. I liked it—and the owner [Mario Simic] was a real hunk." That's how Betty talks about handsome men. Like a teenager.

"And Brad picked me up every night after work," she says. Then they would go to Alphonso's for enchiladas, or down to the beach for crab.

See, see, was her message to nagging friends: I am getting on with my life. I am fine. I'm not crazy, he is! Now, get off my back!

She was fine. Yes, she was.

But Brad wasn't fine. He never would be. True, he was handsome, he was sweet, and his credentials were okay, too. He was educated, a graduate of the USC business school, and, she adds with a certain pride, "He was brought up right." His parents, well-to-do retirees from Pasadena, observed the amenities. He not only knew his wine but even how to swirl it casually in his glass for a few seconds while the waiter stood by, waiting for him to taste it. Betty especially loved his mother, Kay.

Brad was also, during the next long, tortured years, her most faithful friend. "Once, in the middle of it all," she later said, in one of her more subdued moods, "I had tried to talk to my parents about what was happening to me, and they wouldn't listen, so I was lying in bed, and just crying my heart out; and Brad came in, and he just held me while I cried, and he didn't say a word. Nobody had ever done that before ..."

But Brad wasn't Dan. He wasn't as smart, he wasn't rich, and he lacked flair. He spent his days, for God's sake, measuring construction pits and debating the merits of chain link versus steel mesh, supervising a handful of blue-collar workers in his modestly successful little fencing business. Beyond that, his main passion was sailing. Worst of all, he was six years younger than she was. Betty Broderick was no Cher. She was caught irretrievably in the old-fashioned double standards of her upbringing—which said that women always marry men who are one, two, perhaps five years older. No more, no less. Like Dan, three years older—that was perfect. "I know six years isn't that much. But he seemed so much younger. He had no life experiences. He was just so innocent, he always seemed like my eight-year-old."

It was just one more door to a new future slammed shut by her past. She was, and remains, completely embarrassed at her lonely liaison with Wright. It was a comedown. She could see it in the eyes of other La Jolla wives, women whose parties she and Dan used to attend—women who once openly envied her for her husband, so much smarter, more successful, more handsome than their own. One of Betty's most fatal flaws was her inability to forget what other people were thinking. She was her mother's daughter. She was Dan's wife. Image was all.

"I remember once when I had Brad escort me to a major charity event," she said later, still squirming at the memory. "I felt so stupid and failed and old. Here I was, getting fat, in my ugly matron's dress, with this young hunk, this sweet guy, but he was a nobody—and I didn't want to be the other half of a midlife crisis joke. I felt like a fool, and everybody acted as if we didn't even exist. I went overnight from front-row tables to the back of the room."

Have a little sex, it's good for you, her divorcee friends urged her, giggling.

Become a slut, her mind silently retorted. Become a pitiful, aging whore.

"I thought Brad was so cute, I always told her to go for it," says her friend Vicki Currie. "But she just always just pooh-poohed it."

In fact, just to make double sure nobody thought she was being promiscuous, Betty told several friends that Brad was gay.

Brad Wright was not gay. In reality, Wright had finally introduced the proper Catholic girl to sex with a man not Dan, and, according to him, she was liking it fine. "She called me Animal," he said later with a sheepish grin, "and I called her the Dinosaur, she was so old-fashioned." Then, "After she started to get so big, I called her Bear." Once, he offered, guileless as a blushing boy, he even crushed one of her ribs during sex.

Betty was aghast that Brad had told. First she fell into nervous giggles, chattering a mile a minute, trying to escape the topic. Normally so verbal, so unflappable, even on such topics as murder, she simply cannot talk about sex. The same woman who left such sexually explicit messages on Dan Broderick's telephone machine ("... you're screwing the cunt [in the hall] that has her legs wide open for anybody who comes by ...") loses her tongue when it comes to any discussion of her own physical pleasures. To this day, she cannot admit that she has ever enjoyed sex with any man.

But, she insists, sex was always better with Dan, "because Brad wasn't my husband. At least with Dan, even if it wasn't much fun, I felt like it was right."

Even after Dan left her, after she was divorced, after her tubes were tied, after she was finally free of the fear of pregnancy, Betty never crossed the great divide to sexual liberation. She never even made it into the sixties.

But, she agrees with a self-conscious laugh, sex was definitely different with Brad. No black-shrouded nuns sat at the end of his bed, crying "Procreate!" He believed in simple things, new to her—like sex in the daylight. "Suddenly, here was Brad, walking around the house naked! And I just didn't know anything about anything."

After the killings, Betty rewarded Wright for his loyalty. She signed over her new condominium to him outright, in a quitclaim deed—"so the lawyers couldn't get it."

At the same time, a new idea was beginning to crowd into her mind: she was a woman whose whole life had been cast in one direction, that of the professional Wife and Mother. It was all she knew how to be. Therefore, she needed to create a new household, complete with a new husband. If Dan could start over again, why couldn't she?

Who was she kidding?

Even dating was an impossible prospect. It's not hard to imagine her panic. Where does a thirty-eight-year-old mother of four who has no dating experience, no flirting skills, no persona beyond that of being "Mrs. So and So" even begin?

Nowhere, is where. It was as hopeless as pitching a nun into a disco. They will not shimmy overnight.

She stared at her body in the mirror, trying to imagine what kind of man, short of a complete loser in life, could possibly want this used mother of four, this body worn from nine pregnancies, this woman thrown away by another man. No man, that's who, her mind cried. In her view, there wasn't much difference between being thirty-eight, fifty, or sixty-five. Her best days were gone; she was old. She no longer had anything left to offer. That's why Dan had left her in the first place. The fear was so bad. She stared at the liquor cabinet. Why couldn't she drink it away like so many other women? Instead, she went to the refrigerator.

Betty would never realize that she was not alone. She had several divorced women friends, but she could not identify with them; her case was always, in her own mind, so special, so different. These women, long past their own nights, standing naked in front of the bedroom mirror searching for stretch marks and cellulite, had made peace with their lot. This was life. Men carry the clout, men call the shots, that's how it is. Women pick up whatever benefits they are given, women go on.

They tried to reach her with their new wisdom. Come with us, they begged. Don't cry, they told her, patting her cheeks, her hands, her shoulders. Don't cry this way. There is life ahead. Don't be angry. Come with us to the bars, to the restaurants, they said. Let's go get our hair done, and our nails, and let's buy a new dress. Let's go out tonight.

"But she just could not do it," says her friend Candy Westbrook, a vivacious Anne Francis look-alike who now runs a San Diego modeling agency and who had also long since become a lively part of the local dating scene. "She would say it was too humiliating, that it was different for me, because I was widowed, but she was divorced."

Another friend, Melanie Cohrs, an attractive, easygoing La Jolla interior designer, also divorced, tried hard, too, to lure Betty into the San Diego singles scene in hopes that she would meet someone to take her mind off Dan and Linda.

"Finally, we talked Betty into having a singles party at her house," Cohrs recalled, shaking her head, half sad, half amused. "But it was a disaster. Betty just couldn't do it. She wouldn't come out of the kitchen. Here were all these intelligent, dignified professional people in her house, most of them divorced, just like she was. But Betty thought it was all so degrading. She wouldn't talk to anyone; she spent the evening hiding, acting like the maid. She thought any woman who had sex on a casual basis was a slut, and she would tell me so."

Later, from jail, Betty lashed out at all of those who had tried to turn her into a party girl. "It was horrible. I tried it a few times. I went out with Patti Monahan, and sat on bar stools. And I used to wonder what was worse, if they asked me to dance, or if they didn't."

Still, in the privacy of her kitchen, where no one could see, she began answering singles ads, although, to this day, she is embarrassed to admit it. It was no more than a joke, she says. Just a silly lark.

But it wasn't a silly lark. She was desperate.

She scanned the list of men advertising themselves.

Richard. Who was Richard, she wondered? She stared at the ad. Could she? Would she? Richard. He was her age, the ad said. He was Italian. He was in real estate. Los Angeles. Studio City.

She flushed with shame, alone in her kitchen.

She walked around her big, empty house. She went onto the back balcony. She stared at the sea, down the hill. It was so silent. Too late to call anyone. Besides, her friends were tired of her, she knew. Her parents didn't want to hear it. And Brad would only agree with whatever she said. This is how it would be. She would be alone.

She walked back to the kitchen and wrote a short, bright note to Richard.

I don't have to meet him, she thought. I can do this, and let it go. But it won't hurt to see …

She walked to the corner mailbox with the letter and shoved it into the slot, before she changed her mind.

She felt a flash of hope.

Richard answered within a week.

"Good day, Lady Bets," he wrote. "… This is just a short note to briefly introduce myself and say hello. I am forty-three years young, Italian, 6'5" tall, a trim 185 lbs, and a nonsmoker.

"I am a real estate investor who enjoys a wide range of activities, including quiet dinners at home with friends, good conversations, dancing all night till dawn, and caring and sharing with others who also have solid values.

"Perhaps when you are free we can get together for a drink and an informal chat, either in La Jolla or Los Angeles … Looking forward to hearing from you SOOONNN!!! Warmly, Richard."

The enclosed photo showed a handsome man with a receding hairline and a moustache, dressed in Levi's, black patent cowboy boots, and a red plaid Western shirt with pearl buttons, sitting on a black leather couch. His dark eyes sparkled. His smile was friendly. He looked like a perfectly nice guy.

"What kind of creep advertises?" she thought, hating him. And she flung the letter into the bottom of her files, where it still lay years later after she was in jail, displaced wife and mother, accused of murder.

She never had a drink with Richard. She couldn't bear herself for even thinking of

134

it. She hated Dan Broderick even more than she hated the handsome Studio City cowboy named Richard. He was turning her into a pathetic whore. Just like his cunt.

A few months later, however, she finally swallowed her pride and answered an ad in USA Today from an Arabian-horse breeder, who was looking for an "attractive escort" during a business weekend in San Francisco. Oliver was his name. She sent him a photograph and a note; in return, he sent her a round-trip plane ticket with a reservation at the exclusive Stanford Court in San Francisco. "And he had a limousine pick me up at the airport." It was a pleasant weekend, she says evasively, with her usual nervous laugh. "He was real nice and it was all very proper. We went to a play and to dinner. But he was looking for a permanent relationship, and I was still a married woman, so that was the end of that. The only reason I did it," she adds, "was because it was out of town. Nobody would know." In any case, she never saw Oliver again, and she never answered another personals ad. Not until she got to prison would Betty again begin corresponding with strange men.

Chapter 13

A Message to Fuckhead and the Cunt

Dan Broderick was enjoying his new home. His interior decorator was rapidly turning it into the elegant oasis he had always dreamed of, a formal sea of subdued colors, wingback chairs, paisley wallpapers, and moiré drapes in the bedrooms, Scotch plaids and creams in the den, with small framed pictures of spotted hunting dogs hanging on the staircase walls, and antique mirrors in the halls.

Linda was now a constant, open part of his life. She came to the house often, and watched the renovations. But the decor was all his. She never offered an opinion, says Dan's decorator. Dan Broderick's home was his castle. He would marry this woman in due time, but, for now, Linda Kolkena understood that he didn't want to know what fabrics she liked, what pieces of furniture she preferred. And she didn't care. She was happy enough to live in any house Dan Broderick was in.

One afternoon during the 1986 Memorial Day weekend, after dropping the children off at Betty's house, Dan and Linda went shopping for household supplies at the Price Club, a San Diego cut-rate emporium. There he bought himself an answering machine, installed it that afternoon, then left the house.

Betty discovered the new machine within hours, when she called to complain that he hadn't picked up the children on time, thus making her late for her job at the art gallery.

She didn't hesitate. Before his message tape had even finished playing, her mind was surging forward, eagerly awaiting the beep: "This is a message to fuckhead and the cunt," she told the new machine. "You have one hell of a nerve dumping the kids here on the sidewalk and zooming away without making any attempt to communicate with me about my plans for the weekend. Make me sick, both of you. I have a good mind to dump the kids back on you and drive away. Call me. We have a lot to talk about, asshole. And come pick up your four children that you're working so hard to have custody of. Congratulations. You can have them."

A few minutes later, she called again: "Fuckhead, come get the kids. I want to get rid of them, but I don't like driving to your shitty neighborhood. Hurry up and come get them, asshole."

An hour later: "Fuckhead and the cunt, come get the kids."

And, in her last call of the day: "I actually love this machine, 'cause then I can really just say anything I want. Tell the kids that you don't think it's wrong that you're screwing the cunt in the hall that has her legs wide open for anybody who comes by, and you paid for it? God, you got a sense of humor. I love it. You're all fucked."

That Dan Broderick, father of four children, including two teenaged daughters, had bought his answering machine in all innocence is beyond question. But never was a

136

gift more heaven-sent to a man so litigiously minded—for it was instantly as clear as the little red light blinking on his machine that he was now going to be able to prove, with taped evidence, that he had been driven from his marriage by a crazy woman.

He wasted no time in maximizing the potential benefits of his new weapon. Within days of her first bombast into his machine, when Betty tried to call her children, she was greeted by the sweet, perky voice of Linda Kolkena, eerily similar to her own, telling callers on the Broderick family tape that "We're not home now."

Whether it was deliberate cruelty or only gross insensitivity on the part of Dan and Linda, the result was predictable: staggered by Linda's gall, pierced to the quick by sound of another woman's voice on her children's answering machine, Betty lunged at her tormentor through the telephone. Within the next days, she unloaded her pain with messages like these:

"Cunt, what's this we-can't-come-to-the-phone shit? You're not supposed to come to the phone at the house, you're supposed to screw at the house, answer the phone at the office ... Dumb people drive me crazy!" Or: "Cunt, what are you doing on this machine? Don't you have a toilet to live in of your own?" And, "Cunt, what is your voice doing on this machine? ... If it's the Broderick residence, that assumes you're a Broderick, and you're nothing but a cunt. Anyway, where are my darling children?"

Later on, Betty would initially try to excuse all her ugly phone messages as the result of her frustration at finding Linda's voice on the answering machine. That was, of course, never entirely true. Betty exploded into the machine dozens of times over the next three years, regardless of whose voice was on the taped message, just as she had the day Dan installed it. What is true, however, is that Linda, knowing full well how it antagonized Betty, continued to put her voice on the answering machine, off and on, long before she became the new Mrs. Daniel T. Broderick III, legitimate mistress of the household. It was cruel, it was flaunting, it was inexcusable. Not until almost two years later, in response to a plea from Betty's attorney, did a judge finally order Dan to "get the girlfriend off the machine."

Not that it mattered by then. Unloading obscenities into Dan's answering machine promptly became Betty's most gratifying form of self-therapy. The more powerless she felt, the more vulgar her tongue became, and the more satisfaction she experienced—because she also soon discovered that, even more than her earlier petty vandalisms, those nasty little dollops got Dan Broderick's attention. They in fact drove him nuts. He could walk out on her, he could refuse to talk to her—but he couldn't escape her accusing voice, not even inside his own home.

It was, of course, just one more of Betty's pathetic, self-defeating measures, since Dan would only use her messages to bludgeon her even further until the day she finally killed him.

Like the good lawyer he was, he began building his case from the first day she spat into his answering machine. Over the next three years, she made literally hundreds of calls to his house. The overwhelming majority of them were completely innocuous, devoid of any offensive language at all, nothing more than a mother's calls to her children. But the only ones Dan saved—the ones that would dog Betty through countless divorce, custody, and contempt hearings, as well as her divorce trial and two murder trials to follow—were those that ranged from moderately ugly to disgusting. Eventually, Dan even began recording some of her private conversations with her sons.

Regularly, he would walk into his office and toss the latest, worst tapes onto his secretary's desk. "Here," he would say, "transcribe these in case we need them."

"He was infuriated by them, but he was always embarrassed, too," says Stormy (Ann Marie) Wetther, Dan's secretary, who still shudders at the memory of Betty's voice. "Just listening to her gave me the creeps. Her voice was so maniacal—it reminded me of *The Exorcist*. She sounded so evil, especially her laugh. It was a cackle."

Later on, fueling Betty's frenzy even further, her children told her that Dan would also often turn the telephone ringer off, or hide the telephone itself—which naturally only caused her to unleash even viler invective into his answering machine, thus adding to his collection. Neither Broderick could ever resist the bait laid out by the other.

Linda was also apparently an enthusiastic participant in gathering the tapes. "Linda used to love it when Mom would leave a bad message," Lee said later. "She'd say, 'Oh, great, here's another one we can use.'" Sometimes, Linda would also deliberately turn the answering machine on even when people were at home, Lee said, just to bait Betty into leaving yet another foul outburst.

Many of Betty's offending messages were strictly personal, harking back to old grievances between the two of them: "Fuckhead, who do you think you're kidding? Look in the mirror and tell me, who do you think you're kidding? Jesus Christ! You're like a slug with a fancy tie on—too low to kick and too wet to step on. Does that ring a bell? Love to the cunt."

Others were ominous, at least in light of later events: "Stop screwing the cunt long enough to return my calls. Left messages on the machine with the maid, with the secretary, et cetera. I have very important things to ask you. You're making me mad. I'll kill you."

Some were merely the infuriated, baffled wails of a woman stripped of all control: "What's this business about you continually sending the children to a psychiatrist? ... You're the one who had a total mental meltdown. You're now fucking the secretary, acting like a fool, screwing your family all over the map, walking out on them. That's normal? ... Jesus—there's nothing wrong with us! Why don't you go see somebody? You're the one whose mind is a pretzel."

But the most devastating were always those in which she burdened the children with her rage: "Rhett, this is Mommy. I'm out of the shower now. Where are you? You can make a choice today about staying with me or staying with the cuntsucker."

And some were simply painful to hear, her personal agony was so clear: "Cuntsucking asshole! What am I supposed to do now? I just want what's mine. I don't want to see you or the cunt, or the slums, any of your fucking bullshit anymore. Just want what's mine. That's all I ever wanted. I don't give two shits about you. You're not worth spit. Fuckhead, you've turned my life into a nightmare, I can't go to sleep. I close my eyes and I see you and the cunt, and I see you doing all your wonderful things, and, uhm ... you're gonna be real sorry ..."

After the killings, therapists had a field day analyzing Betty Broderick's sex hang-ups, as reflected in her messages. Defense psychologist Katherine DiFrancesca argued that there was nothing unusual in Betty's abrupt switch from a woman whose worst prior epithet was "Damn" to one who began to talk overnight like a besotted B-Team stripper. Language commonly deteriorates in pace with loss of self-esteem, said DiFrancesca. In her view, Betty was no different than millions of other people, male and female, who express their own rageful sense of devaluation by devaluing everything around them—and gutter language is typically the handiest, quickest outlet.

The prosecutor, meanwhile—who naturally disagreed that there was any excuse whatsoever for Betty's mouth—became so engrossed in the theater of playing Betty's squalid messages (all neatly filed and dated by Dan from his earlier contempt and custody battles) that bored reporters began to refer to them jokingly as "The Best of Betty." The entire proceeding eventually began to resemble an obscenity trial more than a first-degree murder case. Even Betty got into the humor of it.

"Hit it, Pearl," she used to mime from her chair every time Deputy District Attorney Kerry Wells headed for the tape player.

In time, Dan would use Betty's phone messages to have her both jailed and fined, filing one contempt motion after another on grounds that her vulgar language was fully as offensive as her prior vandalisms. But that time was not now. Instead, in June of 1986, his eye was on a different target: Dan was getting a divorce, even if Betty wasn't, and he furthermore intended to take the children away from her for good. Toward that end, he took copies of her messages to the children's psychiatrist, Dr. Sparta, and to his attorney—both of whom agreed, he later said, that "until Bets sought psychiatric help," she was too unfit even to be granted visitation rights with her children. His divorce court date was July 16.

Around the same time, in a onetime event the prosecutor would later feast upon, Betty also stopped by a shooting range to practice her aim—which, bystanders later testified, was excellent. Betty said that she was only looking for a hobby she could pursue on her own: "Finding people to go golfing is a pain, I don't play tennis, but shooting is a solitary thing. You just go out and do it."

As he had done the summer before, Dan again sent the children away to camp and then to visit his parents without consulting Betty. She was no longer a factor in any parental decision. She was also growing more aware with every passing day of just how completely dependent she was on Dan Broderick's largesse, even for her groceries. Her whole life had been a continuum of reliance on two men—first her father, now Dan. That dawning realization made her angrier still. Yet, some days, her reaction to her own captivity was almost comic.

"Fuckhead, I want to get my car fixed," she told his machine one day. "It's a mess, and the [insurance] policy is in your name, so you have to do it. Ha Ha. Bye." Then,

139

moments later, laughing, she called back: "The car is also in your name, so you're stuck doing it. Bye. Tootleloo!"

Other times, she wasn't amused at all: "Fuckhead, pick up this phone right now," she hissed into the phone on one occasion. "I'm opening the mail and I see that the insurance on this house has been canceled. I now have no insurance on a major investment. Policy canceled, effective May 31, 1986. What's happening here, fool? Idiot, answer the phone ... The whore won't mind if you answer the phone for a little while ... Sweetie, answer the phone ... this house has no insurance because fuckhead didn't pay the bill."

Dan's collection of Betty tapes grew by the day.

Meantime, judging from a couple of letters Dan wrote Betty in early July, his anger was keeping fully apace with hers. One letter protested her "obnoxious phone messages," which, he reminded, were in violation of his restraining order. "It would be one thing if you were civil, but your lectures and disgusting language are unacceptable." He finished with a furious blast over her alleged attacks on his person and property, coupled with a promise to punish her where it hurt most—in the pocketbook: "A couple of months ago, I agreed to help you remove your Christmas decorations from the storage locker. [But] That was before you ripped the antenna off my car and tried to break the rear window. I don't intend to come near you, voluntarily at least, ever again. I also don't intend to pay for the storage locker any longer."

Money was always the measure. In his second letter that month, Dan was preoccupied with the ownership of their modest little motorboat. "There is no way we can share it," he wrote. "If you and I have learned anything over the past seventeen years, it's that we can't cooperate with one another. If you want the boat, I'll sell you my half for its fair market value as determined by the local Bay liner dealership. If you don't want the boat, I'll buy your half ... Please let me have your decision on this in writing. In the future, I would appreciate it if you would communicate with me in writing."

"Miserable bastard," Betty wrote in the margins of his letter, talking to herself again. "You want everything your way. You have no sense of right wrong true false indecent immoral. God will thank you for it."

But, by the end of June, she at least woke up to the realities of her situation. July 16 was coming up fast. By then, she had also begun keeping a daily diary—which turned out to be the best mirror into her declining mind over the next thirty months.

Most of her early entries were devoted to her frantic, eleventh-hour search for an attorney to represent her at the divorce hearing. According to her jottings, she spent most of that time on the telephone, sometimes calling as many as half a dozen lawyers in one day. As always, she began with only those on her rapidly diminishing list of those with first-rate reputations. She appealed for help to old friends from Gray, Cary, like Brian Forbes and Karl Zobell. But they couldn't help her. They were too close to Dan. Conflict of interest. Sorry. They recommended other lawyers, who recommended other lawyers.

But nobody Betty Broderick wanted wanted her. And, by now, no matter what excuses they gave her, it clearly wasn't just their connections with Dan that made some attorneys turn her down: word was now out in San Diego legal circles about what an unmanageable client she was—how she ran cars into houses, had been committed to a mental institution, wouldn't follow legal advice, etc.. One lawyer told Betty flatly that she wouldn't take the case because she had heard Betty wrote in the margins of court files.

During that period, she tried to lure Dan Jaffe back, to no avail. Once around with the Brodericks was enough for him. She also called Marvin Mitchelson's office in Los Angeles, and tried to reach feminist Los Angeles attorney Gloria Allred. Neither returned her call. She even called Melvin Belli and Gerry Spence, two of the best-known attorneys in America. All her diaries record is that Belli's assistant asked, "Can you afford it?"

But San Diego is a big city with at least seven thousand attorneys in the area. By the end of the summer, she had become a beggar, searching through the suburban San Diego yellow pages, reduced to calling lawyers she would later bitterly dismiss in her diaries as "losers in life, incompetent nobodies." Betty's awe of Dan became her own worst enemy: Dan Broderick would eat these second-stringers alive, she knew.

"I have been totally railroaded by my husband and Mr. Ashworth," she wrote one relatively obscure attorney who had already turned her down. "They have sold my house—refused to negotiate any settlement—now the divorce is final, and I've been robbed of the four children as well. I desperately need qualified counsel. Please let me know in writing why you are unable to take the case." He never answered.

On July 16, she still had no attorney. She would later say that she had requested a postponement until she found representation, but was denied. She also claimed that she had never heard of bifurcation. In any case, she wasn't even in court on the day Judge Milton Milkes not only granted Dan Broderick a divorce by default, but also ruled in favor of all his requests, which included:

—Sole legal and physical custody of the four children.

—No visitation rights for the mother "until she undertakes an appropriate program of psychiatric therapy."

—Reiteration of existing restraining orders, preventing the mother from coming within one hundred yards of his house.

—And, finally, "the issue of dissolution of the parties' marriage shall be bifurcated from the remaining issues in this case with the court retaining jurisdiction to determine all other issues at the time of trial."

What all that meant, in short, was that Dan Broderick was now a legally divorced man, but he still maintained total control over both the Broderick children and the family finances: Betty could no longer visit her children without his permission, nor did she have a court-ordered support settlement. She was still reliant on Dan's voluntary $9,000 monthly allowance. Not least, because of the bifurcation, there was no division of their community property. That would not happen for another thirty months. In short, Dan was free, even if Betty wasn't.

She was in shock. How could she be divorced when she hadn't even been in court? When she had no attorney to defend her? And how, for God's sake, could she be denied the right even to visit her children? Where was the proof that she was an unfit mother? Her little fits of property damage? Her dirty words on a telephone machine? Her brain shrieked. What was more immoral—a married man who shacked up openly with his girlfriend in front of children, or a mother who used four-letter words? Why was she the unfit one?

Men who beat the living daylights out of their wives still got visitation. Crazed mothers who dropped their children out of buildings and broke their bones got visitation. But not Betty Broderick? All because of her three or four nasty, uncreative little words on his answering machine? "Why is a woman not allowed to use those words?" she demanded. "No man would be dragged into court three times a month for saying 'fuckhead.' No judge would've wasted even five minutes on it!"

She was left reeling. And she would never recover. From that day forward, Betty Broderick was no longer responsible for her own actions. Her rage was too great. Dan Broderick had not only taken her children, and her money, he had now also shamed her utterly. She was branded. Betty Broderick: Unfit Mother.

And all by default. What was that? And how could he treat her this way, strip her so completely? What had she ever done to deserve it? How could the courts let him? "Whatever happened to shit like due process and equal protection of the laws?" she was still raging years later. "Bifurcation? Ha—I call it bifornication—and now I know what it means: the husband gets to fuck his bimbo at the same time he's fucking his wife!" She had not only been fired by Dan, but by the laws of society, too.

"I always trusted judges—but how could they possibly be saying that Betty Broderick, of all people, couldn't even have visitation with her children?" she screamed over the jail phone. "Women burn their children with cigarettes, they throw boiling water on them, they let their boyfriends rape them—and they still get visitation! But not Betty Broderick? I was Mary Poppins! I was Mother Fuck of the year, for Christ's sake!"

What Betty Broderick was learning, as so many women have, is that almost anything under the sun can be accomplished in the domestic courts of America—particularly if one of the parties is a smart, determined professional male with the resources and the will to have it his way, and the other is a housewife without means beyond those supplied by the departing husband, and who still lives under the old-fashioned illusion that, in the end, mothers and children will surely prevail in divorce court.

That is no longer how it works, not since the no-fault concept came into being in many states two decades ago, effectively eliminating the former, courtly notion that the party breaking up the family—overwhelmingly the male, according to statistics—should literally pay the financial price. No-fault was, and remains, a windfall for husbands who leave their families and, as virtually every study has shown, a disaster for women, who are no longer subject to kinder, gentler treatment in the courts, whether they are fifty years old with five children, or twenty with no kids. Ideally, in this brand-new world, each party gets half of the community property, fifty-fifty, with appropriate child support awarded to the custodial parent, usually the mother. But that, too, can shortchange mothers. Also, whereas the husband was once liable for the children until they were twenty-one, now, in many states, the age has now been reduced to eighteen. College costs are no longer an automatic element of the father's burden.

No-fault is the direct gift to wives and mothers today of the ambitious innocence of the feminist movement of the sixties and seventies. Back then, activists thought no-fault a fine thing, because, in theory at least, it lent dignity to women as well as men by liberating warring spouses from the traditional mud-slinging of divorce courts. Who cared who was at fault? said feminists. The object was to equalize the sexes in the courtroom, to save the woman from the degradation of begging, of proving either her piety or his perfidy. She no longer needed to gouge him for extra bucks by virtue of his wayward gonads. In theory, the wife would still, as custodian of the family, come out with her fair share.

Back then, few feminists thought ahead to what exactly might result if the philandering husband was no longer penalized for abandoning his family. Not much attention was paid to the potential ramifications of an uninhibited new world in which the male no longer had to live in fear of a wrathful judge pointing a disapproving finger at the prodigal—and charging him for it. In the old days of punitive judgments and chivalrous attitudes toward the fairer sex, infidelity invariably carried a price in court. Settlements were often so one-sided in favor of the wife and the traditional family unit, in fact, that many a man wound up living in a one-room apartment with little more than his toothbrush and his dog, while the wife and kids kept the family home, as well as the lion's share of his income.

But all that became passé.

Male legislators everywhere happily obliged no-fault activists. Between 1970 and 1980, forty-eight states adopted some form of no-fault divorce law. It has turned out to be punishing for the majority of divorced mothers and their children. Studies during the two decades since suggest that divorces are on the rise in the United States, in part because men no longer have to pay the same severe price. Instead, in most community property states, the wife is no longer even automatically granted title to the family home, at least until the children are of age: now it is routinely sold, the proceeds divided. She moves to cheaper housing, generally with the children. He takes his half and moves into a bachelor condo.

In addition, thanks to bifurcation, women in many states may receive no property settlement at all for months or years.

Divorce law reforms, in effect, backfired on women in general. Some statistics now show that divorced men, especially affluent professionals, experience a 70 percent increase in life-style comforts, while ex-wives suffer a 30 percent decline.

But Betty Broderick had little or no comprehension of any of this at the outset of her divorce. Dan, by contrast, understood all of it. For him, it was an optimum situation; for her it would always be a dawning disaster, too impossible to be real.

But, after July 16, one reality after another forced its way through the defenses of her mind. She learned, as most women do, by increments. She was no longer Mrs. Daniel T. Broderick III—yet she was more beholden to him than ever before. No more waltzing into his house to take her children away for the day, or a weekend at her house. Not until she had undergone therapy. Not until she had satisfied the demands of Dan, his doctors, and the courts. All men. No mothers. Her brain began to buckle as it never had before. Where was the justice in this? What did any of these assholes know about morning sickness, cesareans, dirty diapers, crying babies at three A.M.? Nothing, is what.

Plus, she no longer had any control over the money she had worked so hard to help him accumulate. If she misbehaved, if she displeased him, he could reduce her to a bag lady overnight. She was back under Sister Claire Veronica's piano, still as bewildered at her situation as she had been thirty-five years ago.

"The divorce is now final and he has SOLE custody of the kids. We have NO SETTLEMENT and the way things are going, we never will," she wrote in her diary that week, "because now he has no reason on earth to settle with me."

Their success was now only his success.

And Dan Broderick wasted no time in driving these new facts of life home to her. Four days after his divorce court victory, he began laying out his new rules with crisp, implacable efficiency. First he wrote her a brief note, urging their mutual cooperation in providing a peaceful post-divorce transition for their children. On the face of it, it seemed like a reasonable enough letter—but, to Betty, in her still-stunned state, his words were nails pounding into her brain, starting with the first sentence.

She was no longer "Bets." Now, it was "Dear Elisabeth Anne."

"You and I are no longer married," he wrote. "It's now up to us to do our best to minimize the trauma our divorce will have on our kids ... Bad-mouthing one another to the kids, or even worse, blaming them for the divorce, is destructive. I suggest that each of us encourage the kids to love and respect the other and that we refrain from any derogatory comments to or about one another ..."

But, if she thought that letter cold, she had a lot to learn. Dan had only begun. Two days later, only a week after their divorce, he began a serious crackdown:

"I am tired of coming home and finding messages full of obscenities on my answering machine," he wrote her. "As I have pointed out to you in the past, every time you call me, you are violating a court order. That doesn't seem to matter to you. Maybe this will: from now on, when you leave a message or call and use any vulgar or obscene language, you will be fined $100 per offensive word. These fines will be withheld from your support checks. Believe me, I'm not doing this to bait you. I just want to deter you from using language in your dealings with me which any normal, civilized person would find extremely objectionable."

At that point, Betty Broderick lost all capacity for rational conversation. Her outrage was surpassed only by her incredulity. This sonofabitch was richer than God, thanks to her help, and now he was fining her in the same way she had once fined their children for saying "Shut up." Worse, she was helpless as a child. The courts had said so. He could do whatever he pleased to her. He was in complete charge. And now he thought to bludgeon her into submission with his little fines for nothing more than her tongue?

Uh-huh. Right, Dan.

Rarely has a man so misjudged a woman. It was always one of the most fascinating aspects of the Broderick affair that these two people who had lived together for 16 years, literally grown up together, could have remained such total emotional strangers.

Like small brushfires, Betty's sporadic temper fits of the past merged into one blazing, unbroken wall of mental fire. Although Dan and Linda would be the final victims, the first casualty of the incineration was, of course, Betty herself. Never again would she be the same woman. If she had not behaved rationally before, after this summer all reason was borne away forever, ashes in the breeze.

Fuck him and his imperial edicts, his threats, his power, his courtroom chums. Never again would she dance to Dan Broderick's tune. No more "Yes, dear." No more "Yes, Your Honor." At long last, Betty Broderick's tenacious hope collapsed beneath the weight of the hurt, and the hate. From then on, each time Dan threatened her, she reacted with even greater fury. She began literally stealing the children from his house, seducing them to meet her on street corners. He found her language "offensive"? She left even more vile messages on his machine.

But, if she was fire, he was ice. In the next years, he became ever more intractable in his refusal to give her an inch. And neither Broderick was ever tempered by concern for the four helpless children caught in the middle. Although Dan would always accuse Betty of putting the children in the middle—blaming them for the divorce, for even sitting at the same dinner table with Linda—he continued to do his part, too. Now, not only were the Broderick children forced to broker their own weekend visits, in time Dan would also punish both Betty and the children by canceling trips to her house if her behavior that week had displeased him. In addition, his daughters later testified, both Dan and Linda had by now also openly begun to refer to Betty as "crazy," "the large one," "the monster," etc.

Meanwhile, by most accounts, Betty periodically used her children in the same callous way—especially when she thought Dan and Linda were using her as a weekend baby-sitter; then she would also abruptly cancel their visits, saying she had other plans. In time, both Brodericks became such vengeful, selfish people that an outsider can only conclude that no two people ever deserved each other more.

Less than two months after the divorce, on September 9, Dan sent her another letter that made all the earlier ones sound like valentines;

"Dear Elisabeth Anne," he wrote, in a four-point memorandum. "In light of recent events, the following is going to occur:

"1. During our telephone conversation on ... September 4, 1986, just before I hung up on you, you used a disgusting and unseemly word to refer to Linda. Pursuant to my letter of July 23, 1986, that will cost you $100. It will be withheld from the next check I send you."

145

From there, he reminded her that, on September 7, she had also "used an obscenity to refer to Linda" in a message to Kim. "That will cost you $100." In a third offense, she had entered his house and taken photographs of his property. "From now on, each and every time you set foot across the property line of 1041 Cypress Avenue," he wrote, "I will withhold $250 from the check I send you each month. Each time you step across the threshold into the house, I will withhold $500."

And, lastly, he reminded her that "I have been awarded sole legal and physical custody of the kids. You have been denied visitation privileges until you undertake an appropriate program of psychiatric therapy." Even so, he accused, in early September she had enticed Danny and Rhett to sneak out of his house and meet her on a nearby street corner. "You then drove them to your house. This is totally unacceptable." What's more, he knew that she had "tried to pull the same thing" on other occasions.

"I am not opposed to your seeing the kids occasionally," he wrote, "if arrangements are made IN ADVANCE so I know when they are leaving and when they are coming back, and if, while you are with them, you refrain from statements designed to pit them against me or make them feel guilty for not being obnoxious to Linda. From now on, each and every time you spend time with the boys without clearing it with me in advance, $1,000 will be withheld from the check I voluntarily send you every month. Incidentally, if you want to arrange to see the kids, you should talk to them and have them call me ... Please do not try to call me directly. There is too much animosity for that to be productive. Sincerely Yours, Daniel T. Broderick III."

Not long after, he left on a European vacation with Linda.

Among her diary entries that month, Betty wrote: "Rhett always reports Dan and Linda with no clothes on laying on each other in bed. Linda in see-through nightgowns in kitchen in front of girls and friends."

It is both fascinating and painful to read her diaries from the divorce on. They are the work of a woman who has realized, too late, that she miscalculated everything. She was cornered, on the edge of the abyss, with no safety net below. Night after night, she sat at her table, scribbling into her notebooks about the injustice of what was happening to her. But no answers ever came to her at the end of her long, rambling essays. Only rising, repetitive rage. And it was only 1986—three long years before she finally killed.

For a few days, she took to her bed. She was too upset to work, and so she never went back to the Simic Art Gallery.

"Shaking in my bed, feels like an earthquake," she wrote. "Have no one to help me. Kids gone, Gail [Forbes, her neighbor] gone."

But panic sporadically forced her to her feet. In August, she returned briefly to the telephone, searching again for a lawyer. Same old story. She didn't want anybody who wanted her, and vice versa.

Meantime, as is usually the case in bifurcated divorces, court-ordered mediation sessions were now underway to resolve the Broderick property settlement. Attorney J. William Hargreaves was designated to lead the negotiations. But mediation is only as useful as the warring parties want it to be—and, in the Broderick matter, sessions soon failed for the same old reason: Dan wouldn't pay the full $5,000 fees, and Betty refused to split costs since the divorce wasn't half her idea. But, beforehand, in a tactic reminiscent of their old Marriage Encounter days, the Brodericks were asked to write notes to each other describing their feelings. Dan didn't comply, but Betty did:

"First off, let me say how nervous and overwhelmed I am," she wrote. "My entire life, past present and future is on the table now. None of this affects you. Your past present and future are right on track. Bastard. I'm mad as hell ... [the children and I] have been betrayed, abused, humiliated, robbed ... We have been victimized by the one person on earth who was supposed to protect us from harm, not cause it! ... Literally all the money in the world would not keep me in the life-style to which I had been accustomed ..."

As for the children: "When I am assured of financial security—my house, car, social standing, I will begin to discuss custody. For now, I am too enraged by your actions to be around the children or accept any responsibility for them ... I don't know how to raise secure happy healthy children with a firm sense of right and wrong when you are living proof that none of my values are WORTH A DAMN."

Hargreaves, meanwhile, was beginning to sound more like Dan Broderick's personal adviser than a detached mediator. In a handwritten "Dear Dan" note in August—with no copy to Betty—Hargreaves urged Dan to fork over the money for mediation in his own best interests:

"As it is now, having Betty pay would really just be a reduction of her advance, which is your money anyway," Hargreaves told Dan. In a particularly confidential note, he also told Dan that, if he didn't pay for a settlement now, "I happen to know that the alternative to mediation is Bea Snyder [a prominent feminist attorney] representing Betty. Talk to Tom [Ashworth]. But if I were you, I'd concede this point ... I think the court would probably order a significant payment of her fees by you personally in any event, if that makes you feel any better about the situation ..."

But Dan was less interested in Hargreave's advice than in teaching his former wife the value of a dollar: "I will not agree to pay the $5,000 in mediation fees," he wrote Hargreaves, "because I firmly believe that this process will fail unless Bets has a financial stake in its successful outcome."

So much for mediation. Nor did Betty hire Bea Snyder. Betty never wanted a female attorney, although she eventually hired one, because, she said, she was "afraid they would use it against me, call me a crazy feminist or something like that." Closer to the truth, Betty was never comfortable around professional women, because they represented a challenge to her own career choice as homemaker, one she never fully accepted herself.

Shortly after mediation efforts collapsed, Hargreaves volunteered to represent Betty in the divorce. She never wanted him. He did not have a top-flight reputation in town. But, by now, she was too humbled and exhausted by her attorney search to delay much longer. She was also desperate for court-ordered support to end Dan's arbitrary fines. And so, although she was still demanding that Dan pay all her attorney fees, she capitulated in September and sent Hargreaves a retainer of around $800, along with this wistful, wary note:

"Dear Bill," she wrote, "By presenting this check, I feel I have entrusted you the monumental task of validating the twenty years of my life WITH Dan Broderick and securing a base for my future WITHOUT him. I sure hope you're up to the job! Thanks for taking it on! Betty Broderick."

Thus, did Betty acquire her second attorney.

It would, to say the least, be a brief, unhappy liaison. Within months, she fired Hargreaves, who was, she always insisted, never more than Dan Broderick's stooge. Why else, she demanded, had Dan been so quick to pay Hargreaves the same $10,000 he had refused to pay Dan Jaffe? (Which he did, in fact, do, without a murmur of protest.)

Among Hargreaves's failings, as Betty perceived them: he had sat idly by, while Dan got the entire Broderick divorce proceeding sealed from the public; in addition, she said, Hargreaves also so goofed up in a spousal support argument that he forgot to include her taxes in his figures, thus costing her around $4,000 extra a month, which another attorney had to later correct.

For his part, Hargreaves later countered that Betty was impossible to represent. In his view, "she was really impaired. She couldn't understand that life was possible without Dan." He also likened her money lust to that of Joanna Carson—no amount, he thought, would have satisfied her, such was her urge for revenge. On the other hand, Hargreaves also once remarked that he found Dan "obsessive" in his controlling tendencies—it was almost like Dan was "inviting [Betty] in to shoot her." Eventually, concluding the Hargreaves-Betty battle, he sued her for several thousand dollars in unpaid legal fees, and ultimately won.

Dan Jaffe, meantime, was observing all this with rising disgust from his Beverly Hills office. He had kept track of Betty's case, and probably understood better than anybody that Betty Broderick was so opposed to a divorce that, left to her own devices, she would self-destruct. And so, when he discovered that Tom Ashworth and Dan had won a divorce by default in July, he wrote a letter to Ashworth in September threatening, in effect, to file a formal complaint in Betty's behalf.

He was "distressed" to see that Ashworth had accepted Betty's default in the divorce action, he wrote. Although he was no longer representing her, he thought that such a savvy pair of attorneys as Tom Ashworth and Dan Broderick must surely know that they were taking advantage of a woman emotionally incapable of looking after her own interests.

"I am now convinced that the only way this case can ethically and morally move forward, and, of course, legally move forward," he told Ashworth, "is for your office and client to file a motion to have a guardian ad litem appointed for Mrs. Broderick so that there will be someone to protect the substantial interests that Mrs. Broderick has in the matter. She clearly does not understand how her attitudes and actions in this matter severely prejudice her legal position, and it is clear that some individual must be available to make binding and rational decisions ...

"Unless I hear from you concerning the setting aside of Mrs. Broderick's default,"

Jaffe concluded, "I plan to contact the legal powers that be and the Bench in San Diego so that someone is made available to protect Mrs. Broderick's legal rights." Jaffe also complained about his many unanswered phone calls to Ashworth over the last few weeks.

This time, he got an immediate reply. "I am afraid that [Betty] is being less than candid with you," Ashworth wrote. In reality, at least three "competent San Diego attorneys" had agreed to represent Betty, said Ashworth—the most recent being J. William Hargreaves, Esq..

Ashworth slid past Jaffe's suggestion that a guardian be appointed to serve Betty's interests, remarking only that, while her actions at times seemed "self-destructive," at other times she only seemed "calculating." He concluded by saying that, while neither he nor his client had any desire whatever to take unfair advantage of Mrs. Broderick, neither could he, Ashworth, "stand by and permit her to destroy an entire family through her actions." And, finally, he reassured Jaffe, "it is my understanding that she is presently represented by Mr. Hargreaves." In short, according to Ashworth, Betty was now in solid San Diego legal hands.

It was soon after that exchange that Dan promptly anted up $10,000 for the remainder of Hargreaves's retainer.

In October, Dan fined her $200 for two incidents of offensive language and $250 more for a trespass in September. Less the house payment, that left her with a check of around $3,700 for the month.

"Asshole and his sleazy cunt in Europe," Betty wrote on the bottom of his statement, "Don't we love it? [He] didn't have enough money for kids and maid and they called me for help ..." And she wasn't exaggerating—Dan had in fact left his housekeeper with a $50 weekly grocery budget for a family of four while he was gone on his three-week trip, and the woman had indeed finally called Betty, asking for more grocery money. Naturally, Betty would make the most of that detail for years to come— that and dozens of other tales of horrific deprivation and starvation she heard from her emotional kids. They no doubt exaggerated, playing one parent against the other as children caught in divorces normally do. But it never failed. Betty would then fly out to Saks or Magnin's or the local gourmet supermarket to buy them whatever it was they claimed they lacked, from new shoes to pistachio nuts. It was one reason that she was always broke.

Then came her November "allowance," along with yet another letter.

She had been especially bad in October, it appeared.

This time her check showed deductions that not only wiped out her entire monthly $9,000 allowance, but actually left her in the hole—she owed Dan $1,315.32.

Typically, he included an itemized statement, explaining his "sanctions":

—"Offensive language (ten times)" for a total fine of $1,000.

—"Trespass on 1041 Cypress (six times)" for $1,500.

—"Trespass in house (five times)" for $2,500.

The rest was miscellaneous bills—coupled with a gratuitous lecture about her frivolities and his generosity: "By my count, in the twenty months we have been separated, over $450,000 has been spent on you or made available for your use and enjoyment," he wrote. So "if you don't have enough money to pay your bills, you have only yourself to blame." He finished with another financial threat:

"I know your first impulse upon reading this letter will be a violent one ... You better think twice about that. If you make any attack on me or my property, you will never again get a red cent out of me without a court order ..."

In the margins of the letter Betty wrote, "Wouldn't anyone become violent after all his INCESSANT BULLSHIT [underlined 5 times]. How can anyone survive under this kind of assault?"

But she was enraged even before she got the letter, because Dan had told her it was coming. Violence begets violence, particularly after the first few adventures, once the barriers are broken, once it becomes a norm—and especially when both parties are constantly fomenting it. So, that Saturday, "I hopped into the Suburban in my little yellow Ralph Lauren shorts and I banged on his door ... All I wanted to know from the fucker was exactly how he expected me to get through November on minus $1,300," she says today. In reality, she was so furious it's surprising that she didn't run her car through the door again.

Not incidentally, that was also the day of the annual Blackstone Ball, one of her favorite events in years past. It didn't help to know that "while the president-elect of the bar was screwing his wife, he was about to don his fucking top hat and cape and take the cunt to the party that I should have been going to." Betty never did let false pride get in the way of blunt outrage over her lost social status. She was never the type to say it didn't matter. It mattered a lot.

Dan did the usual: he ordered her off his property. She stared at his smooth, clean-shaven face, sniffed his after-shave in the evening air, and grew even angrier. How long had it taken him tonight to get his toilette together? Was the cunt inside, dressing for the gala, too?

She refused to go. He promised that if she would leave, he would talk to her about the money matter at ten the next morning. He was making an appointment with his ex-wife.

She wasn't buying it. She still refused to leave. He threatened to call the police. She dared him. He would do it, he warned her. She double dared him.

One more time, Betty Broderick underestimated her ex—or, at least, overestimated his image-consciousness. By now, his loathing of this infernal woman who refused to play by the rules had become utterly, maddeningly intolerable to him. He called the cops.

They came. They asked her to leave. She again refused. Dan watched as they handcuffed her and took her away.

And that was the first time Elisabeth Anne Broderick went to jail—booked, fingerprinted, and mugged for violating Dan's restraining order. It was six days before her thirty-ninth birthday.

According to her former friend and neighbor, Gail Forbes, Betty called from jail that night, just as Forbes was about to depart for the Blackstone Ball herself, wanting Forbes to call *San Diego Union* society writer Burl Stiff to "tell everyone that while

Dan was enjoying himself at the ball, he had his former wife jailed." Her tone, Forbes later volunteered at trial, was "exultant."

"What bullshit," says Betty, who at first denied even calling Forbes. On the other hand, she qualified, "I was in such shock I can't really remember who I called, but I sure as hell wasn't exultant. I was scared to fucking death in there with those women."

She was in jail for only a few hours. But, she always said, "November 1, 1986, was really the beginning of the end for me, I can see it now ... I could never believe he would treat me that way. What did I ever do to him? What was so wrong with asking how I was supposed to live for a month on no money?"

Even so, amazingly, what she remembered the next morning was Dan's promise to meet with her at ten A.M. to discuss her complaints about the money, the children, the broken marriage.

He didn't show up.

So she called his answering machine:

"Fuckhead, you're right back where you started with not talking to me," she said. "Now you've got to settle with me so I can leave you and the little cunt in your idyllic mansion in the slums there. I'd be more than delighted to do that, but I want my money! So you promised you'd talk about it at ten today. Obviously, you don't know how to tell time. Bye."

Meantime, Dan did not relent about the minus $1,300. That November, Brian and Gail Forbes lent Betty $6,500 to help her pay her bills.

A week after her release from jail, several of her friends gathered at the home of Kathy Saris, a former Miss Massachusetts and wife of a La Jolla dentist, to celebrate Betty's thirty-ninth birthday. It was an awkward, kindly little affair, aimed strictly at bolstering her spirits, alleviating the shame. Photos of the event show a group of attractive women in tasteful, conservative, casual clothes and expensive haircuts. Betty stood out amid them like a marshmallow in spinach salad. Her weight gain had already begun; her round face, framed by its blond bob, wore the expression of a woman who might have been on drugs. She looked dazed, vacant; her forced smile looked both sad and stupid.

"I was a basket case," she says now, bitterly. "I was just a shaking wreck, my whole body was trembling. I can't remember a thing about it, except trying so hard to act like I was fine, faking my smile and being scared to death that if I didn't get out of there, they were all going to see that I was a basket case." Presumably, the brighter ones among them did see.

Chapter 14

Happy Holidays to the Broderick Children

Then it was the holiday season again. She spent Thanksgiving, as divorced people usually do, dropping in on friends kind enough to invite her. Her children spent the day with Dan and Linda. Increasingly, she was taking her pain out on them. She began to blame them for the collapse of the marriage. She raged at them for spending time with Dan and Linda instead of her; she taunted them because they lived docilely in the same house with their father instead of running away to live with her. She had lost all memory of how they had gotten into his household in the first place.

In a conversation with her son Danny, for example, she remarked that Dan had "robbed me of everything I have on earth, including you kids."

No, the boy protested. "He didn't rob you—you gave us to him!" The child, then ten, went on, crying, to beg her to stop using "bad words," so that Dan would let them spend more time with her.

"For two years while I was married to him, I put up with shit in my face and you kids never even knew it," his mother replied. "You never knew he was fucking Linda while he was married to me, did you? ... I put up with shit for two years hoping he'd get over this, and he'd grow up ... he is obviously too weak a little faggot ... You tell your father to grow up and act like a gentleman and this could all be over in an hour."

Betty had forgotten that her children were powerless, that they were only kids trying to get by, that the youngest was only seven, the oldest a confused sixteen. She continued to lure the two youngest, Danny and Rhett, into sneaking out of his house without telling Dan. And it wasn't hard for her to do, because, although they would both get into trouble with Dan for it later, these two little boys always loved their mother enough to try to please her. They later begged the judges to let them to live with her because, as Rhett once put it, "You don't need television to have fun at Mom's house." And, they both complained, Dad wasn't home enough.

"He is always at work," said Danny in divorce court two years later. "I think [Betty] could take better care of us than my Dad ... she is always there, and she knows how to take care of us, and everything we like and dislike, and I just think she is all in all a better parent."

And none of the Broderick children accepted Linda. She was "nice sometimes," Danny tactfully told the judge. "But she can be like real bossy, and acts like she is taking my mom's place." Even Kim, who got along with Linda best later told the judge that she was a meddlesome snitch who was mean to her brothers and too uneducated to be a suitable mate for her Dad.

Whenever the children came to Betty's house, they brought with them new tales of the wicked future stepmother, abusing and depriving them, thereby only stoking Betty's angry fires higher.

"Once, Kim told me that when they went out on her birthday and she ordered steak and lobster, Linda made some remark like, 'Oh, we're really living high tonight,'" Betty fumed years later from jail. "How dare that bitch tell my children what they can or can't eat? They said she would complain about them buying a $5 bag of macadamia nuts, and then go spend $50 on a facial for herself!"

Linda's friends tell a different story. "Betty poisoned the kids' minds so much that even at the dinner table, the boys wouldn't speak to Linda. They would ask Dan to pass the salt, even when it was right beside Linda's plate," says attorney Sharon Blanchet.

Although families and friends will forever argue the matter, each side shifting blame, the reality is that both Brodericks punished their children in terrible ways. Betty could not behave like a mother should, not unless Dan gave her the money she demanded. But he only saw this as emotional blackmail from a woman who was not behaving like a decent mother should. And so he often punished her for her behavior by refusing weekend visits she had counted on, according to the children. On the other hand, Betty charges, "If he knew I had made advance plans, he would suddenly just drop the kids off."

Dan's friends say the opposite was true. According to them, Betty was so jealous of Dan and Linda that she saw every visit by the children as their way of turning her into their baby-sitter—and, in retaliation, would frequently refuse scheduled weekends at the last minute to ruin their plans.

For all their education and intelligence, Dan and Betty Broderick became a tragicomedy in action. Neither one of them could back off. They were a pair of gummy bears, locked in permanent, sticky embrace.

And now jail became just one more ugly element of their story, a new tool in Dan's arsenal, one both foolish and useless.

Instead of being cowed by her new status as both mental-ward patient and common prisoner, Betty only grew more defiant.

"You guys, you're missing a gorgeous roast beef family Sunday dinner like we've always had," she told her children in a phone message. "I hope you're enjoying dog food with the cunt."

Dan, meantime, was flourishing at every level. By now, he was president of the county bar association. He was in love; he was regularly photographed at local bar functions with the lovely Linda. His income was pressing upward, probably well over $2 million annually. His reputation was all that he had dreamed of, back in his Harvard days.

"He was maybe the best-known lawyer in this town. But he didn't act like a big wheel," said Dan's young partner, Robert Vaage, who later inherited many of his pending cases. "And he was a great teacher." Vaage recalled one case in particular in which his opponent, a senior attorney in town, had insulted him in court. But Vaage won, and, when the verdict came in, he wanted to gloat, to rub it in. "But Dan warned me, 'Never bad-mouth people you have to do business with.' And he practiced what he preached. I never heard Dan say a bad word about anybody, Betty included."

In December, Dan punished her again. This time, when her "allowance" check came, it showed deductions of $2,400 for bad behavior. Most of her November violations were for "offensive language" (fourteen times, or $1,400). She had also been fined for being on his property twice (total, $500) and for entering his house once ($500 more). Betty stared at Dan's meticulous invoice with strangling rage—and also vicious humor: clearly, she concluded, it was a better bargain to cuss into his phone than to visit his property; she got a lot more for her dollar.

In the same letter, Dan also informed her that they had finally been advanced to the top of the La Jolla Country Club waiting list, pursuant to their application two years earlier. But "I elected not to make that payment [of about $45,000] ... henceforth, neither you nor I are entitled to use the Club's facilities."

A small thing, perhaps, in the larger scheme of all that was happening to her—but to Betty Broderick, it was devastating. Now she had no country clubs at all. She could not get dressed up in her pretty clothes and go to lunch with the ladies in a place of infinite well-being, to pretend that none of it mattered. Not unless someone invited her. Because Dan had "elected" not to join. Any idea she had that she owned half of their money collapsed under the weight of one central fact: until she got a court-ordered property settlement, it didn't matter what she owned—he controlled it. She was now a beggar. He was king.

Her frame of mind during that holiday month, and her special concerns, were reflected in this early December entry in her diary, written, as always, in her even, clear script in a loose-leaf notebook:

"Overwhelmingly depressed
—kids here (Danny and Rhett)
—house a mess (wallpaper, paint, etc.) missing:
—Casey's party
—Blackstone Ball
—Ireland Fund
—Milliken party
—Armstrong family party
—Loma Larks
—no confidence in attorney
—Huge weight gain, don't fit in any of my nice clothes
—no Christmas money
—girls didn't come or call (they knew I wanted Christmas picture)
—bought Christmas tree I couldn't afford ($77)
—spent all of Gail's $6,500
—no money to survive on
—picked up $340 worth of greens I can't afford
—no garage for car (raining)
—termites in house
—roof leaking."

By mid-December 1986, her diary was a blur of notations about sleeplessness, anxiety, depression, and fear. Finally, she took her first positive step forward and directed Hargreaves to file for a temporary spousal support order. The hearing was set for December 30. "I had to do something. He had simply cut off my money with his fines! Stupid as I was, I wasn't into starving!"

In the same week, the 1985 battle over Christmas money repeated itself. She refused to take the children on their annual holiday ski trip to Utah unless Dan paid her about $7,000 extra for expenses. Nor could she entertain them in her La Jolla home, according to the letter her attorney wrote Dan, since "her home is only partially furnished and cannot accommodate all of the children, unless they sleep on the floor or with Mrs. Broderick."

Dan Broderick's reaction was by now predictable: Up yours. He had offered the same $2,000, and he wasn't about to be the victim of "reverse ransom," as he called it. He was so angry, in fact, that he wrote Betty a letter saying, in effect, that he took her decision as final—no last-minute changes of heart allowed: she could damn well forget seeing her children for a single day at any time between December 19 and January 4.

And forget it she damn well would. She was still trying, nearly two years later, to teach Dan Broderick that "there's more to fucking than fun." See how long the bimbo found him so dashing and romantic with four kids hanging around his neck. Yes.

Betty never would come to grips with either Dan's determination or with Linda Kolkena's commitment to him. It would take more than four snotty kids to derail Linda's dream of becoming the next Mrs. Daniel T. Broderick III.

Dan and Linda took the children skiing that Christmas and seemed to have a fine time.

She was everybody's charity guest that season. But she was in misery. "All Betty could see was the unfairness of what had happened to her," said Vicki Currie. "All she could talk about that Christmas were those fines."

Everywhere she went, she was heaped with unwanted advice: Compromise. Forget it. Move on.

They didn't understand. She hated them for it. She fled home, frustrated, to her diaries and notebooks and legal documents and the refrigerator. "I was happier when I was by myself. They made me feel crazy. And, I knew I wasn't crazy. I thought they were crazy, just like Dan Broderick. Everybody was telling me constantly to just roll over, that black was white. I am not color-blind."

Mostly, she spent the holiday season of 1986 calculating her living expenses for the upcoming spousal support hearing.

According to her figures, she needed $28,500 per month.

She arrived in court on December 30 wearing her usual upbeat, chipper, how-can-I-please-you face. She was the bright student at the spelling bee, the innocently hopeful little girl, laughing too gaily, making too much small talk, as her eyes roamed the room. Waiting for Dan to enter. She was always waiting for Dan. And, she knew, inside, that if only she was charming enough, if she only showed them how sincere she was, both the judge and Dan would treat her well. They would like her. Dan

155

would come to his senses yet. Betty was always a woman who lived somewhere outside herself, forever setting the real Betty aside in some pastel, placid dreamworld, where all things including herself were perfect, where all conclusions were ideal. She is still that way today.

But Dan, her sweetheart, her husband, and her identity in this life, simply brushed past her, tight-jawed and cold, and sat down at the table with his new attorney, Gerald Barry, a partner of Tom Ashworth—who was now presiding judge of domestic courts.

She turned her attentions to the matter at hand—money and independence.

She wanted full financial freedom from Dan. She wanted to pay her own house payments, her own taxes, and every other bill, "like a grown-up woman, not a goddamn child," she snaps today. At the same time, she didn't expect to suffer any decline in her life-style. Half of all that Dan Broderick owned was hers. That was their bargain.

Still, she never even asked for half. Not even close, not during all the long years of their divorce struggle. At $28,500, she wasn't aiming for much more than 25 percent of his monthly income. But, she told the judge, with that much money, she wouldn't feel too cheated.

Dan, by contrast, thought $7,316 was plenty for one woman without children—and that for only a limited period of time, until she got herself a job.

"His lawyer kept talking about need," she said later, laughing bitterly. "Well, obviously, anybody could squeak by on $9,000 a month. Need had nothing to do with it. The point was fairness—percentages. Why was I budgeting while he and Linda were living like royalty?"

She even came to court that day hauling a bag of worn children's shoes and rat-eaten dresses from the rental house to show the judge that Dan was not providing properly for either his children or her. That same bag would show up in divorce court two years later and also in her two murder trials.

She suffered a crushing defeat in that early round. What she got from Judge Napoleon Jones, instead of $28,000, was $12,500. Worse, from that amount, she had to pay $4,000 to $5,000 monthly in property taxes and insurance bills, which Dan had borne before. In short, not only had she failed to win enough money to maintain her current life-style, she now had even less spendable income than she had when she was reliant on Dan's informal dole. Before Betty Broderick had fully even mastered the art of living rich, she was back to square one—worrying about money.

Shifting the tax and insurance payments to her turned out to be an accounting error that the judge would eventually rectify with apologies—but not until Betty had spent several thousand dollars more in legal fees on a new attorney.

At the same hearing, arguing that it was in the best interests of the children, Dan's attorney also succeeded in having the Broderick divorce case permanently closed to the public. According to Betty, Hargreaves barely protested, although she did. As a result, for the next three years, the Broderick matter proceeded in secrecy. Throughout the entire Broderick divorce drama, Betty could howl all she wanted about how she had been fined $8,000 for calling Dan a "fuckhead" or jailed for calling

Linda a "cunt," but few people could believe such an absurdity—and nobody could go read the files or sit in on hearings to see for themselves. Dan Broderick was now free to take his ex-wife to court as often as he pleased without fear of being snickered at, either by reporters or his peers down at the courthouse.

In the subsequent months and years, her sense of helplessness only increased each time she walked into a sealed courtroom to face Dan and his attorney. And the entire community increasingly wondered why the Broderick case rated such top secret status. Not until two years later did another divorcee tell Betty that her own attorney, an associate of Dan's attorney, had once told her that the Broderick case was closed because Betty was a child molester. "I thought I would just die right then, when I heard that—I felt like the wind had been knocked out of me," Betty recalls.

Meantime, now that she had a firm, court-ordered support figure, Dan could no longer fine her even a dime for calling him a fuckhead without being in contempt of court himself. That was the only bright side of her dim month.

The day after the court-ordered $12,500 award, Dan wrote Betty yet another of his legal letters. This one informed her that she was now responsible for payment of all insurance premiums. In addition, in an effort to help her into the world of independent finance, he outlined in meticulous detail which premiums expired on what dates, and provided the exact amounts she must henceforth pay. He also warned her that she had better start budgeting for her taxes. "I strongly suggest that you consult a tax attorney or an accountant about how to handle this right away." It was just one more piece of advice Betty threw away.

A few days later, she received notification that Dan had canceled her medical coverage under his state bar insurance policy, effective instantly. The letter was signed by Linda Kolkena, "legal assistant to Daniel T. Broderick III." "Paid whore," Betty scrawled on the copy.

She was so upset that, days later, Hargreaves wrote a letter to Dan's attorney imploring that "in consideration for the feelings of Mrs. Broderick," all future correspondence affecting Betty be signed by Dan, "rather than having Mrs. Broderick receive copies of such correspondence executed by Linda Kolkena."

Neither Dan nor Linda paid the least bit of attention.

Betty began to focus her attention specifically on Linda Kolkena. If Linda had once been a trivial airhead who would soon evaporate, a stupid bimbo interchangeable with a million others whose worst offense had been putting her voice on the family answering machine, now Linda began to emerge in Betty's mind as a creature far more hateful—and substantive: Linda was now an arrogant, cruel little bitch, deliberately inserting herself into a divorce that was none of her business. Overnight, Betty's prior disdain began to take on the hues of indelible hate. And, certainly, Linda Kolkena proved in the next years to be remarkably insensitive toward the woman she was replacing. Later on, for example, when Dan finally sent Betty the deed to her own house following their protracted divorce trial, it was notarized by Kolkena. Betty tore it to shreds and threw it into a box of documents, which is where her defense attorney later found it in time for her murder trial.

On the other hand, some of what Betty accused Linda Kolkena of doing, she probably never did.

Finishing out the year of 1986, for instance, Betty raced around La Jolla almost gleefully treating everyone to a glimpse of a photograph she claimed Linda had sent her anonymously. The picture showed Linda and Dan at a party celebrating Dan's election as president of the county bar association. Dan, holding a drink, was grinning boyishly into the camera, with a radiant Linda at his side. The photo had been printed in a local legal publication called *Dicta*, and the caption identified Dan as the president-elect and Linda as his paralegal and close friend. Those three words alone were enough to drive a stake through the heart of any recently, unhappily divorced wife. "Since when does any publication editorialize about personal relationships?" Betty fumed from jail years later.

But that wasn't the worst of it. The photograph Betty was showing her La Jolla friends had also been tampered with—just beneath the picture and caption was a neatly typed two-inch-square note pasted in, which read: "It must KILL you to see these two happy together ... EAT YOUR HEART OUT, BITCH!!!"

This photo, Betty told everyone, had obviously been sent to her by "Linda the Cunt Kolkena." Could they believe that the bitch would be so vicious?

No, they could not. They looked at Betty, so desperate for sympathy and support, and they looked back at the altered photograph. Capital letters and triple exclamation points. So like Betty's own notes. Nearly everyone suspected that Betty had sent the photo to herself.

About the same time, Betty also said she began to receive anonymous ads for weight loss and wrinkle reduction in the mail—although, as it would later turn out in her murder trial, she may not have been imagining that those came from Linda after all.

Either way, by the end of 1986, Betty Broderick was already down for the count. From here on, the most remarkable thing about her story is the way she refused to stay down. She just kept getting back up, over and over again.

Chapter 15

Mothers and Daughters

In early January, she returned from a holiday visit with Brad's parents in Pasadena, where she had spent much of her time nursing her friend Kay Wright, who was then dying of cancer. It had been a sad time. By then, Mrs. Wright had become a surrogate mother to Betty, warm and sympathetic in a way her own mother never could be.

Betty's own daughters meantime, weren't doing much better in their effort to cope with life than she was. Kim, a former straight A student, was about to flunk out of Francis Parker in her junior year, and Lee was only a year away from winding up in a drug rehabilitation hospital and quitting high school altogether. Nor were the boys doing well. Therapists expressed concerns that both might be suicidal, Dan's friends later said.

Betty also returned home to a stack of mail that included more notices of insurance and credit card cancellations from Dan, plus a stack of bills. She had said she wanted independence, now she had it.

Her anger was instant, as she stood alone in her big house on the hillside. She stared at her sad, drooping Christmas tree, with its presents to the children underneath, still unopened, and thought of all that she had lost. Property. Status. Money. Dignity. And her children. She hadn't seen them for nearly a month now. They had again spent the holidays with Dan and his office girl on a ski trip. Linda Kolkena had stolen her life. Her husband, her kids, her money. Without working a day for any of it.

She marched to the phone and called his house. She got the answering machine. It was 7:30 on Sunday night. How could they not be home? The holiday was over. They were home. She was convinced of it. The fucker had turned off the ringer again. Keeping her from her children. Again.

She didn't even pause. She gripped the phone in her hand, with its maddening "Please leave a message" recording, waited for the beep, then spat out another of her furious messages, studded with even more references to cunts and fuckfaces than usual.

It's not hard to imagine Dan Broderick's fury when he came home, turned on his answering machine, and heard Betty spewing forth. By now that machine had become a red flag to him, too. He listened to Betty's voice. In his house. Disturbing his peace. Why couldn't he control this woman?

But he knew her game: now that he couldn't legally fine her anymore, she thought she was home free. She thought that he, Dan Broderick, was powerless.

Well, she would see.

He filed another contempt motion—his first based on her language alone.

Three days later, Betty was back in court, defending her mouth to a judge.

In his complaint, Dan argued that her foul language was every bit as offensive as her physical rampages through his house, smashing windows and spraying paint and kidnapping his children. He beseeched the court to find her in contempt of his restraining order and, accordingly, be "incarcerated in the county jail therefore."

Betty argued that, apart from her right of free speech, Dan's complaint was sheer hypocrisy. She had in fact learned the term "fuckface" from the Broderick clan, she said in her formal response:

" 'Fuckface' is considered to be a term of endearment in the Broderick clan. I first heard it from Dan's sister, Christy, during a Scrabble game seven or eight years ago. After getting over my initial shock, I realized that everyone thought it was quite funny, especially coming from such a sweet-looking young lady. 'Dear Fuckface' is how the family starts letters to one another. In using this terminology, I was simply using a family endearment. Other shocking terms of endearment invented and used by the Broderick clan are 'penis breath' and 'dickhead.' These terms ... are used throughout their everyday communications with one another ... They have been doing this around my young children for years."

Dan lost that round. Judge Anthony Joseph declined to jail Betty for using dirty words. Instead, he let her off with a lecture.

But this battle had hardly begun.

Instead, Dan began collecting Betty's ugly messages and filing regular OSCs. Typically, over the next months, he would gather her offending messages for a period of several weeks, then file them collectively in one OSC declaration. Other times, however, he would file a contempt based on one message alone. It all seemed to depend on his mood. It was a replay of late 1985, except now, instead of trying to have her jailed for vandalisms, it was strictly vulgarity: nearly every dirty word she uttered into his answering machine went into his files.

Thus did 1987 become the year of the renewed Order to Show Cause. Dan filed. "I was entitled to explode," she says. "And the truth is, I loved leaving those messages. All I ever had was my tongue. I did it for the shock value. And every time I used that language on his machine, I felt a little bit better for a while. I couldn't stop from doing it."

In April, in court again for more phone messages, she received a five-day suspended jail sentence.

Not until May would Dan finally have his way.

But anger, combined with pressing financial fears, cleared her head significantly during those first months of 1987—at least sporadically.

She began the year by filing two motions of her own—one for increased spousal support and another for modified custody, giving her guaranteed visitation.

But her certainty that she would never get a fair shake from the San Diego courts only grew. At a first contempt hearing, she says Judge Joseph broke into a friendly grin when Dan entered his courtroom and said, "Why, Mr. Broderick, to what do we owe this honor?" Joseph then told her, she says, that "he had great respect for Dan, and would that make any difference to me? I said that, yes, it did make a difference.

But he just brushed it off."

Studying a court calendar for 1987 is a staggering testament to Dan and Betty Broderick's mutual determination to wear the other down. The year was a blur of legal actions, courtroom appearances, declarations, stays, vacated calendars, continuances, charges, and counter charges.

Throughout January, Hargreaves was still seeking access to Dan's financial records. In addition, he was writing his own client beseeching letters begging her cooperation. A February deadline for appealing the $12,500 support order and also new arguments over the custody arrangement was fast approaching. "Please contact me immediately ... Repeated phone calls to you have been unsuccessful," Hargreaves wrote her.

But, by now, Betty had fired Hargreaves—at least in her own mind. Typically, however, she never confronted him with her gripes. Instead, she strung him along while she hunted for someone new. She was now calling Beverly Hills glamour attorneys again.

Nobody surpassed Betty Broderick when it came to docile capitulation to the personalities around her. She was, and remains, constitutionally incapable of telling people to their faces how she feels about them. During her murder trial, for example, she raged constantly at what she saw as the ineptness of her attorney—but only behind his back. When he was around, she turned into a docile little girl. She also gossiped constantly about the hypocrisy of old La Jolla friends who refused to defend her publicly; at the same time, she accused some of her newer friends—divorce reform activists who did try to defend her—of "using my life story to advance themselves." In the next moment, she would then call the same women for friendly chats, or write them intimate letters from jail.

Betty always needed a buffer between herself and the object of her resentments. Only on an answering machine, or in her endless letters, diaries, fliers, and other writings, or in conversation with third parties—usually reporters and other strangers—could she ever really muster the courage to say what was on her mind. It isn't surprising that her victims were in bed. Betty could never have shot two people who were up, dressed, and looking her in the eye in broad daylight.

"Oh, fuckhead, it's me!" she told Dan's answering machine that month. "I took the advice of hundreds of people who told me to call Marvin Mitchelson a year ago. I finally did it. Called him. He's gonna come down here and tar and feather and make even a bigger public asshole of yourself than you've done all by yourself. I'm just going to have to pay him a little for it. This is going to be fun. [singing] The bigger they are, the harder they fall, tougher they talk ... Asshole!"

She ended up being directed instead to another attorney in Mitchelson's circle, William J. Glucksman. As a retainer, he took a $10,000 diamond necklace she was wearing.

At about the same time, she finally decided to comply with the court order that she see a therapist. Dr. Gerald Nelson was the guest speaker at a La Jolla ladies luncheon, and Betty immediately liked his style. Better yet, he was a child psychiatrist. She could visit him to talk about the children, not herself. Her pride would not be sacrificed; at the same time the court's requirements would be met. She began sporadic visits to Nelson's office in Del Mar, a fashionable coastal community just north of La Jolla. In time, Nelson became such a trusted friend that he was one of those she attempted to call on the morning of the killings.

Meantime, Hargreaves's time clock was still ticking. Once again, Betty wasn't handling her attorneys with any maturity. Thus, in early 1987, she had, in effect, two attorneys. Within the next confused weeks Hargreaves finally gave up. Glucksman, who would last no more than a couple of weeks himself, promptly filed for a change of venue on grounds that Betty could hardly get a fair hearing in San Diego Family Court where Dan's former attorney, Ashworth, was now presiding judge—nor in a legal community whose titular leader was now Dan Broderick himself. Like Dan Jaffe before him, he intended to take Dan Broderick to the cleaners. His motion was denied.

Betty dropped Glucksman, she says, because Dr. Nelson persuaded her that she needed a local attorney. He recommended a friend, Tricia A. Smith, whose office was also in Del Mar.

Betty made an appointment with Smith for the next day and wrote in her February 4 diary, "Great!" Smith, a stately, silvery-haired woman with an efficient manner, would be Betty's fourth and last divorce lawyer. She lasted about a year before Betty fired her, too. After that, from 1988 on, like a lamb heading to slaughter, Betty represented herself.

During the chaotic weeks of the joint Hargreaves/Glucksman reign, Betty managed to meet the February 3 deadline for her support and custody motions. She wanted more money plus the children. As it would turn out, of course, she didn't want the children without the money guaranteed first.

Her custody motion was based mainly on Dan's neglectful parenting. Among a host of specifics, she accused him of sending the children to school dirty and of being more interested in his career than in the children's health. When Rhett once got sick at school, for example, Dan had picked him up and taken him to his office instead of home to bed, she complained. Dan had even neglected Danny's teeth, which were crooked and required a retainer, she alleged. "About eight months ago, the retainer broke, and petitioner refuses to take Danny to get it fixed. Now, Danny's tooth is crooked again. Petitioner also refuses to allow me to take Danny to the orthodontist." Atop all else, she said, Dan never attended any school activities and "didn't even know who their teachers were." By contrast to his terrible parenting, she pointed to her own record: "While the children were living with me, I was a FULL-time mom ... For fifteen years my parenting abilities were absolutely fine, from Petitioner's viewpoint. Now, while we're in litigation, if Petitioner's self-serving contentions are to be believed, he has taken a 180-degree turn with respect to my parenting abilities. It just does not make any good sense."

She wanted at least $25,000 in spousal support. "My expenses are admittedly high," she said in her declaration, "but are consistent with the type of living standard I earned during my lengthy marriage to Dan."

She then described the life-style to which she had become accustomed when he left her. Among other items: "We had five vehicles—an MG, a Gazelle, a Corvette, a Jaguar, and a Suburban for me and the kids. We traveled to Europe once a year, took frequent ski trips, cruises, island trips, and often paid the entire expenses of couples traveling with us, always first-class. I entertained frequently and extravagantly ... All of this, plus unlimited ability to charge at every major department store in San Diego ..."

Now she had been fired from her job as wife and mother. "Being forced out of our marriage is like being thrown into a snake pit." She begged the court to "make an order giving me some parity in this matter."

The Broderick divorce would never proceed on schedule. Betty's custody motion was removed from the calendar for an indeterminate period, in order that psychiatrists might evaluate the fitness of the parents, customary in most such disputes over children.

Once again, however, Dan was victorious in advance. While the court order contained a specific proviso requiring Betty to "cooperate in submitting herself for psychiatric or psychological examination," no such language ordered him to submit to the same testing—and he never did.

Just one more insult, added to the many already festering in her mind.

By now, she was such a nervous wreck that she was periodically coming undone in public places, among strangers. Much of La Jolla was gossiping about her, this crazy lady who had burned up her husband's clothes, run the car into his door, and even lost visitation rights with her children. Even so, many mothers, armed with only the sketchiest of facts, were on Betty's side.

Jana Hernholm, for example, a La Jolla mother who knew Betty only casually through their school activities, remembers running into her at a ski resort one weekend and feeling only pity. Betty was not the same cheerful, funny, intelligent woman Hernholm had known. "It was just so sad. Tears were streaming down her face all day ... she couldn't stop talking about the wrongs she perceived. I'd say, 'Just put it behind you,' but she couldn't even hear me ... She was just consumed by it. But it was also just so obvious to me that he was toying with her. He could've stopped it. He could've given her back her kids."

Even so, at about the same time, Betty finally won a round herself. Although the custody matter was tabled, her spousal support motion got to court five days after Betty had hired Tricia Smith. Betty's case began at last to take some shape.

Smith succeeded in getting Betty's monthly support increased from the $12,500 to $16,000. The judge agreed that he "blew it." He had intended, he said, to "maintain the status quo ... [but] in my order, I completely omitted ... taxes."

It wasn't the $25,000 that Betty wanted, but it was the biggest loss that Dan Broderick had suffered in a courtroom in a long, long time.

Betty was delighted with her new attorney. She also recalls with satisfaction how Smith had ordered her to "look rich when I came to court that day." And so, says

Betty, "I wore my brown cashmere Oscar de la Renta with my gold jewelry, and when I walked in, Trish said, 'You do rich good!'"

She even remembers the shoes she wore—"My four-inch Charles Jourdan pumps. I always wore four-inch heels to court so I could look down on that little nerd [Dan]. He was such a little shit, and when I had those shoes on I was about 6'2." I went nose to nose with [Dan's attorney] Gerald Barry. I was right in those heels— 'Don't fuck with me, boys!' Hah. They're so used to looking down on us. Next to my tongue, my height was the only real weapon I ever had—until, of course, I bought the gun," she added with a sour little chuckle.

Within a month Dan appealed the temporary spousal support order. Although he eventually lost, his action only further persuaded Betty that he had no intention of settling with her in any speedy fashion, but was instead stealing time to accumulate ever more debts against her share of their community property. "Tricia told me it was the first time she ever heard of anybody appealing a temporary support order," Betty said later.

Dan's friends denied any such deviousness. "It was such an incredible amount of money for any man to have to pay. We all encouraged him to appeal it," says Stormy Wetther.

At the same time, because the court order failed to specify clearly that Betty's $16,000 was to arrive on the first of each month, Dan didn't send her next check until the end of the month, she says—by which time her own bills were backed up. So she had to pay more attorney fees, she says, to get the order rewritten to clarify the due date, "to add in just that one little thing." To her, it was pure harassment, nothing more.

Meanwhile, Tricia Smith was fast discovering, as Dan Jaffe and others had before her, that Betty Broderick could never suppress her anger long enough to focus on the longer-range goals of winning a fat settlement and, presumably, getting her children back.

February was one of Dan's busiest months in contempt court. Altogether, he filed three separate actions against her. By now, even one bad word was enough to drive him to seek redress.

In March, he filed his sixth contempt.

"... at 9:30 P.M., Citee telephoned my home. I answered the telephone and said 'Hello.' Respondent said: 'Aw, dickhead.' She then hung up," said Dan in his declaration. By now, he was also advising the judge of what specific penalties he thought appropriate: five days in jail and/or a fine up to $1,000.

"And that one wasn't even me! He must have had another fan," Betty still insists, laughing. "For one thing, 'dickhead' isn't my word. Besides, I would never call Dan Broderick one name and hang up—that wasn't my style. Once I got the sonofabitch on the phone, I'd talk until he got mad and hung up."

But as winter turned to spring, her telephone voice grew uglier, especially toward Linda. "I'm so glad you put the machine on, fuckhead. I like talking to the machine, and I'm sure you're just recording every little word for the future, and I'm glad of it ...

because every little word is true ... I don't know how either one of you can do any of this ... She's ruined six lives, and her life was never anything that counted to anyone anyway, so she had nothing to lose, has nothing to lose. Once a cunt, always a cunt. It wasn't like she was an upstanding citizen and had any friends or anything, that anyone cared about her ... It's a shame that your income plummets this year, isn't it, sweetie? [kissing sounds] You're so cellophane ... You think you're so clever, and you're just a classic fool."

Chapter 16

Gripes

March, 1987, was her most lunatic month so far. Her diaries, always a good measure of where her mind was, became wild, disjointed things, painting the portrait of a woman on the verge of a breakdown. Even her penmanship began to lose its neat legibility, turning instead into loose, double-sized scrawls with ever more exclamation points and underlined words. Some pages contain only three or four words. To read these chronicles from beginning to the end is a progressive journey into madness—one reason that the defense could never get them introduced into trial. The prosecutor didn't want jurors to travel to hell on Betty Broderick's express. By early 1987, she had become an insomniac worrying about money, children, and her health—"can't sleep, back pain ... do I have ulcers?" She worried about being jailed for her telephone calls. She was also beginning to distrust her lawyer—"Is she for me or agin me?" Tricia is not giving me the service I need!" In particular, Smith was not returning her phone calls fast enough.

She was enraged in those dark hours of the night, too, about the lack of progress in her case. Dan had yet to personally submit himself to lengthy, legal interrogation by her lawyer. "Two and one half years," she scrawled, "AND NOT ONE DEPOSITION!"

She was also increasingly obsessed with her future.

What job could she do? Where could she go? She had to find something to do with the rest of her life, now that she would no longer be Mrs. Daniel T. Broderick III. But in her mind, all routes were blocked. "Applied for child-care job in Jackson Hole. Kids five, three, and one," she wrote on February 5. "But how do I explain not having mine???"

Then, midsentence, her financial fears would override all else. "Bought medical insurance. $78 per month!" And, on March 5: "Still no money!" His check was late again; it would often be several days late. Her handwriting grew larger and wilder. One day, she called Western Law School—but her main concern was tuition costs, not classes, according to her diary notes.

She couldn't balance her bills, she didn't know what she could afford anymore, and so she hired an accountant to help her. "Mimi here today." Mimi the accountant came once a month to go through bills. Could she afford to keep the gardener? Would she have to sell the house?

Her diaries became ledgers of numbers, columns of figures that never added up.

Something would have to give. In her life-style, of course. Never his. Oh, no.

She became consumed with Dan's expenses, his lavish life-style, versus her deprivations. Her 1987 diaries were filled with notes on every new piece of furniture he bought, the brand name of every fabric, every dish, every rug. His new pool, the new circular driveway, the landscaping. He was a grand gentleman. But she was no longer a lady of means. Linda Kolkena was.

Not least, she burned with anguish over her wrecked reputation. She could see the curious, embarrassed expressions in the eyes of people she hardly knew. She dreamed of revenge, of vindication. She fantasized about how glorious it would be to win a forum that would expose him, not only in San Diego, but to the entire nation. And so, in early 1987, she began to write to her two favorite talk show hostesses, Oprah Winfrey and Sally Jessy Raphael. Her diaries are filled with drafts of long letters she wrote that spring, telling them her story.

"I feel I would be a good person for you to have on your show because women are totally unaware that they are so vulnerable in this legal system," she said in one. "They need to be informed, they need to be scared—they need to force action so we, ourselves and our children, can be protected!"

She later claimed she never mailed the letters.

The diaries went on. On February 10, according to her notes, Kim was expelled from Francis Parker. Next day, "Lee out of school. School calling!"

—Two weeks later: Danny's eleventh birthday. "No visitation."

—On March 4: Went to see K. Hoyt at Bishops about Kim getting kicked out of school.

—The boys told her she couldn't drive them home because they were afraid Dan will have her "put in jail."

—"Kim alone in the house with boys after school ... construction worker ..."

Nor was Betty getting along with Dan's latest housekeeper, a young woman named Robin Tu'ua: "The fat baby-sitter ... a total snot with me."

Not least, she had discovered that "Rhett has lice! Head lice! My son!"

Meantime, her phone messages continued, perpetual fodder for more OSCs.

"Dan Broderick, fuckhead, you'd better get on top of your daughter Lee," she said in one. "She's wild, out of control, drunk, street walker, ugly. Being that you've got sole custody, better do something about it before you have to go to jail for her, okay?" Then, minutes later: "Amend that—jail or the morgue."

At the same time, both her attorney and Dr. Nelson were trying to persuade Betty to aggressively seek full custody of her children. Although Nelson had not yet met the Broderick youngsters, he was convinced that Dan was unable to provide them with a suitable home environment.

In a letter to Betty that spring, he begged her to forget her obsession with winning a financial settlement first: "... The number of bedrooms, the state of your home, and your furniture, is, in my professional opinion, unimportant. The children are surrounded with a luxurious setting, and they are suffering significant psychological and emotional trauma. I urge you ... get your children home."

It would never happen. She would not put aside her anger long enough to focus on the children, although she probably needed them far more at that point than they needed her.

Instead, she continued to demand only that she be allowed freedom "to visit and speak with my kids." Visitation was all she wanted. She remained torn, until the end of this story, between genuine concern for her children and glee that Dan was failing in his mission to replace her.

"Kids home alone," she wrote repeatedly in her diaries. She found Kim's newest boyfriend, a construction worker, especially unsavory.

And, always ongoing were jottings about her latest legal notices—two new OSC filings came on March 13; the divorce trial date had been postponed again; Dan's deposition had been delayed one more time.

By March 26, her nights had become a living hell. "Called Tricia at one A.M.," she wrote, "feeling out of control" because Smith had all her files and wouldn't return her calls. "Up all night worrying."

And then the miscellany:

"Cunt hosting party on MY boat," she wrote on March 15. It was not a grand boat, only a small ski boat. But Dan wouldn't let her use it, she said. It gnawed at her. "Fuckhead, I have the day off, and I would really like to use the boat, my boat," she said in another phone message that would wind up as an OSC. "How do I get the keys? Where are the keys? Will you make another set and deliver them over here so that when I want to use the boat I can use it. Thanks, sweetie. Asshole."

She also noted tersely in her diary that April 12 was their eighteenth anniversary. "Went to LPGA [golf] tournament."

To top it all off, among the various legal documents in her March mail, she learned that Hargreaves was suing her for unpaid fees.

In March, Betty began court-ordered visits to marriage and family therapist Dr. Ruth Roth—where, not surprisingly, she said all the wrong things. She was so indignant to be forced to see Roth for psychiatric evaluation, when Dan was not, that she refused to take Roth seriously. It was a doomed enterprise from the outset. She flounced into Roth's office, dressed to impress in a designer suit and her power pumps, determined not to display a trace of the frightened, passive woman inside. She did a great job.

During her three sessions with Roth, she went out of her way to shock, overwhelm, and defy any reasonable conversation. It would only be the latest among Betty's many miscalculations.

Ruth Roth is not a woman whose ego you want to tamper with. A small, attractive therapist in her sixties with short-cropped hair dyed auburn and a lingering New York accent, Roth is a bristling, no-nonsense type clearly accustomed to being in control. She has been mediating divorce and custody disputes for the San Diego courts since 1976, first in the county conciliation courts then in private practice. She has, she boasts, mediated over five thousand cases in her career—"and 90 percent of them were successful." People who can afford her fees seek her out, rather than opt for public services, she says, for the same reason that "you don't buy a Datsun if you can afford a Cadillac." She is a familiar, well-regarded "expert" in the San Diego family courts. What she says usually goes.

"She just went off on her own agenda," Roth later testified in Betty's murder trials,

168

describing their few meetings. "I tried to maintain control, but I couldn't."

As usual, the best measure of Betty's angry attitude rested in her language. Like anyone else, Betty can clean up her mouth when she tries; she does not, for example, say "fuck" in court. But she apparently had so little respect for Roth that she buried the woman in obscenities.

She told Roth what was by now becoming the standard outline of "the story." How Dan was, from 1983 on, "screwing" Linda while Betty was left in a rental house with rats. How she had "worked my ass off to get us where we were going" only to be left. "Now he has everything and the cunt." She told Roth that he had a violent temper, that he kicked small dogs, beat the boys. Once, she said, he had even beaten Kim, when she was only ten months old. And she talked about the third dead child.

Roth tried to move the conversation on to present realities. But, Roth testified, Betty would not be led. She was "unusual ... very intelligent. I thought she was angry but not psychotic." In fact, Roth said, she thought Betty Broderick was the angriest client she had ever seen.

Even so, she at first thought Betty could still be a good mother if she focused on the children, not her anger. She tried to guide Betty's mind in that direction.

But Betty ignored her. According to Roth's testimony, Betty said she had taken the kids to Dan in early 1985 to "let him see what four kids is about besides fucking!" But, Betty continued, "You know what that cocksucker fucker did? He kept them!!!" Roth blushed primly as she recited these quotes from her notes. Nor did Betty spare Roth her anger toward "Linda the Cunt Kolkena." She had in fact been so intensely explicit in her remarks that Roth later wrote in her report that "She is sex obsessed."

During their first visit, Roth said Betty also threatened to kill Dan. The context was this: Roth had been trying to persuade Betty that the best course of action was to regain custody of her children. But, said Roth, Betty angrily resisted: "I'm not going to be the single parent of four kids. He'll die first. . . . The less I see of them, the better. No kids, no bother . . . you'll see. . . . He's a cuntfucker."

And that was the end of Dr. Ruth Roth's first session with Betty Broderick. Roth promptly called Dan Broderick, she said, to warn him that "I have every reason to believe you may be in danger, that Elisabeth wants to do great bodily harm to you."

In California, this extraordinary breach of doctor-patient confidentiality —called a Tarasoff warning—is not only ethically permissible but also legally advisable in instances where the doctor might later be held liable for a preventable crime. The warning is named after the victim of a psychotic killer whose therapist was later successfully sued for negligence in failing to alert the victim or her family to the potential danger.

But before Betty knew that Roth was confiding in Dan, she returned for a second session—and repeated the same threat almost verbatim, according to Roth.

"I'm not going to be the single parent of four children. He'll die first ... I told you that," Betty told Roth, in apparent exasperation at her denseness. "I'm not letting go of him that easy. The little fucker was mine, and he'll stay mine."

Are you threatening him? Roth asked.

"I threaten the little cocksucker all the time!" Betty told her, laughing. In conclusion, Roth asked Betty what Linda's real name was. "Cunt," said Betty. End of session two.

Roth issued her second Tarasoff warning to Dan that week. But, she said, Dan didn't seem to take it seriously. "He just shined it on," said Roth—who was, by now, having regular telephone conversations with Dan, discussing ways to best handle Betty and protect the children from her.

Later, Betty only laughed at Roth and her Tarasoff warnings. Her talk of killing Dan was just a figure of speech. "I was not sitting there telling Roth that I was premeditating murder. I was pissed off, but I am not stupid, for Chrissake!"

That, of course, was always Betty Broderick's exact problem. No professional therapist who ever interviewed her concluded for a single minute that she was either stupid or crazy.

On her third meeting with Roth, Betty quit.

"She said, 'I'm not coming back, because you're too good,'" Roth testified. "She said, 'You make me forget how much I hate him'."

"I said that because, typically, I was trying to be nice, I didn't have the guts to just tell her the truth," says Betty, "and the truth was I couldn't stand her. She was pushy and arrogant, and she spent forty of her fifty-minute periods talking about herself, telling me how wonderful she was."

She is embarrassed, however, at her failure to clean up her language for Roth. "I was just a mess ... I had simply lost it all, by then."

The only part of Betty's experience with Roth that even remotely pleased her was the fact that the judge had clearly ordered Dan to pay Roth's full fees. But even that turned to ashes because Dan later refused flatly to pay more than half, based on his prior reasoning—if Betty didn't have a financial stake, she wouldn't proceed in "good faith." And so, like Hargreaves, Roth sued Betty for the balance—around $800. The outcome of that little side skirmish in the Broderick divorce war wouldn't be determined for more than a year. But, atop her other pressures, Betty was also fast becoming a familiar face in small-claims court: At about the same time, a La Jolla children's shop also sued her for an unpaid bill for clothing she had bought the boys and billed to Dan—who refused to pay.

After mediation broke down, Dan hired Roth to counsel Danny through most of 1987. Danny, then eleven, was depressed. He wanted to live with his mother. But, he told people, his mother wanted him to hurt Linda—for example, "to pour boiling water on her cunt," making it look like an accident—and when he wouldn't, she was angry with him.

During the later divorce trial, Dan also recalled an incident just before Mother's Day in 1987 when Danny threatened to jump from a second-floor window, after Betty told him on the telephone that he couldn't come see her that day—that he should stay home instead and "have Linda's Day at your Dad's house."

Danny "was in a lot of pain, frustrated ..." said Dan, and so he had taken the boy to the neighborhood ice cream parlor, where he spent an hour talking to him, trying to explain "what was going on with his mom. Why she is acting like this. Why she can't stop it. The thrust of my comments to him was, 'Dan, your mom doesn't have impulse control. She cannot control herself. Some people are like that. She is like a little girl who for some reason wouldn't or can't control her frustration. She is like a little child who can't get her way, so she rolls around on the ground and kicks and screams. She has never been able to do that [control herself].' And," Dan finished, "I think, intellectually, he understood that." He evidently neither mentioned his own role in helping create Betty's anger, nor did he explain to the boy why, if Betty was so naturally uncontrollable, he kept taking her to court anyway.

Betty claims not to remember many of her angry outbursts. What she does remember about that period is being pulled in a dozen different directions by all the stresses imposed on her from every side—from Dan, the courts, the therapists, her friends, her creditors, her family, and her body. She remembers sensations of anger, fear, loneliness and, sometimes, wondering if she was in fact going mad, just as he said.

And she remembers her own white lightning sense of outrage at the unfairness of it all. "All I know is I just never ever had any doubt that none of this was just. All my life, I literally hated it when I would see old ladies with their bags, counting out their pennies at the post office for stamps. I always thought, 'Where are their children, where are their husbands and brothers?' Somebody owed them more ..."

She also remembers small things better than the larger ones—the kids' homework, for instance. They would call her for help, and over the telephone she would try to answer their questions. But both sets of family encyclopedias were then at Dan's house. "Now, you try to do fifth-grade geography, you know—what two rivers come together in the middle of Africa—without books!" So she went out and bought a new $1,000 set of Encyclopedia Brittanica. "But even that didn't help because sometimes they just needed help with lessons out of their schoolbooks." But she couldn't see the book. "So there I am, trying to do algebra and crap long-distance, that I haven't done since we've all done it. ... So I'd say, 'Okay I'll come over, and we'll sit out in my car, because if I have the book I can do this much faster. But they'd always say 'No no no, Mom. If you come around here Daddy will have you arrested'."

Chapter 17

Mothers and Sons

Children are always the biggest losers in divorces, but the Broderick youngsters suffered more than most, even before they lost both parents altogether.

Perhaps the single most glaring example of adult irresponsibility, amid the heat and hate of divorce, is contained in a taped, thirty-minute conversation between Betty and her son Danny in late March, 1987. During the murder trials, the prosecutor played this tape with satisfaction, knowing full well that few jurors could withstand the gut-level disgust it evokes.

On the other hand, the defense countered that the only reason the tape existed in the first place was because Dan Broderick was more interested in collecting evidence against his ex-wife than in protecting his little boy's peace of mind. Otherwise, he would have ended the conversation as soon as he heard the child crying and yelling into the phone. Throughout the conversation, the boy was sobbing, almost hysterical. According to daughter Kim in trial, "Danny never got that upset." Dan listened from the next room. It was the first time he had taped an actual conversation between Betty and one of her children for use in their divorce war.

Both defense and prosecution of course were correct. The "Danny Tape," as it became known, represents the worst impulses of both Brodericks at the expense of their children.

Here it is, excerpted in part:

B: "... He's so stupid he doesn't care ... but that money is mine. I earned it. I earned it for twenty years of hard work and total shit from that asshole.

D: Yeah, but you're never going to see us again if ... don't you even care about your family, besides the stupid money? [crying]

B: I care perfectly about my family. I took absolutely perfect care of my family. I was the best mommy in the whole world and the best wife in the whole world. It's not my fault your father is such a fuckhead ...

D: Then how come you won't just shut your mouth so we can come over there? ...

B: I care plenty about my family. I only worked twenty-four hours a day for seventeen years.

D: So then, well, fine. If it isn't your fault, then why don't you just mind your own business ... [crying]

B: What do you mean, mind my own business?

D: And don't care who he's seeing. He could be seeing a totally different girl, and it wouldn't make a difference.

B: Well, I guess you're a real California kid. Congratulations, your brain is scrambled eggs. You've been living with him too long. You don't have any sense of values, right and wrong, up and down, in and out, black and white, truth or lie. If you stay living with him, your whole head will go scrambled.

D: Well, all you care about is the money ... what else do you care about besides your money and your share of things to own?

B: ... I cared about my family bad enough to put up with him fucking Linda for two years ...

D: It's not only Linda's fault. It's Dad's fault too, and it's your fault, Mom!

B: Why?

D: 'Cause you keep on saying bad words ...

B: Listen, the first Christmas your father took you guys away from me and fucked Linda right in front of you at the ski place, we were married, and I wasn't calling anybody a cunt then.

D: What ski place?

B: In Utah. We were married when he did that.

D: No, you weren't ... yeah, but you were still separated.

B: Well, what difference does that make? We were still married. And you are my four kids that he took away from me for Christmas and put you in an ugly apartment where he could fuck his secretary.

D: He didn't take us away—you gave us to him.

B: On Christmas?

D: No, on Easter. You sent me over there on Easter and a couple hours more, they [the other kids] were over here.

B: Uh-huh. And you've just been having a good time ever since, haven't you?

D: No! We haven't. We're having a horrible time! You keep on saying those bad words, and we're never going to be able to come over there, if you don't stop. And if you don't stop it, it just shows me that all you care about is your money, [crying]

B: Well, this house isn't as pretty as that house.

D: Yeah it is. It's a lot prettier.

B: Well, it's in a better spot. I don't like you in gay town with all the criminals and all the retards and the old folks and the drug deals ...

D: ... If you don't stop saying bad words, we're never going to be able to see you again.

B: Yeah, well, as soon as I get a fair settlement from Daddy ... then I'll discuss custody ...

D: We aren't allowed to be around you, if you're saying bad words, Mom.

B: Well, and the cunt is allowed to be around you, who's been fucking him?

D: What's wrong with that? You guys are divorced, so Dad can be with anybody he wants to.

B: I didn't get a divorce. Daddy got the divorce. I'm still married.

D: I know ... no ... no, you aren't, cause if you get divorced, you both are separated, Mom. And, he, he likes somebody else now. He doesn't like you anymore, and if you ... you gotta stop saying the bad words! [crying]

B: Why doesn't he like me anymore?

D: Because you've been ... he's sick of you because you guys get in all these fights.

B: Why do we get in these fights?

D: I don't know.

B: Because he was fucking his secretary ... He's scum, Danny. He's absolute scum. He's cheated and lied and fucked around ...

D: You don't think being mad for two years is enough though, Mom?

B: No. It took me twenty years of goodness to get mad ... Danny, I'm not selfish. I'm just fair.

D: You want everything. You want half, you want half, and half of everything Dad owns. You want all, all the kids, and you want Linda to go away, so that leaves Dad with nothing.

B: Well, excuse me. First off, you're wrong; I don't want everything ...

D: What do you want? [crying]

B: Second off, what do I care if he's left with nothing? He walked out on his family. He doesn't deserve a family.

D: Oh, okay, what does he care that you're left with nothing? It's the same exact thing, Mom! How do you feel with no one living there. Not very good, huh? ...

B: Well, if you say that one more time, I'm going to tickle-torture you for twenty-five minutes when I see you. That is not true, but I want what's mine out of that fuckhead, who refuses to settle.

D: Yeah, well, you stop saying bad words and it will happen ...

B: For two years since the separation, he could have settled this in the first week. In the first day he could have settled this.

D: No, he couldn't, 'cause you were so naughty you sent us over there.

B: No, from the separation, he could have settled it, and now I would know how much money I was getting to pay the bills and to buy things and stuff and fix up this house so you guys could come live here ...

D: It's fixed perfectly fine for two of us to come live there. I don't know if the girls want to come, but if they do, I don't care, but all I care is that I want to come, and Rhett wants to come, and there's enough room there. There's one big room for both of us. [crying]

B: Danny, you're yelling at me. You don't even like me! You think I'm selfish and mean and everything else. What do you want to come for?

D: Because we both like you, and you're just being a real jerk because you don't want us to come over. All you want is your stupid money. And it's true, Mom. You don't care about us. You just want your money!

B: That's not true.

D: Then how come you won't stop saying bad words?

B: You're my little babies.

D: Yeah, I know, and if you stop saying bad words, you can have your little babies! [crying harder]

B: [laughs] My little baby's growing up. He's got quite a mouth on him. You're a smart kid, Danny. I love it. You're a smart kid. You're a very, very smart kid. You're going to be such a famous guy when you grow up. Whatever you do, you're going to be so successful because you're so smart. You take after your mother.

D: Why don't you just ... no ... you're not very smart, Mom, because you aren't doing anything that you should be doing. You should not, not be so mad after two years. And you should ... if you like us, if you think we're such your little babies, then why don't you want us to come over here? Why don't you stop saying bad words? [crying]

B: [laughs] ...

D: ... Why don't you just stop saying bad words? This whole thing could be settled a lot, lot quicker ... if you keep on saying bad words, it will never be settled, Mom.

B: Well, you tell Daddy to settle quick, and it can be settled before lunchtime tomorrow ... He's got all the money. He's got every single cent the two of us own. When he gives me my half, then we'll discuss ...

D: He gives you money every ... I don't know, but he gives you a lot of money.

B: Yeah, well. It's not enough ... It's not what the law says I own.

D: Yeah. Well, how much do you own?

B: Half.

D: Okay, well, you'd get your stupid half of your money if you'd just stop saying bad words! ... How come you just won't stop saying bad words? ...

B: Because I'm mad.

D: Yeah, well you can't be mad for two years. You're just going to get worse and worse and worse until you get your stupid share of money, and you're never going to get your stupid share of money unless you stop saying bad words! [crying] There's nothing funny about it, Mom!

B: Where's Daddy, while you're yelling at me like this?

D: I don't know.

B: He's probably listening on the other phone.

D: No, he isn't, because I see him walking through this room every once in a while to fix some light bulbs.

B: Where's the cunt?

D: I don't know where, Mom. I don't know.

B: Well, it's not time to come over and screw him yet, huh?

D: No. She's with her family.

B: ... I wonder what her family thinks of her fucking her boss who's married with four kids.

D: Not any more.

B: Well, what did they think of her when she was fucking him when he was married with four kids?

D: Well, fine, you can say what you want, but you're just being a real jerk to all your family. Nobody is going to like you anymore.

B: ... Well, I didn't do any of this, Danny. I was the best mother and the best wife in the whole world ... Daddy fucked all of us. He fucked your whole life and my whole life.

D: Well, you're doing the same thing right now, Mom.

B: Saying bad words has nothing to do with fucking your whole family ...

D: ... You're making everything ten times worse, and it's just going to get worse and worse until you stop saying those bad words. Why won't you stop? [silence]

175

Huh? ... And you always say that you're not doing anything, but you are, Mom! ... Why won't you just listen, Mom? You could make life a lot easier for everybody in this family if you'd just stop saying bad words. You're going to get your stupid share if you stop saying bad words. You're going to get us, the kids that want to come over to your house, and forever, if you would just stop saying those stupid bad words! Why won't you just stop? [crying]

B: [long pause] Because I hate Daddy ... He has robbed me of everything I have on earth, including the kids [crying] ...

D: Yeah, but you ... he didn't rob you—you gave us to him!

B: ... he's handled this like a fucking slug, throwing me in jail and stealing my house out from underneath me!

D: Oh, yeah, do you know why he threw you in jail? Because you came and rammed through his house.

B: After he stole my house from me ... I wish he'd just die. I wish he would get drunk and drive his fucking car ...

D: What's going to make the difference, Mom?

B: Because then he'll be gone off the earth ...

D: You've been mad long enough ...

B: No, I haven't.

D: Oh, yeah. So you want to be mad another two years, and after that another four years, and after that maybe another six years?"

Whereupon the recording ended. Dan apparently ran out of tape. Betty never would apologize or excuse herself for that conversation. "He wanted to drive me crazy, and he did," she says. "I couldn't tell you today what I was thinking—except that every word I said was true."

April, 1987, was another legal firestorm. The month began in court, where Betty was convicted on one count of contempt and given a five-day suspended jail sentence by Judge Joseph.

That was also the month Dan filed his appeal of her temporary support on grounds that it was "a civil form of double jeopardy" for the court to have corrected itself by adding Betty's taxes to the original award.

Her diaries had, meantime, become her best friend, her most faithful listener. She unloaded into them increasingly in the lonely hours of her nights.

"Rhett called at 2:40 A.M., dreaming about lice," she wrote. Lee had arrived at her house at 6:40 A.M. and "scared me to death. Made eggs and bacon." Three years later, Betty would say that one reason she bought a gun was due to her fear, as a single woman living alone, of intruders.

Adding to her April annoyances, she heard from the children that Linda took several friends to Mexico for Secretary's Week. "Cunt week," Betty wrote in her diary, along with an angry note insisting that Linda paid for it with "MY money!" Linda Kolkena was spending her community property funds. It was intolerable. She was paying for the slut's car, her clothes, her facials, and probably even her birth control pills.

During the same period, Danny was bumped by a car as he walked his bicycle across an intersection near Dan's home. He wasn't injured, but he was scared, and no one was home at the time. Dan was gone to a wedding reception, and the housekeepers did not work on weekends.

That was the first time Betty called the Child Abuse Hotline. Apart from embarrassing Dan, however, it was a futile gesture. "They sent somebody out who talked to Mr. Fancy Pants in his big multimillion-dollar house, and apologized for the disturbance, and left," she says.

In the most explosive of the month's events, Dan canceled prior plans for the children to spend Easter vacation with Betty. He based his decision on the advice of Dr. Roth, who, he said in a later contempt filing, had called him at home on the evening of April 9 to say that, because of a conversation with Betty a few hours earlier, she no longer thought it "advisable" for Danny to see Betty over Easter— although the plans had been made only two days earlier with Roth's approval.

Betty was supposed to pick both boys up at school on Friday afternoon for the weekend. But Dan didn't call her directly to tell her the weekend was off. Instead, he directed his attorney on Friday morning to inform Betty's attorney that plans had been canceled. This was obviously cutting it close in terms of timing, which both Dan and Roth knew. They both knew, too, that Betty would not react to their last-minute decision kindly. In fact, according to Dan's declaration, Roth advised him to pick the boys up early that day to "avoid any confrontation if Respondent came to get them too." So he did.

What resulted was a small, absurd scene out of a bad sit-com.

Picture it. Here comes Dan, not in his red Corvette today but in his green MG Midget convertible, roaring up to the school twenty minutes early to whisk his sons away before their mother got there. But Danny was on a field trip elsewhere. So he snatched up Rhett and set out to find Danny.

But, sure enough, here comes Betty—having received the enraging news from her attorney less than an hour earlier—screeching up to the school just in time to spot the familiar little MG soaring away with her ex and her youngest son in it.

She gritted her teeth and gunned her motor. When would this insufferable sonofabitch and his hired flunkies leave her and her kids alone? How dare they?

Within a few blocks, she had overtaken Dan's car.

According to Dan's later contempt motion, she forced him off the road. "She had me wedged into the curb. She rolled down the passenger window and started screaming."

What happened next, according to Dan's account, sounds like an escalated hair-raising escape worthy of an old Steve McQueen movie. "After three or four minutes of this," he said, "I put my car in reverse, hit the accelerator, and backed up at a high rate of speed into the nearest side street. I made a quick U-turn and drove to Presidio Park [where Danny was] as fast as I could ... and was able to get [Danny] into my car and then to my office without further contact with Respondent."

"Yeah. Riiiite, Dan," Betty said later, sarcastically. "What bullshit! I wouldn't hurt

177

my own son. I simply forced him to pull over and explain to me what I had just learned from an attorney thirty minutes earlier! I'd been planning on that week for a month! Poor little Rhett was crying, but Dan wouldn't let him out of the car. I wanted to kill the sonofabitch."

The month never got any better. There was no legal cease-fire. Betty was next served with a new OSC for the car incident, as well as half a dozen answering machine offenses. That hearing was set for late May. Two days later, she was scheduled to appear in court to answer for two contempts from March.

"OPEN the court! He's mentally ill!" she screamed into her diaries on the night of April 22.

Amazingly, at the same time, Betty Broderick was also applying for foster children. "I was looking for some kind of direction," she said later from jail. "And I'd been doing some work with the Children's Home Society, so I asked for kids—I just wanted newborns until they were placed. I love babies, so it would've been great for me, and them. But they [authorities] said no because I had an unfenced swimming pool."

May's mailbox was no better than April's. It was filled with more OSC notices and assorted legal papers—including word that Dan's deposition had been delayed for another month, and the divorce trial itself had been postponed again, until July.

Meantime, her legal bills were steadily mounting, along with her anxieties. In the next months, her diaries were filled with her escalating fears of being left destitute, thrown onto the streets. She was fixated with the idea that Dan might decide to sell the del Cielo house out from under her on a four-hour notice, just as he had sold Coral Reef. "What was to stop him?" she asked later. "His name was on the title of del Cielo, too. He could do anything he wanted—I understood that much by then."

Compounding her insecurities, her attorney, Tricia Smith, was clearly determined not to meet the same fate in unpaid fees as Betty's former lawyers. First, Smith negotiated with Glucksman to retrieve Betty's diamond necklace, which he was still holding hostage for his own unpaid bills. When Betty finally paid Glucksman, he forwarded the necklace to Smith, who did not return it to Betty until she accepted a lien on her house as collateral on Smith's legal fees. By May, Betty was so worried about losing her house that she was writing frantic midnight notes to Smith in her diaries, wanting to know if Smith would please release the trust deed on her house "if I can get $12,000 from Dan to pay you."

As Betty would later say from jail, in a moment of introspection, her obsession with financial security was probably the direct result of her own privileged background. She feared failure, she thought, perhaps even more than a person who grew up in poverty and had nowhere to go in life but up. Her three brothers were all successful businessmen, her older sister was a budget official for the state of Maryland, and her younger sister was a successful entertainment executive in Hollywood. "They're all wealthy, successful people with beautiful families. Everybody lives in big houses and travels, and their kids are all in private schools." Only her sister Clare never married—"But she's got a ten-page resume to make up for it." So, she added matter-of-factly, "Even before this incident [the homicides], I was the only family failure. I

178

didn't have a marriage or a resume. I had nothing but a jail record."

During the spring of 1987, her resentment of everybody and everything only grew. As usual, she focused first on her attorney. She castigated Smith in the pages of her diaries, day after day. Once again, she was being taken advantage of by an attorney—"$45,000 in fees so far," she wrote. All for nothing ..."

Finally, late one night, she wrote Smith a blazing note, firing her. Naturally, she didn't have the courage to mail it.

At the same time, she was increasingly preoccupied with her health. If her mother took to her bed with "the vapors," when she was upset, Betty was equally subject to blending mental with physical maladies. "Can't sleep," she complained again in her diaries. "Back problems. Grinding my teeth. Headaches. Depressed. Anxiety!!!" And her weight was ballooning.

But beyond all else, these spring months were dominated by her escalating obsession with her children. She took note of their every crisis, real or imagined.

Among her spring diary entries:

Kim got another F. Rhett was caught with $124 at school. She worried about Lee and drugs. Lee was "hysterical and wants to run away" because Linda didn't get out of bed to drive her to school, so she had to take her moped in the rain, then ran out of gas, and was late for a final exam.

On May 7, Francis Parker school officials called Betty to say that Rhett was so ill in class he had been isolated from the other children. "Rhett separated from other kids as contagious," she wrote in furious script. According to her diary, she then made her second, futile call to the Child Abuse Hotline.

Next, at a school charity auction, she impulsively bought a one-person package trip to Hawaii for July. But even then she expected Dan to pay the extra money so she could also take the children along, too.

No way, he told her. He and Linda were also planning a summer vacation to Hawaii, and they intended to take the children with them. If Betty wanted to take them on her trip, she could pay for it herself.

May 16: "Rhett sets fire in a neighbor's yard; Kim out of gas on the boat in dark last night ... No adult supervision!" Rhett, meantime, complaining that there was no "fun" food in Dan's house. No snacks.

Dan was starving her children, she now concluded. Everything wrong was his fault. His treatment of her children became, in her eyes, evidence of his unfitness as a parent—just as, for him, Betty's telephone messages were ample proof of hers. Just as he sat at home in the evenings, coldly harvesting his latest nasty answering machine tapes, she sat in her kitchen, scribbling furious notes about his sins into her diaries. But the results were identical: both Brodericks had become obsessive in their determination to collect evidence of the low character of the other.

But, while Dan's vision was still precise, Betty's had faded from clarity to dimness, with total blindness not far away. Now, she could see nothing beyond her own victimization. She was blameless. He was a monster. It was that simple. And it was still only 1987.

Also, amid her May diary pages were firm, large notes about her social schedule.

She was still literally leading a double life, trying by day, despite her awful nights, to carry on as a respectable, proper La Jolla lady. On the weekend of May 9, she discussed plans to attend a Theta lunch, a charity rummage sale, and the Spring Faire, where she was supposed to run the ticket booth. She also noted wistfully that the McGuires had built a splendid new house in Rancho Santa Fe, and that the Bartollottas were in Europe. Both couples were formerly part of the social circle she and Dan moved in—two more bright young attorneys, with wives Betty once listed among her closest friends. Until she killed. Then neither woman would ever utter a single public word in her defense.

But May was mainly the month of Kim.

It began on the Saturday morning of May 2, when the eldest Broderick daughter was scheduled to take her Scholastic Aptitude Test for college. But when she got to the test center, Kim called Betty in a panic because she had just discovered that she had to establish her place of birth, or the test results wouldn't count. Since she didn't have a driver's license, she needed her passport in a hurry. And she didn't know where it was. She thought it might be in her desk drawer at Dan's house—but she couldn't reach Dan at home, she told Betty.

Panic time. Like her daughter, Betty could always switch quickly into frantic mode. What resulted was another round of telephone calls from the furious, accusatory mother in behalf of the frivolous, thoughtless child—all paving the way, needless to say, to more contempts down the road.

"You outrageous fucker! There is a total emergency happening, and your daughter can't get hold of you. Typical! Asshole!" she screamed into Dan's answering machine. Her frustration was doubled because she couldn't even call his private line—he had always refused to give her the number.

"Fuckhead, I'm standing here trying to think of your friends that may know your unlisted number. Guess what. You don't have any friends, [laughter] ... I am previously engaged to be at a beautiful First Communion in the lovely community of La Jolla for my godchild, [sigh] I hate driving over to the slums to get this thing for Kim. Answer the phone, you dumb fucker! You've already ruined the last two years of her life, don't ruin it any further ..."

She next tried to call several of Dan's friends, but only got answering machines. Then, in what would be her first and only effort to contact Linda Kolkena directly, she called Linda's condo. Where she also got an answering machine.

"Oh course you're not home, you're off fucking your boss. We're having a family emergency, and I need the number of your employer. Cunt."

Although there was no restraining order preventing Betty from approaching Linda Kolkena, Dan would nevertheless include this call in his next list of phone offenses, filed in a May contempt action.

Finally, she reached Brian Monaghan, who then called Dan on his private line—and, somehow, the Brodericks managed to resolve the crisis in time for Kim to take her test.

Then, in late May came the matter of Kim and her prom dress. Betty was home alone, reading, she says, when her daughter came running into her house, "hysterical" because Dan had given her only $150 to buy a new dress and shoes for her junior ball.

Betty moved with the speed of a lioness to protect and provide for her child. She screeched up to one of her favorite La Jolla boutiques, Kim in tow, just as the store was closing—and, half an hour later, emerged in possession of an $800 peach satin, beaded party dress and matching slippers. It was, as Betty puts it, "a dress to die for—long sleeves, V-neck, very appropriate for a young girl. She looked like a princess." She paid for it, of course, on a credit card, despite her worries about her $78 monthly health insurance payment.

More than once, in fact, Kim scored new clothes from Betty, simply by crying about how low she had fallen in life, thanks to her chintzy father and his new girlfriend. Money always being the measure in the Broderick marital war, it became a weapon that Kim learned to exploit—which she later admitted in court, as the prosecution's star witness. But she downplayed it all.

"I was always hysterical," she said, looking embarrassed. "And Mom would always buy me wonderful things." But, she added, she always "felt guilty" about Betty's expenditures on her, because "then she would say she didn't have enough money to pay her bills." As for Dan's $150 prom dress allocation, "It was no big deal, really ..." Sure she was upset, she said; but, first, she was an emotional person, and, second, the year before, "Mom had bought me the most fantastic dress. I looked like Cinderella! Dad just wanted me to be ... regular."

At the end of the month, Dan filed another contempt motion over Betty's telephone messages about Kim's passport. The next day, a different OSC was continued to May 28. Altogether, throughout April and May, nine different counts of contempt against Betty were in the system.

Linda had also gotten into the act, filing a statement of her own to support one of Dan's contempt motions. Describing her only direct phone encounter with Betty, she wrote: "At approximately 8:10 P.M., the telephone rang. I answered it as I always do: 'Mr. Broderick's office.' Respondent, whose voice is well known to me and easily recognizable, said, 'The cunt's working late tonight! Put me through to Dan.' I immediately hung up, called Mr. Broderick at home to tell him what had happened, and quit working for the evening."

Betty hadn't been making any friends among Dan's recent housekeepers, either. According to one of them, Robin Tu'ua, in later testimony, after one upsetting conversation with Betty, Rhett had locked himself in the bathroom and emerged with "big clumps" of his hair cut out. Only after that, she said, did Dan unplug the telephones.

Tu'ua also said that Betty had threatened to kill her during that period, after Tu'ua had snapped at Betty for picking Rhett up at school, contrary to court orders. According to Tu'ua, Betty, who was then sitting in her car in front of the house with Rhett, had warned her to mind her own blankety-blank business or else. "She told me she had a gun in her glove compartment ..." Betty had then squealed away, said Tu'ua, who then called the police. They took a report, but nothing came of it. Betty denies the whole scenario. She never even owned a gun, she says, until 1989.

On May 28, Betty went to court to answer for five counts of contempt.

Tricia Smith did her best. She asked for a jury trial, but was denied. She also argued that Betty was not in contempt of any restraining order because none existed—the temporary order issued in November, 1985, she pointed out, had never been made permanent. Judge Joseph discounted that, too, declaring in effect that by virtue of his own acknowledgment of the expired order, he had renewed it.

Lastly, Smith argued that no restraining order could preclude a mother from calling her own children. Such an order, said Smith, would be so "overbroad" in its reach as to be unconstitutional.

But Joseph was fed up with Betty Broderick. He rejected Smith's arguments and imposed a twenty-five-day jail sentence. However, he said, he might suspend some of the sentence if Betty apologized to the court for her disrespectful behavior. Smith begged for a stay of the sentence, long enough to let Betty go home and get her affairs in order. Joseph refused. And so Betty Broderick was handcuffed and hauled directly from court to jail.

And this time, it was for real. Not just a few hours. This time, she was issued a uniform at Las Colinas and slapped into a cell with two other women, both fascinated with this big, hyper blonde with the great makeup and manicure suddenly pitched into their midst. One of them, Betty remembers, was "this old lady who was a heroin addict in for welfare fraud. The other was a young Spanish girl who was pregnant and had been doing drugs since she was eleven years old. I said to her, 'Do you realize how much money you've spent on drugs? It's much better to go to Nordstrom's!' And they laughed." She now laughs fondly at that old memory, too. She was so innocent then.

At first, she was "absolutely petrified in jail," but she soon learned that she had nothing to fear, she says now. "All these big black girls were so protective of me. I got along fine with my room-mates because I cater to everybody—they can have my clothes, my candy, my last bar of soap. I don't allow myself any rights ... I always feel obliged to make conversation, play cards, sleep when they sleep, eat when they eat, all in the name of getting along. I am such a fucking wimp."

She was in jail for six days.

Joseph suspended the remaining nineteen days—but only after Tricia Smith made an eloquent appeal for mercy. She also enclosed the best letter she could extract from Betty, promising not to make any more offensive phone calls:

"Judge Joseph," Betty wrote on June 1 on single-lined prison stationery. "As per your request, I promise to change my ways. I will never again call my children as long as they are living with their amoral, alcoholic, abusive father. This whole thing has been excruciatingly painful for the children and me. They come to me, as they should, with all their heartbreak and troubles. I thought it was my duty, and I know it is my right as their mother, to be there for them ALWAYS. But I will let the self-important Harvard lawyer, president of the bar, beat us all. He obviously loves BEATING

182

women and children. I will do anything to escape this escalating madness."

From there, Betty recited her whole litany of Dan's sins against her and the children. "It makes me sick that you are unable to see through this and do anything to help defend the kids ... Divorce is the 'Great American Tragedy.' ... The lives of women and children are DERAILED by divorce."

She finished with a promise, of sorts, to reform if he would release her from jail. "I understand what you don't want me to do. This has been an enlightening experience which I do not care to repeat. I won't waste my time or anyone else's with these diversionary tactics."

But Betty had barely cleared the jailhouse door before she was retracting every cynical word of the letter she had written.

"The statement you referred to [in court] is no statement of mine," she wrote Joseph in a letter copied into her diaries. "It was dictated by my attorney." Her actual views, she wrote, were these:

"I stand aghast at the gross miscarriage of justice put forth in your courtroom. It is a shame you are so 'honored' by the presence of Dan Broderick that you lost all sense of truth, justice, right, and wrong ... How you could have construed phone calls made to my children at their own separate phone number during times Dan could not possibly have been home as harassing Dan Broderick is a pathetic joke ... Just because Dan is fucking his receptionist, I WILL NOT BE TREATED AS AN INSANE CRIMINAL. I AM GUILTY OF NEITHER."

Her verbal rampage continued for pages. She complained that she had been denied her basic civil rights, including freedom of speech, and she protested the sealed courtrooms as un-American. She had always trusted judges, she added. But Joseph had failed her. "I absolutely refuse to be the victim of your biased and unfair judgment again. Somehow we will have to find UNBIASED judgment in this town or elsewhere. B. Broderick."

She also enclosed a list of seven attachments, ranging from the Webster's dictionary definition of cunt and prostitute, to various clippings from Time magazine and the New York Times dealing with custody issues and lawyers.

In short, Joseph could take her earlier, coerced promise to reform and shove it.

It was Tuesday, June 2, when she got out of jail—and back to her mailbox. There, incredibly, she found another contempt service from Dan awaiting her. Also, amid the wad of legal papers, she learned that: a June 1 contempt hearing, postponed since she was already in jail, had been rescheduled for Thursday, June 4—but then continued to June 8, at Dan's request, at which time she would have to answer for five more counts of contempt dating back two months. But, on June 8, those five counts would be delayed yet again until September 21. Meantime, on June 22, she was back in court, where another contempt was dismissed "with prejudice."

It had now been two and a half years since he left her, and one year since he divorced her. But in the summer of 1987, Dan Broderick still refused to give his former wife, now a jailbird and entirely disgraced in the eyes of her La Jolla peers, even a week's space to breathe or think over her shocking new experience. "I don't know why she didn't kill him then," one of her friends later remarked.

Meantime, Tricia Smith filed an appeal, asking that Dan Broderick be ordered to cease harassing his former wife. It was denied.

Chapter 18

Battered in La Jolla

But the worse it got, the more brittlely nonchalant Betty appeared, the more the old, sweetly appeasing Betty vanished within herself.

"She acted like jail wasn't any big deal at all," recalled Candy Westbrook. "I said, 'Oh, that must have been terrible.' But she just laughed about it. 'Oh, no,' she said. 'Actually, it was kind of interesting. I made some new friends.'" Westbrook mimics her friend perfectly. "It was like, Oh, yeah, I went to jail. Bip bop! Wanna go to lunch?' That's the way Betty would talk. She just wasn't rational anymore."

"It was terrible," Gail Forbes later said. "She was just never the same again. Her language was worse, her attitude toward the kids, life, her appearance ... after that jail sentence, she just seemed to lose interest in everything except what Dan and Linda were doing to her ... She wasn't even as careful about the children as she always had been ... She'd let them play on a big trampoline in her front yard without any supervision. Finally, I stopped letting my kids go over there."

Privately, all over La Jolla, women were trying to make sense of it. Why couldn't this woman just let go and get on with her life? Why was she going, for heaven's sake, to jail?

"Most people simply didn't believe her story. Everyone thought she must be doing something to deserve this, something worse than just saying ugly words," one of Betty's old friends, Judy Courtemanche, later remarked. By then, too, says Courtemanche, herself a divorcee of independent wealth, Betty's conversation had turned to disjointed babble. "There were so many details and accusations, so much she was trying to say about visitation, fines, appeals. The words just tumbled out of her mouth. She didn't make a lot of sense anymore. I felt so sorry for her."

Ann Dick, prominent in La Jolla social circles and also married to a successful San Diego attorney, had known Betty since the seventies, when Betty used to baby-sit her children. "At first, I wanted to doubt her. I had problems with Betty's story. I thought, 'Can she be being manipulated by the very system in which my own husband makes his living?'." But Dick, later a defense witness, decided that, "Yes, she was. If she'd had a Gerry Barry, or if Dan hadn't been one of the most feared, powerful attorneys in this town, none of this would ever have happened."

Cinching Dick's suspicions that something very wrong was afoot, she tried to contact Betty on the weekend she was jailed, she says, "to see if there was anything I could do. But they had no record that she was even there on their computer." Dick remains convinced to this day that Dan used his influence to have Betty's name removed so no one would know he had his wife jailed.

After Betty's release from jail, Dick, Gail Forbes, and a few others realized at last that their friend was in deeper trouble than they had thought. "We realized that she just wasn't capable of thinking rationally anymore," says Dick. So several women toyed briefly with the idea of taking charge of Betty's affairs—particularly her unpaid attorney fees. But Betty showed little interest, says Dick. And so the women eventually abandoned their good intentions. "It finally just became clear to us all that what Betty needed was thirty days of in-patient evaluation, not amateur psychiatrists," says Dick sadly. "We decided that if we wanted to really help her, it would be an eight-hour-a-day job——and none of us had the time. So we just let go."

And, by the end of June, Betty was back at it again.

"Hey, girls, get the cunt off the machine," she commanded on June 28. "... she is a joke. You must be home. Hmmm. Anyway, I'm checking on the [chicken pox] spots, especially Lee and Kim, and wondering if Danny got them yet. Kim, be careful with yours. Don't ruin your pretty face. And get the cunt off the machine. She has no business being on this machine. Such trash."

Later the same day, with rising frustration:

"Kim ... you just called me two minutes ago. I know you're home ... why don't you, instead of crying, talk to Daddy like a human being and ask him what the hell's wrong with him? Why he's such a prick all the time? If he gets his cheap jollies out of being such a prick? ... Kim, instead of getting all crying upset, just try to deal with Daddy. I know it's impossible, I know it's hard. Try to deal with him like a human being. Maybe one of these days he'll turn into one by mistake ..."

Whatever else may be said about Betty Broderick, she was not one to compromise her ideas. Years later, while awaiting her second trial, she attempted in one of her more thoughtful letters from jail to explain her own personality, her refusal to abandon her anger, and her sense of fair play, even when it would have served her better to back down, shut up, and take whatever Dan was willing to give her.

"Compliance leads to self-hate. Defiance saves self-respect," she wrote. "And '87 was the first time I was fighting back since I banged the car into his door, and then he puts me in jail for calling him names! Well, when I was at least trying to fight back, I felt better able to cope. I wouldn't have stood in line to go to the gas chambers at Auschwitz either. If you're so overpowered you're going to die anyway, I'd a hell of a lot rather die protesting. Besides, I had every right in the world to be angry! I was gang raped, and they want me to LIKE them? Ha! Ridiculous! Taking it in the chops time after time and doing nothing in self-defense—you only turn your anger, frustration, despair, hate inwards and hurt yourself even MORE. Nice girls don't get angry—they go slit their wrists OVER THE SINK so they don't leave a mess. Well, I just decided I didn't want to be a nice girl anymore. I wanted the life I built, I deserved, I earned. MY LIFE was worth fighting for!"

And so she fought on, with Tricia Smith helping her. During those long, hot summer months of 1987, Smith seemed at times almost valiant in her uphill effort to save Betty, not just from Dan, but from Betty herself.

In another victory, Smith won an amended support order from the courts, making Betty's temporary $16,000 spousal support retroactive to December 1, 1986. Amid the continuing, distracting contempt filings by Dan, Smith was also still trying to move the case toward what should have been its only object from the beginning—a divorce trial to resolve property, support, and custody issues. But, for reasons each side would later blame on the other, that goal seemed constantly to slip from focus.

In June, Barry asked for a sixty-day trial delay, and Dan's deposition was postponed again. Smith, meantime, began in the summer of 1987 to threaten Dan with contempt actions of her own. On June 8, she dispatched four separate letters of protest to attorney Barry, making clear her suspicion that Barry and Dan were deliberately delaying trial proceedings in order eventually to dilute Betty's share of the Broderick community property, either by accruing undue debts, or, perhaps, even by hiding assets.

First, she complained that Dan was purposely creating future financial confusion by paying Betty's June support with various community property checks. "With Mr. Broderick's sophistication, it appears that his only motivation for doing this would be to confuse the issues," she wrote. "I find this surprising, after you have assured me on countless occasions that Mr. Broderick wishes only to equally divide the property and get on with his life as quickly as possible."

Second, Smith complained that Dan's $37,000 Corvette had been sold in violation of the court order preventing either party from disposing of community property without the consent of the other. She requested immediately one half of the proceeds of the sale.

Third, she protested that, contrary to court order, which authorized Dan only to deduct Betty's house payment, he was still also deducting payments for property taxes, the lease on the Suburban, and auto insurance. Betty resented this gratuitous control over her finances, and wanted it to stop. If it didn't, Smith said, "Mrs. Broderick has instructed me to file a contempt of court pleading against Mr. Broderick."

And, fourth, Smith was aggravated that, contrary to court orders, Dan still had not paid her $12,000 in legal fees. If she didn't get her money in ten days, she would file a contempt action herself, she threatened.

Barry's return letter was cold and blunt: Smith would get her fee only when a court order had been drafted to suit his language requirements— which had not yet been done, he wrote.

Secondly, Dan was making the various insurance and car payments at the request of Betty's prior attorney, Hargreaves, who had sought those deductions in 1986, Barry said. He challenged Smith to file a contempt action. Since Dan's name was on both the car and house, he said, Dan had every reason, for purposes of his own liability, to see that the bills were paid—the implication of course being that Betty couldn't be trusted to do the responsible thing.

Regarding the support/community property checks, there was no intent to confuse or delay, said Barry. Even so, in his only concession, he agreed to see that the practice was discontinued.

And, concerning the Corvette:

"I am advised that the Corvette automobile is an asset of the corporation, and as such no restraining order has been violated," said Barry. Betty's share of the Corvette should properly be adjudicated, said Barry, during the divorce trial—by which time, of course, Corvettes would be the last thing on Betty's mind.

She couldn't even keep her eye on the target through the summer. By the end of June, her diary entries were chillingly disconnected. At one minute she was worrying about her children, in the next she was obsessed with Hargreaves, who was still pressing his case through the local legal arbitration panel—which Betty had decided to address herself, despite the fact that one of the three panelists, Ned Huntington, was a close friend of Dan's. It was the first but by no means the last time she would decide that she could argue her own case better than any attorney could, and for free. She spent hours preparing her defense. She was becoming a Sears Roebuck lawyer. But she could not remain fixed on any one thought. Too much else was on her mind. Linda.

Always, at the heart of it all was Linda. Betty would never come to terms with the visions in her head of the lithe, lovely young woman tripping around the house in her shorts or her nighties, sitting down to breakfast, flushed and radiant from the night before, with Betty's teenaged daughters and young sons. But she could never admit it.

"Cunt eating off the wedding china," she wrote in her June diary instead.

But, now, it wasn't only her wedding china that she wanted back. She wanted everything she had left at Coral Reef before, in the days when she thought her marriage would not end. She wanted her demitasse collection. She wanted her old forty-five record collection. She did not want the cunt listening to a single one of her Lettermen records. She brooded. She simmered. She found no release.

But at least little Rhett was pleasing her. Only recently, he had run away from a school field trip near her home, and come to her. Such a sweet little boy. He ran into her arms, in the middle of the day. Later, when the frantic teacher discovered where he had gone, and that Betty hadn't even bothered to turn him in, she was furious. But Betty wasn't apologizing.

"He just wanted to see his mother," she later said blandly in defense of Rhett, and herself. "His father won't let him see me. He had to run away." Poor little boy, with his runny nose, his allergies, always crying. That night, as always, he wanted to sleep with her; and they curled up together, and for just a little while, she felt all right. She didn't even write in her diaries that evening. Her eight-year-old calmed her.

June 26 was Linda's birthday. She was twenty-six. Danny told his mother he couldn't come to her house for the weekend because it was Linda's birthday, Betty wrote in her diaries, digging her pen so deep into the paper that it left tracks many pages below.

The loneliness grew. Outside her house at night, she could hear La Jolla teenagers laughing, the tires of their BMWs and Mercedes convertibles squealing as they sped toward the beach. She couldn't sleep anymore. Now her diaries talked constantly of her nocturnal ways. She was always up, wandering around her empty house, walking onto her pretty balcony with its blue awnings, its patio tables waiting for the carefree luncheons, the omelette brunches, the ladies' teas that she never hosted anymore.

Nobody wanted to come. She didn't have the energy anyway. She watched the moonlight on the sea. Such a perfect location she had found for their new dream home ... She wanted to kill him.

"But don't ever take 'I'll kill him' out of context," she said years later, from jail. "Don't ever leave out the ever-present prelude. If he doesn't stop attacking me ... I was frantic, frightened, cornered, helpless ... I always said, 'If he doesn't cut this out, I'm gonna kill him. If he doesn't cut this out ... If he doesn't stop this ... if, if, if... I was literally screaming inside and out. It was my cry for help, that kind of talk. I just needed him to stop."

Throughout the summertime, Ruth Roth continued to be a part of her life. Despite Betty's objections, Roth and Dan had decided that Lee could drop out of Bishops and attend La Jolla High in the fall. "So my daughter left one of the best private schools in the city to attend a public high school," she wrote in her diary.

Then, as always, back to her financial fears. "No money!" she wrote on Friday, July 3, after a trip to another empty mailbox. Now she would have to wait until Monday for her check. The bastard never sent it on the first. She couldn't even schedule a regular day to pay her bills.

Now, too, she was having to rent a car while the Suburban was in the shop for repairs. "Owe $420 on rental," she worried into her notebook.

Her July check didn't arrive until the seventh. Just another way of letting her know who was in control. Her credit rating depended on his largesse. She couldn't sleep. "Up all night with anxiety attacks." Tricia was gone on vacation. "Shit!"

She spent July 4 at home alone. It was a bleak day. She devoted part of it to work on the Hargreaves arbitration. She "read a book" but didn't even bother to list its title. Then, out of habit, or perhaps just to be among people, she went to a shopping mall. She cruised Nordstrom's, but didn't find anything she wanted to buy. On the way home, she paused briefly to watch a fireworks display at the local park. But the sight of all the picnicking families depressed her too much to stay.

Her diaries were now the work of a woman who could no longer find anything positive about life to jot, even in passing. Her remarks were often flat, flavorless; even her handwriting had gone lame, lacking its usual exclamations and underlined words. She no longer recorded her club meetings, her charity lunches. Only once that summer was there one small note that harked back to her earlier, happier life:

"Rhett in play. The Crybaby Princess."

Everything else related to her misery. "Jail is definitely preferable to being here all alone without anyone to talk to," she wrote.

* * *

But, one night in July, her rage returned in full force. In wild, furious script, with many underlined words and others scribbled out, she wrote a letter to her former husband. Although it was mid-1987, her mind was still in 1986:

"Dear Fuckface,

189

"Due to your manipulations, I am once again without a car. The only reason you put me in a leased car and leased house was so that when you walked out on your family I was not left with one cent of equity or ownership in anything ... I hope you are very proud of your crafty manipulations, but I certainly hope you don't think you're fooling anybody. . . .

"I wrote a check for $945 to start a lease on a new car. I could not BUY a car because thanks to you I had NO MONEY, NO INCOME, NO JOB, NO CREDIT RATING, ETC. After the deal was done, the check written by me, and the car delivered, you had the nerve to once again add your name to the lease. Our divorce had been final for four months, we had been separated for a year and a half. What was the point of that? You are a grossly sick person. I hope to God someday you seek help with your inferiority complex and your neurotic need to CONTROL everyone around you. Now that I have court-ordered support with an allowance in it for a car payment and an insurance payment, I will go out and get a car with my name on it and insurance with my name on it so I don't have to pay high rates for your many drunk driving arrests ...

"For a while, I had hopes you would snap out of your craziness, but you seem only to get worse. Where will all this end? You will never get rid of me until you settle fairly, and you don't want to settle because you'll be relinquishing CONTROL of me ... You wanted out—so please get out. Go away, etc., but you cannot take all that's mine with you!"

No signature, just a happy face, in parentheses, and this line: "If I cared about you I'd rewrite and correct this—but I don't."

Dan simply popped this letter into the same "out" basket where he kept all the other future contempts.

On July 15, he filed two more contempts for her calls in June and July.

On the same day, according to her diaries, Betty called the ACLU "in total desperation." But they told her divorces weren't their thing.

Tricia Smith was meanwhile girding herself for a big day. After several delays, Dan's deposition was finally scheduled—firmly, it seemed—for July 20. But Smith had still not received the full financial documentation she had first requested in January—and needed to conduct a thorough interrogation. In legalese, this is called "discovery." On July 15, she wrote Barry yet another letter, again itemizing the information she wanted—everything from a listing of Dan's property titles, partnerships, stocks and securities, bank accounts, and expenses (both personal and corporate), to data on his cars and household furnishings. She did not get it all for another six months.

Compounding Smith's problems, when the day of deposition arrived, Betty was nowhere to be found. She had instead left the day before for her preplanned vacation in Hawaii. And so, after all these months, there, finally, sat Dan, Gerald Barry, and Tricia Smith in Smith's office, waiting for Betty, who apparently hadn't even told Smith she was leaving town.

Betty, of course, shifted the blame to Smith and Dan. Smith hadn't notified her of the scheduled deposition, she later insisted—plus, Dan knew she had a trip

190

scheduled for that week. Besides, she added lamely, "Dan had canceled three times already, so I didn't have any reason to believe it was really going to happen. And, if I had canceled that trip, that I'd already paid for, he wouldn't have shown up."

Betty hadn't advanced an inch in her thinking since 1985. Then she thought that Dan couldn't leave her if she gave him the children. In 1986, she thought he couldn't sell the family home without her signature, or get a divorce if she refused to appear in court. Now, one more time, she had run away, rather than face yet another step toward the Broderick family's final dissolution.

And so there she lay, that July week, alone upon the beaches of Waikiki, this overweight bleached blonde with a too-bright smile and sad blue eyes, self-consciously covering her flab in a color-coordinated swim wrap, as she watched strangers pass: young lovers entwined in passionate embrace on their beach towels; laughing children romping in the surf; and, worse, handsome, tanned, middle-aged couples with gray streaking their hair, glancing at each other with the affectionate ease she had always dreamed of for herself and Dan someday.

So much had changed since her trip to Canada two years before. Then she had been Mrs. Daniel T. Broderick III, mother of four—beautiful, rich, and self-confident, waiting for a tempest in the teacup to pass. Now who was she? She was fat, divorced, without children, with a jail record, traveling on credit cards, and worrying about bills. She wasn't a home-maker, a school-teacher, or even a daughter in good standing anymore.

"It was a horrible trip. I was so out of place, wherever I went. I never knew how to introduce myself to strangers," she said. "I had kids, but I didn't have them. I had a divorce, but I didn't have a settlement. I wasn't Mrs. Anybody anymore. I was Betty Nobody. And strangers look at you funny if you just tell them that." So she spent the trip isolated, hiding out in her motel rooms, burying her face in books in public places.

Throughout, she took meticulous notes on everything she did, saw, ate, and bought—right down to the hour she had dinner, what entree she ordered, and what it had cost. But nowhere did she ever write about her impressions of anything. It was a diary, pathetically dead, of motion without emotion. No person was present in it. By now, her compulsion to record her every move was, in itself, verging on a sickness. She seemed to be verifying her presence on earth only through mindless chronology. "Walked on the beach. Rented a car. Drove around island. Had lunch."

But her rage had not abated. Before she returned from Hawaii, she sent Dan a postcard: "Aloha. Here's the great beach [happy face] warm water, great events, lovely people, all families. Not a single forty-plus man with his office cunt. All NORMAL HAPPY FAMILIES!"

He promptly filed another contempt.

The rest of the summer was more of the same. Smith left town again in August. Dr. Sparta filed a damning report with Child Protective Services on the detrimental effects of Betty's behavior on the children.

And the parade of Dan's contempt motions continued. On August 4, in another contempt filing, Dan asked that the suspended jail sentence be reimposed. On

191

August 12, two contempts for messages from June 28 and July 10 were set for an October hearing. On August 25, those two messages, plus two new ones, were combined for a new hearing, rescheduled for September.

The messages now at issue included: the Hawaiian postcard, the June calls relating to Kim's passport, and Betty's July 20 letter to Dan containing her fading hopes that he would "snap out of it."

And, at the end of the month, her motion for visitation rights with her children was removed from the calendar. No new court date was set.

Her resentment toward Tricia Smith grew. In what Betty regarded as the largest betrayal yet, Smith, increasingly concerned over her unpaid fees, finally wrote directly to Dan, proposing that he send her the full $222,000 check for the recent sale of the Fairbanks Ranch lot; she would serve as the broker, she suggested, dividing the monies between Dan and Betty—after she subtracted her own fees from Betty's half. Dan initially hesitated. He didn't want to get involved in any spats between Betty and her attorneys, he told Smith. But eventually he agreed to a modified form of what Smith wanted. As he later said in divorce trial, he saw no reason why not. Smith told him that Betty had agreed, and, besides, the check couldn't be cashed without Betty's signature anyway.

And Betty had of course signed. But that hardly counted to her. She was instead blinded by the principle of the thing. Once more, in her mind, attorneys had worked behind her back. She would never forgive Smith for it. "Why is my attorney writing letters to Dan Broderick?" she still demands. "And I was not even sent a copy of it? Tricia Smith was just like all the others—she wanted to fit in with the In Crowd, at my expense."

Chapter 19

In Limbo

By now, Linda had become far more than an office frill for Dan Broderick, according to coworkers. She was instead an indispensable element of his flourishing law practice. Among her duties, she screened and interviewed all potential new clients, wrote reports, interrogatories, and orders. By the time she died, said Stormy Wetther, "she had an incredible grasp of the medical and legal issues. She knew the cases almost as well as Dan did."

She was also Dan's biggest cheerleader. Wetther remembers one case in particular that Linda loved to talk about. It had been a "bad baby" case, wherein the doctor was accused of gross errors during the delivery, leading to a paraplegic child who was seven years old before the case went to court. Dan had asked the child to take off her shoes and socks before the jury. It took the little girl so long to perform this minor task that Dan won a settlement of more than $2 million. Linda cried when she talked about it, says Wetther. "Linda was always so sensitive. It was so easy to make her cry."

Linda also had a fetal heart monitor strip framed on her wall—another "bad baby" case—that one, she told visitors, worth $3 million.

Meantime, she was becoming more beautiful, more stylishly glamorous by the day. Her salary was supposedly around $37,000 to $40,000 annually—plus the assorted travel and entertainment perks that came from being Dan's woman. With her money she became, among other things, a clotheshorse, just like Dan and Betty.

"She loved clothes," says Wetther. After her death, her friends divided up her clothing—"and she outfitted at least five women," says Wetther, who was, at that moment, wearing an impeccably tailored white two-piece linen suit that had belonged to Linda. Maggie later showed up for lunch in a green pants suit that had been Linda's—as well as her emerald and diamond wedding ring.

Linda was also extremely generous to her family with her "increased income," says Maggie. She sent her parents to Holland on their first visit home in years, and once to Hawaii. She flew Maggie to San Diego every St. Patrick's Day for the festivities, and periodically brought Maggie's two children to San Diego for trips to the zoo and Sea World.

Friends later recalled, too, that Linda—like Betty—never forgot a birthday, an anniversary or any other occasion for celebration. "I remember once waking up on my birthday to find the room literally filled with balloons and 'Happy Birthday' signs," says Wetther. Linda had worked on them all night. She was just really a sweet person."

But not all was bliss with Dan and Linda personally. Betty was exacting a price in her downhill slide to hell. Like a contagion, her stress had long since infected the other household, too.

Linda wanted to get married. She wanted to start a family. She had been waiting for five years, and now that Dan was finally divorced, she wanted her happy ending. But Dan was reluctant to rush to the altar again.

Meanwhile, all four Broderick children rejected the notion of the girlfriend as the new wife, their stepmother. Kim once even extracted a promise from Dan, she later said, that he would never marry Linda.

The Broderick children were always the chief barrier between Linda and Dan. Linda told everyone how mean they were to her. "She tried so hard to make them accept her," said Brian Monaghan, "but those kids would come back from a weekend at Betty's just loaded with hate."

"If Danny or Rhett even smiled at her, she would tell us all about it, it made her so happy," said Sharon Blanchet. "She saw the slightest trace of warmth as some sign that maybe they would eventually accept her ... She even referred to them as 'our kids'."

But they weren't "our kids," and they never would be. Even Kim, who got along with Linda best, criticized her later to the divorce court judge as a "phoney friend." And Kim definitely didn't think Dan should marry Linda, because "she never went to college. I don't know if she even graduated from high school. Personally I don't think she is right for my Dad." But she had a clear view of why Linda so appealed to her father. "Linda absolutely adored him," she said later. He could make the dumbest jokes, and she'd laugh and wonder why we didn't think it was funny, too."

But she modified her views. After the killings, she told reporters that Linda had been her good friend. "The truth is, I liked Linda, She was always nice to me," she said one evening after her mother's trials were over. "I just didn't want Dad to marry her—I didn't want him to get married to anybody. We were so close, and I didn't want it to be spoiled."

Linda's friends, meanwhile, continued pressuring her to walk away from Dan Broderick. This thing had been going on without resolution for too long.

"Linda was so stressed out," says Maggie. "She lost weight ... She used to carry Maalox and Gelusil in her purse—at twenty-six, twenty-seven years old. Her nails were bitten to the quick. She said Betty was driving them crazy... And she couldn't do anything to please those kids ... The emotional battery in this case was never against Betty, it was against them."

Maggie worried about her little sister increasingly. "But she was so young, Linda thought she could fix it all, once they got Betty out of their lives," says Maggie. "All she wanted was to be Dan Broderick's wife and the mother of his children. She would do literally anything to please him. She even gave up garlic, which everybody in our family loves, because Dan disapproved."

At the same time, Linda's loathing of Betty Broderick only grew. Apart from feeling sabotaged by Betty with the kids, Linda never had a whit of sympathy for a woman who was getting $16,000 a month. Never once did it apparently occur to her to actually approach the woman she was displacing simply to say, "I'm sorry." Instead, like most of Dan's friends, she only saw Betty as a greedy, wicked witch. "Linda couldn't understand what else she wanted—none of us could," recalls Wetther.

But, unlike Dan, who tried to keep his private life private, Linda told everyone what a crazy bitch Betty was, what bizarre things she was doing and saying. She mimicked Betty so well, Laurel Summers once said, "that you'd think Betty was there." Nor was Linda shy about using Betty's exact, graphic language. "Dan would never repeat Betty's messages," says Mike Reidy, "but Linda would deliver them verbatim."

Linda also complained constantly, says Sharon Blanchet, that Dan was being too soft on Betty, too lenient. She wanted him to file more contempts, seek more jail time. Blanchet, Wetther, Summers, and Cuffaro all agreed with her. Women were always hardest on Betty whether they were friends of Dan and Linda, or her own closest friends, most of whom either testified against her, or fled altogether during her trials.

Linda's open advertising of the ex-wife's sins apparently led to periodic friction with Dan—and their quarrels evidently began to surface publicly. A secretary in Dan's office building, for example, swears that she once saw Dan pour a pitcher of beer on Linda in a crowded local bar, with the angry remark, "You need to cool off." Dan's friends heatedly deny that he would have ever done such a thing.

But, according to housekeeper Sylvia Cavins, Linda and Dan were in increasing harmony on one point: both began calling Betty hateful names, albeit not obscene ones, in the privacy of their home. "The Large One" was a favorite—and, Cavins said, Dan started it, not Linda. They also joked that "Betty had some kind of disease," said Cavins. "I can't remember what you call it—there's a name for it, when you're round-faced, wide-eyed ..." Nor did Cavins think Linda was particularly upset by Betty's vitriol. "Betty used to call [Linda] a seventeen-year-old Polack. Linda just thought it was funny."

In fact, said Cavins, Dan always recoiled from Betty more than Linda did. She recalled one particular St. Patrick's Day—always Dan's favorite holiday, she said, "and he went to every pub in town." But that night, she remembered, he walked into the house with "weeds all over his beautiful clothes." When Cavins asked him why he was so messy, "He told me he had come home in a taxi and thought he saw Betty out front, and, he said, "I just couldn't face her, so I rolled down a gully."

By the autumn of 1987, Betty was writing pages like this in her diaries:
—Trapped by fear! AS USUAL
—Afraid to send settlement offer because he will make it backfire
—Afraid of T. Smith
—Afraid to go see kids
—Afraid of Judge Joseph and jail
—Afraid to call media."
She was afraid of everything.

She had never been idle, she was never the type to curl up in a ball at home with a bottle of wine or a bag of hamburgers and withdraw. But, always the extrovert, always active, she was now staying in bed later and later after too many nights walking the floors. Her muscles hurt, her jaws hurt, her stomach hurt, her back hurt, and she cried too much. The malady of the divorce had moved beyond her head and into her body.

Finally, like an alcoholic who has at last hit bottom, she went in search of others in the same boat. Her accountant had come by the house that day with a leaflet she thought might interest Betty, advertising an organization called HALT (Help Abolish Legal Tyranny).

At first glance, she recoiled. It smacked of radicalism, by its very name. At the same time, the literature told her, HALT was a national public-interest consumer organization with a membership of more than 150,000, dedicated to helping reform the legal system to better serve the average citizen in a quicker, cheaper way. HALT was mad at lawyers.

And so she dialed the telephone number. She learned that, by coincidence, the monthly HALT meeting was that very night in neighboring Del Mar. A nice, clean, respectable neighborhood. Maybe it would be okay. Maybe they weren't just a bunch of militant crazies. So she went "just to investigate what they were all about."

She walked into a room of twenty to thirty ordinary-looking people with friendly smiles. Both women and men. Her heart was pounding. She was afraid of them.

"I was scared and I cried. But I stood up and told them that my case was exactly why they existed," she said later. "I told them about the sealed courtroom, and it sent them to the moon; I told them about no visitation, I told them about the fines ... and for the first time ever, nobody said, 'Oh, well, dear, you just have to get on with it.' Instead they paid attention, they knew exactly what I was talking about!"

The day after her first meeting, half a dozen HALT members went to court with her. She had told Tricia Smith not to come. By now Betty had decided it was a waste of money to pay Smith to represent her in the contempts when "I might as well lose for free."

Judge Joseph didn't send her to jail that day. Instead, the hearing was postponed. Dan didn't even show up. But this time, she at least had friends with her, willing to challenge the sealed proceedings. And, for a long time, HALT stood by her—especially Ronnie Brown. A quiet, serious woman several years older than Betty and a former military wife, Brown lived nearby, and so the two women got into the habit of taking sunrise walks together on the beach. Ronnie was always a terrific listener, Betty said later, long after most of her old La Jolla pals wouldn't even return her phone calls.

Thanks to her new friends in HALT, Betty seemed temporarily to become more focused on the task at hand—getting the divorce settlement she wanted. Her offensive calls to Dan dropped off. She was not hurting herself so deliberately anymore. At last, it seemed, Betty was moving with her mind instead of her mouth. By mid-September, she was calm enough to permit Tricia Smith to submit her first divorce settlement offer to Dan; Smith also filed a motion to keep Linda's voice off the answering machine and prevent Dan from unplugging the children's telephone. It was Betty's first seriously aggressive counter-attack.

The divorce settlement Smith proposed was a straightforward one-and-a-half-page document:

196

Betty wanted a cash amount of $1 million, nontaxable, plus $25,000 per month for ten years, whether she remarried or not. She wanted title to her house and her car. She wanted the household furniture in her possession, plus all funds she had already received from Dan from their various community property assets. She wanted him to buy a $1 million life insurance policy, with her as beneficiary, until his spousal support obligation was fulfilled.

In exchange, she would pay half the children's college expenses. She would forfeit any claims on his law practice, or any other property mutually owned, including his pension fund, his residence, the boat, the ski condominium, the limited partnerships with his brother, and so on.

Both parties would waive any rights either might have to Epstein credits. Lastly, Dan would pay all of her legal fees, past and present.

She was, in short, proposing a $4 million package deal to end the war.

But the hook was—Dan would keep the children. Betty, the one-time perfect mother, wasn't even seeking custody. Dan and Linda could have them. She wanted only guaranteed visitation. Betty had decided, she told friends, to travel, find a career, to enjoy life without the stresses of being a single parent. Translated, she had opted for the final revenge, although she would never admit it.

"I loved my kids enough that I just wanted to deal with them well, to give them quality attention when I could," she protested years later from jail, "and I was so completely without self-confidence at that point, I wasn't fit to mother them full-time. I needed to heal myself."

Gerald Barry's reply—and Dan's—was swift and sure.

"The offer contained in your letter of September 21, 1987, is rejected," Barry wrote to Tricia Smith. That was it. The one sentence was all he wrote.

To this day, some of Betty's old La Jolla friends still believe that it was the insidious influence of HALT that created the monster who eventually killed. She might as well have joined forces with the Daughters of Bilitis or the PLO. In reality, the exact opposite was probably true. Without the support of people who didn't think she was crazy, she might have snapped even sooner.

But Betty's HALT friends were never able to touch, much less allay, the source of her rage. She always felt too unique to really relate to them. "I just wasn't like them," she would say later. "Nobody went through what I did. I was up against the most brilliant, powerful lawyer in San Diego. I agree with all the reforms HALT favors— lawyers are destroying our society with their escalating fees. But that just wasn't relevant to what was happening to me."

That September Betty made her first bid to be heard in the San Diego press. She was reading her morning *Union* on September 8, when her eyes fell upon a quote from the president of the San Diego Bar, advancing a "fast track" plan to unclog the local court system. A chief feature of the reform was to use arbitration and mediation counselors in place of judges whenever possible. "There is nothing worse than a courtroom tied up for six months with a complicated case involving the dueling rich,"

Daniel Broderick told reporters. Betty picked up her pad and pen and wrote a letter to the editor. Given her mood, the letter was surprisingly restrained. She had read the article with "great interest," she said. However, "I was sickened by the hypocrisy of the statement made by Daniel T. Broderick III, San Diego County Bar President ... Mr. Broderick himself has gone to great lengths to stymie the courts and the wheels of justice for the past TWO YEARS by resorting to every trick in the book, and some that haven't even been printed yet, to complicate what could have been a quick and simple divorce settlement and turn it into a legal nightmare. By virtue of our jointly owned assets, this could have been a case of the 'dueling rich,' but I have amassed legal fees of over $60,000 so far with no end in sight and it is rapidly ceasing to be so. Disgusted and discouraged, (Mrs. Daniel T. Broderick III) Betty Broderick. La Jolla."

It is unclear how Dan learned of Betty's letter, but he did. His response was instant and intense. Given his past insistence on sealed court proceedings to protect the children, the two-page, typed letter he wrote to the editor of the *Union*—marked personal and confidential—was startlingly personal, filled with the most intimate, tedious details of his marital problems. He even enclosed four of her nastiest phone messages.

"I have not tried to put off the resolution of our divorce proceeding in any way," he wrote. It was "Mrs. Broderick, not I" who had chosen to proceed in court instead of mediation. He then told how Betty had been committed to a psychiatric hospital for running her van into his front door. He told of her several contempt convictions for obscene telephone calls to his home.

"She has vowed on countless occasions to do everything within her power to ruin my reputation," Dan wrote. He concluded by asking the *Union* not to publish Betty's letter because "it is a gross distortion of what has occurred ... its sole purpose is to embarrass me and the Bar Association. If it appears in print, it will do both without justification."

Meanwhile, Linda had gotten into the act, too, calling her old boyfriend, Steve Kelley, the *Union*'s editorial cartoonist, to ask if he could help stop publication of Betty's letter. But Dan's protest was enough. The letter never got published.

* * *

At the end of September, Dan and Linda went off on a two-week Caribbean cruise. It boiled in Betty's mind, one more stab to the heart. The Caribbean. Scene of their honeymoon. Why couldn't he take the cunt to Tahiti or Hawaii?

She also had a final court date that month—this one to answer four more counts of contempt. She didn't appear, but, since Dan was gone, the hearing was only postponed. It still galled her years later. "If I didn't show up, they would've had a warrant out for my arrest"

Attorney Hargreaves won that month, too—an arbitration panel (consisting of lawyers) ruled that Betty owed him several thousand dollars in unpaid fees.

By then, Dan's complaints against Betty were so backed up on Anthony Joseph's calendar that the judge was now looking at answering machine messages dating back to May, plus Betty's July letter to Dan. Thanks to Dan's refusal to back off, and Betty's refusal to shape up, Joseph had become an almost monthly monitor of one ex-wife's nasty blasts into her ex-husband's telephone. By now Joseph also well understood from experience that, as soon as he dealt with Dan's latest batch, more would be awaiting him tomorrow.

Finally Joseph reached his limit. Both Betty and Dan Broderick were insulting him. He was angry. He exploded. He was not going to hear any more of it. He erased his entire Broderick calendar, dismissing every one of Dan's backed-up contempts—but, again, with prejudice against Betty. Which meant that, if she misbehaved again, she might still be jailed: a total of twenty-four days in suspended sentences from contempt convictions six months old still hung over her head.

Even so, for the first time in two years, she was able to go home to look at a clean court calendar.

Now she could concentrate on the divorce settlement. Or, at least, she might have.

Instead, she ignored Joseph so completely that within weeks Dan was threatening a court order denying her even the right to talk to her children on the telephone, due to the increasingly outrageous things she was saying to them.

Chapter 20

The Big Four-O

She moved through that autumn in her own desperate, quixotic fashion. The children were at her house most weekends, but she was too distracted to care. Fall was always the worst time of her year. Football games, trips to Notre Dame, Larry's Oktoberfest party. Family traditions. All gone. Her diary entries were often listless.

October 12: Attended the chamber orchestra with Judy Bartolotta—who told her about upcoming plans for the Oktoberfest.

Same weekend: took Rhett and the Forbes children to the San Diego Zoo. It was "a fun day."

But two days after Dan and Linda returned from the USC-Notre Dame game, she again took her bitter anger out on her children in a phone call—and, again, Dan taped it for his contempt files. Betty asked Danny what plans he had made for the upcoming weekend at her house. He told her he just wanted to "stay there and take care of the dogs." This exchange followed:

Betty: "Well, I'm really not even interested in seeing you guys and having anything to do with that fucked-up family until you get your act together over there. Try to be normal ... I'm too embarrassed to tell anybody I know you guys.

Danny: Why? It's not our fault.

Betty: Because Daddy's fucking his office cunt is very embarrassing.

Danny: I know, but why are you embarrassed to tell them you even know us?

Betty: Well, because you're living over there, you obviously approve.

Danny: We don't, Mom. That doesn't mean anything.

Betty: Well, then, why don't you come over here and live over here and get out of there?

Danny: Well, it's not that easy.

Betty: Yeah, it is that easy. It's exactly that easy, you know. You can just move here, and it's that easy. There's nothing going on in that neighborhood anyway, right?"

Days later, Dan enclosed a transcript of the above conversation in a letter to Tricia Smith, along with a plea for her to help him control his ex-wife.

"... This kind of abuse is directed at all four of my children on a regular basis by their mother," he wrote ... I am [asking] for your help in putting a stop to it. As you know, I have done everything I can to minimize the contact between your client and the children, but there is only so much I can do without making the situation even worse. If I try to prevent them from calling her or interfere with her calls to them, I'm afraid it may cause even more stress in their lives than the calls themselves do." And, in a bitter footnote:

"It's interesting that the afternoon of this call, [Betty] brought her four puppies to

Rhett's class for everyone to see and play with. That night she went to Danny's school for an open house. How anyone could say the things she said to Danny in the morning and then try to project herself as a loving, concerned mother that same afternoon and evening, I'll never understand." Nor would he ever even try.

Betty, meantime, was preparing for her first public appearance to tell the world what a louse Dan Broderick was. The event was a large seminar sponsored by HALT to discuss women's problems in divorce court. It featured dozens of women speakers ranging from the prominent to the obscure, and it was well attended by the press. Hundreds attended.

"I am the former wife of the President of the San Diego County Bar," Betty began, in a soft, nervous voice. Her comments were brief, no more than three or four minutes, and centered mainly on her problems in obtaining an attorney because of her ex-husband's status in the legal community. She also spoke about her contempts and fines. She finished by saying she felt hopeless and overwhelmed.

Her remarks, she says, went unreported, despite the heavy press coverage and her own prominence. Her paranoia increased. Dan, she was positive, had somehow used his influence to suppress her, just as he had killed her letter to the Union.

Still, Betty had gotten her first taste of public attention and TV lights, and she liked it. By the time she went to trial for murder three years later, she had become a master in seducing journalists with her angry, clever wit and defiance. But, back then, in the fall of 1987, she was still quiveringly timid. "I wanted to call the press a lot of times," she said later. "I was thinking by then that just the threat of going public might make him settle with me—but I was afraid of making him madder."

Then it was November, the month of the Blackstone Ball—just one more event that she would probably never again attend. It had always been nearly as important to her social life as the USC-Notre Dame game. It was to a Blackstone Ball that she had worn her first Bob Mackie evening gown, years ago, when Mr. and Mrs. Daniel J. Broderick III were still planning a future together.

But now, the Blackstone Ball was only another source of pain. She would never again remember it as more than the anniversary of her first arrest the year before.

But, this year, she kept her peace—until the morning after, when she awoke, furious, and made another foulmouthed call to Dan's machine, accusing him of neglecting the children by staying out all night drunk. She also called the Child Abuse Hotline again, without result.

By degrees, the angry wall around her vulnerabilities grew thicker as ugly new events steadily nosed out the sentimental memories of bygone times. Betty Broderick, whoever she once was, receded faster by the day.

November 7 was her fortieth birthday. She crossed the Great Divide with minimal numbed fuss. A friend, Judy Backhaus, staged a birthday luncheon for her at George's at the Cove, a fashionable La Jolla Village restaurant.

But it was an even worse experience than her birthday party with the girls the year before. "I didn't know where I was or how old I was or what the hell I was doing," she later said. "I needed the Betty Ford clinic by then—but they don't take codependents. I needed people to bolster me. Even jail was better—the women there understood a lot better about shithead husbands than my La Jolla friends did."

She went home to her diaries: "Solitary confinement is the cruelest punishment known, short of the electric chair," she wrote. And: "Dan is punishing me for knowing the truth about what a weakling he is."

At about the same time, she went to school one rainy afternoon and attempted to pick up her sons, instead of having them ride home on the bus. But since school officials had no prior approval from Dan, they refused to let the boys leave with her until they got his permission by phone. He refused.

"I was embarrassed to tears," she recalls. "There I was, standing face-to-face with people I had known for years, and they wouldn't even let me take my own sons home."

* * *

Her financial fears, meantime, had become all-consuming. Mimi was now making regular visits to help with bills and taxes. At the end of 1987, Betty hired a second accountant to deal strictly with her taxes, thus freeing Mimi to deal only with her ever-accumulating bills. At one point, her credit card charges alone exceeded $200,000. There was no rhyme or reason to any of it—only more evidence of a woman out of control.

Adding to her anxieties, Betty had finally begun to pay attention to her lawyer's lectures about Epstein credits. She understood at last that her community property was eroding—that every day the divorce trial was delayed, she was losing money. And the more she understood about Epsteins, the more convinced she became that Dan had planned it this way all along. In time, she even decided that the crack in the Coral Reef house—which clearly existed—was only Dan's first step in a long-standing plot to abandon his family and, in the process, cheat her of equity in her own home.

"He didn't want to give me anything! He wanted to drag the settlement out. Every day he stalled, he was stealing from me, and shifting money to Larry."

Her desire to fire Tricia Smith was also growing more apparent with each passing page in her diaries. "T. Smith is NO HELP. Case doing NOTHING," she wrote. Money, money. So much money with so few results. All she was doing was enriching attorneys to defend her against Dan's incessant contempts.

Yet she kept making her inflammatory calls.

In a different, less antagonized household, some of those calls might have been almost comic—like this one left on November 15 for Lee, who had apparently taken Betty's car without permission: "Lee Lee, bring that car back!" Betty ordered. "Oh well, nobody'll even get this message anyway 'cause the cunt's around. She'll probably erase it. I need to talk to Rhett about getting beat up this morning. I need to talk to Danny about his wonderful report card. I need to talk to Kim about finishing our conversation of yesterday. And I need to talk to Lee about getting my car back. In that order. Good-bye."

But, in Dan Broderick's eyes, nothing about Betty's mouth was humorous. Lately, her tirades were almost always over some matter concerning the children, some failing on his part. Either he hadn't delivered them when he promised, or, conversely, he brought them when she wasn't expecting them. And she continued to be furious that he would not reimburse her for the money she spent on the children for clothes, toys, and trips. In Betty's view, she deserved some form of child support, even if it wasn't court ordered. "What a cheap fucker you are," she hissed in another message, a week later.

Obviously sensing trouble down the road, Tricia Smith began protecting her own professional reputation by meticulously documenting Betty's instructions to her in writing.

In one letter, Smith wanted the record to specifically reflect that, in the custody matter: "You have instructed me not to try to negotiate any time for you with your children over Thanksgiving or Christmas. You have also continued to instruct me not to file any custody or visitation proceedings on your behalf for a more equitable and equal sharing of the children." If any of the above was incorrect, Smith asked Betty to notify her immediately.

But Smith's understanding was correct. Betty would punish herself, and her children, to the bloody end, rather than let Dan win.

Just before Thanksgiving, the children told Betty that Dan was about to have the annual family portrait made for his Christmas cards. Anyone who has ever been the unhappy half of a divorce knows how that small detail, carelessly tossed out in passing by children, pierced her heart. Another family tradition gone. Another year without her. She was so alone. She was going mad. She thought about it all day. She thought about what clothes she would dress the children in if she were still part of the Broderick family portrait. She remembered how wonderful the boys had looked three years ago when she bought them identical blazers and slacks for Dan's fortieth birthday party. She thought of the matching red velvet dresses she had bought Kim and Lee when they were little girls. She had always loved to dress them in twin frocks … But then her nostalgia vanished in a blur of hate. She remembered how she picked Rhett up at school one rainy, cold afternoon and he wasn't even wearing a sweater. She had taken him to Nordstrom's and bought him one. She remembered so much. Dan, with his perfect clothes, his rose boutonnieres … Linda with her new condo, her upscale new wardrobe …

Adding irony to injury, she also discovered, that very day, that Scott's, a local children's store where she had shopped for years, was suing her for $879.11 in clothes she had bought for the boys because Dan refused to pay the bill. Humiliated again.

She picked up the telephone and demanded that Dan return the clothes he refused to pay for. "I don't want fuckface using the clothes for his goddamn family portrait, and to purport to the community that he's dressing his children well, when he won't even pay for half the clothes," she said. "So I'm coming over to get the clothes that I own. So if you would please put in trash bags the several thousand dollars' worth of clothes I've bought in the last two months ... I will give them to poor children whose fathers don't have enough money to clothe them."

By now, Dan could no longer control his temper any better than Betty could. He promptly filed another contempt. At the same time, he sent another letter to Drs. Roth and Sparta, saying that "I have reached the point where I feel I have no choice but to ask the court to enjoin the respondent from any further contact with our children."

Betty spent Thanksgiving doing exactly what she had done the year before—darting around La Jolla, dropping in on old neighbors from Coral Reef, people who remembered her fondly from the days when she played with their babies and let the popcorn fly over their tiny, delighted heads.

As Christmas approached, Dan wrote another conciliatory letter to Tricia Smith. He hoped, he said, to work out some arrangement allowing Betty to spend part of the holiday season with the children: "I know the kids would like this, and I assume the respondent would as well."

Smith, who sounded exhausted herself by then, even in formal letters, replied, upon orders of her client, that, no, thank you—without sufficient funds to entertain the children, Mrs. Broderick would not be able to accept them.

Tricia Smith then practically begged Dan to back down and fork over the extra money, anywhere from $3,000 to $5,000—not his standard $2,000 offering. Sounding as much like a marriage counselor as an attorney, she pointed out to Dan that he was a wealthy man, so dollars weren't the real issue. If he would only make the gesture, Smith wrote, everybody would be better off, himself included: "The benefits to you are great and those to your children are even greater." And, "The small amount of money it would cost you in relative terms cannot be significant to you."

Dan's response was stunning in its iciness. Gone was the friendly fellow who had said only weeks before that it would be good for the children to spend Christmastime with their mom. When it came to dollars and cents, Dan Broderick lost all delicacy.

"By my calculation, after your client has paid monthly real estate taxes, income taxes, car payment, house payment, and utilities, she is left with over $5,000. No one in their right mind could contend that that is not enough for one month's food, clothing, entertainment, and gifts, even the month of December. Basically what the respondent is asking me to do is pay her to spend time with the children over the holidays. This is preposterous, whether or not I can afford it."

Even the boys' dogs became weapons in the adult war. A pair of tiny Shi-Tzus, Betty had bought them for her sons at $500 apiece years earlier, before she and Dan separated. When they bred, she either gave the puppies away or let the boys sell them at $100 apiece for their piggy banks. Danny and Rhett loved them. But, after the separation, they did not stay long at Dan's house. He hated the two yapping little dogs underfoot with their claws wrecking his magnificent hardwood floors. Topsy and

Muffin were not permitted inside his house. Instead, they stayed in a makeshift dog run in the gulch below his backyard lawn. Finally, Danny and Rhett took their pets back to Betty's, where they were allowed free run of the house. Betty liked dogs.

But, on Friday afternoon, December 18, she resented those little dogs, too. She was planning a weekend trip to Pasadena. Why was she responsible for hiring someone to care for these dogs while she was gone? Why shouldn't he share responsibility for his children's pets?

And so, in a typically acerbic streak of Betty humor, she tied red Christmas ribbons around their necks, loaded Topsy and Muffin into her Suburban, and drove over to Dan's house one morning where, in purposeful defiance of the restraining order to stay off his property, she marched up the sidewalk, opened his front door, and deposited the two little pooches in his foyer. She watched with satisfaction as they went scurrying across his costly Persian rugs, their toenails clicking on his glossy floors, sniffing at everything. Fuck him and his restraining orders and his hatred of dogs. She hoped they pissed on every chair leg in the house.

It would of course net her another contempt a few weeks later.

For the third Christmas in a row, Dan and Linda took the children skiing, while Betty spent the holiday in Pasadena with Brad and his dying mother. For Betty it was a trip of mixed emotions. On the one hand, she felt loved as usual. On the other hand, she was beginning to loathe herself in nearly every respect. "I remember this huge party at the Jonathan Club, and I wore my gorgeous black velvet skirt—but I was getting so big. Thank God it had an elastic waistband ... When I saw the pictures later, I looked like an elephant. Brad's parents tried to make me feel like a part of their family. But I just wanted my own family."

Before she left La Jolla, she also made reservations to go to Tahiti in January.

"What do you do when you're totally down the drain?" she asks today, wryly. "You go to Tahiti, of course. That's what people do in the movies. So I got out the credit cards and said, 'Hell with it ...'"

Why she didn't get out the same credit cards in order to entertain her kids that Christmas was a question no longer even worth asking.

She put her final signature to the year of 1987 with a vengeance by mailing a two-page, single-spaced Christmas letter to dozens of Dan's and her friends and relatives throughout the country. Her letter was accompanied by two photographs: one was the picture of Dan and Linda laughing together at a cocktail party, which she alleged that Linda had sent with the "eat your heart out, bitch" note attached. The second photo was of Betty and Dan on their wedding day. Across the Dan and Linda picture she printed the message: "Crash or No crash, It's a certainty that 1987 is the Year of the Bimbo."

Her letter said:

"I heartily apologize to you all for my lapse in correspondence the past several Christmases. I was only following the rules: 'If you don't have something good to say, don't say anything at all.' The last five years out here in sunny California have been living hell. Our darling family has been ravaged by Dan's classic midlife crisis with a nineteen-year-old receptionist. In '83 and '84 I valiantly tried to carry on and shouldered the burden of the trauma myself, figuring the whole disgusting mess was too asinine to be true and he would get over it. Instead of getting over it, he escalated the whole thing into a legal nightmare as well. During '83 and '84 he had completely rearranged our finances and our whole lives, lowering our life-style and putting us in a rented house and car. It was only then that he made his decision and walked out."

From there, she went through the details of Dan's infidelity and her divorce in painful, shameless detail. She described her frustrating attorney search, leading up to the day that "big-shot San Diego lawyer went into court and got a FINAL divorce decree giving me no monthly support or any division of community property and he seized sole custody of our four children, granting me NO rights to any visitation." She told how he had her arrested for "stepping foot on his property" on the same night he "donned his top hat and cape and attended the annual Bar Association Dance with his office girl ... The legal saga continues. I have amassed over $70,000 in legal fees!!! I have sold my jewelry, I have liens on my house, lawsuits by lawyers against me for fees and outstanding IOUs. I had no idea this could, and does happen in divorce. Dan says, 'The law says you own half—there is no law that says I have to give it to you!' He has used every legal trick and loophole to draw out and unnecessarily complicate things, so I will DROWN in legal fees and harassment. He is VERY GOOD at this, the nature of his noble profession.

"All I can say is I'm sorry—I really am. I'm sorry for all our friends and relatives— we really enjoyed each other lo these many years.

"I'm sorry for my children, whose lives have been shattered.

"I'm sorry for Dan. I hope he can buy what he's looking for.

"I'm sorry for myself. I have lost everything that matters to me.

"I'm sorry for the world that the family and traditional values of love, trust, respect hold so little meaning in the eighties.

"See why I haven't written? The NATURE OF BETTY WAS HER FAMILY. I gave it my all—truly. I have no idea where I go from here, but if I have any good news, I'll be sure to share it. I still have my inveterate 'Shutterbug,' thank God. My pictures are a constant source of pleasure. I still love to cook, travel, read, ski, dance, laugh, etc., etc., but find myself at such odds personally, socially, and financially. My imposed exile from my family is very hard to deal with.

"Please write back and tell me your good news. Because of all the moves and upheaval, I haven't heard from any of you either (Dan does not forward my mail sent to Coral Reef). And send pictures!! I display and save every one of them. Remember a picture says a thousand words—no time to write—send the picture anyway.

"I'd say come visit—but I don't even want to be around this mess— why would anyone else? Trial is set for end of July '88—six years from the start of all this!

"I hope 1988 brings love, peace, happiness, and prosperity to us all. Love, Bets."

It was finally becoming clear to everyone except Dan that Betty Broderick's telephone manners could not be corrected by the threat of jail. Her suspended jail sentences hung over her head like a club, ready to drop on a daily basis. But she no longer cared. "Fuck them. You bet I'm in contempt of court—utter contempt," she declared.

She was now beyond the point of humiliation. Jail had not conquered her. She had not been broken by the cacophony of inmates at Las Colinas shrieking "Fuck you, Muuuuuther fuccccccker" in the background as she made calls to her polite, embarrassed La Jolla friends. She had not bent beneath the indignity of communal toilets in tiny cells; she did not fold beneath the sheer fright of deputies shouting commands at her, ordering her to put her thumbs in her waistband as she passed them by en route to breakfast in the crowded, loud prison commissary. She had endured handcuffs and jail buses; she had been fingerprinted and mugged and issued a plastic ID bracelet. Betty Broderick had seen the other, sordid side of life— she was now, in fact, a part of it.

But all she had learned from this loss of dignity and reputation was: she could survive it.

None of it, she said years later, was any worse than the hell in her head as she paced her del Cielo home alone at three A.M.. Long before she went to jail on two murder counts, Betty Broderick had already become institutionalized in many respects. And she exhilarated in her own curious, newfound ability not only to withstand but even to enjoy it.

"There's nothing more liberating than to realize that you don't have to live up to anything anymore," she said later. "After he sent me to jail, my image was already gone, so I didn't have to pretend anymore. I had nothing left to lose. I know it sounds crazy, but I suddenly felt free."

Thus, in his single-minded drive to control her behavior, Dan Broderick was only compounding the problem he was so determined to conquer. Inadvertently, he was only helping to create, over the next months and years, the final, heedless, broken creature who would one day shoot him to death in his bed, her hasty bullet striking as close to his heart as she could get it.

But Dan never would see it, never sense the danger. Instead, until the very eve of his death, he was still behaving like some legal Evel Kneivel rocketing his bike across the dark, deep chasms of his ex-wife's fraying mind.

By 1988, it was a radically altered Betty Broderick abroad in the streets of La Jolla. This one was well beyond caring how she was perceived by others. Her social image was already in shreds. All personal vanity was gone, buried beneath the layers of fat. Her language was now so routinely crude, even in polite gatherings, that old friends like Brian and Gail Forbes lectured her about her foul mouth, especially in front of their children— but what did she care?

By then, she was pacing the floors of her house all night, eating straight from refrigerator containers, and scribbling wildly in her diary. By then, those notebooks had literally become the "Diary of a Mad Housewife," except there was nothing even remotely amusing in Betty Broderick's proliferating pages. Now her mind gave her no rest; the late-night demons besetting her were relentless, vicious, and growing ever larger.

"Pressure from Hargreaves's seizure of $2,800 I badly need to pay bills. My credit cards at limit. I NEED THAT MONEY. T. Smith NO HELP AT ALL!" she wrote on January 7. Then, in another of her stark little lists, she complained again about everything from "skin entirely broken out" to her weight—"182 NEVER HIGHER! Fingernails bitten to the quick. THE STRESS IS KILLING ME!"

On another page she wrote a short, ominous note to Dan, which— although never mailed—the prosecutor would later select, alone among the hundreds of pages of Betty's diaries, as evidence of premeditated murder, while the defense argued that it was merely a collective, colloquial reflection of her crumbling state of mind:

"There is no better reason in the world for someone to kill than to protect their home, possessions, and family from attack and destruction," she scrawled. "You have attacked and destroyed me, my home, my possessions, and my family. You continue to repeatedly attack and steal and destroy. You are the sickest person alive. A law degree does not give you license to kill and destroy nor does it give you immunity from punishment. No one will mourn you!"

Then, abruptly, furiously, she would undergo an utter personality change, rising from her bed, dressing, and flinging herself again into the shops and restaurants of La Jolla with a vengeance, to spend money she didn't have. One day in January she hit I. Magnin's, where she charged $1,000 in cashmere sweaters. "They had a sale. I had never owned a cashmere sweater," she said later, vaguely. "I can't remember what all I bought. Maybe I bought the same one in every color ... All I can remember is that I would've paid $1,000 for ten minutes of relief—and by then, the only time I felt halfway normal was when I was either eating or signing charges. Those things I could do alone, and they made me feel like everything would still be okay."

But shopping was an emotional high of limited duration. By the time she got home, she was tired, depressed, frightened and enraged again. She threw the bags into corners, where, according to friends, they still lay, years later. "It was amazing," recalls Candy Westbrook. "She had all these wonderful clothes all over the house with the price tags still on them."

Compounding Betty's miseries, according to her diary, mutual friends of hers and Dan's were finally being forced to choose. And most chose Dan and Linda over her. Among the most painful occasions of 1988 was Brian Forbes's fortieth birthday party. By then, Gail Forbes had decided that, if Betty couldn't move on with life, she would. And so, according to Betty, Gail told her that she would not be invited to Brian's birthday party because she would make other guests, many of them friends of Dan and Linda, "uncomfortable."

Betty didn't say much about it in her diary, beyond a one-sentence notation that "I'm sick of solitary confinement, all alone."

But years later, from jail, she still remembered that event vividly. "I'd even bought Brian a birthday present ... I got him a $60 massage at a place in La Jolla, because he loved massages ..." But, as a consolation prize, she added bitterly, the Forbeses later invited her to a private family spaghetti dinner with their children. "I was so insulted and hurt." Even so, she still went.

208

It was fast becoming a social trend: Betty Broderick was no longer invited to the main events, only the kitchen dinners. She was too much of an awkwardness for her friends to accommodate. Just a month earlier, during the Christmas season, that fact had been pounded home to her even harder when Lynn and Mickey McGuire, a legal couple who had been friends of hers and Dan's for years, staged a combination Christmas open-house party to celebrate their palatial new home in Rancho Santa Fe.

"Lynn is my friend. But Mickey pulled rank, and so she called me, very upset, to say that Mickey had absolutely forbidden her from inviting me to their party because he had invited Dan and Linda ... So Lynn told me I couldn't come." As it turned out, she added, "Dan and Linda didn't even come, they had too many other party invitations that night. It wasn't even important to them. But it was important to me ... I just felt so bad about myself, I was getting so heavy, I was just such a mess. I needed people not to throw me away. But they did."

In the same month that his ex-wife was fantasizing about her forthcoming Polynesian escape and dreaming of rejuvenation, while simultaneously wishing into her diaries that she could kill him, Dan only pressed harder. At the same time she was about to strip herself of legal representation by firing her fourth divorce lawyer, Dan Broderick—who was now chairman of the bar association's Judicial Evaluations Committee which rates candidates for judgeships—hit her with yet another contempt motion—this one for eight offenses, including her Hawaiian postcard and her unauthorized deposit of Topsy and Muffin in his living room. He also asked the court to throw her back in jail to serve out the remainder of her suspended nineteen-day jail sentence from June. A hearing was set for February 24.

"It sounds cold," agreed Dan's friend Sharon Blanchet, "but what else was he supposed to do? A restraining order is a restraining order, and you can't make exceptions, just because it's the kids' dogs, or whatever. Otherwise, the whole purpose of the order is lost."

Bon voyage, Betty.

She did not enjoy herself in Tahiti. Pictures from that trip show a large, pale woman, wrapped in a pink and white floral Tahitian pareu, or sarong, sitting at a hotel restaurant table, surrounded by happy tourists. She wore the uncertain, dazed smile of a woman who didn't know where she was.

It was another nightmare trip, she said later, even worse than Hawaii had been. "I didn't want to be a single woman wandering around the world ..."

And she returned from Tahiti to the same unhappy world she had left. No one met her at the airport, she noted in her diary, and her mailbox was stuffed with more legal papers: Ruth Roth's suit against her was proceeding; so was the suit by Scott's, over the boys' clothing; and there was another OSC notice. Her house was also a complete wreck from teenage parties held there while she was gone. A fire extinguisher had been squirted over her carpets and couches, ruining them. Lee's friends, she guessed sourly. By now, it was increasingly clear to everyone that Lee

Broderick, then a tall, too-thin, pretty girl of seventeen, was bound for the wild side of life, at least for a while.

The two Broderick daughters were always very different, even from childhood.

Kim, then eighteen, was the peacemaker, the pleaser. Like her mother, she preferred evasion and conciliation to confrontation. She was the one who obeyed the rules and studied hard, at least in grade school. After the separation and divorce, she—alone among the Broderick children—quickly adapted to Dan's household rules. For a time, she was the Little Mother—and she liked it. It didn't stop her, however, from crying to Betty about what a cheap, mean man her dad was, when it suited her purposes. She never meant a word of it, of course—she was only a young girl playing both sides.

Lee, by contrast, was the rebel, defiant and stubborn. In that sense, she obviously took after her mother, too—at least in her mom's later, go-to-hell incarnation. The two daughters were flip sides of the Betty coin.

"Fuck you," Lee would scream at Dan, when he nagged her about grades, hours, and life-style. When he hectored her too much, she simply went over to Betty's house for the night, or the weekend. Once, after the divorce, she threw a glass at Dan's car. To hell with his rules, his controls. And Mom was, of course, always happy to receive her, partly so she could use it against Dad the next day.

But, eventually, even Betty, who wouldn't have been able to distinguish a line of cocaine from spilt salt in those days, began to suspect that something was wrong. Too many young people were coming and going at all hours of the night. And they all were laughing too loudly. Their eyes were too bright.

In La Jolla, as in every affluent American community riddled with adult neuroses and pampered, neglected children, drug abuse is of course a common youth problem. The only difference between Lee Broderick and her teenaged La Jolla friends was that she had perhaps a better excuse than most to challenge convention: None of their fathers were having their mothers jailed; none of their mothers were racing around town rattling on about cunts, fuckfaces, and the poverty of $16,000 a month.

It would be a few more months, however, before Lee became such a problem that both Dan and Betty Broderick were obliged to suspend their own wants and needs long enough to deal, however temporarily, with hers.

Betty, meantime, had begun to attend meetings of Al-Anon, a recovery group for codependents of alcoholics and addicts. She went, she said later, in order to better understand the addictions not only of Lee but also of Dan. But she had thought Al-Anon was mainly a gathering for wronged wives. Once she learned that Al-Anon is less interested in addicts than in the flawed personalities who choose to live with them, she didn't hang around long. It is just another sad "What If" of this tale that Betty was never able to forget the sins of Dan and Linda long enough to concentrate on her own self-destructive reaction to them.

Tricia Smith, meanwhile, was getting nowhere with the divorce case. In January, 1988, she wrote Barry, again demanding financial records that she had been seeking for nearly a year. "I am writing this letter to make one last, final demand for the discovery which has still not been forwarded to me in this matter," she wrote. "Although I have been extremely patient, you and your client seem to be attempting to avoid supplying me with the material requested." She concluded by threatening to seek legal sanctions if she did not receive the materials within thirty days.

Included in the list of items she sought were all of Dan's tax returns through May '87; copies of all checks he had paid on various "partnerships" he had entered into—particularly with his brother Larry—and for which he would later seek Epstein credits; all data on his pension plan, loans, and contributions from 1984 to the present time; lists of all cases Dan had begun from the date of the 1985 separation to the present; plus much more. Tricia Smith was ready to go to war.

But Betty couldn't—or wouldn't—wait any longer. By the end of January, she was driven—either by financial fear or fear of success—to self-destruct once more. First, against Smith's best advice, she fired an appraiser who was scheduled to evaluate Dan's law practice for the divorce trial. He cost too much, and Dan would doctor his books to fool him anyway, she reasoned.

Then she fired Tricia Smith, too—although to this day, Betty insists, waffling, that she and Smith just "drifted apart by mutual agreement ... Tricia was tired of the uphill battle against Dan Broderick. And the divorce was never moving forward."

But, before Smith bailed out, she went to court with Betty one last time to argue against eight pending contempts.

She begged the judge not to put Betty back in jail. She argued once again, and with eloquence, the triviality of Betty's offenses, the absurdity of two educated adults engaging in this kind of time-consuming warfare at the expense of taxpayers.

She lost.

Joseph found Betty guilty of all eight counts of contempt and imposed another eleven-day jail sentence. But he suspended it. This time, he had no intention of throwing Betty back into jail, since that approach clearly was not working. Instead, he fined her $8,000 and authorized Dan to deduct $1,000 per month from her $16,000 support check in payments to the city of San Diego until her debt to society was met.

In Smith's only victory, she finally got Linda's voice off the answering machine. "I believe Linda Kolkena and her sexuality is the reason for the failure of my marriage," Betty said in her declaration. "I become enraged and emotional when I hear her voice. My inner feelings come out in expressive language."

Betty explained that she usually talked to each of her children three to four times a day. "It is not unusual for more than ten or fifteen phone calls to go back and forth ... I believe Mr. Broderick unplugs the phone or puts Ms. Kolkena's voice on the phone purposely to harass and enrage me. He has been requested not to do so many times by my attorney ... At the last contempt trial, the court even requested that he voluntarily, without court orders, take Ms. Kolkena's voice off the machine. Despite these requests, he has refused to do so."

Joseph ordered Dan to get Linda's voice off the answering machine. "From this day on, there is no need for Linda's voice to go on any telephone answering machine that is available to Mr. Broderick," he said. "Anyone else in the household can record that message, including Mr. Broderick ..."

At the end of the hearing, Tricia Smith formally notified the court that, henceforth, she was off the Broderick case "at Mrs. Broderick's request."

Chapter 21

The Beat Goes On, Harder

Dan and Linda spent most of February traveling, first on a ski vacation to Colorado with the children, then to Switzerland by themselves. In the months before they died, they traveled often, to Hawaii, Greece, the Caribbean, San Francisco, New York, New England. By now, they were also one of downtown San Diego's most attractive, enviable new couples, regulars on the legal social scene, familiar faces in the evenings at Dobson's and other downtown bars.

Linda was spending most of her time at Dan's house—although friends say she usually skipped dinners there, in order not to upset the boys, arriving instead at nine or ten in the evening after they were busy at their schoolwork or in bed.

Linda's friends were delighted, because the day seemed to be soon at hand when Dan would cease dithering and marry the young woman who had put up with so much for so long to remain at his side.

Betty, meantime, sat at home, marking each of their trips into her diaries and remembering how much she herself had always wanted to travel the world. She had had so many plans, once upon a time. She had made it to Europe three times—but none had been the romantic, glamorous adventure of her girlhood dreams.

Every time she went over to Dan's to pick up the children, resentment gnawed at her—not only over the huge amount of money he was spending to refurbish his home, but also the style in which he was doing it. His taste was her taste.

If he wasn't home, she would walk out back and stare at his new swimming pool with hate. It was the same Bill Blass pool she had saved clippings about for so many years. The only difference was Dan had done his in green tile, instead of navy blue.

Sometimes, too, she would stroll through the house, appraising the value and nature of his furnishings. Occasionally she even took her camera and photographed the elegant rooms for her future divorce trial. While she was struggling on a budget, he was spending hundreds of thousands of dollars on his own home. Not fair.

"It was an Ethan Allen showroom, all the right pieces, but no warmth. He thought he was King Edward! And he did his whole goddamn house in my colors! My favorite colors were blue, Williamsburg blue, and cranberry ... I always thought, why can't they get their own taste? Why can't they get their own life?"

She wasn't supposed to go into the house at all, of course. "Dan told us to dial 911 for the police whenever she came inside," said Sylvia Cavins, a pleasant, earthy woman in her fifties, who alternated with her daughter, Linda David, as Dan's housekeeper for two years, until the killings. "But I just hated to call the police on her," says Cavins. "So we didn't do it. Still, we'd always watch to make sure she didn't damage anything and get us in trouble with Dan."

Dan was, both women agree, a stern taskmaster, an impersonal householder with an unrelentingly businesslike manner who would usually leave them memos on what he wanted done, rather than discuss matters in person—and when he did, it was always a formal encounter in his den, with him behind his desk, the housekeeper sitting in the chair before him, wondering what, if anything, she had done wrong. They called him Mr. Broderick. And they were nervous every time Betty was in the house, since, like Betty herself, they were violating his rules.

Yet it might have gone on, the ex-wife sneaking around in the house, checking everything out—except one day Betty betrayed their trust. When Linda David, on duty that day, turned her back, Betty crept into a hallway and found a letter on a table written by Linda Kolkena to Dan's parents.

"She opened it, and she read it," says Linda David, angry still, "and so I called her later, and I told her I didn't appreciate the position she was putting me in, and that she couldn't come inside anymore."

Betty denies reading the letter—lamely. (It is just another curious detail of her personality that, while she will admit to so much, periodically some small, embarrassing detail will arise that causes her, if not to lie outright, then to selectively forget.)

In return, Betty often took her anger at Dan out on his housekeepers. Nowhere does her class consciousness show more unattractively than in her remarks about these various women who were hired to feed, clean, and chauffeur her four children, as well as run Dan Broderick's household. They were, variously, "losers," "drunks," and "sluts." One was "that big fat girl with the foreign name." None of them "were the sort of people I wanted my children exposed to. My children had a mother!"

But, the housekeepers would later get even for Betty's condescension. Four became prosecution witnesses at her trial. Some were credible, others were not—but it was all part of the courtroom soap opera to come. (One would tell in detail about the Boston cream pie episode in 1985. Another would say that Betty threatened to shoot her in 1987. Another would tell how somebody, presumably Betty, had furiously crossed Dan's face out of a family photograph hanging in a hallway. And two of them, including Cavins, would testify that Betty frequently threatened to kill them both.)

By now, divorce activists were Betty's closest companions. Ronnie Brown, and later on another friend, Dian Black, wanted to form an organization that, unlike HALT, would focus strictly on divorce law reform. Both were committed to the notion that no-fault divorce laws were the single worst disaster ever to befall mothers and children. And they wanted Betty Broderick to join them, to lend her name and her story to their organizing efforts.

And, despite herself, Betty was becoming something of an activist. Experience had educated her—perhaps for the first time in her life—to issues larger than herself. She had glided through nearly sixteen years of marriage without ever hearing the term no-fault, much less bifurcation. Like most women, she had simply assumed that divorce meant "you split everything down the middle on the day of the divorce, and that's it."

But now, she had a divorce and no settlement. Dan had both his freedom and full control of all their assets. "Yet it was his fault our family was destroyed!"

Finally, she decided to write her story for publication, as a call to arms to other women. While Dan and Linda were enjoying Europe, she went to Deer Valley in February with the children and spent a week working on her memoirs. What resulted was a ninety-page manuscript, which she titled "What's a Nice Girl to Do? A Story of White-Collar Domestic Violence in America."

After the title page, she wrote:

> *"Don't get in the mud and fight with the pigs.*
> *You only dirty yourself and the pigs like it!"*

In her introduction, she promised that hers would be "the story of how one man had the power to break all the rules."

What resulted instead was such a furious, personalized account of a "wonderful wife and mother," wronged in every respect by a "foaming-at-the-mouth mad-dog attorney," that it had scant relevance to the average woman in divorce. Dan came out as something lower than a barnyard pig, yet more powerful than God. Betty herself verged on saintly. Not until her postscript did she even get around to addressing no-fault divorce laws, which "leave the door open for this kind of emotional terrorism, without any threat of repercussions to the oppressor."

She got a lot off her chest by writing it, but, beyond that, Betty's book, like her diaries, served the interests of no one, except the prosecutor, who later seized on the manuscript as further evidence that Betty Broderick had been premeditating cold-blooded murder for nearly two years before she finally got around to doing it.

Of special interest to the district attorney was the last paragraph of Betty's tome: "I wish I could finish this tale of woe," she wrote. "I tried to finish it five years ago, when I burnt his clothes and threw him out. As things are today, I have ulcers, insomnia, a chronic bad back from the incredible stress, and have gained sixty pounds. The home I'm living in is still a mess, even though I've spent a lot of my own money on it. It's still in a beautiful spot, but it still has Dan Broderick's name on the deed. I am facing the crooked judge and jail again—I am without an effectual attorney, but have thousands in outstanding attorney fees ... At this point, February 20, 1988, I have nowhere to turn—if this is the way domestic disputes are settled in the courts, is there any wonder there are so many murders? I am desperate. What is a nice girl to do?"

Nothing ever came of Betty's book. Later, in fact, she would deny that she ever intended it to be more than "a diary for my children, so they would know what happened." She would never see herself as symbolic in any way of other women.

Not until three years later, long after Betty had been jailed for murder, finally Ronnie Brown did organize a local group, the Alliance for Marriage and Divorce Reform, which is reportedly thriving—and which never mentions Betty Broderick.

In March, only weeks after the court levied its fines, the Brodericks clashed once again over how best to educate their children.

Danny was already enrolled at Francis Parker, one of the best San Diego private schools, but Betty wanted him in the even more elite Bishops School in La Jolla. Dan resisted, arguing that Danny was happy at Francis Parker and that there was no reason to uproot him.

Ignoring him, Betty managed to get Danny on the highly competitive list of youngsters accepted for the Bishops entrance exam.

But, on the morning of the exam, March 12, Danny didn't show up. Instead, Dan had taken both boys with him to ride in the St. Patrick's Day parade.

The result was guaranteed. Betty was about as livid as she had ever been:

"Listen, you fucking, insane asshole," she screamed into his answering machine. "This is Saturday now at about 1:30 or something. I've been calling for days to get this weekend straightened out. You fucked your son over by having missed the Bishops exam. I am not accepting Rhett by cab, which is unsafe, so that I can be your maid and baby-sit while you continue your drunken afternoon with your office cunt. You are so insane. Will you please go get help. You're sick."

Worse, in another measure of just how stunningly irrational she had become, she also sat down and wrote a rambling, twenty-page letter of outrage, studded with profanities, to the one person in town—not counting Dan Broderick himself—who was least likely to sympathize with her: Dan's attorney, Gerald Barry:

"Dear Mr. Barry—Your fucking asshole client is at it AGAIN—déjà vu," she began. "He has been using the routine restraining orders as SOLE CUSTODY orders since fall of '85 when he had no custody order at all. As with the delay tactics, you would think that after THREE YEARS of being treated like mindless, worthless shit, I'd get used to it, but somehow I just can't."

From there, she raved on about random offenses committed by Dan, including his refusal to let Rhett come to soccer practice or games when she was a volunteer coach.

She finished her letter by telling Barry that, as she wrote, she was drinking from a coffee cup with the word STRESS printed on it, along with a definition. In typically ribald Betty Broderick style, she quoted from the cup:

"STRESS: the confusion created when one's mind overrides the body's basic desire to choke the living shit out of some asshole who desperately deserves it."

She wrote Barry several more letters over the next two months.

In one, she ventilated her anger at the legal system, which "bludgeoned, attacked, and generally fucked over" its victims, especially her. She blamed it, as usual, on Dan's stature in town: "The Emperor has no clothes, and all your courtesans are applauding and protecting a naked man."

Then, her mind snapped back to her gnawing resentments over the present: "Dan is living like a king. Spending money like he won the lottery. The disparity between our two living arrangements is TOO GREAT. I want it resolved. Betty Broderick."

Her lunatic letters to Barry continued through May. Now Gerald Barry had every reason to see, with his own eyes, that this was obviously no longer a steady, rational woman. But not since Dan Jaffe had urged two years earlier that a guardian be

216

appointed to protect Betty from herself had anyone in the legal system come forward to suggest that this deck was shamelessly stacked.

She grew unsteadier by the day. She continued her erratic, credit card shopping sprees. On one day in March alone, she spent $1,000 at Custom Shirts of La Jolla. She walked into department stores and boutiques and bought armfuls of clothing for herself and the children. But, by now, shopping for herself was no fun because she had to visit the large-sized salons of her favorite stores. "The clothes were just so ugly," she says. "And I looked like shit in them."

Nothing in her life provided relief anymore.

The children were a growing aggravation. Lee was now living mostly with Betty. "Out all night!" cried Betty into her diary. Once when Lee took her car without asking, Betty called the police and reported it stolen.

At the same time, she was even angrier at Dan for not providing both girls with cars. "Lee was riding this piece-a-shit moped all over town," she later said. "It was unsafe. And it looked like hell. My girls weren't cut out for that kind of image!" She ended up leasing cars for both girls herself.

Then she made plans to go to New York to visit her family again.

"Felt like I was dying," she wrote in her diary that week. "So unhappy, so lonesome. Kim and Lee partying, wrecking my house ... won't clean up house or return missing things." In a striking indication of her growing obsessiveness, she even listed the "missing things" in a neat column: They ranged from "fire extinguisher, spotlighter, and bathing suit" to "champagne (Tattinger), Godiva chocolates, and Girl Scout cookies."

Her diaries make no mention of how her week in New York went—and today she says even she can't remember.

At about the same time, a small-claims court judge ruled that Ruth Roth should take her bill back to Dan Broderick for payment, as per the original court order. It had taken Betty months in time and effort to score this small victory. "It was pure harassment," she said later. "Dan knew that bill was his. But it cost me a lot of hassle, just going down to small claims court to prove it—and that's what he wanted. He was deliberately trying to drive me crazy!"

And, certainly, she was beginning to sound crazier by the day.

On March 23, she wrote a curious, testy letter to Tricia Smith, pretending that she hadn't fired her after all:

"Dear Tricia—I was sorry to hear ... that you will not be helping me clean up the pile of vomit called my life. I wish you had had the courtesy to call or write me yourself. I know you're very busy, but it would only have taken a minute. Thank you for the help and support you gave for the last year. Too bad we didn't get anywhere."

Then, according to her diary, Oprah Winfrey's show called, wanting her to appear on a program about messy divorces. She refused because, "I didn't want to be part of a circus."

Otherwise, it was a fairly quiet month. Dan filed only two OSCs—one accusing Betty of throwing rocks at his car.

April is one of the reasons that La Jollans like to call their little community surrounding the beautiful cove "the Jewel," after the Spanish la joya, although most historians think the name derives from the early Como Yei Indian word hoy a, meaning cave.

It is, at that mild time of year, one of the prettiest places on earth. The air is clean, the lushness of orange, purple, and pink flowers cascading down the hillsides clash gloriously against the brilliant blue sea and cloudless sky. Lovers and old people sit for hours in the sunlight, watching the waves beat their timeless songs upon the great, eerie, ragged rock formations rising from the sea along the shoreline. Gardeners smile, Mexican maids beat rugs in the ritual of spring cleaning, and the ladies of La Jolla whisk about with new energy, working out at Personalized Fitness and getting new spring hair colors and faces at the local beauty factories. Parties get planned, Jonathan's worries about the quality of the incoming caviar and strawberries, Las Patronas matrons worry that only five months remain to ready the Jewel Ball. April in La Jolla is when all the juices are flowing, in lords and retainers alike.

And, certainly the teenagers at La Jolla High School feel their youth—and many of them do drugs in celebration. Lee Broderick was among them. But one day at lunch hour she got caught by campus security officers, snorting coke in a car with some of her buddies. The school called Dan to tell him that she would probably be suspended for at least three days, and that a parental counseling session was in order. He agreed to be present at eleven the next day. But that night, Lee ran away. Three days later, she was still missing.

Betty reported her disappearance to the police.

Dan didn't. He was fed up.

He heard of Lee's whereabouts for the next six months, only through Kim—she was living with other teenagers in a beach community south of La Jolla. Dan did nothing to track her down. "I did not try to contact her during that period," he testified later in the divorce trial, because, he said, his younger daughter knew his rules. Furthermore, this incident was only the latest among many, he said. Lee had run away from home several times before. She disobeyed his curfews. He had warned her repeatedly, he said, that "this is not appropriate behavior ... So I ultimately told Lee, shortly before she left permanently, that 'You cannot do this again and run away any more. If you have a problem, come home and let's discuss it, but don't stay out all night.' At that time she was just sixteen years old. But Lee does what she wants."

And so, for the next six months, Lee Broderick was a child without a home. Betty talked to her off and on, but Lee wouldn't return to either parent. She had said sayonara to the madness of family life.

Kim, meantime, wrecked her car that spring, without injury. She also became pregnant by the construction worker Betty so disapproved of.

That weekend, Betty went on a Presbyterian church retreat. She returned neither calmed nor focused.

"Tax man says I owe $38,500!" she wrote in her diaries on April 14. In hindsight, it was just another of Betty's bad decisions that, in her attempt to gain independence, she had demanded responsibility for her finances—but then she hadn't taken responsibility. The IRS commanded her attention no more than the San Diego courts did. Taxes were lower on her list of monthly priorities than her bill to the local florist. She neither budgeted for, nor paid for, them.

"Dan in Mexico with cunt," she wrote the next day, with growing hate. "Left only $40 for Kim. Lee missing; boys here."

Then Lee surfaced again, with a bang. She crashed her car, and it was finally clear even to Betty that her daughter needed professional help. She persuaded Lee to check into the McDonald's Center, where La Jollans with drug problems usually go if they can't get a bed at Betty Ford.

Betty was torn between shame and concern, between fear of what people would think, fear for Lee, and her own refusal to believe her child could be a drug addict. Lee, meantime, protested that it was just a one-time thing, that she wasn't hooked on anything. But wiser heads at the drug recovery home were telling Betty Broderick that Lee needed treatment. And so Betty signed her daughter in for what was supposed to be a month-long recovery program.

"It was the most horrible thing I've ever had to do," she says. "I didn't know what to do! There I was, all alone, trying to make this life decision, and I didn't even know where Dan was! It was definitely one of the high water points of my life. I was shaking, I was so nervous—I was in worse shape than Lee was."

At the same time, her mind had already whirled ahead to consider the potential benefits of this family crisis. Maybe this would bring Dan back home. "I thought that if he attended the family sessions, then maybe, finally, he would be able to identify a little bit with his own drinking problems," she admitted years later from jail. "I thought maybe it wasn't too late, after all, to save our family—that maybe Lee's problems had some higher purpose."

But Lee stayed at McDonald's only three days before she walked out and called her mother from a nearby pay phone to come rescue her.

"She told me that she wasn't one of them; she said she was in there with all these hard-core addicts and alcoholics, and that it was a ridiculous waste of time and money, that she didn't belong there. She told me she wasn't a drug addict. And," says Betty with a rueful sigh, "I believed her." So she picked Lee up in the parking lot of a shopping center and took her home, where Betty's friends, Gail Forbes and Lynn McGuire, tried to help her design a home treatment program for Lee. It was hardly enough to see Lee through.

But, in those days, Betty didn't have the time or self-control to focus on one young girl's unhappiness. She was too busy trying to survive herself.

Nothing changed. By now, Thomas Murphy, then presiding judge of family courts, was beginning to wonder why the Broderick matter was still cluttering his court calendar. He ordered a series of new settlement conferences to get the case moving. He also introduced a new expert into the mix. Clinical psychologist Dr. William Dess was assigned, not to interview either the children or the parents, but simply to review all the existing mental health reports for purposes of making a custody recommendation to the court.

The conferences went no place, of course. As usual, Dan blamed Betty, Betty blamed Dan. After five tries—with one or both Brodericks failing to appear—the sessions were dropped. But Dr. Dess would remain in the picture for many months to come.

Meantime, Betty had yet another contempt hearing on May 4. She wondered if she would be jailed this time, or fined again, or both.

She was fined—partly because Dan had changed his mind about wanting to have her jailed. Instead, because Lee was in trouble, he appealed to Judge Joseph at the last minute not to jail the mother of his child in crisis. This annoyed Joseph in the extreme. He lectured Dan for misusing the court process. "He told Dan, 'Don't you ever come back here again unless you want her jailed.' And I never forgot it," Betty said later. "I knew if Dan ever filed another contempt, I was going to jail again for sure, because Joseph was so pissed that day."

Even so, angry or not, Joseph complied with Dan's wishes. Instead of jail, he fined Betty another $1,000, atop her existing $8,000 fine. He also agreed with Dan that Betty should pay another $16,000 in Dan's attorney fees to Gerald Barry, at a rate of $1,000 per month. However, Joseph decreed, her monthly deductions should not exceed $2,000. Once she had satisfied her prior $8,000 fine, then the full $2,000 monthly deduction could be directed toward payment of Barry's fees. In other words, Dan could work it out however he liked, at a rate of $2,000 per month, until $24,000 had been extracted from his unruly ex-wife.

Later that same day, a dazed and enraged Betty Broderick disgraced herself further at her children's school. For reasons that she can no longer remember, she had gone to Francis Parker and wound up in the office of Principal Dave Glassey, where she lost all control. Whatever business she had was forgotten as she exploded into tears and furious rhetoric, studded with her by now commonplace crudities. She told Glassey and an assistant what a rotten bastard Dan Broderick was, what an unfit father, what an immoral human being, what an alcoholic, abusive asshole he really was. She told them all about "the cunt" too.

It must have been some scene—big, mad Betty in her power pumps, towering over two circumspect administrators, raving. She finished by giving Glassey a copy of her "book," and then telephoned Dan to call him more names in front of the principal and the assistant. Glassey, who appears on paper to be a very prim, proper man, would later tell investigators that he had finally been obliged to reprimand Mrs. Broderick for her language. Francis Parker is even more image-conscious than Dan and Betty Broderick were.

A few weeks later, Dan mailed Betty his latest divorce settlement proposal. This time, he offered to give her $9,000 per month for one year, reduced to $5,000 per month thereafter, continuing for seven years (or less, if she remarried). That came out to a total package of $528,000 for eight years (or, less than half of his annual

220

earnings at the date of separation in 1985). He offered nothing as her share of their community property. Instead, his proposal suggested that he had lost so much money on their various investments that she actually owed him hundreds of thousands of dollars in Epstein credits for her share of the community debts that he had paid since their separation—more than enough wipe out her interest in his law practice. All that remained negotiable, in his view, was her half of his pension plan, which might come to $250,000 or so, but that was yet to be calculated.

"Bullshit," Betty wrote in the margins of his proposal. End of discussion. She would see him in court. The Broderick divorce trial was now scheduled for July.

Meantime, in another small victory for Betty, Dan's appeal of her $16,000 in temporary support was denied.

She continued to lament her weight. She seemed to be gaining every day. But she wasn't even trying to diet anymore. Instead, she was now beginning to think about more cosmetic surgery. She could have a face-lift. She could have liposuction. Some doctor could suck the fat off her stomach, off her thighs, off her chin and neck. She could do that. Her friends all did it. She studied the brochures as she gazed out to sea and had another pastry from French Gourmet and wondered what Dan and Linda were doing tonight.

She had been living alone in the del Cielo house for nearly three years now. She had put in a pool, and a pool house. She had spent thousands on its interior. But her fixation on the differences in life-style between herself and Dan only grew.

"Tiny kitchen," she complained to her diary. "I need a family room!"

Then, obsessively, fearfully, proudly, she recorded her latest shopping sprees, even the smaller ones: "I go to Price Club. Dump $200 for party stuff," she wrote on Memorial Day weekend. Also, "spent $450 at Saks."

Only Lee could now interrupt her self-obsession. Her daughter had not reformed; even Betty Broderick, who barely even touched her dinner wine, could sense that.

At the end of the month, she overheard Lee on the telephone, discussing "rocks" with someone. Betty didn't know what a rock was, "but I knew it was something bad from the sneaky way they were whispering."

Betty didn't know what to do with her daughter, who didn't know what to do with her mother—and the father didn't want anything more to do with either one of them.

By summer of 1988, in fact, Dan Broderick decided to punish his wayward daughter in the same way he punished her mother—through the pocketbook. He wrote Lee out of his will.

"I was genuinely concerned … that if I died and she got a fourth of my estate, it would go up in smoke … that she would spend it on drugs or give it away or just squander it," he later explained in divorce court.

But then it was Kim's hour. Dan and Betty's firstborn had grown up. It was her high-school graduation day.

Betty looked through her closet for the most attractive thing to wear. By now, all her clothes were matronly three-piece outfits with flared skirts and jackets, mostly in shades of beige. Beige with white polka-dots. Beige with pink stripes. She had become an ad for the Mature Woman. How had it happened? she wondered. Only two years earlier, she had worn size eights and tens, and could still zip up a pair of thirty-two-inch jeans. Now she looked so bad. She smiled at herself in the mirror. She looked like Miss Piggy. She hated herself. She hated him.

He would be there, at his daughter's graduation. It would be the first time in years that they had both attended a family function simultaneously. She was nervous. She wondered what she would say to him, what he would say to her. Their daughter, the little girl who had been conceived on their St. Thomas honeymoon 19 years ago, was graduating from high school. Surely, at least today of all days, he would talk to her. He would be nice. Surely.

She dabbed at her plump, pale face and fluffed her yellow hair one more time. She felt hot. Her panty hose were too tight. She snatched up her purse, and her camera, and drove to the Francis Parker Middle and Upper School campus. To see Kim graduate. And to see Dan.

And there, across the wide lawn, she saw Linda Kolkena. On Dan's arm. The pretty, slender, young Linda Kolkena. Flashing her wide, brilliant smile at Kim's teachers, at all the parents, at Betty's friends, mothers she had known for years. Acting as if she had every right to be there. Holding his hand.

"Oh, I didn't care at all," chirps Betty today, perky as a mechanical songbird. "I just thought it was, you know, just so tacky of him to bring his girlfriend to our daughter's graduation—and she was dressed completely wrong, such gaudy jewelry for daytime ..."

Linda's friends later defended her decision to attend the graduation. "Linda knew it would be hard on Betty," said Sharon Blanchet. "But Linda and Kim were friends, and she thought she should go. Besides, Linda had every right to go. How long were she and Dan supposed to live their lives based on what would or wouldn't upset Betty?"

"Mom never forgave me for inviting her," said Kim years later. A few weeks afterward, she remembers, Betty was supposed to visit her in her new apartment. Kim had cleaned and prepared lunch and was waiting. "And then she called me and said, I'm not coming. I just remembered how much I hate you!'"

During graduation ceremonies, Betty sat on one side of the audience, Linda and Dan on the other. Afterward, Betty says, still bitter, Kim went first to them. But, typically, she attributes Kim's motives to—what else?—money: "They gave her a diamond bracelet, I gave her a leather appointments book—which side would you go to?"

To this day, Betty cannot admit what she did next: she followed Dan and Linda around the reception, taking their pictures.

"She told the kids that she was photographing Linda's jewels for the divorce trial," says Blanchet, shaking her head. "Well, Linda's 'jewels' amounted to a string of pearls and a ring Dan gave her. Anyway, she followed them around, and it was so obvious—she embarrassed everyone, it was horrible. Linda said she even followed them out onto the street as they were leaving."

Betty furiously denies it. "I did no such thing," she insists. "I just took pictures of everyone. I love to take pictures." In fact, she says she "can't even remember if I took a picture of the cunt."

She does remember vividly, however, overhearing the remarks of a teacher who walked up to Dan and Linda—and confused Linda with Betty.

"It was a teacher I had once had to the house, in 1984, for a lovely dinner, along with his wife ... and I hadn't seen him in years," says Betty, with typical, forced nonchalance. "And, of course, I wasn't as heavy back then—so he thought Linda was me. He called her Mrs. Broderick. People were always doing that because she had the same blond hair. Anyway, it bothered me, and so I made a point of walking over to him later to tell him, 'I'm Betty Broderick, not her.' The poor man, he was so embarrassed." But not Betty. She had long since left shame far behind.

"Why should I have been embarrassed?" she asks, brightly. "Don't you see—there could never be more than one Mrs. Daniel T. Broderick III in La Jolla. That was my name—that's why Linda Kolkena wanted me dead; you can't replace a woman who's still alive."

But a few weeks later, contradicting all that she had said, Betty scrawled this angry note into her diary: "Kim keeps coming to my house to steal things. She is now looking to remove the cunt's pictures I took at graduation."

Kim later came along and scribbled her own angry retort on the same page: "Bullshit, Mom. I have no interest in those pictures! I WANTED TO SEE MINE! WHY would I want pictures of her?"

During the same month, two more divorce settlement conferences failed to materialize. By now, yet another judge, Federico Castro, was involved in the Broderick case, and, at Dan's request, he ordered Betty to seek vocational testing—routine in many divorces involving wives who have not worked outside the home for most of their adult lives. As the very term implies, this is a court-ordered effort to get the weary old mom out of the house and back into the job market, so that she can contribute to her own support. Betty was insulted at the very notion of taking "rinky-dink tests to tell me if I should go work at a department store selling cosmetics or into assembly line work. I'm a college-educated woman. Why can't they ever order women to 'professional testing'?" Moreover, she saw it as just another delaying tactic. Why had it taken Dan so many years to even bring it up?

In her only satisfaction, Castro at least ordered Dan to pay for the counseling—and the choice of the counselor was left up to Betty. With the help of her HALT friends, she settled on a woman who was said to be sympathetic to middle-aged women in her position.

Even so, she was so angry at the belated, insulting nature of his demand that she went to Dan's house the next day to complain about it. But, she says, he refused even to speak to her. He was working in his yard, squatting next to some plants, and, "He wouldn't look up or even answer me. I wanted to wring his neck!" Meantime, Linda was upstairs, "looking out a window, shouting, 'Dan, Dan, do you want me to call the police?'," said Betty, mimicking Linda's voice, just as Linda had once mimicked hers.

223

In the end, the vocational testing plan was dropped because Barry withdrew the request abruptly without explanation. That infuriated Betty as much as the original court order itself. Once more, Dan was jerking her around at will, with the help of obedient judges. First, she had been ordered to take the tests. She had complied; she had spent time with a counselor. But now that Dan had changed his mind—either because he didn't want to pay the $5,000 fees or didn't like the choice of counselors— the court order was voided, withdrawn, erased. Why? How? "Why isn't he in contempt?" she demanded.

What's more, she says, compounding the degradation, the judge once even asked her if she had a boyfriend. "And I'm like—why does that matter? Dan Broderick has been living with his secretary! Does anyone ask him if he has a girlfriend? And if I had said yes, [the judge] would have said, 'Well, go home and have him support you.'" Little by little, Betty Broderick, sheltered for so long, was learning about double standards in the real world.

Meanwhile, the divorce trial was delayed again, from July to December 28, for reasons that were not clear. Dan filed no OSCs that month.

Chapter 22

Muhammad Ali and the Housewife

Sooner or later, the San Diego media was bound to get wind of the steamy, sordid Broderick divorce story. It was the *San Diego Reader*, a small weekly newspaper devoted mostly to features on community personalities, arts, and culture, that first heard of the Broderick case and assigned reporters Paul Krueger and Jeannette De Wyze to look into it. They called Betty one day in May, 1988, to see if she would like to discuss her divorce.

Oh, yikes. She paused for maybe three seconds before her fears of Dan Broderick dissolved beneath the exhilarating realization that, at long last, here was a potentially powerful ally—the press.

She invited Krueger and DeWyze to her house as soon as they could get there—whereupon she told them her whole angry, bitter story in an outpouring of wit, intelligence, and passion that left them fascinated and confused, wondering if it could possibly be as bad, as unfair, as she said.

She cast Dan in the worst possible light, starting virtually from the day they were married. Then, just as the reporters were shaking their heads in pained disbelief, she suddenly turned into a stand-up comedienne, making them laugh with her self-mocking rendition of her original suspicion that he was only going through a midlife crisis:

"I mean, he walked out literally three months after his fortieth birthday party. With a red Corvette and a nineteen-year-old. Da-da da-da! Are we the American joke, or what? If you weren't my husband, I'd think you're real funny. He's revving up his Corvette to go pick up his girlfriend, he's got a new leather jacket, he's wearing those Risky Business sunglasses ... I said, 'You're on the cover of Midlife Crisis Magazine. I love it. Cool, man, cool.'" She told it all her way—leaving out, of course, her part in any of it.

Krueger and De Wyze, good reporters both, called Dan Broderick.

At first Dan didn't want to talk to them. When he finally did agree to an interview, it was because he believed that once he had spoken with the two reporters in a quiet, reasonable fashion, they would see that this tawdry domestic dispute was not a story worth their time.

His voice on their tape was pleasant, soft and easy, with a winning, gee-whiz tone to it. But he was still the premiere attorney. Like a man giving a deposition, he stipulated that he would truthfully answer all their questions. "You can take that to the bank." He would say nothing that couldn't be corroborated, he told them. He then turned on his own tape, as they taped him.

They first quizzed him about Betty's claim that she couldn't find first-rate legal representation in town, because of his influence.

He denied it. The real reason his ex-wife hadn't been able to find an attorney, Dan speculated, was that "She's an uncontrollable person, who most lawyers are afraid they can't work with."

Like Betty, Dan told the story all his way.

He told Krueger and De Wyze how this "perfect mother" had used their children as a weapon against him. "She just dropped them there at Coral Reef. 'Here. They're yours. You want to be apart from me—well, see what it's like raising a family by yourself.' There was not a stick of furniture in the house ... And whenever she wanted to, she started on her rampages, throwing stuff through the windows, and breaking mirrors, spray-painting the walls. I mean, unbelievable things! And she would always say that I provoked her, that she was upset with me because I did something or other. One time, I had taken the kids to get haircuts and she was expecting them at a soccer game. I didn't know they were supposed to be at a soccer game. I mean, I'm not that kind of person, that I'd just take them to get a haircut, just to spite her. I came back, and there was hundreds, maybe thousands, of dollars in damage. I mean, windows broken and chandeliers cracked, and our stereo was smashed. I mean, it was unbelievable stuff ...

"So I filed for divorce. I got a court order ... basically a stayaway order ... And, mind you, by now she's living in a $650,000 home in La Jolla that I bought for her ... just for her ... because I had the four kids. And even with the court order, she kept coming in and spraying stuff, and I remember a Boston cream pie that my girlfriend made for me ... She came and just took it and smeared it all over the bedroom, with my clothes ... I mean ... absolutely crazy stuff. My little kids would watch this, and they'd be crying when I'd come home—they couldn't control it, I couldn't control it ...

"So I called her and I said, 'I'm going to list the Coral Reef house. You're living in your house over there in La Jolla. I don't want to live here anymore. It's got bad memories associated with it ... I've got to get to someplace where you don't feel like you've got the perfect right to come in and do this.' I really didn't want to bring a court order and get her thrown in jail, for my kids' sake ... although I felt like I probably could have. I mean, it was going on like every other week ... every time I'd walk into the house, I'd wonder what I was going to find. It was that bad ..."

But she told him, "It's my house. I don't want it sold," said Dan. He had tried to reason with her. "Well, how much money would we have to be offered before you agree to sell it? ... Neither of us are living in this house. It's empty now." But: "She said a million dollars wouldn't do it."

And so, he said, sounding exasperated, he called his attorney and got the house sold without her consent. When De Wyze pressed Dan to discuss details of the divorce settlement itself, he digressed instead into a lengthy defense of his own integrity. He assured the reporters that he had submitted to Tricia Smith all requested documents supporting every detail of his finances—"every tax return, every check, every credit card receipt." He continued to defend his honesty by recounting what he had said to Smith:

"Look, if I'm lying, I'm committing perjury, and I lose my license to practice law; maybe I'll go to jail if I've defrauded the Internal Revenue Service because I haven't ... reported all my income, and if you catch me, I deserve what I get. I mean, it may be kind of a stupid Gary Hart challenge, but I know that in my case it's not going to come back to haunt me, because I have been absolutely honest about it ... I've paid all my income tax. I mean, I report all my income. [Betty] has accused me of hiding money in Switzerland ... I have not hidden a dime anywhere."

The reporters next asked him about the unusual arrangement of the father winning sole custody, with no visitation for the mother.

Even on tape, it's easy to see Dan Broderick's face sadden, darken. His voice changes from jolly to grave. This, he said, was a matter he was very reluctant to discuss, in the interests of protecting his children.

At the same time, he didn't hesitate to show the two reporters a transcript of Betty's most outrageous taped conversation with Danny. He was having it both ways. He wanted to be dignified, above it all, yet he was determined to show them just what a foul creature Betty had become. What followed was a schizoid Dan:

"I showed you the transcript of one telephone conversation that my ex-wife had with my son Danny ... That is like the very tip of an iceberg. It's unbelievable. And the psychologists who're taking care of these kids and seeing them—I mean, they've just been horrified. They've never seen anything like this, ever. I mean, it's like a magnified case of 'Mommie Dearest', from the Joan Crawford show ...

"I mean, it's just extreme mental cruelty, I guess would be the best way to put it, or psychic abuse ... She gets at me through them, is my sort of armchair, amateur psychologist's view of what's going on, but it's terrible."

"Why do you let them go over there then?" asked De Wyze bluntly.

For the next few minutes, it was Dan Broderick at his most appealing. He sounded both bewildered and pained as he tried explaining to these two strangers that, basically, he didn't know what the hell he was doing anymore, he had no idea of how to help these young children survive the Broderick divorce nightmare.

"As for my boys, that's a good question," he told De Wyze and Krueger. "The psychologists have told me that I'm being irresponsible ... for letting them go over there [to Betty's house] ... [But] they want to be with their mother. Honest to God ... And they always ask me, can they go see their mom, can they spend time with her, can they be with her ... and 'She'll be good, she won't do this, she won't be mean, she won't bring us home.'

"And I feel like maybe it's better for them to see some of her, and have at least some kind of relationship, than none at all, but I'm very ambivalent about it. I mean, it's a real good question. Why do I? A lot of people ask me that. And I ask myself that. I'm trying to do the right thing. I do not believe it would be in their best interests to live with her, and I—honestly, I don't think it's in their best interests to spend any time with her. But I can't separate them from her altogether ... So I'm doing the best I can ..."

Why, Krueger pressed, did the kids want to be around their mom, then, if things were so bad?

"It's just the obvious thing," said Dan. "They miss their mother ... I guess that's the way people are with their parents. They are the people they love. It's like a moth attracted to a flame. They can't help it. I mean, that's kind of a superficial analysis, but that's kind of the impression I get."

Why has this whole divorce dragged on so long? asked De Wyze.

Dan said he didn't really know, but suggested that it had something to do with recent changes in court procedures.

But don't you want to get it over with, asked Krueger?

Whereupon Dan Broderick delivered what would ultimately become the most widely quoted paragraph of this interview with the *Reader*.

"It's never going to be over for me. I know that. I mean, I'm resigned. It's not going to end until one of us is gone. I mean, it's just not going to. I mean, the ultimate trial is going to resolve some community property issues. But it's not going to end this thing. And so it's going to be a very unpleasant experience, and it's one that I am not looking forward to, going down there [to trial] and having this ... I mean, I would much rather she had a lawyer."

De Wyze wanted to know what he meant: "It's not going to be over until one of you is gone, because she will probably be asking for support for life?" Was that what he meant? "That's not only what I meant," said Dan. "I mean that, too, but I mean, it's going to be ... she can't let go of it. She cannot let go of it ..."

"Why does she do this?" asked Krueger.

"Well, she's filled with hatred," said Dan. "I left her, and she's mad about it." Whereupon Dan proceeded to tell the two reporters that, actually, Betty had always been hell to live with.

It is one of the saddest aspects of most bitter divorces that even the lovely memories of better days usually go up in the flames of later, jaded emotions; differences and spats that were once upon a time no big deal suddenly become ammunition for older, wearier spouses bent upon self-justification and escape. Like arsonists, they go about the repositories of their pasts, flinging gasoline into the mind's most precious, irreplaceable stores, and tossing matches in after.

And Dan Broderick was no exception, any more than Betty was. The "private man" described by friends had vanished entirely. In the end, neither of these two left themselves a single tender memory.

"We had a tumultuous marriage ... I mean, just a real compatibility problem," Dan told Krueger and De Wyze. "A lot of things that are exaggerated now have been evident from the very beginning ... all our married life." But he "just thought that was the way she was ... something that I could try to accommodate ... traits of her personality."

"In hindsight," Krueger asked, "do you believe, then, that she was, then or now, diagnostically something other than completely sane?"

"Yes, I do," Dan promptly replied. "I've got no question ... I don't know what label to put on it ... there's something there, though, I'll tell you that ... driving a truck into the front of my house. And, I mean, these outbursts and this web of deception that she weaves ... And I think she would pass a lie detector test ... Reality is eluding this woman in so many ways ... I cannot put a label on it, and I won't try. But there's something, I'll bet you anything. But we're never going to find out."

However, he also allowed that he himself had to bear some of the blame. "I was far from the kind of good loving husband I could have been ... I mean, there were problems in our marriage. Some were her fault, some were my fault ..."

De Wyze wanted to know why he had filed so many contempts against Betty.

"Yes, I understand you want to talk about that," said Dan. The reason for them, he said, was because Betty was committing "incredible violations of court orders ... not just once, or twice. Not just one warning or two warnings. I mean, repeated warnings: 'Stop this. You can't do this. Leave the guy alone.' And she would come back and do it again. And pretty soon the judge had to say, 'Well, ma'am, this is a law-abiding society. You cannot act like this. Stop it.' And he put her in jail."

Krueger asked Dan if Judge Joseph hadn't chastised him at a recent hearing for reversing his request that Betty be jailed, due to Lee's recent problems. "It seems to me that I could make the argument that you manipulated the proceedings to get your peace of mind," said Krueger.

Dan disagreed, sounding only faintly annoyed. "I certainly think it's a fair use of the court process," he said, "to go in and say, 'Judge, please try to control her behavior. But if you want to hear what I have to say about it, don't throw her in jail for it. Do something else to get her under control, because jail would not work, because one of my children' ... I mean, I don't see anything wrong with that. That seems to me to be a perfectly legitimate request for someone in my position to make."

But, he agreed that "the judge was upset with me, and I was surprised by it, but I still feel that it was an appropriate thing for me to do." The courts exist, he pointed out to Krueger, to heal "these shattered families"—rich or poor. In a word, Dan Broderick was blameless. He did not see himself as one of the "dueling rich" clogging the court system.

Asked about his fining system, he pointed out that no court-ordered support payment was in effect at the time he imposed those "sanctions." Moreover, he said, "I've spent a whole bunch of money [on Betty] out of the goodness of my heart."

He finished the interview with another comment on his perception of Betty's motives. "I don't think there's a lawyer in America who's going to be able to satisfy her, because nobody can get what the law won't allow—and that is everything I have. That's what she wants," he said. "She'd like me to be destroyed, she wants me out of business, she wants me to be held up as an object of ridicule ... She's on a mission from God. Just go check out what she told you."

And so, Krueger and De Wyze did. They checked it all out—and, contrary to Dan Broderick's expectations, they decided the story was worth printing. That's when their honeymoon with Dan came to an end. He promptly threatened to sue the *Reader* if the paper proceeded. His threat was enough to kill the story. "We couldn't afford to take on a big fish like Dan Broderick," said De Wyze. "So we gave up." In August, the editor of the *Reader* wrote Betty a short note, informing her that the story was dead "because we thought we would be subject to charges of invasion of privacy."

Dan had won again. Not until he was dead would De Wyze and Krueger be free to write a full-length account of the Broderick divorce case.

* * *

Power. He had it, she had none. He won every time. First he sealed the courtrooms, and now he was imposing his own personal gag order on her outside the courtroom too. She was as frustrated as she had ever been.

She went home and drew up a three-page, twenty-point leaflet that she entitled "HOUSEWIFE'S REVOLT." Under that, in even larger letters, were the words "I PROTEST." She then listed all that she protested, item by item. Most of it was the same litany that her remaining friends could now recite by heart:

"Dan Broderick legally kidnapping my children and holding them hostage for four years. The day he claimed sole custody NO VISITATION I could find no attorney because of his being President of the San Diego County Bar Association. There was not one word of testimony given by anyone as to my being less than a perfect mother always."

She itemized all that had happened to her, from the four-hour notice sale of her house to her twenty-eight-day jail sentence for calling him names on a machine with his "live-in office girl's" voice on it.

She concluded by saying, "At this point (forty), I have lost, without contest, my home, my children, my possessions, my social standing, my life savings, and my only source of income. I have a jail record and am over $300,000 in debt. I am not a lawyer, but I don't think this is what the California divorce laws are all about." She signed it "Betty A. Broderick."

It was a leaflet designed to humiliate Dan Broderick completely in the eyes of anyone who read it. Friends of Dan and Linda later insisted that Betty had distributed her flyer throughout La Jolla and even downtown, outside Dobson's and other bars, stuffing it under the windshield wipers of parked cars. "I never saw one," Helen Pickard said later, "but some people said they saw them attached to telephone poles in La Jolla."

"That's a fucking lie," said Betty later, scandalized, as she sat in jail for two murders. "Do I look like a crazy person? I gave one leaflet to Dan Broderick and to a few other people, so I can see how he might have thought that—but then he told everybody I was passing them out. It's not true. It would take a wacko to do something like that."

Chapter 23

Linda Wins

June 26, 1988, was Linda's birthday. She was twenty-seven. And, just as he had done nearly twenty years earlier when he gave Betty a portrait of himself on her birthday, Dan Broderick now gave his new love the best gift he could think of. Himself. At long last he proposed.

It was not a quiet proposal at home, or over a candlelit dinner on the bay. Instead, Dan offered his hand to Linda at Dobson's, the most raucous, collegial public place he could find, in the heart of his downtown legal kingdom with all his Irish American drinking buddies looking on. He gave her a pretty emerald and diamond ring, while she blushed and spilled tears of joy, and their friends all laughed and cheered and ordered fresh rounds for the house. Not incidentally, Dan and Linda also announced that they were planning "a new family." Five children at least.

It had taken him six years. But, finally, Linda Kolkena's years of patience had paid off. She would be the new Mrs. Daniel T. Broderick III.

Betty was out of town that week. She had taken the boys to British Columbia on what was supposed to be a fishing trip of two or three weeks. For the first time since 1985, her need for a vacation with her children had outweighed her stubborn refusal to do it unless Dan gave her extra money. This time, she gave up and agreed to pay for it out of her monthly support. So Dan let them go.

But within a week, she cut the trip short and returned home. "NO MONEY," she wrote in her diary, in large, slashing letters. On the same page, in small, tidy script, she also noted, "Dan announces he's getting married. Asshole!" That was all.

But she then called Dan's partner, Bob Vaage, and told him, in reference to the society announcement about Dan's proposal to Linda on bended knee, "By the time I get through with Dan Broderick, he'll be down on both knees!" Wacky Betty, at it again.

"I did it to be funny," she said later, embarrassed. "I didn't think that Dan Broderick on the floor of a bar doing anything was newsworthy—that was his natural position when he was drunk."

"Mom was real quiet when I told her that Dan had proposed to Linda," Kim recalled later. "I was real surprised. I thought she'd be mad enough to kill him then. But she really didn't show any reaction at all until she found out they were going to start a new family."

For her own part, Kim hadn't been too happy about it herself. Her father had reneged on his promise to her that he "wouldn't marry anybody ... I guess I was just afraid, like Mom always said, that if he had a new family, he wouldn't love us as much anymore."

Two weeks later, while Dan and Linda were in Hawaii with her children, Betty checked herself into the care of a La Jolla plastic surgeon for an $8,000 overhaul.

She had her forehead lifted, her eyes lifted, and her stomach tucked. In particular, she told the doctor, she wanted him to erase all signs of her C-section scars.

"I didn't know whether to laugh or cry when I went over there," recalls Candy Westbrook. "There was my friend, with staples still in her head, fat as a pig, and she'd just had her stomach tucked. I wanted to say, 'Betty, this is crazy. Why don't you just go on a DIET?' But I didn't have the heart. She was so completely nuts by then. Just nuts."

"It was like everything else I tried," Betty said later. "It made me feel better for about an hour." Worse, she didn't look any better either.

The same month the mother was getting herself redone, her oldest daughter, Kim, was getting an abortion. According to Betty, Lee stole several hundred dollars from Betty's bank card account to help her sister pay for it.

Adding to Betty's pain, although Kim did finally confide to her mother that she was getting an abortion, she also said she preferred to take a girlfriend with her to the clinic, rather than Betty—but, Betty later discovered that the girlfriend had been Linda. "I went ballistics!" She says. But she never told Kim how she felt. Even today, Betty can't admit to the depth of her hurt about anything, not in any real way.

"I went to Linda," Kim later explained, sadly, "because every doctor I knew hated Dad, and I thought, 'Oh, God, if I get maimed ...' Linda named a good doctor and offered to drive me over. It wasn't that I liked her more than Mom ... but she was closer to my age, and when you're getting an abortion, you just don't want to go through it with a parent!"

But Betty got her revenge, Kim added bitterly. She used the abortion as another example of Dan's irresponsible parenting. "Mom told everybody about it. The whole world knew!"

Betty denies telling more than one friend. Instead, she says, she counseled Kim on alternatives to abortion. "I was willing to raise the child ... it would have actually been great therapy for me. By then, I had no purpose in life at all. I would've loved a little baby."

Compounding the deteriorating mother-daughter relations, Kim also came to Betty's house one evening and stole a batch of Betty's taped phone messages—which Betty herself had recently stolen from Dan's Jaguar, when Kim drove it over.

"What would you do?" asked Betty later from jail, laughing. "There they were, in his glove compartment, all ready to go to his secretary for transcription, so he could use them against me. So of course I took them. Then Kim, the little bitch, came over, because she was so afraid Dan would be mad at her, and ransacked my house, and took them back to him.

"It's scary how much she's like Dan," Betty says today of her oldest daughter. "She only thinks of herself, and she will say whatever her audience wants to hear. She's going to end up in a mental institution by the time she's forty if she doesn't learn some basic honesty." Mothers and daughters. If Betty hears, in her analysis of Kim, echoes of herself, or her views on her own mother, it doesn't show.

Not much could break through Betty's personal preoccupations by the summer of

1988. But Lee's life-style was increasingly forcing its way in. Betty was positive that her daughter, still living mostly with friends, was now back into the drug scene. "Some of her friends were right out of *Nightmare on Elm Street*." She brooded, she worried about what to do, and, of course, she blamed Dan, who had washed his hands of the whole mess.

She returned to her ongoing diary letter to him, and wrote: "Writing Lee out of your will was the most ridiculous, asinine, immature, vindictive thing I have ever heard of. As usual, you use money to CONTROL everyone. You're winning again. Will you be happy with her head on a plate or body on a slab at the morgue? Probably not even then, because she didn't jump to your commands."

But Betty then actually pulled herself together long enough to take some constructive action. She hired private investigators to track down her daughter. They found her at a La Jolla street celebration in August and prodded her into a car where Betty was waiting. She talked her daughter into going to a drug hospital in nearby Encinitas. This one, unlike McDonald's, was a locked-down facility. Once in, Lee was there, in theory, for a month-long program.

The hospital promptly called Dan for both money and a discussion of Lee's treatment, and he went to see his daughter for the first time since she ran away five months earlier. Lee's doctor recommended that she be sent later to a boarding school out of town, away from the influence of her La Jolla pals—an idea Dan supported. But Lee didn't want to go and asked her father if she could come live with him again instead.

Dan agreed, he said later in divorce court—but with three conditions. "I said, 'Well … you can come and live with me, but, one, you will have to stay away from drugs; two, you will have to come in at a reasonable hour at night; three, you're going to have to be nice to your brothers and not abuse them verbally,' like she tends to do. I said, 'When you're ready to live with me, you understand those three conditions—let me know.'"

This time, Betty was even more hopeful than before that Lee's hospitalization might bring Dan to his senses. "But," she says, "he wouldn't even come to the programs for parents. He was too busy."

Even then, Betty could not accept that Linda had won. The former Mrs. Daniel T. Broderick III would still have taken her husband back in a minute. "Well, maybe … but only for the sake of the children," she admitted snappishly from jail years later.

In any case, ten days later, Lee persuaded Betty once again that she was not a true addict, and talked her mother into taking her home again.

Chapter 24

Down

Lee went on her merry way, Betty continued her decline.

She was isolating herself more and more. Sometimes, that summer and fall, she would "just stay in her bedroom all day and cry," according to her maid, Maria Montez. Other times, she would sit in a depressed slump and flip through hundreds of family pictures, which she kept in Rolodex files all over the house. She also had boxes of family memorabilia—including every card Dan ever sent her. They were always the same—large cards with preprinted messages for birthdays, Mother's Day, and anniversaries. His only personal touch, apart from buying the card itself, was to write "Dear Bets" at the top and "Love always, Dan" at the bottom.

And then there were the boxes and boxes of her children's cards and school papers. "To Mommy, Happy Birthday, Love Kimmy," said one, written in the childish scrawl of maybe a sixth-grader. Among the most touching items in her collection was a Halloween essay Rhett had written the year before in third grade: "Every year on Halloween, my mom makes sugar cakes but the special kind are the ones with spiders on them they are not made out of sugar but out of chocolate fudge," the child wrote. "... This year I'm going to have fun fun fun. I'm going to invite [his friend] Evan to my mom's house or Evan is going to invite me to dinner ... If I go to my mom's house ... me and my mom and Evan would all go trick-or-treating ... I'll go to Mom's if Dad lets me go. It's a maybe ... The end."

When she tired of this sentimental journey, she would add to her burgeoning library of clippings from magazines, newspapers, and books. The themes were lately always related to women as victims and survivors.

The loneliness was crippling.

Finally, she reached out and took a stranger into her house. Her new friend was Lucy Peredun, another displaced divorcee with a small daughter. She lived in Betty's pool house for six months. The arrangement was that Peredun would do light housework in exchange for free room and board—"but I think Betty mostly just needed a friend at that point," said Peredun, later a defense witness.

At about the same time, Betty also met Dian Black, another divorce reform activist and paralegal who, in the months to come, would become a loyal friend. A pretty, vivacious woman in her late thirties and mother of two, Black had become an ardent advocate of self-education among women facing divorce after going through a long, ugly custody battle herself. When she heard about Betty, she called her. During the next year, Black spent many evenings listening to Betty's troubles over coffee. Sometimes, she could even drag her out to a movie. Other times, says Black, "She just wouldn't answer the phone for days."

Sporadically, Betty also plunged into self-help efforts, most of them irrelevant to her problems. She took a graphology course that summer, for instance. She joined the Lifetime Health and Nutrition Center, at a cost of $436; then she discovered 'Course in Miracles', a Christian inspirational group which mattered enough to her that, even after she was in jail, she asked for special permission to keep the literature in her room.

But none of it was enough to stop her suicidal free-fall.

Next she began turning her anger on the very people in charge of her fate. Betty's reckless recourse to her yellow writing pad had started months earlier with her letters to Gerald Barry—but from July through September, she expanded her forum to include Dr. [William] Dess, and Judge Murphy himself. It was mind-boggling to behold. Her hateful calls to Dan's machine actually dropped off for several weeks because she was now more preoccupied with telling the "system" how fucked up she thought it was. She behaved like a drunk, without being one.

She wrote long, rambling letters to the judge about Kim's abortion, about Lee's drug problems, and she complained violently about the Broderick divorce file—which had suddenly vanished a few months earlier. The judge thought it was due to some clerical blunder; Betty was convinced that it was just another element of a judicial conspiracy to suppress all evidence of what Dan had been doing to her behind closed doors all these years, The Good Ole Boy Network in action again. Lending credibility to her suspicions, the massive file was eventually recovered—but, coincidentally, not until a few weeks after the Broderick divorce trial was finally concluded in 1989.

She also wrote to Barry again, blasting him for refusing to discuss the divorce case with her. To court-appointed psychologist Dr. Dess she complained that "we have wasted four months" in resolving her joint custody motion. Most of her letters were studded with references to cunts, sluts, assholes, fuckheads, and drunks. Not surprisingly, Dess's first report that fall endorsed the status quo: no visitation. Although he had never met Dan, Betty, or the children, Dess was persuaded from his review of the data supplied by Drs. Sparta, Roth, and others that Betty Broderick was bad for her children. And his opinion was decisive. It did not matter that, in interviews with the judge, all three minor Broderick children had said they wanted to live with their mother. Judge Murphy ruled against changing the custody arrangement, pending the final divorce trial in December.

In another letter to Dess in September, Betty wrote:

"I am still waiting for the statement of a SINGLE FACT that led you to your grandiose conclusion ... In your letter ... I fail to find a single name or fact that leads to your dramatic and totally erroneous conclusion. If I have to tell this story again, I'm going to vomit. How dare you submit such BULLSHIT to a court of law?"

She listed eight reasons why Dan should not have custody. Her husband, among other things, was "a raging alcoholic" and "an abusive, obnoxious, coldhearted, detached father" hated by his children, whom he has "always scared to death by smashing, kicking, etc. when he doesn't get his way." In addition, he "has been openly fucking his office girl since 1983."

From there, she went into an unbelievable seventeen handwritten pages, reiterating her entire story. She even told Dess about the rats and the dogs. The letter is exhausting to read; writing it must have taken her hours. But, by now, Betty's

235

appetite for telling "her story" had become seemingly insatiable. Fury is awesome fuel.

"[He] is a pathologically SICK person who is and has been systematically destroying my four previously happy, healthy, well-adjusted kids, and FOOLS LIKE YOU ARE ALLOWING IT," she told Dess. "There is not a single fact against me as a mother. I am madder than hell at lying, cheating, scumbag Broderick—I have every right to be and would be crazy if I weren't."

Her handwriting got larger and larger as the pages continued. "AND I HAD NO LEGAL REPRESENTATION," she wrote in huge underscored letters on one page, "BECAUSE MR. BRODERICK WOULD NOT RELEASE MY FUNDS TO RETAIN COUNSEL."

She then defined her own view of morality. "You don't need a law degree to know you're getting fucked—I am an intelligent, strong, ethical, terrific person and mother. I know what's right and wrong in this world, and I am willing to stand up for the RIGHT. I am proud of being an example to my children ... Mr. Broderick did not become what he is because he was married to a whiny, weakling of a wife. He knew what I could do for him. He knew I was a better, stronger person than he. He picked the right girl to marry—but he picked the wrong girl to fuck!"

She concluded her letter thusly:

"Now I bet you proper legal assholes are totally shocked by my language. Why won't she just step in the gas chamber and shut her mouth like all the other women before her? BECAUSE IT'S WRONG. Betty Broderick."

And those weren't her only indiscretions of the season.

In August, she walked into Dan's house to pick up her children, and found a brief letter from Dan to his parents lying on a hallway stand. She opened and read it.

It began as just another routine letter to "Dear Mom and Dad" from a son who dutifully reports home on a regular basis, even when he doesn't have much to say. He apologized for taking so long to write. His practice was going well. The kids were fine. He told them what a good time he and his sons had recently had in Hawaii. He reported on Danny's reptile collection—"[He] has several aquariums filled with various species of lizards and snakes." Kim was leaving for the University of Arizona in another week—"It's hard for me to believe I've got a baby daughter leaving for college." He reported on the progress of his home remodeling. The kitchen was a mess, but in three weeks the house would be done. He hoped they would come visit, since it had been four years.

Then he got to the real point of his letter:

"I have some exciting news to share with you," he wrote. "Perhaps you have already heard, as I have been so derelict in not writing sooner. I have asked Linda to marry me. I hope you'll both be happy for me and wish us well. I can understand that you may have mixed feelings about this because of her age, the fact that she is the educational equivalent of Al Kinzler [apparently a neighborhood character from his youth], and, well, she's Dutch, for God's sake, but she makes me happy, she loves me more than I've ever been loved before, and she loves me just the way I am and

236

has no intention of trying to change me ..."

Betty couldn't leave it alone. "It wasn't even Dan's handwriting!" she says today, by way of explaining what would become another display of Betty Broderick mirth and wanton indiscretion. "It was Linda's handwriting. He had dictated a letter to his own parents!"

She went home and parodied Dan's letter—and mailed it to the senior Brodericks in Pittsburgh, these people she had known for so many years, but who had stopped speaking to her when their son did.

"Letter found in Linda's handwriting!" she explained at the top of the page. "Let ME rewrite this letter for Dan."

Then:

"Dear Mom and Dad,

"I'm sorry it's been so long since my last letter. The kids are a mess, we just got back from a very expensive week in Hawaii. They had a horrible time because they really HATE the office cunt I always force them to be with. The boys are miserable living in the slums in a house that says 'do not touch' for children. They have no friends, no activities, and watch TV all day. Kim leaves for Arizona next week. It's a shame with her great looks and brains she's wasting herself there. With all the upset of the divorce her previously straight A's were down to D, F, and incomplete by graduation. I'm happy though. Arizona is real cheap. (Oh, and I forgot! Linda took Kim to get an abortion last week.) It's not one bit hard to believe I have a daughter going to college. Most guys forty-four do—but I HATE being that old. (Notice no mention of Lee in original. She had failed out of the public school I foolishly allowed her to attend, is using drugs, and is wanted by the police for grand theft. I guess she's ticked off I threw her out of the house, threw all of her belongings in the trash, and vindictively 'wrote her out of my will.' *Teenagers!*)

"My kitchen will be redone soon, that will make the TOTAL renovation of my house complete. I have spent the maximum amount of money possible to impress everyone with my importance and make sure there is nothing left that Bets can possibly get half of. Ha! Ha!

"I have some really sickening news to share! After fucking her since early '83, I've asked Linda to marry me!! (If I was Al Kinzler I'd be insulted.) She loves me just as I am—rich and foolish—and won't try to change me ..."

One thing you can say about Betty—she left a helluva paper trail.

Dan's father was not amused. In a formal, typed return letter to his son that month, he congratulated Dan on his engagement. He thought Linda seemed "a classy girl and I hope makes for you a fine wife."

Then he got straight to the matter of the "latest missive from Bets," which he had enclosed:

"Aside from the abominable language, this is overladen with venom and vitriol," he wrote. "I did not show it to your Mother ... I send it along to you only because it may possibly be of use to you in your legal problems with Bets. Her obscene ranting and raving leads me to believe she is truly a demented psychopath; and very probably should be committed. Were I you, I would be concerned for my own and Linda's safety." The elder Broderick urged his son to "take whatever action is appropriate" to protect himself.

He signed off with, "All best wishes. Sincerely," then the one handwritten word: *Dad*.

That fall, Kim began college at the University of Arizona—yet another disappointment to Betty: her daughter had neither the grades nor the interest to enter a more prestigious school.

After a brief return to La Jolla High School, Lee, meantime, had dropped out for good, in favor of correspondence courses. Dan later accused Betty of "paying other children" to do Lee's homework for her. Lee also found a boyfriend, a John Travolta look-alike and would-be model, moved in with him, and they both went to work at a steak house in the Village. In addition, she accumulated so many speeding and traffic tickets that she lost her driver's license. The Broderick sons continued at Francis Parker, not Bishops. It was now their fourth school season without their mother.

But, interestingly, according to her diaries, Dan had apparently made an overture to return the boys to Betty. "Fucking asshole says boys can live here now! Three weeks after Bishops started! No money for clothes or vacations ..." she wrote on September 26. She naturally rejected the whole notion, since nothing had changed. No divorce settlement, no kids. She would never bend. No matter how much it hurt. And it hurt. It was destroying her, in fact. She was a mother without children, a wife without a husband, a woman without a life. But it had been going on so long now that some days she barely noticed how narrow, how obsessed, and how empty she had become. Now she was consumed totally by notions of her "fair share," of the "bargain" Dan had broken, of his refusal to "settle" with her. Her threats to kill him increased, too. But nobody paid much attention. It was just Betty's flamboyant way of talking.

But, in fact, Dan was still trying to reach an out-of-court settlement—on his terms. In late September he sent her yet another proposed property settlement plan. (He was still working on the alimony issue, he advised; and he did not mention the custody issue.) This one was a five-page document. The bottom line was: he was now prepared to give her a cash settlement of $180,563.

He calculated the value of his law practice at $1.4 million and the pension plan at another $478,163. Both these figures were based, not on current value, but on their value at the time of the separation, which Dan and the courts consistently set at February 28, 1985, the day he walked out. At that time, according to Dan's calculations, their community property also included about $57,000 more in various small partnerships. He meticulously added in the value of his bank accounts on the day he moved out, too: His personal checking account then held $260, his personal savings account another $46. The reason for these scanty accounts, he later explained at the divorce trial, was because he kept most of his money in his law firm account.

The total of all these numbers came to $1.9 million. That, said Dan, was the value of their community property—at the date of separation.

He therefore owed her, he estimated, exactly $967,716.

But then, he began his subtractions for money she owed him.

He claimed $948,581 in Epstein credits. This was the sum of all debts he had paid on their community investments prior to the 1985 separation, he told her. Her half of those Epstein debts, he said, was $474,291.

In addition, he was charging her another $200,438 for cash advances since February 1985. This included the $140,438 down payment he had made on her house at Calle del Cielo, plus the extra money she had received on Coral Reef, plus another $20,000 paid to her and Hargreaves in 1986.

Thus, between Epsteins and cash advances, her debt to him came to $674,729.

If she accepted his proposed property division, he also calculated that she would owe him an additional $112,334, because that was the difference between the value of the assets she would receive and his.

Which brought her total debt to him to $787,063.

That left her with $180,563 cash due from him. He would keep his law practice, and his house. She would keep her house, the furniture already in her possession, the piano, and the Warner Springs ownership. He would keep their investments in Colorado condominiums, office buildings, and lots in the fashionable ski resort of Telluride, nearly all of them money-losers, according to Dan.

Betty studied the document in astonishment.

What kind of fool did he think she was? How did the pension plan shrink to $480,000 when it had been worth at least $650,000 two years earlier, by his own admission? What about the hundreds of thousands he had lent his brother Larry?

Why was she obliged to pay half of the losses on his bad investments when she had no control over them? How was the piano now worth $12,000, when they had only paid $8,000 for it in the first place? And so on. A million other items swirled and clanged through her head. She even remembered the long-gone $37,000 Corvette. Where was her half of that? No. Wait. Now she remembered—Barry had called it a company car. Right.

Where was he getting these values from?? What a lying, cheap sonofabitch. Still, Betty didn't pick up the telephone and start another search for an attorney. She didn't hire an appraiser. She didn't even call a Telluride realtor and ask what the going price was for lots in the area where she and Dan had invested. She didn't do anything.

Even now, after all she had been through, Betty Broderick hadn't the foggiest notion that it was finally hardball time.

Dan, meantime, was busy ingratiating himself with Dr. Dess. In a brief but strikingly personalized note to Dess that month, Dan thanked the doctor for his efforts, but warned him that his recent letter to Betty "will undoubtedly trigger a venomous attack on your integrity and competence." He also confided to Dess that many of Betty's "former friends" had called him over the last three years in frustration, wondering how to persuade her to seek psychotherapy. But, he concluded, "I firmly believe that there is no hope for her or for anyone whose life is dependent upon her for stability or the development of self-restraint."

If William Dess had never met either Dan or Betty Broderick personally before forming his earlier opinions, he had now, on the eve of the divorce trial, met both of them through their respective letters. In their own ways, one so diplomatic, the other so destructive, both Brodericks had done everything conceivable to color his final judgment.

Throughout the fall, Betty hurtled heedlessly onward. She complained to her diaries of back pains, stress, insomnia. The boys were with her most weekends, including Halloween.

Then, at the end of October, Dan wrote Betty a polite two-paragraph letter, asking if she wanted to share the children with him over the Thanksgiving and Christmas holidays. This was not the same man who had just written William Dess, basically calling his ex-wife hopelessly unstable, if not nuts, and worrying about her damaging impact on his children. This time, he even gave her two full weeks to reply.

But she didn't even open the letter. It was the Notre Dame weekend again. She knew he was going. Taking the cunt. Now his fiancee. Soon to be his wife. He was looking for a free baby-sitter again. Either that, or Dan was nearly as emotionally inconsistent as Betty. She returned the letter to his office with "WIFE-BEATER" slashed across it in big, embarrassing letters.

It annoyed Dan Broderick in the extreme. As soon as he got it, he dictated a letter to Dr. Gerald Nelson, whom Betty intended to call into court in her behalf on the custody matter, to say that he had "reluctantly come to the conclusion that there is just no way I can voluntarily surrender custody of my sons to my ex-wife. I honestly don't believe she is emotionally capable of taking care of them in her present mental state."

Dan had met with Nelson a few weeks earlier to discuss the custody situation. He had not been impressed—mainly because, as he would later say in divorce court, Nelson immediately told him to give Betty however much money she wanted, in order to promptly resolve the custody dispute, which was only hurting the children.

"Basically he [was] saying if she gets everything you have, then maybe, maybe, she will be able to bury it and be with the boys," Dan said. "And I went back and thought a lot about that, and I didn't think that opinion was worth the air he used to give it to me ..."

A few days afterward, he wrote Nelson another letter thanking him for his efforts to solve "this intractable problem," but saying, in effect, no thanks, he would see Nelson in court. No way would he relinquish custody of the boys to Betty. He cited her "wife-beater" comment to Nelson as one of the latest reasons why. "Aside from the fact that I never, in all the years I was married to her, laid a hand on her in anger, I view that method of communication as bizarre to say the least."

In retrospect, it was perhaps almost inevitable that Betty Broderick would eventually kill in the month of November. It had become her most nightmarish month, as a glimpse at both her household calendar of 1988 and her diaries would later show. Always a holiday-oriented person, so occasion-minded that she never forgot a birthday or an anniversary, she had measured out her life in sentimental dates. But now, with chilling care, she was remembering new anniversaries in her diaries, circling them with big black slashes on her calendars.

Especially in November. November 1, she wrote in her 1988 diary, was the second anniversary of her first jailing after she had gone to protest the minus $1,300 check. November 7 was now not only her birthday "but the fifth anniversary of slitting of wrists." His birthday, on November 22, was now "fifth anniversary of clothes burning."

Even Christmas was no longer Christmas, the time of her once glorious parties, filled with laughter and fun and accolades from all. Instead, in Betty Broderick's mind, it would forevermore be "the real date of our separation, the first time he went public with Linda the Cunt Kolkena in front of my young children on that ski trip."

It was just one more layer of Betty Broderick's personality that had been stripped away and deadened by this interminable scorched-earth divorce war. But it was a loss that remained in the interior of her mind, invisible to everyone but her. Betty kept a lot of herself hidden in those last months.

Now her focus had turned to Kim, who was being nickle-and-dimed to death, in Betty's view, by her stingy father. It began when Dan put Kim on a budget at college. It was time she learned some financial responsibility, he said.

Kim wailed to Betty. Dad wasn't giving her enough. She was living like a bum. She didn't have enough clothes. She had no travel money. Once she even told Betty that she had no food. Dan Broderick was whistling in the wind if he thought he was going to teach a child of his and Betty's financial discretion overnight. But, typically, he was stubbornly determined.

Matters came to a head when Kim ran up a $400 phone bill one month. Dan refused to pay it—"Get acquainted with the U.S. Postal Service," he told her. And so her phone was disconnected. She promptly ran crying to her mother, who immediately paid the bill, cursing Dan Broderick to hell as she did.

The result of Betty's habitual rush to the rescue was of course predictable: Kim's phone bill was just as large the next month. And, again, Betty paid. She was no more responsible than Kim was, and, years later from jail, she even admitted it.

"I was always spending money I didn't have. I went into more and more debt on my credit cards, etc., because I paid Kim's phone bills. But I just couldn't cut her off. I wanted her college experience to be comfortable and fun. Dan and I had the best undergraduate educations our parents could afford, so why shouldn't our kids, too? I felt so bad that Kim didn't have a car that I even bought that for her, too—which, of course, she crashes before the first payment was even due ..."

Betty was also driven by the same strangling old resentments of Dan's life-style. Every dollar her children didn't get, Linda Kolkena did. It infuriated her that while Dan was doling out $300 or $400 at a time to his daughter, he was spending a fortune on himself and Linda. His home remodeling had cost at least $300,000. His sports cars and wardrobe were lavish to the point of ostentation. And now Linda Kolkena was wearing designer labels, too.

When Kim came home for Thanksgiving break that fall, Betty took her on a

241

shopping spree to San Francisco. "I bought her shit from one end of the town to the other, all on credit cards, just so she would feel good. So she wouldn't feel deprived because her parents were divorced. She went back to school with suitcases full of ski jackets and all kinds of gorgeous stuff ... we had fun ..."

Later, in jail, prior to her first trial, Betty Broderick only sounded bewildered at the news that Kim had joined the prosecution camp and was calling her mother, among other things, a spendthrift who made Kim feel guilty by spending money on her that Kim knew Betty didn't have.

"The little bitch! Now she says that. She was happy enough to get all those beautiful clothes and my money at the time. Besides," added Betty, suddenly sounding drained, "I thought I was doing her a favor. I was turning myself inside out, getting further into debt, thinking I was doing it for her good. Now she's going to punish me for it?"

Indeed she was.

On November 14, her diaries reflected more of her escalating miseries and fears:

"storm electricity out

"court at 8:30 A.M.

"HARASSMENT TRAUMA [huge letters, half the page]

"skin a mess   10 lbs. in a week   nails bitten to blood

"no sleep anxiety depression."

A few days later, she resentfully wrote that not only were Dan and Linda turning her into their baby-sitter, but all her old friends were, too. For the first time, this woman who once thrived on the sounds of children laughing and playing around her house was furious that two of Danny and Rhett's friends were there: "Matt Currie here (parents had party). Evan here (parents had funeral). Betty is kids dumping ground! Shit!" Her handwriting slanted wildly across the pages, as tilted as her thinking.

On Thanksgiving Day, she cooked a meal, according to another bleak little diary notation:

"Thanksgiving! gold ware. new china. Candles. Crystal. turkey mashed gravy stuffing broccoli corn yams rolls and butter champagne. Nightmare!" The day after Thanksgiving, she was obsessed with her health: "Comatose time. Severe anxiety. Back out. Down left leg severe pain. Blurry vision day and night. Insomnia (black circles). Headache. Skin breakout. Severe depression and fatigue. Major anxiety over total situation."

That day, too, she noted that she had called the Battered Women Services Hotline, the Women's Legal Center, and a local women's resource center. But apparently none of them could help, assuming they could even understand what this exploding woman was trying to tell them. By the end of the month, some of her diary entries were almost illegible.

And then it was December again, another Christmas without a family. She was fighting with Lee again.

"Lee calls me a 'fucking bitch' after I spent $1,000 on skis!" she wrote angrily on December 3 in her diary. On December 12, Kim had an appendicitis attack. Dan flew over to see her. Betty blamed it on the stress he had caused Kim over money.

That same day, she wrote that she had missed her Investment Club meeting. "Too depressed." The next day, she skipped the St. Germain Silver Tea. "Too depressed."

Still, she proceeded as if there was no tomorrow. The only thing she had done in her own best interests all year was make several visits to Dr. Gerald Nelson—sixteen sessions, according to her records. She was at least complying with the court-ordered "program of therapy" as a condition of any custody change.

And, finally, the Broderick divorce trial was about to begin. Four years after Dan left her, Betty Broderick was at last going to get her day in court. The property settlement would be adjudicated; her monthly support would no longer be court-designated as merely temporary; and she fully expected to regain custody of her three minor children.

But then, in mid-December, she got word that yet another postponement was in the works. According to Betty, she stormed into Judge Murphy's office "in my sweats, and I told him he would have to arrest me on the spot, that I wasn't leaving until I got a trial date. Dan Broderick was going to marry Linda Kolkena before he had even settled with me, and after that, it would have become impossibly confusing. Who owned the pension plan, who owned what? Me or her? She would've gotten more from being married to him a week than I got after sixteen years."

Barry was there that day, she says. And both he and Murphy tried to persuade her to reconsider, to wait until she got an attorney.

But Betty didn't want an attorney. She had decided months ago to represent herself in her final legal battle with Dan Broderick. She would appear "*in propria persona*," or "*pro se*," as it is known in legalese, when one party decides to go to court without an attorney. Her reasoning was simple: nobody knew what a sneaky cheat Dan Broderick was better than she did. She could expose him herself. "And there was so much history to this case. No attorney could've caught up with it. Besides it would've just cost me another small fortune in attorney fees."

That was her official line. What she never would admit was that she also didn't want any pin-striped stranger standing between her and her former husband, the father of her children, the man who had promised to love her until the twelfth of never.

At long last, Dan would have to talk to her. She would have him cornered on a witness stand. He would finally have to publicly explain how he had left her, the perfect wife and mother, for the office cunt, and why. He would have to explain, on the record, why he had the mother of his children jailed, why Rhett's ears were dirty, how many times he had gotten drunk, how many piano recitals he had missed. She didn't care about money. She wanted to talk. She wanted Dan Broderick to say he was sorry. She wanted him to stand up in the middle of the trial, admit the error of his ways, and come back home where he belonged.

That Christmas, the children shuttled back and forth between the two houses. For the first time in four years, Dan and Betty Broderick didn't engage in a punishing standoff over money for ski trips because, for the first time in four years, Betty was too preoccupied preparing her case to bicker over the small stuff.

Chapter 25

Divorce Trial

She stared into her closet that Christmas, pulling out all her frumpy, boring matron's suits. She studied herself closely in the mirror for the first time in months. Sometimes it shocked even her, how much she had changed in two years. Her complexion was splotchy, her face webbed with fine lines of strain and exhaustion, her jowls drooped with weight. She looked years older than she was. She could not look good for this, her first close encounter with her former husband in years.

The most she could hope for was an air of self-assurance. For that, she pulled out all her four-inch pumps. She wore her big shoes to court every day.

She spent the holiday season at her kitchen table, poring over her stacks of legal documents from years past, stealing snatches from arguments Tricia Smith had made two years earlier, sorting through receipts, and, beyond all else, thinking of all the questions she would finally be able to ask him, all the answers he would have to give. She jotted her case down on her yellow legal pads. "Where were you when baby died?" she wrote at the top of one list.

Friends begged her to come to her senses. What was she doing, walking into that courtroom alone, with $1 million in Epsteins and her children at stake? Hire a lawyer, they urged. Any lawyer was better than none.

No. She was through with that rat race. She was sick of it all, plus she had to hurry, before he married the office girl.

She arrived in the courtroom of Judge William J. Howatt, Jr., on December 27 accompanied only by her friend Ronnie Brown.

In his first order of business, Dan's attorney, Barry, asked that the Broderick divorce case remain closed to the public for the sake of the Broderick children. Betty objected, "on principle," as she had for years, but lost. Howatt did agree, however, that Ronnie Brown could remain, for moral support.

And so, up went the heavy brown paper, covering the small window pane on the courtroom door so passersby could not even see who was sitting inside. A large sign was posted. *CLOSED*.

Betty asked if the missing divorce file had yet been located. No, it had not been found. However, Howatt told her, the court had reconstructed a partial file, with the help of Mr. Barry's records. She had not been asked to provide her own input.

Trial commenced.

Barry's opening statement was a brief summary of the issues to be resolved: property settlement, child custody, and spousal support. However, he alerted Howatt, "a problem of major proportions" would involve a substantial amount in Epstein credits, as well as sizable deductions for cash advances made to Betty in past years.

He thought spousal support might entail significant argument, too

Howatt then asked Betty if she would like to make an opening statement now, or wait until she began her case.

"Isn't this the beginning of the case?" she asked, confused. "I can make an opening statement ... I don't have one prepared but I can make it." It was a question. He didn't reply.

So she stood, and, in her best "Welcome to the Francis Parker Mothers Club" fashion, told the judge, in part:

"I'm happy to be here, finally, to get some resolution of this case ... I'm trying to get back some semblance of normalcy in a life that's been under siege for six years ... We have millions of dollars' worth of property, none of which has my name on it. In most cases I have no knowledge of what it's worth, what we paid for it, what the debts are. I have no idea about the property. I have lists that Mr. Broderick has submitted. My support—I would just like to be able to go on living ... I hope that we can settle something. Thank you."

The trial lasted eight days. It was lamb to the slaughter from the git-go. Dan Broderick and Gerald Barry danced together with the easy grace of Fred and Ginger. They were smooth, practiced, professional, and poised. Their goals were clear, their preparation exhaustive, their demeanor subdued and mature. They were good lawyers.

It was a testament to Betty Broderick's extraordinary tenacity, instinctive intelligence, and chameleon personality that she was able to pull herself together enough to perform in divorce court as well as she did. It was a measure of her madness that she even tried. It also speaks volumes about the judicial system that this woman who had been jailed, committed to a mental institution, and now was clearly walking the ragged edge, was even allowed to proceed in her own behalf.

Like a candle in the wind, she was, at one minute bright, even brilliant, in her thoughts; in the next moment, her intelligence flickered dimly, illuminating nothing except her own pathetic decline.

Throughout the proceedings, she shrugged, apologized, and played her same old game. She was still Miss Goody-Two-Shoes, cute and coy, trusting to the end, as she had all her life, that things would work out, once she had charmed the men in charge with her own innocence.

Thus, she accepted Dan's financial figures almost without question—and trusted in Judge William J. Howatt, Jr., to see that justice was done. After all these years, Betty had learned nothing. This judge did not come to her rescue, any more than the others had. Only rarely would he even tip her on how properly to frame a question to escape Barry's unrelenting objections. He accepted evidence that she didn't even know she may have had a right to protest. Nor would he give her lessons in Epsteins.

Unfortunately for her, none of the three men in this courtroom was sympathetic to her ingratiating ways. Nor did it help that she was so incongruously packaged—wide-eyed helplessness, confusion, and a little-girl voice, wrapped in the hulking 5'10" body of an Amazon who dwarfed most of the men around her, former husband included. It was just another one of God's bad tricks that, given her personality, Betty Broderick wasn't born a petite 5'2" china doll.

What Dan and Gerald Barry wanted, basically, was to deny Betty Broderick almost everything she wanted. In specific, they asked the court to agree that Dan had accumulated nearly $1 million in Epstein credits, half of it payable by Betty—and they wanted the judge to value Dan's law practice, not at its current 1988 worth, but at its value at the time of separation in 1985, four years earlier. They wanted a property settlement based on their figures, which showed that, sadly, Dan Broderick had suffered significant losses on nearly every investment he had ever made during the course of his marriage to Betty. Not least, they wanted the judge to reduce her monthly support from $16,000 to $9,000, at most—and that for no more than a year. After that, Dan wanted to pay her $5,000 monthly for a limited time, perhaps two more years, followed by nothing at all, since, by then, Betty should have found a job and, as Barry put it, become "a contributing member of society."

And, finally, they wanted Dan to retain custody of the two boys on grounds that the rage Betty felt over the divorce had rendered her an unfit mother.

Betty's goals were just as clear as Dan's. She wanted the same $4 million package she and Tricia Smith had sought nearly two years earlier: $25,000 a month for ten years, plus $1 million in cash. Neat and clean. She didn't want to haggle over the value of pianos, boats, Corvettes, Colorado condominiums, or any other items of community property.

She also wanted the three minor children. It was not she who was the unfit parent, she said, but Dan. He was not only a controlling, insensitive, neglectful father, he was also an alcoholic who wouldn't face his problem. He had cruelly harassed and manipulated her into her indiscrete rages by using the children against her—and then punished her for it. He had been lying and cheating her ever since he met Linda in 1983, and his brother Larry had been helping him shuffle assets out of her reach. He had deliberately delayed the divorce settlement in order to accumulate even more Epstein credits. He had been buying time. He wanted to leave his wife and family, "but he didn't want to pay the price for it."

Barry's case came first. For the next day and a half, Barry marched Dan systematically through the Broderick family finances and custody issues.

The financial figures Barry presented were roughly the same as those in Dan's September settlement offer—except now Betty's share had shrunk even further. Most of his losing investments, Dan said, were connected to his Colorado ventures with his brother Larry. He blamed the decline on the collapse of oil prices in the early eighties, which had caused real estate in Colorado, "an energy state," to collapse. "I don't like it. I'm sure that Bets doesn't like it. I know my brother doesn't like it. But that's it."

To cite just one example, a Denver office building Dan partially owned had lost about $60,000 during the last few years, he said. He was charging Betty Epstein credits for half that loss. Other properties in Colorado—lots in Dillon, the Keystone condo—would also cost her in losses. Even the property in Telluride, now one of America's most fashionable ski resorts, was worth only about $700 per acre—half its earlier value—according to information provided to Dan by his brother.

Howatt accepted this secondhand appraisal from brother Larry without question—although, later on, he would not permit Betty to introduce even a letter from her accountant on grounds it was hearsay unless the witness was present and sworn.

According to Dan, among his few investments to actually appreciate in value since he left Betty was the Warner Springs unit near San Diego, bought in 1984. He estimated that, although Warner's had a remaining debt of $8,000, its equity was around $16,000. He proposed that Warner's "go to Bets ... because she uses it and seems to enjoy it." He, meantime, wanted to keep title to all the disastrous Colorado investments with his brother Larry.

In effect, Dan testified that his only real wealth was in his law practice. And he intended to give her half of that—based on its 1985 value. The actual value of Dan Broderick's law practice as of December, 1988, would never even be introduced into this trial, because Betty never pressed for it.

But an expert appraiser called by Barry was firm in his testimony that, as of the date of separation, Dan's law practice was worth only $1,495,000.

There would be few terms more significant in this entire trial than "date of separation." Gerald Barry referred to it in every other breath—for what it meant was that, although Epstein credits on debts Dan was paying continued to accrue right up the present, the value of the community property assets was frozen "at the date of separation" four years earlier.

When it was Betty's turn to examine the appraiser, after first excusing herself one more time for her ignorance, she actually got to the heart of the matter quickly. How had he arrived at his numbers? she asked. Where had he gotten his information on the number of cases settled before and after the separation?

From Mr. Broderick and Mr. Barry, said the appraiser. They were the sole source of his working data.

And why hadn't he valued the practice to the present? Betty asked.

Because, he said, neither Mr. Barry nor Mr. Broderick had asked him to do so.

But then, as would be her maddening wont throughout the trial, Betty simply dropped the line of questioning and sat down. The witness was excused.

Cash advances came next. Dan wanted reimbursement for every dollar he had given her, above and beyond court-ordered payments, since he left—including the $140,000 down payment he had made on her del Cielo house. Which brought that total to about $210,000, atop the nearly $500,000 in Epsteins.

Not until years later would Betty even think to wonder why she had to reimburse Dan for the down payment he made on her Calle del Cielo house, when he didn't have to repay her equally for the down payment on his Cypress house, since they weren't even divorced at the time of either house purchase. Enter again the magic phrase—"at the time of separation." Although both houses had been bought prior to their divorce, from the day Dan moved out, it was all his money, not hers.

Concerning Betty's monthly support, Dan thought her itemized expenses were outrageous. No man, whatever his income, should be asked to pay his ex-wife $16,000 a month, much less $25,000, he protested. "It seems unbelievably high to me. I can pay it. I can pay it at least right now. [But] when I consider how many people live on so much less than that and that this is just for one person—one able-bodied, intelligent, well-educated person—it seems to me that it's an awfully large amount of money for me to have to pay every month."

Besides, he pointed out, since he left Betty, he had already paid her a whopping amount of money: $192,638 in voluntary monthly support alone; then, in response to the court-ordered $16,000 in 1986, another $402,500; for a total of nearly $600,000 in support alone over a four-year period. Adding in the cash advances, plus distributions from various sales of their assets, such as the Fairbanks Ranch lots, the total he had paid her so far was well over a million dollars—$1,083,387, to be exact (minus, of course, $24,000 in court-ordered fines and Dan's attorney fees).

As for Betty's claimed monthly expenses, Dan thought them ludicrous— $1,000 for a gardener? He thought $300 was plenty. Her food and household supply budget of $850 "should be more like $500"—it didn't cost him that much, he said, to feed himself and four children for a month. Her $200 monthly phone bill should be reduced to $50—his monthly average, with three children, he said, was only $51. As for her $2,000 clothing budget, Dan said he spent only $586 a month on himself and four children. Thus, $500 for her was more than fair. Not least, he also thought her $4,500 monthly mortgage was unreasonable, too. He didn't see why a single woman alone needed such a large, expensive house. She should move to more modest accommodations.

Turning to his own resources, he agreed that, even at the time of separation in 1985, his annual income had been $1,332,444. But, by the time he was finished with overhead and taxes, he argued, the amount wasn't nearly so grand. In reality, his net monthly income was only about $65,000, he said. From that, he paid himself $36,000 every month—but, after taxes, that actually amounted to only about $22,600. Simple arithmetic, of course, says that would have been nearly impossible, since Betty's monthly support alone came to $16,000. And Dan eventually conceded that, sometimes, whenever his checking account ran low, he would "take a bonus from the corporation." It was a shell game.

Even so, by the time Barry was through, a casual listener might have wondered how poor Dan Broderick scraped by. Moreover, Dan added, he expected to have to tighten his financial belt even more severely very soon. Not only because he was now sending a daughter to college, but also because "I'm getting married on April 22. I'll be starting a new family. I anticipate there will be additional expenses in connection with that."

Barry then turned to the custody issue. Dan wanted the two boys, but not seventeen-year-old Lee. That was clear from the outset, although he didn't state it so baldly. Instead, he told the judge, sounding saddened, Lee "has no use for me ... she does not value my advice. She basically thinks I'm a worthless, ignorant individual who has no concept of what's good for her or what's not. The last time I saw her was about three weeks ago, when she came over for money and I wouldn't give it to her. Her mother and sister tell me that she uses the money I give to her for drugs. She walked out of my house. This was in early December, and she used a few four-letter words, called me an asshole, and got into her mother's car. And as she was leaving, she threw a glass at my car ...

"Lee is in deep trouble and she needs help," he continued. "But ... she has a strong enough will that she will resist help until she gets it herself. No one has custody of Lee ..." Nor did he think Lee was even close to being willing to obey his rules. And, he finished, pointedly, "She will not come to my house if she is going to use drugs, and if she does not come home at a decent hour, and be disruptive and cause problems for my sons. That's not going to happen."

His two sons were a different matter. He wanted full custody—"for their benefit." He agreed both boys had initial adjustment problems, being separated from their mother. But now, Dan thought, both were "normal and doing well."

And so was he, as a single dad. He saw them off to the school bus each morning, he said. He was home "99 percent of the time" to help them with their schoolwork, play basketball, visit ice cream parlors, watch TV, play checkers or video games. In between, the housekeeper was always there to supervise and prepare meals. If they were "with their mom on the weekend," he said, "Bets" would pick them up, usually on Friday evenings, and then return them home on Sunday evenings.

It sounded almost like an Alan Alda movie. In this picture there were no unpleasantries, no children threatening suicide, or running away. No hidden telephones in closets, no children acting as go-betweens in visitation because their parents didn't speak—and certainly there were no pretty young girlfriends in the mix. Instead, in this wishful picture, everything was neat, clean, and civil. The real mom might have been a sepia photograph sitting on the mantle, forever lovely and young and cherished, dead, perhaps, from childbirth or some tragic accident or sad disease, long before her time. Forever "Bets."

But Bets was still there, sitting in the courtroom, big and belligerent and only biding her time until she finally got her chance to confront Dan Broderick with six years of rising, blinding resentments.

And, at last, it was her turn to cross-examine the witness.

She began on a typically apologetic note.

"I don't have any firsthand knowledge of any of these numbers that have been put before me, nor do I have at my disposal accountants, lawyers, paralegals, or secretaries. I have no exhibits to put in front of the court." She couldn't stop. "I don't type," she went on. "I don't own a typewriter. I have never worked in an office," she told the judge. "I don't know the law or really the rules of trial. But I will try to play the game as best I can," she finally finished, "if you will just tell me as I go along."

Howatt didn't answer.

Thus did Betty Broderick step, like Alice in Wonderland, through the looking glass and into the world of no-fault divorce. The tone of the next six days was set from the minute she opened her mouth to ask her former husband her first question.

It would always be hard to know who to feel sorrier for: Dan, pinned into the witness stand like an impaled butterfly while his ex-wife stalked before him, spitting out questions built on six years of rising rage; or Betty, the needy, naive woman-child, now presiding so wantonly over her own destruction for no larger gain than the immediate satisfaction of interrogating the infidel at last.

"Mr. Broderick, when did this case really start?"

"February 28, 1985," he said.

"Is that when you estimate this case started?" she challenged.

"Well, the case actually started in October of 1985 when I filed the [divorce] action," he said.

"When did this divorce actually start?" she persisted.

"At our separation, if that's what you mean," said Dan, trying to satisfy her.

"No, no," she lectured. "When did this divorce start?" He was tired of her interrogation already.

"I guess April 12, 1969, to tell you the truth," he said. Their wedding day.

It would be the single most hurtful remark he made in trial. Years later, she would still feel the sting of it. "How could the sonofabitch take away all the good memories, too?" she once asked from jail, on the verge of tears. "Just because he wanted to leave me for Linda Kolkena, why did he have to erase our whole life together? We had so many good times ..."

But that day, she stayed on track. "No ... All right. What I'm trying to get at," she told him, "is when did I first become aware of your affair with Linda Kolkena?"

Barry objected. The question was irrelevant. Howatt agreed and delivered his first lecture to Betty about the nature of no-fault divorce proceedings.

"In California," he told her, "as you may have become aware, the issue is not one of whose fault the divorce was, because it is no longer a fault proceeding. We do not have the issue of finding fault with one party as opposed to the other. We are only here to decide the questions of division of property, the assets of the community, your interest and his interest in those assets, and the determination of the appropriate parent for custody of the children."

Betty argued it. "I understand those facts," she said. "But I [also] understand that my interest in the community was improperly manipulated for two and a half years purposely and with malice before this case was filed by an expert attorney. That's very important to my case!" Her questions were aimed at showing, she said, how Dan had begun to cut her out of their community assets from the time he began his affair with Linda.

Okay, said Howatt. "Let's start ... and see if there is anything that you can develop with regard to the assets. You have to relate to the assets, okay? And not to any alleged affair or liaison." He also told her to stop talking so fast and interrupting him and the witness. Betty agreed—and then resumed exactly where she had left off.

"Do you remember what my reaction was when you hired this girl?" she asked next.

"Your Honor," Barry protested, "I don't want to make it difficult on Ms. Broderick, but I don't see the relevance of the question."

"Again," Howatt told Betty, "we are dealing with the area of fault."

She vowed to move on to the matter of the houses.

But Betty would never really move on until she felt like it. When she wanted, she could be dense as mud and tenacious as an army of cockroaches. "Do you remember me telling you to get rid of Linda Kolkena, meaning off your payroll, by October 1, or get out of my house?" she asked.

He remembered.

Barry objected. Sustained. Again Howatt lectured her. Lay off the alleged affair!

Betty ignored them both. Instead she went into an interrogation about the events on his thirty-ninth birthday when she had gone to his office, found party remnants, and, that night, ordered him to move out of the house. Dan evidently looked to Barry for rescue.

"Don't look at your attorney!" Betty snapped at him. "Answer the question!" She was clearly beginning to enjoy herself. At long last, she was in charge.

Barry objected again. Why couldn't the judge make her stop? "Okay, okay," said Betty, waving Barry away. "Let's change the whole subject. Let's talk about the financial structure of our family. Would that make you happier?"

"Yes, ma'am," said Gerald Barry.

But she did not go directly to family finances or anything else. Instead, for the next three days, it was free-form. Whatever came to mind, she asked.

Eventually, she would wear down every man in this courtroom. Gerald Barry's objections, which were constant at first, became increasingly sporadic, arbitrary, and listless. Sometimes he would protest, but other times—even when Betty was interrogating Dan about his alleged drug and sex habits—he would just let it go. Let her get it off her chest, let her mouth run its course; in the end, she would pay. And, unless Barry objected, Howatt usually let her follow whatever meandering path she chose. Not that his efforts to control her made any difference anyway. During the course of the trial Howatt probably lectured her fifty times about no-fault laws, all in vain. By the end, his black robes of authority were as tattered as a beggar's rags, his grave preachments reduced to the comic rat-a-tat chorus of a Woody Woodpecker cartoon.

In the next days, the Brodericks bickered over nearly everything from wallpaper to investments. But the personal attacks were the nastiest. She called him an irresponsible drunk who engaged in immoral sexual conduct in front of his children; he said she was so consumed with hate that he had told the children their mother was mentally unbalanced.

As it now stood, he said, when the children asked to visit her, "I have to say, I don't know when you will be able to see her. It depends when she gets over this thing.'"

And just when had he begun accusing her of being mentally ill? she demanded.

Hadn't that begun in 1983—only after he met Linda? His reply was hard.

"I don't know when I first came to the conclusion that you had an emotional problem," he said. "It might have been '83, it might have been '69. It's been a long time, Bets."

She ignored that. And just what was "this thing?" she asked.

"This 'thing' is really the whole heart and soul of the case," he shot back. "It is the antipathy you feel toward me—and I understand that, I might say. I understand your anger. I understand your hatred. I understand. The thing is, you're using it against them [the children]. You are venting it in front of them and directly to them ... When you can come to grips with this hatred and hostility you have for me and direct it in other ways and not around them, then we will be at peace—and until that happens, this is never going to end."

She argued with him. "This thing," in her opinion, was the fact that he had legally bludgeoned her for years.

"No, ma'am ... When this court makes its decision," he retorted, "that will not end this problem that you have. There will be hundreds of other incidents that will trigger hostility on your part ... unless or until you get the kind of help you need to channel your anger in other ways ... Honestly, I don't think, Bets, that you have a legitimate basis with being unhappy ... I don't think there is any amount of money in this world that is going to be sufficient for you. You want me, you want my money, you want my death or my ruination in this community. You want me destroyed, and over and done with, and unless and until that happens, you are not going to be happy."

She acted as if she had not heard him.

She returned instead to the subject ever-present on her mind. Linda.

Hadn't he said in the past that the children never saw him do any more than kiss Linda Kolkena on the cheek?

"I said ... put my arm around her and kiss her on the cheek, that is all they have ever seen," Dan replied.

"You're totally unaware," she asked, "of Danny and Rhett looking in the door at Linda and you in bed together with her legs up in the air many times?"

"That has not happened," he said. For some reason, Barry didn't object. The bizarre exchange continued.

"Are you unaware of their reports to me that they have done such?"

"The door to my room is locked, my bedroom, if that is what you are referring to. I don't know what the boys have told you. They tell you what they think you want to hear." Which was probably true. It was Betty whose mind and eyes were so painfully locked on his bedroom, not the children's.

"And are you aware of the reports from the older girls of Linda parading around the house in see-through nightgowns?"

"Linda does not and never has done that, and I can't imagine the girls would tell you otherwise," he said.

But their friends also said so, she countered, taunting.

"This is an outrage!" he finally exploded. "That does not happen."

252

It was ugly, it was silly, it was sad, and it was sometimes even laughable—except, even in January of 1989, there was always the cast of death overhanging it all, in remarks by both him and her, and even two of the later witnesses. In hindsight, it seems eerily obvious that both Dan and Betty Broderick knew, at least on some instinctive level, that they truly were wed until death did them part.

Betty Broderick's interrogation of her former husband had not begun so harshly. For the first couple of hours of her cross-examination, she had in fact dwelt only on the early years, on their mutual dreams, their plans for a glorious future together. She was trying to call him home from across a courtroom.

Her initial questions were at times pitiful in their pleading nature. It was "Dan" throughout. Didn't Dan remember how they had lived, during that first year of marriage? On her salary, driving her car—that they had even spent her small savings?

No, he didn't remember. It was like pulling teeth from a chicken to get Dan Broderick to admit that he and his young family had suffered any hardship at all during his student days. He simply didn't recall those years as being all that tough. He didn't remember that Kim had no crib. Only reluctantly did he even finally remember that, yes, "We got food stamps once or twice." He also remembered her various odd jobs—including one department store sales stint she did at nights during Christmas season. But he saw it as no hardship. He had, in fact, been carefully reviewing their taxes since 1970 for this trial. "I reviewed your W-2 on that," he said. "Your total income from [the sales job at] Lord and Taylor was $187."

Betty finally gave up. Dan would never recall their early years with gratitude, sentimentality, or generosity.

He also freely admitted that he often did not consult his wife when he made investments with his brother. Betty tried to pursue that line of questioning, but Howatt wouldn't let her. She argued in vain that it was critical, that she shouldn't be held accountable for any of their Colorado losses, because "If I had had any control, I would have sold them!" Forget it, the judge told her. That's not how divorce court works. What's done is done.

She next tried to develop, in vain, her theory that Larry and Dan had been deliberately shuffling, hiding, and manipulating assets to ultimately cheat her, ever since Dan began his affair with Linda in 1983.

"Did Larry know about your affair with Linda since the beginning?" she asked Dan.

Objection. Sustained. No-fault again.

"It's not relevant? With the manipulation of these huge sums of money?" Betty asked, shocked.

"Not his affair, if there were one ... Whether there was or wasn't is of no concern to me at all," said Howatt.

"It is plenty of concern to me!"

"I am sure that it was," Howatt agreed.

No, no. Never mind that he was seeing another woman and lying about it, Betty told Howatt. She was now talking dollars and cents. All these delays, all these debts,

253

all these Epsteins were, in her opinion, deliberately contrived by the two brothers to guarantee that, by the time a property settlement was finally reached, Dan would owe her virtually nothing.

No, Howett told her—she could not pursue the Linda-Larry connection any further, not without hard evidence.

Betty Broderick's frustration was understandable. But so was Howatt's. Even had he been so inclined, he could not, by law, allow her accusations. Such are the glories of no-fault divorce laws. Betty Broderick wasn't permitted to make a case for serious financial deception because it was too closely related to sexual deception. And she didn't have the legal skills to slip around the barriers.

"I'm trying to illustrate the manipulations of saying one thing and doing another!" she protested.

"No," said Howatt, again.

In an ideal world, the entire proceeding would have been halted and Betty Broderick ordered to go hire herself some help, since she was clearly not competent to be representing herself. But that was always Betty's catch-22, even in her later murder trials: the same system that had challenged her mental stability ever since 1986, to the extent of even stripping her of visitation rights with her own children, still found her competent to look after her best interests, alone, in divorce court—and, later, to testify in her own behalf for shooting two people. Her much-alleged mental instability was used consistently as a club against her, but never as a factor in her favor.

And nobody saw the contradiction with more bitter irony than Betty herself. "When it serves their purpose, you go from totally sane to totally crazy, one way or the other," she said years later from prison. "And then, just when it might be to your benefit to be insane, it's 'Oh! she got cured. As fast as she was declared nutty, we declare her sane again.' All those years, they were all calling me crazy, crazy, crazy. Now they are all saying, 'Oh, no. She's not crazy,' because they wouldn't want me to get off because I was crazy, even though they drove me crazy. God, I love lawyers."

Nearly two years before, Tricia Smith had argued eloquently in temporary support hearings that Betty Broderick was entitled to enough money to maintain the life-style "to which she had grown accustomed." Granted, the sums involved were huge, atypical, beyond the grasp of the average person, Smith had said—but it was all relative. This case wasn't about dollars, it was about percentages—and her client was entitled to a fair percentage of Dan Broderick's $1 million-plus income. It was unfair, she argued, for a wife of sixteen years to suffer a diminished standard of living simply because her husband had chosen to dissolve the partnership.

Never had Betty Broderick needed Tricia Smith more than now. She was trying to make the same points, but her methods ranged from inept to embarrassing.

She asked Dan to recite the "major gifts" that he had given her. When he hesitated, she prompted him: "such as the lynx coat, the diamond necklace, the bracelet, the pearls." Yeah, he said—but they were Christmas presents mostly—his point being, he had not lavished her with gifts at random.

"Do you think that the two of us are well-known for our clothes?"

"I don't know about that."

"Yes, you do."

Don't argue, Howatt said.

"Is it true that I'm well-known for my clothes?" He didn't know.

"You don't have a recollection of mention in the newspaper of the different clothes that I would wear certain places ... Do you remember [*Union* society writer] Burl Stiff being sweet on your plaid jacket?"

No. He didn't remember that.

She would not be stopped. For the next half hour she tried to force Dan Broderick to admit that she had, through her social activities, advanced his career, via the society pages in San Diego.

"When your name and picture appeared in the newspaper, didn't you receive a lot of comments about it ... Didn't you become more well-known all over the city because of the publicity?" she demanded. "You don't think a lot of your cases came to you from social contacts around La Jolla?"

No, he didn't. "When my name appeared in the paper in connection with a case that I was involved in, or as a result I had achieved," he told her testily, "I think that did have a significant impact ..." Otherwise, he thought her La Jolla social functions were irrelevant. "Ninety-nine percent of my work comes from other lawyers."

She switched subjects to his chintzy ways after the separation. The country clubs. Even more galling to her than his arbitrary cancelation of their Fairbanks membership was the humiliating way he had dealt with her club expenses while she still had privileges, before this divorce trial finally occurred to legally divide their supposedly communal money.

Wasn't it true, she asked, that each time she had used club dining facilities, Dan had docked her support check for the amount she spent—despite the fact that he had to pay a $300 monthly minimum even if nobody used the club?

Yes, he agreed. He had charged her for every lunch or dinner she had, although, it was true, she never came close to surpassing the $300 monthly minimum he had to pay anyway. But, whatever her bill, "I deducted it from your monthly support payment." "When I used the club, I always had the kids with me. ... You would rather pay the minimum than allow me to use that minimum for free?" That's what it amounted to, he said.

Howatt cut her off before she could press the question further.

Next she wanted to describe the frustrations of her search for a leading San Diego divorce lawyer to take on Dan Broderick. But Barry objected. Sustained. Irrelevant.

By now, Betty was obviously beginning to wonder what was relevant. She couldn't talk about Linda, or Larry, or anything to do with "fault." Now she couldn't talk about the problems she perceived in finding a decent local lawyer either? All these arguments and delays over her attorney fees were "done purposely to delay and drag this case on to create all these Epsteins!" she told Howatt.

No, he said. The history of her attorney search was not relevant to the property/custody issues at hand.

"It's going to be relevant if I lose!" Betty snapped. "I have $80,000 expended in attorney fees, and here I sit without an attorney ... Tell me, please," she asked Howatt, "how does it impact the whole Epstein mystery that this [divorce trial] is four years down the road? If I was successful in having Mr. Taffe come in with both feet on October, 1985, would there have been any such thing as a dollar of Epsteins?"

"There may well have been," said Howatt. "There are a lot of cases, not yours alone, that take a substantial period of time to resolve." Although she might feel personally frustrated by the history of her case, he added, that had nothing to do with the issue of Epstein credits. "They either are or they aren't there. It is that simple," Howatt told her. "He either paid them or he didn't pay them. They are either legitimate Epstein credits or they are not."

But wasn't it true, she persisted, that the years of delays in her trial had increased the Epsteins? "It's my simple understanding that if the property was separated ... closer to the time of separation or filing for divorce, then this whole book worth of Epsteins wouldn't have existed. Isn't that correct?"

Howatt finally agreed. "It is possible," he said, "that if the divorce was concluded earlier, these Epstein credits would not have accrued."

She arrived in court on the third day of trial, her mind roiling. Custody. Epsteins. Where? How? What? She felt like hell. She was getting the flu. Or was she? She had felt lousy for so long. What should she ask first? Custody. That was the goal now. Concentrate.

She was determined to make Dan admit that the issue of her mental health was simply his contrived, face-saving excuse for abandoning his family. Betty would never forgive him for calling her crazy.

When exactly had he first told her children she was mentally ill? she demanded. Craftily, she tried to sneak around Howatt and the no-fault issue by avoiding any mention of Linda this time. "When I would confront you with questions about a certain other party, wasn't your answer that I was sick?"

But Dan was craftier. Could she be more specific? "Were you seen at several parties around town with Linda Kolkena in 1983?" she blurted out. Objection. Sustained. No-fault.

Poor, doomed Betty. Her frustration sizzles on the transcript pages.

This wasn't an issue of fault, she protested again. It was a critical custody issue, because Dan's only grounds for trying to keep the kids was "that he is claiming my needing psychiatric help ... He has been using this big image of me as a mental case to establish custody since '83 ... That's what he based his custody on ... that 'You are sick.' I've never been accused of a single thing that I can rebut and disprove. Nothing. There is no basis that I can say, 'I'm not a drunk. I'm not a prostitute. I have never used drugs. I've never messed around. I have never smoked. I have no complaints.' I cannot rebut this custody. It's only based on my being a mental case. I'm trying to prove that I am not a mental case. I'm trying to establish by these questions why I

256

might have been a little angry at certain things that had gone on in our marriage ... why I have been forced to be so angry at the manipulations of Mr. Broderick from 1983 right up until today."

Howatt was unmoved. Dan's "outside activities, shall we say, are not really assistive to your present ability to parent."

"Do you consider that you have any health problems, Mr. Broderick?" she asked next. She had decided to turn the tables on him, expose Dan Broderick's own mental health problems.

He had recurrent headaches and a heart murmur, he told her.

"You don't consider that you have a drinking problem?" No, he didn't. And did he take drugs? No, he said—nothing stronger than Tylenol.

"Have you never done dope?" she asked.

He surrendered. She had the goods. "When I was in medical school, two or three times, in your presence, I smoked marijuana," he said. And "since I graduated from medical school in 1970, I have probably smoked marijuana—when I said 'smoked it,' I mean 'puffed it'—about three or four times, maybe a total of five times. The last time was seven or eight years ago. That's it."

She pressed on. Did he do cocaine, too? Absolutely not, he told her. "I have never seen cocaine ... I know that's hard to believe, but I have never set eyes on it."

This path was leading her nowhere, of course. But at least she had a good time embarrassing him.

At the end of the day, Howatt pressured Betty to hurry up. How much more time would she be needing—"another thirty minutes on the figures that you are going through and two hours on custody, or what?"

"I don't know. I don't know," she answered, flustered. "I don't even know what I'm going to ask him yet on custody. It just seems a pretty huge issue to me. Once I get Mr. Broderick off the stand, my case is over ... I don't really have any other witnesses to anything, except my children."

The next day was all downhill for Betty. Her every effort only resulted in more opportunities for Dan to describe the struggle of a hardworking, single father trying to raise four children alone after their mother abandoned them.

To support her argument that Dan was a negligent father, she had brought to court the same bag of evidence she had been hauling around for two years: ripped, dirty boys' tennis shoes with the soles flapping, girls' shoes with rundown heels, a swimming suit with the rear end ripped out, and other items of rag-tag clothes. Her evidence also included an ordinary tree stick, which she said was Rhett's Halloween costume a couple of years before.

Howatt's impatience erupted as he eyed Betty's rag bag. He thought her assortment of scruffy children's clothing was worthless and told her so: "I accept the fact that the children have holes in their clothing. I am sure you did as a family. I am sure Mr. Broderick as a child did. I did as a child. I used to like to get my sneakers so they would pop when I walked ... and it used to drive my parents nuts."

257

The key thing, he continued, was who was best going to provide for the children's needs? Further, he said, "I grant you—and [Dan] has granted from the very outset—that, were it not for what he perceives to be your fixation to anger with him and the manner in which you use that in dealing with the children, that you would be far and away the better parent to have the custody ..."

"Okay," said Betty passively.

"Now," said Howatt, "let's deal with the stick. What is the story with the stick?" If there was sarcasm in his tone, it didn't show from Betty's eager response.

"The stick is a Halloween costume. That is Rhett's Halloween costume for the parade at school in 1985 or '86! All the kids have costumes, and they parade around. And this is the saddest thing I have ever seen in my life, and this is not the kind of thing that my kids should be subject to. I am going to keep that forever."

She then asked Howatt again when the boys could come talk to him. Howatt didn't see the necessity. They were so young. But Betty insisted. They, after all, were the real custody issue, "and they have been asking me on a daily if not hourly basis when they can come in here ... and I think psychologically it is very important for them that they feel the least tiniest bit that they had something to say about their future." Barry didn't object, and so Howatt finally agreed. Then, in the rarest of moments in this trial, Dan and Betty Broderick briefly behaved like civilized adults concerned with the welfare of their children. In a polite exchange, they discussed when the boys should come.

Not in the morning, said Dan, because Danny had two finals at school. After school, however, would be good.

But be sure, Betty reminded him, not to "mention anything to Danny," lest he worry throughout his tests.

"Sure," said Dan. "That is a good suggestion."

She spent the rest of the day struggling with Epsteins. She accused Dan of deliberately dragging out payments and encumbering properties in order to increase her Epstein debt to him. Why else, for example, hadn't he paid off the Warner Springs unit? Even the piano still had a $900 debt. And why hadn't he paid off his Harvard loan of $157 per month sooner? Why did she owe him half of payments made on that loan for almost two years after he left her?

Dan denied any preconceived plot. He made monthly payments on many bills, he said. He had been paying Harvard $157 a month since 1974, and had continued to do so simply out of habit. And the amount she owed him wasn't large—only around $2,000. Besides, he said, "I had never heard of Epstein credits until long after our separation."

Betty tried to dispute him on grounds that his first attorney, Ashworth, is a well-known expert on Epsteins, but Howatt interrupted her. "You misunderstand the whole point," he told her.

"I do?"

Yes, said the judge. For instance, "It may have been of significant tax consequence in 1984 to have the interest deduction" on a $157 per month student loan payment "given the large amount of income" involved in this case. It was up to him to decide which Epstein credits Dan was claiming were legitimate and which were not. Meantime, "The most significant answer that you received so far from Mr. Broderick is ... that he never heard of an Epstein credit at the time you separated, and didn't hear about them until afterward presumably ... You are looking for skeletons where there are none."

But then Betty found one.

It came in the form of two financial statements Dan had not included in his seemingly exhaustive courtroom accountings.

"Dan," she said innocently, "as I was looking over boxes and boxes of papers, I happened upon two bank withdrawals you made the month you left, one for $175,000 [on February 22, 1985—six days before he left her], virtually closing the account, and one from a different account for $80,000 [on February 5,1985], again virtually closing the account. Where did those monies go?"

He fumbled. He shuffled through his papers. He couldn't tell her just now, he said, where that $255,000 had gone. But he knew that "if I go to my books, I can tell you exactly ... by two o'clock. I just don't know, looking right now, where this money went to, but I will have a paper trail where it went and what for."

But she could see that the $175,000 was a wire transfer.

"Dan, do you ever wire transfer money to your brother Larry?" Yes, he agreed. Sometimes.

Betty knew where the money had gone.

On the day he had wired that money—wherever it went—she continued, "Did you have any idea you were walking out on February 28?" No.

"But, yet, you closed out an entire $175,000 bank account?"

The account wasn't closed out, he said. When he left her, it still had $22,968 in it. What's more, he added, in a sudden moment of selective clarity, he was certain that on the same day he had transferred the $175,000, "There was also a deposit ... of $60,445." How he knew all this when he couldn't even remember where he had sent $175,000 was never clear.

Betty pounced. Wasn't it possible, she asked, that if he had withdrawn this money to pay Larry for assorted Colorado debts, he had been raiding her community property, prior to the date of separation, and then double charging her later for the losses?

Betty was never as stupid about finances as she pretended to be.

Dan resisted. The Epsteins he was claiming, he said, "were all payments made after our separation, so this would not be involved in an Epstein credit claim."

She was not persuaded. It struck her as unusual that so much money would disappear, she said, "just days before you walked out."

Dan promised to find out where the money went and let her know after the lunch break. It was the only time in the entire trial that Betty had Dan Broderick on the run.

After lunch, he reported that the $80,000 had been withdrawn to cover a tax obligation from 1984, and that the $175,000 had indeed been a loan to his brother Larry's company, Englewood Forest Products—but Larry had repaid the loan at 13 percent interest forty days later, he said.

Betty wanted to know how that missing money affected the value of his law practice.

It had not been included in the appraisal, Dan said—and it should have been. His figures would be immediately adjusted upward, thanks to her vigilance. "I totally forgot about the whole transaction until you asked me about it this morning," he said.

(What he also forgot was a $450,000 loan he had made to his brother in 1988 from his pension fund—and which wouldn't be brought to light until long after he was dead, when the Broderick boys finally sued their uncle for their share of the unpaid balance.)

In another of her more lucid moments in trial, Betty then asked Howatt at which point in time he would value Dan's law practice—at the time of separation or at the present time of trial, four years later?

Howatt evaded the question. A community asset, such as Dan Broderick's law practice, "can be valued either at the date of separation, or at the date of trial," he told her.

But how would he make this important determination? Betty persisted.

Howatt would make that determination "at the end of the case," he told her, "based on the facts and circumstances that have been presented to me ..."

Betty was puzzled. So far, she pointed out, there was nothing in the record even evaluating the current worth of Dan's law practice. "That is true," said Howatt. He was volunteering nothing. "So that would be my responsibility to go get?" asked Betty. "Correct," said Howett.

But just as it began to seem that Betty Broderick was perhaps about to turn into a tiger, clearly targeting her prey, she again reverted to a purring pussycat.

Well, she simpered helplessly, "Do I have to go and get it through an expert—or do I just ask Mr. Broderick?"

Reading through these trial transcripts today, it is easy to imagine the pregnant pause that must have followed that bombshell question.

"Well, you ask him the question you want to ask him," said Howatt, "and to the extent he knows how to answer we will hear what he has to say."

She tried. But she didn't know how. She asked Dan to explain why the value of his practice—"all the cases and hardware and computers and cars and pension and everything"—seemed to come out to less in value than what he made in a single year.

Barry objected. Sustained. Argumentative.

"Jeez," she hissed. And gave up.

Court was then recessed so Judge Howatt could interview the two Broderick daughters in individual sessions. Betty beamed. She was counting on her children.

Tall, skinny, pretty, nervous Lee, then seventeen, went first.

What did she think about living with her dad? Howatt asked.

"Me and my dad just don't get along," she said. "I think he is incredibly

260

unreasonable, I can't deal with him at all, he drives me insane." She was especially angry because he hadn't invited her over for Christmas or on a trip to Hawaii the summer before.

What else was on her mind, Howatt asked?

Money. "I think I should get something. I feel like I've been cheated ... I'm going skiing this afternoon and I had to work for three weeks every day, every night, to get enough money to go, and my dad is writing my sister a check ..."

Her father, she told Howatt, "doesn't think he owes me anything. He doesn't approve of the way I am living my life, and he doesn't want to give me anything if he doesn't have control over me, and he doesn't, because I am living with my mom."

Generally speaking, Howatt asked, what did she fight with her father about?

Well ... she hadn't lived there in some time, Lee said, but their last argument was over a haircut. "I wanted to get a haircut and my mom wouldn't pay for it because my dad has sole custody and she doesn't have enough money, and if I want my hair cut, go pay for it myself. And I was saving money for skiing, and I couldn't afford it. So I went to my dad's house and asked him very nicely if I could get my hair cut, and he said no. And I got really mad and said why not? He said, 'I don't think I should have to pay for your haircut, that is your responsibility and you take care of it yourself.'"

She also thought her mom was being "ripped off" because she got no money for Lee's support. She liked her mom, she said, because "She doesn't have to control everything." Dan, by contrast, "thinks I am completely on drugs, but I am not. I think he is scared of me actually ... He does not like to be around me. He gets nervous ... like I am ... a crazy weirdo ... He just doesn't want to be bothered by me at all. He doesn't let me in his house ..."

Her brothers didn't like Dan either, she said. Why was that? asked Howatt.

"Because they think he is mean, and they just don't like him ... I never really asked one of them why. I just think it is because he messed up the family and he wouldn't let them go see my mom. That is what they really want to do every weekend ..."

Did all the children blame Dan for the breakup?

The boys did, she said. But not her or her sister. She and Kim understood, she said, that "there is nothing either one of them can do, if they fight all the time when they were married." And, she said, "They fought a lot." At the same time, she added wistfully, "I remember them being happy a lot, too, when I was really little. They didn't fight at all. But then they started to fight really bad, like all the time ... They just like broke bottles and stuff, and yelling and screaming ..."

She sounded tired of the whole thing. "I want to just turn eighteen and get my own apartment and go to school and just have everybody leave me alone."

Then came Kim. She was nervous, too. Her first words came in a disjointed, confused tangle. But in the end, she turned out to be a better witness for her father than her mother, much less her little brothers.

"I think personally that my brothers should be able to live with my mom," she began. "That is what they wanted me to come and give my opinion on, because they don't like my dad's girlfriend, and my mom is kind of a little crazy. She does irrational

261

things and has a very bad temper, but I don't know, maybe that will stop after the divorce is settled. But I don't think that they should have to live with my dad and Linda if they are really going to be miserable, and, from me talking to them, that is how they sound they are. But," she added, switching again, "they have also been brainwashed by [her mother]. So I don't know."

And how did she feel about Linda? "Well, she is nice to me, but I just think it is really fake," she said. Kim Broderick's frustrations, her divided attitudes, leap off the page.

For her own part, she would not want to live with Betty, she said. She recalled bitterly how her mother had "kicked us all out ..." Then, "When she realized it wasn't that hard for him and he was doing fine," she wanted them back—in Kim's opinion, just to hurt Dan. "As soon as we were adjusted and enjoyed it, she said, 'I want you back'."

Even now, when the kids were at her house, Betty felt like Dan was "getting away scot-free ... If she gets mad at them, she will throw them back there [to Dan's house] ... She can't deal with little kids, and she has no stability whatsoever ... She's wishy-washy."

Her father, she said, was "very strict, but he is not that unreasonable." She liked him and got along with him well, she told Howatt, and thought he was trying hard to be a good parent, although "he is not very emotional or sensitive ... I mean, I can't go to him and sit and cry [over] little problems ... boys, or something like that. But if it's something big, I can talk to him. He's not always understanding at first, but, after, he is fine. He gets mad and yells, but he is nice ..."

As for Lee, she thought Dan "was being way too hard on her." On the other hand, she said, equivocating again, Lee "has gone way overboard. She has thrown things. You can't throw glass bottles at people's cars when you're mad at them." And, she added, Lee was "into bad things ... She is stoned all the time. She is always smoking pot ..." But she liked her sister, she said. "She is just different than me." She also thought, firmly, that "someone should be giving her [an] allowance" so she didn't have to work so hard. "And my dad doesn't give her any money ..."

Midway through the interview, Kim changed her mind about the boys living permanently with Betty. "They would be happiest at my mom's for short-term, but long-term they wouldn't." Contradicting her earlier statement, now she told Howatt the boys were happy at Dan's. They only told Betty that they hated him to get her attention. Her next statement was even more damaging: "He makes them go to school, and he makes them do their homework. At Mom's house there is none of that ... they just have to cough a little and she will say, 'Okay, you are sick.' She doesn't like following rules and stuff like that."

She also said that she was no longer having quarrels with Dan over her college expenses because, just three days earlier, he had raised her allowance from $200 to $300. She didn't know why.

Did she think Betty's animosities toward Dan were over money, or the girlfriend? asked Howatt.

Both. But mostly money, Kim thought. Money was all Betty talked about.

"Everyone that calls on the phone ... 'Hi, well, la, la, la ... I don't have enough money for this, and I am $40,000 in debt.' I mean, she is always talking about money, and it's disgusting. It really annoys me, because ... it seems like she gets a lot. She spent a lot of it on me. She took me to San Francisco ... She just doesn't think ... She is very impulsive."

She then changed her mind one last time about custody of the boys.

Now, she told Howatt, she thought the boys should go to Betty only "if my dad gets married" to Linda. Otherwise, they should stay with Dan. "He is stable. He has them on a routine. They go to bed at a certain time, eat at a certain time ... At my mom's house, it's chaotic ... It's fun at my mom's ... you can go any time or blast music. You don't do that stuff at Dad's. You don't make a mess. You sit in the living room. At my mom's, you jump on the furniture and do whatever you want."

But, she added before she left Howatt's chambers, in a lasting note of wisdom, she thought both of her parents were "too traumatic about the whole thing, and both of them should have tried to leave all of us kids out of it a lot more, rather than make this a six-person divorce. They wanted all of us in it the whole time ... and, you know, if they had just talked to themselves, they could have ended this a lot earlier and not had so much hurt feelings and disaster."

Time was running out, and Betty knew it. She became a beggar woman in court, rifling through trash heaps of domestic minutiae, hunting for the last scraps of neglect on Dan's part or excellence on hers that she could either remember or imagine. The trial transcripts became increasingly poignant as the end grew near.

She wanted to discuss that Saturday morning, years ago, when she had gone to pick up Rhett for his soccer game, only to discover that Dan had taken him away, so enraging her that she had broken a window at Coral Reef. But Barry objected. Irrelevant. Sustained.

"I am just trying to point out the many instances that he forcibly manipulated the kids away from me," she protested.

It didn't matter, said Howatt, since Dan had already "admitted, point-blank, that he purposely, decidedly, and with complete intention, precluded the children from visiting with you or on occasion spirited them away and sequestered them from you."

"So I don't go incident by incident?" she asked.

No, said Howatt. "He admitted that is what he did, and he has given us a reason for it."

"It is not important, the magnitude and the amount of times he did it?" Betty persisted, incredulous.

No. The court didn't care how many times he did it. To the court, one incident was the same as a thousand. Betty Broderick wasn't going to build a painstaking picture of her rising rage for this judge. Not until she finally got to criminal court on murder charges would she at last be allowed to do that.

Gerald Barry's redirect of his client was short and sweet. It focused on Dan's integrity, and his trust in his brother Larry.

"Did you make any of those investments with the feeling that you would be divorcing your wife?" Barry asked.

Whereupon, Dan delivered a final grand slam: "The honest answer to that is this: since very early in our marriage, very early, I have felt that our marriage was going to end in divorce, and that is a fact that Bets and I have talked about since very early in our marriage. And so, certainly, during these years when I made these investments ... I anticipated that one day this marriage of ours was going to fall apart. [But] I did not make any of these investments with a view toward that."

Barry then hauled out his heaviest artillery—Betty's vulgar taped messages and conversations with the boys. He wanted to play a few of them.

Howatt asked if Betty had any objection.

"Yes, I always object to these tapes," said Betty, who had already heard them so many times before in various court proceedings that they were like a Greek chorus in her head by now, unending harpies. Herself.

"What would be the basis of your objection?" he asked.

"What is my multiple choice?" Betty retorted sarcastically. Her temper was apparently wearing thin.

"I'm sorry," said Howatt. "I can't give you a multiple choice."

The tapes played.

The language was the same that Betty had been using for years now, but, although Dan' had heard the words many times before, his shock appeared undimmed by time. "She will call me 'cuntsucker,' 'fuckhead,' 'asshole,'" he said. "I mean ... words that I never even heard about."

Barry rested his case.

But before Betty could begin her final questioning of Dan, the media arrived, in the person of *Reader* reporter Paul Krueger, who demanded admission to the courtroom. Why, Krueger wanted to know, was the Broderick divorce trial closed to the press and public?

Howatt didn't have a ready answer. "Unless you can give me something on which, so to speak, to hang my hat," he told Barry, "I am going to have to open up the hearing." Barry didn't have a ready reply either. This was a surprise. He needed time to define his arguments, he told Howatt. He also accused Betty of contacting the press.

She denied it—but she was glad that somebody had. She assumed her friends in HALT had done it, she told Howatt, because "They, as well as I, feel that my basic rights have been denied from the very beginning—that this is a sealed proceeding that nobody can witness. They feel it is really unfair to me, and so do I. Because when these proceedings are over, no matter what the outcome, Dan tells everyone I am crazy, and being that I have lost every one so far, I am real unhappy what has gone on in this system ... Whenever I say anything to anybody, his pat answer is, 'She is wacko'."

Howatt wasn't interested in her complaints, only the bottom line: "Well, are you against closing the hearing to the media? Yes or No?"

"I am for opening the courtroom to whoever wants to come," Betty told him firmly.

Howatt pressured her to reconsider. "Do you want the press to be able to come in and report the intimate details of these proceedings?" His "basic concern," he said, "is the best interest of the parties—and that includes the children." Also, he pointed out, the proceeding had obviously not been totally closed, since her friend Ronnie Brown had been allowed to remain "so you had somebody you could hold on to for support, so to speak ..."

A lifetime of insecurity surfaced in the next word Betty Broderick spoke. "Well ..." And her voice trailed off.

Howatt, who had so far been loath to advise Betty Broderick on nearly anything else, wasn't finished. He asked if she wanted to see "your whole life and times [printed] in what amounts to a tabloid ... Maybe that is an unfair characterization," he qualified, "but [the *Reader*] is certainly a newspaper of some circulation in the community ... and to make this kind of information available not only to the children through that medium, but ... to their friends and associates, either through their parents or through their own reading of the paper ... it's up to you ... If you consent to having the hearing closed, it will remain closed," Howatt told her. "If you feel that it is not in your best interest to have it closed ... I will force Mr. Barry to prove to me the authority on which to close it."

Betty hung in. "I would like Mr. Barry to prove the authority," she said.

Barry brought out the same letters from the children's psychologists that Dan had used with such success to block the *Reader* story Krueger and De Wyze had tried earlier to write. The only difference was that, now, Dan could not also threaten to sue for invasion of privacy. This was now a First Amendment issue.

"Your position is unchanged?" Howatt asked Betty again. It would have taken a stronger woman than Betty Broderick to withstand much more of this pressure.

Still, amazingly, she persisted. "If I am such the guilty, horrible, awful person in these whole proceedings that Dan paints me to be," she demanded, "why is he so afraid of anybody knowing the truth?"

Howatt defended Dan. "Certainly, as an adult, he can live with the choice that he has made, making a new relationship and dissolving an old one," said the judge. "The difficulty is not with him but rather the children."

Howatt then sympathized briefly with Betty's plight. "The system has failed you," he conceded, "because it has not afforded you the means or the opportunity to resolve the conflict in a reasonable and timely fashion." Even so, he promptly added, he didn't think that was any excuse opening such sensitive proceedings to the press.

Betty countered that there was no reason for anyone to construe her position as "in any way persecuting or endangering the children" because her children already knew "everything about everything."

She was not bending. It was astonishing.

Howatt asked her again the same question she had already answered several times: Did she want the proceedings sealed or open?

"In fairness to me," she said again, clearly, "I would like them open.'

"Okay," said Howatt. "I will abide by your decision then." At which time he recessed court in order to interview Danny and Rhett in his chambers. Assuming, he asked her in a remarkably snide aside, that she still wanted the children's interviews to be held in private?

"Yes, sir," she said meekly.

If Betty Broderick wasn't worried before about aggravating the judge who would dictate her financial future and decide whether she could have her children back, she surely was by now. For one of the first times in her life, she had stood up for herself before an authority figure, and taken a decidedly unpopular position. She had not been nice.

Danny Broderick, then a twelve-year-old seventh-grader at Francis Parker, was a very bright, thoughtful little boy, and, when he walked into Howatt's office, his mind was made up, his opinions were firm: he had nothing bad to say about his dad—but he wanted to live with his mom and visit Dad on weekends "because that is when he is there. He is never there the other times, he is always at work."

What was it like, living with Mom? Howatt asked.

"It's a lot of fun, and we do a lot of things, and we just know how to have fun with her, and she knows how to have fun, too ... And she makes good meals, and she knows what we like ... Our dogs are over there ... that is about it. And we have a swimming pool there, just like at my dad's house. We have a trampoline. We have a little pool room down by the pool and basketball hoop, like my dad's house ... and a volleyball kind of thing. And it is right by the beach, too, so I like that a lot better ..."

And what kind of fun things did he do with his dad?

"We see movies and go out to dinner once in awhile, and I play basketball with him every so often after work, and we play catch with the football ... and do basically what you would think a working parent would do—a hardworking, long-working parent," he added. He sounded so grown-up. Danny Broderick had thought it through, what he was going to say to this judge, what he would stress. His biggest complaint was that his father wasn't home enough during the week. Dan was usually there when the boys left for school in the morning, and he usually got home around 6:00 or 6:30. But then, after dinner, he worked in his den. "The thing that we mostly do together is homework, and that is not even every day." His conclusion was that it was "boring," living at his father's house.

Howatt wanted to know if his mother ever got angry with him.

Yes, said Danny. But "she has never slapped me or anything." By contrast, he said, his father "gets angry a lot, and he usually spanks us ... hitting me in the behind."

"Do you like your mother better than your father?" Howatt asked.

"I wouldn't say better," the little boy responded, "but I think she has better qualities."

As for Linda, he said that she was okay, but he really didn't like her very much.

Was there anything else he wanted to tell Howatt? Nope, said Danny. "Just basically that I want to live with my mom ... Every day I think about living with her, so that is all."

All the Broderick children had been sworn before they testified to Howatt. Now, looking at Rhett, the nine-year-old, fourth-grade baby of the family, Howatt asked if he knew the difference between truth and lies. Sure, said Rhett.

"Have you ever told a lie?" the judge asked.

"A whole bunch of times," said Rhett. "But not to my parents. To my brother."

Like Danny, he knew exactly what he wanted to say: "I think my mom should get me, she has more experience with kids." And his dad was "mostly at work." He loved it at his mother's house. "We go to places like Warner Springs, and we just read stories, rent movies, and she makes me and my brother's favorite food." At his dad's house, he watched TV, played video games, and played with his toys.

He fought with his brother a lot, too, he said. Danny kicked him, he announced, on "an average" of seven times a day.

And did they fight at his mother's house, too? Howatt asked.

No. "My mom keeps him distracted too much ... She invites over friends that he likes, and she makes them his favorite food, and she rents his favorite movies." Mostly, he said, they only got to watch PG and cartoons, although "every once in awhile we can trick my dad and my mom into getting us an R movie. My mom says no R movies if there's any violence." Just recently, he said, his mom had turned off 'Action Jackson' because "she said it was too violent." Otherwise, he said, at Mom's, it was mostly "cartoons and movies like 'Rumpelstiltskin', with real actors and stuff ... 'Cinderella'."

His routine during school days, the little boy said with comic precision, consisted of getting up "at 6:18" to his alarm clock, getting dressed, and going to school. He didn't have breakfast, except "every once in a while I have cereal, and usually there is a chance I will drink some Sundance"—fruit juice mixed with sparkling water.

He never took his own lunch to school, he said. "Usually there is nothing in the house that is good except meat that has to be cooked, and junk, too, that my dad wouldn't allow me to eat for lunch."

After school he watched TV, did his homework, and watched more TV.

"Is there something special that you do at your mom's that makes it a nice place to be?" asked Howatt. "Yeah. You don't need TV to have fun." He didn't have any friends in Dan's neighborhood either. They all lived in La Jolla.

What did he get in trouble with his mother for?

"She only yells at me when I cuss, because I don't really do anything real bad, except every once in a while my brother kicks me and I call him a bad word." His mother never spanked him. "She just slaps me on the face a little hard." His dad spanked him on the rear. Dan only got angry, he said, when he and Danny fought, and once when he climbed down the laundry chute.

Why did he want to live with his mother instead of his dad? "Because Mom is there when I need her." And what about Linda?

He didn't like her. "She always tells on me, like when I cuss at my brother. She goes, 'Dan, Dan, Rhett said a bad word to Danny.'" Anything else that Rhett wanted to tell him?

Rhett thought. "Well, when my dad gets really mad, he starts breaking things. He tries not to. Like once my brother and I were wrestling ... I pushed him ... and his elbow went through the window, and my dad came in and he had a fit, and he looked like he was ready to punch another window ... Once me and my brother were fighting, and he was really sick of it ... and he threw Danny across the room ... first he threw me and then he threw my brother on top of me, so then I got squashed, and then he got really mad and he spanked us."

How about his mother? Did she get angry like that?

No. Only with Lee for sneaking out and staying all night, and cussing at her. So, "Like every four months, [Betty] kicks her out of the house, but then she [Lee] comes back thirty minutes later and Mom forgives her and everything is good again. But the next day she [Lee] starts at it again."

Kim, he added, was rude to his mom, too, but nice to his dad. Anything else Rhett wanted to say? No. "Except for I want a new video game."

Betty worried all night. She arrived in court the next day a nervous meek. Now the *Reader*'s attorney was there, too. The magnitude of the drama she had provoked was terrifying.

Gerald Barry made a last-ditch effort to keep the press out, now arguing that open hearings would not only be harmful to the Broderick children, but also unfair to Dan, since Betty had been allowed to ask such " "outrageous" questions as "Are you a cocaine user or addict?" Had he known the hearings might be opened, said Barry, he would never have allowed such questions to go unchallenged.

Betty began to waver. "I am now being put in a position that appears that my choice is to hurt or not hurt my children ..." That wasn't true, she told Howatt. Nevertheless, she had decided to drop her demand for an open trial and "leave this to your discretion, Your Honor—anything you choose."

No dice, said Howatt. It was not his decision to make. It was hers. She could not shift the burden on this one. "What I need from you is a final determination, either yea or nay?" he said. "Do you want it open or do you want it closed?"

Then, lest she waffle, he basically threatened to punish her in his final ruling if she didn't make the correct call. Hers, he said, was "a terrible dilemma," which he outlined thusly:

On the one hand, he said, if she decided to demand an open trial, "there is the inference that may be drawn from your action that that is not an appropriate parenting decision and could adversely affect your position in the custody matter." Whereas, if she suppressed her "primary need to have the hearings opened ... you act in a manner which can be inferred as appropriate in a parenting way ..." although she might be sacrificing "your own personal needs and welfare, as you believe them to be." So which would it be? Her interests or the children's? Betty not only folded, she groveled.

"I thank this court from the bottom of my heart for its understanding throughout this entire case," she said. "I think since this case is 99 percent over, it is a rather moot question at this point. And at this point, I definitely do not choose to have it open."

"Thank you very much," said Howatt.

Two mental health experts testified in the custody matter, one for each side. Dan's advocate was the court-appointed psychologist, Dr. William Dess. Dr. Gerald Nelson, who had been treating Betty personally over the past seven months, testified for her. Nelson was the only trial witness she called.

Although Dess had met none of the Broderick children and Nelson had met only Lee, each was unequivocal in his opinion about what was best for the four youngsters.

Based on all he had heard about Betty's behavior from the children's various therapists, Dess was so appalled that he recommended against even visitation unless it was in a supervised setting, such as the YMCA or the YWCA "to start out with." In his view, all four children were suffering "significant emotional problems" related to the divorce, and only Dan could provide the requisite stability needed for them to heal. He didn't think Betty should be allowed anything beyond "extremely limited" contact, especially with the two young boys. Only once before "in ten years of doing this," he said, had he recommended such drastic measures concerning a mother.

Not that he thought Dan Broderick was the perfect father, Dess added delicately. "Some people have commented that Mr. Broderick at times might tend to be a little rigid and is not the most affectionate person in the world, and may not have been overly involved with the children during the marriage." Even so, said Dess, he was a better alternative than Betty. "He is consistent and, to my knowledge, has not taken a vendetta to run down Ms. Broderick to them ..."

Dr. Nelson was equally convinced that, if Betty got both a suitable financial settlement and her children back, her extreme behavior would end and she would once again become the exemplary parent Dan Broderick himself remembered. Like Dess, Nelson agreed that the Broderick children had been severely damaged by the divorce. But he thought that Betty was "the only person who is going to take the time to bring them to therapy, to spend time with them, listening to them, talking about the pain and anguish they felt ..." Nor, in his opinion, did Betty show any evidence of "serious psychopathology."

Howatt intervened, in defense of Dan. How could Nelson say that Betty was the one parent who would tend to the children's mental health needs when Dan had been sending them to therapists for years?

"What I am saying," said Nelson, "is that the children need a parent. They don't need a psychotherapist. They need a parent who is going to be full-time and take care of them, and Mr. Broderick is unable to do that because of the pressures of his work ... basically, I don't get the sense that he knows the children very well."

He allowed, however, that Betty "is a very difficult person. She is very strong-willed and determined to get her way." On the other hand, "I think she is a very loving and caring person ... where she gets into trouble is through this rage at her husband.

"I think it is rather sad," he concluded, directing his remarks at both Dan and Betty, "that two competent, capable, bright people with your training have let your children suffer ... I think that the community has failed you in helping you work out this problem ... It is a tragedy."

In his cross-examination, Barry asked Nelson about a remark he had found in Nelson's notes, saying that Betty was someone who "plays at therapy." What did that mean? "It's basically a person who uses therapy in a manipulative way," said Nelson. "That is, her goal is not to seek relief of symptoms or good mental health or growth, but to use it to get her children back and to work through her divorce with her husband."

Betty was polite and brief in her cross-examination of Dess. She established that they had never met, and that, in preparation for his testimony, he had not spoken with Nelson or any other doctors beyond those recommended by Dan and Gerald Barry. She also got him to agree that, based on what he had heard, she had once been an ideal parent— "until this thing broke open," he added, "and you felt wronged."

"In your psychology practice," Betty asked, "is there any allowance in human experience for anger?" Yes, Dess said. "But it does not rationalize your behavior."

Despite their differing recommendations, Dess and Nelson had one attitude in common: neither thought the Broderick case was a conventional domestic dispute; both spoke in tones laced with foreboding, hinting of violence and even death.

Before Dess left the witness stand, he asked the court to take note of his concern about the potential dangers in this situation if Betty did not get what she felt was an equitable settlement. "I have heard things that refer to drastic action," he told the judge. "I am concerned about perhaps her health ... about the possible reaction ... towards Mr. Broderick ... I don't know what to do about that, other than to say that, however this comes out, I hope that ... some type of a cool head will prevail ..."

Nelson sounded the same ominous note, in response to a question from Howatt, who asked him flatly what significance he attached to Betty's obscene phone calls, as well as reports that she had "on occasion threatened to kill Mr. Broderick"?

Nelson agreed that Betty's behavior often indicated "lack of impulse control, poor judgment, immaturity ..." Nevertheless, he insisted that she could still be the better parent, once the pressures were relieved.

"She is not mentally ill," said Nelson. "She is perfectly rational. If she murdered Mr. Broderick, as she has threatened ... she could never be called incompetent in terms that she was psychotic or mentally ill. This lady knows what she is doing. She is very bright, very determined to get her share of the assets and to get her way."

Needless to say, Nelson's remarks would come back to haunt Betty during her murder trials.

Nor was the talk of death done. In her final courtroom exchange with Dan, Betty herself raised the issue of her various threats to kill him. How could he take such talk seriously, she asked. "Haven't you heard me say that to the children and everything when I am so mad? Did you think that I was going to kill you?"

Dan turned grave. "Bets, we shouldn't play games about this. There are many times when people—myself—[say] 'I am going to kill that guy,' or 'I'm going to kill

270

you,' and not said it with conviction ... but you have threatened to kill me hundreds of times, and I have taken those threats very seriously on many occasions, and you shouldn't try to trivialize this. I don't think that was the way you said you were going to kill me on the phone. I thought you said it with conviction, and I think you said it many more times than you know you have."

The Brodericks spent the next several minutes, in an open courtroom, engaged in serious, eerie discussion about the merits of her murdering him.

"Being that you canceled me out of your insurance years ago, do you think killing you would be a way for me to get a settlement out of this case?" she asked.

"Killing me would probably be one of the most self-destructive things you could do, and when I go, there goes the income stream," he said. "So it would be a bad move. But that doesn't alter the fact that you have threatened, and I have taken it seriously."

She abruptly dropped the topic to ask him some minor question about the Christmas ski trip of 1985. Before finally letting him off the stand for good, she wanted to know, again, what had been the final straw in the destruction of their marriage? "Did it have anything to do with Linda Kolkena?"

"Linda Kolkena has nothing to do with the end of that marriage," he told her.

Full circle. It was the same answer he had been giving her for years—and it remained just as unacceptable to her in January, 1989, as it had been in the summertime of 1983.

* * *

Then it was time for Betty to present her case. But she had no case. She had only her life story, with no attorney to lead her, only herself to tell it. So she took the stand and started talking.

Her first remarks were vintage Betty. She apologized for herself yet again—"I am still very nervous and totally overwhelmed by the task I have taken upon myself here." Then, in an extraordinary display of the distorted realities of her mind, she told Howatt, "All these accusations of calling Mr. Broderick horrendous, horrible names, were made in '85 and—when I was under tremendous stress and pressure. And I hope I am appearing in front of this court with the benefit of four years in distance, and the knowledge of many, many different books." It was as if the last two years, her phone calls and letters of only weeks before, no longer existed.

She then made a small, nostalgic little speech, filled with anger and pain apparent even on the printed transcript pages:

"Mr. Broderick was low enough to put in front of this court that our divorce started the day we were married, and I will argue that, I guess," she began. "In 1969, we were two young, bright, ambitious people. Our only assets were the wife's car, wife's degree and well-paying job, and wife's savings account."

She talked about her background. Parts of her self-analysis were remarkably astute and candid: She had gone to all-girls schools, "and I know it sounds funny

271

now, but they were more or less finishing schools that only prepared women for marriage. We were taught ... that to be married to a very, very successful man meant that in the early years of your marriage you did accommodate [the man's] work schedule ... that [by doing so], you would reap the benefits then of a successful man's income. All I ever wanted was a husband and a family, and that was it."

And so her needs and Dan's had converged harmoniously for a long time, she said. "He needed a wife that could wait on him, have sex with him, have his family for him, and run his home for him, while he worked all the time. I needed a successful husband to fulfill my financial needs for the house and the kids. We had a very symbiotic relationship, as long as I was totally submerged in my babies, and we were in the formative years of the practice. We were equal partners until we became wealthy—and Mr. Broderick at that time considered his earnings his sole property."

Now that they were divorced, she only hoped that Howatt would see that she got her fair share. "We have so much money, more than enough to keep Mr. Broderick and his new family happy, and me and the family we have now happy."

She was so quiet, so submissive. All anger had gone out of her, now that she was on the stand, sitting there alone, with three pairs of male eyes on her. It was the sort of exposed vulnerability few women ever suffer in such raw form. She was stripped, for the moment, of all but her abiding faith in this judge to help her.

Why did she think she should be the custodial parent? Howatt asked.

And so she was next obliged to sell herself to him as a mother.

"Because I'm there all the time, and [she and her children] have this incredible attachment and communication ... And I think that is a real important thing, that they feel they have someone who cares. I don't think they feel that way about Mr. Broderick at all, and I don't think you can pay anyone enough to feel that way about your children ... You know, the maids will do their job ... but it is just a job to them. My children have been my life. They are the only thing that matters to me. The house and the cars and the boats and the furs and the diamonds and all that crap doesn't mean anything to me."

But at the same time, she added, she needed decent support in order to raise her children properly. "If I got the children, I wouldn't want them to have to give up their private schools and their health and car insurances when they come of age, their ski trips, their summer camps, their music lessons, things like that ..."

In a note of irony that only she could not see, she also told Howatt that her children needed her for proper lessons in conduct—for example, "Nobody has ever taught these kids telephone etiquette." Only recently, too, she had discovered that Kim had no knowledge of the "trivial kitchen skills. She can't even poach an egg ..." Nor did Kim become a debutante, "as she naturally would have if she was in my home with all of her friends in La Jolla ... [who] went through that process. Although it appears trivial and silly, I think it is an important part of someone's self-esteem, a feminine self-esteem, as she grows up."

She again likened her situation to being fired from a job she did well and being replaced by an incompetent. She couldn't do Dan's job, so why was he proposing that he could do hers? She was begging. The transcripts are painful to read.

And so it went, until she finally wore down and, with an air of confusion, rested her "case."

Barry hardly bothered to cross-examine her. He asked her a few minor questions about financial transactions and sat down.

The Broderick divorce trial concluded on January 6, 1989.

Closing arguments were quick. Barry begged the judge to recognize that Dan Broderick's former wife "really knows no spending limits" and that her $27,000 monthly expense account was "emotional blackmail." Dan Broderick had risen to his wealth through hard work and his own "God-given talents," said Barry, and he was already being more generous than most men in even conceding that his former wife might require as much as $9,000 monthly for a year with $5,000 for a couple of years afterward.

Moreover, Barry argued, it was for Betty's own good that she be put on a financial tether. "If you make an artificially high award, you really cripple her," he told Howatt. "In effect, it provides a lack of incentive to contribute to herself." Besides, Barry added in a moment of blatant, cynical flattery, Betty Broderick was clearly a woman of considerable abilities—only consider her fine performance in this divorce trial. What professional attorney could have done better?

As for the property division, Barry reiterated his argument that the court should value Dan's practice as of 1985 and accept all the Epstein credits he had claimed—including the Harvard loan, since it had clearly "enhanced" the Broderick community wealth. In Barry's final analysis, Dan owed Betty a total of $29,366 in cash, plus another $28,000 from various partnerships. Concerning custody, Barry asked that Dan be awarded the two boys, but with visitation rights to Betty—Dr. Dess's recommendation to the contrary just wasn't realistic, given the boys' obvious affection for their mother, he conceded. In a rhetorical sleight of hand, Barry also managed to include Lee in Dan's custody request, while strongly implying at the same time that she should obviously be given to Betty.

Betty's financial proposal took no more than five minutes to present. It was the same one she had been seeking since 1987: $25,000 per month for ten years, whether she remarried or not, plus a $1 million cash payment, tax free. Given that—and only given that—she also wanted all three minor children back, with visitation to Dan.

Miscellaneously, she also reiterated her demand that the court should order Dan to buy a life insurance policy of "at least $1 million ... so that I would have some security ... should his death take away our earning capacity ..." And she wanted full reimbursement for her attorney fees during the past four years, a total of around $78,000.

She thought that her requests were more than fair. "I think I have been incredibly nice and generous in letting Mr. Broderick calculate [the value] of everything," she told Howatt. Even assuming that Dan's figures were not deliberately deflated to cheat her, the income levels involved were still so high that "I don't think necessity should be the basis for anything ... we have to look at proportions and an equitable life-style." In an acerbic parting shot, she also noted that Mr. Broderick's "God-given

273

talents," as described by Mr. Barry, had been vastly enhanced by his medical and law degrees, which she—not God—had helped to pay for over many years of struggle in her youth.

But now she was past her prime, she told the court. At this stage of her life, she could hardly hope ever to match her husband's earning power. She would in fact be lucky to find profitable employment anywhere.

"Everybody wants a kitten, and no one wants a cat," she remarked.

The men chuckled.

Court was recessed until January 30, when Judge Howatt would render his decision in the Broderick matter.

Betty Broderick during her second trial, November 13, 1991
(© Jack Yon / U-T San Diego / ZUMA Press)

Dan Broderick, in his office, May 17, 1988
(© Don Kohlbauer / U-T San Diego / ZUMA Press)

Dan and Linda Broderick's house, where the killings took
place, and where Betty rammed the front door with her car
(© Lillian Kossacoff / U-T San Diego / ZUMA Press)

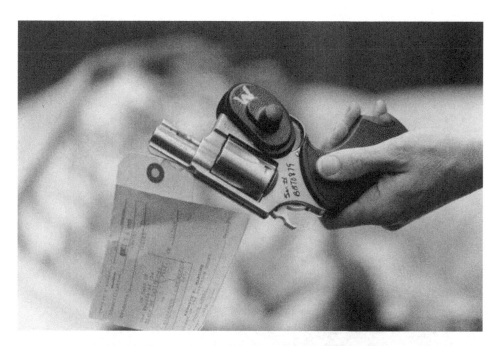

The gun used to kill Dan and Linda Broderick
(© Michael Franklin / U-T San Diego / ZUMA Press)

Dan and Linda Broderick's headstone at Greenwood Cemetery, San Diego
(© Debbi Morrello / U-T San Diego / ZUMA Press)

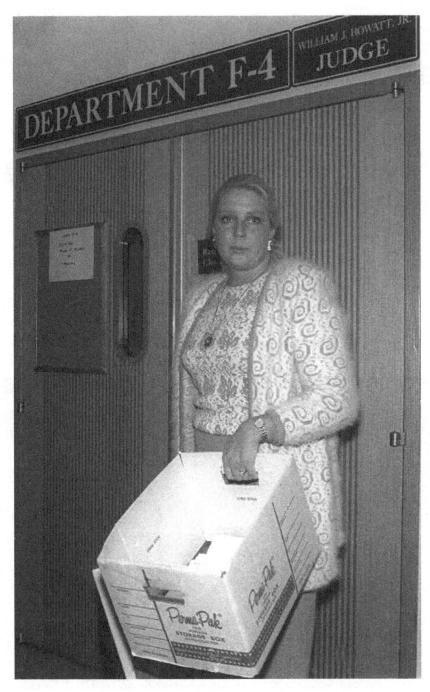

Betty Broderick attends her divorce and child custody hearing
in San Diego Family Court, March 03, 1989
(Joe Klein / ZUMA Press)

Betty Broderick pleads not guilty to murder, November 15, 1989
(© Jerry McClard / U-T San Diego / ZUMA Press)

Betty Broderick testifying in court about the moment she shot Dan and Linda, November 5, 1991
(© Michael Darden / U-T San Diego / ZUMA Press)

Prosecuting Attorney Kerry Wells holds up a photograph from which Dan
Broderick's face has been crossed out, November 4, 1999
(© San Diego Union / U-T San Diego / ZUMA Press)

Betty Broderick is led away after her conviction, January 14, 1992
(© Don Kohlbauer / U-T San Diego / ZUMA Press)

Chapter 26

What Would a Jury Say?

Throughout January, she seemed almost euphoric. Everywhere she went, she told her friends how well she had performed in court, how even Gerald Barry had praised her skills. She also showed everyone a lengthy article about the trial in the *Reader*, which openly suggested that the sealed courtroom was the improper result of Dan Broderick's influence in the legal community. At long last her story had made it into the press—and the press was on her side. The *Reader* had not blamed her at all for her part in keeping the hearing closed. Beneath a photo of Betty in the corridor, the story also pointed out that Dan had "managed to avoid being photographed" by coming and going each day through a rear door used by judges, "despite a county policy that allows such maneuvers only when there's a security problem or the possibility of violent altercations." Reporters Krueger and DeWyze also quoted Dan's remark to them in their interview a year before: The divorce trial, Dan had said, "is going to resolve some community property issues, but it's not going to end this thing. It's not going to end until one of us is gone."

It was a remark Betty studied with interest. Years later, she would say that she took it "as a direct threat—proof that I had been right all along: he was trying to kill me." It was perhaps at that moment that Betty's mind, already so paranoid and ravaged, turned from flip and furious to true thoughts of death. His or hers? Who knows? But, certainly, some new die was cast.

At the time, she was too buoyant that month to reflect anything beyond her own certainty of impending victory. She was going to win. She knew it. Her reputation would be restored, her worries over money removed. She would have $25,000 a month, plus all three children, plus a $1 million nest egg. Finally, the world would see that she had been right all along about Dan Broderick. She would be vindicated. No more Crazy Betty.

She felt so good she stopped writing in her diaries. She wrote no more hateful letters. She made no obscene phone calls. The divorce was over. She even took a job, not for the money but for the pleasure, at the La Jolla Pre-School Academy. Each day from seven A.M. to two P.M., Betty Broderick was once again surrounded by squealing, adoring babies. She began to think about a new diet. Some of her aches and pains vanished; for a few nights that month, she even managed to sleep straight through—no two A.M. anxiety attacks, no pacing about the house in the dark, waiting for the sun to rise. She began to remember what it felt like to be normal.

But what if she was wrong? The fear still flickered. She called her parents that month and begged them to come to San Diego to be in court with her for the verdict. She even offered to pay their airfare. "I just wanted my family there, to show the judge that I wasn't a solitary person, that I was part of a family that cared." But they wouldn't come. The aging Bisceglias hadn't been back to visit their daughter since

281

1986, when she left them sitting at the dinner table to drive her Suburban through Dan's front door and wound up in a mental hospital for three days.

"But then, a few days later, [her sister] Clare calls and invites them to her fortieth birthday party, a big bash in Beverly Hills, a lot of heavy Hollywood types—and, suddenly," she says bitterly, "they agreed to come to California."

The memory of Clare's birthday weekend still hurts her.

Because she was feeling new confidence in herself, she decided to go all out for the occasion. She got the boys for the weekend, took them to the barber, and assembled their best dress suits. She flew Kim in from Arizona. And she went on a major shopping spree with Lee. "And Lee got gorgeous—perfect black dress, $200 shoes, $100 earrings ... I was trying especially hard to puff her up because of all she'd been through." She then piled her perfectly groomed brood into a van and drove to the Beverly Hills Hotel, where the Bisceglia clan was gathered.

It was a strained, unhappy weekend. Betty spent too much money trying to impress everyone. She still remembers a bill she paid in the hotel's star-studded Polo Lounge. "I took my turn and bought Sunday breakfast for everybody—strawberries and champagne for twenty people. It was horrendously expensive, but at the time, I still thought I was going to be fine—and all of it was a chance to try to get back in my family."

It didn't work. She begged her parents again to return to San Diego with her for court on Monday. But, again, they refused. "My mother wanted absolutely nothing to do with it, whether I won or I didn't."

She drove back to San Diego, hurt, angry, and filled with rising anxiety over the impending verdict. That night, too, she had an argument with Lee, who wanted to go out after ten with a shaggy-haired boy Betty didn't know. Betty told her that, if she left, she couldn't come back. Lee went, and didn't come back.

Court the next day was short but not sweet. Dan got nearly everything he asked for. Betty got nothing she wanted.

Howatt accepted all of Dan's numbers. He valued Dan's law practice at the date of separation; he agreed that Betty owed Dan nearly $750,000 in Epstein credits and cash advances; he accepted Dan's valuation of the pension fund and every other item of property, right down to the $12,000 piano.

Betty got half the pension fund—or around $240,000, which she couldn't touch until she was sixty-five without massive tax liabilities; she got the piano, the Warner Springs unit, and her house—all with their outstanding debts included.

When the final math was done, Dan owed her $33,606.02 in cash—but Howatt cut that by another $5,000, which was still due on the $16,000 that Judge Joseph had earlier ordered her to pay on Barry's legal fees.

Which brought her net cash award down to a grand total of $28,606.02—$1,000 less even than Barry had proposed. Dan got sole legal custody of the boys—but, for the first time since 1986, Betty was at least awarded formal visitation rights on alternating weekends and holidays, plus the full month of July. An earlier request she had made to keep them until Monday mornings, in the event that she was denied custody, so she could serve her traditional Sunday dinners, was denied. The return deadline was six P.M. Sunday.

Betty was awarded custody of Lee, however, plus $1,500 in monthly child support until Lee was eighteen—but only on condition that Lee remain "a full-time student in high school."

Howett also ordered Dan to take out a $1 million life insurance policy, payable to all four Broderick youngsters—but excluding Betty. In the event of his death, she got nothing. Nor did Betty get her $80,000 in back attorney fees; she was responsible for her own legal costs, said Howett.

The only item of consequence that Dan didn't win entirely was spousal support. Howett kept it at $16,000 each month. But even that was qualified, contingent upon "further order of the court, remarriage, or the death of either party." Further, the order noted, "It is apparent to the Court that Wife must ultimately take some responsibility for contributing to her own support ..."

Lastly, Howett re-stated the one-hundred-yard stay-away restraining order, preventing either party from "attacking, harassing, molesting, or in any manner bothering one another."

She drove home with a screaming mind. Not $1 million. Not even half a million. $28,000. A joke, an insult, an outrage. And only one child? She gets Lee, the troublesome one, the one he doesn't want, but not her boys? How dare the judge let him pick and choose among his children that way? What did they think she was, a garbage dump for Dan Broderick's refuse, his cleaning lady? She was supposed to mop up the mess he made by leaving his family?

Dan had gotten every single thing he wanted. The verdict was no more than a literal reading of Gerald Barry's wish list. Except for spousal support.

Spousal support. She wanted to stop the car and vomit, just thinking about that, her rage was so great. How could the cheap sonofabitch even suggest $9,000 a month, then $5,000, and then nothing? After all she had done to help him get where he was? All those years of having his babies, cooking his meals, hostessing his parties, taking his shirts to the laundry?

Yet she was supposed to be grateful for $16,000? Ha. And how long would that last? "Until further order of the court." Which meant "until Dan Broderick decides otherwise, until he goes in again and appeals it," her mind cried. And when would that be? Three months? Six? A year? Where was her security?

And what did it mean, "until remarriage"?

It meant that if she found someone to marry, Dan was completely off the hook. He was getting married within weeks—but if she did the same thing, she got absolutely nothing from her sixteen years of investment in Dan Broderick.

Unbelievable. She felt like gunning the motor until the car hit five hundred miles an hour and aiming it directly at his goddamn house again. There was no solution. The divorce was finally over, but nothing had changed. Four years it had gone on. Yet, today, she was still just as dependent on the bastard as she had ever been. She couldn't make any plans, she couldn't budget, she couldn't relax. All she could do now was worry about when the ax would fall again. And fall it would, she knew, the minute she displeased him.

And what about her reputation? She was still a mother denied her children. An unfit mother. Unfit. Unfit! Now everyone would know. She was disgraced again. She felt dizzy. He had cheated, he had lied, he had treated her savagely. She had done nothing but call him childish names.

Yet she was the loser, the victim—and the fool. She had trusted in a judge to see through it, to laugh at Dan's deflated property estimates, his alleged losses. He made millions, yet he sounded like he was practically broke. And the judge let him get away with it.

She burned to sue him, in front of a jury, not only for criminal fraud but also for damages. What about defamation of character, slander, intentional infliction of emotional distress, mental cruelty, loss of consortium—all the stuff Dan Broderick pleaded in his own malpractice cases to win millions for his clients. He made juries weep over how mean people had been to them.

What would a jury say? What would twelve ordinary citizens say, she wondered, if they heard what Dan had done to her? They would of course side with her, just as the *Reader* had, once those reporters had heard the full story. The idea embedded itself, dangerously, in her brain, where it still remained nine months later when she slipped into Dan's house on the morning of November 5, 1989, with her gun.

The first target of her fury was Lee. The next time she spoke to her youngest daughter, she told her to stay away, that "$1,500 isn't worth what you're putting me through. You're killing me."

So Lee moved back to Dan's—and one more time became her parents' Ping-Pong ball of first choice. But, evicted by her mother, she found there was no room for her, either, in her father's house. Instead, she lived for the next few weeks in Dan's small pool house out back, which had no toilet. Nor would he give her a key to his house, she later testified, for fear that Betty might get it. So "if nobody was home, I'd have to go down in the arroyo" behind the house to relieve herself.

Betty fell into a few weeks of almost eerie, purposeful calm, of the sort terminal patients sometimes display. For once, she didn't instantly run around town telling everyone how cheated she had been—she, in fact, initially even refused to tell several friends what she had been awarded in trial. Part of it was pride—she didn't want anyone to know how far she had fallen from the grandeur she had anticipated. But, by then, too, even Betty had finally begun to see that few of her La Jolla friends sympathized with an ex-wife who was getting $16,000 a month in support.

For the next month, she was seemingly in control of herself, friends say, and even cheerful. "It seemed like she was putting it behind her and getting on with her life," says her friend Dian Black. "She was angry about the settlement, especially the kids, but she didn't talk about it much. She was more fun than she'd ever been."

But, inside, Betty Broderick was hardly maintaining. Quietly, from the thin, the cluttered, private confines of her kitchen, she called the district attorney in January to ask if she could file criminal charges against Dan for cheating her through his deals with his brother. They told her no. "They said criminal charges only applied if it was a business partnership, but not to divorce court. Well, to me, marriage is a business partnership." But she accepted it.

Methodically, she shopped around for new attorneys to appeal the divorce settlement and begin new custody negotiations. This time, she quickly found and hired two locals without fuss or struggle: Herman Hauslein, to challenge the divorce settlement, and custody attorney Walter Maund, whose orders from her were explicit—Get the children back before the fall school begins.

To her surprise, after all the time and money just expended in divorce court, Dan didn't contest Maund's mission. Instead, he suddenly entertained the idea of negotiations, speaking through his associate, Kathy Cuffaro.

But Betty knew why: Dan had just announced his wedding date. He and Linda would be married on April 22—ten days after the twentieth anniversary of his marriage to Betty. Even the date festered in her mind. How could he remarry in April? Why didn't the sonofabitch complete the cruelty by marrying Linda on the exact same date, too? Either way, he dearly didn't want their kids. He never had. He was going to start a new family. He wanted to unload his old family on her. Betty the baby-sitter. Betty the solution. Betty the sap. Right.

She continued about her business. She joined a women's self-help group and became active in HALT again; she attended a 'Course in Miracles' seminars; and she continued working at the preschool—although by now she was seriously looking ahead, worrying about what "real career" she might pursue. Law? The stock market? Real estate? But photography had always been a special interest of hers, and so she called Michael Campbell, a La Jolla portrait and society photographer she had met at a function months earlier, to ask his advice. She ended up as his unpaid assistant "to see if I like this stuff, and if I was any good ..."

She went to a wedding with him and a couple of local parties, acting as his Girl Friday. They eventually talked of going into business together. Nothing ever came of it, but Campbell's relevance to the Broderick story did not end there. As it so happened, he was also the photographer Linda had commissioned to do her wedding pictures. He had already done Linda's formal wedding portraits. To this day, it is unclear whether Betty contacted Campbell with that knowledge in mind—which she vehemently denies—or by sheer coincidence. Whatever the truth of the matter, Linda Kolkena was instantly convinced that Betty was plotting somehow to sabotage her wedding—and so, this time, it was Linda, not Betty, who did the wrong thing.

According to Campbell, Linda called him in a panic to say he shouldn't have Betty working for him, that Betty was crazy, that she had been both jailed and institutionalized, that she had run a car into Dan's door, etc.. Linda was worried that Betty would destroy her wedding pictures, she told Campbell. Or steal them. Or look at them. In her mind, it was a nightmare that this horrible woman could be anywhere so near to her magic hour.

Campbell didn't know what Linda was talking about. He hadn't heard any of the sordid details of the Broderick divorce because Betty never told him about it, he says. He did know, however, that Linda had insulted him personally. He was a professional. Nobody touched his pictures, much less an unpaid amateur like Betty. What was the

285

matter with Linda Kolkena anyway? According to Linda's friends, later, Campbell told her that she was the one who sounded crazy, not Betty.

Even so, Betty was humiliated. "I lied to him—I told him I never ran that car through anybody's door. I just sort of pooh-poohed the whole thing. But, my God, can you imagine how I felt? That car thing was four or five years earlier. I was trying to get all that behind me. She was hounding me. Why didn't she leave me alone? I thought after she got the prize and married the sonofabitch, she'd leave me alone. What was the point of her doing this now?"

There was no real mystery to it, of course. Linda Bernadette Kolkena was in so many respects just like Betty had been twenty years before. A first-time bride with old-fashioned values, she saw her wedding day as the one perfect moment in life to be treasured forever. Despite her youth, despite the changing decades, Linda, like Betty, cared about every traditional wedding detail. Her friends would give her showers, and she would take them on a "bachelorette" party. She spent weeks searching for the perfect, flowing white wedding gown, finding the right florist for her bridal bouquet, the right musicians, the right stationer for the invitations, the premier confectioner for the cake. This was her fairy tale forever. And wedding photographs were a critical part of it. Like Betty, Linda Kolkena would also one day have a bound wedding album to show her children.

For weeks before her wedding, Kim said, Linda walked around the house humming lyrics from "Chapel of Love," the Dixie Cups's 1964 hit tune: "Going to the chapel . . . gonnnnnna get maarrrrrried . . . gooooing to the chapel of looooove ..."

Unlike Betty Broderick, however, Linda was not marrying a young man her own age, but another woman's former husband, the father of four children, three of whom would barely speak to her. She had been reviled on an almost daily basis as "the cunt," "the home-wrecker," "the whore." She had cried to her friends, she had complained, and she had waited patiently for nearly six years. Linda Kolkena had paid a far greater price for her man than most young brides ever do. Her wedding day would forever be tainted with hate—and it went both ways.

That she hated Betty Broderick was by now as understandable as it was sad. She was too young, too romantic, too selfish to take pause, to consider the older woman's side. Despite any guilt she may have felt over the adultery, she could not bring herself to show Betty compassion, much less apologize for the lies, to attempt a peace council. Instead, she only followed Dan's lead, until, finally, as the years wore on, and the invective mounted, she felt only loathing for Betty Broderick. Crazy Betty. A witch from hell, to be despised and feared, standing between her and happiness.

That Betty hated Linda was of course just as understandable—and not only because Betty remains convinced to this day that Linda Kolkena, in combination with white Zinfandel and middle age, ruined her "perfect marriage." There were all the extra insensitivities over the years, too, minor cruelties that added up: the notarized house deed, signed by Linda; the insurance cancelation letters, signed by Linda; Linda's voice on the answering machine, before Dan was even divorced. Never mind the wrinkle ads and the legal party picture that Betty alleges Linda sent. Linda

Kolkena's documentable acts were needless, heedless, and deadly enough. And Linda wasn't done yet.

As the wedding approached, Betty Broderick's tenuous hold on composure began to disintegrate entirely. "At first, she seemed fine," says Helen Pickard. "But then the wedding began to eat at her. She was obsessed with every detail of it. It's all she could talk about. She would say, 'Can you imagine that Linda's going to wear a strapless dress?' But then she went shopping for new wedding clothes for the boys. She even talked about buying Dan and Linda a wedding present."

"Yes, I was going to get them this gorgeous standing-on-the-floor silver champagne bucket that I saw in a catalog," Betty said later from jail. "It was fancier than I like, but Dan loved fancy. So I was going to buy it and say it was from the kids, because I knew that, if it came from me, he would send it back." She never did buy the ice bucket.

Instead, one Saturday in mid-March, she burgled Dan's property.

As usual, the circumstances are in dispute. As Betty tells it, she went to Dan's house to pick up the boys and noticed a large envelope on the front steps. Dan's housekeeper later insisted that the envelope was on a hallway table inside the house.

Not that it matters where it was. Either way, Betty picked it up, snooped inside, and discovered that it was Dan and Linda's wedding list, ready for the printer—twenty-two pages, more than a hundred and fifty names, including about a dozen judges, among them Ashworth, presiding judge of family court. Also Dr. Steven Sparta. None of her other divorce court judges were on the list, but, even so, Betty saw it as more evidence of the San Diego legal conspiracy against her, proof of conflict of interest. Worse yet, dozens of their mutual old friends were invited. How could they go?

She stole the list. She didn't see anything wrong with the theft. "Why should I?" she asked later. "If you're stupid enough to leave it on the front door stoop, you get what you get. Anyone would have picked it up. It was just a lark, no big deal." But that wasn't all she stole.

Strolling through Dan's house, she also spied a pile of T-shirts lying on a table: "First Annual Cabo Chicks Bachelorettes Party," the logo said. How sweet, she thought. How trashy. How cuntlike. The kids had already told her Linda was planning a pre-wedding party for around fifteen girlfriends in Cabo San Lucas, Mexico. She wondered how much that would cost Dan, to fly a whole fleet of bimbos to Mexico. She took one of the T-shirts too.

For Linda it was the final straw. The divorce was over. Why wouldn't this bitch leave them alone?

Never mind, said Dan. They would deal with it Monday. The right way. The legal way.

But Linda was fed up.

There are two versions of what happened next—Betty's and Linda's. One protects Betty, the other justifies Linda. In substance, neither adds up to more than just another tawdry episode in the Broderick matter.

According to Betty, she was at work at the preschool that Monday morning when she received several telephone calls—but the caller hung up each time. "So I knew something was wrong. I'd heard that thieves try to determine when you're not home, and very few people knew I even had that job." So she went home early, around one P.M., to check. There her housekeeper, Maria, told her that a pretty young blond woman had been in the house that morning, rummaging through her papers. The woman had told Maria she was a friend of Kim's, picking up something.

Betty knew instantly who had been inside her house. Linda Kolkena. Incredible.

But she didn't have time to think about it, because, at the same time, she says, she found a message on her telephone machine, saying that she was summoned to appear before Judge Howatt at 1:30, on a complaint over the stolen wedding list. Another four-hour notice, just like the house sale. Well, they wouldn't do it without her this time.

She scrambled and made it to court just in time—for Howatt to order her either to return the wedding list by the next day, or forfeit her $16,000 monthly support payment until she did. He also ordered her not to call anyone on the wedding list or reveal their names.

Her head throbbed with frustrated rage. Why had Dan made such a fuss over a stupid prank? Would his controlling gestures never end? "Just six weeks after I thought I had a final divorce settlement, they're suddenly telling me that if I do anything to piss off Dan Broderick, the whole deal's off. No money. Behave or starve, bitch—that was the message. After all those years, absolutely nothing had changed."

But, she insists, vaguely, she returned the list on time, as ordered. She can't remember who she gave it to, however—just "some court clerk."

Linda's friend, Sharon Blanchet, tells an entirely different story. According to Blanchet, Betty never returned the wedding list. And, says Blanchet, it was not until two days after the court deadline passed and Betty still hadn't complied that Linda finally decided to raid Betty's house and take it back herself. Friends who knew what Linda planned to do tried to talk her out of it. "I told her it was stupid, that she was just giving Betty ammunition," says Blanchet. But Linda was too frustrated to be stopped.

The next day, she drove to Calle del Cielo—alone, according to Blanchet. She was nervous as she pulled up in front of Betty's house. Linda Kolkena had never even had a conversation with Betty Broderick, beyond one brief exchange in passing at the door of Dan's house years ago. Otherwise, she had only heard the voice reviling her on Dan's answering machine. Betty both repulsed and scared her.

But it was early morning. Betty was at work. She had called the school to make sure. Nobody would be home. The front door was unlocked. She entered the house and paused, momentarily taken aback at the spectacular ocean view through the wide sliding-glass doors. She looked around at the living room. It was larger than the entire house Linda Kolkena had grown up in. What in God's name was this woman complaining about? But, as she moved through the house, she was even more fascinated by the disorder. It was March, but Christmas wrappings still lay in wadded heaps on the floors, she later told friends. She walked past a dressing room. Clothes hanging on chairs, on doorknobs, clothes everywhere, many with the price tags still on them. Clothes never worn—many in sizes so small that Betty couldn't have fit into them in years. And throughout the house—on the coffee tables, on the mantles—she saw pictures of Dan. Betty's pretty white wedding album from 1969, when Linda was only seven, still lay on the coffee table. Chilled, she glanced over her shoulder. But, no. She was here alone.

She found the kitchen nook, which she knew from conversations with Kim served as Betty's office. Entering, she was amazed yet again. Boxes and boxes of legal documents, piles of papers everywhere, magazine and newspaper clippings stuffed into folders, lying on the floors, stacked on counters. It was chaos. She was never going to find her wedding list in this clutter.

But, lying atop a pile of documents, she did find Betty's 1988 autobiography: "What's a Nice Girl to Do?" She flipped to the last page and read the final sentence: "If this is the way domestic disputes are settled in the courts, is there any wonder there are so many murders? I am desperate ..." Ninety pages of pure hate. Dan should see this. So she stole it.

But, as she was leaving, she got caught. Suddenly, standing in the doorway was a small, stout, dark Mexican woman with a long black braid down her back. Maria Montez glared. Who, Montez demanded, was she? Linda smiled weakly and lied: a friend of Kim's, she said. Then she fled. With Betty's manuscript.

But when she showed it to Dan, Blanchet said later, he was less interested in its contents than in his fiancée's outrageous behavior. What in hell was Linda doing, breaking, entering and stealing? He ordered her to return Betty's property at once. And, as docilely as Betty had been in the years before her, Linda obeyed.

Despite the risk posed to her own license as a practicing attorney, Blanchet accompanied Linda on her return trip, "to stand lookout outside," she says, while Linda entered Betty's house a second time to replace the stolen manuscript. Again, Linda knew Betty wasn't at home because she had called the school to make sure that Betty was tending to infants that morning—and not at Calle del Crelo, waiting for her.

Whichever story you believe, this much is clear: Betty Broderick left court on that Monday with a swimming head. Why? "By 1989 they had everything," she said later. "They had the money, the kids, they're getting married. They have killed me already. Yet they're still coming at me! Why?"

Driving home, she settled it once and for all in her mind: because they wanted her dead—that was why. They wanted to drive her so crazy she would kill herself and not be around anymore to mar their perfect images.

That's what she was thinking as she left court that day. God, how many trips had she made to this building? Twenty? Fifty? Her brain felt like the heart of a tornado. She was the victim again.

"I'm being assaulted on my answering machine, at my home, at the job where I was just trying to get on my two feet and go forward with my life again," she said later, thinking back. "And they were literally destroying my reputation. For years, I lived with gossip, about how I had bullets and bombs, how I was sneaking into their bedroom at night and stealing things and threatening to kill them. Linda Kolkena had been telling that stuff to everybody ... my own kids told me. She was even spreading bullshit around about me threatening to bloody her wedding dress. It was so humiliating! The little bitch had been watching too many soap operas."

Besides, "I'm living alone in this big house with sliding doors, and anybody could get in, and I had been robbed a couple of other times. And I just said, I'm not living like this anymore."

And so, midway between downtown and La Jolla, she pulled off the freeway at one of San Diego's largest gun shops, went inside and placed her order for a .38 Smith & Wesson handgun. Amazing how easy it was. Her past record of misdemeanors didn't even matter. It cost her $357.33. She fired it once in the indoor range. She liked the way it felt in her hand. She knew guns from her childhood. She enjoyed the kick. She was pleased that she hadn't lost her eye after all these years. She filled out the permit forms. It didn't matter that she had been convicted four times for contempt of court and spent a week in jail. In California, only convicted felons are denied guns. The friendly salesman told her she could pick up her gun in a couple of weeks.

She finished the drive home with a lighter heart. Self-defense. That's what this was. She had taken control.

Whether Betty returned the list or not, Dan sent her a full support check that month. But the Brodericks finished out March in court again, where custody of Lee was returned to Dan. Betty didn't contest Dan's declaration that she had thrown her daughter out of the house.

Chapter 27

Mr. and Mrs. Daniel T. Broderick III

She picked up her new gun at the end of the month. At the same time she bought three boxes of bullets, ranging from cheap target ammunition to hollow points, which are designed to expand on contact and create maximum damage. They are widely favored by police officers in the field. But Betty said she didn't know the difference. "You know me—I just asked for whatever was top of the line." The gun was loaded at the store, she says, and never fired again, until November 5.

She made no secret of her purchase. To the contrary, like a boastful child with a new toy, she practically advertised it. She immediately showed it to her sons in what she says was an educational effort to keep them from ever touching it. She even took them to the shooting range and let them fire guns so they would understand their lethal power. She also told both Kim and Lee she had it, and showed it to Maria, warning her, too, never to touch it.

In the beginning, she kept the gun in its case, hanging in a closet. Later she moved it to a lingerie drawer near her bed—all in an effort, she says, to keep it from her sons.

"But, of course, the boys didn't listen to me. They were fascinated with that gun. It was like hide-and-seek." One day, she found them out in the yard with it. And so after that, she says, "I started carrying it in my purse all the time, to keep it away from them."

During her trials, the prosecutor would argue that the boys were not "fascinated" with the gun at all, but, instead, so afraid that Betty intended to shoot Dan with it that they were trying to hide it from her the day she caught them with it in the yard. Either way, the children all told Dan that Mom now owned a gun.

But even then, despite the gravity of his earlier comments during the divorce trial, Dan didn't seem to take Betty's threats to kill him any more seriously than he had done two years before, when Ruth Roth issued her Tarasoff warnings. That was just Bets talking—she would never "kill the golden goose," he told friends.

Linda was not so sanguine. She had long begged Dan either to install an alarm system or get guard dogs, friends said. But Dan would not run scared from Betty Broderick. In his only concession—and with an apparent eye to protecting his front door from another assault—he had occasionally hired security guards for a few hours at a time in the past when, according to the children, "something had happened in court that he thought might upset Mom." According to later testimony, he also had the locks on his front door changed four times. But that's as far as he would go.

Finally, Linda acted on her own. She called Scott Presley, a professional bodyguard, and hired him to stand guard full-time for three days prior to the wedding. Presley and his partner set up surveillance in a van in front of the Broderick house—but, says Presley, angry still, neither Dan nor Linda ever alerted him that Betty

Broderick was an armed woman. In fact, he says, Dan specifically ordered him not to bring a gun to the stakeout. "So we figured she was just another La Jolla bon-bon we could take out physically if she showed up to make some kind of scene. Dan Broderick risked our lives. Linda had street smarts, she was a working-class girl with enough sense of danger to at least call us. But Dan was just another cool dude in a sports car. If he was scared of his ex-wife, it sure as hell didn't show," says Presley. "He paid us to sit there for three days—but he didn't even provide us with a picture of her. So one night at some party, we approached a big blonde who turned out to be some fancy lawyer's wife. It was a crazy assignment."

To this day, Presley regrets that he didn't at least urge Linda to go out and buy a cheap alarm herself. "For five dollars, they could both be alive today."

Meantime, gallows humor was rampant among Dan and Linda's wedding guests. Linda had told everyone about the bodyguards and Betty's alleged threats to shoot her and Dan at the wedding. People nervously joked that, if a car backfired on the day of the ceremony, guests would be hitting the ground, ruining their finest party clothes. A handful, however, didn't think it so funny—Gerald Barry among them. He didn't attend the wedding out of fear, so the story goes, that if Betty did go on a rampage, he would surely be among her first targets.

"It was crazy," recalls Blanchet. "We talked about it, but most of us never really believed it. How can normal people take something like that seriously?"

Betty, meanwhile, was sinking fast in the springtime of her husband's second marriage. On April 4, she quit her job at the nursery school. "I love the job, the teachers, the kids, and the location," she said, in a handwritten resignation note with an unhappy face at the top. "But the pay is ridiculous ... I need something I can really devote myself to, and L.J. Pre-School Academy isn't it."

And Dan, virtually up to the day he walked down the aisle with Linda, was still exercising his legal clout. On April 7, he went to court again to win a switch in the visitation schedule, so that the boys would be at his house on the weekend of his wedding, not at Betty's as scheduled. As usual, he didn't call to discuss it with her. The change in visitation was simply presented to her after the fact. Fait accompli.

On the weekend of April 8, Linda took her girlfriends to Cabo San Lucas for her bachelorette party, while Dan and several of his friends went to Denver for a bachelor party at brother Larry's house.

Betty stayed home with the children and tried to ignore the calendar. Then it was April 12. Her twentieth wedding anniversary. Her marriage for fifty years. Until the Twelfth of Never.

Somewhere around that time, too, she ran over a light alongside Dan's driveway as she was dropping the boys off. He naturally photographed the damage. According to his photographs, she had also driven onto his lawn that night, aiming her car directly at his door. Evidently, she was thinking of smashing into it again, but reconsidered. Not that it mattered—within weeks, she would be answering for it in court. Betty no longer got any breaks from Dan for rational second thoughts. Dan, the lawn lover, was as angry about his mashed grass as he had been years earlier over his splintered front door.

Kay Wright, Brad's mother, also died that month. A few weeks before, she announced that she wanted her death to be a celebration of life for her friends. In preparation for the final party, recalls Dian Black, Betty spent days traipsing around La Jolla, buying up old records with Kay's favorite songs, which Betty then spliced onto a single, long-playing tape. 'Forever Young' led the selection. "I'll never forget it," says Black. "One night I was at Betty's house and she was playing the record, and suddenly she wanted to dance. I had never seen Betty relaxed enough to dance anywhere, much less with another woman. She was always so inhibited about everything, but that night she wanted to dance, and so we did. Just me and her in her house, dancing to 'Forever Young.' She was so sad about Kay. But she didn't cry. She just said, 'Kay's going out in style.'"

Then it was Dan's wedding day.

"No more cheap whore. Now she's Mrs. DTB3," Betty wrote in a single line on a notepad the night before.

Her remaining friends worried about her. Among them was Helen Pickard, who had watched and listened for months, longer than most others would. Pickard, mother of three, had been divorced a few years earlier. Since there was no major money to fight over, hers had been a peaceable settlement. Afterward, to support herself and her children, she had organized a successful janitorial service, cleaning office buildings. She rose each day at four A.M. to supervise her crew and, in time, made all her affluent La Jolla friends with maids smile at her growing expertise about the best toilet bowl cleansers and floor scrubs. Helen Pickard never would really understand Betty's bitter complaints about getting only $16,000 per month in her divorce settlement. Even so, she liked Betty and was in the habit of stopping by her house each morning for coffee—partly because Betty was the only other woman Pickard knew who was always up at dawn. Over coffee, Pickard heard "the story" over and again, and she tried to counsel Betty to shape up. When Betty stole the wedding list, Pickard urged her to return it, just as Sharon Blanchet had tried to persuade Linda not to steal it back. "I just felt sorry for this poor girl [Linda] who was only trying to get married," says Pickard.

Then, the day before the wedding, Pickard says, Betty called her to say that "She was going to buy a new watch and have the date of Dan and Linda's wedding engraved on it 'just for fun.' She was laughing, but I thought it was creepy. It worried me." So Pickard called another of Betty's former friends, Jeannie Milliken, whose husband, the judge, was performing the wedding ceremony, and the two agreed to set up a beeper system for the day to monitor Betty's movements: Helen would spend the day with Betty, "and if she got away from me, I could let Jeannie know."

But, Pickard stresses, "I never thought she would kill them. I only went over there because I was afraid she might do something to embarrass herself—like drive by and honk, make some sort of scene. You know Betty's crazy sense of humor." Also, says Pickard, "I just felt so sorry for her. I knew if it were me in her position, that would've been the hardest day of my life. I just didn't want her to be alone." Pickard stayed at Betty's from seven A.M. until eleven that night. She tried to get Betty to go with her to

Palm Springs, "but she didn't want to go, because she was certain that some of the Brodericks would be coming by to say hello. It was so sad. She was still referring to them, even then, as 'my family.'

"But she was cheerful, the way Betty always is—a little quieter than usual, sort of melancholy, but definitely in control," Pickard recalls. "She didn't cry or rave. But she kept returning to the topic of the third child who died. I don't think she ever got over that, and, for some reason, she always blamed Dan for it ... Then she got out her wedding album, and we looked through it. At one point she said, 'You don't feel sorry for me, do you?'

"And I said, 'No, I don't, because you can do anything you want in life.' I told her, 'You're getting to be boring. If the legal system is so bad, go be a lawyer. If you want to be a pinnacle of La Jolla society, go do it!' Betty was so smart, so talented. There was nothing she couldn't do well. I would have given anything for even half her gifts."

As the sun set over La Jolla, Pickard says she told Betty, "Okay, now. This day is over. You'll never have to go through with it again. Go on now, get on with your life.' But I just don't think she had any faith in herself. She had no identity, beyond Dan's."

Pickard recalls the day as mostly excruciating. It was an agony, she says, watching Betty watch the clock, as time dragged on and on. But finally, late that evening, one of the Brodericks did come to see Betty. It was Nancy, Dan's third sister, "And it was just heartbreaking," Pickard recalls, "to see how thrilled Betty was that at least one person in that family hadn't forgotten her." The three women went out to dinner at a Mexican restaurant in the heart of La Jolla Village. And finally Betty Broderick went home to bed. April 22 was over.

Years later, after Helen Pickard had become a prosecution witness, Betty remembered that day with nothing but angry humiliation. "Helen Pickard was never my friend! She was not my confidante, she knew nothing about what went on in my life. She just barged in every morning, and I tolerated her. I was perfectly fine the day of Dan's wedding—I didn't need a baby-sitter! In fact, I was planning to do something with him [Black]. But because I'm the wimp I am, I didn't throw [Pickard] out when she showed up because I'm a polite person." Betty is still rewriting history to suit herself, to this day, only more so.

The next morning, she drove over to Dan's house to pick up Kim for breakfast. Of the Broderick clan gathered inside, only Dan's brother Dennis came outside to greet her. "He gave me a big hug and a kiss, without hesitating for a moment. He was happy to see me." She was so grateful she later wrote him a thank-you note.

She pumped Kim and her other children for every detail of the wedding, alternately gloating and brooding. She couldn't get enough.

The ceremony had been brief. Afterward, Dan had raised the flags of both Ireland and the Netherlands on his flagpole. He had been radiant, so happy, said housekeeper Sylvia Cavins later, that he had hugged her and, for the first time in the eighteen months she worked for him, "told me to call him Dan, instead of Mr. Broderick."

But Kim didn't tell her mother any of that. She instead told Betty only what she

294

knew she wanted to hear. The boys had refused to smile for the photographer. Good. And, according to Betty, Kim had laughed at the Kolkena family for being "so low-class—she said they jumped up and down, and yelled and clapped at the end of the ceremony. She said it was so embarrassing!" Betty loved it. And that wasn't all. "Then, later, they all went to some sleazy, disgusting Mexican bar down in Old Town," said Betty, still relishing it years later from jail, "with Linda still in her wedding gown!"

But the facts remained the same. He had married her.

And the little things gnaw at Betty still: He had worn a proper, rented morning coat to Linda's wedding, after he had ruined Betty's beautiful wedding in his ugly street suit and brown shoes. "He wore the same exact rented gray thing that he would never wear to my wedding."

Then, there was the matter of Linda's wedding china pattern—a flowery design of the exact type that Betty says Dan forbade her from choosing for their wedding. "The sonofabitch told me no flowers. But this service for twelve, Limoges, that they got had little tiny pink and blue flowers all over it. It's very, very girlish and it looks very luncheony. I couldn't have flowers, but here this little bitch goes out and buys flowers. Flowers, flowers everywhere. He forgot to tell her no flowers."

Meantime, Dan and Linda still had Betty's wedding china, moved to Cypress from its storage days at Coral Reef. Now she wanted it back, as soon as they returned from their honeymoon.

And that was the final blow—their honeymoon. Where did they go on their honeymoon, but back to the Caribbean. Worse, they took a cruise on a large, elegant sailing ship almost identical to one Betty had dreamed of sailing for years, once she and Dan got rich. Dan had taken his new wife on Betty's magic ship, to the exact same part of the world where he had honeymooned with her. And no way did she think it was just simple male thoughtlessness and insensitivity. "The bastard did it on purpose, he wanted to hurt me."

Meantime, proud as Dan Broderick was of his beautiful new wife, young enough to be his daughter, he was also a bit self-conscious about it, it seems, judging from several telegrams he sent to his pals back in San Diego from the honeymoon ship. Nearly all of them made not-so-veiled references to sexual exhaustion:

"Marriage consummated. Linda with child. Name under consideration—General Michael I. Neil Broderick. Your proud servant, DTB," read one he sent to Mike Neil. "Getting weaker," said one to Mike Reidy. Others were signed, "Your victorious servant, Danny Boy." And so on.

While Dan and Linda were gone, Betty attended the funeral of a woman she and Dan had known for years—the wife of an attorney and mother of three, who had died of cancer. "I was so glad they were gone, that I wouldn't have to see them there—that I could go." But she left depressed over more than the woman's death. Her whole ruined life was reflected in that funeral. "Every friend I ever had was there, all crying in the church about this wonderful wife and mother. They were lauding her for that. And that's what I was! Yet they would barely even say hello to me. It was like I was invisible. Why was I different?"

Among her first acts, the new Mrs. Daniel T. Broderick III promptly put her voice back on the family answering machine.

In one of her next acts, Linda refused to return Betty's wedding china, despite entreaties from both Kim and Lee, Gail Forbes, and even Sylvia Cavins. Dan himself was ready to return it—why did they want it anyhow?

Absolutely not, said Linda. She was sick of Betty Broderick's incessant demands. Betty hadn't asked for the china in the divorce trial, and she wasn't getting it now. Period. In fact, Linda told friends that she would rather break it, piece by piece, than give it back to Betty.

"It was childish, I suppose," said Sharon Blanchet later. "But Betty didn't want it before—and then she did want it. Linda just got mad. It was the principle of the thing. It was the same with the answering machine. She said, 'How long do we let her rule our lives?'"

Betty, of course, instantly broadcast Linda's latest meanness. After the killings, gossip became so distorted that one friend of Betty's doggedly insisted that Linda had, in fact, dropped the china, a piece at a time, from a second-floor balcony onto a driveway, right in front of Betty's eyes.

"That never happened," Betty said later. "But Linda Kolkena was definitely on a power trip after she married him. That china was just cheap junk. I only wanted it for sentimental reasons. There was no reason for her not to give it back." Not long after the wedding, Betty also began telling friends about a new spate of anonymous fat and wrinkle ads she said she was once again receiving in the mail from various San Diego-area postal depots. Linda, of course. Nobody believed her.

Dan, meantime, resumed his old fining system, although it was now clearly illegal.

"Dear Elisabeth Anne," he wrote in May, "Enclosed please find your alimony check for the month of June 1989. Note it is in the amount of $15,903.77. I have withheld $86.23 for the cost of replacing the light fixture you destroyed with your car when you drove up the front walk a couple of months ago and $10 for the cost of replacing the bricks that you chipped. Sincerely yours, Daniel T. Broderick."

And again in June: "Dear Elisabeth Anne: Enclosed please find your alimony check for the month of July 1989. Note I have deducted $340, which is the cost of the family portrait you defaced when you brought Rhett over with an earache ..."

Betty denied damaging the portrait, which had an X slashed through Dan's face— but even if she did do it, she said later, "He wasn't allowed to fine me. That was court-ordered support. He was supposed to take me to small-claims court, or send me a bill or something. He was writing his own rules again."

Why these two newlyweds didn't finally back off, why they couldn't see the dangers ahead in their continued determination to conquer a woman already ragged beyond reason, remains one of the enduring mysteries of the Broderick story.

Chapter 28

Down, Down, Down

Still, Betty tried to keep up pretenses. That spring, she put $5,000 down for a social membership in the La Jolla Beach and Tennis Club, which mainly entitled her to restaurant privileges. "She was so proud, just to be seen there again, among all the right people," said Pickard, Betty's lunch guest at the club one day. Colleen Stuart recalls similarly poignant scenes. Once, during the summer, Stuart remembers, she went to visit Betty at her house. "And it was the saddest thing I ever saw. She had all these lovely tables set up on her patio, with blue cloths and matching sun umbrellas. It was like a restaurant waiting for business. She even had fresh flowers on every table. She had all these expensive invitations engraved in gold printed up. Boxes and boxes of them. They said, 'Mrs. Betty Broderick cordially invites you to lunch on such-and-so day.' She was trying so hard to just go on without him. And she was being so Betty—so cheerful, upbeat. It was awful. Betty could never just break down and cry in front of anybody. The only two emotions she knew were anger and fear ..."

But, Betty's defenses were failing her at an alarming pace. Her once-bright mind was now so clouded that, increasingly, she could not match the trappings of acceptability with appropriate social behavior. Heads turned at the beach club as she grew louder, more obscene, angrier than ever before, pillorying Dan over her Caesar salad. Now, everywhere she went, she talked of nothing but Dan and Linda, how they were trying to destroy her, drive her to suicide.

"I thought that after the wedding, once she realized that it was really over, she might get better," Candy Westbrook said. "Instead, Betty only went crazier. She couldn't even put away their wedding pictures. She pretended that it all still existed. I always wanted to take that damned wedding album out and burn it."

But Betty was always such a deceptive personality. She had been balancing inner rage with outward routine for so long that, at times, if it was important enough to her, she could still dress up, tone down her fury, haul out her natural wit, and entrance almost anybody. Sheer habit kept her afloat. Thus, throughout that summer, while she was driving her few remaining friends away in droves with her foul rantings, she was also visiting, at the recommendation of her new custody attorney, yet another psychiatrist, both alone and with the boys—and, by all accounts, she performed well enough to persuade him that her sons should be returned to her, despite her anger at Dan.

But, at the same time that she was charming her new doctor, she was now also an armed woman. She had secretly begun carrying her .38 revolver with her wherever she went, inside her purse, along with a cellular telephone in case the children needed to reach her. That summer, she went to Neiman Marcus trunk shows, to the Valencia for lunch, to charity functions, always wearing her bright smile and her haunted, glittery eyes, and carrying her little Smith & Wesson. She was also huge now, she had aged ten years in three. Her old friends cringed at the sight of her. This woman bore no resemblance to the one they had once known. Yet nobody, her doctor included, could apparently see how bad it really was inside Betty Broderick's poor head.

Some days, she couldn't function at all. Instead, says Dian Black, she would sometimes just hide out at home for days at a stretch. "Betty always had this thing— she couldn't stand the idea that she was imposing on anybody. She never wanted to be seen unless she was in an upbeat mood. Betty would never let anybody help her work things through. She just didn't understand that friends are for the bad times, as well as the good. Somehow she just never learned to trust anybody to accept her for all that she was. Betty thought she had to be perfect all the time. I used to call her the 'Happy Hostess.' If she didn't answer the phone, I knew she was in a depression and just wanted to be alone. And I tried to respect that." In retrospect, adds Black, second-guessing herself as everyone closely involved in the Broderick story does, "I wish I had gone over there and kicked the door down. I just didn't realize how far gone she was."

Increasingly, too, Betty stopped taking early morning walks on the beach with her friend Ronnie Brown. "I didn't have the energy anymore to walk anywhere," she said later. "I'd just drive down and sit on a bench." More often, however, she watched the sunrise alone from within her house, where she obsessed the finances of her life as never before. Gerald Barry had been right—she couldn't keep her house on $16,000 a month, that was clear. The overhead alone, in mortgage, taxes, and insurance, ate up nearly $10,000, not to mention gardeners, pool cleaners, and Maria, her maid. Bills spilled off every countertop.

She would have to sell. She would have to move to some tacky condominium.

It was so unfair.

So she pushed it out of her mind, and reached impulsively instead for the thick stack of mail-order catalogs sitting by her telephone, and called Boston, or New York, or Philadelphia, and ordered something new. Something pretty. Something soothing. A crystal goblet, a new clock, a lawn chair. A toy for some child's birthday, a precious little gift for some couple's anniversary. It didn't matter. It felt better to buy.

But it couldn't last much longer. Her credit cards were reaching their limits. Her income taxes loomed. She hadn't budgeted to pay them. She didn't know how. She didn't want to know how. She was in big trouble. Hell with it. She didn't care anymore. Maybe she would have the drapes replaced this week. By the time she went to jail, Betty owed the IRS nearly $40,000.

Meanwhile, Linda was even ordering stationery like hers. Ivory and navy blue. Tiffany. Was there nothing Dan and Linda could do that was their own idea? Did they have to copy her taste in everything? The little bitch had even posed for a Christmas picture in an outfit almost identical to one of Betty's traditional favorites—black velvet skirt, white frilly blouse, with red-and-green-plaid accents. The slut. In her Christmas clothes.

Her head hurt. Her back hurt. Her jaw hurt. All her old physical ailments were back. And she couldn't sleep anymore. "I'd go to bed and turn around, and goddamn if it wasn't one A.M. when I woke up. I was up and down all night—again."

And what about the children? Walter Maund was getting nowhere. More delays. More legalese. She couldn't even remember what his hourly rate was—$100? $200?

She made another pot of coffee. Gourmet almond mocha. Her skin was turning yellow from all the coffee. Why couldn't she be like so many other women—knock off a bottle of brandy every night, or pop half a dozen Valium a day? It would be so much easier. Instead, she was stuck with coffee and the refrigerator. There was always so much food there it was hard to choose. A roast beef sandwich now? At three A.M.? Ice cream? Or a slice of chocolate mousse pie? Or all three? Then she could sleep.

She also read constantly in those lonely hours of the night—but not for simple pleasure or enlightenment. That Betty was long gone. Now she read only for validation, explanation of her collapsing life, justification of her own extreme behavior. Her library became an eclectic collection of clippings on cheating lawyers, midlife crisis, and victimized wives. Boxes of legal documents, personal files, and books were stacked high by the summer of 1989. Filed articles ranged from "The Confused American Housewife" (*Psychology Today, 1976*) and "Extramarital Relations: Gaining Greater Awareness" (*Personnel and Guidance Journal, 1982*) to "Gender Roles and Coping" (*Journal of Marriage and the Family, 1984*) and "A Fear of Lawyers," (*New York Times, 1987*). Also "Scared to Death" (*Hippocrates, 1989*), "When He's Unfaithful: How Some Women Cope" (*McCall's, 1989*), "Gender Bias in the Courts" (*Creighton Law Review, 1989*), and "Divorce: Be Prepared" (*San Diego Woman, 1989*).

Atop the pile lay a copy of Phyllis Chesler's book, 'Women and Madness', personally autographed to "Dear Betty, With love in sisterhood. Phyllis Chesler."

She had also saved a package of cocktail napkins reading, "It's Better to Divorce than to Murder."

Notably absent from her reading materials by then were any letters or leaflets indicating a job search of any sort. She had given up on that. Now she had decided she would become a bon vivant instead. A jet-setter. She could afford it if she sold the house and had no children.

Then came July—Betty's first court-ordered summer with her sons in five years. "That was the happiest I had been through all of this ... I was actually able to make advance plans with those kids for the first time." Nor did she balk over money. Betty paid full costs without a peep.

They went camping in Canada. For once, there was no stress, no six P.M. Sunday deadlines to be back at Dan's, nobody's expectations to meet except their own. They ate hearty breakfasts in clean air, they fed blue jays, they took river trips, they went fishing, they hiked down quiet mountain trails. They talked to each other, they laughed. They did simple things. Betty didn't talk about Dan or Linda or money or the custody fight. She just enjoyed watching her children laugh and love her.

She felt good. She hoped that the exercise would work off some of her weight. And she began to think about the fall. Who was she fooling? She didn't want to be a lonely, sad divorcee pretending to gaiety in St. Tropez or Acapulco. She wanted her children back. And, surely, Walter Maund could get her them for her by the coming school semester. She would carve Halloween pumpkins again, and help with homework, and go back to coaching soccer and attending PTA meetings. Yes.

For once, money was not first on her mind. She wanted to be a mother. And, yes, even still, a wife. His wife.

Before they returned to San Diego, she found a shop that sold polo shirts from New Zealand. She bought one for each of the two boys—and one for Dan. "I never hated Dan, you know. I hated what he was doing, but not him," she later said from jail, quietly "... and I knew he would like that shirt. They're pretty hard to find, and it was real good quality."

After all these years, was she still thinking that he might yet come home?

"Oh, I had no ... I don't know," she said, flustered at the sad, bald question. Then, tiredly, all fire temporarily gone, "Yeah, I guess I still entertained the hope that maybe, even when he was fifty or sixty, he would finally wake up one day and see the reality for what it was." That's as close to honesty as Betty Broderick has ever publicly come to her real feelings. "But what are you going to do? I can't make him do that," she finished. Using the present tense again, a year after he was dead.

Then she and her sons were back in La Jolla, land of plenty and gimme more. Back to weekend schedules, and 6 P.M. deadlines, and, worst of all, to the news that Walter Maund, a mild, polite man, had not made any progress in custody negotiations with Dan. Betty went into an instant rage. One more time, she had paid lawyers and gotten nowhere. She blamed Maund. She blamed Dan. She blamed, period.

Inflaming her nearly as much, the minute she returned with the boys, Dan flew them to Hawaii for a vacation with him and Linda. They didn't even have time to savor their month with Mom before Dad was dazzling them with volcanoes and hula dancers—and, forcing them to spend time with his new wife.

Betty reverted to her madcap ways with a vengeance. Colleen Stuart remembers inviting her to attend a black-tie concert at the Four Seasons Hotel that month. "But she was so ashamed to be part of a female couple that she showed up in a pair of sweats with a black tie and her camera. Her only way of attending was to make a joke of it. I was so embarrassed for her. It was almost like she had decided she was such a loser she might as well act like a clown."

At about the same time, Betty was hit by that most devastating of all rumors: Stuart told her that, as local gossip had it, the Broderick divorce trial had been sealed for years because Betty was a child molester.

By late summer, she was carrying her gun in her robe pocket when Dan came to pick up the boys.

It's a sick picture: there was Dan Broderick, unaware, parked in front of Betty's house, waiting for his young sons, or standing casually on the curb—and, at least once that summer, even walking inside the house—where his fat, disheveled former wife waited, filled with hate and pain, pacing about in her robe, with her hand in the pocket caressing her gun. Sadder still, both boys knew she had it.

"Once I was over there when Dan came to pick them up," recalls Helen Pickard. "And Danny was standing on the porch with his arms around Betty's waist, real tight. At the time, I thought it was sweet. Later on, after I heard about the gun, I realized that maybe he was trying to keep her from doing anything."

But this particular vision of Crazy Betty came out only later, in trial. Then Betty admitted it. Yes, she testified, "The last several times I saw Dan—two or three times, I had the gun in my pocket." The reason, she explained, was because "I was deathly afraid of Dan Broderick. I was afraid of him attacking me, maligning me, threatening me ... to take the children, to lose the house, and that I would never see another red cent from him, threatening me in writing for years ... He was inside my house ... and I was in my robe ... and I had the gun in the pocket. It was for protection."

But, later, from the jailhouse telephone, she had a different, more bizarre explanation: "Danny was always asking me if I was going to kill Dan," she said blithely. "So I put the gun in my robe just to prove to him that Dan could come and I wouldn't kill him. It was like saying, 'Now see, silly. I'm not going to shoot Dan. I had the gun, and I didn't do it.'"

That's how insane life in Betty Broderick's household had become by the summer of 1989. But she could not see it, not then, not now. From jail, a year after the killings, she was still less interested in the gun than the robe she carried it in—"a pink satin A-line Princess with a zipper down the front, and I loved it, because I could gain all the weight I wanted."

At the end of August, Betty had what she calls her "first legitimate date." She had decided, she says, that "since the divorce was finally over, it was okay, in my mind, finally to go out, publicly. I was trying to force myself to get a life. I wanted the word to get around that I was dating." To Betty, Brad Wright would never really count.

Her "first date" was a local surgeon and widower she had known for years, who took her to a symphony. Like a teenager, she spent the day shopping for something new to wear. But now she couldn't buy in any of her usual department store designer boutiques because their sizes stopped at twelve. She ended up wearing an orange and turquoise silk ensemble from the Mother of the Bride department at Bullock's, and "I looked like hell ... you can't look good in any of that stuff. I just felt so bad about myself."

Even so, she was ashamed to be seen with the plump, balding, aging man who was her escort. He was simply not handsome enough for this 180-pound bottle blonde with a jail record, a ruined reputation, and a dead-end ahead. "He was real nice," she says. "But I've never gone out with anyone ugly before. I've always been half of a good-looking couple."

Thus was one more avenue of relief closed to Betty Broderick by her own inability to let go of the past and reckon with the present. She and the doctor never dated again.

Before the month was out, she provoked Dan into dragging her back into court again, this time in a fight over Rhett. According to Dan's later contempt declaration, he had taken Rhett to Betty's house on a Wednesday, out of sequence in the visitation plan, because Rhett wanted to go to Sea World the next day with the children of some friends who were visiting Betty. The plan was that Betty would return Rhett on Friday, in time for a weekend boating trip Dan had planned to Catalina Island. What followed was the classic cat-and-mouse, up-yours game so many divorced couples play, with their children in the middle.

When Dan's housekeeper went to fetch Rhett, he wasn't there. Betty's maid said everyone had gone to Tijuana for the day. Steaming, Dan waited until Saturday morning to call Betty. When he did, according to his subsequent contempt filing, he had been treated without courtesy. "When Respondent answered the phone, I said, 'Is Rhett there?' She said: 'Don't you even say hello? How rude! I'm not one of your employees,' and hung up."

He didn't call back until Monday, when Rhett still hadn't been returned. This time, he later complained to the court, when Betty answered the phone Dan had said, "Hello. Is Rhett there?' Respondent replied: 'No, he's not.' She then made an offensive noise into the receiver and hung up."

Betty was ordered to return Rhett immediately or be held in contempt. But Rhett was no longer even in California. That weekend, Betty had put him aboard a plane to New York to visit with her parents for a week. As she later explained it, Rhett didn't want to go home because his siblings were gone elsewhere for the summer, and he would have been home alone with the housekeeper.

Dan was furious, but, according to his associate, Kathy Cuffaro, he refused to crack down harder on Betty "because he didn't want to stir her up anymore. He just wanted peace in his life." Instead, he settled for a court order forbidding Betty from approaching the airport the day Rhett returned to San Diego from his visit with Frank and Marita Bisceglia. It was just one more dangerous aggravation, in the mind of Betty Broderick, to now be forbidden from even approaching a public place.

Poor Walter Maund, meantime, was struggling uphill in his custody negotiations. Compounding his headaches, Betty was still leaving an occasional nasty blast on the Broderick family answering machine. And she had stopped visiting either the new doctor, or her old friend Dr. Nelson. What for? she asked. She wasn't the crazy one—Dan was.

Even so, Dan's friends say he was seriously thinking of returning custody of the boys to Betty, with conditions. But Linda objected. "Although it would have been so much easier on her to let them go, Linda said to Dan, 'It will destroy the kids if we let them go live with her.' She was convinced Betty was sick," says Blanchet.

As a result of all the bickering, the custody hearing was again postponed, until October—after yet another school term had begun.

Betty finished out the month of August adding to her clip file. Most notably, in light of later events, she saved a *Time Magazine* issue featuring "Death by Handgun" on the cover. Instead of clipping it, she stashed the entire magazine. It was as if Betty Broderick was literally watching herself happen, defining her mind and mapping her future course through selective readings. She sought what soothed. She no longer even bothered to keep up her voluminous fashion and interior design files. Now, her mind, like her conversation, was drawn strictly to legal injustice, wronged women, cheating husbands, crooked lawyers, weapons, death, and very little else.

School season again. September. Maund had failed her. Her fifth fall without her children. The boys were back at Francis Parker, not Bishops. Kim was back in Arizona, complaining again about the puny budget Dan had put her on. And Lee, Dan's banished child, was working as a hostess in a steak house in the heart of La Jolla Village—a common servant, now seating her former classmates at lunch every day. Betty was humiliated for her child, for herself, for her ruined family.

Meantime, the kids told her that Dan was planning another one of his all-expenses-paid extravaganzas. Count Du Money. This time he was footing the bill to Greece for his two office associates, attorneys, Cuffaro and Bob Vaage, and their mates. Plus, of course, the new Mrs. Daniel T. Broderick III.

At the same time, Betty had finally put her del Cielo home up for sale. Realtors trooped through her pretty house. She showed them all the improvements she had made over the last five years—the new pool house, the new kitchen and bathroom, the beautiful pool, the Jacuzzi, her gorgeous landscaping, her rose gardens. She walked them along the back patio with its blue-and-white awnings, its spectacular ocean view. Inside, warm lamps glowed, soft music played, fresh flowers were on every table. The towels were fluffed in the bathroom, the air was fragrant. It was a model home. After all these years of bitching about what a "tear-down" Calle del Cielo was, Betty now walked through the rooms like a woman in mourning, admiring the corpse she had so beautifully dressed for the funeral.

She wanted $1.5 million. The house was worth that for the ocean view and sunsets alone, she thought.

From there, she took one of the most depressing drives of her life. She knew where she was going. Down the hillside, with the Pacific spread before her, past the quaint little La Jolla Shores shopping district nestled among the palms, within the sounds of the surf. Smaller than La Jolla Village, half a mile away, but so much cozier, quieter, with its little groceries, delis, gourmet markets, and patio cafes. How many mornings, she wondered, had she walked down there to sip her chocolate coffee and walk on the beach at sunrise, calmed by the perfection all about her? Classy. That's what this little neighborhood was. She was born to be here. With a rich, handsome husband and four perfect children.

At the corner, she took a hard right and drove north, leaving all perfection behind her. Now she was winding inland, heading toward the UCSD campus, toward the sprawling shopping centers, high-rise office buildings, fast-food restaurants, and gas stations on the northern edge of La Jolla, abutting the noisy, steaming, ugly freeway to LA.

She pulled up in front of a large condominium complex across from a shopping center on a street called Morning Way. Years before, she had tried to persuade Dan to invest in this complex. It was a complete winner, she had argued at the time—a steady source of rental income from visiting professors, students, and other transients. But now, she, Betty Broderick, was going to live there herself. Amid the transients. Amid the displaced.

Now, each day when she left her driveway, she would face not the vast Pacific, but a cinema complex, a pizza parlor, a drugstore—a concrete jungle of smog, noise, and swarming people with pressured faces, sitting in bumper-to-bumper traffic.

From within the condominium grounds, the neat, dun-colored buildings were arranged in a horseshoe around a small, well-manicured courtyard, typical of hundreds of others in Southern California. Now, from her front-room window, she would look out each day onto another apartment exactly like her own. No sun would ever shine directly into any of her rooms. She could have a two-bedroom unit for around $200,000.

She wanted to cry. No more lovely luncheons, living here. No more Christmas parties. There was hardly room for ten in the living room, and no yard at all. "It was the biggest comedown of my life," she said later from jail. "It was even smaller than most of the places Dan and I lived in when we were first married."

The mystery, of course, was why she was now moving into such a small condo when her custody war had not yet been conclusively lost. If she had won the children, Dan would have been obliged to pay her more money in support. She might have made ends meet after all. But, by then, she was too depressed, confused, and angry to think anything through. "Yeah, it would have been a problem," she said later, vaguely. "When the kids came over on weekends, they'd have to sleep on couches and stuff ... But I'd decided I wasn't going to get them back anyway, and I couldn't stand being a part-time mother anymore, or a housewife alone. What's the point of standing around in the kitchen all day crying? But I really don't know what I was doing, I wasn't really thinking anymore."

Dan and Linda and their friends were about to leave for the Greek Isles. But before they did, Dan sent a letter to Betty's attorney, outlining plans to leave his sons with his housekeeper and, on weekends, with Laurel Summers, Dave Monahan's paralegal girlfriend.

What? Sometimes, lately, Betty actually felt dizzy looking at Dan's latest legal communiques. Leave her children with housekeepers? And, worse yet, "another bimbo?" When they had a real, live mother living fifteen minutes away? She felt another familiar wave of nausea, born of shock and rage. Why? Why did he hate her so? Why was he so punishing?

In another of her few counterattacks, Betty went to court in late September, demanding the right to care for her own children while Dan was traveling. And she won. Judge Castro gave her the boys for the time Dan was in Greece. But it was not a clean victory, because, in defending his own plans, Dan argued that Betty couldn't be trusted to send Rhett to school, that she encouraged him to "play hooky." Thus, in an insulting caveat, Castro, taking Dan at his word, added in his order that "Respondent shall be responsible for making sure that the child, Rhett, shall attend school during the period she shall have custody ... failure to comply ... shall cause the immediate suspension of further visitation."

Worse, because Castro had given her the boys for that week, visitation weekends for the remainder of October were also revised—the upshot being that Betty suddenly found herself with a substituted weekend that fell on the same date she and Brad had planned to take a three day, prepaid trip to Acapulco. So she had a choice of either keeping her commitment to Brad, or not seeing her sons for several weekends in a row. She spent the rest of the month worrying about what choice she would make.

Throughout those final months, she continued to call her parents, trying to "just get them to listen to me." But, she says, they wouldn't. "I would tell them my life was destroyed, I was going crazy, Dan was killing me, I was losing my house, and they'd just say, 'Oh, well, and other than that, Betty Anne, everything's fine?'"

Although her obsession with her own financial insecurity continued, she now seemed just as preoccupied with the future of the children. Why hadn't Dan bought the $1 million insurance policy for them, as Howett had ordered in January? She inquired about it so often in calls to the insurance agent that, later on, both the Broderick family and the prosecutor would suggest that she had deliberately delayed killing him until the policies finally went into effect in September.

Autumn in La Jolla reflects itself only barely. Here and there a few leaves change color, the air clears and cools, the ocean shifts from royal blue to a deeper shade of blue-gray. But the bougainvillea, impatiens, and hibiscus still bloom, lawns remain thick and green, the towering palms still stand in sultry, tropical silhouette against the horizon. Golden teenagers still surf at the Cove, patio cafes thrive even at night. Only fashion and boredom dictate even a wardrobe change, from silks and cottons to richer, heavier cashmeres and light woolens.

But to Betty Broderick, no matter where she lived, the seasons would always change in her mind as sharply, as poignantly as they did in her youth. She could smell the shifts in the air, even if they were happening not in her lush La Jolla gardens but two thousand miles east. She could still feel the chill in the wind as she skipped home, in her childhood, from Maria Regina, the fallen leaves crunching beneath her feet; she could remember the thick plaid Pendleton skirts she wore and the feel of her angora sweaters curling around her neck as she soared through the streets of Eastchester in her little green MG toward Mount Saint Vincent's College.

And she would never forget the sharp bite of frost in the October air, more than twenty years past, as she had strutted so brightly, so smartly, so confidently across the Notre Dame campus in Great Bend, in her pretty, stylish fall clothes with her long blond hair swinging so free—to find herself that night sitting in the crowded, noisy, dim little college pub, across from the slender young man she would one day marry. She would never forget the yellow and rust chrysanthemums of fall, the thunder of Notre Dame football fans cheering, the clingy, sexy excitement of being young and desirable and so certain, then, that she was worth every bit of it.

Two decades later, although her self-confidence was long gone, Betty would still connect autumn with the cozy, laughing pubs of Notre Dame and Manhattan, where, during their courtship—before the marriage, the babies, the struggles, and the studies changed it all—she and Dan had sat in worn tavern booths, drinking grog and looking at each other across tables with eyes of love, as they listened to "their song."

Lovely, with your smile so warm, and your cheek so soft, There is nothing for me but to love you, just the way you look tonight. . .

Rhett and Danny were excited when they told their mom, one October evening, that they were going to the Notre Dame game with Dad and Linda later that month. Kim was going, too. Only Lee had not been invited. Only Lee would not see where it was that her parents had fallen in love.

For once, Betty did not say anything inappropriate to her sons. For once, words failed her. It hurt too much.

"It made me so sad," she later said wistfully from jail. "All of my friends, mine and Dan's, friends that we knew before we were married, people we had grown up with— here all of them would be, all of us old enough now to have our own children in Notre Dame ... but there's Linda Kolkina in the room where I should have been, with my children, my extended family, and all my friends for my whole life ..."

She always wondered what the other wives thought, when they saw Dan there with Linda and not her. "I bet they were looking at this young thing that's just adoring Dan, and didn't have any kids to worry about—and they're all forty-something. They must have been thinking maybe their husbands are going to go off and bring a young chickie home next year, too, and they're going to be gone. Just like me."

But Betty refused to show the depth of her pain. Instead, cussing Dan to hell, she cheerfully went about the business of outfitting Kim in a fabulous new wardrobe for her autumn at Notre Dame—a stunning Armani leather jacket in Kelly green, plaid Ralph Lauren slacks, cashmere sweaters. "If I couldn't be there, then Kim would be me. She was a reflection of me. I bought her all the clothes I would have liked to wear, if I could have gone."

She spent the Notre Dame weekend at Warner Springs, as depressed as she had ever been, feeling "so left out." She sat in the bar, drinking a Coke, and cried over her broken marriage to a woman she didn't even know, while everyone else watched the football game on TV. She told the woman how she had once been "a Notre Dame wife" herself until her husband, a brilliant lawyer, had left her for his secretary and used his connections to ruin her. "It was the saddest thing, that's why I still remember it," the woman later told reporters.

Naturally, Betty took her frustrations out on her attorney, the beleaguered Walter Maund, who had written her a letter earlier in the month begging her to resume seeing her therapists in order to present to the court the picture of a "new" Betty Broderick. Maund reminded her that both doctors continued to believe that she was the best parent, and "It is important for us to support this attitude."

Instead of taking his advice, Betty wrote him a scorching reply: "I greatly resent your letter ... if I need to go to a therapist, it is because of lawyers like you who take my case and take my money and DO NOTHING FOR ME." She attacked him for dragging his feet on the custody case since March, for permitting one delay after

306

another, and further declared that "I am not interested in presenting a 'new' Betty Broderick. I am terribly fond of and in fact quite proud of the same one I've been and always will be."

She concluded by ordering him to "get this case to court, Walter! The endless delays are torturous to the children, me, and my finances ... The holidays are almost here again. The kids feel I've let them down again by not getting this into court."

She spent the next week moving into her new condo while realtors continued their search for a buyer for del Cielo. A friend from a Bible study class Betty had attended a year earlier remembered later in trial how sad Betty had been as she walked through her house, trying to decide which pieces of furniture might fit into her small new apartment. She was especially worried that a large red-velvet easy chair would take up too much space. "She called it the kids' Santa Claus chair," her friend recalled.

Betty did most of the moving herself, with the help of a couple of neighborhood teenagers she had hired, and a rented truck. Some nights she stayed at the condominium, again sleeping on the floor just as she had done at del Cielo years before. One night, after moving boxes by herself all day, she tried to light a pilot in the water heater, and it ignited in her face, burning her hand and singing her eyebrows and eyelashes. She wasn't hurt, but she sat on the floor and cried.

She was lonelier than she had ever been, trying to adjust to life in this strange, cramped new place. Her one-time roommate, Lucy Peredun, had long since moved on, and now Betty would only need Maria once a week or even less. She was desperate for company; any stranger would do. So she decided to look for another roommate.

At the end of October, she answered a "room wanted" advertisement in the *La Jolla Light* placed by a divorced, struggling woman in ill-health named Audrey. But, after a four-hour session with Betty in late October, during which time Betty recited her entire "story," even Audrey decided she couldn't handle the stress of living with Betty Broderick. Betty was "in pretty bad shape," obsessed with her former husband and "desperate for someone to talk to," Audrey later told defense investigators. Only two days before the homicides, Betty had called Audrey, wanting to meet for coffee. Apparently none of her old friends were available that day.

She decided to go to Acapulco with Brad at the end of the month. But she had a miserable time, she says, partly because she felt so guilty about the choice she had made. In addition, Betty Broderick was hardly in any condition by then, either physically or mentally, to blend into a flashy Mexican seaside resort scene.

"It was one of those places where everybody there was either part of a married couple, or an aging man with his little bimbo. I wasn't either, so I didn't fit in anywhere. I just sat in my room all day and read books while Brad went sailing."

That was how Betty Broderick spent her last free weekend.

Chapter 29

November, 1989

Tuesday was Halloween. Dan had said the boys could come to Betty's house that night so she could take them trick-or-treating. She carved a pumpkin, decorated the house with witches and goblins, and made a batch of Rhett's favorite "spider" cookies. They were growing up so fast. By next year, Danny would regard trick-or-treating as beneath his adolescent dignity.

But later that day, they called to say that they couldn't come over after all. So she spent the evening handing out candy to other people's kids.

Then it was November again. On the seventh she would be forty-two. Sixth anniversary of her suicide threat. On the twenty-second, Dan would be forty-five. Sixth anniversary of the clothes burning. Six years it had been going on. Six.

She moved more of her things to the condo. She made appointments for the following week with realtors and her accountant. She complained bitterly and obscenely about Dan and Linda to anybody who would listen. She lunched, she went to the market, and she shopped, always carrying her big brown purse with the .38 inside. She toyed that week, too, with the idea of buying herself a new Mercedes convertible two-seater that had caught her eye, mainly because of the color—"the most gorgeous turquoise metallic, a deep blue-green." Maybe that would lift her spirits. Besides, once she sold the house, she could afford it. Yes, she decided, she would go buy that car soon. Next week.

Then, toward the end of the week, her attorney forwarded two letters he had just received from Dan's attorney, Kathleen Cuffaro.

Later, in trial, Betty couldn't remember whether the letters arrived on the same day, or separately. But she thought they both came on Friday. She opened them, scanned them, and, she says, threw them on a kitchen counter for closer study later. But she instantly got the gist: One letter was threatening to throw her back in jail, the other said no to her custody proposal.

Cuffaro's first letter, dated October 27, included three transcripts of Betty's latest phone messages. As Betty's messages went, these were actually fairly mild, even tedious after all these years, containing, among them, a total of only three "cunts" and one "little fucker." All were explosions of frustration because she couldn't reach the boys.

But, Cuffaro wrote, since the divorce decree in January, Betty had committed at least twenty similar acts of contempt "of which we have documentary proof." If Betty didn't cease her "odious behavior" immediately, Dan was prepared to file contempt charges—and, if that happened, Cuffaro said, "I firmly believe … another jail sentence will be imposed." In conclusion, she noted that, contrary to reports by Betty's doctors, she saw only evidence that Betty's "emotional disturbance and mental disease" was worsening, not improving.

The second letter, dated November 1, was a scathing rejection of Maund's latest custody proposal, which had suggested a permanent, unconditional return of Danny and Rhett to Betty. In essence, Cuffaro told Maund to forget it: Dan was prepared to discuss returning the boys to Betty only on a trial basis, with the strict condition that the arrangement could be automatically terminated by him, unilaterally and without court action, if Betty violated any court orders ... "or if she further involves Danny or Rhett in her pathological obsession with their father and his wife."

In conclusion, Cuffaro suggested that Maund "try again to come up with a proposal that is consistent" with prior custody discussions with Dan. She also wanted to know precisely how much child support Betty would be demanding during any prospective "trial period."

On Friday, Betty also took Lee shopping. It was Nordstrom's big midyear sale. Betty mentioned Dan's latest legal papers to Lee, and said he was about to send her back to jail. But she didn't dwell on it at length, Lee later testified. That evening Betty picked up her sons and went to a football game with them. It was her first weekend visit in nearly a month.

On Saturday, November 4, she took them for haircuts. She went to Jonathan's and spent almost $400 on gourmet groceries.

When Helen Pickard dropped by for a cup of coffee that day, Betty also told her about Dan's latest threats to jail her, Pickard later testified. Betty complained, too, Pickard said, that she couldn't accept the children for Thanksgiving "because Linda still had her china."

That afternoon, she went to Rhett's soccer game and sat in the bleachers crying, because "The poor little guy hadn't played enough to be any good. But he was trying so hard," she said later from jail. "It just broke my heart." She also took a walk on the beach with the boys, where she ran into a young surfer friend of Kim's, and hers. She told him how much she hated Dan Broderick and would like to kill the asshole. The boy had heard it all many times before but, he later told the jury with visible reluctance, her language was bluer than usual that day. "She was one pissed-off lady."

That evening, Brad came over for dinner. She can't remember what she cooked, or what time she went to bed, but it was early, around 6:30, she thinks. She had promised to take Danny and Rhett to Tijuana the next day. Brad and the boys stayed up, watching TV. Brad spent the night, sleeping in a guest room. Rhett later came to bed with her. She had fallen asleep in her clothes.

Dan and Linda spent their last night having dinner at a local Mexican restaurant with several close friends. They were still exuberant about their trip to Greece and thinking about an Outback expedition to Australia next, says his friend Cuffaro, who dropped the couple off at home, for the last time, at around 11:30 Saturday night. It was, she adds wistfully, a very happy evening. Dan was drinking peach schnapps. And both Dan and Linda were radiant. They were talking about having a baby. According to

309

Linda's ovulation calendar, Monday was the peak day of her cycle.

Betty couldn't sleep. As usual, she was up and down all night, catnapping fitfully. When she talked about that night later—in several different conversations during the months before her first trial—her thoughts came in a confused, sometimes contradictory tangle, and always in her eerie mix of present and past tenses.

"I was just so depressed for months and months—Maria had become a nurse. I wouldn't pick up my towel after a shower. I wouldn't move, I wouldn't do anything. I wouldn't water plants, I wouldn't cut my roses. I had gorgeous roses. It was too much of an effort to go down and cut them. I couldn't even open my eyes. My eyes were always like half drawn. I can't even describe the feelings of such tiredness—just bent over in the middle, with this big heavy weight on your chest. I think the weight on your chest feels like a horse's hoof ... It's like you can't even breathe, and it's just awful. I could carry on conversations, but I had no retention whatever. You could tell me that yesterday I made a deal to go out to lunch with you, and I'd have no recollection of even talking to you.

"... I felt like I was being literally pounded into the ground. Literally. And it was that kind of pounding, when you hear the big buildings and those machines go *'Boom! Boom! Boom!'* I was getting pounded. And the only thing you think of is freedom and escape from the pain. You know—just make it stop.

"The kids were there that weekend, and I cried, looking at them all weekend, because I hadn't seen them in so long ... because he went into court, took my weekend away. So I hadn't seen them in a month. Then when I finally got the boys— it was Sunday morning when this happened —and I was going to have to give them back at around 5:00. And I felt like I hadn't even seen them, because there was a soccer game and this and that. And Danny Broderick was invited to go to Disneyland, and this really broke my heart—he told his friend no. He said, 'Mom, I couldn't go, because if I went to Disneyland, then I'd never get to see you.' And I thought, 'Oh, great, the guy's going to have to give up his social life to see his mother?'

"I was crying at Rhett's soccer game ... Usually when I see my kids, no matter how depressed I was, I was perfect. It was like two people. I was like a split personality—from a lunatic to a perfectly happy person the minute I have the kids. The only thing that made me happy was my kids slamming in the front door, yelling 'Hi, Mom!' And they'd slam in the front door, and the door would fly back and go boom against the wall, and that would make me instantly happy. I would feel fine. But this is the only weekend I've ever experienced where I was crying with them the whole time. I was crying because I hadn't seen them in so long, these legal papers were threatening me, she [Linda] was going to start the bullshit about the machine again ... She wouldn't give me the china and that stuff, and I was moving, and I was under a lot of pressure physically, moving all by myself. I was just really, really under tons of pressure. Kim was upset and hysterical that Dan wasn't supporting her ... It was all falling on me.

"I couldn't even breathe ... so depressed that to take a breath was an effort, much

310

less to do aerobics or all those things. I used to be such a high-energy person ... And now I was dragging around like a dead man. I'd go to bed dead tired, feeling like I could sleep for six weeks, and then an hour later I'd wake up. And then I'd walk around the house and I'd drink coffee, I drank coffee all day and all night. It was decaf, a lot of it.

"It was just incredible anxiety and depression, at the same time. The depression would make me tired, but I was so literally shaking with anxiety, just free-floating anxiety, that that would wake me up. It wasn't a specific nightmare or a specific thought. So I'd walk around, I'd read newspapers ... And I'd sit in the kitchen, I'd turn on the lights ... If I was alone in the house, I'd put on music, and I'd turn on a lot of lights ... I'd watch Nightline ... or go back to bed and try to sleep."

On the night of November 4, "I was so pooped that I went to bed in my clothes that night. The same outfit I was wearing when I turned myself in. A pink linen pantsuit ... pink and white checks ... So I was sleeping in the outfit. I just kind of lay on top of the bed. I know it sounds crazy. But you are not talking to a normal person here ..."

So she lay in bed, at seven P.M., alone, thinking. About everything.

"I just felt so unjustifiably punished for something I never did. I mean, I still don't know what I ever did to deserve being treated like this in the courts. I felt just the victim. They will not live to see that. No!"

She dozed. "And then I wake up. And then I turn on lights, and I walk around the house ... walked around the house and thought, 'Oh, great,' because it's like two o'clock in the morning. And then I go back to bed again.

"Danny wanted to go to Tijuana the next day ... I said okay, but if we go, you're going to have to call Daddy and make sure he knows we might be late coming home, because if we go to Tijuana and we've got to be back by 6, it's going to ruin the whole afternoon worrying about how long it's going to take us to get through the border. So the plan was that in the morning we would call Dan—who, of course, wouldn't answer the phone."

Thoughts of the children pressed in. Rhett had been four when it started. Now he was ten.

"My kids are getting older and older, and he is violently mistreating them at this point, having thrown the girls out without education or cars or rent. The boys wanted nothing through this whole thing but to be with me. They're approaching teenage years, where I am very nervous about drugs and car accidents and marijuana, and I don't want my boys to go to shit while Dan's not watching them, and I don't want to get them back at eighteen, damaged goods, like I got the girls back. I wasn't going to give him the chance to ruin my sons. I wanted my sons back, and I couldn't get anywhere. When this [the killings] happened, I had no date in December to even look forward to—it was just sometime in December. And when you hear that, you know it's going to be sometime maybe next April. It was such a professional setup.

"My last hope was Walter [Maund], that he was going to get the boys. He wasn't going to get me more money, but he was going to get the boys; and I was going to sell the house and go to the condominium, and we were going to live much, much

311

poorer; but the boys approved of the condominium, and we were going to go live there. And then, Dan started putting Walter Maund through the hoops, and it was real evident, the day this [the killings] happened, that we were getting fucking nowhere.

"... And I'm not walking away from my boys knowing that he was harming them. I'm not doing it. I will kill for it, goddamn it! I never thought—I'd heard—you know, women always say, I'd kill for my kids. Well, I'm a Scorpio, goddamn, and I will kill for my kids. I will. Goddamn it. I never knew I had it in me, but ..." And then came the letters:

"The letters that I got the night before this are absolutely definitive proof that he was going to throw me in jail again, and he was going to fine me again. He was going to say I was crazy again—it was the same cycle! And the battered woman syndrome is a cycle. You see the abuse coming because you've lived through the cycle several times ... I knew exactly what was coming next, because I had already lived through it in '85, '86, '87, '88, and here it was '89, doing it again.

"That morning—you have to take all that I suffered and that I didn't react to and that I didn't stand up for and I didn't fight for—all those hours from spring of '83, through '84, through '85. The humiliations that I put up with and the stories that I heard that I was a fucking child molester and crazy and everything else, and no Christmas for five years. No birthdays with my kids. You build all that up in a pressure cooker, put that in a pressure cooker for six years and see what happens ... Any person alive would have done exactly what I did, only probably four or five years sooner."

She thought about suicide, too. She wanted so much to just lie down and never wake up.

"When I went to bed that night, with Rhett in bed ... I mean, it was practically an uncontrollable urge to just do it that night. I mean, it would be the most welcome thing to be dead. The life, the pain ... I told you, I couldn't stand up, I couldn't breathe. No one loved me. Doesn't that sound trite now? But it was true. I mean, what is life if no one gives a flying fuck whether you're dead or alive?

"And I wouldn't have been the first ex-wife that killed herself. They either take to the bottle or slit their wrists or go on pills, or they get carted off in a straitjacket, or they blow their own brains out. And I was suicidal for the last two years of this whole thing, because I couldn't believe what was going on. You lose your equilibrium on earth.

"Without a jury he put me in jail twice. And now he was turning the clock back to '85 and [putting] me through the whole thing again. And Linda's going to put the answering machine back on to just literally fuck me over? Is it so much to ask that I can return the phone calls to my children on their own phone line, which isn't bothering anyone? I had fought this in court for five years, I'd spent over $100,000, and my life had been destroyed for the last seven years by that cunt, and she is going to do this with me now? And I was like, oh, no. Oh, nooo! I have had enough! I am dead. I am out of here. I am not doing this ever again in my life—never again am I going in a sealed courtroom to get gang raped by Dan Broderick and his lawyer and

312

his friend the judge ...

"But you don't just lay there thinking of killing yourself—you only think of how to stop the pain. You know 'Alice Through the Looking Glass'? You know that dark tunnel she fell down? That's you. Going to hell and coming out God knows where, but I could not even see the light at the end of the tunnel. I was just in a dark, dark, dark free-fall tunnel to hell. And I just had to make it stop. The pain is so awful and the darkness is so dark, that you just need it to stop. You don't plan it—because once you start planning it [suicide] and thinking about it, then of course it doesn't make sense.

"And I couldn't do it with the kids around. I just couldn't. And I kept thinking, and why kill yourself? I mean, damn it, what did you do? I mean, they want you dead, and that will put an end to it, killing yourself. Even if I did kill myself in their house, you wouldn't have seen any funeral on TV. They would have swept my bones in the backyard and told everyone, 'See, we told you she was crazy.'"

In the darkness, she sat up on the edge of the bed, clammy, her heart pounding. The terror was overpowering. Every nightmare movie she had ever seen had come true. She was it. She was going mad. She had gone mad. Maybe she should drive to a hospital and sign herself in. Maybe doctors could quiet her heart. Maybe kind nurses in white would stroke her hair and calm her mind and make her well again.

But why? Why? What had she done?

They had everything. "I mean—they get married, and they go to Greece, they go to New England, and they're traveling, they've got everything, including my children. They've fucked me happily, and they're still going to go back and say I can't even call my kids? Ha, ha, ha, ha. No, no, no. Oh, no, no, no! Six years of it. I have a long, long, long fuse, but they got to the end of it. I mean, I took shit and shit and shit and shit and shit daily since 1983! No judge, no court ever said I can't call my kids. Linda could just do this herself, and it was her who would take the time to do this ... and, I'm telling you, it's a spark to a stick of dynamite to tell me I can't talk to my kids. Betty Broderick can't talk to her kids because Linda Kolkena decided I'm not going to talk to my kids? Oh, no. Oh, nooo!

"Any normal person would have, a long time ago ... done something to say I'm not taking this anymore, you sonofabitch. Any man would have beat the living crap out of him six years ago."

Around four o'clock she was up and awake for the final time. She was not going back to bed again that night.

She went to the kitchen and tried to read the newspapers. But she didn't care about the news. Instead, she picked up the two Cuffaro letters and studied them again, letting them sink in more fully this time—especially the one that, to her, was a direct promise of jail again. "Because the last time the judge had us in there, he got red in the face and screamed at Dan Broderick, because Dan had brought me on contempt in front of this judge about eight times, and the judge said, don't you dare come back in this room with these contempts unless you want her to go to jail. So if Dan came back with another contempt, I was going to jail for sure—or, at least, that's

313

what I read into that letter.

"I was just so tired of being the defenseless, helpless victim of these two maniacs. What the fuck do they want from me? They want me to go away and never speak to my kids again? No. They will not live to see that. I will not live to see that. I mean, my heart starts racing, my blood pressure goes through the sky. This case was not about your husband marrying a younger girl, and it was not about money. It was about the kids."

She tried to describe the interior of her head at that point:

"I was so depressed, I felt so completely helpless ... and it didn't help that I was turning forty-two years old. I looked like shit, I felt like shit, my life was going down. Down, down, down. And they're still coming at me. I went crazy. I went absolutely crockum. There's a scene in the 'Superman' movie where he flies around the earth real fast, and he screams this bloodcurdling scream that the whole world—well, that's what I felt like. I felt like standing up in my kitchen and doing a primal scream so loud that the whole fucking world would wake up and go—'what's that?' It's Betty Broderick going over the edge.

"But, you know, nice girls don't do that ... I just literally did the Superman scream inside ... I wanted to cry real bad, sob and cry. But when you've been as far along as I was, and cried and shook and threw up so many times, you can't cry anymore. You just want to die. I mean, as I sit here, I can't explain to you the real physical feeling of death inside, just absolute death."

"I just had to get out of there. I just had to make it stop. Oh, it's literally physical. I feel like a fool talking about it, because there really are no words for it, but the morning that this happened, I was literally holding onto things to walk around. I was like—I mean, I looked like I was a cripple or something. And you have this tension headache, of course, that you've had for the last six years. And my back was always out, and my shoulders were slumped, and my stomach was slumped, and my frown in my face was just—your whole face kind of falls. You feel like a bloodhound ... if someone measured me, I would have probably measured out at 5'6". Because I felt like I was being literally pounded into the ground."

She went to the car. But, before she left the house, she wrote three lines on the bottom of one of the Cuffaro letters. Her penmanship was steady, her thoughts exact:

"I can't take this anymore. 1. Linda Kolkena the cunt interfering with what little contact I have left w/ my children. She's been doing it for years. We've litigated it CONTINUALLY. 2. CONSTANT THREATS of court, jail, contempt, fines, etc., which is very scary to me and no matter what the evidence, I always lose. 3. Them constantly insinuating I'm crazy."

"It was the letters that did it ... It was basically those three things. ... I was just sitting there writing it down, saying I just cannot stand this. And I had no reason to believe it was ever going to stop or get better.

"It was daylight when I left my house ... like five or six or something. I don't know. I don't know what time it was. All I know is I don't go out in the dark anywhere. I'm

314

scared to death of the dark ...

"But even when I left my house in the morning—when I left that house, I wasn't going to his house. If you asked me, where are you going, you saw me going down the street, I would have told you I was going down to the 7-Eleven to get coffee and then go down to the beach like I always did. I did that all the time. I don't even know how I went to his house or why. When I backed out of my driveway, I didn't know I was going to his house.

"I figure that the point that I had to make the decision to go talk to him—which is really the decision that I made, just go talk to the sonofabitch—had to be by the 7-Eleven ... it must have been at that turn that I said to myself, 'What good is getting coffee and chocolate and walking on the beach another morning after all these years going to do? It's not going to make him stop, it's not going to make it go away, it's not going to make me feel better. I'm going to go talk to the sonofabitch. I'm going to make him stop.' But I don't remember really doing that."

And what made her think Dan Broderick would be inclined to talk to her at six A.M.?

"I didn't know as I went from step to step, but if I had confronted him and he said, 'Okay, you're going to go to jail for being in contempt because you're on my property,' I would have shot my brains out right in front of him. I was going to kill myself. ... I would have just shot myself right in front of him. I had to make it stop. And I told you I was not going to shoot myself in front of my own kids in La Jolla. What kind of headline funeral would that make? Everyone would say, 'Well, you know, Dan was right. She was crazy.' That's exactly what he wanted me to do. And so if I had to do myself in, I was doing myself in as messy as possible right in his house. But they still would have thought I was crazy, I guess, huh?

"The importance of it was that when I backed out of the driveway and I left my house that day, I really was going down to get the coffee, to do what I always did. ... I did not get in my car and get a gun and back out of that driveway to go kill Dan Broderick ... And that's the honest to God truth—I'm not making up a bullshit story here to save my ass."

Then she was parked in front of his house.

"I don't remember getting there, and I don't remember leaving there."

She took the gun out of her purse, picked Kim's keys out of a box on the car seat beside her, and walked around to the back door of the house. It never occurred to her to knock on the door.

"Knock on the door? Ha ha ha. Are you kidding? He wouldn't even talk to me if I knocked on the door ... Years before, I knocked on the front door in broad daylight and said, 'I need the keys to my car that Lee stole,' and he wouldn't open the door ... Knock on Dan Broderick's door? That sonofabitch? He wouldn't even have gotten out of bed. He would have just called the cops.

"But I never thought it through ... Most things never even occurred to me. I mean, there's a million things—Why didn't you do this, why didn't you do that? It's because I didn't even think. There were a million things I could have done differently, but I wasn't thinking ahead. I was just doing. You know? I was a doo-doo. Actually, if I had planned it, I could have planned it much better."

She crept through the house, up the stairs, and into their bedroom.

What happened next is anybody's best guess. Betty's version would change dramatically throughout two murder trials. It's possible, of course, that she can no longer remember what actually happened in that bedroom. It's equally possible that she remembers every bit of it.

Either way, in all its confusion and inconsistency, here is what she said before her first murder trial:

It was dark. But she could see him. She could see them lying there together. "I was standing there with it [the gun] in my hand, so he thought I was going to shoot him, and he put his hands up like in the cowboy movies. Put your hands up, your two hands up, like stick them in the air? What do they say? 'Stick 'em up.' That's what he did."

She fired in panic, she said.

"But I have no memory of doing it. If I had a memory of this, wouldn't I be having screaming nightmares and shit? I can't imagine myself doing it, so I don't know. The whole time I was there, I never knew what was going to happen. I couldn't fathom ever in my life—I had never even struck anyone in my life ... I had no plan. I had no plan of action, I had no plan of anything.

"And I have never seen anything in that bedroom ... I've never yet—have you? Do you know of any pictures out there of gory stuff? I have not seen a thing. I haven't heard or seen a thing that would like give me nightmares or traumatize me. I mean, I have no bad memory of that."

Then she ripped the phone out of the wall.

"I know they've been making a big deal about that phone from the beginning, but it was never a big deal to me. I mean, when I did it, I didn't really think about it ... there were about ten other phones in the house right up on that floor in other rooms. I didn't cut the wire to the whole house or anything ... All I thought about was, 'This is what they do in the movies.' And I didn't even know that he was hit, because he spoke to me so clear. I didn't think the guy was hit. I thought he was going to pick up that phone ... He was right next to the phone, and the phone was on the floor when I got there. I mean, the phone was on the floor right next to him. On the floor. And I thought, 'Oh, my God, he's going to pick that phone up.' So I—I just did it because Dan was right there, and he spoke to me—he said, 'Okay, you got me, I'm dead,' or something like that ..."

She also hit Dan's hand with her gun as she stepped over his body to grab for the phone cord—which was not actually pulled out of the wall. Betty broke the cord in two at the center with her bare hands. But that detail didn't emerge until her second trial. In the second trial, too, Betty said that Linda was awake and cried out, "Call the police," causing her to panic and fire.

But that was two trials later.

If it was dark in the room, how did she see him put his hands up?

"Because," she said in the summer of 1990, "I was close to him. I don't know ... [My attorney] says I could have imagined the whole goddamn thing ... I still don't know why it was dark. I don't know if I closed my eyes, or if they had drapes down. I don't understand this myself. I didn't even look at the room. I don't know."

Did she say anything to him? Or Linda? "No," she said tersely.

Then she fled the house.

"... And the truth is, I had no idea if I hit anybody or anything when I left there ... I was just like—'Boy, you really did it this time.' I thought Dan would get up and be after me ... That's why I didn't go home. I thought that sonofabitch was going to be after me, or at least call the police and have them after me. But I thought he personally was going to come after me. That's why I was scared to go home and went to Lee's and was hiding and everything, because I had no idea I hit anybody. And that's the truth ... I didn't know that they were dead until later, when I heard it on the radio or something."

When police came, they found Linda, wearing black-and-white polka-dot shortie pajamas, face down on the bed, her long, blond, bloodstained hair mostly obscuring her face. Her body was in a diagonal position, as if she had attempted to escape the killer by moving toward her husband. The covers had been flung away. The most prominent police photograph presented later in court showed her rump and long, slender, tanned legs, flung out limply behind her. She looked like a rag doll, thrown aside by a bored, temperamental child.

Dan was lying on the floor at the side of the bed, on his stomach, in boxer shorts, half hidden in a tangle of bedding. He, too, had apparently been attempting to flee his assailant, or else fallen off the bed after being shot.

Linda had been shot first in the chest, frontally, the coroner later testified. As she reflexively moved away, turning, a second bullet had lodged directly in the back of her head. The first bullet "went through the breastbone and ... the [second bullet] went through the brain stem ... severing all communication with the brain."

Dan had been shot once in the back. He had not died as swiftly as Linda, judging from the large pool of blood and saliva beneath his face. Nor was his wound necessarily fatal, said the coroner. He might have survived anywhere from "a matter of minutes" up to "maybe half an hour ..." With immediate medical attention, he might have even lived.

Betty's two remaining bullets missed their targets, but not by much. One lodged in a wall, the other hit the bedstand near Linda's head.

For somebody shooting in the dark, experts later said, she had been remarkably accurate.

317

Part Four

Betty

Chapter 30

I Need Help

Dian Black, not an early riser, sleeps in a bedroom heavily draped against the morning sunlight, and so she doesn't know exactly what time it was when Betty called. She guesses it was around seven A.M. when her husband shoved the phone into her hand, mumbling that it was Betty, "and she's upset about something."

Black groaned and put the phone to her ear, trying not to wake up. *Now what?* she thought.

"I need help," was the first thing Betty said to her. It wasn't the words, it was the tone of voice that caused Black to wake up despite herself. "She sounded so awful, I'd never heard her that way before ... she was crying, and I could hear her making these sort of retching sounds," Black said later.

"She said she'd been to Dan's house, and she'd fired shots, but she didn't know if she'd hit anyone." Black sat up and tried to concentrate. What lunacy was this? "I thought she'd had a nervous breakdown or something," she remembers. But Dian Black is a good and loyal friend. She opened her eyes, forgot sleep, and reached for a pen and paper.

She tried to find out where Betty was, but "she could only tell me she was in a phone booth somewhere in Clairemont ... she was so disoriented she couldn't tell me what street or anything, she finally said there was a Coco's [restaurant] across the street." Black got her to read off the number of the phone booth she was standing in, and told her to stay put. Black next called Ronnie Brown and told her to call Betty back, to keep her on the phone until Black was able to find her.

Black also called Brad Wright at Betty's house. Danny answered the phone. Fumbling into her clothes, struggling to keep the alarm out of her voice, Black asked the boy to awaken Brad. After telling Wright what Betty had said, Dian Black set out to find her; but when she finally located the phone booth, Betty was gone, so Black went back home to wait.

It never occurred to Black to call the police, she said later, "because I guess I just didn't believe her—I thought she'd just flipped out ..."

Brad Wright was also initially confused, uncertain as to how seriously he should take these latest disjointed ravings of his girlfriend, now somewhere abroad in the city. He dressed hurriedly and trotted a few doors down the street to the home of Brian and Gail Forbes. The Forbeses and their five children were only beginning to stir, on what should have been just another lazy La Jolla Sunday. Gail had the coffee on.

But, as she listened to Brad's account of his conversation with Dian, Gail Forbes instantly understood that this was, most likely, no false alarm. She, more than most of Betty Broderick's friends, had been seriously alarmed for months at the deterioration she saw. She had warned Dan to watch out, and finally earned Betty's undying animosity by agreeing with Dan that Betty should not have even visitation with her children, unless it was supervised.

Now, she seized the telephone and called the police to report a possible homicide—only to realize, midway through her call, that none of the three adults present knew Dan Broderick's actual street address. They only knew how to get there. And so she got a polite brush-off—the San Diego police dispatcher was singularly uninterested in an unconfirmed crime at an imprecise address.

Thus it was that Bradley Wright and Brian Forbes, two tanned, fair-haired men given to Polo shirts, chinos, and tennis shoes—who had, neither of them, ever in their lives been witness nor party to a violent crime, either in society or in war—climbed into Wright's new Porsche and sped toward the central city to discover, on the second floor of a pretty antebellum mansion framed by towering eucalyptus and cypress trees, the bodies of Dan and Linda Broderick, sleeping in their own blood.

It would affect Forbes far more than Wright. Two years later, sitting on the witness stand, Forbes, a small, balding man, circumspect in a gray suit and white shirt, would still look stunned as he described that morning. He remembered every detail, down to how fast he and Brad had made the drive across town. He told how he had banged on Dan's front door "with an open hand," how he had shouted for Dan, how he had finally been hoisted through a laundry room window by Brad, how he had rushed up the stairs, "calling their names, in case they were awake ... so that we wouldn't surprise them ..." It was clearly the most dramatic moment in Brian Forbes's life, one he would never forget. "They were greenish," he said during the first trial, of the bodies he found. By the time of the second trial, he had grown more graphic: the pool of blood and saliva under Dan Broderick's head, he said, looked like "cookies-and-cream ice cream."

For Brad Wright, it was a lesser moment, this first encounter he had ever had with Daniel T. Broderick III. After reporting the incident to the police, he went sailing for the rest of the day. "Why not?" he asked later, looking blankly surprised at the question. "I knew Betty wouldn't be calling the house [looking for me], because she knew I had a [sailing] race that day."

Betty, meantime, was still waking people up, changing lives forever. After rousing Dian Black, she had called her daughter Lee, who was also asleep. "I shot your Dad, I shot the sonofabitch," she said, according to Lee's later testimony. Like Black and most others dragged into this incredible day, Lee sleepily wondered if her mother had finally gone completely mad. Either way, it was clear that a crisis of some sort was at hand. She and her boyfriend, Jason, got dressed and waited. Fifteen minutes later, Betty arrived. She was crying, babbling, and generally hysterical, Lee later said. When Lee made her a cup of tea, she vomited it up.

But Betty was coherent enough to persuade both Lee and Jason that, this time, Mom was serious. Disjointed as her babble was, it was still filled with riveting specifics.

She told the two dumbstruck teenagers that she had to do it, according to Lee's testimony. She cited Dan's remark to the *Reader* that "It wouldn't be over until one of us was gone ... I couldn't let him win."

She told her daughter, too, that she felt "empty and dead inside and that she was so miserable she couldn't go on another day." She also mentioned again, Lee said, that she had received "a paper that was gonna put her in jail."

She told Lee and Jason that she had tried to enter through Dan's front door, but the key wouldn't work. So she had gone around to the back door, where the key did work. She had crept through the house, gun in hand, and climbed the stairs to the master bedroom. There, she told Lee and Jason, she had fired blindly into the darkness. "She said she fired the gun once, and it fired five or six times. She said she wanted to kill herself, but she didn't have any bullets left," Lee later testified.

"Is he okay? Did you hear him yell, did you see any blood?" Lee asked her. Betty replied that it was "completely dark," so she couldn't see, she didn't know—but, Lee continued, "She said she thought he was okay, because he said, 'All right, you shot me. I'm dead.'"

Betty also told Lee that she had pulled the phone out of the wall, Lee testified, "so that he couldn't save himself."

At that point, Lee said she had reached for the phone to call her father herself to see if he was all right—but then she realized that she couldn't. "I wasn't allowed to have Dad's private number," she told the court.

And so, she called her sister, Kim, in Arizona instead—and Kim, from that distant place, tried to will her father into answering his telephone by ringing him repeatedly. When he wouldn't answer, Kim then called San Diego police and several hospitals, trying to get some information. But she could learn nothing. By that time, of course, Brad Wright and Brian Forbes were already at the house, along with the San Diego police—and an all-points bulletin was out for Elisabeth Anne Broderick.

Betty, meantime, sent Lee and Jason off to her house to "check on the boys." While they were gone, she sat on the edge of their bed—her purse at her feet with its emptied .38 lying atop the cosmetics and wallet, in full view—and made several telephone calls.

She called her father. "She said, 'Dan's driving me up the wall, he's driving me crazy, I feel like committing suicide,'" Frank Biscelgia later testified. "I said, 'Betty Anne, calm down, everything will be all right,' and before I knew it, she hung up," the old man recalled, his tone still filled with wonder.

She also called Dr. Nelson, but couldn't reach him. At some point that morning, too, whether earlier or later, she also called her friend Patti Monahan, to tell her, according to later testimony, that "I shot the fucker, I finally did it," and, among other vivid details, that "It's true—they do shit their pants. I could hear him gurgling in his own blood."

Lee and Jason arrived at Betty's house to find it surrounded by police looking for her mother—but they didn't tell her that her father was dead.

Lee lied to them. She hadn't seen Betty, she said. "I told them I was just there to get some laundry."

She and Jason then returned home to find Betty now collected enough to say that she wanted to turn herself in. After another phone conversation with Dian Black and Ronnie Brown, everyone agreed to meet at a La Jolla shopping center, in front of a restaurant called the Magic Pan.

There, they all piled into Jason's Volvo and drove to the police station—where they sat for the next hour, parked in front of the building, discussing what to do. Nobody was able to move out of the car. "We just sat there, debating ... It was just so nuts," Black recalls. "We were all in a catatonic, frenzied state ... we knew she needed to go to the police ... but Betty was pretty much out to lunch, so we just sat there ... We still didn't even know what had really happened."

Finally, Dian Black and Ronnie Brown decided that, regardless of whether Betty had shot anyone or not, she needed a lawyer before she walked into the police station to surrender. "She was in deep shit—I knew that much. I knew she had gone into Dan's house and fired a gun," says Black, "and I just kept thinking, 'God, he's going to be so mad that he's never going to let her out of jail after this!"

Secondly, Black hit upon the idea that somebody should go to Betty's house to get all her court records, her diaries, her autobiography, her letters. To anyone who hasn't been through the snarls of the domestic courts system, that might have seemed a paranoid, useless thought, Black agrees. But to her, it was completely rational. "I knew what Betty had been through. I knew that her file had suddenly vanished, that all her court records were sealed for all those years. So I wanted to make sure that at least her own personal records were safe, so her attorney could at least reconstruct what had happened to her. Those files were the only evidence she had. I didn't want them to just be able to lock her up and throw away the key without anybody ever knowing the full story."

So Lee and Jason agreed to try again to raid Betty's house. Before they left, Lee later testified, her mother removed the diamond necklace and watch she always wore "and she put them on me." And, on a scrap of paper, at Black's suggestion, Betty wrote her will, leaving all that she owned to her four children. On the back of a photograph of Jason, she also wrote out a list of instructions about the location of various safety deposit box keys and other valuables. But, even then, says Black, "She was so out of it" that she had to be led like a child.

This time, as Jason and Lee approached Betty's house, they were apprehended by police and taken to headquarters for questioning.

With the help of her attorney boyfriend, Ronnie Brown had, in the meantime, finally located a lawyer, Ron Frant, who was willing to come to his office on a Sunday to meet Betty Broderick.

It must have been quite a scene, these three women cruising around town, now in Black's Nissan Sentra with its dark tinted windows, waiting for Frant to arrive at his office, two wondering if one was a killer or only a hysterical divorcee who had gone over the edge. So far, they had heard no news on the radio to help them decide. Not until Black stopped at a pay phone to check in with her husband did they learn that, according to a radio bulletin minutes earlier, Dan and Linda Broderick were dead.

Neither Dian Black nor Ronnie Brown is cut out for this sort of thing. They are nice

324

women, not harborers of murderers. Shivering with shock, fear, and dawning astonishment at their own role in this day, they drove their friend to Frant's office, hugged her, cried, and split.

"Ronnie and I were so scared by then we couldn't even talk anymore," Black says now. "I expected to be surrounded by the SWAT team any minute—guys with Uzis, you know? 'Come out with your hands up!' It still seems like a bad movie, that whole day."

A little later, attorney Frant escorted his client to the downtown San Diego Police station, where she officially surrendered.

And that is the story of how Elisabeth Anne Broderick, once so pretty and bright and full of fun, became the fat, blowsy, dull-eyed killer who was arraigned on two counts of first-degree murder on November 7, I 1989—her forty-second birthday.

Chapter 31

Showtime

Oh, no. No need to worry about her, she assured everyone who asked during her first days in jail. She was just fine. A-OK. It was as if the killings hadn't even happened. Betty was still the happy hostess of Dian Black's memory, busy setting everyone else at ease, getting out the place mats, pouring the coffee, offering drinks—hiding herself, saying and doing all the right things.

Whether she was chillingly indifferent to her crime, as the prosecutor would later argue, or simply so psychologically ruined that she was incapable of comprehending what she had done, or just so angry that she didn't give a damn, will always be arguable. But this much is beyond dispute: to this day, two trials later, Betty still frequently speaks of Dan Broderick, and sometimes Linda, as if they were still alive and well and tormenting her.

"He's such a shit!" she exploded one day, nearly fifteen months later, after reciting some past example of his sins against her. "I'd like to kill him!"

"But, Betty," her listener replied, "you did."

Silence. Pause. Then a small, confused laugh. "Yeah, well ... but I didn't get revenge ... he didn't suffer enough."

In time, she would at least tacitly acknowledge that she had killed a man she had once loved. But she would never express even a whit of remorse for it, not to her children, not to her parents, or her friends, nor, later on, despite her attorney's desperate pleas, even to the two juries deciding her fate. She would never abandon her claim that she had killed in self-defense, that she was a victim of emotional battery, driven to protect herself and her children.

It was, of course, the thing that always set Betty Broderick apart, that made her, at least for a moment in time, the object of national fascination. Such purity of purpose, whether it is based on fact or fancy, principle or paranoia, is a rare thing in this or any other time—especially when the potential price is life in prison.

For the next two years, like a chameleon, Betty would adapt to whatever her prison audience required. She would ingratiate and conciliate. To one of her first roommates, a street corner prostitute, she apparently sounded sufficiently tough. "She said she must not be as good a shot as she used to be because she had five [bullets] but only got three in," the inmate later testified in court. Betty only laughed, dismissing her former cell mate as no more than "a snitch, trying to cut a deal with the prosecutor to save her own ass." Betty hardened fast. Within weeks, she was as conversant in jailhouse jargon as a woman who had spent her youth in juvenile hall instead of among the nuns at Sister Maria Regina's.

But to a later more celebrated, educated roommate—San Diego's highest-profile madame—she was a different person, more interested in small talk about schools, families, and the future. Like a pair of college roommates, the two women did each other's hair and makeup.

Then there was her eerie radiance. Like a rubber band finally snapped, she seemed almost relaxed. But her energetic mind was a constant tangle of ideas, couched in her usual wit and humor. She fretted over her magazine subscriptions, she worried about her hair coloring, she chattered endlessly over the phones about people, gossip, new babies, divorces, politics—everything except the only thing that really mattered. She even began to worry again about her weight. As Betty herself would later say, "I loved the first year, I needed jail, I needed the chance to hide away in my little cell ... to provide my own therapy. It was like R and R."

Meantime, to her friends in the outside world, Betty was a case study in escalating madness. Dian Black recalls, in particular, a weekend not long after the killings when she went to see Betty, and "she showed up [at the visitors' window] with these little pieces of tinfoil in her ears, and she asked me how I liked her new earrings. She was laughing, like it was all a big joke." On another occasion, Black recalls, "Betty sounded positively hurt when she heard a prisoner refer to her as 'a murderer.' She wasn't in touch with what she'd done at all."

In the months after her arrest, San Diegans were treated to nonstop details of Betty's $16,000 support settlement, her lavish shopping sprees. Her pretty pink-and-lavender Bob Mackie gown began to sound like a closet of fifteen; Dan's Jaguar and MG sports cars might have been Ferraris and Bentleys. The fact that they had taken a few trips to Europe and a Caribbean cruise rendered them overnight jet-setters. Their inexpensive little ski boat began to sound like an Onassis yacht. Their houses became "mansions," and, in time, even the original Broderick tract home on Coral Reef was sometimes described as "luxurious." Never mind that the Brodericks had only barely advanced from their Sears Roebuck installment payments to Neiman Marcus credit cards before they self-destructed.

In disaster, both Brodericks became larger than life, San Diego's favorite ongoing drama. To the middle-class majority—all those who live out their lives on finite budgets, weeding their own gardens and shopping at JC Penney's—here, once again, in the example of this pretty, privileged pair of overachievers crushed beneath the weight of their own uncompromising needs and greeds, was soothing validation of their own condition. There was always more than a little lip-smacking satisfaction in most local debate over the Broderick "tragedy."

From the beginning, Betty was a dream come true for the local press. Media switchboard operators all over town accepted her collect calls. She became a news addict, gorging herself on her own headlines. She couldn't get enough, and neither, for a long time, could San Diego.

First to be favored with Betty's phone calls was a reporter for the *Los Angeles Times*. But the reporter, a young woman about to be married for the first time herself, soon lost sympathy with Betty and later wrote a decidedly unsympathetic story for the *Times Sunday Magazine* headlined "Till Murder Do Us Part," which she then sold to a

TV movie maker, whose depiction of Betty was even more unflattering. Betty railed and swore that she had been cheated, deceived, and misrepresented.

But she was hardly deterred. Betty never met a reporter she didn't trust on sight. It was a measure both of her naivety, as well as her confidence in her own powers of persuasion, that, for the next two years, she continued to talk to nearly any reporter who asked, even in the midst of her trials. Her attorney finally gave up begging her to please, please shut up.

"If this case is presented right, I should walk on the whole thing," she told one reporter. She thought "a few hours of community service" was appropriate, "if I have to do anything." She called the *La Jolla Light* to complain about her fears of osteoporosis due to the poor medical care in jail. Before it was over, she would be issuing press releases from jail, written on her yellow legal pads, informing the world that "I am not an ordinary prisoner. I am Betty Broderick, and this case raises major issues which include ..."

Ruined once, Betty Broderick was, in short, ruined twice, this time by her own media appeal. It was never a fair match, Betty's relationship with the press. She was so eager for an audience, and the press was so cynically eager to give it to her that, very quickly, she became one of the most overexposed, over-reported killers in San Diego County history. Consequently, most of the San Diego media soon began to display a tired, cynical bias against her, well before her first jury was ever selected. The afternoon newspaper, the *Tribune*, in particular, began to mock her openly as no more than a frivolous scatterbrain. In May of 1990, for example, months before her first trial, columnist Alison DaRosa printed this snide little item under the caption "Sitting Pretty":

"Elisabeth Broderick, accused of murdering her ex-husband and his new wife, doesn't like the way she's looked in recent newspaper photographs. So she hired a professional photographer to capture her at her best. She curled her hair, applied makeup, and pressed her clothes; the photographer brought studio lights and backdrops."

In fact, the photographer in question was on assignment from the *Los Angeles Times Sunday Magazine*, and Betty hadn't even wanted to pose for him. She was enough of a photographer herself to know that "They can make me look like some crazy ax killer, like Lizzie Borden, if they want to." But she did it, thanks in large part to her own attorney's persuasion. Betty could never just say no.

Black humor became the local media order of the day.

Columnist Tony Perry of the *Los Angeles Times* referred to her so often that he eventually began most of his entries without introduction, writing simply "More Betty"—a typical tongue-in-cheek item being, "Don't tell Betty Broderick, but the number of attorneys in San Diego Country increased 42 percent from 1986-91, the largest jump of any urban county in the state."

The whole city, in fact, at times seemed caught up in sick irreverence over the Broderick case. During Halloween of 1990, for example, another columnist reported that a couple had shown up at a party dressed as Dan and Linda—in pajamas with bullet holes.

Nightclub comics made hay with Broderick jokes. One local club balladeer, Michael Angel, even got the lyrics to his little ditty, "Brenda Bombay," printed in full in a local newspaper:

You always wanted to be special, you always wanted to be known.
And sometimes life is just not fair, but you wouldn't leave it alone.
'Cause you just couldn't stand to lose, and let him get away with abuse.
And so you thought you'd even the score, as you headed out your front door ...
But you just can't take another life, then claim to be the battered wife.
'Cause when it's finally said and done, you still hold the smoking gun.

By November, 1991, midway through her second trial, a couple of local radio disc jockeys were also gleefully promoting a "Betty Broderick Christmas Album." Song titles, according to a newspaper column, included:

"Frosting the Old Man with a .38 Snub-nose," "I'll Be Home for Christmas with an Uzi," and "I'm Dreaming of a Short Sentence." Topping their offerings was a song titled "The Twelve Days of Christmas," including these lyrics:

On the fifth Day of Christmas, my true love gave to me:
Five rounds of lead
Four obscene phone calls
Three (bleep) yous
Two extra chins
And a car driven through the front door.

And late-night talk show hosts never had it so good. Some devoted hours to the killings, fielding furious debates into the wee hours of the morning between Betty sympathizers and those who wanted to see her gassed: was this the tale of a vengeful woman scorned, as so many headlines suggested—or was she driven to kill in self-defense by one powerful man's psychological abuse and a nation's disregard, legally and culturally, of a woman's rights, as her mushrooming mail insisted? Was this former housewife and mother a case study in the imbalance of power between the sexes, of gender bias in the legal system, especially divorce courts? Was she a symbol of all that feminists would remedy—or was she just a selfish, vindictive narcissist? Was she an emotionally battered woman, or was Dan Broderick a battered man? Were the Brodericks merely an example of the much-touted, materialistic "me-generation" of the eighties, somehow different from all the generations that came before? And what blame, if any, should be assigned to Linda Kolkena? Was she just an innocent young woman who took love where she found it, or was she an insensitive bitch? And so on and on.

Betty Broderick had unwittingly tapped a mother lode. And this was not yet even the season of 'Thelma and Louise', the controversial 1991 film about two female buddies who, fed up with sexism in all its forms, got their guns. But the saga of Betty Broderick was always Hollywood-bound.

Not until the end of her second trial, however, would anyone ever publicly raise the issue of her sanity. Then it was the frowning jury foreman, speaking to a swarm of reporters, who introduced the question:

"Clearly [Betty's] reactions were never something a normal, reasonable person would do ... But since no insanity defense was offered," he said, shrugging helplessly, "we just had to decide how Betty Broderick perceived the world ... That was our biggest problem."

By then, Dian Black, standing at the edge of the crowd, could only shake her head sadly. Privately, she had been complaining for two years to Betty's attorney that "this woman is not competent to stand trial without therapy first! She needs help to understand what she's even done!"

Always, caught dead center in the fishbowl of public fascination, were the four Broderick children. Pawns first in their parents' long divorce war, they next became ammunition in their mother's murder trials. Nor would the emotional abuse they suffered at the hands of manipulative adults pursuing their own agendas end, even after the final verdict was in.

In the first bizarre twist to the tale of the children, within days of the killings Rhett and Danny, then ten and thirteen, were sent to live, not with relatives of either of their parents, but, instead, to another broken home, Kathy Schmidt Broderick, former wife of Dan's brother Larry and mother of Larry's three minor children. For months, Betty was forbidden by the courts from contacting her sons, either by phone or letter.

But daughters Kim and Lee, then nineteen and eighteen, remained free agents, and, for a brief moment in the wake of the killings, they seemed united in the idea that, even if Dad was dead, they had a duty to support Mom.

Two days after the shootings, on her forty-second birthday, both wrote her remarkably loving notes.

"Mom, I don't know what to say. I love you so much," wrote Kim. "Everything will be okay! I'm taking care of Danny and Rhett as well as I can. I'll try to do what's best for them, but some things are out of my control ... Be tough, Mom ... I love you and I'm here for you whenever. Call me if you can ... I'll take care of things, Mom. We will all be fine. I love you—Kim."

And, from Lee:

"I guess this is not the best birthday you have ever had. This is going to be hard for everyone, not just you. I hate to see you spending this holiday season without any friends or family. We all love you, Mom ... There is [sic] a lot of people on your side. You are not alone. ... I will come and visit whenever I can. Love you, Lee. P.S. Danny would like me to tell you that he misses and loves you. I'm sure Rhett would say the same, but I just couldn't ask him."

But that small moment of emotional harmony between the sisters would not last. Within a few weeks, Kim moved to Denver, where she was soon agreeing with Uncle Larry that her mother should be denied both bail and contact with her brothers. But

Kim always insisted that her decision to become the prosecution's star witness was her own. What turned her stomach, she said later, was her first conversation with her mother after she was in jail. "I expected her to be saying, 'Oh my God, what have I done?'" Kim said. "But she never even apologized for killing Dad. Instead, she said she'd done it for us, that she couldn't stand the way he was treating us. She wasn't sorry at all. She was laying guilt on me, she wanted me to be glad she did it, and when I wasn't, she called me a traitor." She finished on the verge of tears.

In time, Kim also became a star player in the media circus. Before it was over, she would blast her mother on such TV programs as *20/20*, *Maury Povich*, and *Oprah* for leaving four children homeless. She loved her mother, she said, but "I think she should be punished for what she did." Her photograph would dominate half a page in *People* magazine, along with the deadly quote: "I didn't like it that Dad got restraining orders against her, but what could he do? When he tried to deal with her, she screamed obscenities. Now at least he's living in peace. He's probably better off."

Lee, meantime, remained in La Jolla. She visited her mother regularly on weekends, bringing her Estee Lauder cosmetics, moisturizers, hair coloring, magazines, and other items Betty regarded as essentials of survival.

Unlike Kim, Lee refused to cooperate with the prosecution and, thus, became even more ostracized by the Broderick clan than she was while her father was alive. "She's a thief, a drug addict, she's just like her mother," Larry Broderick once hissed in a telephone interview. For a time, Lee was not even permitted to know her brothers' telephone number in Denver. Later on in trial, the DA went nearly as far, once even suggesting that Lee might have somehow been involved in her mother's crime, for insurance purposes. Through it all, Lee Broderick marched with her head high, her expression frozen, her feelings hidden. And, unlike her sister, Kim, she consistently had only one firm answer for the media hordes: "No comment."

* * *

From her cell at Las Colinas, Betty was still obsessed with the same issues that had so tormented her before the killings—money and litigation. Two murder charges had done nothing to dilute her loathing of lawyers. Within weeks, she was fighting with her second criminal attorney, Marc Wolf, whom she had hired to replace Frant, on grounds that Frant "mostly did drug cases." But Wolf was no different than all the others, she complained. Robbing her blind. She accused him of hiring a public relations firm against her wishes and, worse, racking up a $160,000 bill in less than six weeks—and she fired him. (Wolf consistently refused comment on his flamboyant former client.)

Betty turned over control of her finances to Brad and also gave him her condo. She pressed her appeal of the divorce settlement and launched a new court action, demanding contact with her sons. In a small victory, she was finally allowed to write to them on a limited basis, her letters subject to censorship by a Denver therapist selected by the Brodericks.

It was a legal war Betty would fight mostly on her own. Although two of her brothers were willing to take Danny and Rhett, the Bisceglia family was never an effective presence in San Diego family court during those early months. Instead, most of Betty's family members were so shamed and shocked by the killings that they kept the lowest profile they could, hoping that their friends, neighbors, and coworkers would never associate them with the infamous San Diego socialite killer. When publicity finally caught up with them in Eastchester, the elder Biscegligas were devastated. In custody hearings—again behind closed doors—the outraged Broderick clan, led by Larry, his brother's designated executor, simply ran over them.

Compounding Betty's outrage, she was convinced, with some cause, that Dan's brother Larry and his former wife, Kathy, were financially exploiting her children. Not only was Dan's estate paying Kathy Schmidt Broderick $50,000 or more per year to care for Betty's two minor sons, plus another several thousand dollars for private school tuition, Larry Broderick also billed the children another $50,000 as compensation for his duties as executor of Dan's estate. In addition, according to later court documents, Larry also failed to repay a 1988 loan for $450,000 from Dan's pension fund, further eroding the inheritance of the three Broderick children named in Dan's will. According to friends, he was also on the verge of declaring business bankruptcy.

Further, Dan's old law firm, Gray, Cary, Ames and Frye, submitted legal fees of nearly $400,000—so high that the court-appointed San Diego banker in charge of protecting the Broderick children's interests legally protested with such vigor that Gray, Cary eventually agreed to cut its bill by about 40 percent.

That same banker also took trenchant note, in his first legal challenge, of Larry Broderick's various other steep expenses, all charged to the Broderick children— everything from a new Jeep Wagoneer to travel costs and dinner tabs in luxurious restaurants, ostensibly to discuss estate matters.

Betty was both livid and vindicated.

"I couldn't get an extra cent from Dan Broderick while he was alive to cover what I spent on the kids for food, clothes, and entertainment. Now they're paying hired help $5,000 a month to keep them? At the rate these bloodsuckers are going, by the time my boys are old enough for college, all their money will be gone! Why doesn't somebody do something to stop it? It's grand theft."

Eventually, someone would. Two years later, the same bank, acting in behalf of the two Broderick sons, sued Larry Broderick for $295,000— their share of Larry's $450,000 unpaid loan to his brother's estate.

But this was still 1990. Kim was receiving around $3,000 a month— while Lee, the disinherited, got nothing, although she would eventually be entitled to one-quarter of the $1 million court-ordered insurance policy from the 1989 divorce trial.

Money was always the measure with the Brodericks, in death as in life. In another twisted note, the Broderick estate later even thought to bill Betty for twenty-five days of her November, 1989, support payment— every day beyond November 5, when she killed Dan.

Nor did the Brodericks show much more generosity toward Linda Kolkena's family. Although Linda was also beneficiary of $1 million in Dan's life insurance, the Brodericks challenged Linda's family's right to that money on grounds that, since she had died anywhere from one to thirty minutes sooner than Dan had, her entitlement legally reverted to him. Her family, in short, was entitled to nothing beyond what Larry Broderick and family chose to bestow. According to Linda's sister, Maggie, her ailing father finally received around $200,000. The Kolkenas did not contest it. Adding to the insult, according to a report by Paul Krueger in the *Reader*, a local mortuary even billed the Kolkena family for her share of funeral costs—around $7,000.

Linda Kolkena Broderick was never much more than incidental in the Broderick story, the forgotten second victim, the "new wife," who had also died. In the beginning, even her maiden name was frequently misspelled both in the press and in court documents—Kokino, Kokine, etc.

But Dan's friends were the worst offenders. In their most stunning display of insensitivity, when the American Ireland Fund staged a tribute to Dan at a $250-per-plate black-tie dinner during the summer of 1990, complete with speeches and slide show photographs of Dan Broderick with his children. Linda Kolkena's name was not once mentioned, her picture never once shown. Several of her girlfriends in the audience cried in anger.

As her sister once quietly observed, fighting back tears as she spoke to a gathering of reporters outside the courtroom during the first trial, "Linda has become nothing more than a parenthetical in this case, a cheap bimbo, a gold digger, a dirty four-letter word ... Why? I don't understand why. Doesn't my sister's life count, too?" The gathered reporters could only avert their eyes, until Maggie Seats finally gave up and left. She had only been in town for the day, on business. Unlike the Broderick and Bisceglia clans, none of the Kolkenas could afford to leave their jobs to attend the trial full-time, to establish a courtroom presence in Linda's memory. Maggie's impromptu little press conference barely made a mention in the next day's paper. Even the prosecutor, Kerry Wells, didn't have time to see her, she said later.

When Betty wasn't on the jail phone, she was churning out personal letters on her yellow legal pad—letters that convey, better than anything else can, the increasingly detached state of her mind. Those she wrote to her two daughters were particularly eerie. This was not a mother in jail on charges of murdering their dad. This was a dutiful, concerned mother enduring an inconvenient period of temporary separation, nothing more.

To Lee, on November 27—three weeks after the shootings—Betty wrote:

"Please take care of my cameras. They are very valuable to me. You can use them but be careful. No sand, no water, no dropping. If I ever get out I may still be a photographer. Also, the cellular phone—sell it or just cancel [it] for now, $35 a month even if you don't use it.

"Are the furs in storage? Who has my TV from condo kitchen? ... My roommate's birthday is Dec. 9, a Saturday. I want to get her 'Presumed Innocent' in paperback with a ribbon tied around and a nice birthday card. Could you do that?"

Then the woman who had been too helpless to help herself at her own divorce trial gave her daughter some brisk, efficient financial advice on what to do with the $250,000 she stood to gain from her late father's life insurance policy: "Every single day that money is not in an interest-bearing place, you're losing money. HONESTLY, EVERY DAY COUNTS!! Especially with such large sums of money. You're going to be an heiress, like you only read about. You'll be able to fully live off the interest alone, and when you start earning money you can leave the interest in there. NEVER touch the principle ... Your money can only do two things, GROW and GONE. Depreciable things like cars, clothes, trips SPEND your money never to be seen again. ... In your case, I would look into several HIGH-INTEREST CDs—FDIC INSURED   CDs earn you MORE money on top of MORE money. Be smart about this! Most people never get such an opportunity in their lifetimes."

Then, it was back to Betty as usual. "How are your nails? Did you go back to Kristi—she probably hates me, thinking I went someplace else. Tell her my nails are all bitten."

And finally, she worried about what Brad was up to. "Now that I'm locked up, girls are coming out of the woodwork asking Brad out. What a riot! My only rule is not in MY condo, MY bed (God forbid), or with MY money! [unhappy face] Keep an eye on him."

Her letters to Kim in Denver were decidedly different in tone, an awkward blend of breezy chitchat, laced with ill-concealed anger:

"Dear Kim, Are you freezing!! Are you having any fun?" she wrote prior to the 1990 preliminary hearing, which she knew Kim would be attending at the prosecution's request. "Does the DA pay for your plane ticket? They should, if they want you!! Tell them you want the $$—don't make anything easy for them to PROSECUTE ME!! The fucking bitch [Kerry Wells] thinks I won't stand up to her and her lies. Ha! Ha! Ha! I've been through too much for too long to tolerate any more legal bullshit from ANYONE ever!!!

"How are your classes? I hope you don't miss anything coming here. How is sewing, cooking, piano?" She then offered maternal warnings about one of Kim's boyfriends. "Please don't ever speak to [him] again for any reason—the guy is trouble. Get tough, Kim—stop letting people manipulate you ..."

In a later letter, her tone was edgier: "How is the campus? Pretty? Are there places to hang out and meet people, like coffee shops, etc.? Keep a lid on your drinking—I always worry because you are the child of an alcoholic, and without you controlling it, you have genetic tendencies in that direction no matter what you do ... Are you eating well? Start cooking—it's really fun! I'll send you recipes ...

"Do you really not want me to be able to speak to the boys? Creep ... They should be allowed to speak to me and send me notes and letters ... Give the boys long, warm hugs from me ... Tell Kathy to take good care of my boys until they come back to their Mommy ... Love you and miss seeing you! Mom XOX."

She wrote Kim several more letters during the winter, most filled with small talk. Kim rarely answered. By summertime, 1990, Betty's letters were plaintive. "Kim, it's terrible going too long without talking to you!" she wrote. But, again, instead of addressing the issue most on Kim Broderick's mind, she launched into a discussion of where Kim should take a $10,000 watch Betty had given her for repairs. "Only an A+ jeweler should touch it. Neiman's will do it here for you ..." By fall, less than a month before her trial, she wrote this: "Dearest Kimby—PLEASE write me or leave "This machine will accept collect" on your machine. Lee Lee and I get along great BECAUSE we talk all the time. We don't AGREE all the time—but at least we talk everything out. You are my number one baby—I miss you the most—don't hide—nothing goes away or gets better by ignoring it!!!" XOX. I can't wait for you to come home! Love, Mom."

But she wrote to Brad most often, sometimes issuing only brisk housekeeping commands, but at other times expressing love and gratitude.

"I have lots of time to think and dream in here, and since I've never been one to fantasize and I don't dare look to the future, I've had lots of time to smile and remember all the incredibly wonderful things we've done together," she wrote two weeks after the killings. "There is no point to this letter ... just thank you for being there when no one else was, thank you for being strong when I was weak, for taking care of me and mine even now ... I love you." Although Brad always called her Betty, she signed it "Bets"—Dan's pet name for her in bygone times.

For the next two years, Brad Wright would continue to be Betty's banker and loyal, all-purpose gofer. He never seemed to mind—even when she once hit upon the idea of turning him into guardian of her boys by marrying him from jail. "Why not?" she asked a reporter over the jail phone. "If I tell Brad, 'Get out here, you're getting married at two o'clock today,' he'd do it in a second! Then he'd be their legal stepfather, and he could have the money Kathy's getting. He would be a good, kind father, too, better by far than the shithead they had."

Meantime, mail continued to pour in to her from women all over the world. The tone was usually the same: "All your prior emotions are still alive and well in me," wrote a typical middle-aged divorcee who got a raw deal. "I only wish I had your nerve ... you are wrong when you said that nobody won. THEY lost. YOU won. You no longer have that sick, tense, enraged feeling in the pit of your stomach, wondering what 'they' are going to do next. They are no longer admired around town, while you're treated as though you don't exist. You are no longer humiliated nor do you have to deal with their harassment. Your future is not wonderful, but they have none—as they deserve."

In time, she got so many letters that she began to get in trouble with her jailers for the clutter in her cell. "You're supposed to fit all of your belongings—everything—your shampoo, your soap, all your legal papers, everything, in a shoebox," she complained. "And I can't do it. I look at all this mail, and I ask them, 'What am I supposed to do? Eat it?'" For this kind of lip, she was periodically punished during the next two years, thrown into isolation for days at a time—"where they give you torture food, like hockey pucks of alfalfa and hay—all because I'm getting too much mail from women who got fucked over, too.'"

But, in truth, Betty was always more thrilled by her male correspondents. And she would never learn to distinguish between the legitimate men who merely wanted her to know that not all husbands were as cruel as they thought Dan had been, and those—the majority—who simply got their jollies in the dark of night by corresponding with the black widow who had pumped two people full of bullets.

One regular correspondent, Bill, from Los Angeles, wrote her about his tennis game, the six books he had read last week, and the wonderful new French restaurant he had just discovered, "very renowned by the movie set." Ending one letter, he wrote: "It is past midnight, I am off to the bed, and I will close with love, kisses, erector sets, toys, and visions of sugar plums. MAY I VISIT YOU??? Are you allowed platonic conjugals? Here is a kiss, put it where you wish. X."

Betty always said, indignantly, that "Of course I know these guys are flakes, why else would they be writing to a woman in prison?" But she answered every letter faithfully.

At about the same time the San Diego press was getting bored with Betty, the national media got wind of her story. Among those first on the scene, naturally, were the TV tabloids. *Hard Copy* lobbed the opening salvo, on the eve of Betty's first trial in 1990, in a lurid segment complete with actors playing the roles of Linda and Dan seminude in bed, in the moments just prior to their deaths. At the end of the program, the hostess called Linda "a home-wrecker." As it turned out, that pretty well summarized the position later adopted by most of the national press. Despite the jaundice of the San Diego media, most national accounts of the Broderick case in the months to come were sympathetic to Betty to a sometimes astonishing degree. Most, like the *Ladies Home Journal*, approached the story from the standard angle of a woman scorned.

Friends of Dan and Linda Broderick were staggered by the onslaught of positive publicity toward the beast who had shot their friends to death. They struggled, mostly in vain, to comprehend the Betty Phenomenon.

"Betty is incredibly bright. She used to tell Dan that she would ruin him, make him pay," Sharon Blanchet remarked, after Betty made the *Barbara Walters* show. "She always said she would make *Oprah* and *60 Minutes*. And she's doing it. She's created all of this by sheer force of her own personality. The facts have nothing to do with it."

Chapter 32

The Cast

San Diego County District Attorney Edwin L. Miller, Jr., was privy to all of Betty's fan mail—prison correspondence was at that time routinely copied for the prosecutor to read. And so he knew that what he had on his hands was the specter of a feminist *cause célèbre*; an educated, articulate, flamboyant woman who would wrap herself in the rhetoric of emotional and legal battery, who would defend her crimes by trashing not only Dan Broderick but also the entire legal system within which Edwin Miller worked. Judges, divorce attorneys, that stable of court-appointed "experts"—all would be on trial, right along with Betty Broderick. She held every promise of becoming a virtual feminist star upon Edwin Miller's crime-infested firmament.

He moved with speed, and decided flair, to defuse the menace. He not only named a woman to prosecute the case, he picked the head of his Domestic Crimes Unit. A woman who dealt routinely with battered women and abused children. A woman who had seen the very worst: wives with broken bones and faces swollen or slashed beyond recognition, babies with cigarette burns, starved into whimpering helplessness, sodomized literally to death. One wife was so terrified of her husband that it took her two years to report his murder of their six-year-old daughter and lead police to where the child's body was buried. Another case involved an eighteen-month-old baby who had literally been strangled to death by forced fellatio, before being stabbed and tossed into a garbage dumpster.

These were the people whose world Deputy District Attorney Kerry Wells, Miller's choice, inhabited.

The press, naturally, loved it. Woman against woman. A catfight. What could be finer?

Wells would, in fact, prove to be a controversial choice, either brilliant or disastrous, depending on who was doing the critique.

On the downside, she was young and relatively inexperienced in trial work. A Los Angeles native and graduate of Southern California's Whittier College of Law, admitted to the bar in 1980, she was thirty-seven when she was assigned to one of the most sensational murder cases in San Diego history. Most remarkably, she had never prosecuted a murderer during her ten years in the district attorney's office.

On the plus side, she was well respected among her peers as a smart, efficient, hardworking, no-nonsense professional. In addition, Wells's personal profile was right for this case. Here was no stereotypical, unattractive spinster who might alienate a jury by her perceived inability to relate to a wife and mother in crisis. Instead, Kerry Wells was married (to another attorney), had two small sons of her own, and, not insignificantly, she was also pretty—reed thin, with short, curly, strawberry blond hair, and a complexion meant for Ivory soap commercials. At first glance, Miss Topeka came to mind. In court, she often wore Peter Pan collars trimmed with lace, and fragile strings of beads or pearls. Her gold earrings were never larger than dimes, her suits were always simple and tailored, usually gray, beige, or blue. When she smiled, she showed dimples and looked like a girl of eighteen.

Which is not to say that Kerry Wells spent much time smiling during the two long years she spent trying to bring Betty Broderick to justice.

To the contrary, Wells displayed such a complete, gut-level loathing of this pampered woman who dared equate herself with the battered women of Kerry Wells's experience that, in time, it became Wells's most glaring flaw. Her disgust was so personal, her dislike so intense, her moral outrage so pure that it became instantly apparent to both jurors and reporters alike. Everything about Betty Broderick, from her vulgar language to her witty, unrepentant interviews with the press, repulsed Wells.

But in the beginning, as she faced mobs of reporters and TV lights outside each court hearing, Wells was almost charming, simply because her natural shyness showed. She seemed afraid of these clamoring hordes; she had never dealt with such noisy aggressiveness before, and so, initially, she blurted out a few bits of herself, spontaneously.

"I've worked with battered women," she said one afternoon, exasperated, looking bewildered. "And this woman is not one! Betty Broderick is making a joke of a serious, important issue."

But, as the days and weeks wore on, Wells lost her natural appeal. Instead, as she gained her bearings, she grew ever grimmer, so tight-jawed, humorless, and moralizing that, by the time the first trial was done, reporters were laughingly referring to her as "the Church Lady," after Dana Carvey's character on the television show *Saturday Night Live*.

Her disgust with reporters feeding the ego and celebrity of this double killer was withering. She lost all patience with questions about even the most obvious circumstances of the case—Dan's infidelity, his fines, his controlling ways, jailing Betty for profanity.

Yes, yes, she would snap—Linda refused to give Betty the wedding china. "But is that any reason to kill them?" And, yes, so Dan had lied about his affair. Yes, he had thrown her in jail and fined her. Yes, Betty Broderick "had a right to be angry—Dan Broderick was not perfect." But, she always finished in angry frustration, "Is that any reason to kill them?" It became her standard line, her answer to everything. But, increasingly, she refused to provide any answers at all.

Instead, in time she simply ignored the press altogether, whisking by with the cold disdain of a woman passing through a swarm of flies.

And, in court, she displayed not a shred of female compassion toward Betty Broderick, even when it might have served to soften her image to advantage in front of the jury.

"I can't help it," Wells once remarked, of her own angry attitudes. "She's a cold-blooded murderer, and she lies about everything! I don't understand why anybody is buying her story! I don't understand why this case is attracting all this attention! This is not a feminist issue! This is not a case of psychological battery!"

In one of her first public acts, Wells arrived in court on April 3, 1990, to inform reporters that, in the matter of Elisabeth Anne Broderick, the state had elected to seek life without possibility of parole—not the death penalty. The decision had been made, she said, out of consideration for the Broderick youngsters, who would probably be trial witnesses. The district attorney did not want to expose them to the "horrible trauma" of participating in a proceeding that could lead their only surviving parent to the gas chamber. Wells said this with pursed lips, jutting chin, and cold eyes. She did not look like a woman who was pleased with the decision Edwin Miller had made. But that perception turned out to be only more of her icy public persona—because many months later, she admitted in a relaxed moment that she had serious personal qualms about the death penalty.

Throughout the two-year Broderick drama, Wells always seemed caught between conflicting, kinder, personal impulses, and the do-or-die professional ambitions of a woman walking the tightrope in what is still mostly a man's world. During the first trial, the stress eventually appeared to affect even her health. She grew thinner and paler by the day. A friend said she couldn't keep down food and was drinking cans of liquid nutrients throughout most of the first trial to keep her strength up.

"Her office was nothing but Maalox bottles and soda crackers," said investigator Bill Green, laughing despite himself. "It got to the point that I couldn't even bring a jar of pickles into the office or she'd throw up."

Betty, meantime, was only warming up. Observing her chief antagonist in life, now that Dan was dead, she sounded more like a quipster for *Mad* magazine, or *Spy*, than a woman on trial for multiple murders: "Why doesn't Kerry Wells get her bony ass home and wipe noses, and do the soccer and the Little League and the piano for twenty years, and then when her husband leaves her, come back to prosecute me?"

Nor was she satisfied simply to taunt Wells in the media. A few weeks after she was jailed, one of Betty's former cell mates sent her a postcard—a close-up photo of a penis with sunglasses perched across its hairy base. Betty sent it to Wells with a note: "See what I have to put up with?" Wells grimly reported this to the judge at the next hearing, as reporters grinned into their notebooks. Journalists covering the Broderick trial couldn't believe their good luck. The battle lines were drawn. The Church Lady versus Crazy Betty.

And that was before they even got to know defense attorney Jack Earley, who would spend the next two years blaspheming the dead with almost as much gusto as Betty did. By the time the case was over, it was hard to tell whom the Broderick camp despised more, the killer or her lawyer.

Initially, there was little about forty-one-year-old Jack Earley to suggest a gunslinger ready to take on the San Diego legal establishment on behalf of a female killer pleading the novel defense of psychological abuse. The flashiest thing about him was the ice blue Jaguar he rode into town the day he met Betty Broderick. He came from Newport Beach, another fashionable coastal community an hour north of San Diego,

339

where he had been in private practice since 1982. Murder was his specialty, and, beyond responding to the obvious human fascination involved in such cases, Earley, like many criminal defense attorneys, also harbored a genuine philosophic aversion to the death penalty—which, in the beginning, is what most observers expected the state to seek for Betty Broderick.

In appearance, he was a pleasant-looking, preppy young man given to dark, conservatively tailored suits, loafers, murky maroon print ties and button-down shirts, usually in pale blue; he wore dark-rimmed glasses over hazel eyes which were definitely not mirrors to his soul; his best feature was his head of thick, wavy dark hair—which would display many silver threads before he was done with Betty.

His personal style was equally ordinary. In court and out, he was calm, methodic, deliberate, plodding. Unlike Kerry Wells, he was also consistently friendly and relaxed with reporters, but his emotions were always hard to find; spontaneity is not a part of his makeup. Ask Jack Earley what he thinks about the weather, and he will think it over. He seldom snaps, but his smile is also always a pause delayed. It takes time to discover the cynical, black-hearted wit lurking beyond the public persona.

Earley is one of life's nonreactors. He listens, he calculates. Beyond all else, he is, as most good criminal attorneys are, a tactician. He doesn't defend homicide on any moral grounds—nobody can. But he has a solid grip on the psychological tools needed to persuade a jury that, sometimes, in this mercurial world of conflicting human passions, homicide might be an excusable solution.

A native of Virginia, Earley graduated from Southern California's Loyola Law School and worked for several years as a public defender before going into private practice. He had handled at least thirty murder cases. His clients had ranged from a frightened old lady who shot wildly into the darkness of her home, killing a teenaged burglar, to some of the most depraved examples of humanity imaginable—such as the rejected boyfriend who threw acid on his former girlfriend before dismembering her; another spurned lover who took murderous revenge not on the girlfriend but on her seven-year-old son instead, beating him to death; the daughter who hired a couple of teenagers to kill her aging father for his insurance.

Of this lot, Earley had lost only three clients to life without possibility of parole, and of six death penalty cases, none to death row. One reason for his success was that, in Earley's experience, the average accused killer (as opposed, for example, to a bank robber or embezzler) is far more docile, more willing to do precisely whatever an attorney tells him or her to do—unless, of course, the accused is so certifiably insane that it doesn't matter anyway, since he/she will never be brought to trial.

Jack Earley, in short, was confident that he knew his killers.

But that was before Jack met Betty, after being contacted by her friend Dian Black.

He remembers his first visit with Betty well. He was at Las Colinas for three hours, listening to "the story"—her account of the pressures that had driven her to kill. "She didn't really like me at first, because I didn't cry about her story, like a lot of [other attorneys] did." And, he adds dryly, "I was very tired when I left. I could see that she would be a very difficult client, because she was so intelligent. It's a lot easier when they're stupid."

Betty remembers her first impressions of Earley, too. She thought he was "a doofus," a dull, colorless man "who had no idea in hell of what it was that I went through! He looked bored at everything I said! I just didn't think he got it!" Translated: Jack wasn't Dan.

But she hired Earley anyway, primarily because she had no better alternative. At the time she had a cash fund of at least $750,000—including proceeds from del Cielo, which had been sold shortly after the homicide for about $1 million. Earley agreed to take the case, she says today, for a flat fee of $250,000, although he would later bill her for twice that. He says the other half went to "pay her own bills—she insisted we pay her bills." She, of course, accuses him of lying. Betty would never trust Earley any more than she trusted any of her other attorneys.

Earley and his client bickered over dollars steadily for the next two years, occasionally with such passion that at times the whole affair seemed less like a murder trial than a TV sitcom. "Why must I pay this (department store) bill, when I can't even pay my investigators?" Earley griped one afternoon, sitting in his office, glaring at a stack of Betty's credit card charges.

"Because I'm no deadbeat!" Betty screeched over the phone later. "I'd rather my money went to department stores than to another fucking lawyer!"

"This is going to be an antagonistic relationship, I sense it," Earley said, deadpan.

But, contrary to Betty's original cynicism, Jack Earley grasped the elements of her story at once. In fact, in those first months of 1990, he bristled about San Diego like a tomcat stalking the biggest fight of his career. He threatened to sue for a change of venue on grounds that Betty could never get a fair trial in Dan Broderick's town. He promised to challenge every single judge on the San Diego bench on grounds of potential bias. At the same time, he was becoming an overnight feminist, reading at least snatches of every important book on battered women he could lay hands on.

"She was emotionally abused, Dan Broderick used his influence to batter her relentlessly ... He was determined to drive her so crazy she would kill herself," Earley said in the first weeks, flushed with enthusiasm as he tested his argument on reporters. "It was Chinese water torture ... drip drip drip, until finally she snapped. Betty was just a simple housewife, and suddenly she was thrown into the ring with a gladiator. He had all the advantages, all the skills. These courtrooms were Dan Broderick's domain—he controlled them and her money, too. How long could any intelligent woman stand up against that without snapping?" By the time he finished, Earley looked ready to weep.

Earley's plan, from the outset, was to retry not only the entire four-year divorce case but also Dan's prior two-year affair with Linda, if he could. It all depended on whether Wells would open the door to character assassination by trying to demonstrate through a parade of attorneys and judges what an exemplary human Dan was.

"Oh, how I hope they will try to defend his character," said Earley almost

341

prayerfully in early 1990, with a wicked little grin. "If I can just get Kerry to get down in the mud with me, Betty's going to win—because we can show that she was always a decent, good mother, and he was a falling-down, cold, vindictive drunk ... I want all the hearsay in, all the smut, all the dirt, all the character evidence to come in."

His strategy, too, was always to focus more on Dan, less on Betty—"She's not sympathetic enough because she's so angry," he said matter-of-factly. His primary goal, always, was to make Dan Broderick look so mean, so selfish, so unlikable that no jury could regret his death. "The key," he once remarked, "is to help jurors see that maybe the victim deserved it."

It was Linda who worried him more. "She's harder," he fretted. "It's harder to make a jury dislike the new wife as much as the man who abused the old wife ..." And so, he concluded, annoyed as a plumber confronting a mystery leak, "Betty's probably going to have to serve more time for her than him."

Earley also quickly concluded that the press might be among his most useful tools. And, although his first big print splash, the *Los Angeles Times Magazine* cover story, was negative, he wasn't discouraged. "I don't care if the piece is positive or negative—the very fact that a major newspaper finds Betty's story worth a magazine cover is a plus. It lends her case legitimacy, no matter what the content is."

He was also enjoying his own new-found celebrity. He even grew his hair out a little. He liked it almost as much as Betty did when the *Ladies' Home Journal* called. He was even happier when 20/20 came to town and Oprah later flew him to Chicago for a live performance. None of his other clients had ever landed him on national TV.

But it didn't take long for Earley's media strategy to backfire, simply because, as he soon learned, he could never control his own client. He couldn't stop Betty from calling reporters on her own and saying whatever came to mind—and he had zero luck in persuading her to tone down her self-justifying outrage. Once she made headlines by telling a reporter that it was God's will that guided her bullets. "Either God or my Good Fairy," she later elaborated.

In the beginning, before Earley became a wiser man, he used to say, "Betty has simply got to admit, at some point, that something horrible has occurred here." But within a matter of time, he was only grinning weakly at his own optimism. At times during the next two years—especially after visits with Betty at Las Colinas—Jack Earley wore the bewildered, half-dazed expression of a man who could not believe he had ever been stupid or venal enough to take on Betty Broderick's defense. "If I had it to do over, I would not take this case, not for any amount of money. She's the hardest client I've ever worked with," he said, sighing, prior to the first trial. "She simply will not take advice."

Even so, this much is beyond dispute: Jack Earley was probably one of the few attorneys in California with the temperament to deal with Betty Broderick for two months, much less two years, without quitting in frustration, or at least smacking her.

Through it all, Earley did his best to hang on to his emotional battery defense. But he was increasingly discouraged not only by Betty's stubbornness, but also by the stark facts of his case. His client had bought a gun, driven across town, climbed the stairs, and not only shot them in bed, but then ripped the phone out of the wall.

342

Although Earley seemed genuinely to believe his own drip drip drip theory, he was also a practical man. It would not be easy to convey to twelve jurors in two or three weeks the accumulating pressures one woman suffered over seven long years—particularly when that woman consistently displayed more defiant anger than shattered, weeping remorse.

Thus, he gradually toned down his rhetoric. He stopped talking about hiring such nationally noted experts on battered women as Charles Patrick Ewing or Lenore Walker. Instead, he said, he had concluded that it wasn't in Betty's best interests to introduce such well-known names into her trial because "The prosecution will be able to anticipate our case in advance." (If he had asked them and been refused, he would never admit it.) Instead, he said, he would bring a lesser known witness to testify to the battery issues.

Earley also began to back off his earlier, fiery promise to pioneer emotional battery as the central defense in Betty's case. Instead, he worried increasingly that it might be a mistake to even introduce the term into his own arguments because "it's a buzzword. It's too radical." It might be counter-productive, he thought, to brand Betty's trial with any intense feminist ideology that could alienate a potentially conservative, middle-class jury. Instead, he decided it was wiser to simply tell Betty's story and let the jurors draw their own conclusions.

By the eve of the first trial, Earley sounded like a man bound for a funeral. "This is not a good case," he once remarked gloomily. "The best we can hope for is that she won't get two first-degrees. Twenty years [for second-degree convictions] is a lot better than looking at life with no possibility of parole."

At least once, according to Betty, he also tried to get her to agree to a plea bargain, accepting two second-degrees. "I told him to fuck off," she says. "First he tells me we have a good case, now he tells me to plea-bargain—after he's got all my money? Well, I don't think so. Noooooo. Not at all!"

Earley did apply for a change of venue, but, as he expected, it was denied. He also abandoned as just another futile gesture, his vow to challenge every judge in town. Instead, by springtime 1990, after only two challenges, he agreed to accept Judge Thomas J. Whelan, a veteran deputy district attorney who had just been appointed to the bench in January.

Whelan looked the part of a judge more than most. A big, ruddy-complected man with silver hair, his face was homely and tired, marked by old acne scars, but with features that had settled into the kind of quiet, kindly resignation of one who has done some hard living and not found it all that bad. He never raised his voice; sometimes he seemed almost to be sleeping on the bench, lying back with his eyes closed. Everyone agreed he was a Spencer Tracy look-alike. The only glitch in this perfect picture was the old-fashioned hair oil he favored, and he also usually wore his pants an inch too short.

A devout Catholic and family man whose wife is a teacher in La Jolla—at the same parochial school Kim and Lee Broderick once attended—Whelan was the sort of judge that most jurors like and trust on sight—which turned out to be just one more problem for Jack Earley.

Although Whelan would change his mind by the second trial, at the start of the first one, he seemed determined to conduct this case in the most open way possible, particularly given Betty Broderick's long-standing claims that the San Diego courts had always been biased against her. In early pretrial hearings, Whelan meticulously documented his every ruling on attorney motions with not one but half a dozen case citations. "I don't even want to have sidebar conferences [private sessions with the attorneys] unless it's absolutely necessary," he told reporters. Like everyone else, they, too, instantly liked this friendly, down-home judge.

Whelan also announced at the outset that he intended to conduct a murder trial—not a rehash of the Broderick divorce. Therefore, he ruled in pretrial evidence hearings that the financial terms of the Broderick divorce settlement would be off-limits in the criminal trial. It was inappropriate, he said, to retry the two-year-old decision of a divorce court judge in a murder trial. He would permit a copy of the financial settlement to be entered into evidence for the perusal of any juror who might be interested, but that was it. Nor, he ruled, would either attorney be allowed to editorialize on the divorce settlement in the courtroom.

Further hobbling Earley, Whelan also ruled that neither side would be permitted either to defend or attack the character of Dan and Linda Broderick, unless a direct correlation to Betty Broderick's state of mind at the time of the killings could be shown. In other words, witnesses such as the secretary who had lectured Dan about his deception with Linda would not be permitted, since Betty didn't know about it.

Throughout both trials, the question of Betty Broderick's sanity remained the great unspoken, the issue nobody wanted to address.

In California, as in many states, there is no longer any such defense as "diminished capacity" or "temporary insanity"—but did Betty qualify for something in between? Was she competent to proceed in her own defense? Had she been driven over the edge to the point that no trial should be conducted at all? Was she responsible, or not? Mentally well, or not?

No satisfactory answer was ever provided, either by the defense or by the State of California. Kerry Wells of course, was never even remotely interested in any diagnosis of Betty Broderick's mental health beyond one that read: Narcissist. Selfish. Evil. Jack Earley's concerns were more complex. In the first place, despite the fact that Betty couldn't, or wouldn't, cooperate with him in her own best interests, she was apparently too coherent, too angry, and too charming ever to be a candidate for the local asylum. "I've had people in to see her. And nobody will find her incompetent," he said prior to the first trial. Nor was he attempting any intensive therapy in jail. The last thing he wanted now, he admitted, was some therapist breaking down Betty's furious mental defenses before trial, "because then I might have a basket case on my hands, instead of a woman able to testify in her own behalf."

Earley was far more interested in Betty's physical appearance than in her psyche. He wanted to get her on a diet; he wanted the woman who would take the witness stand in her own behalf in the fall to look as close as possible to the striking, slender woman that she been when Dan Broderick walked out.

"I don't want the jury to look at her and think, 'What a fat pig, no wonder the guy left her,'" said Earley. "I want them instead to see a lovely, intelligent woman who is now in the process of healing after all the horrors Dan put her through. I want her to wear makeup, I want her to dress well, I want her to have her nails done ..."

And so it went. Betty Broderick, mad enough to kill, stood trial not once but twice as a competent, rational, sane adult, despite the fact that the common standard for sanity in this country is simple: Does the defendant know right from wrong? Ask Betty that question and, to this day, she will say the same thing: it wasn't wrong. "I had to do it! He was trying to kill me and my kids! I'm not the crazy one. Dan Broderick is. My mental health isn't at issue—his is!"

Despite the multitude of enduring questions that the Broderick case raised about sexual politics, circa 1990—and despite the fact that this was ultimately a drama decided by men—"The People of the State of California versus Elisabeth Anne Broderick" was always courtroom theater dominated by two strong women.

Over the next months, it was sometimes almost funny watching Jack Earley trying to cope with the prosecutor and his client, two emotionally charged women, each dealing with the matter of murder on trial for the first time, one swathed in quivering moral outrage, the other serene in moral rectitude—both chewing away at poor Earley, who could never really comprehend the blistering passions of either.

Betty plucked at Earley's sleeve constantly, alternately whispering, smiling, and pouting, passing him endless busy notes of reminder and advice, while Wells pointed her finger at him and glared. Earley blinked, he sighed, he shrugged, he tried to ignore it all—but, despite himself, he became the straight man in a miniseries, reflecting, day after day, the temperamental differences between men and women.

Nor did he get any help from Judge Whelan, sitting upon his bench with closed eyes, wearing a small smile of bemusement, saying so little that, some days, he was an almost invisible courtroom personality. Whenever Earley did flare—usually when he thought the judge had favored Wells in some ruling—Whelan's reply was always the same. "Knock it off, Mr. Earley," he would say, quietly, but with the firmness of a street fighter you didn't want to push too far. Wells would lift her chin in triumph, Earley would sag into his chair, blinking through his spectacles, whipped again—and, invariably, Betty would smile at him with the apologetic timidity of a woman who was so very sorry for whatever discomfort she had caused.

Completing the cast of leading characters who would coexist in Whelan's courtroom like some irascible little Addams family, were Marion L. Pasas and William L. Green, chief investigators for the opposing sides—and, as anyone closely observing a criminal trial soon learns, leading architects of the case itself. Courtroom attorneys, like TV anchormen, can be no better than the behind-the-scenes reporters who shape their stories for them; likewise, criminal investigators, the unsung heroes of every trial, can only pray for attorneys with enough courtroom flair to showcase their work in a winning way.

A San Diego native and onetime probation officer before she became a private investigator and jury consultant specializing in death penalty cases, Marion Pasas was hired by Jack Earley to canvas the city for witnesses who would remember Betty as the exemplary mother and wife she had once been and, hopefully, in the process, trash Dan and Linda Broderick for gradually destroying her.

She also served, once the trial began, as chief baby-sitter of Betty. Sitting daily between Earley and Betty, Pasas was responsible for preventing the defendant from distracting Earley while he argued for her freedom, as well as intimidating her into behaving properly before the jury—which is to say, like a remorseful woman on trial for murder, not a social hostess. An attractive, stylish woman with a striking mane of curly silver hair, forty-six when she joined the case, Marion Pasas does not fail at much, but she failed miserably in that small task. Finally, like Earley, she surrendered to the reality that Betty was unlike any client she had ever seen.

"Serial killers are easier to work with," she once remarked in exasperation, "because they know they're in deep trouble. They just do what you tell them. But Betty just never saw herself as a person on trial for murder, so she could never understand the importance of her demeanor. When somebody she knew walked into court, she just had to wave and smile. She thought it would have been rude otherwise."

Pasas's counterpart on the prosecution side, William Green, was a twenty-five-year veteran of the San Diego police department who had been working for twelve years as assistant chief of pretrial investigations for the district attorney's office. A mild-mannered, relaxed man also in his mid-forties, trim and balding, divorced and without children like Pasas, Green still sports the neatly clipped, de rigueur cop's moustache—and also the quietly cautious, confident manner of a professional skeptic.

Like Pasas, Green spent his summer canvassing the city—but in search of the exact opposite point of view: he wanted witnesses who would recall what a harridan Betty had been, how she had driven Dan Broderick away, then mercilessly abused not only him and Linda but, more importantly, her children, too, in the years before the homicides.

Green enjoyed the novelty of this new assignment. Unlike most cases he works, "It was a dream in the sense that people would return calls, they lived where they said they did, their phone numbers didn't turn out to be bogus."

But Green was under less pressure than Pasas to produce. Witnesses were never as critical to the prosecution, simply because Kerry Wells always had the added, invaluable assistance of Daniel T. Broderick III, whose meticulously collected evidence against his ex-wife from their four-year divorce war, including all her nasty phone messages and letters, would become central to the state's case.

"It's not fair," Jack Earley sometimes groaned. "Kerry doesn't have to do a thing to build her case—Dan's doing it for her, even from the grave."

"The sonofabitch! He still has his hand around my ankle from the grave. He'll never let me go," Betty agreed.

Marion Pasas was also in charge of the clothes detail. At least a month before the trial began, Betty began worrying about what she would wear. She eventually submitted to Marion a detailed list of twelve different outfits she wanted, complete with matching shoes and jewelry. She wanted "the white Adolpho with the matching white snakeskin pumps," and her "gold set." She wanted the blue Escada with the cowl neck, and the brown lizards." She wanted a beige cashmere St. John ensemble with silk leopard-print blouse. And she wanted three colorful Diane Fries print party dresses with matching Bruno Magli pumps in red, turquoise, and mauve.

"I can't believe this," muttered Pasas. "She is not wearing Diane Fries to court, period."

But Marion Pasas is a kindhearted woman, so she let Betty have most of what she wanted. "What the hell," she said, sighing. "It may be the last time she ever gets to wear these things." She went to Betty's storage garage to search for every single item Betty wanted, right down to the matching pumps. Betty's daughters and friends had already raided most of her prettiest clothes. But the shoes remained. Size elevens. At least fifty boxes, all neatly labeled by color and leather type. Betty definitely had a streak of Imelda Marcos in her when it came to shoes.

Rummaging through the crammed garage, Pasas also found Betty Broderick's wedding dress, packed in a cardboard box. The waistline looked about eighteen inches around. A lovely thing with a high neck, bordered in lace, with long sleeves. "Why," asked Pasas softly, holding the dress up, "do you suppose she kept this?"

The San Diego County Superior Courtroom where the Broderick trials occurred was one of the smallest in the building, with only thirty-six seats. It was ugly and oppressive, a windowless place lined with cheap wood paneling, tan tile floors, and furnished with brown chairs, all cast in gloomy fluorescent lighting. Behind the judge's bench on a shelf sat a scale of justice and a large hourglass that nobody ever turned over. The judge was flanked by the flags of California and the United States, with a dreary poster of George Washington off to one side.

For her first day in court, Betty wore a fitted royal blue two-piece suit and blouse by Louis Feraud. Her hair was a hard yellow in the artificial light, curled too tight on jailhouse rollers. She looked like a queen-sized Barbie doll in a bad wig. Her manner was that of a woman taking her seat at a charity luncheon. No shame, no timidity showed. She kept smiling at reporters, making little waves, rolling her eyes, mouthing hellos.

At last, the bailiffs opened the doors and the first of two panels of sixty jurors marched in.

They were not a visibly affluent group, these silent, somber people who came forth to do their civic duty on this warm autumn day. Many were elderly, the majority men. Most were dressed in cotton dresses and slacks, T-shirts and shorts. Only two were middle-aged, conspicuously well-groomed women; only a handful of the men wore ties. These were not people who spend $95 on chewy pralines at Neiman's when they felt depressed or stressed.

They stared at Betty, she stared at them. She smiled, timidly. A middle-aged woman in the front row, short and fat, wearing a magenta cotton housedress, her hair bleached a bad blond, smiled back, gently. Next to her sat an old man with white hair, whose eyes were cold with judgment. A teenager in shorts giggled nervously as she settled into her chair.

It was an awe-inspiring moment. Somewhere in this mixed crowd would be twelve good men and women to decide the rest of Betty Broderick's life.

Jury selection began on September 27, 1990, and lasted three weeks— half as long as the trial itself and, as Judge Whelan later remarked, more time than most criminal cases take in their entirety.

Jurors were first given lengthy questionnaires, compiled by Wells and Earley, probing their views on everything from divorce and abortion to the integrity of the legal system. One question Earley insisted on had to do with the attitudes of potential jurors toward women who use vulgar language.

"I'd like to start 'em out with three Hail Marys. 'And now repeat after me fifteen times—cunt-fuck-cunt-fuck,'" Earley later cracked dryly.

Earley's idea of the perfect juror, he joked, was "a Catholic wife and mother, married forty years, who doesn't believe in divorce, but who reads Lear's, belongs to NOW, and has a daughter married to an Irish American drunk." That, or a panel of divorcees whose husbands were behind in child support.

At the same time, the defense knew Kerry Wells would be looking for twelve conservative males, who thought of feminists as "libbers," had perhaps left a wife— but otherwise had never suffered so much as a traffic ticket due to their law-abiding ways. Either that, or women too young ever to have received a single bad blow in life from even a boyfriend. Alas for the defense, the deck was stacked heavily from the outset, by luck of the random jury pool draw, in Kerry Wells's favor. The majority of those in the pool were Republicans who read *Reader's Digest* regularly, went to church, and had great respect for American institutions. Most professed to have no attitudes on divorce, infidelity, abortion, or alcoholism.

If Earley wanted a little bitterness, a little anger in his people, Wells guarded against any hint of it. She was hunting for people who see no gray zones in life, only black and white.

In the end, only thirty-three people were automatically excused from the prospective panel of one hundred and twenty—sixteen for bias and nine for hardship. After that, serious jury selection began with voir dire (literally "true talk" in Latin), which is that phase of the process when attorneys question the potential jurors directly on their personal attitudes toward issues raised by the case. Each side was entitled to twenty "peremptories," or dismissals without explanation. It is similar to a poker game in that, once the peremptories are exhausted, the attorneys are stuck with whichever twelve jurors are left seated in the box.

Thus, there is no more critical phase in jury selection than voir dire. Both sides weigh every potential juror's words carefully and even watch their expressions with the vigilance of chicken hawks in a barnyard, searching for hints of hidden personality clues that may either sink or save the defendant.

In one of the silliest little ploys on the part of the prosecution, aimed strictly at making Wells look heroically lonesome in her uphill fight against crime, her jury consultant, an elderly, stern-faced man in gray, sat not at the table with her but in the audience instead, where he would signal his feelings about each juror, pro or con, by either tugging at his ear or rubbing his nose. It was so transparent that, in time, even prospective jurors would glance at him to see if they had been nixed or not.

If Kerry Wells wanted no feminists on the jury, neither did she want any male chauvinists who saw women as wilting lilies to be protected. She wanted people who believed that women can be as cold and ruthless as any man.

"Do you think a woman is capable of committing a crime of violence for jealousy or revenge?" she asked each. "Did it necessarily have to be an emotional act? Can you convict, even though you might not like the victim?

"Do you think there are any differences between men and women?" Wells asked a pretty social worker of around forty. "Of course," said the woman, looking almost insulted at the question. Dismissed by Wells.

"How would you describe yourself?" Wells asked a tired-looking, gentle-mannered woman in her thirties.

"Understanding, I guess ..." said the woman thoughtfully. Gone.

Earley, meantime, basically laid out his entire case by asking potential jurors about certain homilies, platitudes, and clichés. Among his favorites, he asked repeatedly if they had heard of the following expressions:

"Good ole boy network." Did they know what that is?

"Hell hath no fury like a woman scorned." Did they believe that?

"Don't speak ill of the dead"?

"Straw that broke the camel's back"?

"Who you know is more important than what you know"?

On the first day of jury selection, Betty apparently toyed briefly with the idea of a plea bargain. "What's the best offer Kerry will make?" said one of the dozens of notes she slipped to Pasas. Others were less substantive. "My mother gave me a sweet sixteen party. No boys allowed!" she wrote in one, apropos of nothing.

But, throughout the process, Betty rarely volunteered an opinion on her potential jurors, Pasas said. She also spent time reading William Styron's book 'Memoirs in Madness'. She underlined nearly the whole thing.

By the end of jury selection, Pasas had become increasingly concerned that Betty was "losing it," that she might in fact be legally incompetent to proceed (or ICP) in her own defense. During the interrogation of a prospective juror, a pathologist, for example, Betty kept writing "Empty Caskets" on a notepad, then showing it to Pasas. She did this several times. "I don't know what she was talking about," said Pasas. Later, Betty explained that neither Dan nor Linda had actually been buried. "They were cremated ... Their bodies weren't even in those expensive caskets. It was all for show. Dan Broderick would've approved."

Then, abruptly, it was over. The Betty Broderick jury was sworn in. She smiled sweetly at them.

Those who survived to judge were six women and six men, ranging in age from nineteen to sixty-two. Four were Catholics; only two listed any college. The majority were homeowners; all were white except one Hispanic man. They were a calm, pleasant, serious-faced group of people, mostly of the sort you might find at the church pie sale on Sunday or playing checkers in the park.

The youngest, Nicole Prentice, worked in a suntan parlor. The defense worried that she might relate to Kim or even Linda, but figured she was too young to influence anybody else. The two oldest jurors, at sixty-two, were David Southwick, a handsome, craggy-faced highway worker, married forty years, and Eloise Duffield, a sweet-faced, silvery-haired grandmother and retired preschool teacher who spent most of the trial looking shocked at all she heard. The defense counted on her to despise Dan's treatment of a once wonderful mother like Betty.

Other jurors were mostly so mild in personality that neither side knew how to peg them. One was a sixty-one-year-old mother of eight, employed by Pacific Bell. Another was an auto shop teacher, fifty-seven, once-divorced. Another was a thirty-nine-year-old construction worker, married to a legal secretary; he said he didn't like attorneys, which pleased the defense. On the other hand, he had been involved in a bitter custody dispute, which pleased the prosecution.

The panel also included an American Airlines flight attendant, forty-five, married with two children. The prosecution liked her because she was an airline attendant, as Linda had been. The defense liked her because she had once been spirited enough to force the airline to reinstate her after being dismissed for pregnancy. One of the two jurors with some college was a bearded building contractor, thirty-six, married without children, who remarked in voir dire that murder stories bored him.

Another, Terilyn Berg, forty-four, married and mother of three, managed a naval base cafe. In her most memorable remark of voir dire, she said she had never even heard of the Broderick case because "when you're busy feeding hungry kids, you don't pay attention."

Roque Jesse Barros, Jr., thirty-one, was a social worker who dealt mostly with abused children. The defense worried that he might see Betty as a child abuser. He wouldn't even have been seated, except Earley mistakenly gambled that Wells wouldn't accept the jury panel as soon as she did.

Lucinda Swann, twenty-six, married but without children, employed by the San Diego Air Pollution Control District, was so shy in voir dire that her subsequent choice as jury foreman startled both sides.

But in the end only one juror would really matter: Walter Polk, fifty-nine, a naval aviation repairman, married for forty-three years with six children. Balding and bespectacled, Polk was the only juror to wear a suit and tie to court every day. Pasas was drawn to Polk from the outset, partly because he cynically remarked during voir dire that he thought the news media, starting with Dan Rather, often "made news" instead of reporting it. Unlike other prospective jurors, Polk also freely admitted that he had discussed the Broderick case at work and with his wife and found it fascinating. Polk was also an ardent gun-control opponent and member of the National Rifle Association, which Pasas also liked. "Strong foreman potential," she wrote at the bottom of his questionnaire. Ironically, Bill Green later said that Polk had also been a heavy favorite with the prosecution, partly because he seemed too circumspect a citizen to sympathize with a killer like Betty.

The tedium was over. On Monday, the Betty Broderick trial would finally begin. Apparently Betty's celebrity affected even Judge Whelan. After court that day, he told *Union* reporter John Gaines that he heard Meryl Streep had been out to Colinas to see Betty.

It was, of course, not true. But the remark went a long way toward establishing what the tone of this trial would be, even from the bench. The judge himself was seemingly star-struck.

By now, the defense camp was obsessed with worry over Betty's ability to testify in her own behalf. Some witnesses for the prosecution, like Gail Forbes, were making bets that Earley would never dare to put Betty on the stand. That was, of course, a ridiculous bet—Jack Earley couldn't have silenced Betty in court even if he had tried. She would have fired him, rather than be denied the opportunity to at last tell the world her story. Earley knew that.

If only he could get her to cooperate, to at least say she was sorry, he moaned with mounting frustration and anxiety. "I need her to grovel!" But he knew she never would. It was catch-22: he was asking Betty to renege on the very emotions that made her kill in the first place. It was contrary to her own argument of self-defense.

"Oh well," said Earley after one especially futile jail visit, shrugging. "I finally just told her, 'Betty, do what you want—but the captain doesn't go down with this ship.' She just laughed."

* * *

It was Saturday, October 20, the weekend before trial, and the Las Colinas visiting room was, as usual, crowded, mostly with young men in jeans carrying small babies, and mothers. Nearly everyone was either Hispanic or black. Babies cried, mothers wept and wailed, sometimes one of the husbands screamed an obscenity into the two-way phone, divided by thick Plexiglas.

Betty bounced up to a chair behind the glass wall in her gray prison sweats, threw a friendly grin at another inmate, and began chattering away into her receiver. She had not lost much weight, as Early had hoped, and, contrary to Marion Pasas's firm instructions, she had had her bouncy Shirley Temple curls cropped short by Danielle of La Jolla the weekend before. But she still looked good, compared to the putty-faced, obese woman with three chins and ragged pony tail who had been jailed for murder nearly a year before. Her skin was pink, her blue eyes were clear, she was wearing careful makeup, and no roots showed.

But nothing about her suggested a woman even remotely in contact with reality, with the fact that, come Monday morning, she would begin an ordeal that might end in a life sentence. She was instead zanier, funnier, and more defiant than ever, but with a strange new overlay of cunning about her. In one minute, she would say something clever, making her visitor laugh out loud; in the next she was literally winking as she confided, "I can play to Eloise Duffield [the elderly juror] ... I was humble for sixteen years! That's how I got in here! I can do that bit!"

Then, like a scattergun aimed into thin air, her mind turned to her wardrobe. She had settled on her brown St. Johns cashmere for opening day at trial, she said. "I'm a little fat for it—but it'll be great on TV ..." She had decided against her blue Louis Feraud suit, she said, "because it's so matronly."

Then she was insisting again that she had done her children a favor by killing their father. "I feel like I'm a hero to my kids ... They may not think that right now ... but they'll eventually understand, even if it takes them a few years."

If she was afraid, it didn't show. Instead, she only seemed high as a kite—wired, excited—anticipating her day in court. She was plotting her performance like an actress, bent on playing the wrong part, perhaps, but an actress still, rehearsing old lines in her mind. It didn't take a trained psychiatrist to see that Betty Broderick was gone, lost to the real world. More than ever, it was impossible to have a conversation with her. She was unable to listen to even the most trivial remark. Instead, she interrupted, rushing on with the monologue in her head. Like a stuck record needle, her mind was relaying the same, tired snatches of her story, just as it had done for months—but tonight it was worse; she had regressed even further, to the most basic elements of her original story, and, unlike times past, she could not be quieted, drawn back into the present even temporarily.

She expected that Wells would try to make her look at the death scene pictures, she said. She was bracing for that, it bothered her. "Oh, nooooo, no, thank you," she said, shaking her head like a prim, proper lady who had just been invited to peep into a skin flick parlor. "Why should I look at them? I don't have any mental picture of [it], I don't remember it, why should I start having nightmares now, a year later?" Besides, Brad had told her the scene "wasn't that bad, not that much blood." But, even so, she promised smugly, "If Kerry Wells makes me look at them, it's going to backfire on her, because I may throw up on her. Unless," she added, "I laugh."

And why would she laugh? "Because," she explained, gone to lunatic euphoria, "it's all over! Whatever happens, it's over. I don't have to worry about anything anymore!"

And so on. There was nothing to do but listen. "I think I have a great case, if Jack would get his ass in gear! I think we can win," she said merrily.

Walking out into the balmy Santee desert air was like escaping a pressure chamber. It's not easy to describe thirty minutes sitting eighteen inches from Betty Broderick's face, looking through the Plexiglas into her eyes. It would be different if they were small, evasive eyes full of stupidity. But these were beautiful blue eyes, filled with direct, alert intelligence. They shone with anger, they went frigid with hate, they bubbled with humor. All they lacked was that occasional sideways evasiveness that comes with guilt.

You cannot stare Betty Broderick down for shooting two people to death.

Chapter 33

Trial Time

It was chaos in the corridor outside Department 27 on the Monday morning of October 22, 1990, when the matter of *The People of the State of California versus Elisabeth Anne Broderick* went to trial.

Reporters and television crews clotted the hallway. Every major media outlet in San Diego County was there. Besides the media, some two hundred members of the public were queued up along the wall, hoping to gain one of the few remaining seats in the tiny courtroom. Most were women.

The Broderick and Bisceglia siblings flew in from all over the country, in rotating shifts, to attend nearly every session of the trial. It was one of the most twisted, sorry spectacles of the whole drama, watching these two groups of successful, educated people setting up their separate camps in the courthouse corridors daily, avoiding each other like strangers in an elevator—one family motivated by grim, tight-lipped anger and pain, the other lost in an agony of confusion and guilt. In years past, these two clans had behaved according to the norms of most contemporary extended families. Now, that fragile structure had collapsed into bitter dust. Seldom has a crime better demonstrated just how shallow, how transitory, latter 20th century middle-class American family relationships can really be.

Only rarely, in the three weeks of the trial, did one of the Brodericks make the twenty-yard walk across the invisible line to display a trace of compassion for the hapless family of the woman who had killed their loved one—but when it happened, everyone in the corridor crowd noticed.

"Hi, Frank," said Terry Broderick one morning, bashfully. One of Dan's younger brothers, now in his thirties and a stockbroker in San Diego, Terry was suddenly across enemy lines, standing in front of Betty's brother Frank, a big, friendly, shy Nashville businessman, who was sitting, sad-faced, with his wife, Maggie, one of Betty's college classmates. "I'm Terry," reminded young Broderick, holding out his hand. Frank Bisceglia looked at first stunned, then touched to the point of tears, then awkwardly embarrassed. So was Terry. The two men shook hands, muttered a few inanities about the weather and San Diego. They had nothing to discuss, the chat was only seconds long, but the handshake was worth a million words.

In court, the two families sat on opposite sides of the aisle. At recesses, the Broderick siblings were constantly surrounded by a pin-striped gaggle of Dan's attorney friends. Adding to the crowd were three of Betty's former, closest La Jolla lady friends—Gail Forbes, Helen Pickard, and Patti Monahan—all now prosecution witnesses. They showed up regularly, ostensibly to comfort Kim, who was usually weeping by recess. During court sessions, they sometimes hung around the halls, schmoozing with TV technicians and shooting the breeze with whoever else from the Broderick camp happened along. At lunch, everyone would go off together. An unseemly air of thrill overhung it all.

Brad Wright, Dian Black, and Ronnie Brown, who came to court nearly every day, sat with the Bisceglia family. Lee attended only sporadically, but also sat with her mother's family. So sharply divided were the camps that the two sisters only rarely defied the pressures, even to go off for lunch together alone.

"Good morning, ladies and gentlemen," said Kerry Wells to the jury. "This case, to put it in the simplest possible terms, is about hate, revenge, and murder. It is about a woman who had so many things going for her that she could have done so much with, like a million-dollar home in La Jolla, like a $16,000-a-month income, like intelligence and education, friends, four beautiful children. But none of it was enough because she was so consumed by hate."

Wells delivered her opening arguments from a podium, with a loose-leaf binder containing her entire speech before her. Her voice trembled at the start. She wore a severe gray suit. Her only concession to feminine decoration was a tiny coral rosette hanging on a thin chain just below her collar. If she had any makeup on, even lipstick, it didn't show. She looked pretty. Most of all, she looked innocent, earnest, and outgunned sitting all alone at her table, while Jack Earley, Marion Pasas, and Betty Broderick sat at the defense table. It was a strategic decision of the most calculating sort, of course. As in jury selection, Wells's aides were simply sitting in the audience.

Her opening was brief—maybe thirty minutes—matter-of-fact, and untheatrical. She began with a tight focus.

"This case is not only about murder—it is about premeditated murder," she told the jury. This case was about evil—not male-female domestic relationships, not about divorce. Betty Broderick had killed out of lowest, meanest jealous rage and had wantonly hurt her children in order to feed her own selfish needs. Period.

Betty Broderick had driven across town to Dan and Linda's house, said Wells, and she had taken a gun, loaded with hollow-point bullets, which "are designed to kill." She had used stolen keys to let herself in a back door. She had crept up the stairs to their bedroom. She had not even walked directly into the bedroom through the main door, but instead crept around through a back entry, "where she would be the least likely to be seen by anyone sleeping in the room."

During all this time, Wells pointed out, "she clearly had the opportunity to think about what she was doing, stop, to turn back—but she didn't."

She recounted how Betty had repeatedly threatened to kill them: "Killing Dan and Linda Broderick was something she had thought about a long, long time," she told the jury.

And so, "She snuck into Dan and Linda's home in Hillcrest in the early morning hours while they lay there sound asleep, at their most vulnerable. She shot them dead." If this wasn't a case of first-degree murder, Wells said, she didn't know what was.

But that wasn't the end of Wells's argument. She then stepped beyond her first-degree murder scenario and into the swamps of divorce court. She spent the next half of her opening statement heaping blame on Betty for the failure of the marriage

355

itself.

"... It wasn't the loss of love or the emotional loss that made her so mad," Wells asserted. "The defendant has said that she was never in love with Dan Broderick, that she married him because she knew he was going to be a money-maker ..."

Therefore, in Wells's scenario, when Dan finally left, Betty was consumed with hatred simply because "she felt she was being gypped out of her investment in him as a money-maker and the prestige of being Mrs. Daniel T. Broderick ..." To Kerry Wells, it was that simple: Betty Broderick was determined "to make him pay for being the one that left, and she didn't care who she destroyed in the process."

She then focused on the "intentionally destructive" nature of Betty's actions over the years—everything from the vandalisms (car through the door, Boston cream pie, etc.) to the "obscene, vulgar, and ugly" phone messages.

Especially the latter. Betty's messages would turn out to be Wells's favorite and perhaps most lethal weapon in trial. In pretrial hearings, Earley had argued heatedly that they should be inadmissible since they were taken out of context; they were but a handful of rash remarks made over a period of years in the course of literally thousands of messages, he protested. Wells insisted that the messages instead showed premeditation. Earley had also argued that Betty's thirty-minute 1987 conversation with Danny should not be allowed in court since the recording was made without her knowledge—illegal in California. Wells countered that Betty clearly knew someone was listening in. Earley further argued that if the selected tapes Dan had edited out of hundreds of Betty's phone messages from 1986 to 1989 were relevant, then Betty's own diaries from those several years should be equally admissible in their entirety, as rebuttal. Why was it fair to play dozens of Dan's hand-picked tapes to the jury as evidence of Betty's state of mind during those years, asked Earley, without giving her own personal writings over three years equal weight in establishing her deteriorating state of mind?

He lost. Whelan ruled for Wells on both counts. The tapes were legitimate evidence, but the diaries were irrelevant. The latter could be quoted selectively by expert witnesses, but would not be admissible in their entirety.

In a pattern she would maintain throughout the trial, Wells then played a few of Betty's messages, standing by with arms crossed, lips pursed in distaste. Before the trial was over, she played so many of the tapes that reporters and even a few jurors began to listen with expressions of boredom.

But the first time around, they carried plenty of shock value, mainly because of the deliberate, purring nonchalance in Betty's voice. As her words filled the courtroom, Betty busied herself writing on her legal pad, her expression as intent and unperturbed as that of a woman writing thank-you notes.

Wells wound up quickly. Puckered as a woman spitting out a mouthful of castor oil, she told jurors how vile Betty had been in her language to Dr. Ruth Roth: "The little fucker was mine and he'll stay mine." Wells talked about how Betty had "dumped her children" on Dan's doorstep. She skimmed over the years of litigation, the contempts, the jailings, and the divorce trial. Instead she merely reminded the jury that Betty Broderick had walked off with $16,000 a month—"that's $192,000 a year!" She also credited Dan Broderick for his own success. He was a "unique" person who had worked hard for his wealth. Before she was done, Wells even brought up Dan's drinking habits, defending them as purely social.

Jack Earley couldn't believe his good luck. Just as he had hoped, Kerry Wells was going to "get down into the mud" with him. He fairly skipped to the lectern, with visions of miscarriages, drunk driving arrests, unheated Boston basement apartments, Avon products, and red Corvettes dancing in his head. Gone was the worried Jack Earley of only twenty-four hours before. Now he was a man possessed of pain and indignation at all men who treat their wives the way Dan Broderick had treated his.

His opening argument lasted nearly three hours.

Unlike Wells, Earley used no notes to guide him. Instead, he shambled over to the jury and, peering at them solemnly, his tone flat, began his story.

No two attorneys were ever more different in style. As Earley shuffles around the courtroom, ruminating, searching his mind for his next thought, peeping through his glasses and sometimes looking a little like a bewildered, myopic Mr. McGoo crossed with Lieutenant Columbo, he is ingratiating in the extreme. But his extemporaneous approach takes its toll on syntax, which he sometimes murders.

Here, for example, are the first few paragraphs of his opening:

"Good morning, ladies and gentlemen. I'm going to start by an apology on something that you will probably see, that the evidence will show through the trial, that is at least a problem with time," he began. "There is a lot of details in this case, there is a lot of evidence for you to have, and so to be able to put it in context and put it in order, there is going to be some time that is taken, some meticulous time. There may be times where it is frustrating, or frustrating for you, as the evidence is trying to be presented in logical order so that you can have it at the end.

"One of the things that maybe we're not used to here in California, and the evidence is going to show, that what Elisabeth Broderick started to deal with in this case was a snowstorm. You are going to see a snowstorm of paper, a litigious assault that started sometime in 1985. You're going to see that there was a person who, while raised in the East Coast and knowing how to deal with snowstorms, had no training, no background, with the snowstorm of white paper that you will see, which takes eight volumes for the court to hold, not counting her paperwork or the paperwork that she was given. You will hear about Daniel Broderick, who was a very prominent, very well-known lawyer. He was very liked by the legal community; he fit in, and he had what people said was meticulous—somebody that you didn't want to be his opponent, because he negotiated sitting on your chest, someone whose reputation as a lawyer was the most important thing to him, more important than his family, more important than his children, more important than anything. He would do anything to protect it."

With Jack Earley it is better to paraphrase. To his credit, he sounds a lot better in person than on paper. Jurors later said that they understood what he was driving at, even when he digressed into East Coast snowstorms. He also has an astonishing memory for detail, and he is a very good storyteller, thanks mainly to his intensity. "This guy grows on you, doesn't he?" remarked *Union* reporter John Gaines about two hours into Earley's presentation.

Slowly, ploddingly, Earley marched jurors through the entire history of the Broderick marriage, from start to finish, from young students in love, to immense wealth in La Jolla, to Dan's decision to leave Betty for the younger, lovelier Linda. He left out virtually no detail of Betty's story.

He never once mentioned the phrase 'battered woman's syndrome.' But he strongly implied that this was a tale of psychological battery that so eroded Betty that she finally snapped. She had been undermined on a daily basis, by both Dan and the legal system, until, finally, "she found herself in a pit with no handles." At one point, he even compared her to Martha Mitchell, late wife of former Nixon Administration Attorney General John Mitchell, of Watergate fame. "They said Martha was crazy, too," he told the jury—until history proved otherwise.

Then, operating on his theory that "juries like a little showmanship," Earley unveiled a big photo display of Betty, Dan, and their children in happier days. As he continued speaking, he tore away picture after picture, with theatrical flourish, demonstrating all that Dan had robbed her of.

"You have to understand her life," he told them. He worked his way up to the time when Dan met Linda, lied about it, then finally left Betty in a rental house.

Rip. Gone was a photograph of Betty in her home.

Earley then explained that she had never given her children away but only taken them to stay temporarily with their father, due to rats, her New York trip, etc.. But, rather than settle with her, Dan had simply used them as a weapon against her.

Rip. He tore away a picture of Betty with her children.

Then Dan filed for divorce and, Earley said, even attempted to serve her with divorce papers at a Bishops fashion lunch—at the same time he was telling everyone she was crazy.

Earley ripped away a photo of Betty at a social function, surrounded by pretty, well-groomed women.

Finally, by 1989, said Earley, she was completely defeated, humiliated at being fined, jailed, denied even visitation with her children and rendered financially subservient. Meantime, she had grown fat and unattractive. She was a wasted woman, stripped of all anchors in her life.

Rip. Gone a final picture of beautiful, slender Betty in tight jeans in 1986. In its place, cleverly concealed until now, was the worst photo of Betty that Jack Earley could find—the obese woman with vacant eyes and triple chins, who had been booked at Colinas for murder only three years later.

"She was someone who was left without family, children, home, who she was, where she was going," said Earley, gazing dolefully at the single ugly photograph left on his flannel-board display.

So she went to Dan's house on the morning of November 5, 1989, he said, "thinking of all the things that are bothering her," just wanting to talk to him. She took the gun with her, explained Earley, only as a way of forcing him to talk to her. It was just a grandstanding stunt.

But then, Earley said—suddenly mumbling so that reporters had to strain to hear, and even then nobody got it clearly—"It was said, 'Call the police!'"

So she panicked and fired.

She shot, in "a heightened state," Earley continued blandly. But she had no memory of it at all; instead, she had intended only to kill herself if Dan wouldn't talk to her. And she had snatched the phone out of the wall, he said, only in a reflexive action, developed through years of fear, "so that he couldn't call the police because she had violated the restraining order."

Earley never did explain his murky remark about someone in the bedroom saying "Call the police." Which would later prove to be a stroke of genius on his part.

In conclusion, he begged the jury to look not at the mere facts of the killings but also at Betty's mental state. "What was she dealing with, what made her do this? If she is guilty of a crime, what crime is she guilty of?" He then shuffled back to his chair and sat down—without saying what he himself thought the answer to that question should be.

The jurors stared, confused. Reporters looked at each other to see if they'd missed something. For the first time all day, even Betty Broderick lost her steady expression of polite, sweet attentiveness and stared at Earley in bewilderment.

Chapter 34

The Prosecution

And now, after all the months of talk, it was time to see exactly what Betty Broderick had done. On the second day of the prosecution case, Wells introduced the deceased to the jury.

She marched into court with large color photographs of the death scene and arranged them on an easel three feet from the jury box: Dan was lying face down on the floor, half hidden by the bedcovers; Linda was sprawled face down across the bed, blood streaking her long hair. It is always startling, how fragile all living creatures seem in death. Brian Forbes was right—they did have a greenish hue. The pictures also clearly showed that, in order to reach the phone cord, Betty practically had to step on Dan.

In the back row of the courtroom, the Broderick family cried. Kim was the first to leave. Lee, across the aisle, followed minutes later. So did Betty's sister Clare. But Dan Broderick's brothers and sisters, a tough lot, stayed, with tears running down their faces.

In the days to come, Wells would haul her grim pictures around the courtroom, shuffling through them like a deck of cards, displaying first one, then another, depending on the witness on the stand. When not using them, she stacked them with deliberate carelessness along the tables and walls—virtually shoving them under Betty's nose. But Betty showed no reaction at all.

Earley maintained a steadily grim expression until he got back to his office that night. Then, in an irreverent, cackling explosion of tension: "Looks to me like it was every man for himself up there that night. Obviously, Dan wasn't trying to shelter his new bride. He was trying to dive under the bed to save himself."

Among Wells's first witnesses was a ballistics expert who explained why Betty's hollow-point bullets hadn't done more damage to Dan and Linda. Betty had, in a word, been cheated by the gun salesman—hollow points are effective only in guns with a longer barrel than a .38. Betty's teeny-weeny ladies' gun was never designed for such deadly ammunition. Betty listened, frowning.

Wells also called a police consultant to say that, so far as he could tell, these were not panic shootings. "It looks to me like fairly well directed shots, given the accuracy," he said. In fact, he added dryly, causing jurors to smile, most police officers shooting in a panic are notoriously inept. "Cars get shot, trash cans, buildings ... to be frank, about the only thing that usually doesn't get shot is the suspect."

But Wells had barely gotten her case under way before she was undermined by one of her own witnesses, a homicide detective who testified that he had found the telephone Betty ripped out of the wall lying in the hallway that morning, with its cord neatly wrapped around. But police photographs on display directly in front of him proved otherwise: the phone had been thrown wildly into a corner, its wires in a tangle. It was the closest the Broderick trial ever got to an "Aha! Gotcha!" When Earley triumphantly thrust the evidence photos in front of the officer's reddening face, he could only stammer that he had obviously been mistaken.

Wells rebounded quickly, as she would do throughout this trial whenever she was in a pinch, by marching to the tape recorder and stabbing the button with a vengeance. For the next fifteen minutes, effectively erasing all memory of the overeager cop, jurors listened to a dozen or so of Betty's foulest phone messages. Snatches included:

"I want to get rid of the kids ... stop screwing the cunt ... drunken, selfish, cruel-hearted ... you're gonna be sooooo sorry. Fucking the secretary. Fuckhead ... cunt ... Cuntsucking asshole! What am I supposed to do now? I just want what's mine ... I'll kill you."

Wells then brought out her star witness—Kimberly Curtin Broderick, first child of Dan and Betty Broderick. She was then twenty.

No prosecutor could have asked for a more credible weapon. The pretty, wholesome-faced young woman with the dark eyes and long, glossy brown hair pulled back in barrettes who took the stand on this autumn day of 1990, wearing a demure black dress with gathered skirt and schoolgirl flats, was the fulsome, all-American girl, likable on sight. When she cried, half the jurors looked as if they wanted to cry with her. And she cried often.

The crucifixion of mother by daughter lasted for the better part of two days. It wasn't so much what Kim said about Betty—it was the fact that she went the extra mile, reaching for details to damn her mother, without applying the same scrutiny to her father. Dan was dead, and Kim wanted Betty to pay.

Wells began her questioning with the morning of the killings, when Betty had called Kim at school.

"You know I had to do it," Betty had said, Kim testified. "I had no other choice. One of us had to die ... it was either him or me ... I couldn't let him win."

During a hearing months earlier, Kim had said that when Betty called, her voice had been "shaking, she was scared." Now, Kim described her mother differently. "She was calm, she told me to calm down, to get a plane home."

For the rest of the day, Wells walked Kim through the most trivial details of her life with Mom and Dad, both before and after their separation. Wells's goal was to depict Betty Broderick as the most selfish, temperamental mother, unloving wife, and wanton spender any jury had ever seen. She wanted Kim to testify about everything from an incident when she was maybe seven years old, when Betty had once thrown a ketchup bottle at Dan, to Betty's anger at Dan's $150 limit on Kim's junior prom dress.

And Kim followed Wells's lead with chilling docility. She became, on the witness stand, a teenager who had never seriously griped to her mother about Dan, Linda, or virtually anything else. She had not inflamed her mother with her complaints. None of the issues raised by Betty—from Kim's college budget to her treatment at the last Notre Dame weekend—had been any "big deal," Kim said. Her mother had

361

exaggerated everything.

Wells moved on to the crime, drawing the daughter ever closer to pulling the noose. Her initial nervousness gone, Kim went forward with increasing willingness.

Yes, she testified, her mother had threatened to kill Dan and Linda "a lot of times." In fact, a month before Dan and Linda's wedding, Kim said, Betty told her she was going to put three or four bullets in their heads. Not until Jack Earley's cross-examination did Kim qualify this by admitting that her mother frequently said she was going to "kill" Kim, her sister, her brothers, and just about anybody else who aggravated her on any given occasion, including the dogs.

But, she insisted to Earley, her father had taken Betty's threats seriously. In hindsight, Kim also thought Betty had deliberately stolen her keys to Dan's house.

At Wells's prompting, Betty Broderick's oldest child even provided the jury with an additional motive for her mother's crimes: Two months before Dan had died, Kim testified, the court-ordered insurance policy of $1 million for the children had gone into effect, and Betty had told her, she said, " 'If I kill him, we'll all be rich.' She said that a lot," Kim added.

According to Kim, Dan was never the mean, controlling, drunken, insensitive man that her mother described. To the contrary, it was Betty, as Kim remembered it, who had always been the temperamental, violent one. "I saw scratches on his back. She made moon marks on him. She'd stick her nails into your arms—all of us."

Concerning Dan's drinking, Kim remembered that when the children were little, "Dad drank six-packs." Later on, it was occasional wine with dinner. But, after the divorce, she said—in direct contrast to what her sister Lee would later say—he was a near teetotaler. Except for St. Patrick's Day, she added with a wiltingly gentle smile. Then he would "get high." But, even when he did drink, "He was really funny and nice ... Dad wasn't good with emotions at all. He had a hard time saying 'I love you' and hugging you. But when he was drunk, he had no trouble at all. He was really loving and affectionate."

The jury watched with faces of purest compassion. They were suffering along with this demure, wounded young victim of such adult folly. It was tangible. Wells, sensing it, forged on with growing tenderness. Jack Earley began angrily objecting to every other question. Sidebar conferences were called increasingly. But it was a losing game for Earley, because, each time court was stalled for a conference, there sat Kim, biting her necklace, looking at her hands, and more often than not, crying softly to herself as she tried to avoid eye contact with everyone—except her mother. Amazingly, sometimes she would cast a furtive glance at Betty and smile like a little child lost, and Betty Broderick always would smile back, and nod, with sympathy.

Wells returned to Betty's ugly phone messages, her purpose now being to lay the legal groundwork necessary to get Betty's 1987 conversation with Danny admitted into court. Kim was ready with all the right answers.

Her mother's language had always upset the boys, she said—but she recalled vividly the night of Betty's conversation with Danny, because Danny never got that upset. It lingered in her mind.

And so the tape played, all thirty awful minutes of it. It no longer mattered that Dan

362

had deliberately taped it, that he was just as guilty as his wife for the pain being inflicted on his son. Dan was dead; Betty was on trial for murdering him. All that mattered now were the two voices filling the hushed courtroom: the young, heartbroken son, screaming and sobbing in frustration; and his coy, teasing, taunting mother, refusing to behave like a grown-up—to leave little Danny Broderick alone on a balmy California evening to go out and play, the way children are supposed to do.

Danny: "... Don't you think being mad for two years is enough, Mom?"

Betty: "No, it took me twenty years of goodness to get mad ... He's scum, Danny. Absolute scum. He's cheated and lied and fucked around ... that money is mine. I earned it for twenty years of hard work and total shit from that asshole ..."

Danny: "... What else do you care about besides your money and your share of things to own? ... Stop saying bad words! ..."

Betty: "For two years while I was married to him, I put up with shit in my face and you kids never even knew it. You never knew he was fucking Linda while he was married to me, did you?"

Danny: "No." [crying]

Betty: "No, and I put up with shit for two years hoping he'd get over this, and he'd grow up, and he is obviously too weak a little faggot ..."

Danny: "But now, you know, if you care about your family, you would stop saying bad words."

Betty: "... I'd rather be a lady and wonderful person and call a cunt a cunt. ... I wish he'd just die. I wish he would get drunk and drive his fucking car ... then he'll be gone off the earth."

And so on. Several jurors visibly flinched, listening to an adult abusing a boy so badly in her efforts to force the child to take her side. Betty scribbled in her pad, ignoring it all.

With that, Kerry Wells wrapped up her day. If there had been any lingering doubts about Wells's willingness to use the Broderick children to win a conviction, it was gone. The only remaining mystery was whether she would also call Betty's two young sons into court to testify against their mother.

For the defense, it was one of the worst days of the entire trial. Walking into the mob of reporters waiting in the corridor, Earley offered one of his best blank faces and remarked, dryly, "I'm extremely pleased with the way things are going. I think we've got them on the run."

Dian Black, meantime, looked ashen as she left the courtroom. The Danny tape had stunned her. "I can't believe what I heard," she said weakly. "That was just so— sick! I had no idea she was capable of doing stuff like that to her kids." Then, bewildered: "Why is this trial even happening? If that tape doesn't prove she went nuts, what does? She needs help!"

On the phone that night, Betty sounded perky as ever. "Well, I didn't think it [the tape] was that bad," she said, impervious to either shame or reason. She was more

363

interested in the prim, schoolgirl outfit Kim had worn to court that day. "She never dresses that way," said Betty, laughing. What's more, half the clothes Kim was wearing to court every day were her dresses. "I think I'll ask Jack to introduce a motion that Kim can't testify against me wearing my clothes." It was still all theater to her, nothing more.

Kim arrived in court the next day, demure in a lace collar, less nervous, more aggressive than the day before. At times, throughout the day, she volunteered condemning details without even being asked.

Wells knew she was at risk of alienating the jury if she spent much more time encouraging the daughter to condemn the mother. But she couldn't resist. Throughout the trial, Kerry Wells never knew when to quit overworking a good thing.

She next got Kim to say that Linda's refusal to return the wedding china was no big deal. "Mom didn't like it, she bought new china." Wells even asked Kim why Betty had married Dan. Because, Kim promptly replied with authority, her mother said she felt sorry for Dan, and "he had asked her so many times, she finally gave in."

And their fights? "She was always mad at him!" Kim replied.

And why wouldn't Dan talk to Betty after the divorce? Because, whenever he would get on the phone with her, Kim said, "she'd scream and yell and cuss, so he'd hang up and say forget it."

And so it went.

Wells took Kim through the entire family history since the separation. Kim cried about the night Betty took her to Coral Reef. She recalled all the subsequent vandalisms, and even volunteered a few new ones: once, for example, she told the jury that Betty had written 'Fuck You' in lipstick on a mirror. And after the divorce, she said, Dan had been a wonderful father. But Betty always undermined him with the boys. For instance, she said Betty had once made Rhett cry by calling him "a spineless wimp" when he was afraid to run away from home. As for her own quarrels with Dan, she shrugged them off.

Wells then invited Kim to embarrass her sister. What about Dan's conflict with Lee, leading him to write her out of his will?

With a shy smile at her sister, sitting in the front row, Kim obliged.

Well, she said, Dad hadn't meant to be mean to Lee. He was "just upset ... Lee got caught doing drugs at school ... and she stole things." So Dad was only trying to shape her up—through her purse.

Jack Earley's burden, in his cross-examination of Betty Broderick's daughter, was to somehow discredit her, embarrass her, reveal her distortions—but with gentleness in the extreme. Eloise Duffield, he knew, would not like him a bit if he was too mean, too sarcastic toward this young victim of such a terrible family tragedy. Of all the jurors, Eloise Duffield, the sixty-two-year-old mother of four who sat in the back row of the jury box generally observing all she saw with tight-lipped disapproval, had become Earley's daily weathervane. The smaller her mouth grew, the more he worried. "I just can't tell if it's me she hates more, or Kerry," he brooded.

His tone was pleasantly bland, as he addressed Kim. He looked like a kindly schoolteacher, correcting a messy history paper. For the next couple of hours, Earley tried to make Kim admit that she had helped inflame her mother's ragged emotions throughout the divorce with her complaints about Dan's treatment of her and Linda's meddling. Hadn't she often called Betty from college, crying about how Dan was cheapskating on her budget? Hadn't she complained constantly to Betty about the worn-out state of her wardrobe, and Linda's interference? Weren't there some contradictions in her testimony? Earley asked mildly.

Rummaging among his evidence boxes, he even produced a pair of Kim's high school shoes, which Betty had once presented in divorce court as proof of Dan's negligence. They were black, short-heeled pumps, so run down that at least half an inch of the white plastic spines were showing.

Kim Broderick, brown eyes flashing, was ready to take him on. With a slight smile of condescension, she said those shoes had not bothered her in the least. Instead, it was her mother who had been so shocked by the sight of them that she had confiscated them and said, "You are forbidden to wear these."

As for her complaints to Betty about Dan's rigid budgeting of her monthly college expenses, "I was laughing about it," she insisted. Mom simply mistook her mock tears for the real thing. Mom was like that.

Earley sparred with Kim over everything from Dan's grocery budget to the names he and Linda called Betty in front of the children. Kim agreed that Dan and Linda had both called Betty fat and crazy. But she would volunteer nothing more. It was like pulling teeth. Kim Broderick was not going to offer anything to help her mother.

Finally, Earley obliged her to at least concede that her father was also given to his own temper fits. Yes, Kim said, testily, Dan had once hammered a defective lawnmower to bits, he had thrown a sliding glass door off the bedroom balcony on another occasion, and once he had tossed an aquarium out a window, although, she added defensively, no fish were in it. "It was already broken."

At last, Earley could stand her defiance not a minute longer. He began taunting her—and, at the same time, flashing forbidden character evidence before the jury.

Would it change your mind about your father, he asked, if you knew he had written a blackmail letter to Wilma Engel? That he had poured beer on Linda in a bar?

Kim looked shocked. "Dad wouldn't do that." She was on the verge of tears. All she wanted, she finally snapped in a breaking voice, was to see that "the other side of this story comes out, too."

Earley had overstepped himself, and he knew it, and he backed off fast. Eloise Duffield was beginning to shift in her chair, her mouth now the size of a dime.

But in the corridor afterward, Kim, for once, was not crying. Instead, surrounded by Broderick siblings and the La Jolla ladies, she was laughing angrily as she held up her foot. See, she said—all her shoes were run-down, even this pair, because she was pigeon-toed.

Later, Kim Broderick sat in a bar near the courthouse, nursing a Coke and bumming cigarettes, as she remembered the day in 1985 when her mother left her at Dan's house. The memory still brought her close to tears.

She was only fifteen at the time. "And I never understood that he was having an affair. I didn't know a lot of things that were making Mom so mad," she said. "But even now that I'm older, I still don't understand why she had to take it out on me! She never explained anything," said Kim bitterly. "She just dumped me at his house and drove off!"

Her father relied on her to help him out, she said. He asked her what he should bring home for dinner, he asked her to help him figure out how to cook it. She liked it—which is why, she admitted with blushing candor, she didn't want him to marry Linda. "I didn't want Dad to marry anybody ... our relationship was getting so good, I didn't want somebody else to interfere. I knew he wouldn't need me as much anymore."

She recalled her parent's fights in her childhood. Her mother, she said, was always "so jealous about the craziest things." Once when she was very small, for example, the family was watching a country-western music special on TV, when Crystal Gayle came on "with her hair down to the ground, and Dad was talking about how pretty it was ... And Mom went nuts. She yelled at him about how ugly it was and how it must have dead ends, and that he shouldn't talk about other women in front of her."

And, yes, she said, as she got older she played both sides against the middle. Whenever Dan wouldn't give her money for something she wanted, she would "go running to Mom, hysterical." But she never expected the day to come when she would hear her mother telling her over a telephone not only that she had just shot her father but "that she had killed him for me! That she couldn't stand the way he was treating me!"

Her face colored as she fought back tears. "What did I ever do to deserve that guilt?" she asked in pitiful exasperation.

And so, maybe if Betty Broderick had been able to apologize to her oldest daughter for shooting the father she loved, if she had been able even once to say that she was sorry for hurting her children, if she had been able to explain honestly, even five years later, why she had left Kim at Dan Broderick's empty house that spring night back in 1985—how frightened she herself had really been beneath her anger—it might have made a difference. Maybe. But Betty never could do any of that.

Two of Betty's relatives were also in town that day—her youngest brother Mike, an electronics company executive from New Jersey, and her cousin Connie Lawler, a svelte airline executive married to a New York City criminal attorney. That evening they visited Betty in jail. Neither had spoken to her in over two years. But it was easy to tell what they were hearing, just watching Betty, as she spoke to them by turns from the visitor phone. She was flushed, radiant, animated, on fast forward. She was telling them "the story."

Both emerged from the visiting room looking stunned. "That's not the Betty Anne I know," said Lawler, aghast. Not once in thirty minutes had Betty asked a single personal question about family, as the old Betty would have done. Instead, said

Lawler, she had raved like a loon. "She's manic! Why isn't someone helping her?"

Mike Bisceglia looked shocked enough to cry. Then, angrily, he wanted to know why Jack Earley wasn't attempting some sort of psychiatric defense? "Betty Anne could have a chemical imbalance, to make her do something like this." He swore to discuss it with Earley.

But, next day, both Lawler and Mike Bisceglia were gone, and Betty Broderick was a woman alone again, with only Dian Black to complain futilely in her behalf.

Just as Kerry Wells loved Dan Broderick's tapes, she also loved his housekeepers. They became another of her favored trial weapons. Before this drama was done, she would call four of them to testify to Betty's hate of Dan and Linda, her threats to kill them, and whatever other assorted items they could think of to inflict further damage.

Linda David, Dan's housekeeper for six months in 1987, portrayed Betty as a calculating, vengeful woman who never really loved her husband. She said Betty had told her she only married Dan because she knew he would be a money-maker. After the divorce, David quoted Betty as saying that she knew Dan and Linda only wanted to be left alone but that it would never happen. "I'll either make his life a living hell or I'll kill him."

Sylvia Cavins, David's mother and Dan's housekeeper for the last two years of his life, talked about Betty's greed, which annoyed Cavins in the extreme. "I told her once that some men support their families [for a year] on what she got for a month," said Cavins, who also lectured the boys similarly. Once Cavins said she had even taken the two Broderick sons on a tour of the ghetto and told them "they shouldn't believe it when Betty said she was having money problems." In her coup de grace, Cavins also testified that Betty had threatened to her personally to "put four bullets in Dan's head, one for each of the children" at his wedding. Furthermore, said Cavins, Betty predicted that she would get away with it, "because when the jury found out what Dan did to her, she said they would let her off."

The other two housekeepers were nowhere near as impressive as Cavins and her daughter, either in appearance or manner. One was Marta Shaver, a nervous, high-strung, middle-aged woman with an immovable cap of auburn hair that looked like a wig, who had been Dan's first housekeeper for a year. The other was Robin Tu'ua, an angry Amazon, as tall and heavy as Betty, but with a decided eye to her own sex appeal. Her colored blond hair fell to her waist, and she wore as much makeup as Tammy Faye Bakker, albeit more skillfully applied. She described herself as Dan's "governess," after Shaver left.

Shaver was so theatrically rehearsed, particularly in telling about the "total devastation" of Betty's Boston cream pie caper, that Earley finally sniped that she should take her tale to Hollywood. Whelan yelled at him to "Knock that off!" ["Let's be logical about this," Betty said later, laughing at the whole episode. "How could I have possibly gotten that much mileage out of the cunt's crappy little pie?"]

Tu'ua admitted once eavesdropping on a telephone conversation between Betty and Rhett, in which, she said, Betty had told the crying boy that he couldn't come visit her until he got rid of Linda. Betty's language was so crude that "I would prefer not to repeat the words," said Tu'ua primly, adding that Betty had once threatened to shoot her, too.

Wells's next witness was Betty's old friend Patti Monahan, whom Betty had telephoned on the morning of the killings, allegedly to utter the gruesome line, "It's true, they do shit their pants, and I could hear him gurgling in his own blood."

But, by trial time, Monahan said she could no longer remember exactly what Betty had told her, except that she had been "very graphic."

Monahan's memory lapse was a nuisance for Kerry Wells, but not a significant one. Over Jack Earley's impassioned objections that it was double hearsay, Whelan allowed Wells to trot Monahan's boyfriend onto the stand to testify that, even if Patti couldn't recall, he remembered exactly what Patti said Betty told her that morning. And so the grisly quote—which Betty always heatedly denied—was entered into testimony.

There wasn't much Earley could do after that—except, in one of the more bizarre footnotes of the entire trial, enter into evidence a crime report clearly stating that Dan Broderick "had not defecated before he died."

On cross-exam, lacking much alternative, Earley settled for humiliating Monahan as best he could. He obliged her to reveal publicly that, after twenty-two years of marriage, she was receiving only $2,700 a month from her own successful attorney ex-husband.

"Do you think a wife deserves half of the community property?" Earley asked.

"Well, I don't know," Monahan said hesitantly. "I never gave it a thought ... I didn't think of percentages ... I only thought about what it took to lead a full, lucrative life, and what a woman needed to be happy ..."

In criminal court, as in divorce court before, Lee Broderick was always the odd child out. Of all the Broderick children, perhaps none was more cruelly used in the ugly struggle between her parents than Lee. Before she was even eighteen, Lee Broderick had been bounced around, bartered, branded bad, and generally treated like everybody's most annoying, unwanted pest, instead of like a young girl with more reason than most to stray from the sweetheart path.

After the killings, she became even more of a pariah, at least among the Broderick clan, because she consistently refused to say that her father was a complete saint and her mother a total bitch. Lee never departed from the idea that it was a two-way street.

But, as would later become amply clear in court, Lee Broderick never really belonged to either side. To the contrary, she may have been more hurt than any of the other children by her father's death, simply because she never got the opportunity to win back his approval, to make peace, to feel his hug one more time, as she had when she was a child. So many of the early Broderick family photos show a beautiful little girl with chubby cheeks and sparkling eyes, of maybe four or five, sitting on her handsome young dad's lap, the two of them always touching, his arm around her, her arms around his neck, or just holding hands, always looking at each other with such uncomplicated love.

Wells called Lee to the witness stand, ostensibly to establish the events of the morning of the killings. More likely, she did it for the sake of appearance, to dilute any notion among jurors that she was afraid of Lee's testimony.

Lee was very nervous that morning, pacing the courthouse hallway with her boyfriend. Looking at her, it is easy to believe that Betty Broderick once weighed 110 pounds at 5'10". Lee is the same physical type that Betty once was, tall and almost painfully thin. She is also very pretty, with dark eyes and hair like her sister, but with sharper, more angular features. Her style of dressing is also different. She wasn't making any attempt to look like Little Bo Peep on the witness stand. Instead, she wore a tailored brown plaid miniskirt and brown blazer, with a string of pearls.

"How do I look?" she asked, looking miserable.

Wells approached her with caution, asking a series of perfunctory questions about the morning of November 5, when her mother called her.

In a quivering voice, Lee recited the same details she had reported so many times before. It was all routine by now, she had told the story to so many police officers, investigators, and family members.

It was only when Lee repeated for the jury that her mother had said she "pulled the phone out of the wall so he couldn't save himself" that Jack Earley looked as if he might swallow his lips. It was a devastating line that Lee would later amend in the second trial: Her mother had not said why she pulled out the phone—it was only Lee's assumption that she had done it "so that he couldn't save himself." But that was a year later. For now, the damage was done.

Like Kim, Lee also agreed that Betty had often threatened to kill Dan. Oh, yeah, she said, with a shrug. "She had talked about it for a number of years."

Throughout her testimony, after her initial stage fright passed, Lee's voice was matter-of-fact, detached; this was not her life, it was a movie she had once seen. Not until later, when Pasas and Earley were yelling at her outside, did Lee Broderick even realize how damning her innocent remarks had sounded.

Wells, increasingly confident that this witness wasn't going to explode in her face, asked Lee about the night Betty had run the car into Dan's front door. Wells's tone had warmed notably.

"Oh, yeah, she was definitely trying to do some harm to him," said Lee. Wells also got Lee to remember that, during a shopping trip to Nordstrom's on the weekend of the killings, her mother had been angry about the letters she had received from Dan's lawyers the day before. Wells almost smiled.

"Did you love your father?" asked Wells, before sitting down. "Yes," said Lee, flushing.

Earley looked as puckered as a man who had just eaten a wad of raw garlic as he took up cross-examination of the daughter he had expected to be his best foil to Kim. But since he would be calling her back as a witness in his own case, he was interested for now only in damage control.

He reminded her—and the jury—that one of the earlier theories was that she was somehow to blame for her father's death.

Lee agreed. "I was told by my lawyer that they were going to try to make it look like I had something to do with it." But, again, she showed no real emotional reaction.

Earley got her to explain that her mother constantly threatened, as a manner of speech, to "kill people." Oh, sure, said Lee, looking surprised at the question. Mom was always saying she wanted to kill "a lot of people" when she was mad.

And, yes, on the night Betty ran her car into Dan's door, he had refused to talk to her during the hour before. He had said, "Talk to my lawyer. Get out of my house." So Betty had left, and then returned to do her damage. When the police came, Lee added softly, apropos of nothing, they had taken her mother away "in a straitjacket."

On the subject of Betty's personality, Lee agreed that Betty always hid her true feelings. "She always tries to pretend like everything's okay. But she can only fake it so long ..." Lee also said her mother often told her that she "was scared of [Dan] and wished he would stop beating her up [in court]."

Earley sat down. Lee would be back. Meantime, his gloomy expression said, he couldn't wait to have a word or two with her in the woodshed.

There was never much apparent order to Kerry Wells's case.

Now, departing from Patti Monahan and Lee, both of whom at least had some information bearing directly on Betty Broderick's state of mind at the time of the killings, Wells headed once again into the morass of domestic fault.

It remained one of the central ironies of Betty Broderick's murder trials that the woman who couldn't get what she regarded as a fair divorce settlement in 1989, thanks to no-fault divorce laws, was now, in criminal court, going to prison for life if Kerry Wells got her way, based strictly on fault—not only for the killings, but also the domestic tensions leading to the divorce itself.

It was Betty's fault, Wells argued, that the marriage had gone sour; it was her fault that Dan had left her; it was her fault that Dan was obliged to lie about his affair with Linda. "She threatened to commit suicide, way back in 1983," Kerry Wells once declared. "He was afraid to tell her the truth!"

Wells called as her next witness Betty's former friend Helen Pickard, who turned out to be as enthusiastic in condemning Betty Broderick's personal habits as Kim and the Forbes couple.

Betty was smart, charismatic, charming, said Pickard—but she was also a self-centered, extravagant, thoughtless woman who had picked on her husband for years. The children, said Pickard, were never the real issue. Dan and Linda were. And money.

"She talked about them incessantly ... she couldn't let go of it," said Pickard. "And she didn't want the children until she got a financial settlement ... that definitely had to come first." Betty was "real close to money ... She worshipped it. It was her main goal in life. She was an alcoholic spender," said Pickard, delivering a line that would be the next day's headline.

On the Saturday before the murders, Betty had been "extremely upset" about

Dan's announced plans to begin a new family, Pickard said. "Her last question to me was, 'Is Linda pregnant?'"

In perhaps the most damaging blow of all, Pickard also recalled a telephone call she received from Betty in jail less than three weeks after the killings. Betty told her that she'd never been happier, and that Linda had been "destroying my life, my children, my social standing," said Pickard—and so Betty had destroyed Linda instead. "And, then," said Pickard, voice breaking, hand fluttering to her throat, "She laughed!"

Jack Earley, for once, did not belabor his cross-exam.

Instead, he walked up to the lectern, and, with an expression of utter disdain, remarked, "You've described a pretty disgusting person whose main concern was money, whose only redeeming quality was her pretty clothes ... And yet, for whatever reasons, this was your friend?" It wasn't a question. It was a statement. He then turned on his heel and sat down, without giving Pickard a chance to respond. So there she sat, open-mouthed and blushing, confused that, suddenly, it was all over.

But her discomfort didn't last long. In the corridor outside, her friends waited. Kim hugged her. Gail Forbes did, too. The media clucked about, asking questions. Within five minutes, Pickard was making jokes about Jack's picture display of Betty in earlier days. "I looked better at twenty-nine, too," she quipped. There was no charity here.

Wells finished the day by reading to the jury her favorite selection from Betty's diaries; the November, 1988, notation said that:

"There is no better reason in the world for someone to kill than to protect their home, possessions, and family from attack and destruction. You are the sickest person alive. A law degree does not give you license to kill and destroy, nor does it give you immunity from punishment. No one will mourn you."

Earley protested again, in vain. That issue had already been resolved. Wells could pick and choose, but the jury would never be allowed to read Betty's diaries in their entirety.

"I'm gonna keep Betty on the stand a week!" he swore after court that day, as angry as he ever got. "I'm going to take her through every one of those diaries, line by line, to show that one quote in its context!"

So far, the week had been a complete rout for the defense. And it wasn't over. As Earley well knew, Wells had more damning testimony to come. "You know," he said, straight-faced, "Maybe I should just argue that no case is this good. It's too good to be true. Therefore, it can't be true."

Marion Pasas didn't think any of it was funny anymore. Betty was wearing her down with her upbeat, frivolous courtroom manner. That day, clowning around during the morning session, Betty had stuck her tongue out at the courtroom photographer. "Even the bailiffs warned her at one point to remember that the jurors were watching her," said Pasas. "This whole case is so bad, it's like a landslide that won't stop!"

Pasas studied her dagger red acrylics. Her yearning to bite one was tangible. A thumbnail had broken off. As she regarded the ugly, naked stub morosely, she lapsed into a nostalgia trip of the sort that perhaps only another criminal investigator can really understand. One of her very favorite clients, she reminisced, had been "an enforcer for a drug dealer. He did a murder for hire; he put fifteen holes in a snitch. He was ugly, but he was perfect in court," Pasas remembered fondly. "He never did anything, he never said anything. There was nothing he showed to the jury that was unlikable!" He got eleven years.

But Betty Broderick might get life.

Pasas would never believe Betty Broderick deserved the long prison term she was bound to get. She liked Betty. Lately she had even been acting as her caterer. For the first time in a year, Betty could now have something for lunch besides the standard jailhouse bologna sandwich and apple—but only if Pasas remembered to bring it. "So every day, I try to remember. Sometimes I take her a fruit salad, and real coffee, or brie and French bread. She gets so excited, especially when I bring her coffee—and she loves Payday candy bars. She's always so grateful when I bring in that bag." Pasas was making herself feel lousy, because yesterday she had forgotten. "She's always real sweet about it. She tries to pretend that she really doesn't mind ... but I can see how disappointed she is." Pasas's earlier frustration over Betty's maddening, self-destructive courtroom behavior had evaporated entirely. She was now too depressed with herself for letting even one day pass without bringing this woman who would be going to prison for so many years a fresh piece of fruit, a cup of coffee, and a candy bar with nuts. "Tomorrow," she said, "I think I'll get her a crab salad. And some grapes. She'll like that."

Melancholy had spread to the Broderick camp, too, during this first week of trial. With each morning's headlines, with every evening newscast, the friends and family of Dan and Linda Broderick were obliged to relive their pain. Not far from Pasas's office, in one of San Diego's most fashionable new Italian restaurants, attorney Sharon Blanchet was going through it all in her mind once again over dinner. It was just so unfair that Betty had killed them. So impossible. So unreal still, after all this time. She remembered the evening before Dan and Linda were married like yesterday.

"Linda had bought Dan a pocket watch," Blanchet said. "But the night before, Maggie dropped it, and it broke. And I remember thinking instantly, 'No more time.' ... I know it sounds silly," she said with a self-conscious smile, "but I'll never forget it. That phrase just ran through my mind—it came out of nowhere: 'No more time.'"

The last day of Kerry Wells's case was yet another mixed bag of witnesses. First she called Steve Frantz, a local attorney, who recalled meeting Betty at a shooting range in 1986. He remembered her, Frantz said, because she was such a terrific shot. She hit the bull's-eye every time.

Next, Wells summoned Brad Wright, ostensibly for the purpose of asking him about the weekend events surrounding the crime. But, just as important, Wells wanted to establish firmly in the eyes of the jurors that, for all Betty Broderick's complaints about Dan and Linda, she herself also had a good-looking, virile young lover, right up to the night of the killings.

Wright's manner was thoughtful, cautious, mature. Yes, he agreed, he had been

Betty's "boyfriend" since 1985. Betty blushed like a girl and smiled sweetly at him throughout his testimony. Here, for the first time in her life, was a man—unlike father, brothers, and husband—who had always been willing to stand beside her, publicly and without shame, no matter what.

That's loyalty. And now, Kerry Wells was trying to crack it. It was laughable. There was always about Brad Wright an almost childlike naivety, a thing way beyond guile, which rendered him incapable of seeing ordinary events in the same way that most adults do. His wall of innocence was impenetrable.

So far as he could tell, Wright told Wells, Betty was just fine the night before the crimes. He recited the routine of the evening. Dinner, TV, and bed. When he heard Betty's Suburban firing up at around dawn, he thought nothing of it, because she was an early riser. He thought she was off for her daily walk on the beach. He went back to sleep. The next he knew, Danny was waking him to say that Dian Black was on the telephone. He and Forbes had then gone to discover the bodies. After which, he had gone sailing. Jurors gasped at that news, reporters snickered. Otherwise, Wright was useless to Wells. She tried in vain to make him say that Betty would sometimes cancel weekends with the children whenever "she found out Dan and Linda had plans." Wright blinked at her, befuddled. To the contrary, he said, Betty was always canceling weekends with him because of her plans with the children. They always came first.

Wasn't it true, Wells demanded, that Betty had told the "kids to stab Linda?" Wright offered one of his best, boyish smiles. He had sure never heard that one before, he said. Wells finally gave up.

Finally, Wells called Dr. Ruth Roth, the marriage and family therapist who had briefly attempted in 1987, at the behest of both Dan's and Betty's attorneys, to mediate the Broderick divorce dispute.

Never in her entire career, declared Roth, had she confronted a case so unsolvable as the Broderick matter. Not because of Dan Broderick, but because of his strange, wild wife. In her three sessions with Betty, Roth found her entirely uncontrollable.

She told of Betty's threats to kill Dan before she would become a single mother of four; she told about her Tarasoff warnings to Dan.

But, Roth said, despite Betty's anger at Dan, she had still repeatedly tried to persuade Betty to take custody of the boys. In Roth's view, it simply made more sense for the "stay-at-home mommy" to have custody of the children, with the working father visiting. But Betty wouldn't hear of it.

With a prim apology to the jury for her language, Roth then read Betty's precise words to the court: "I'm not going to be the single parent of four kids. He'll die first ..." And, "The less I see of them, the better. No kids, no bother ... he's a cuntfucker."

During one session, Roth testified, she and Betty had gotten into a squabble over Betty's terminology. Referring to her notes, Roth thought that at one point, Betty had accused Dan of "sucking." But, she told the jury, deadpan, Betty had gotten furious and yelled at her: "I said fucking, not sucking. He fucks, she sucks!" Almost everyone in the courtroom fought back smiles except Kerry Wells.

Not until the second trial did Jack Earley become organized enough to realize that, besides her three sessions with Betty, Roth had also interviewed Dan once during her mediation efforts—but, she said during the second trial, she hadn't taken any notes on Dan. It was, Roth admitted, the only time in her career that she could recall not taking notes on a client. She couldn't remember why she had made that exception for Dan Broderick.

It was enough for Earley. With a slight smirk, he sat down—but not before reminding the jury that, in all the long years of the Broderick divorce war, which included numerous psychiatric reports on Betty and all four children, there was never even one thin file on Dan Broderick's mental health. Only he had not been formally evaluated, ever.

With that, the prosecution's case was concluded. Now it was Jack Earley's turn.

That night, he looked frazzled, distracted and rigid with worry, as he headed off to Las Colinas for one last session to "prep" his client for her testimony. Betty would be his first witness in the morning.

For weeks, the defense team had discussed it, worried it, analyzed it, and fought their own doubts about whether or not she could do it. And now, at the eleventh hour, the question was still alive.

"I'm telling you, she's ICP," Pasas told Earley one last time.

"Uhmmmmn," he muttered. "Well, let's see how it goes tonight ..."

While he was gone, both Pasas and Earley's assistant attorney, Lisa Bowman, sat in tense anticipation in their offices, waiting to hear whether it was red alert, or an aborted mission.

Would Earley decide to give it up? Would he take one last look at his angry, remorseless client and decide that she was too out of touch to defend herself? Would he file for an incompetency hearing?

The two women worked silently through the evening, preparing the defense. Pasas poured over her thick stack of witness interviews, writing out questions for Earley to ask and making last-minute phone calls to witnesses. Bowman worried over her charts and graphs, and time lines showing the "litigious assault" Betty had suffered over the years.

Two hours later, Earley called Pasas from his car phone.

"I think she can do it," he said.

"Oh, shit," said Pasas, putting down the phone with a sigh. It was all systems go. Ready the nukes. Betty Broderick would hit the witness stand in the morning.

Chapter 35

The Defense

The hallway was more jammed than usual on October 30, the day Betty Broderick took the witness stand in her own defense. Court-watchers, some carrying lawn chairs and brown-bag lunches, had arrived at the crack of dawn to be first in line the minute the doors were opened.

The press was out in double force. One local TV station would even interrupt its regularly scheduled soap operas and talk shows during the next four days to present Betty's testimony live—and, as later ratings would verify, it was a smart decision. Half the housewives in San Diego, it seemed, were pleased to pass up a few episodes of 'As the World Turns' and 'Sally Jessy Raphael' to follow the saga of Dan and Betty and Linda.

Elisabeth Anne Broderick, wearing a muted beige plaid suit with gored skirt, took the stand. After all those frustrating years of trying to tell her story, she at last had the full attention of the city of San Diego, and beyond. The floor was finally hers.

She looked pale and scared. Her bottle-blond jailhouse hair looked yellow as a lemon rind, her curls lay too close about her head, without style or order. She was so nervous she even forgot to smile.

"Good morning. When were you born?" asked Jack Earley.

"November 7, 1947, New York City." Her voice trembled.

Earley's tone was flat, his expression blank. He is not the sort of attorney who dithers with such amenities as setting his client at ease. But he is methodic: for the rest of the day, his droning questions would move Betty Broderick through every single aspect, large and small, of "the story:" from her Tupperware parties in college, to her face peel in 1983, to the day she burned her husband's clothes over Linda Kolkena, to her attorney search, to her shock at being denied even visitation rights with her children, and much, much more.

Most striking about Betty's first hour of testimony was her own demeanor. The transformation was astonishing. This was not the same furious, funny, blasphemous Betty Broderick who had been on the jailhouse phones all summer. This Betty showed no emotion beyond nervous timidity. No edge of hate shaded her tone. No disrespect for the dead was evident. This Betty was docile, visibly struggling to be as pleasing as possible.

But the strain in her voice was apparent, the struggle within her so evident that everyone in the courtroom sat braced, waiting for the break that was bound to come.

Earley got her through most of their struggling student years—the part-time jobs, the unheated apartments, the harsh pregnancies, the bus rides to the laundromat with Kim on her hip—before she finally broke down.

"During that period of time," asked Earley, "how was Dan dressing?"

"Dan's always been very meticulous about his clothes," said Betty, lapsing into her unconscious, chilling present tense. "... He loves clothes, he looks very well in clothes. He always looked much better than the average student. He always wore a jacket and tie to class, where the average student was wearing T-shirts and jeans in those years ..." Her voice paused, lingered, wavered, and finally broke. "He was very dapper. Dapper Dan, we always called him ..."

It was a delayed reaction. Seconds later, she was strangling in tears, her face reddened and crumpled in pure agony. In the days to come, Betty Broderick would cry many times, but never again would she be as convincing, as spontaneous, as pitiful as she was in this one moment, sparked by her own brief memories of Dapper Dan.

But she regained her composure quickly. Within the next hour, she even succumbed to her obsessive need to take notes. Might she have a pencil and paper? she asked Judge Whelan in her bashful little-girl voice. Whelan looked startled, shrugged, and passed the problem on to Earley, who only looked embarrassed. Betty instantly dropped her request, once she saw that it was somehow out of line.

Within the next thirty minutes, however, she breeched protocol again when she noticed Eloise Duffield, who had an admitted hearing problem, straining on the edge of her chair. With a solicitous expression, Betty asked the juror directly if she was speaking loud enough for her to hear.

Never a conventional killer, neither would Betty Broderick be a conventional defendant.

Throughout the day, as Earley led her from Harvard, to the Plum Tree Apartments, to La Jolla, Betty never once betrayed a trace of anger toward Dan Broderick—only the naive innocence of a woman who never once suspected that her happy home was going to hell, even before Linda Kolkena came along.

When Dan first began going out drinking with the boys on weekends, she tried to understand, she said, "because the guy really did work so hard." But she was admittedly unhappy because he was never home. She wanted to move back East to be near her family. But Dan wouldn't agree. His career was going well, and "he did not want to start from zero anywhere else ... He begged me to stay here."

So, in 1976, at her urging, they had gone to the Marriage Retreat, where he had written her his letters, promising that once he reached his material goals, everything would be better. (Betty's own letters from that weekend retreat could not be found until the second trial.)

Earley was of course eager to get Dan's letters entered into evidence, since they were solid proof, written in Dan's own hand, that Dan Broderick had always been a man far more interested in things than in people—and one, too, who had scoffed at the Catholic Church as "uncool." There were at least four Catholics on the jury.

Thus, Earley prodded Betty to discuss them in detail, to establish that they had been of immense significance to her throughout the marriage, that they were a major factor in her later depressed state of mind.

As Betty summarized the contents of those old letters, a flicker of something akin to pain crossed her face. She reiterated them in their essence: Dan had agreed he wasn't "the kind of husband or father that he wanted to be or that I should have," but, first, he wanted to be "a very important man ... very prominent and very rich ... and as long as he had to concentrate on those goals, he didn't have time to be home with the family ... And he said that 'We're almost there,' if I would just give him more time ..."

From there, Earley walked Betty through her many social and school activities to show that, while she was always an active mother, Dan was a consistently absent dad, always busy at work.

In his quest to portray his client as a hardworking, long-suffering housewife and mother, married to a selfish ingrate, Earley found no detail too minor to reveal, from the cars the Brodericks drove to the trips they took, especially after 1982, when the good times really began to roll. His goal was to inundate the jury, newcomers to this whole story, with so much evidence of the mental anguish visited upon an unsuspecting wife by her materialistic, philandering husband's prolonged lies and vanities that, in time, the homicides might seem a nearly inevitable outcome. It turned out to be a smart strategy.

Kerry Wells took copious notes. The deeper Earley went into these life-style items, the deeper she would also later descend, until, finally, the whole spectacle seemed less like a first-degree murder trial than some wacky, tacky Hollywood parody of 'Divorce, Yuppie Style'.

Meanwhile, having apparently noticed one juror frowning in puzzlement, Betty turned to Whelan and asked if the jurors could "ask questions if they don't understand?" Her tone was so solicitous, so naive, that several jurors smiled as Whelan patiently explained to her: no.

Earley moved on to 1983, the beginning of what Betty always called "the Linda problem." For the next two hours, the jury listened to the saga of one more marriage gone sour, all because the husband had found someone who made him feel better than his wife did.

Until Dan met Linda, Betty said, their marriage had been normal. But, after that, she said, he had become a changed man virtually overnight, suddenly aggressively critical of everything about his life: Yet he lied to her—he denied that any other woman was involved. Instead, she told the jury, beginning to cry, he blamed her. He said "A lot of it was my fault because I was old, fat, ugly, boring, and stupid ..." She was bewildered and crushed because "I was thirty-five years old! And I wore size eight, which people know can't be very fat for someone nearly five-eleven ..."

Through her sobs, she then recounted her last-ditch efforts to compete with the younger, carefree woman: She had become just one more Aging Wife, trying frantically to "fix it" in every way she knew how. It was the one certain point in her testimony that probably caused every housewife in San Diego to put down the iron and turn up the volume on the TV set.

"If your husband is telling you that you're not pleasing to him anymore, you try to do whatever it is better, that he does not like," she said, choking on her tears, her voice a thin, reedy wail. "You know—if the problem is you're not a good cook, you take cooking lessons. If you are not a good housekeeper, you keep house better. If you are old, fat, ugly, stupid, you try to be younger, you try get wrinkles taken off your face that weren't even there!" In another segment that would make the evening TV news, her face reddened and crumpled, she shrieked in frustration, "You even get your tooth fixed!" she cried, halfway opening her mouth, pointing a finger toward some lower tooth. "I have this one tooth with a tiny little millimeter, something, crooked ... I tried to be perfect. Absolutely, flawlessly perfect for Dan Broderick ... I was very proud of him, I wanted him to be proud of me ..."

But none of it had worked. She next told the jury of her anguish on the night Dan announced that he had hired Linda as his assistant. But even then, she said, wiping away her tears, she had been torn. Certainly, she wanted Dan to hire help. "As I've said earlier, Dan was always under a lot of pressure working ... You don't make that kind of money by not working hard. None of it is luck ... He would fall asleep with the legal file on his chest and wake up in the morning and do it again." But Linda Kolkena? Who couldn't even type? No.

From there, guided by Earley, she described the next year in agonizing detail: the ultimatum she had given Dan, either to fire Linda or move out; the day he came home with the new Corvette; her later suicide try; the clothes burning. But through it all, she told Earley, Dan insisted that she was imagining everything, "that I was crazy, losing it, that I should get help." And so, she said, at Dan's urging, she had gone to see a therapist for the first time, because "I wanted so much to believe him." She cried again. Jurors looked pained, Earley looked pleased.

But, just as a couple of female jurors seemed on the verge of tears themselves, Betty suddenly conceded that she wouldn't have been so upset about Dan's affair, except that "it was becoming a little too public for me, a little too embarrassing to me, that he was being seen everywhere with her."

So much for heartbreak.

By midafternoon, the jury was up to speed on events through 1987, from the car "bamming," to the bifurcated divorce without visitation rights, to the rats in the rental house. Betty told about Dan's fines, and being jailed when she went to protest the minus $1,300 check. "I couldn't believe it. I didn't think I was being unreasonable, to ask for money to keep me going through the month."

She admitted to some of the vandalisms—the Boston cream pie, a broken window, the spray paint. All done in anger at her own helplessness, she said.

Then, the jury got a first-hand glimpse of Betty Broderick's temper, aimed at her own attorney. Earley had asked her an innocuous question about Dan's cancellation of her credit cards. "Do you remember, when was that, in relationship to the Notre Dame game?" For whatever reasons, it annoyed her. Earley was "putting the cart before the horse on some incidents," she suddenly snapped. All these details and incidents of her life were being taken out of order, were being confused in the telling, she continued in a sharp, nonstop mini-lecture. ".... When the soccer game

378

happened, I didn't know about the divorce yet! When the cake was smushed around, it was because he was still lying about Linda! He hadn't told me the truth yet, so I was highly, highly agitated about a lot of different things ... I didn't know what was happening with my house being torn down, my kids were at his house, he was starting to pull the plug out about letting me see my kids, go to my own house. I was in a tailspin. It is all very mixed up in my mind, but it is all close together!"

Earley waited, listening soberly until she was done—then asked her exactly the same question again. His flat manner seemed to both alert and calm her. This time she answered politely, promptly.

The day ended with more of the same—a barrage of details, large and small. She told about receiving "anonymous, harassing things in the mail ... ads for wrinkle cream and weight loss."

The photograph from the legal newspaper *Dicta* was most hurtful, she added, because "Dan being president of the bar was something he and I had talked about since we had come to town." She studied the picture Earley had placed before her. Others in the photo were old friends of hers, too, she said, "So it was not only my husband, it was our whole social circle ..." But she did not leave it at that. She kept talking. Pasas stiffened and began to pick at the tails of her hair. Earley stood, looking helpless to cut her off.

"This is him being admitted president of the bar association," Betty told the jury. Then she read aloud the caption printed by the publication itself, which clearly upset her even more than the attached "Eat your heart out, bitch" note:

**It says, 'With them is Linda Kolkena, paralegal,' and,"—she paused—" 'close friend of the president elect'!" The hate in her voice as she read those last six words was the closest she had come on this day to blowing it. "Tick, tick, tick," said *Union* reporter John Gaines under his breath. Earley hustled to snatch the picture away from her.

If seats had been for sale, bailiffs Jose Jimenez and Rita Long could have made a bundle on Betty's second day on the witness stand. As theater goes, everybody knew that this was it, the must-see performance of the entire trial, because, surely, Jack Earley would finish with his domestic history today and get to the killings.

Wells arrived, looking as if Dracula had drained her during the night. Even Earley and Pasas skipped their usual morning amenities with the press. Earley was taking no comfort in the fact that Betty had handled herself well so far. If she was already sniping at him, what would happen when Kerry Wells got hold of her? His client would lash out in a fatal display of unlovability. He knew it.

Betty looked calm, cheerful, and curious. Her complexion was rosy, her hair was fluffier. Her stage fright was gone. Today, she watched the audience with as much interest as it watched her. She winked at a friend. She smiled at the jurors as they filed in. Not least, in perhaps the truest reflection of her new confidence, she had chosen to wear the one dress Marion Pasas had begged her not to wear—a two-piece gold satin sweater combination with a flowing pleated skirt, more suitable for an afternoon tea at the Valencia than a murder trial. She wore pink lipstick and blue eye shadow. She looked like rainbow sherbet.

But her serenity didn't last. Because today Jack Earley was intent upon establishing Dan Broderick as just about the meanest, most violent drunk in San Diego. He wanted to lay the groundwork for an upcoming expert witness who would declare that Betty Broderick had not only been emotionally abused but physically and sexually battered, too—something Betty had always denied in press interviews.

Did Dan Broderick have a temper? Earley asked. Yes, said Betty. When he got mad he would "yell, scream, and smash things."

Earley then tried to get her to say that Dan had hit her, too. She wouldn't. Earley pressed. "And had he ever hit you while you were married?" he asked. "Yes." Period. Earley looked visibly annoyed. He had clearly spent hours discussing these questions with Betty. She knew where the defense strategy was supposed to lead, and, presumably, had agreed with it. But now, Betty was about to be Betty. Having agreed, or suggested agreement, she folded on Earley at the critical hour.

The most he could get her to say was that, yes, sometimes "I would be bruised and marked up a little." Whether she was overstating or understating the facts, it was clear to everyone in the courtroom that she hated this line of questioning. Earley pressed on. At last she agreed, with visible irritability, that Dan once gave her a black eye.

"I explained before that Dan was a very, very high-pressure person, mostly self-imposed," she said curtly. "But he was always wound very tightly, and if he got upset about something, he had an outrageous temper and a lot of strength that you would not think he would ordinarily have, and he would ... there is a long, long list and record of breaking and smashing, yelling and screaming when he was in a fit of temper ... After he finished smashing stuff he would say, 'Just be lucky it was not you, next time it might be you.'" And what was Dan like when he drank?

"It was a progression of moods and things," said Betty, irritably. "It would start at a party just being fun ... and as he drank more and more, he would be more and more fun, doing really silly things, like flipping down staircases, falling out of chairs on purpose, Alligators and Turtles stuff. As the night went on, he would pass out ... When he woke up the next morning is when most of these bad tempers would take place."

But Earley also wanted her to say that Dan had forced drunken sex upon her, too. "At night ... when he came home from drinking, would he also be nice, would he be forceful, or ...?"

Betty cut him off: "He would be very, very drunk many, many times coming home staggering, not making any sense, and I would just be real careful not to get him mad ... As I also said yesterday," she added sharply, "this was an ongoing problem!" Her tone of voice told Earley that was enough. She wasn't here to embarrass either herself or the man she had married, defense strategy be damned. Wells almost smiled.

Earley then turned to Linda Kolkena's offense against Betty. He did the best with what he had, to save his client despite herself.

First he told the jury of the two snide little notes Linda had written to Dan on a stack of Betty's bills: "This is for the fat one," and "Now we know how she keeps her girlish figure." He pointed out that Linda had been the one to sign the letters canceling Betty's insurance policies, immediately after the 1986 divorce. Earley then produced the deed to Betty's house, which Betty had received after the divorce, notarized by Linda, in letters as big as Betty's own name. The defense team had later found the deed in Betty's files, ripped to shreds. Earley liked this item so well he had taped the torn pieces of the deed back together so that the jury could see this example of one woman's needless cruelty toward another.

Then, there was Betty's perception that Linda was ruining her reputation. "It seemed I was the topic of Linda Kolkena's conversation most of the time," Betty said. "She told a lot of stories on me. Humiliating, embarrassing, flatly untrue things ... 'Betty was crazy, Betty was sick ... Betty had come to their house in the middle of the night. Betty had taken things from their nightstands ...' Things like that." About the only detail Earley forgot to mention was the wedding china.

He moved inexorably onward, toward the crime, to the state of mind that led to the killings.

"During the beginning months of '87," Earley asked Betty, "what was your feeling about your life and what was going on around you?"

Her answer was disjointed. She felt, she said, that she had been reduced to a beggar and a jailbird, without cause. From November 1, 1986, forward, she said, her face crumpling into tears again, "I was a basket case ... I was thrown in jail ... I don't remember being in jail. I know that I was there. I was handcuffed, mug shots, and everything else. I was literally in shock. To me, that was the left, the right, and *bam!* I never got up after November 1, 1986. I was just down for the count. I couldn't deal with anything ... The *left*, to me, was the kids' situation, not seeing the kids; and the *right* was the sale of the house out from under me with no control; then, *right between the eyes* was cutting off all the money—being absolutely, totally unreasonable ... just, you know, 'Die! Get out of my life! Get out of my life, go away, I owe you nothing. I have everything, you have nothing, and that's what you deserve!' I never recovered from that. I still never have recovered from that ...

"So much of my life was all wrapped up in my husband, home, and my children, that when all three of those things were gone, there really was not anything else." Her voice trembled, but she did not cry. "I would just get up in the morning, and I would have nowhere to go, nothing to do. I didn't have to go grocery shopping, do laundry. I didn't have to drive the kids to school. I didn't have to do all the things that I always did. I was just lost," she finished, shrugging, with one of her apologetic, uncertain little smiles.

In the best of all worlds, Jack Earley wanted Betty Broderick to admit that she behaved deplorably toward her kids, that she had hurt them with her mad phone calls, and that she should have taken them back, financial settlement or not.

He was of course dreaming. Betty refused to admit that she had been irresponsible toward the children—but she at least tried to explain her behavior. It was, she said, always grounded in fear.

"When Dan first walked out, I was left with four children, with no security in a home or a car, no money in the bank, no plan of where I was going to get anything. I knew I was not capable of supporting these kids ... I just needed it all decided before I took on the responsibility of our children ... I was too nervous, too scared, totally distrustful of Dan Broderick ... To me, he was capable of giving me the four kids and just cutting off everything ..." And, she finished, she wasn't emotionally capable of handling even herself anymore, much less four children. "I wasn't handling anything!"

Earley led Betty through all the mounting pressures on her in the final, fatal year of 1989, at last arriving at the weekend prior to the killings, when she had received the two letters from Cuffaro.

"I felt like I was dying ... the legal stuff was killing me," she said. "My back had been hurting me for the last two years. I had not slept for the last two years. My skin was the worst that it had ever been, from stress. I had headaches from biting my jaw so tight ..."

Then, early the next morning, she said, she saw the legal letters "out of the corner of my eye" and decided to read them carefully. "But I knew it was not good news, because I have never gotten good news from a legal envelope." Her face began to crumple and redden again. With Betty, the facial collapse always came before the tears.

"I was sick of it!" she shouted. "It was just more of the same, more of the same, more of the same! Threats! Manipulation! ... And I was really mad at myself for not being able to get the kids back. Dan was delaying, putting Walter [Maund] through the same kind of hoops that he put Tricia Smith through ... He was going to divert us through contempt orders, criminal court. It was just the nightmare starting all over!"

She began to cry harder. "Another thing was that it was two days away from my birthday," she said. "I was just standing in that kitchen saying, you know, 'Jesus Christ! I'm turning forty-two years old! I have been put through this bullshit since I was thirty-five, seven years of my life wasted!'"

Her voice echoed off the walls as she rushed on, in a stream of consciousness, outlining her last thoughts before she got in her Suburban and drove across town to Dan's.

"... I haven't been able to get a job, or make a decision about where I'm living, or help my kids, or do anything! And I kept hearing him say it would never be over ... I was just a mess! Everything came down on me, and I just couldn't stand it another minute ... them telling people I'm a child molester, that I'm crazy, an unfit mother! I just couldn't stand it another minute," she said, nearly shrieking now. "I would rather be dead! I had no life left! That is how I felt!"

She got in the car to go down to the beach. But, instead, she said, "I thought that I am just going to go over there and talk to him and tell him that I just can't stand this anymore, it has to stop. It is ruining everyone, ruining me, ruining the kids ... I just thought the whole thing was so senseless ... They were married. They had everything! Why couldn't they just let me and the kids have a life?" Her voice was steady now, the tears .gone.

"What were you going to do when you got over there?" Earley asked.

"Just talk to him, like I had before, just tell him, 'If you don't cut this out, I'm just going to kill myself.' I wanted to kill myself right in front of him ... Just splash my brains all over his goddamn house!"

It was purely coincidental, she said, that when she got to Dan's house, she discovered a house key that had belonged to Kim, laying in the front seat of her car in a box of miscellaneous keys she was moving to her condo. Then she remembered that she always carried her gun in the center compartment of her handbag, which she said had been locked in the car, when she got into it earlier. It was only on the spur of the moment, as she parked in front of Dan's house, she said, that she decided to take the gun with her, "as a show of force—a way to make him listen to me." How this incidental fit into her earlier talk of suicide was never clear.

When she arrived in the bedroom, Earley asked, "Were Dan or Linda up?"

"I didn't meet either of them up, no," she said.

The audience waited with interest. In his opening, Jack Earley had said, one of them cried, 'Call the police.' Now, surely, the courtroom was about to hear that she was provoked, frightened, spooked into her heinous act.

"What happened when you went into the door?" Earley asked.

"I pushed the door open a little more than it was. I just stood in there. And it looked like Linda moved, and she went toward Dan, and Dan went toward the phone."

"Did anyone say anything?" asked Earley. What followed was an exchange that would come back to haunt him in the second trial. But it sounded good now.

"I don't know," she said. "... I don't know what happened because it was dark to me. I don't know if their shades were down or if I was in shock ... it was dark. I didn't see, I didn't hear. Everything happened that fast."

"What did you do?" Earley asked.

"I went into the room to talk to them or to wake them up or something. They moved, I moved, and it was over." Did Dan speak, asked Earley?

"I hardly really remember being there at all," she said. She was calm now, her red face gone. She was concentrating. "I told people afterward that I thought that Dan said something. I thought that he did. I thought that when I got around the bed, I had a gun in my hand, and he said, 'You got me.' I don't know. This is all what I thought later, that he was saying to me, 'Don't shoot'."

"What did you do?" asked Earley.

"I grabbed the phone out of the wall and ran out." The reason she did that, she said, was because "I didn't want him to call the police and have me arrested."

"Once you were in jail," Earley asked, "can you describe what your feeling was?"

She responded quickly, almost smiling.

"When I was first in jail, I don't remember being there ... And then I started coming

383

out of it a little, and then I slept. I was able to sleep for the first time in what seemed like interminable years to me. I was happy to be locked in a dark, safe little world where nobody could get me."

"Are you happy about what you did?" Earley asked. "Well, of course not," she snapped. "No. Not at all." "Do you feel responsibility for the things you have done?" "Yes." Period.

"Has that been an easy thing for you to get in touch with?" he asked. "No." Period.

"I have no further questions, Your Honor," said Earley.

It was nearly three P.M. Little more than an hour of the day was left—but it belonged to Kerry Wells. At last, after all these months, Wells would have the opportunity to exchange her first words with the woman she wanted to imprison for life.

Chapter 36

Kerry and Betty

Betty spent most of the recess crying, said Pasas, who sat with her in the tiny holding tank beyond the courtroom. When she returned to court, tears still streaming, she looked worse than she had before. Her mascara was smeared, her face was swollen, she had eaten off her lipstick; even her curls had fallen flat. She carried a wadded ball of Kleenex in her hand. As she took the witness stand, she kept her face down, looking at no one.

Kerry Wells marched to the lectern with barely a glance at the weeping killer and commenced:

"We have covered quite a few subjects over the past couple of days with you," she said crisply, without preliminaries. "And I have quite a few questions to ask you. I may not be going chronologically, and if I am talking about something that you are not following, you make sure to let me know. Okay?"

The transformation in Betty was instant. Her face cleared, the tears stopped, her eyes focused on the slender young district attorney standing rigidly before her. Betty Broderick knew the time for crying was done. Now was the time for concentration. Concentrate.

In ten minutes, even the puffiness disappeared. For the next two days, this would be a game of wits, two women vying for control. It was alternately funny, embarrassing, and absurd. And, it was always a battle of styles.

Wells seemed too disgusted with Betty Broderick to even look at her. Instead, each time she approached the witness stand with an exhibit, she stood behind her, arms folded across her chest, chin jutting, literally looking down her nose at Betty through her sliding spectacles, so that Betty was obliged to twist around in her chair to face her inquisitor. Earley promptly objected that it was rude, and Whelan agreed. Wells had at least to face the defendant.

Wells's first purpose was to portray Dan Broderick as a reasonable man who had done everything in his power to leave his wife peaceably—and fairly—to begin a new life, but had been thwarted every step of the way by a vengeful woman determined to destroy him rather than let him go. The only reason Dan Broderick had gotten a restraining order, then begun levying his fines, filling his contempts, and finally jailing her was because he was "at his wit's end" trying to control this wild woman who, as Wells often remarked, "lies about almost everything!"

But Betty consistently defied the portrait Wells was trying to paint. At times the raw edge of her rage and ego showed; sometimes she retorted with irritability, sarcasm, or condescension. But, in the main, the harder Wells hammered at her, the more docile and obsequious Betty became. She was usually only polite, confused, and, beyond all else, eager to make Wells understand. She wanted Wells to like her.

But Wells never did figure out that an ounce of sugar would get her a lot further

385

with Betty Broderick than all her pounds of salt. By contrast to Betty, Wells only sounded harsher by the hour, increasingly unsympathetic not only to Betty, but also insensitive to the larger women's issues which Betty Broderick symbolized to countless aging, divorced women everywhere.

Wells began with Dan's fining system, which was a mistake. For one thing, she was not in firm command of the chronology of the long Broderick divorce war. Plus, by now, as even many of Dan's friends would admit, his informal fines were not among his most attractive tactics. But Wells was determined to defend them from the outset.

"It was the vandalizing of the [Coral Reef] home that led up to Dan ultimately fining you in your alimony, wasn't it?" Wells demanded.

No, Betty corrected her—the fining didn't start for at least eight months after the Coral Reef house had been sold. And the fines were never for vandalism—only for her language.

Wells was good at hiding her own confusion. Never mind, she snapped. The point was still the same: Dan's fines, whenever they occurred, were lawful, were they not? No court-ordered support was in effect at the time, was it? He was paying her $9,000 a month out of the goodness of his heart, was he not? He was merely withholding money to which she was legally not even entitled—wasn't that true? "If he really wanted to be a real jerk," demanded Wells, "he didn't have to pay you anything, did he?"

Betty stared at Wells in momentary bewilderment. "Right," she finally agreed, quietly. Dan Broderick really didn't have to pay her anything.

Wells's apparent lack of empathy for any long-term wife and mother who had been suddenly left dependent on the largesse of the departing husband always verged on the startling. Betty Broderick's talk of "fair share" seemed alien to her, at least in the courtroom.

Next Wells plopped a thick stack of checks down in front of Betty, showing that Dan had been paying all her bills during their separation, and writing her personal checks, too. His checks were written to nearly every major department store in town. Wells selected one to show Betty. It was made out to Saks Fifth Avenue.

"Did you shop at Saks?" demanded Wells.

Betty looked at her with such innocent surprise that half the courtroom smiled. "I shopped everywhere," she said.

"And what is this bill for—$425?" Wells demanded sarcastically, waving another bill. "A fur?"

"Huh? $425?" Betty repeated, staring at Wells in astonishment. "For a fur?"

Earley buried his smirk in his papers.

Undaunted, Wells next waved a check for $3,000 under Betty's nose. It was made out by Dan to Betty. And what, Wells demanded to know, in the smug, theatrical manner of one who has just uncovered the smoking gun, had Betty written on the bottom of that check? "What did you say?"

Whereupon, Elisabeth Anne Broderick, who had never wanted a divorce at all and, certainly, in early 1985, didn't believe that one would ever really occur, was obliged to read her private little note to her husband aloud before the court. She blushed, her voice was soft.

"Thanks, sweetie," is what it said.

Presumably, in Kerry Wells's eyes, she had just exposed more of Betty's lies—because she still wasn't done. She handed Betty another check with another written notation, and asked her to read it. "Thanks, hon," Betty recited, almost whispering.

"Mrs. Broderick," challenged Wells, "you made the impression that you were being left destitute in February of '85 ... that you did not have any money ... That is not true, is it?"

"It was true. In my eyes, yes, it was true," said Betty vaguely. But she was no longer focused, her eyes drifted into her lap. Her mind was at least temporarily lost, somewhere back in 1985, amid those still hopeful little love notes she had written on two checks so long ago, in her pathetic bid to woo back home again the man who was, at that time, still her husband.

Nearly every woman on the jury looked pained, and so did a few of the men. Particularly Walter Polk.

Not that Wells failed entirely. Far from it. Time and again, she showed the jury examples of Betty's assorted evasions, exaggerations, and outright lies. Time and again, she pushed Betty into corners where this woman— who can even tell you today what her street address was in Boston in 1970 and recite the phone number, too—could only shrug helplessly and innocently claim, "I can't remember."

The sale of the Coral Reef house was a good example. Wells wanted Betty to admit that not only did she know that Coral Reef could be sold without her permission, but that she had also been represented in negotiations by a competent attorney, Dan Jaffe.

Betty denied it all. Jaffe had never been her attorney of record, she said, since Dan wouldn't pay his retainer. Nor did she recall Jaffe ever urging her to sign any papers concerning the sale of Coral Reef. She remembered only that "he was upset that he had come all the way down to San Diego" but did not get his retainer.

Wells later summoned Dan Jaffe to testify that he had spent the day trotting from the office to the car in order to consummate the house sale, a deal he thought was excellent for Betty. But she wouldn't agree. Instead, she had driven him to the airport, saying she would think about it.

* * *

Whether Betty was deliberately lying or truly confused remains among the lingering enigmas of this tale. Either way, it was a pattern throughout both her trials. At times, she recalled too little when it would have benefited her so much more to openly recall it all, if she honestly could. And there were so many of these damaging, transparent little memory lapses. At heart, it always seemed to reduce to a matter of her pride. Some things, usually small things, simply seemed to embarrass her too much to face.

387

To this day, Betty's personal ethic remains her own private puzzle. Throughout two trials, she would admit to major offenses—including double homicide—but deny other obscure, largely irrelevant incidents. Yes, she would readily agree, she threw a champagne bottle through a window—but not the umbrella. Yes, she stole the wedding list, but she never defaced a photo of Dan and his father. No, she hadn't taken photographs of Dan and Linda at Kim's graduation—but, yes, she had taken pictures of even their bathroom at his Cypress house.

In the end, it was pick and choose. When was she lying, when was she telling the truth? Had she truly forgotten some things in her stress and anger, or was she merely being manipulative, as the prosecutor insisted? None of it was relevant to the fact of murder, of course—only to Betty Broderick's credibility.

But all the trivia added up. Not least, by her own inconsistencies, Betty also saved Wells from looking like a fool for even pursuing some of these childish incidents.

"I keep telling Betty, just tell the truth about the little stuff," Earley said later, tiredly. "But some things she just will not admit to. It's going to take her some time."

The first full day of Kerry Wells's cross-examination of Elisabeth Anne Broderick was surreal, out of this world, from beginning to end. It bore no resemblance to a murder trial. It was now an obscenity trial, it was divorce court, it was two women, both wives and mothers, sparring all day long over everything from how best to care for children and husbands, to the price of clothes, to the precise time Betty Broderick first learned the meaning of the word cunt. It went on from 9:00 A.M. until 4:15 P.M., when court was finally adjourned—at which time, the TV cameras captured it all in one classic scene for the five o'clock news:

There on the witness stand sat Betty Broderick, wearing her Madonna smile, completely composed, her expression a blend of satisfaction and sympathy for the poor prosecutor—who was sitting at her table, bent over, clutching her head with what was obviously a triple-strength Excedrin headache. Five minutes before court adjourned, in fact, in a sidebar conference with the judge out of hearing of the jury, Whelan had asked her with some concern, "Are you okay?" No, Wells had responded. "I'm feeling horrible, that's okay."

"Hee hee ... I actually felt sorry for her," Earley chortled later, happier than he had been in days. "I wanted to go over afterwards and ask if she was going to make it, but I was afraid she'd hit me."

Wells had begun the day with obscenity. She was determined to show that Betty was lying when she said she spewed vulgarities into Dan's answering machine only because she felt it had been deliberately placed there, with Linda's voice on it, to block her contact with the children. Wells wanted to prove—and she did—that Betty's invective occurred whenever the mood struck her, even when her children were on the line. Wells often seemed more preoccupied with demonstrating that Betty Broderick was an abusive mother than a murderer.

She spent half the morning playing more than a dozen tapes of Betty's uglier messages.

"I'm embarrassed to say I know you guys ..." said Betty in one, because if her

388

children lived with Dan and the cunt, "then obviously you must approve."

Betty listened without expression. She would never betray a trace of shame or guilt over these messages—only anger at Dan and Linda for driving her to such extremes.

"I was very upset that the children were horribly dressed, had no manners," she told Wells matter-of-factly. "They were not the children I was raising. They were out of control ... they were very good children before this all started." She denied telling Rhett to "go beat up Daddy." Why would she say something like that? she asked Wells, seemingly genuinely confused. Rhett was too small to beat up anybody. Triumphantly, Wells played another tape.

"You've got to learn to stick up for yourself," Betty said to Rhett. "You've got to speak up to Daddy and the cunt ... He's ruining your lives and killing you ... [he] treats you like a little piece of shit, and he's a coldhearted bastard fucking an office cunt ... what kind of a parent is that? ... Go fight. Beat up Daddy ..."

It became a minor ritual: Wells would march to the recorder, punch the button, play a Betty message, shut the machine off, then turn to Betty Broderick, grim-faced, with arms crossed, and call for an explanation which, of course, was never there. Betty could no more rationalize her language or her memory lapses than she could explain why she had run her Suburban into Dan's front door. Either you understood impulsive rage, and the memory failures that sometimes go with it, or you didn't. That was it.

Next Wells was in hot pursuit of the word cunt. It was a mindless chase, resulting only in one conclusion: Betty didn't remember when the word had entered her vocabulary. But Wells was so determined to prove one more Betty lie that she seemed not to notice how ludicrous she was making the State of California look.

Wasn't it true, Wells demanded, that Betty had always claimed she never even heard the word cunt until Gail Forbes used it after being shown the *Dicta* picture Linda had allegedly sent—which was not until December of 1986? Yet here it was, on one of Dan's tapes, seven months earlier. How did Betty explain that? Wells waited in triumph, arms crossed.

Betty only shrugged. She had been through so much, she said, she couldn't remember sequences very well. "I don't know precisely when I got that picture," she said. All she really remembered was that it was Gail Forbes who taught her the word cunt. "But maybe I'm mixed up when Gail said that." She offered Wells one of her sweetest smiles of helpless apology. She was sorry not to have the correct answer for Sister Claire Veronica.

Wells glared at her icily. "Mrs. Broderick, isn't it true," she then demanded in one of the trial's more indelibly preposterous moments, "that you were referring to Linda as 'The Cunt' from the very beginning of this separation?"

Wells then played some more tapes. Betty listened without reaction. Wells finally shut the recorder off. Well? If Wells was searching for a vein, she had missed again. Mildly, Betty tried to explain herself.

"This ordeal strung out for so many years, that by the end, for two, three years, that was my common, everyday conversation," she told Wells quietly. "I always called Dan a fuckhead and her cunt. I never used their names. I always said he was fucking the cunt. That is just what I always said ... I know, out of context here and stuff, it sounds obscene. [But] It was just water off a duck's back way back then, because that was just the long-established facts. That is the way that it was." She shrugged.

"Did you think that was truly water off a duck's back, when it came to your children and how they were responding?" Wells asked through gritted teeth.

"Yes," said Betty, exasperated. "... I said some nasty, disgusting, puke-out things," she said, because "I was puked out!" But, she insisted, "It was not shocking to anyone, especially not to Dan or Linda, my children."

Wells moved on to Linda, always the last item on everybody's agenda in this trial. Back to the tape recorder.

"Oh, no, cunt, it's you again," said Betty into the machine in July, 1986—just before she had received her bifurcated divorce. "... Your mere existence is a filthy statement on human life. You're like the scum of the earth. People like you are not new ... they've been around since the beginning of time. Same old story ..."

Wells peered at Betty with pursed lips. She looked like a woman who had just finished cleaning out a Roach Motel.

"That was a message you left directly, specifically, to Linda Kolkena, right?"

Yup, Betty agreed tiredly. It was one of the first messages she ever left on Dan's new machine ... "That machine was answered by Linda Kolkena when she came home. She heard the messages, she made those recordings, she edited out what she didn't want ... It was her operation. And the only purpose of this answering machine was to make his case against me. Other than that, he had nothing against me ..."

Wells asked next if Betty hadn't often threatened to kill Dan and Linda before their wedding. Little in trial seemed to anger Betty more.

"No. That is one of the biggest black lies going around this town for a year before that wedding!" she said hotly. "The night they informed my children they were getting married, they started this nonsense about me coming to the wedding with a machine gun and killing everyone, that they were going to hire helicopters, armed guards ... How do you think that made me feel?"

She agreed with Wells, however, that Rhett had kept asking her if she was "going to kill Daddy?" But, she said, it was an idea planted in the child's mind by Linda and Dan, not by her.

Wells marched to her tape recorder. In this message, Betty had told Dan: "Lee Lee told me that you are afraid of me. You better be afraid of me."

Betty smiled at Wells, amused. "Around the wedding time," she said, "the girls told me that 'Daddy is afraid of you.' I thought that it was very funny. I said, 'Good, I hope he stays afraid of me.'"

But, before the wedding, then, Wells pressed, hadn't Betty threatened to kill Dan? Betty looked almost surprised. "Oh, yes," she said. "I have done that probably through my whole relationship with Dan Broderick."

It was so disjointed, so irrational, so nuts. The jurors looked dazed. Nobody was taking notes anymore.

"You made jokes about it," asked Wells, "[that] you were bigger than he was, he was a wimp, you could beat him up?"

Betty stopped the game. "Dan Broderick," she told Wells icily, "was never afraid of me."

In the final analysis, Betty blamed Linda more than Dan for conducting "a smear campaign against me ... She was just making a real ass out of me in public by telling people that I had said and done these things that I had never said and done. The boys will tell you that."

At which point Kerry Wells delivered her lowest blow of the day—and also the most unfair one, since Jack Earley had never been allowed to interview the two Broderick sons.

"Mrs. Broderick," said Wells, her tone one of elaborate, pointed condescension, "I've talked to your boys."

Earley objected, and Whelan sustained him, although it was too late: now the jury knew, by innuendo, if nothing more, that Betty's sons were saying something pleasing to the prosecutor, whatever it was.

Wells wound up the morning session by trying to humiliate Betty over the bizarre Christmas letter she had sent to the Broderick family after Dan left her, containing the picture of Dan and Linda, along with their own wedding picture. Betty denied remembering that she even did it. When Wells pressed, Betty exploded in embarrassed frustration, in an emotional monologue bound to lead the five o'clock local news.

"I honestly don't remember these things," she wailed. "I was operating under the most outrageous stress levels that any human being could be under! ... I don't remember being in court. I was a crazy person! He was telling people I was crazy—[and] I went crazy! I was like this," she shrilled, suddenly going into a startling, absurd mime on the stand, rolling her eyes upward, shaking her head, flapping her hands, and sticking out her tongue. "You see pictures of me like this, you know—like I'm some kind of electrified crazy person!" But the fact is, she said, calming, "I honestly, sincerely don't remember these things. If it was not for my sporadic scribblings and stuff in the diary, this would all be a blank to me. That is the only way I can piece things together."

Then in another of those ingratiating little remarks that always left Wells white-lipped with insult, "But keep trying," Betty urged helpfully. "And when you hit on something that I can remember, then I'll remember more."

The level of interrogation degenerated steadily, drifting ever further from the murders at issue. Wells next turned her attentions to what a bad wife Betty Broderick had always been, from the very start of the marriage. Her apparent purpose was to justify Dan Broderick's infidelity, if not his deception, too, by blaming Betty for virtually driving him out of the house. Wells didn't have much to work with, beyond the minor domestic spats Kim had described, plus remarks from a few former friends that Betty had sometimes nagged Dan over his personal vanity and workaholic ways. But Wells did her best. This was full-dress divorce court now.

Wasn't it true, Wells asked, that theirs had always been a troubled marriage, well before 1983 when Dan finally told Betty of his unhappiness? "Have you ever stated that you felt the marriage was a disaster from day one?" she asked.

Betty at first denied it, then amended herself to say that, yes, she had made that remark—but only because "If I was pregnant in the beginning, that, to me, was a disaster from day one ..." Also, she added, she may have later said she had always hated her marriage, "in retaliation to Dan saying the marriage had been a disaster since April 12, 1969, in the divorce trial."

"Had you threatened Mr. Broderick with a divorce on many occasions early on in your marriage?" Wells asked.

"... Occasionally, yes," Betty said, shrugging helplessly. "If it was a big fight or something ... I guess so."

Wells then marched her through everything from throwing ketchup bottles to tossing stereos. And what about the Brodericks' 1983 trip to Europe with Judge Milliken and his wife, Jeannie? That was the year Betty suspected that Linda Kolkena was now a part of her marriage, and Wells had obviously been briefed by the Millikens that it was a testy vacation.

"What was your treatment of him like during that trip?" demanded Wells.

Betty looked confused. "I don't know what you're referring to," she said.

Wells rose to full height, removed her spectacles, and, in yet another classic moment of this murder trial, demanded to know: "Were you nice to him?"

By now, nobody in this little courtroom would have been surprised if Wells next had asked: "And isn't it true that you also wore hair rollers and icky, gooey face creams to bed with Dan Broderick every single night?"

"Do you take any responsibility for any of the problems that occurred during the marriage?" Wells demanded.

Betty looked at Wells levelly. "Yeah," she said, pointedly. "I take fifty percent."

Wells turned to the matter of Betty's alleged black eye. Betty stiffened visibly. She didn't remember when it happened, she said vaguely. Maybe a few days before the Blackstone Ball. "I don't remember. It was with his elbow ... It wasn't any big deal. I didn't go to a hospital or anything ... there was no blood ..." But, she added firmly, "I was always afraid of him, and so were the children."

But when had this black eye occurred? Wells persisted.

Betty looked ready to either scream or cry. "I don't know," she stammered. "Sometime in 1987?"

"After the separation?" asked Wells, incredulous.

"No, no," said Betty, as close to crumbling under pressure as she would get in this trial. "I don't know. I don't know!" Whether she was lying, or just embarrassed, her misery was real. She did not want the matter of a black eye to be an issue in this trial. But, she knew, Jack Earley did. She was caught between taking her lawyer's advice and preserving her own personal ethic.

Wells wanted her to retract the black eye altogether. "It wasn't a black eye, was it,

Mrs. Broderick? You had been crying because you had a fight before the Blackstone Ball. You had mascara all over your eyes because you had been crying. He did not give you a black eye, did he?"

Betty's composure was gone. Her eyes practically begged Wells to back off this one topic. "Unless there were major, major injuries, like blood, broken bones, and things," she told Wells softly, "I didn't consider at the time that I had been improperly handled."

But Kerry Wells, supposed expert in battered women syndrome, would not back off. Whether Betty Broderick was actually a battered woman or not, prevailing wisdom suggests that most battered women hide it in shame. But Wells now taunted Betty with her silence. If Betty had been physically battered, why hadn't she discussed it before now? If Dan gave her a black eye, why didn't she write about it in her book? Why had she even denied it? "In fact, you have told reporters that he never touched you, haven't you?" demanded Wells.

Betty finally snapped. "That's not true, is it?" she said sarcastically. "We have five children. He obviously touched me." Reporters stirred happily. Hell with murder. The catfight was heating up.

Wells moved on. What about this alleged suicide try in 1983? Betty had slit her wrists and taken every pill in the house? Was that correct? Yes, said Betty, meekly. "We didn't have many pills, but, yes." Yet she had not seen a doctor later? No. "Dan was a doctor. He taped them up."

And did she have scars from that incident? inquired Wells politely. If so, "Can I see?"

What followed, in a murder trial replete with classically absurd scenes, was yet another one.

Wells marched to the witness stand. Betty showed her wrists. "They're there and there and there," she told Wells, helpfully pointing them out. "This one is better," she explained, pointing to her left wrist, "because I'm right-handed."

Wells peered. Then, having finished her inspection, she violated all the rules: "I'm sorry, Your Honor," she told Whelan. "For the record, I don't see what the witness is showing, but I won't pursue it."

Earley leapt to his feet, yelping at the impropriety of Wells's editorializing. Whelan only shrugged. If Earley wanted his client to show the jury her wrists so they could search for scars themselves, that was fine with him.

It was fine with Betty, too. She popped out of her chair, eager as a child at last liberated from some formal, adult dinner table, and began walking down the row of jurors, holding out her wrists for them to see, chitchatting confidentially every step of the way.

"I used a man's razor," she told Southwick and others in the front row. "I'm right-handed, I cut myself three times here. I'll show you ... That is a scar," she said, as she made her way down the jury box. "That is another scar: that would be the third one on that hand. On this hand ..."

Wells finally howled in objection. Whelan almost smiled. "Don't talk to the jury,

Mrs. Broderick. Just point it out with your finger."

Betty smiled apologetically and shut up. By then she had gotten to the last juror anyway. She scampered back to the witness stand, looking completely pleased to have at last been permitted to make some small personal contact with these twelve silent strangers. Whether they saw scars or not was anybody's guess. They remained, as always, inscrutable.

Not that it mattered. All this little sideshow added up to was more work for Jack Earley, who was now obliged to hunt up a cosmetic surgeon, who would later testify in a five-minute appearance that there were in fact discernible scars—at least on Betty Broderick's left wrist.

Compounding the absurdity of the suicide scars scenario, Kerry Wells wanted to have it both ways. During the first trial, she wanted there to be no scars on Betty's wrists, no serious suicide attempt. But she had revised her thinking before the second trial: One reason Dan Broderick had been obliged to lie about his affair with Linda for so long, she then argued, was because "He was afraid she would kill herself—after all, she'd tried it once."

And why had the supposedly perfect mother dumped her children on their father after he moved out? Wells asked next. Like so many other questions, it was one Betty could have answered with honesty to her own benefit—had she not been so saddled with guilt over her own failure to do the picture-perfect thing.

And so she waffled, she evaded, she never really answered. Her shame was transparent. She burbled on about her father's birthday party, and the rats. But she never told the whole truth. Instead, she said, again, "I really don't remember a whole bunch of this stuff from way back there ..."

Eloise Duffield puckered, so did even the younger jurors. Earley burrowed into his papers, waiting for this squall to pass. He had, of course, begged Betty just to be honest—"But she just can't admit that she used her kids."

Typically, Wells couldn't drop the topic while she was ahead.

"Do you remember telling people that you dumped your kids off at Dan Broderick's house because if you weren't going to be Mrs. Dan Broderick, you weren't going to take care of the kids?" she demanded.

Yeah, said Betty. She remembered that. Then, in a gush of spontaneity, in a voice of anger and pain: "I did want him to be more involved with the children," she said, fighting tears. "He was thinking of needing 'his space,' having his second childhood, wanting to be alone ... he had left me with the kids ... with the rats and everything. He didn't offer any help. I was overwhelmed. I wanted help. I wanted him to know how hard it was, how difficult, how time-consuming it was to do the job I was doing with those kids. I wanted him to get involved!"

It was a touching speech. Wells was untouched.

"You wanted to punish him, didn't you?" she accused. "Make his life miserable by dumping four kids in an empty home, full-time?"

"If that's what you want to say," said Betty tiredly.

Earley finally rose to his client's defense. "If bringing your kids to their father is

394

'dumping them,'" he objected, "that is [Wells's] definition. Calling that house or Dan Broderick a 'dump site' is argumentative." Sustained.

So far, apart from the theater, not much new had emerged from the rhetoric of the day. Wells did, however, stumble over one somewhat surprising little item. For a year prior to her trial, Betty had always insisted that she never once exchanged a single word with Linda Kolkena. But now, in court, that turned out to be untrue.

"Didn't you have a confrontation with Linda once when you were in the [Cypress] house? You went in the house, and you were not supposed to be there, and you were yelling at her and scared her?" asked Wells.

"I let her in the house in 1986," Betty agreed. But she denied any confrontation. "I said, 'I just wanted to see who you were.' But I don't know that that scared her." Wells pressed. Hadn't Betty used "vulgar language, obscene words at that time?"

As always, Betty pleaded memory lapse. "It was a very long time ago."

Asked about the encounter later, Betty only laughed it off, over the jail phone. "It was a two-minute exchange. The little cunt was so inconsequential, I just forgot about it."

Wells had so far danced around the legal mire. But now, it was time to step directly into the swamps, to confront head-on Jack Earley's argument that Betty Broderick had been driven to kill in large part by five years of "litigious assault" unleashed upon her, a common housewife, by her "gladiator" husband.

Earley's own charts showed more than thirty legal filings, nearly half of them for contempts alone. But Wells's point of view was always uncomplicated: No matter how many contempts had been filed, Betty had been convicted of contempt only four times and jailed only once—thanks to Dan Broderick's tolerance.

Betty's position, by contrast, was equally implacable: All of those contempts were strictly designed to delay the divorce proceedings while Dan accumulated ever more Epsteins, at the same time she was obliged to spend thousands in attorney fees to defend herself against them.

Wells began by stating that Betty had been convicted only four times.

What was she saying? asked Betty, incredulous. She was cited countless times.

"Well, that may be true," said Wells. "I'm talking about contempt actions now, when the notice was filed for contempt, and you actually had a hearing about it. There were only four of those, right?"

"Wrong," said Betty.

"How many are you saying there were?" asked Wells.

"A lot more!" said Betty. "Twentyish," at least. "I would go down to court on contempt actions, we would show up in the courtroom, there would be Judge Joseph; but Dan wouldn't show up ... Just drop it, change it, or move it."

"You were held in contempt at that first hearing, is that not true?" Wells asked.

"Which hearing ...?"

"April 2, 1987."

"Concerning what, is what I need."

"Concerning a phone message that began, 'Dear fuckface, I'm not paying one single payment on a car that has your name on it ...'" said Wells.

"I don't know," said Betty. "I would have to look at these whole things; I have to see them in perspective of the other things. If you know the answer, tell me the answer."

Wells showed her the contempt filing. Now did Betty recall that hearing? "Not really, no ... This is the hearing where they took my jewelry and my purse, dragged me off to jail?" asked Betty, befuddled.

"No," snapped Wells, exasperated.

"... because I don't remember things when I'm very much upset," Betty said again.

"That first hearing ... you were not sentenced to any jail time at all, were you?" demanded Wells, doggedly trying to advance her scenario that Betty had been warned time and again before the ax finally fell. "... You were held in contempt, [but] you were not sentenced to jail?"

"That is not the sequence at all," said Betty. "... That is not the first contempt hearing there."

"Are you saying that the first time you were held in contempt that you were sentenced to jail time?" asked Wells, sneeringly.

"I don't know," said Betty, faltering. "I don't think so ..." Wells's jaw muscles flexed. She wanted to believe Betty was deliberately evading, but, by this time, everybody else in court could see that Betty Broderick's mind was a genuine blur when it came to the contempt actions.

"Isn't it true," Wells persisted, "that the first time that you were held in contempt, you were simply warned. You were told this is contemptuous behavior, don't do it again, or you will be sentenced to jail time?"

"There were so many contempt things," Betty explained, apologetically. "But this is not even close to the first one in your hand. There were other ones where I represented myself first, then I was ordered to be represented by an attorney, then Tricia Smith came with me. Dan didn't show up. [That hearing] was put off. He didn't show up again, that was put off ... I don't know where these things fit in!"

Wells switched her approach. But wasn't the reason for all the delays on the court calendar, all the postponements, because Dan would purposely remove a contempt action from the calendar "in hopes that things would stop—is that not true?" Wells demanded. Betty didn't know.

Wells finally gave up and moved to the third contempt conviction— skipping over the second one in May, 1987, which resulted in the six-day fail term.

She didn't get jailed for that third one either, did she?

"Is this is the attorney's fees one, or the dog one?" Betty asked.

"On the third contempt action, three out of four, you were not sentenced to any jail time, correct? On the dogs one?"

"Oh, we're still on the dogs," said Betty, brightening like a schoolgirl with the right answer. "Okay. Right. No jail time on the dogs."

Wells clutched for professionalism in the face of this lunatic dialogue. It was not easy to find. "When I say, 'the dogs one,'" she said, gathering herself to a full posture of dignity, "that helps refresh your recollection ... [but] there were several different things that you were held in contempt for during that hearing, correct? ... It didn't just have to do with dropping the dogs off at Dan Broderick's house?"

Yes, it did, said Betty. All she remembered was returning from Tahiti and being slapped with a contempt for dropping off two dogs. "My daughter was there, she thought that it was funny ..."

"You thought it was funny," countered Wells, rifling through her files for the pertinent phone message, which she read aloud: "I hope that the puppies are shitting all over your house," Betty had said.

Patiently, Betty corrected her again. No, no, she said. The message Wells was reading "is years later, when there were puppies! When I put the dogs over there, they were dogs. But we had puppies several times."

Wells looked ready to faint. All in life she wanted at this moment was simply to make clear to the jury that, of all the contempts filed, Betty Broderick had only been convicted four times and jailed just once. Nor was she jailed on the fourth conviction, was she? Wells challenged.

No, Betty agreed. That was the one, she thought, where she was fined $16,000 in legal fees for Gerald Barry instead. And the one before that, she was fined $8,000 "for dropping off the dogs."

No matter how Wells tried to work it, it was not coming out right.

But those fines, she reiterated, were because Mr. Broderick had argued against jail, correct? demanded Wells, almost screaming now.

Betty couldn't remember. But, she said, with an ingratiating little smile, if that's what Kerry Wells said, it must be correct.

Throughout the trials, both attorneys were constantly sneaking in remarks that they knew were taboo, given Whelan's pretrial rulings. The game was to slip the jurors as much forbidden information as possible before being hushed by an objection from the other side.

And, before long, it was clear to everyone that the attorney who was slowest to object, who let the most pass without yelling bloody murder, was Jack Earley. By contrast to the sharp-tongued Wells, perpetually coiled as a cobra ready to strike, Earley was more like a sleepy, black snake napping in the sun. Wells had long since discovered that she could get away with a lot before Earley would stir.

And so, now, she decided to play a little more dirty pool: her new goal was to suggest to this jury that—despite all the grumbling they had heard about the Broderick divorce settlement, for all the mysterious absence of detailed financial figures in court, for all of Jack Earley's innuendos that Betty Broderick had been terribly cheated in the final judgment—she had actually been treated with complete fairness. She had won all that she deserved.

Wasn't it true, Wells asked Betty, that she had been awarded alimony of $16,000 per month? That she got her house, another $239,000 in the pension fund, plus all her furniture and the piano—"all of those things that you had requested, you got ... correct?"

Earley blinked, amazed, then leaped to his feet to shout an angry objection. Whelan of course upheld him—but, again, it was too late. The jury had heard big, big numbers, however incomplete they were.

Earley, on the other hand, would never be allowed to tell jurors precisely how ungenerous he thought Dan Broderick had been toward the mother of his four children. Never would Earley be able to explain to the jury precisely why it was that Betty had wound up, from an estate worth at least $2 million, and probably far more, with a cash settlement of only $28,000. Worse, he would never craft an illicit insert into his own arguments to compare with the brutal efficiency Kerry Wells had just displayed.

Wells had also figured out that certain small incidents—such as the scene at Kim's graduation—embarrassed Betty Broderick enough to make her twist the facts, or lie, in an effort to salvage her pride. She finally understood Betty's extreme sensitivity at being called Crazy Betty, too.

Now she attempted to exploit both those themes. Even if Dan and Linda were telling people she was crazy, asked Wells, why did Betty find that so surprising? After all, she was behaving in a crazy fashion, was she not? For example, wouldn't the fact that Betty had driven her car through Dan's front door "lend to such a rumor?"

"That might have been an instance where he drove me crazy, yes," Betty said quietly, eyeing Wells with new wariness.

So why was it all Dan and Linda's fault that rumors were going around that she was crazy? Did Betty take any responsibility herself for her own public image? Hadn't even the children's doctors agreed? Hadn't it been Dr. Ruth Roth, not Dan, for example, who canceled an Easter vacation on grounds that Betty was unfit?

Wells finally scored.

Sure, Betty spat sarcastically. It was, technically, Ruth Roth who said she shouldn't have her children that Easter weekend—but Roth was only another of Dan Broderick's hired guns. In reality, said Betty, nobody decided anything about her life except Dan. "Things were always ultimately in Dan Broderick's control," she said bitterly, sarcastically. "[But] he would tell the kids that the judge sent me to jail, the judge fined me. Dan—oh valiant soul—had nothing to do with it ..." Her anger, still so alive, chilled the air. Earley squirmed and looked at the clock, praying for recess. But, in the next moment, Wells lost her lead.

Hadn't Betty finally lost most of her friends because of her obsession with Dan?

Betty's face crumbled. Yes, she said, mumbling, all anger gone, she had lost most of her friends and quit most of her activities because she knew that she was no longer "good social company."

The courtroom was so still, Betty's thin voice so soft that reporters were straining to hear. Tears ran down her face. In her tenacity, Wells had hit home again, but, in the process, also helped create the indelible image of a pathetic, confused woman in ruins. Wells would never learn—at least not in this trial—when it was in her own best strategic interests to back off.

She finished the day on her harshest note so far. Obviously relying again on her interview notes with the Broderick boys, she asked: "Didn't you tell Danny that you were going to kill his father, and he should be happy about it because he would have all sorts of money after you killed his father?"

No, said Betty. Wells smirked.

She had talked to Danny, she again announced, pointedly.

Wells then accused Betty of telling her sons that if she killed Dan, everyone would be rich on their share of his $1 million insurance policy. "You don't recall [Danny] responding to you that the money would go to Linda, and you said, 'Well, I'll kill her, too?'"

Absolutely not. Betty's voice was calm, confident, traced with contempt.

"Did you ever make statements to Kim or Lee during [the fall of 1989] that 'we should just kill him now, we would get all the money, we would be rich?'" Betty looked as bewildered as she had been earlier about the $425 fur. Why would she say something like that? she asked Wells, "Because we wouldn't be rich."

Wells gazed at Betty with loathing. Would it refresh Betty's memory, she asked, to listen to tape-recorded interviews with her boys, made shortly after the killings? It was not a question, but a threat.

Betty paled slightly. "I'm not calling my boys liars," she said. "That was the day after. Everyone was very upset. The fact that the boys told you those things does not mean those things happened."

Earley stirred angrily. What the Broderick boys had said about Betty, he objected, was no more relevant than what they also said about Dan—and, Earley told the jury furiously, before Whelan or Wells could shut him up, "They talked about beatings from their father and all kinds of stuff!"

The day was finally over. It had been, if anything, a draw. If Wells had demonstrated that Betty Broderick was subject to selective memory lapses and great confusion, she had also failed to dislodge her from her position that she was a victim who had been driven to kill by unrelenting harassment.

Afterward, Jack Earley was a happy man. Betty had been too controlled, too articulate, and too detached from her acts of death to wrench many hearts. But Earley didn't care, because, in his view, Wells was worse: cold, harsh, unsympathetic, unsisterly in the extreme. "Kerry is doing me the biggest favor I could ask for—she's literally numbing the jury to the impact of Betty's language," he said. "And she's also showing the jury just how confused Betty was, even by 1987."

He was especially tickled that Kerry herself was now tossing off "cunts" and "fucks" in court as casually as "gollys" and "gee whizzes."

But Earley's jubilance didn't last. Tomorrow was the last day. Tomorrow Kerry Wells was finally going to get around to asking Betty Broderick exactly what had happened on the morning of November 5, 1989, and why.

Wells began her last round with Betty on Friday morning in much the way she had started two days earlier—poised over the tape machine, ready to swamp the jury with more obscenities, more evidence of child abuse.

"Do you recall telling [Danny] that you were not interested in having anything to do with him," asked Wells, "and when he asked why, you said, 'Daddy fucking his office cunt is very embarrassing, and you obviously approve.'" She was ready to play the tape.

Earley demanded a bench conference, where he again protested that Wells was so overdoing the obscenity tapes that it violated evidence rules against overkill. "This is not an obscenity trial ... there [have already] been tons of statements in tapes about her referring to Linda Kolkena as the cunt, the father as the fuckhead."

Wells argued that the tape was essential to prove that Betty was once again lying. Whelan listened gravely as the two attorneys gesticulated and whispered animatedly. From the audience, no one would ever have suspected that the weighty decision facing this silvery-haired, dignified-looking judge was whether to permit one more "cunt," one more "fuck" into his courtroom.

He ruled for Wells.

Triumphantly, she marched back to the tape machine and, one more time, Betty's chirping voice rang through the chamber—and, of course, Betty had said precisely what Wells said she did.

Betty listened without expression, then shrugged it off. "I don't remember these conversations," she said remotely. "I was obviously very depressed and upset about the situation ... the visitation and custody problem ..."

"Would you also tell Rhett that his father was a coldhearted bastard fucking an office cunt?" Wells demanded. Betty didn't remember that either. "If you have a tape of it, I probably told Rhett that," she said. "... I know that is what I felt."

The rest of the morning was a random chase to nowhere. Wells played more of Betty's taped messages—only to meet with more of the same shameless responses—and roamed over various visitation and custody disputes. The audience stirred restlessly. Jurors looked bored. Would Wells never get to the main event?

Finally, she did begin to approach the killings, starting with Betty's gun.

Wasn't it true, Wells asked, that "you would put the gun in your pocket whenever Dan Broderick was coming over to pick up the kids at the end of a weekend?"

Betty agreed. "There were about two or three times that I had the gun with me when Dan came to my house ... the last several times I had confronted or seen Dan Broderick, I had the gun with me ..." But she was carrying the gun, she explained, only for protection.

"You were actually just hoping that there would be a confrontation so that you would have an excuse to kill him, weren't you?" Wells accused.

No, said Betty. She never planned to shoot him.

And hadn't Betty been "angry" at Dan's announced plans that he intended to have a new family with Linda, asked Wells.

Angry? Betty paused for a moment, trying to wrap her mind around the question. Angry? Versus depressed, hopeless, defeated, jealous, resentful, fearful, sad, bitter, crazed?

Angry?

"I frankly didn't care," she finally told Wells. "... The [only] comment I made was, 'If they were going to have more children, why did they have to take mine?'"

Wells next suggested that Betty had waited to shoot Dan until his insurance policy for the children went into effect in September. Hadn't she specifically asked the insurance agent to let her know when the policy was implemented?

Sure, said Betty—she was very interested in that policy. "I was hyper ... wondering why it took him so long to follow through with the court order. If he ever let it lapse, I wanted [the agent] to let me know."

The insurance policy debate lasted several more minutes until, finally, Betty cut it off by asking Wells, in so many words, why she thought anybody would kill for a measely $1 million? Divided by the children four ways, it was peanuts.

Wells dropped the topic and got on to the killings. From there, it all moved fast, if not logically, to its baffling conclusion.

The closer this trial moved to the actual issue at hand—first-degree murder—the more Betty seemed to shrink in both tone and stature. Her voice grew quieter, more tentative. Even physically, she seemed to be contracting, sinking lower and lower into her chair, withdrawing from this bad thing that was about to be thrown at her, she knew, within minutes now.

In her final hour with Betty, Wells set out to strip her of any defense that she had acted in the heat of passion, sparked by reading the Cuffaro letters on Sunday morning. Although there were two letters, Wells focused only on the one referring to a possible jail sentence if Betty didn't shape up—and remarking on her "mental disease."

"You've changed your story about when you read this letter, haven't you?" asked Wells. "You knew that it was not going to help your defense if you had read it on Friday because it would give you time to calm down, correct?"

"I've never changed my story, because there is only one story," Betty retorted. Wells would not believe it. How could Betty say that she had gotten a legal letter from her attorney but not really focused on it?

Betty looked ready to explode. "I had been in this thing for seven years!" she shrilled, reddening. "I didn't open a lot of legal mail!"

Wells next tried, in vain, to force her to admit she had stolen Dan's house key from Kim weeks earlier—that she had planned murder all along.

Betty's face crumbled, and she began to cry. But, as usual, her words were more persuasive than her tears.

"I didn't have a plan! I just wanted to die ... I didn't want to live anymore!" she wailed into the silence of the courtroom. Her only thought, she said, was that Dan had to talk to her, that this legal nightmare had to end. He had to return her children. Through her sobs, she challenged Wells to "just read that letter—it's a horrible letter! They were just fucking me over! And what did they have to gain?" For purposes of this hour, Betty had given up on polite language. Her face was red and creased as a Danish cabbage. Wells looked utterly disgusted. The jurors looked transfixed.

401

And how was it that she just happened to have the gun in her car? asked Wells. It was such a logical question that it caused Betty to stop crying. Wells hated it when Betty cried; she thought it was such a phony, manipulative ploy. In fact, every time Betty even started to tear over, Wells would instantly call for a recess—but Betty invariably thwarted her. "No, no, I'm fine," Betty would tell Whelan apologetically, wiping her eyes with a Kleenex and instantly drying up.

The gun was in the car, inside her purse, Betty told Wells, because that's where she always kept it, for safety, when the boys were at her house. It was pure circumstance that she had it on the morning she drove to Dan's.

Wells let it go.

If she had only wanted to "talk" to Dan, Wells asked next, why hadn't she simply knocked on the door instead of sneaking into the house? Betty gave the same tired answer: "Because Dan wouldn't have opened it."

She had gone through the kitchen door and crept up the stairs, gun in hand, only to make him either listen or to kill herself. That, she said, was her only plan. And, "I was very scared ..."

And, at that moment, Betty Broderick looked very scared again, as she waited for Kerry Wells to ask her the next, obvious question: What had happened then?

But Wells didn't ask.

Instead, she skipped over the killings entirely. She asked a couple of trivial questions about Betty's calls from the Clairemont phone booth afterward, and then sat down. The People's cross-examination of Elisabeth Anne Broderick was done.

It was one of the most stunning—and, in hindsight, inept—tactical decisions any prosecutor could have made. Wells would never explain it later, beyond remarking vaguely that "we thought the jurors would see through her." But, obviously, Jack Earley's sly little remark in his opening statement, about how someone had shouted 'Call the police,' had worked. He had floated the bait, and Wells swallowed it. Wells was clearly afraid that, if she pursued Betty into the bedroom, where Wells had always insisted two helpless people were executed as they lay sleeping, she would only provide Betty with an escape hatch—an opportunity to say that she had been frightened, attacked, assaulted, or somehow otherwise provoked into firing her gun. Rather than risk it, Kerry Wells, prosecuting two counts of first-degree murder, simply left court-watchers, reporters, Whelan, the jurors, and, not least, Betty Broderick herself gaping in surprise.

Wells had spent two days on the divorce and nasty language, but not even five minutes on murder.

Nobody was more shocked than Jack Earley that Kerry Wells had skipped over the killing scene entirely. "I can't believe it—she bought my entire defense!" he later crowed in delight.

Best of all, no more nightly pilgrimages to Las Colinas now that Betty's testimony was done. No more futile, frustrating two-hour sessions, trying to wheedle her into displaying remorse for her crimes. It was over. "Now," Earley trumpeted, grinning ear to ear, "I don't have to talk to Betty anymore at all!"

Chapter 37

Jack's Parade

After Betty stepped down from the witness stand, there was even less pattern to Earley's case than to Wells's. For the next three days, about two dozen witnesses came and went, some of them on the stand for no more than ten minutes. It was a crazy quilt parade: schoolteachers mixed with young boyfriends, a maid, a police consultant who said panic shootings are common, the gynecologist who talked with Betty and Dan in 1984 about having her tubal ligation reversed. A neighbor of Dan and Linda's came to say he heard five rapid-fire shots, (indicating Betty hadn't shot at leisure); and three mental health experts testified that Betty was unwell at the time of her crime. Earley also called two of Betty's judges, mainly for pure meanness, since they were so protected by position, and Judge Thomas Whelan, that he couldn't ask them anything of real interest.

And scattered among them all was a long line of La Jolla women, friends of Betty's with the courage now to testify in the most sensational San Diego murder trial of the decade. They constituted the bulk of Earley's defense, although their testimony didn't add up to much more than a group statement that Betty Broderick was once a cheerful, fun-loving woman and devoted mother who had fallen apart after her husband left her and behaved in shocking ways.

But Earley's first witness after Betty—Dr. Don David Lusterman, the family psychologist from New York who specializes in infidelity—was perhaps the single most thoughtful, credible witness in the entire trial. His manner was quiet, calm, and unassuming. But Lusterman's strength was apparent from the minute he opened his mouth. He was an academic, a student of the human psyche, and a counselor who had worked with hundreds of couples damaged by infidelity. He was in court not to advance the cause of Betty Broderick, but merely to explain his findings. He had, in fact, never even met her.

There was nothing pedantic, obscure, or quirky about David Lusterman's opinions. He spoke in the universal language of purest common sense. Anybody who has ever been touched by a faithless relationship—or even considered how he or she might react in such a situation—could only agree with every word he uttered.

Lusterman also described Betty Broderick's early reactions to Dan's affair with Linda so perfectly that she cried quietly throughout most of his testimony. Even from across the room, this mild, detached stranger was addressing her feelings in a way that nobody else ever had. However remotely, it was perhaps the first real therapy she had ever received, either since 1983, when she first realized that Dan was having an affair, or in the aftermath of the killings.

Lusterman referred to the cheating spouse as the "infidel," to the cheated spouse as the "victim." And because it is almost always the male who is the infidel, said Lusterman, he consistently referred to the infidel as "he," to the victim as "she." At long last, somebody who didn't even know Betty Broderick was agreeing that, at least when it came to the infidelity, and the lies accompanying it, she was the victim, just as she always said.

Lusterman's testimony was simplicity itself: It is never the infidelity per se that is so devastating to the victim, he said, but the accompanying lies—and the longer the lies go on, the deeper the damage inflicted on the self-esteem of the victim, who has spent months, years, deceiving herself, trying to believe that what she knows to be true is really not true at all. Once the truth finally comes out, the victim commonly loses all confidence in herself, he said. If she had bought into the same lies day in, day out, for years, over breakfast, over dinner, every time he said he had to work late, then what was her judgment worth, as a parent, as a human being? It was, in Lusterman's mind, one of the most crippling of psychological blows—and no doctor could really heal it. Instead, he said, it was up to the infidel to begin the healing process by admitting the truth and apologizing for his lies. Those are the first keys to recovery for the victim, because, otherwise, her feelings, her suspicions, and her pain remain unvalidated. There is no "closure."

And, so far as Lusterman could tell, Dan Broderick was a classic case study in how not to handle infidelity, once it is out in the open. Instead of apologizing to Betty for the lies and hurt, once he told her about Linda, she was still the crazy one. He wanted to send her to a hospital, all because he had finally admitted that he had lied to her for years ... Dan never helped her let go of the rage because he never admitted to the lie," said Lusterman. "And when the infidel flees from all blame, it only binds the boil ... She was trying to establish her own sanity in the face of his lies ... but if he doesn't come through with some honesty and validation, she's totally canceled out."

Not incidentally, Lusterman found nothing unusual in Betty's subsequent obscenities, vandalisms, and other acts of violence. She had no other outlet for what he called her unrequited "hot rage." And not only Dan, but also her own family and friends denied her any right to her anger. What she needed was for people to say she was entitled to her rage, that she wasn't crazy. "You can't just expect victims to step over that phase."

Nor did it surprise Lusterman that, even up until Dan's wedding day—and after—Betty was still in an apparent state of denial, still deluding herself that he might yet come home. Victims of infidelity who have never really been confronted with the truth often resort to such illusions, he said. Likewise, divorce commonly means nothing to them, for the same reasons. In lieu of truth, pretense is always a viable alternative. In fact Lusterman added, in what was perhaps Kerry Wells's least favorite line of his entire testimony, he found it quite conceivable that Betty Broderick's denial might have lasted right up until the time she walked into Dan's bedroom and found him in bed with Linda.

There wasn't much Wells could do about this quiet, reasonable man, and so she

404

didn't try. Instead, she rose, and, with as much courtesy as her facial muscles would permit, asked:

"What if [the victim] had a narcissistic personality disorder?"

Lusterman only shrugged. He hadn't met Betty. Narcissism wasn't his specialty. He didn't know if she had other problems or not. He only knew that victims of infidelity very often react to the prolonged stress in ways that may look crazy—"But that doesn't mean they are."

And what about the influence of "plain old jealousy?" Wells asked.

""It's not the same," Lusterman told her. In fact, he thought it was "a vast oversimplification" to equate jealousy with the extreme mental abuse suffered by victims of infidelity who have been lied to for so long.

Wells started to argue that Dan Broderick had tried to be honest with Betty. But she thought better of that and sat down. The sooner David Lusterman got out of the courtroom, she clearly decided, the better.

Then came the rest of Earley's miscellaneous parade. Two teachers and one administrator from the elite Francis Parker School defied the school hierarchy's unspoken taboo against cooperating in this sordid case to testify for the defense anyway. All three praised Betty as one of the most attentive, active, best-loved mothers they had ever seen. Their reviews of Dan as a father ranged from fair to awful.

A school admissions official testified that, after the separation, both boys sometimes came to school in cold weather without jackets; that Rhett often arrived with shockingly dirty hair, ears, and clothes; and that both boys were occasionally sent to school so visibly ill that they were put to bed in the nurse's room until one of the parents came to fetch them—usually Betty, since the school could rarely locate Dan.

One teacher testified that when she once called Dan to discuss her concern about Danny's "acting out" in class, "I felt intimidated by his manner. He felt there should be no problem. It was something he didn't want to hear." Another teacher had nothing negative to say about Dan, but lavished praise on Betty, who, she said, would often come to school to have lunch with Rhett, and all the other children would swarm to her. "They were always more attracted to her when she came in the room than to me."

Wells tried to blame Rhett's colds on allergies. But the teacher said that if Rhett had allergies, Dan had never mentioned it to her. What's more, the woman added sourly, Rhett would then arrive at school the next day in exactly the same condition; so if he did have allergies, evidently nobody was doing anything about it. Wells finished by trying to excuse Dan as a busy, harried single father doing the best he could. If it ever occurred to her, in her own heart, that maybe he could have done better, it never showed.

Both P.J. Hathaway, Kim's sometimes date, and Jason Prantil, Lee's boyfriend at the time, were summoned by Earley, primarily for the purpose of impeaching Kim's testimony. Earley wanted both young men to agree that, contrary to her remarks on the witness stand, Kim had complained incessantly about Dan's poor treatment of her, thereby incensing Betty even further.

He failed. Both agreed that Kim had indeed griped loudly about what an insensitive cheapskate Dan was. But, as the curly-haired, blond Hathaway said, with a disarmingly grin, shrugging, so what? Didn't everybody have the same bitches about their parents? Prantil was no more helpful. Earley was wasting his time, trying to get these young people to tattle on each other.

Since Wells had already called two of Dan's housekeepers, Earley, determined to fight fire with fire, next called Maria Montez, who had worked for the Broderick family since 1976—and for Betty alone since 1985. After the separation, in fact, Montez and her son had moved in with Betty for several months, mainly because, Montez said later, Betty was so lonely. "I felt so sad for her. Sometimes she would just stay home all day and cry and cry," Montez said in her broken English. Nor was Maria Montez a fair-weather friend. Even after the homicides, she sometimes made the hour-long bus trip from her two-room home in one of San Diego's poorest Hispanic barrios to visit her former mistress in jail. "We understand each other," said Betty. "Don't ask me how. I don't do Spanish. But Maria and I know what we're saying to each other, even if nobody else can figure it out. We've been talking in half Spanish, half English and sign language for fifteen years."

Alas for Earley, Maria Montez, however well-meaning, was an ineffective witness, partly because she testified in Spanish with a translator at her side—"This is too important," she said. "And I want to be understood"—but also because she had nothing substantive to offer beyond her obvious affection for Betty Broderick. Still, in a trial centered largely around money and shallow social values, that was no small contribution, as Earley well knew. Montez, with her long black braid and gold front tooth, dressed in a cotton smock, was an affecting sight as she marched determinedly to the witness stand to do what she could for the woman who had befriended her for most of her adult life.

Maria had nothing bad to say about Dan Broderick. She only knew that the children loved Betty more, and when Mr. Broderick was home, "they were silent." Later on, after the divorce, she testified, they would sometimes hide in the bushes when Dan came to pick them up because they didn't want to go home with him. "And the only time Betty was happy was when the children were there," she said.

Montez's testimony was so benign that it was surprising to see Wells take her on. But Kerry Wells could never resist a target, no matter how innocent it was. And, in fact, Wells scored. She got Montez to admit that Betty had lied about Dan burning his own clothes. Montez also testified Betty said the reason she didn't have the children anymore was because Dan had taken them away by force one night and then called her "a drunk and a prostitute," which is why she couldn't regain custody.

Earley also hauled Judges Anthony C. Joseph and William J. Howett, Jr., into court. Both men initially resisted on grounds that it was improper, since they were, after all, judges. But Whelan, going the extra mile to avoid charges of legal cronyism in this, of all cases, ordered them to show up if Earley wanted them—although he also restricted Earley from asking them about almost anything except the missing divorce files. Earley would not be allowed to ask either judge to defend his decisions in the Broderick divorce matter. Both said they had no idea how the Broderick divorce files had vanished, but, in any event, they didn't need the files to render fair judgments. Joseph was puckish, obviously annoyed. Howett, a big, rumpled man, was more easygoing.

Earley was engaging in a pointless exercise, and he knew it. But he didn't care. In a case grounded in allegations of litigious assault, Earley was, at the very minimum, at least stripping judges of some of their precious veneer, simply by forcing them to sit there in front of the woman they had jailed and judged, and be judged themselves by twelve jurors. To her credit, Betty did not betray the faintest smirk of satisfaction.

But, again, Wells won the round by abruptly proposing to Whelan that the entire sealed divorce file [since recovered] be introduced into evidence. Since both Earley and his client seemed so concerned about those formerly missing files, she challenged, then why not let jurors read the entire five-year file for themselves?

Why not indeed?

Earley backed off his fiery rhetoric as fast as an alley cat confronted by a hungry coyote at the trash can. Wells had called his bluff. He objected. He didn't want the divorce files admitted into evidence.

"Dan was a very smart attorney," he explained later, sheepishly. "He wrote so many letters [to Betty and her attorneys] just for the record—he just sounds too reasonable. And the average juror wouldn't be able to see through that."

"What the fuck?" Betty yelled later over the jail phone, amazed. "I've got nothing to hide! What is Jack doing? I've been bitching about those goddamn sealed files for five years, and now my own lawyer makes it look like I'm sneaking around. Shit! What are people thinking now—that I was a child molester?"

What outraged her even more, she said, was the fact that Earley, as usual, hadn't even consulted her beforehand.

Then came Earley's procession of La Jolla ladies, nearly a dozen of them, ranging from casual associates of Betty Broderick to close friends. Some were divorced, some were married, mostly to lawyers. Some were socially prominent in La Jolla and San Diego, others were independent career women. Several were there because they had known Betty Broderick since the seventies when she had been a second mother to their children at her day-care center.

Most looked the La Jolla part—attractive, well-groomed, carefully dressed—and most were also visibly nervous as they milled about in the courthouse corridor, awaiting their turn on the witness stand. Like some of Betty's other, oldest friends who had jumped ship, refusing to get involved—Lynn McGuire, Judy Bartolotta, Kathy Saris, and Chris Michaelson—all these women could easily have avoided a subpoena, too, simply by promising to be uncooperative. But, for their own different reasons, they wanted history to record that they didn't run.

"I don't want to be here. I don't want to see myself on the evening news," said Melanie Cohrs. "But I feel like it's my duty. What she did was so very wrong, but Dan did some terrible things to her, too."

"He was evil, I'm not sorry he's dead," said Wilma Engel, still remembering the hateful letter she received from Dan years earlier for daring to criticize him.

"I think he drove her to it," said Ann Dick, a future Las Patronas president. "If he had given her enough money and the children, this whole tragedy could have been avoided."

But all these remarks were made out of court.

Once on the witness stand, none of the women who came to testify for Betty were allowed to say anything of real significance, partly because Wells objected constantly to any questions leading to even implied criticism of Dan Broderick—but also because Jack Earley didn't exploit them to the fullest. Each had anecdotal material about Dan Broderick's coldness, Betty's fears, Betty's demise. But Earley's only apparent goal seemed to be to move as many attractive, articulate women through the courtroom in cameo appearances as fast as possible to demonstrate to the jury that Betty Broderick once had a lot of respectable friends. Despite Pasas's meticulous interview notes, Earley barely seemed to know the difference between Candy Westbrook, a friend of both Brodericks since 1975, and Melanie Cohrs, a local child abuse activist who had watched Betty's disintegration up close in the final two years. Pasas held her head, watching her months of work go down the drain as Earley shuffled around the courtroom, basically treating each of these women like assembly line clones. Nearly every woman who came to court for Betty later expressed dismay at Earley's failure to utilize them to advantage. Even prosecution witnesses, such as Gail Forbes and Helen Pickard, would have contributed to the portrait of a woman in steady decline, had Earley asked them the right questions on cross-exam. "I never understood it," Pickard said later. "I was called by the prosecution, but I had a lot of good things to say about Betty, too. I thought I was going to get to tell both sides."

In fairness to Earley, however, Wells was vigilant as a hawk, on her feet objecting to even the most harmless questions as irrelevant. And Earley's blitzkrieg strategy probably had an emotional impact on the jurors, because, seeing Betty again for the first time in a year as they took the witness stand, most of her friends smiled at her across the courtroom with enough spontaneous warmth to convince any observer that, whatever she had become, Betty Broderick must have once been a very different person to draw so many respectable women into court to help her.

Before Wells cut her off, Cohrs testified that Betty was, in the last days, so paranoid, so confused, and so obsessed by the litigation that she had lost all capacity to even understand the legal documents in her mailbox. Once, Cohrs said, she had dropped by to find Betty hysterical about some new legal paper she had received. Cohrs read it—only to discover that it was not a threat at all, but, instead, something routine about scheduling. By then, however, said Cohrs, the mere sight of a legal letterhead was enough to reduce Betty to hysteria. "When I told her what the letter actually said," Cohrs said later, "she just couldn't absorb it."

Cohrs had more to say, particularly about the tears she had seen Betty shed when Dan canceled the children's visits at the last minute. But Earley didn't ask. And, certainly, Wells gave Cohrs no openings for extemporaneous commentary in her cross-exam, which lasted only seconds. All Kerry Wells wanted was for these women in their suede suits and patent leather flats to disappear.

None of the others got much further. Wilma Engel barely got seated before her testimony was over. Ann Dick managed to lob in a couple of minor barbs on cross-exam, when Wells asked her if Betty was preoccupied with money. "No more than I was," retorted Dick, "having put a husband through law school, too. There's a certain amount of gain we are all interested in." Further, said Dick, it was unfair to focus only on Betty's spending. "You can say that about both of them ..." Dan, she recalled, was always outside on weekends polishing his new sports cars.

Two more women came strictly to testify that they had seen Betty with a black eye—on different occasions. One sweet-faced matron, married to an attorney at Gray, Cary, testified in a nervous voice that she had seen Betty with a black eye back in 1978, on the afternoon of the Blackstone Ball, when Betty, then the decorations chairman, had arrived to help arrange the orchids. Another La Jolla mother whose children Betty had once baby-sat, recalled a separate incident, when Betty had heavy makeup over what looked to her like a black eye. Betty told her she had stumbled and fallen.

Other women came to testify to Betty's spirituality, and to her soccer coaching days. Candace McCarty met Betty in 1984, when Betty joined a Bible study class at the local Presbyterian Church which McCarty was leading. And, at the end of every Bible class, said McCarty, "Betty individually blessed her children, and her marriage, and her husband ... "I always thought she was a very spiritual person."

Beverly Jean Morris, a no-nonsense third-grade teacher and soccer coach—and the only non-La Jollan of the lot—strode briskly to the witness stand in a purple jogging suit and tennis shoes, where she curtly announced that "Coach Broderick" was a real pro, despite the fact that her own son, Rhett, was often absent from practice and games. At times, said Morris, Coach Broderick would arrive for duty "close to tears—but she always maintained her composure in front of the children." As Morris marched out of the courtroom, she flashed Betty two thumbs up, along with a solemn nod of salute. Except for Wells, nearly everybody in the courtroom laughed, including the judge.

And so it went. More women followed. Judy Backhaus, another of Betty's old friends, remembered once catching her eating raw cupcake batter. By then, Betty was already exceedingly overweight. Littering the kitchen were dozens of loaves of bread. "I said, 'My God, are the Marines coming?'" Backhaus remembered. "Betty said she couldn't remember anymore what kind of bread the kids liked, and they were coming [for the weekend] so she had bought a loaf of every kind, just in case."

Marilyn Olsen, wife of a La Jolla developer, seemed angrier than most about Betty's legal problems. To her, Betty had been victimized by the legal system, thanks to the clout carried by Dan Broderick—and Wells couldn't cut her off.

"Well, that's the whole story, isn't it?" Olsen challenged Wells sharply during cross-exam. Olsen then delivered a quick, efficient little speech about the failings of the American legal system, which leaves women and children to survive divorce as best they can. In the end, Olsen thought, given her treatment by Dan, Betty had behaved predictably, "like a rat in a maze—panic and attack."

By midafternoon, the jurors looked numbed. It had been a dizzying day of revolving-door witnesses—so many that even reporters were bickering over their head counts.

But none of it had added up to much, beyond the sad portrait of a formerly beautiful, energetic, likable, bright woman who had collapsed into crazy behavior, lost her children, and finally killed. No real motivation was established, beyond the fact that Dan Broderick, like millions of other men abroad on this earth, had cheated, lied, and finally left his wife for another younger, prettier woman. Beyond that, there was little amid this blizzard of well-meaning testimony from her friends to set Betty Broderick apart from any other rejected, deceived wife in the same boat who did not kill.

Next came Lee Broderick, not yet twenty years old, looking nervous and scared, as before, to testify this time for the defense. She was here today to do what she could to help balance the picture her sister, Kim, had presented.

Jack Earley began with a question about what life was like at home before the separation.

"Well, we had lots of friends, parties, good times … everybody liked to come over to our house," Lee said. "I thought we had a happy family."

And what about Kim, Earley demanded. Wouldn't she get very upset over money? Lee smiled uncertainly, her eyes flickering across the courtroom, lighting first on her mother's expectant face, then on her sister, who smiled back with understanding.

"Well, Kim gets very emotional very easily," Lee agreed with a bashful smile. And, yes, Kim complained about money problems a lot.

Lee went on to say that she had heard both Dan and Linda refer to her mother, as "Fat, disgusting, beastly, the Beast, the Monster … on the rampage, on the warpath." But, she said, neither of them used obscenities, like her mother did.

As many a wise man has observed, it is never the big things in life, like death and divorce, that get to us—in the end, it's always the small stuff, adding up. And for the duration of the Broderick trial, Jack Earley subscribed with deepest passion to this notion. Thus, he turned next to still more domestic trivia. Furniture, for example.

Lee agreed that "My mom would ask my dad for furniture and stuff, but he wouldn't give it to her." She recalled in particular a certain table Betty had wanted from the garage—but her father said no, "because he had files stored on it." Betty was "real mad" about that, Lee said.

Likewise, she said, Linda refused to return her mother's wedding china, because "She said Mom didn't get it in court, so she wasn't going to get it … she hid it."

How about Dan's drinking? Earley asked.

"Yes, he would drink with his friends on weekends," said Lee. And "sometimes he would come home drunk." Earley pressed in vain to get her to also say that, on at least one occasion, she had to drive Dan and Linda home, even before she got her driver's license, because they were both too drunk to drive. Lee had told Earley and Pasas that in earlier interviews. But in court now she wouldn't say it. Lee Broderick wasn't going to go the extra mile to disgrace her dead father.

She did agree, however, that Dan had a violent, unpredictable temper. "Nobody wanted to disobey him or make him mad when he was home from work," she said. Period. Earley looked ready to leap across the room and strangle her. Only weeks before, Lee had told him in detail how Dan had gone on angry rampages, once even ripping the seat out of their boat. But now, when it most counted, she would volunteer no colorful details at all to further damage Dan.

And how about her own treatment by her father, Earley asked next, sourly, tauntingly. Hadn't Dan treated her poorly? Written her out of his will?

Lee only looked sad. Yes, she agreed, she and her father had not gotten along at all. He wouldn't even give her a key to his house, she said, because she moved so often between his house and Betty's. "He was afraid that my mom might copy it," she added. It was another damning little detail Earley didn't need.

In the end, Lee failed Earley entirely. She provided no vivid details of emotional abuse, Dan's violence, her mother's despair, or her sister's duplicitous ways. She wouldn't even criticize Linda.

But instead of revising his approach, instead of swapping his hammer blows for a powder puff, Earley spent a few more minutes trying to force Lee Broderick to tell the court what she had told him in private. He failed. The girl only withdrew more and more.

Finally, with a flounce of almost childish pique, Earley sat down. Sensitivity was never his strong suit.

Kerry Wells was almost smiling as she rose for cross-exam.

Wasn't it true, she asked, that Lee's father was afraid of Betty?

Oh, yes, Lee instantly agreed, looking surprised at the question. Dan would want to know "if he needed protection," she told Wells. He would frequently ask Lee if her mother was in a bad mood. If she was, "We'd tell him, and he'd get armed guards."

In fact, Lee added, the only reason she had learned her mother had a gun was because her father had asked her to find out; so she had asked Betty, who had then shown it to her. She reported back to her dad that the gun was no joke. It was real.

Lee also agreed with Wells that, despite her dad's temper, she had never seen him hit any of the children—and the only time she ever saw him strike her mother was on the night Betty had run her car into his front door.

On the other hand, Lee refused to agree with Wells that her mother sometimes rejected her sons on weekends, merely to disrupt whatever plans Dan and Linda might have. No, said Lee, firmly. That was never true. "My mom would always rather be with my brothers than mess up their plans."

Wasn't it true, Wells next asked, that the only reason Lee was having problems with her father—the reason Dan Broderick had been angry enough to write her out of his will—was because she was in fact seriously messing up with school and drugs and had even run away from home? Lee agreed, with a shamed smile, that, yes, she had been a rebel child "for a significant period of time." If Jack Earley had tried to lay guilt on Kim for inciting Betty to murderous rage with her complaints about Dan's mistreatment of her, Kerry Wells was matching him step by step in her exploitation of Lee's guilt for displeasing her dead dad.

It only got worse for the defense.

In her coup de grace, Wells then asked Lee if it wasn't true that she had begun a rapprochement with her father during the last months of his life, after she had gotten her high school equivalency certificate and otherwise begun to stabilize.

Lee Broderick paused for several seconds before answering. When she did, her voice was unsteady, but her smile was one of pathetic puppy-dog happiness. Yes, she told Wells, flushing, "One of the last conversations I had with my dad, I told him I had passed my general education exam ... and he was gonna put me back in ... [the will]." She looked ready to cry. So did half the jury. So did a couple of reporters.

And, asked Wells, in the gentlest voice she had used during the entire trial, wasn't it also true that her dad had "been kind of bragging about you to his brothers and sisters ... about how well you were doing? Right?"

Yes, said Lee, no longer able to raise her eyes above her lap.

Satisfied, Wells turned the floor back to Earley, who did not grace it. He was in fact steaming.

But wasn't it equally true, he asked Lee, that a lot of what she had heard about her father's alleged forgiveness, his supposed plans to reinstate her in his will, had surfaced only lately, after the killings? Wasn't it furthermore true, he demanded, that, even as late as summertime 1990, she wasn't even permitted to have her brothers' telephone number?

Lee meekly agreed that, true, she hadn't been allowed to have her brothers' phone number. Beyond that, she said, mumbling now, she really didn't know anything more about anything.

At recess, Wells walked up to Lee, who was standing in the corridor wiping her eyes, and congratulated her. "Good job!" she said, with one of her rare, tight little smiles.

Then, before Lee even had time to absorb the meaning of Kerry Wells's applause, Marion Pasas, white with anger, walked up and, in a moment of meanness which still shames her, accused Lee of "stabbing your mother in the back." Lee fled the courthouse, to the street corner outside, where she stood alone, sobbing. It was Jack Earley, whose temper fits seldom seem to last more than five minutes, who shambled after her to say that it was all okay. He even patted the anguished girl on the shoulder, which is, for Earley, an awkward thing to do.

Then along came Kim. The two Broderick sisters stood on the street corner, clinging to each other and crying. They then left together, before the morning session was done, to go wherever two sisters go when their mother is on trial for two murders.

That was November 7—Betty's forty-third birthday. Earlier that day, Kim had passed her mother a card in court:

"... Too bad it's not a good birthday this year, too bad we can't sing in court. Next year will be much better," the card read in part. Kim told her mother again that she loved her and missed her and couldn't wait until she got out of jail. "Remember when I was a little girl and at all my birthday parties I used to cry?" she added, in a final note, "I guess I was hysterical even then ..."

Weeks later, Betty was still puzzling over that card. Her feelings were as confused as her daughter's, just as ambivalent. If Kim wanted to testify against her mother, but still be forgiven, the mother was angry but willing. That has not changed to this day.

Even after the first verdict, Betty still sat in her tiny, hermetically sealed jail cell, studying that birthday card, trying to understand. One evening, from the jail phone, she read it aloud, again.

"... Now, this is a person who's been told that if she testified against me, I'd get at least fifteen years, and maybe life without parole, and she's giving me a birthday card saying next year it's going to be much better?'" She then laughed gaily, as she always does when she is hiding pain.

Three weeks after her murder trial had begun, and more than one year after the killings, her parents finally came to visit their daughter.

But only her father came to court. It was near the end of an afternoon session when the old man stepped off the elevator with two of his sons. A small, trim man with wavy silver hair and brilliant blue eyes ("He looks just like Paul Newman," Betty always brags), neatly dressed in a camel blazer and gray slacks, Frank Bisceglia, nearly 80, looked shy, uncertain, and, like all the Bisceglia family, so sadly shamed as he blinked into the crowd milling in the corridor. Some faces he recognized—especially Gail and Brian Forbes. He had spent many friendly evenings sitting around his daughter's dinner table with them in La Jolla.

What happened next verged on the obscene. These people, whose only purpose in court that day was to help convict his daughter, rushed to greet him. They offered their handshakes, they welcomed him, they inquired into his health, and his wife's. It would take Frank Bisceglia another year before he gathered his wits and anger enough to tell them all to go to hell.

But now, bewildered and overwhelmed by the whole situation, he only murmured politely to everyone, while his two sons moved their big, solid bodies between him and the reporters, who were creeping in fast with elephant ears.

His wife could not face coming to court, he said, although he did not put it so bluntly. Like his daughter, Frank Bisceglia always tries to put the best face on things. "Mother is having lunch at the hotel," he explained vaguely. And, he added, "All my children told me not to come today, too, but ..." He shrugged. He wanted to see Betty Anne.

"Things will all work out for the best," he said to those gathered about him. "Betty Anne is a good girl. I'd like to give her a spanking when this is over."

413

It was one of life's small, poignant scenes when Betty turned to discover her father sitting in the front row behind her. Her smile was instant and absolutely radiant. She looked both shocked and thrilled. But, in the next second she flushed, and suddenly, shyly, turned away, returning with great, exaggerated purpose to her busy scribblings on her legal pads.

Her father sat quietly for the next two hours, with watering eyes, listening to one witness after another, including Gail Forbes, denounce his child.

That weekend, Frank and Marita Bisceglia visited their daughter for thirty minutes at the county jail. There was never much hope that the meeting would be anything other than confused and painful, just one more small scene in this family tragedy—and it wasn't. There sat two proper old people in their retirement years, smiling as brightly as they could manage through the smudged glass at their once perfect, golden-haired daughter, as they tried to operate the awkward jail phones, while other visitors shoved and pushed and chattered noisily about them. And while Betty Anne, reduced to brittle, festive laughter and frenetic babble, tried to make them understand that which they could never understand—the insupportable pressures in her head and heart that finally led her to shoot two people to death in their bed.

Later, Betty appeared almost angry that her parents had at last come to visit her. Her father was still "a sweetheart," but her mother seemed only to evoke the same old antagonisms. "The bottom line is always the same—look what I've done to her!"

A few months after the "incident," Betty said she had once again tried in a phone conversation to make her mother understand. "I said to her, I said, 'Mother—I mean, it was—this was literal self-defense, you know, me or him! This was it! This was—and there's no other story for it—from my heart, honestly, this was self-defense.'"

But, she says, her mother only cried and hung up.

Now Betty sounded ready to cry herself, but didn't. Instead, she switched to her usual rapid-fire, defensive chatter, as she sarcastically recited all that she should have said to her mother:

"... Like, 'I'm so sorry at this late date in my life that, for the first time ever, I've disappointed you. I'm so sorry, Mother, that I didn't kill myself and keep the women's club happy!'

"I wanted to say to my mother—I mean, this is my mother's almost last chance, being that she's in her seventies and I'm in my forties that ..." She lost her train of thought and started over. "You know, she writes me letters like—'Whatever happened to my gorgeous towhead daughter, who was the great Girl Scout and the president of her class?' And I'm like— 'Fuck, Mom, I'm still here! You know? I'm still here! It's the same little wonderful girl you used to know, and you're making me feel like I should feel bad that I'm still here!'"

But, she finished, wistfulness blended with eternal resentment, "I don't say any of that to her, of course—she'd have a heart attack."

Her voice broke, she couldn't go on. But, typical Betty, she didn't just hang up. She lied politely and said, "I gotta go, the guards are taking us in now."

The next day Jack Earley produced the expert witness he had selected to put it all in context, to finally explain, once and for all, what combination of forces had ultimately driven Betty Broderick mad enough to kill.

His choice was Daniel Jay Sonkin, Ph.D., a marriage and family counselor in private practice in Sausalito, California, a fashionable bedroom community near San Francisco. Sonkin had coauthored two books on male batterers, edited a third, and was a regular paid witness in criminal and civil cases involving domestic violence. Earley hired Sonkin, he said, based on "high recommendations" from a battery of experts around the country.

A horse-faced young man, maybe forty, with long, glossy hair, shagging modishly to his collar and parted in the middle, Sonkin was from the Dale Carnegie school of charm. From the minute he took the stand, he turned his body to the jury and spoke exclusively to them throughout. His manner was ingratiating, collegial, and, at times, breathtakingly flip: "Yeah," he quipped at one point to some remark Wells had made about Betty shooting Linda, "She didn't like her." Grinning, he looked to the jury for approval, which was not forthcoming. They glared at him stonily.

Which is not to say that Daniel Sonkin wasn't a good witness. To the contrary, he did all that he was hired to do, plus some, during his nearly six hours on the witness stand. In fact, he did his job so well—and with enough seeming certainty that Betty Broderick was indeed a battered woman in every respect—that by the time the second trial rolled around, Wells would manage to get him excluded altogether.

Sonkin's message was clear: having spent around eight hours talking to Betty Broderick, her parents, and her sister Clare, as well as immersing himself in the literature—her diaries, her autobiography, Dan's Marriage Encounter letters, and court records—it was his firm opinion that Betty was not only an emotionally abused woman, but also one who had been sexually and physically abused during the entire sixteen years of her marriage to Dan Broderick.

In Sonkin's opinion, Dan Broderick was clearly "a functional alcoholic" who often came home at night and forced drunken sex on his wife. Betty had told him so.

As for the physical abuse, while Sonkin agreed that, in Betty's case, the battery was not extreme, he pointed out that even one or two black eyes can last a lifetime in terms of fear. It's not just the hitting that matters, he said—it's the loss of trust that goes with it, and the lasting fear. The bruises may go away, but the emotional anxieties, the dread, never vanish.

It was a dazzling smorgasbord of choices: if the jury didn't buy emotional abuse, then try physical battery, and if they didn't like that, how about sexual assault?

True, Betty denied any physical battery; but Sonkin could see through her evasions, he said. Based on what he had heard and read—and he obviously accepted as gospel truth every single thing Betty said about Dan—it was obvious to him that Dan Broderick was a classic male batterer. Betty's own consistent denials that she had been physically or sexually abused only further persuaded Sonkin that his diagnosis was correct: One of the chief characteristics of battered women, he said—really intelligent, well-educated women like Betty—is that "they are ashamed, so they deny it."

But such denial was typical of most battered women, he said. Betty was only masking her feelings.

Among other clear indicators of battery, he continued, was Betty's ongoing view of Dan "as nearly omnipotent ... In many cases where battered people kill," he said, "they don't even believe the person has died." He cited Betty's continuing references to Dan in the present tense as a perfect example.

Wells began to hold her head and rub her neck as she listened to this yuppie from Sausalito, whose credentials she later snidely derided as "mail order." She objected constantly, with more anger than she had shown so far in this trial. Each time, Sonkin smiled at her pleasantly, almost condescendingly.

Nor did Sonkin trace any of Betty's problems to her upbringing. As far as he could tell, Betty's family was fairly normal. The only reason she had withdrawn from them as the years passed, he thought, was because like most battered women, she couldn't bear either to lie to them, or to tell them the truth. Instead, as Sonkin saw it, the problems tracked back to Dan's family. He had heard [from Betty] that Dan's father was physically abusive to his mother and that most of the Brodericks were heavy drinkers. "Violence begets violence." It was generational.

In Sonkin's final diagnosis, Betty was severely depressed, overwhelmed, suffering "stress disorder ... [T]hat's the diagnosis we use in battered women."

You could almost hear Kerry Wells's brain cells, like a bowl of Rice Krispies, going snap, crackle, and pop as she rose to cross-examine Daniel Sonkin. She paused, visibly trying to control herself, then spoke in a voice trembling with indignation.

But doesn't she lie? Wells asked, close to shrill.

Sonkin calmly agreed that there were "numerous inconsistencies" in Betty's statements.

Wells then walked Sonkin through the various medical reports on Betty, noting that none mentioned complaints by Betty that she had been either suicidal or battered. She read at length from the 1986 California mental hospital report, which had been based largely on a standard psychological test Betty had taken before she decided not to cooperate any further—and which concluded that she was a "borderline personality ... histrionic and narcissistic."

As every expert knows, said Sonkin with a tolerant smile, psychological testing is entirely subjective. "People read them like horoscopes; they are not valid for court." Also, he added, at times of severe trauma, "a lot of battered women come up looking borderline."

(Borderline personality disorder, as defined by leading psychiatric manuals, refers to "a pervasive pattern of instability of mood, interpersonal relationships and self-image, beginning by early adulthood." Among the chief characteristics of a borderline may be some or all of the following: unstable personal relationships, "alternating between extremes of over-idealization and devaluation"; impulsiveness in such self-destructive areas as sex, spending, substance abuse, binge eating; mood swings ranging from depression to anxiety; lack of temper control; self-image problems; chronic feelings of emptiness or boredom; and "frantic efforts to avoid real or imagined abandonment.")

But, although it was she who had introduced the topic, Wells was not interested in exploring borderline personality disorders any further.

Instead, she moved on to Dr. Nelson's remark from the 1989 divorce trial that Betty "is not mentally ill. If she murdered Mr. Broderick as she has threatened to do ... she could never be called incompetent ... This lady knows what exactly what she is doing."

Sonkin dismissed Nelson's remarks with a cynical shrug, as the casual commentary of a doctor who was obviously only "trying to help her get her kids back ..."

Wells next tried to make Sonkin recant his view that Betty was a battered woman, and admit that, instead, Dan Broderick had been the battered partner in this marriage. Dan had no history of hitting anybody, she pointed out—but Betty had called Dan names and had attacked his property. Furthermore, she challenged Sonkin, if Dan Broderick was so violence prone, why didn't he just "punch her out" when she went to his house to confront him?

Because, said Sonkin, irritably, "he used the courts" instead. And, no, he said flatly, regarding Wells with open contempt, he didn't think that Dan Broderick was the victim in any respect.

"Don't battered women classically remain passive?" Wells demanded, almost shouting. "If she's afraid of him because he's been beating her for sixteen years, why would she go over and taunt him?"

Because, said Sonkin, looking tired of Wells's hectoring, not every woman is alike. Some battered women behave passively; others don't. Betty didn't.

Wells finished with Sonkin by demanding to know why, if Betty Broderick was so "depressed," could she still control herself enough to conduct her own divorce trial? Sonkin repeated his view that Betty Broderick was not crazy, but, instead, only an extremely intelligent woman under severe stress. And so, of course, she could pull herself together at times. But it didn't mean much, Sonkin said. She was still a physically, sexually, and emotionally battered woman. With that, the defense concluded its case-in-chief.

At last, after all these months, it was nearly over. That night at dinner with Sonkin, Jack Earley, Marion Pasas, and Dian Black resembled three survivors of a shipwreck, finally sighting land from their little raft, after weeks of too much sun and saltwater. Their mood was almost zany, an explosion of hilarity, exhaustion, and relief, with a heavy overlay of gloom. They had fought the good fight, all three of these people whose lives had been so entangled with Betty Broderick's for so long, but now they were girding for the worst. And if they all three sounded a little nuts tonight, it was understandable—six months or more, locked in embrace with Betty, takes its toll on the sanest of people.

Earley's gallows humor was at its best. It was driving him crazy, trying to read the faces of the jurors: when one plump juror smiled at him on the way out at recess, he could never decide whether it was because she liked him or because she was "just anticipating her next Butterfinger from the hallway vending machine." And what about the young one, the sun-tan parlor employee, the consummate California child—would she even survive until the end of the trial? Every day she came to court looking more and more like a piece of parchment. Maybe she would soon just disintegrate into a pile of dusty flakes and hair and fingernails in her chair. Everybody giggled.

Dian Black, meantime, who had been on this roller coaster ever since she picked up her telephone at seven A.M. on November 5, 1989, only looked dazed—Betty kept telling her over the phone that she wished this trial would hurry up so "she can get home in time for Thanksgiving."

"She shouldn't even be on trial. She's crazy! She needs therapy," said Black, for maybe the one thousandth time since the trial had begun. She had begun to sound like a Greek chorus.

For her part, Pasas was sympathizing with Betty's sexual repression. "What a slut," Earley wise-cracked at Pasas.

Daniel J. Sonkin, a mere newcomer, could only look bemused and a bit shocked at all the madcap irreverence—because, as it turned out over dinner, he seemed truly to believe all that he had said in court that day.

He felt genuine pity for Betty, he said. He thought she was "pathetic" in her incessant need to please. Every little detail about her behavior seemed to pain him—asking for a pen and paper in court, for example; asking Whelan if the jurors could ask questions, then asking them if they could hear her. Even her constant smiles at friends in the audience had nothing to do with arrogance, he thought—instead it was just a trained behavior pattern, hiding the repressed personality beneath.

"She's so easy to dislike, to be disgusted with ... because she's just not in touch with her feelings." But, he argued with more unaffected, winning passion in private than he had in court, Betty was just one more battered woman, without self-esteem, starved for unconditional love, which she had never received, not from Dan, nor from her parents and friends.

"That's why she was so great with kids—they didn't ask for more," he said, gazing sadly into his spaghetti.

Sonkin's remarks had sobered the table. Nobody spoke for a while. Finally, Jack Earley, in an uncharacteristic moment of melancholy, said softly, "You know, I don't think Betty can get well. She just needs to get old." Besides, he added sadly, "What would she do if she did get out?"

As testimony wound down, nearly everyone looked exhausted. Pasas, always so meticulous about her appearance, had a run in her nylons. Earley had a pimple on his nose. Only Kerry Wells arrived in court looking refreshed. In a rare display of good humor, she even smiled at the assembled reporters as she strode by. The message was clear: she was ready for the kill.

She called a string of cleanup witnesses, including a receptionist for Dan who described the vulgar messages Betty periodically left at his office, and two of Dan's first housekeepers, who told how he had suffered at the hands of his vicious ex-wife.

In addition, came the Forbes couple. Describing Betty's call to her from jail on the night of the Blackstone Ball, Gail searched for the most devastating word she could find to characterize Betty's mood: "Exultant," she said. Brian, in his second appearance, testified, among other things, that Betty had used such foul language in front of his children, he was forced to reprimand her. With that, Forbes, distinguished senior attorney at Gray, Cary, Ames and Frye, stalked somberly from the courtroom. It was always hard to match up this proper, pious little man on the witness stand with the grinning Brian Forbes in a photograph Betty had once taken at a party in pre-Linda days: Forbes was wearing a white lace woman's bra wrapped around his head like a cap, with Dan laughing at him in the background.

"What a fun bunch of guys," Betty said later from jail, sarcastically. "Brian Forbes has always had the foulest mouth of anybody I know."

The trial ended on the fifteenth day of testimony with mental health experts, compliments not of Jack Earley—who would have been happy to leave the jury mulling over Daniel Sonkin's allegations of abuse and David Lusterman's analysis of infidelity—but of Kerry Wells, who called as her final witness San Diego psychiatrist Melvin G. Goldzband to explain the inner workings of Betty's mind. Although Earley had not even raised the issue of his client's mental competence, Wells was determined that these twelve jurors would not retreat to the privacy of the deliberation room harboring even the faintest concern that maybe this woman was simply crazy, incapable of formulating a premeditated plan to kill.

Goldzband took the witness stand armed not only with all the data Kerry Wells could provide, including Betty's diaries and autobiography, but also with a private three-hour interview with the defendant herself. That fact, in itself, presented an interesting footnote to poor Earley's ongoing uphill struggle with his unmanageable client. It wasn't that Earley had instructed Betty not to talk to Goldzband. According to the rules, the prosecutor is entitled to a psychiatric interview with the defendant if the defense intends to introduce similar testimony. But Earley insists he told Betty not to speak to Goldzband until either he, Bowman, or Pasas was there to monitor the interview. Instead, Goldzband went to the jail on his own, and Betty cordially invited the enemy agent in for a friendly chat.

And so, Goldzband could now hang Betty Broderick with her own words. And he did his best. All that hampered him was his own style. A small, graying, avuncular man who had been in the "expert testimony" business for thirty-five years, Goldzband tends to condescend—he delivers the gospel truth with expansive, exaggerated patience to people who might be too slow to get it. He grated on the jurors' nerves, as it later turned out, and was thus dumped in the second trial for a slicker, more expensive hotshot from Los Angeles with a national reputation.

Style aside, his opinions were interesting.

First his diagnosis: "My impression of this lady is that she's got mixed personality disorder, (a less severe condition than borderline disorder) mainly with facets of narcissistic and histrionic traits," he told the jury. But he thought the narcissism was primary.

Wells wasted no time in getting to the point: did that mean she was crazy?

No, said Goldzband. Absolutely not. Betty suffered from no psychosis. Instead, he

419

said, these terms refer merely to "personality traits—the way people are."

For example, narcissism, most simply defined, merely means self-love. Most people possess narcissistic traits to some degree—but in the average person this is a simple measure of self-esteem. In severe cases, however, individuals become "so totally self-oriented" that they see themselves as the center of the universe and as virtually perfect.

Histrionic personalities, by contrast, are people who thrive on attention, who enjoy being "center stage." They are actors, said Goldsband, who derive "enormous ego gratification from being noticed." Among their characteristics, they "exaggerate, do things in big, broad strokes" to enlarge their own self-image. Again, many histrionics are delightful, amusing people, he said—if the trait is subject to some self-control.

But in Goldzband's opinion, Betty was a textbook example of both traits at their worst extremes. It was her total self-love, her sense of being "pretty near perfect" that led to her murderous rage when Dan rejected her, he thought.

"She wanted Dan. She wanted not to be rejected. If there had been a settlement, that would have merely cemented her rejection, and she couldn't tolerate that," he said. "This is a person who, by virtue of her narcissistic needs, feels grossly rejected when her husband selects someone else to live with ... she is perfect. It is inconceivable to this lady, because of her investment in the concept of her own perfection, that she could be rejected ..."

But, when that rejection comes anyway, when the severe narcissist's perfection is "besmirched," he continued, "rage is often the answer ... If attention slips away, they will do something to refresh it ... they have a vast repertoire." Even Betty Broderick's handwriting in the diaries, her later obscene letters to judges and doctors, were characteristic of "a person who writes in headlines."

Furthermore, "Her attitude toward her behavior is that it's constantly justifiable." The notion that she is in any way at fault, said Goldzband, is "totally alien ... [she has] no empathy with feelings of others, beyond the superficial social level." However, she "may appear charming on a casual level," he said—and, in fact, he later remarked expansively, Betty was "the most charming, intelligent murderer I have ever dealt with."

Goldzband did agree that Betty had been depressed at the end, but he dismissed it as an insignificant factor. And he scoffed openly at the notion that Betty Broderick was a battered woman in any respect. He in fact chuckled at the very question.

Typically, Betty spent the day pretending that she was barely even listening as her mental condition was publicly dissected. Instead, she scribbled busily into her legal pads, interrupting herself only periodically to whisper vigorously, with her standard smile of implacable, impossible serenity, into the ear of Marion Pasas, who, in turn, looked more tempted than ever to bring her dizzy client down to earth, just for once, with a smart whack to the chops.

* * *

Earley countered with clinical psychologist Catherine DiFrancesca, a total personality opposite from Goldzband. Although she had done psychological evaluations for the county courts for years, DiFrancesca had none of the stagy traits of a professional witness bent upon wooing the jury. A small, dark-haired, bespectacled woman in her forties, dressed in a neutral suit, she was soft-spoken, somber, and utterly without affectations. She spoke not to the jury but directly to whichever attorney was questioning her. So matter-of-fact, so expressionless, so crisply professional was DiFrancesca that it was impossible to detect whether she even liked Betty.

But DiFrancesca clearly had sympathy for the hell in Betty Broderick's head. Compared to Goldzband's ready, self-assured pronouncements, DiFrancesca was consistently unwilling to speak in absolutes. While Goldzband was quick to lay blame, she was quietly persuaded that it should be shared.

After spending about twelve hours with Betty in nine sessions that year, DiFrancesca diagnosed her as suffering from a borderline personality disorder characterized, first, by histrionic traits, with narcissism secondarily.

These were subtle but significant distinctions. Unlike Goldzband, who placed narcissism first, DiFrancesca thought that Betty's histrionic need for approval and applause far outweighed her narcissism. If anything, DiFrancesca believed that Betty Broderick suffered from insufficient self-esteem rather than an excess of it.

At the heart of Betty's personality problem, DiFrancesca said, "She never did have a strong identity of her own ... she saw herself as Dan Broderick's wife, the mother of his children, but she didn't really see herself beyond that."

DiFrancesca did not think Betty saw herself as perfect. Instead, in DiFrancesca's mind, it was the exact opposite. "Some narcissists only wish they were great. [Betty] only wished she were as smart as Dan Broderick ... She only wishes she were [perfect] ..." But, in reality, it was always Dan Broderick she aggrandized, not herself, said DiFrancesca. It was through her perceived role "as aiding and abetting his life, and his career," said DiFrancesca, that she gained any sense of self-worth.

And she had functioned well for many years—although most borderline personality disorders usually manifest themselves by adolescence— because, said DiFrancesca, her support systems were in place. She was secure. Her collapse occurred only after—and because—she was abruptly stripped of her role as a wife and mother. Then her social status had been taken away, too. Thus, she found herself with no personality—no self—left. Once her anchoring forces were removed, she became increasingly "maladaptive as the stress and the years progressed." The picture of Betty DiFrancesca drew was reminiscent of an empty soda bottle—a mindless, helpless thing—buffeted about at sea until the forces of nature finally slammed it to smithereens upon the shoals.

DiFrancesca also thought that, toward the end, Betty suffered from severe depression, caused by stress, sense of loss, feelings of helplessness. "And you cannot just snap out of a major depression."

Nor did DiFrancesca find Betty's overnight vulgarities surprising. She routinely witnessed that sort of decline in women who feel devalued. The only real difference was that "Most are able to control it ... Mrs. Broderick couldn't."

And nothing, she said, better demonstrated Betty's total emotional erosion than her subsequent lack of empathy for her own children. But by then, DiFrancesca thought Betty suffered from such feelings of personal failure that she couldn't even see the effects of her actions on her children.

Betty's spotty memory didn't strike DiFrancesca as deliberate or manipulative, either. It was typical of histrionic personalities, she said, that they often simply fail to concentrate, or they repress whatever is unpleasant.

Wells did not badger Katherine DiFrancesca on cross-exam. If Betty was so powerless, so out of control, Wells asked politely, then why was she able to perform so well throughout 1989? How did DiFrancesca account for that?

People with Betty's personality traits commonly cover up their real feelings by putting on happy faces, replied DiFrancesca. They keep all the misery inside, which is why the dangerous pressures build.

Wells asked about Betty's boasts at being "the perfect wife, [and] mother."

"No," DiFrancesca told Wells firmly. "I think she has very real, significant problems with self-esteem. She tries to bolster herself with talk of being a great wife and mother, but in reality, I think she feels very empty."

Both sides then rested their cases. Only closing arguments remained.

Over, too, was the biggest mystery of the trial: for three weeks, everyone had wondered if Wells, in a bit of last-minute theater, would call the Broderick boys to testify against their mother.

Many months later, after the second trial, investigator Bill Green explained why that never happened.

Before the first trial, he and Wells had gone to Denver to interview the two sons, he said. They had begun their interview with Danny, the older boy, in his bedroom. "The kid started out sitting up on the edge of the bed," recalled Green, still looking pained at the memory. "But the more we talked to him, the more he withdrew. It was actually physical. First, he lay down on the bed. But, within a few minutes, he was actually curled up in a fetal position."

He and Wells had looked at each other and, without a word, got up and left the boy alone, he said. "And that was the end of it. We never even discussed bringing those kids into court again. No trial is worth that."

Wells and Earley haggled with Whelan over jury instructions. They bickered over everything from broad language to single words. Should medical testimony, for instance, be couched in terms of mental disorder or mental disease? Wells didn't want disease mentioned, but in the end, Whelan chose to include both terms.

Although Earley knew he would lose the point, he also argued, for the record, for a self-defense instruction on grounds that Betty had "felt her emotional integrity, as well as her physical integrity, was under threat." That was equivalent to a physical attack, said Earley. No, said Whelan.

Going to the other extreme, Wells argued that manslaughter should not even be presented as an option to the jury. In her mind, it was either murder or acquittal, with no in-between.

Whelan overruled her. He would offer jurors all five traditional choices, at least in the death of Dan:

—First-degree murder, meaning the killings were premeditated with malice aforethought.

—Second-degree murder, meaning the killings were committed without premeditation or immediate provocation, but with malice.

—Voluntary manslaughter, meaning the killings were committed in the heat of passion, with provocation, but without malice aforethought.

—Involuntary manslaughter, meaning that the killings were basically accidental, the result of negligence, as in, for example, a traffic accident.

—And, finally acquittal—not guilty on all charges.

But Whelan had to think it over that night before he decided to include a manslaughter instruction for Linda, too. Initially, he was reluctant, he told a flabbergasted Earley, because, even now, at the trial's conclusion, "I still don't see where the provocation [for killing Linda] was." Lucky for Betty that Tom Whelan was on the bench and not in the jury box.

On the telephone from jail that night, Betty was more defiant and acerbically funny than ever. She hadn't called to talk, she had called to vent.

"By the time DiFrancesca saw me, I'm surprised I was only borderline. I was like a dead person. I was a zombie. I didn't have any personality left whatever. I was just boo boo bah bah."

Also, she said, laughing cynically, "I was dying to ask all those psychotherapists, have you ever tested anyone who came out normal? What is normal? Can you take these tests and come out normal? You can't. But I'm not nuts enough to get off on it. If you're going to argue on nuts, argue on nuts! Get me off on nuts. And then you send me to the mental institution for two months, and when they find out I'm perfectly normal, I go home like a hundred other people.

"All the psychological testimony drove me crazy ... What am I? Narcissistic, and histrionic, and manic depressive, or pissed off?"

And: "You know what's really ironic?" she asked. "Their criteria for a narcissist was so perfectly Dan Broderick, it made me die! It was exactly Dan. Self-centered, megalomaniac, Mr. Importance. When it came to selfish, he made goddamn near everybody look bush-league."

After court that day, she said mockingly, she told the bailiffs, "I'd like to go look in the mirror and see if my hair looks okay, but I wouldn't want to be nar-ci-cisssssss-tic." She laughed again. These idiots wouldn't know a narcissist if they saw one.

Chapter 38

To the Jury

It was a full house with a long waiting line on the day of closing arguments. The summations were mostly echoes of the opening statements.

Wells was, as usual, organized, focused, and precise; she finished her plea for two first-degree murder convictions in about an hour.

Betty Broderick, Wells told the jurors, had "ambushed" two helpless people sleeping in their bed. It was "a double execution." There was nothing rash or impulsive about her act. She had been threatening to kill them for literally years. "This was not a manslaughter case ... The law does not allow a person to charge into other people's homes with a loaded gun, to confront them, catch them totally off guard, unprotected, helpless, and kill them both, and then say, 'But, gosh, I didn't really mean it. I shouldn't be responsible.' She is responsible for murder, period."

What's more, Wells argued, Betty Broderick never thought she would pay for her crimes. She cited housekeeper Cavins's testimony that Betty had said, "No jury will ever convict me." After the killings, she had told Kim, "Don't worry, I'll be out in a couple of days." Betty thought that "she had a free ride, that the world would say she was justified."

"It was always 'Me, me, me!'" said Wells, rigid with anger. Narcissistic, histrionic—what difference did all these terms make? To Wells they all added up to the same thing: "I call it selfish and cruel, not narcissistic."

Wells scoffed at the defense argument that Betty had gone over to Dan's house that morning, gun in hand, to force him into a discussion. "Hogwash," she said. What rational person could believe that Betty had seriously expected to have a conversation with Dan Broderick at 5:30 in the morning? "What's he going to say?" Wells asked sarcastically. " 'Oh, good morning. What would you like to talk about?'" If Betty had wanted a discussion that morning, Wells asked, then why wasn't there one? Certainly, she held all the cards that morning.

And what fool would buy the argument that Betty had been thinking of suicide that morning, rather than murder? This was cold-blooded, premeditated murder in the first degree, pure and simple, she said.

Then, in perhaps the most tasteless moment of the entire trial, Wells even attempted to defuse defense medical reports indicating that Dan Broderick had not defecated in death. Maybe the reason Betty had made her crude remark to Patti Monahan that morning was because she herself had defecated. "Maybe that's why she went to a Clairemont gas station—to clean herself up," said Wells. Even reporters looked shocked. "Jeez, I feel like I'm on some kind of weird drug trip," muttered one.

Betty, for once, was not hiding in her yellow legal pads. Instead, she studied Wells intently, smiling slightly but with decided contempt at this stupid woman who was publicly suggesting that she had soiled herself over Dan Broderick.

Jack Earley, as usual, shuffled about for nearly three hours in his best bewildered, doleful fashion, likable as ever, but at the same time confusing the bejesus out of everybody with his extemporaneous ramblings about this tale of human nature at its worst—a nebulous mass of details, some glaring, some subtle, about a sixteen-year marriage gone bad, followed by six years of an ugly power struggle, complicated by the Other Woman.

Betty was pushed over the edge, Earley argued, by Dan Broderick's "crazy-making" tactics. She was a woman who had trusted her husband—only to be told that she was "crazy" when he began his affair with Linda, and to be increasingly abused after the separation, said Earley sadly. "He knew how to push her buttons." Dan's only miscalculation, he added, had been in expecting that she would eventually kill herself, instead of him.

Earley begged jurors to read between the lines, to notice all the 'Alice in Wonderland' inconsistencies and distortions in the prosecution's case. Who, asked Earley, could seriously believe that Betty Broderick had self-destructed from simple jealousy and anger of the sort that millions of other people suffer but survive? Who could really accept that only Betty Broderick was at fault, that she caused it all, while "Dan Broderick never did anything wrong?"

And don't forget, he begged, how she had tried, more than once, to get on with her life. She got a job in 1989. She was trying to get her children back; she went to a therapist. "She was trying to set her life right ... She was trying!"

But then, he said, it had begun all over again. Dan changed visitation orders to suit himself, custody hearings were delayed, he even began fining her again. Then she got the final, threatening Cuffaro letters. "Was that conciliation?" he asked.

Then Earley tried to do for Betty what she wouldn't or couldn't do for herself: apologize. "This," said Earley, his voice suddenly filled with sadness, "was an act of craziness, emotion. There is no excuse for what people do to each other. But I ask you to place responsibility where it belongs. She was acting on emotion. She was a victim of emotion. Put it in context in laying responsibility. Use your common sense."

But he didn't tell them what conclusion they should reach, what verdict he thought was appropriate. He did not ask them to set his client free, nor did he even make a plea for manslaughter. He merely trusted in them to make "the right decision."

And sat down.

The defense had rested without even saying what nature of killing these were.

Reporters stared at each other, pencils still poised for the final line that never came. Jurors frowned, Betty glared. Even Judge Whelan, lying back in his chair, as usual, with his eyes closed to Earley's lulling monologue, had a delayed response. It took him an extra minute to realize that Earley was done, to pull himself upright and bring the day's formalities to an end.

Later, Jack Earley was blunt in his explanation. He couldn't ask for manslaughter, he said, even if he had wanted to, without outraging Betty, who expected him to argue that she should be set free, that jurors should ignore Whelan's legal instructions. But how could he make that ridiculous request, even for show? Betty had, after all, shot two people to death, and Jack Earley had a reputation to defend. "And it's hard to humiliate yourself in front of your peers."

The next day, in her first act of defiance since the trial began, Betty arrived in court wearing her gray jail sweat suit with SD JAIL printed across her back in large black letters.

In her second act of defiance, she turned and whispered openly to reporters across the railing: she was protesting Whelan's refusal to admit either her full set of diaries or the entire Broderick divorce file into evidence. This was a kangaroo court, she said. Jurors would never know the full truth, only selected portions of it—so she was making the only statement she could.

Wells, who could not abide any act that might supply Betty Broderick with even a whit of juror sympathy, insisted that Whelan explain that Betty's jail clothes were of her own choosing. She didn't want Eloise Duffield or any other juror worrying that this poor woman had been condemned to prison already. Whelan declined.

An hour later, the jury had been formally instructed in its duties, obligations, and options, and dispatched to the deliberation room. It was Thursday, November 15.

The press promptly set up a rotating watchdog system outside the jury room. Earley seemed cheered that the media appeared to be hunkering in for the long haul.

"Please God," he wisecracked gloomily at lunch, "just don't let them come back today. If they only stay out overnight, I can at least save some face. It's the ones who return in two hours, laughing, that you never forget."

When the jurors had not returned by Friday night, Earley was euphoric. "Heh, heh," he chortled, in his little makeshift office. "Now it's Kerry who's gonna throw up and snap at her kids all weekend, not me."

Betty's spirits were eerily high that weekend. Dian Black had gone to Colinas to visit on Saturday, wearing a T-shirt that read "Free the La Jolla Narcissist."

"I loved it," said Betty, giggling excitedly over the phone. She was talking almost too fast to understand. "I thought it was soooo funny!"

That weekend her two daughters also came to see her. Kim repeated her view that her mother deserved punishment, but Betty was too thrilled that she even came to visit to care.

But by Sunday, some of the gay, giddy edge was diluted by the reality that tomorrow was Monday. Those twelve strangers, after a weekend break, would be back to their deliberations. Now an edge of nervous irritability underlay her chirpy, cheerful tone.

"I hope that jury doesn't come back at all Monday, Tuesday, or Wednesday, and then we've got a hung jury," she said. "Or, if they come back, of course, I hope they come back with the only logical thing to do. Send me home. I've had enough of this bullshit!"

The jury did not return on Monday. By now, excitement in the courthouse corridor was reaching a new pitch. Clearly, there was dissension in the jury room. The day passed with reporters taking bets on whether it would be a verdict of first or second degree. Only Marion Pasas thought otherwise. "Maybe it's just wishful thinking," she said, "but my bet is that they're undecided, that we're going to get a hung jury."

On Tuesday, day four, the jurors returned.

This was not one of those fabled juries, where people come back crying in distress, or looking frazzled. This jury hadn't been out long enough to be tired. Instead, they mostly looked annoyed and embarrassed as they filed into the jury box.

They were unable to reach a unanimous decision, Swann told Whelan.

He quizzed her. Was she sure? How many times had they voted?

She stuttered nervously. She couldn't remember whether they had voted three or four times. One of the other jurors prompted her. Well, maybe they had voted half a dozen times, Swann amended.

But nobody really seemed to know for sure. The only thing they did know was that, no matter how long they stayed in that room, they weren't ever going to agree on whether Betty Broderick had committed murder or manslaughter or some combination of both.

And the reason was Walter Polk, the quiet, proper little man in his impeccable brown suits and ties—the juror both sides had counted on to go their way. Polk had also taken Terilyn Berg, the forty-four-year-old housewife, along with him. In the final vote, it was ten for murder, two for manslaughter. But, according to jurors later, they might as well have returned the first day, because Polk was implacable from the first hour that he would never vote for murder, no matter how long they deliberated. He later told reporters that he thought Dan had been so ruthless and relentless in his treatment of Betty that his only real question was, "What took her so long?"

* * *

Whelan declared a mistrial and dismissed the jury.

Betty, dressed for the last day of trial in the same royal blue suit she had worn the first day, smiled uncertainly. What did it mean? she whispered to Pasas.

Pandemonium ensued. Earley, first looking shocked, then delighted, waited in the courtroom—"out of etiquette"—until Wells finished with the mob of reporters in the corridor. He had won by default.

Wells seemed on the verge of tears. She was, she told reporters, "obviously very disappointed ... I thought the evidence supported a verdict ... I see the issue as her sneaking into people's homes and shooting them in their sleep. I call that murder ... it [the loss] is horrible."

When she finished, Earley came out and, buoyed by his victory, announced to the world, for the first time, what he thought the correct result should have been: "The proper verdict would have been voluntary manslaughter." Even involuntary manslaughter, carrying a sentence of two to four years, would not have been unreasonable, he added.

He said he would continue to represent Betty: "I will be there. She wants me as her attorney, and I like her as a client." He promised to argue for bail for Betty prior to the second trial—but added that he would also be amenable to a plea bargain, if his client was.

In addition, if all twelve jurors would agree that they had ruled out first-degree murder, then Earley said he would argue that it shouldn't even be an option in the second trial, on grounds of double jeopardy. The threat of a life sentence without parole could be eliminated entirely.

Jack Earley had never in his wildest dreams expected to get a hung jury. Privately, he was a man in shock. Once the elevator doors closed behind him, he sagged against the wall, laughing helplessly, giddily. "Oh, my God. This means I've got to deal with Betty for another whole year!"

But, within the hour, as he sat in a bar next to his office, celebrating his victory with a Scotch and water, reality was sinking in fast. Why should he stay on this case? At the moment, he was on top, a winner. Plus, Betty was now indigent and could no longer pay his $260 per hour fees. Why should he accept the county's cheaper rates to do it all over again? Besides, the next time around, he was gloomily convinced, he was sure to lose, because the prosecutor now knew his entire defense. Next time, Betty very well might get two first-degrees. "It would've probably been better for Betty if she had gotten two seconds this time," he said. Still, Jack Earley had rarely been happier. "Poor Kerry," he chortled. The fact remained: he had at least won Round One.

* * *

That night, the Broderick case was the talk of the town. In bars everywhere, debate raged—mostly along gender lines.

"The legal system is top-heavy with males," a female secretary told a *Union* reporter at Dobson's, one of Dan's favorite haunts. "I think this is a good day for women."

"This is every man's biggest fear," complained a male executive in the same bar, "that your ex-wife can shoot you and get away with it!"

But the most poignantly bitter comment of all came from *Union* cartoonist Steve Kelley, Linda's onetime boyfriend. In his published drawing the next day, he showed two tombstones run down by a Suburban van with a license plate reading, not "LODEMUP" but "JURY."

Jurors tracked down by reporters described the chaos in the deliberation room. They couldn't even agree as to what the original vote had been. Some said it started out with seven voting for murder, five for manslaughter. Others said it was eight to three with one abstention.

Either way, although ten eventually agreed on murder, they never got far enough in their deliberations to determine whether it was first or second degree—and for one victim, or both. The main debate, said juror Charles Henderson, the auto mechanics teacher, centered around whether Betty had killed with malice or because she had been suddenly provoked. But, he said, only a couple of jurors thought she was capable of first degree premeditation. "The majority of us felt that there was no real premeditation ..." At the same time, he added, "I don't think anybody really and truly thought she was going over there to kill herself ..." On the other hand, "I felt she was provoked ... Dan was in a position where he could pull all the strings and she felt powerless ..."

Several other jurors said that Earley's strategy of putting Dan Broderick on trial had worked. "That was clearly a defense tactic, and it had its effect. I think that's partly why we hung up," said juror Michael Byrd.

Others said they were put off by the prosecution's witnesses—such as Melvin Goldzband and Ruth Roth. Both "experts" went too far overboard, said one juror, in declaring that, despite all their years of experience, the Broderick case was the worst they had ever seen. Their credibility, he said, "went to zero."

But, in the final analysis, it was only Walter Polk who really mattered.

In Polk's view, killing was out of character for Betty—but Dan's behavior was excessively cruel. Polk thought that "any normal person with normal intelligence and normal personality, after a lengthy period of time of mental abuse, would be driven to shoot somebody, kill somebody, or do some harm to them. It happens every day ... every human has a breaking point ... with humans or any animal, you push them to that point and they're going to bite back."

Linda barely came up in deliberations, he said. In Polk's view, Linda wasn't even the target. "She was just in the wrong place at the wrong time ..." Earley "presented a brilliant defense", Polk thought, "and Kerry Wells presented a fantastic prosecution—but she failed when she took Betty to the bedroom door and dropped it." Polk also thought it regrettable that Earley couldn't argue self-defense on grounds that Betty was a battered woman. The laws should be changed to better protect abused women, in his opinion.

However ironically, Betty Broderick had been saved, at least in the first round, not by a woman but by a gentleman from the old school.

A week later, Earley lost in a bid to have Betty freed on $250,000 bail. Larry Broderick had flown in from Denver to testify that Betty was "an evil monster in a harmless-looking package." He was convinced, he told Whelan, that if she should be released on bail, she would show up in Colorado in an attempt to see her sons. At which point, "I fear, we fear, and the court should probably assume, that there will be bloodshed." Whose blood he didn't say.

Earley called Broderick's performance "grandstanding" and untrue. There was not a shred of evidence, he argued, that Betty Broderick had ever threatened to kill Larry Broderick, much less her boys. She was, Earley said, no longer a danger to anyone and should therefore be released on bail.

Whelan disagreed. Bail was denied.

Betty would spend the next year in Las Colinas.

Earley's hopes of having first-degree murder eliminated in the next trial on grounds of double jeopardy were also dashed when only nine of the jurors agreed to sign affidavits saying that they had discounted first-degree murder in their deliberations.

Finally, amid much speculation that Kerry Wells might be removed from the case for failing to win a conviction, she was reassigned to prosecute Betty a second time.

"It ain't over 'til it's over," she later told reporters, beaming in happy relief, "and Betty Broderick isn't getting rid of me till it's over."

Chapter 39

1991

Betty sailed through her second year in jail with uncanny good cheer, doing exactly what she had done the year before: talking on the phone to friends and reporters and responding to her sympathy mail, which had only increased after the hung jury.

Although she complained periodically about boredom and "no fresh food, no decent water, no exercise, lack of cosmetics, and ugly jail clothes," she really didn't seem to mind. Her tone was consistently upbeat, alert, and optimistic.

Nothing about her suggested despair at her situation or remorse for her deeds. If anything, she only grew more articulate in her anger, more confident of her position. Outwardly, at least, instead of weakening, she grew stronger, harder, tougher. "Of course I'm better," she said gaily one day, "because I've had a chance in here to think, to heal. I provide my own therapy, because at last I've got peace. No stress." Las Colinas had been "like a vacation." Although it "wasn't Michelin five-star," she cracked to one reporter, "the price is right."

She was, in sum, institutionalizing completely. Her roommate for many months was a woman later convicted of first-degree murder for pushing a young girl off a cliff to collect insurance. The two of them got along fine, said Betty, "except she cheats at cards." She read books and newspapers and watched TV. World news interested her only moderately. When the United States invaded Iraq in January, she was puzzled. "If we can get close enough to photograph [Saddam Hussein], why can't we just assassinate him?" she asked.

And her zany sense of humor was untouched. On April Fool's Day, she called several friends and told them, "I've escaped. I'm at the 7-Eleven. Come and get me." She called to invite a reporter to lunch. "Pick me up at the back fence. Bring wire cutters." She even called Gail Forbes, "just to hear the shock in her voice," she said, giggling. And she mailed out several copies of a Gary Larson cartoon, showing a grumpy-looking housewife standing at a window, calling her dog. But the doggie door was nailed shut. "Here, Fifi ... Faster, Fifi," the woman was urging as the dog raced up the sidewalk. Betty had marked out "Fifi" and written in "Betty."

She worked her press connections faithfully all year. Two of her favorites were Cynthia Queen of the *La Jolla Light* and John Gaines at the *Union*. But she would soon outgrow local reporters, because, throughout 1991, she was getting bigger and better press all the time. In March, the *Ladies Home Journal* printed its story, a sympathetic piece entitled "Hell Hath No Fury," which was widely reprinted abroad. For the first time, Betty Broderick began receiving international fan mail from "Ireland, England, France—even the Philippines and weird little places like that."

And it had only begun. By autumn, *Mirabella* magazine printed an even more sympathetic piece with a cover headline taken from Walter Polk's one-liner, "In Hot Blood: Why Did Betty Broderick Wait So Long to Kill Her Husband?"

Earley, nearly as eager to cooperate with the media as Betty, was a happy man. All that soured his spirits was the TV movie underway. Nobody ever called him or Betty for their views. Instead, consultants included Larry Broderick and Sharon Blanchet.

Only Betty's weight clearly reflected the continuing fury, the tangle of untreated emotions inside. Although she had lost a few pounds before her first trial, during the long months between trials she put it all back on, and her skin broke out. "It's all the junk food they serve us, plus the inactivity. I'd kill for a walk on the beach." Even now, Betty hasn't learned to exorcise such casual threats to kill from her conversation. "Old habits die hard," she once said, chortling at the double entendre.

Dan's friends, meantime, continued to pay tribute to his memory. The American Ireland Fund began a drive to collect money for a library in his name in the Broderick ancestral village of Listowel, Ireland. The San Diego County Bar Association established a Daniel T. Broderick III Memorial Fund—reportedly collecting around $50,000—to refurbish a meeting room in Broderick's name at the bar headquarters building downtown. An oil painting of him, plus a long plaque listing names of donors, were part of the planned decor. The fund created a minor controversy in the legal community. One tax attorney wrote to the bar association magazine complaining that, in his view, the money would be better spent assisting all who suffer from domestic violence." Meanwhile, the Trial Lawyers Association established an annual Daniel T. Broderick III Award for "professional integrity."

* * *

Then, in April, Earley abruptly offered Kerry Wells a surprising plea bargain—he publicly agreed to accept a twenty-year sentence on charges ranging from manslaughter and kidnapping to burglary and assault. The kidnapping apparently referred to Betty's failure to return Rhett on schedule during the summer of 1989, the burglary to her theft of the wedding list and Linda's T-shirt.

The offer was seemingly no more than pure, perverse hyperbole on Earley's part, aimed strictly at evoking public sympathy. See—he was a reasonable man with a reasonable client, both trying to save everyone further emotional pain and the taxpayers the cost of another long trial. But it was so obviously untenable that he hadn't even consulted Betty about it in advance. All Wells could tell reporters, sounding more bewildered than indignant, was that Earley's offer had been rejected since it "didn't appropriately describe the crimes that were committed."

Betty read about it in the next day's newspaper, and her response was predictable. "Is Jack fucking crazy? He thinks I'm going to plea-bargain to kidnapping my own kids? And twenty years? Get real! I should be doing community service, just like Ollie North."

Otherwise, Earley took the year off from Betty, spending his time defending other less celebrated killers instead. Betty had not yet been granted the right to call her sons, much less see them—but that was no longer Earley's concern. Until Betty had run out of money after the first trial, another lawyer from his office had been handling the custody aspects of the case, which seemed never to move either forward or backward. But now that attorney had withdrawn, so—just as she had in her divorce trial—Betty was once again representing herself against Dan's attorney friends in pro per. Or, alone.

Kerry Wells, however, got no break from Betty during the year between trials. After the first trial, she was deluged with unsolicited advice from Broderick family and friends about how to better prosecute Betty Broderick the second time around. Most notably, in June, she received a remarkably presumptuous letter from Dan's brother Larry, laying out a thirteen-point program for improving her performance. These opinions, Broderick wrote, were the consensus of both the Broderick family and also several of Dan's attorney friends, including Dave Monahan, Ken Coveny, Ed Chapin, and Brian Forbes. All had studied Betty's testimony in transcripts provided by Monahan, conferred by telephone, and critiqued Kerry's case. The suggestions contained in his letter, Broderick said, were based on "what I believe would have the most positive impact on a jury of lower-middle-class, less-than-average-intelligence jurors." Among his points of advice:

"Virtually every lie that Elisabeth tells on the stand should be refuted, regardless of how long it takes." Also, Dan and Linda must be "humanized." Their friends should be paraded before the jury and each "should take the opportunity to ramble on a little about Dan and Linda ... Make the defense object. Make the court rule in their favor. Part of each anecdote or story will find its way into the minds of the jury."

He wanted Wells to prepare a chronology of "Elisabeth's escalating violence" to show that "her violent reactions and responses were always unreasonable." In addition, Wells should more precisely chart all the legal actions Dan had taken, to show how many were filed strictly in response to motions or actions taken by Betty.

He also advised Wells not to appear alone this time around, to "bring to the courtroom as much help as you can. The idea being to communicate to the jury that Elisabeth is a heinous murderer and a serious menace to society, and that the state is serious about putting her away forever ..." Also, he added, none too subtly, Wells could obviously use the help herself.

In addition, he didn't want Wells to skip over the murders this time. Instead, she should thoroughly dissect the events of that morning. "[Elisabeth's] whole story from beginning to end ... as to her plans to commit suicide ... is simply not believable. If she intended to commit suicide, why didn't she leave a suicide note for her kids?"

As for Dan's character, "You have raised the point that if we attempt to present Dan as a man of character and high moral standard, we would run the risk of Dan's character being assassinated by Wilma Engel, certain doctors who ran into Dan... and/or certain attorneys who felt Dan had gone overboard in his role as an advocate. In that connection, please be assured that both Dan's family and friends are willing to take our chances in this regard ... versus what might be said by scoundrels produced by the defense ... If Dan was the man we know he was, surely the doctors and attorneys who could be called by the defense could be dealt with easily ... [and] the Wilma Engel letter is not damning in our view, especially if we can get to who she was talking to on the airplane ..."

And, last but not least, "I would be inclined to play the tapes and have the boys testify as late in the trial as possible, so as to have the greatest possible lasting impact on the jury."

By summertime, Wells was a tangle of nerves, trying to figure out what to do differently this time, whose advice to take, which way to go. She was even being nicer to reporters, mainly because she wanted to pick their brains. She wanted a performance review from those who had sat through the entire first trial.

"Do you think I should be tougher on her?" she asked this reporter in a long phone conversation. Or should she try to kill her with kindness? But how could she do that? "I just get so angry every time I ask her a question, the way she twists and lies! But it's the way she treated her children that gets to me the most—that's why I have no compassion for her at all."

Should she focus harder on first-degree murder, or should she go even deeper into the divorce war trenches with Earley? Should she ignore Betty's lies, or expose every single one of them? "How can I not respond to some of the outrageous things she says?" Wells asked. "She lies about everything! How do I let the jurors know that it's all lies?"

She didn't mention Larry Broderick's letter—which didn't surface until Earley got a copy of it during the next trial—but she admitted that the Brodericks were griping that she hadn't better defended Dan's character. At the same time, Kerry Wells knew from experience that family and friends are always idealists about their loved ones. She knew that, if she opened that door, Jack Earley would romp through it with glee—and with worse than Wilma Engel's perceived blackmail letter, or a few angry doctors to complain about Dan's strong-arm negotiating tactics. Even Wells conceded in private that Dan Broderick was no saint, especially when it came to his treatment of Lee— nor did she approve of his lies to Betty about the affair. "But what was he supposed to do! He was afraid she would kill herself!" she said, exasperated.

And what about the narcissism? Did that work? Did she overdo the tapes?

She wasn't getting any answers, but it didn't matter. She was getting relief simply by talking about her dilemma. That summer afternoon conversation was one of the few times during two trials that Kerry Wells let down her guard with a reporter long enough to reveal that, beneath the cold, brusque facade, she was just one more ordinary, vulnerable, confused human being under major pressure. And her worst pressure of all concerned the two young Broderick boys: should she call them to the witness stand to testify against their mother in the second trial? At least one of them would say, she knew, that Betty had threatened that Saturday night to kill Dan the next morning.

But how could she do that to children, she asked? On a more practical level, would it backfire? Would the jurors hate her for it? "Will I take the fall?" Or would their testimony be worth it?

434

"I've thought about nothing but this case for two years," she finally said, sounding exhausted. "I have to hold on to my faith in justice. This time, I just hope the jurors will reach a decision—any decision—whatever it is ... I just want it to be over."

Then, toward the end of the summer, Danny and Rhett came to San Diego for a short vacation—and the judge ruled that Betty had a right to visit with them, under supervised circumstances, away from the jail, with the boys' attorney and a social worker present.

It would be Betty's first opportunity to exchange a word with her sons in nearly two years. Rhett was now twelve, Danny fifteen.

She was so nervous the night before, it was painful. "Oh, don't be silly," she said, laughing shrilly, her words as staccato as hail on a thin tin roof. "They're my babies. They love me, it's going to be like we were never apart!" And then she wouldn't discuss it anymore. No big deal.

Later, one of those present at the visit said Betty was so tense that she actually arrived with a list of questions clutched in her hand, reminders of things to ask her sons. It was, said the observer, a sad little meeting, filled with awkward small talk, a few hugs, and no tears. Mainly, Betty had behaved. She had not said anything inappropriate. "It was perfect," Betty later reported gaily. "It was as if we had never been separated. Fuck, I can't wait to get out of here and home to my boys. They need me. Danny's getting so tall ..."

Then it was September. Jury selection was scheduled to begin again in three weeks.

Betty was hyper on the phone that night, but it was a happy excitement. One more hung jury and they would have to let her go, wouldn't they? "How many times can you try a person? What about double jeopardy?"

Earley only shuddered after every conversation with her. She was so much more confident now, more the victim than ever. Time had only sanded away the initial ragged, hysterical edges, which at least had lent her a certain pathetic vulnerability during the first trial. Never mind remorse—now the tears and confusion she needed to display on the witness stand, Earley knew, would be harder to come by than ever. Betty had been allowed too much time to think—and to bask in the public glory. Most recently, even the TV news show *20/20*, anchored by Hugh Downs and Barbara Walters, had made arrangements to interview Betty at the jail. She was thrilled. She had hit the big time. She seemed on top of the world that week.

But so did Earley. For all his concern about the impact of Betty's swelling ego on her upcoming testimony, he wasn't about to turn down Barbara Walters either. He was, after all, a young man yet, with a full career ahead, long after Betty Broderick had become but a faded memory.

Then came the most lurid episode since the killings themselves—and one almost impossible to see as anything short of a systematic setup, given the fact that it was now only days until Betty's second trial began. Now, according to local newspaper headlines, Betty Broderick, after a year of making no jailhouse news at all, had suddenly turned into a vile, vicious prisoner attacking deputies and, moreover, rubbing her own feces over prison walls.

"Betty Goes on a Rampage," read a page-one *Tribune* headline of September 5. "Broderick Injures Three Deputies in Jail Scuffle." The story included a color photo of Betty in her underwear, and received more prominent play that day than the collapse of the Soviet Union.

According to the jail officials, Betty fought with several deputies who had come to move her from her cell to an isolation unit for four days as punishment for an earlier infraction of rules. One press account said she had refused a deputy's order to move from a bench; a later version said she had tried to wrest keys from a deputy to unlock her handcuffs. The details were never clear.

Whatever the case, when the deputies came for her, Betty, clad only in green jail panties and a sweatshirt, clung to her top bunk and, they later said, kicked them as they attempted to break her grip. According to one female deputy, Betty kicked her hard enough to cause her to hit her head on a television set. Another claimed that she suffered a strained shoulder after Betty grabbed her arm.

But, even more sensational, Kerry Wells promptly reported to Judge Whelan that, after Betty was subdued and placed in the isolation cell, she defecated and then smeared her feces over the cell walls and door.

Nor was that the end of the story.

In a move even jail authorities later conceded was rare, the scuffle had been videotaped. A police dog had also been brought to the cell that night.

In the next astonishing development, the jail then released the video to an attorney for one of the injured deputies—who in turn promptly gave it to San Diego reporters (after first trying in vain to sell it to TV networks, according to the *San Diego Union*). In addition, the attorney, James J. Cunningham, also filed a claim for at least $25,000 in damages in behalf of the wounded deputy. He had done so, he said, to "get in line" for any money Betty might later receive for movies, books, and interviews.

* * *

Thus, in the days just prior to Betty Broderick's second trial, prospective jurors all over San Diego County were treated on the nightly TV news to the spectacle of a large, frightened-looking, half-naked woman cowering in her bunk, holding on tight, as several pairs of hands snatched at her. One deputy even seemed to be holding a Taser gun.

But the struggle itself was murky. No deputies were seen on the film to be receiving injurious blows as they finally overpowered their prisoner and hauled her away to isolation. Likewise, the specter of Betty defecating in her isolation cell and then flinging feces around was never shown on any film. No evidence was ever produced. Just more sensational hearsay.

Jack Earley naturally raised holy hell. It was a complete setup, he raged to the media and the judge, a completely premeditated, staged scuffle designed and timed deliberately by jailers to damage his client's chances for a fair retrial—just one more example of how stacked the San Diego legal system was against Betty Broderick, not because she had killed but because of whom she had killed.

Earley demanded a trial delay until the negative publicity died down, and he also asked that Betty be transferred from Las Colinas because he feared for her life. "The word is out on the street with deputies that if you have trouble with Betty Broderick and you get it on videotape, you're going to be able to sell it ... to make money, you're going to be able to sue," he told Whelan.

Meantime, San Diego Country Sheriff Jim Roache issued a press release, denouncing attorney Cunningham's actions as inappropriate and unprofessional. But Roache had no good excuse for why the video had been released by the jail in the first place to an attorney hustling a buck. According to a sheriff's legal advisor later, the tape was turned over to Cunningham because he presented a subpoena for it as part of a worker's compensation claim. "It was just one of those things," he told a *Union* reporter. "It fell through the cracks."

For her own part, Kerry Wells pled complete innocence. She had only brought the matter to the court's attention because of Betty's upcoming interview with *20/20*, she said. She wanted Whelan to issue a gag order prohibiting Betty from discussing the incident to elicit sympathy from potential jurors.

Whelan refused Wells her gag order. At this point, said Whelan, with mild irony, any concern over publicity was irrelevant at best. "I fail to see what more she could say."

At the same time, he also refused Earley's requests for a trial delay and a transfer of Betty to the downtown jail.

Betty was angry, she was defensive—but, most notably, after all this time, she was at last completely and openly humiliated. What her own foul, childish taped conversations with Danny and Rhett playing in a silent courtroom couldn't do, what six days in jail hadn't been able to achieve in La Jolla's ladies circles four years before, what all the years of being called Crazy Betty hadn't done to her pride, what even two homicides hadn't achieved, had now finally been accomplished. She had been shown in all her vulnerability, with "my Jell-O thighs" thrashing and quivering in white, grainy light on television for all the world to see. She looked like a beached whale clinging to that bunk. And she had been accused of squatting, defecating, and then flinging her own excrement on the walls. It was the final disgrace, and she could not handle it.

For once, all her natural glibness failed her: it was all lies, she sputtered. She didn't kick anybody, she only reacted in fright. There were so many of them. Plus, "I hadn't done anything. Who thinks I'm stupid enough to try to grab some deputy's keys?"

But she could barely put together a coherent sentence as she tried to explain the feces incident: It was true, she said, strangling on embarrassment. She had lost control of her bowels while they were dragging her out of her bunk. "They scared the hell out of me, so I, uhm, yeah—pooped in my pants ..." Then, when they took her to the isolation cell, which has a small window in the door, "The goddamn toilet was overflowing. So I took off my panties and I—they—I looked up, and there they were—all watching me through the little window ... and they were taunting me. One of them said—they said, 'Look, she's fucking her finger.' It was disgusting. I've seen them do this before. They're sadists. Once I saw them set up a bunch of black girls in a cell with one white gay girl ... Anyway, yeah, so ... I got mad. I took off my panties and I threw them at the window, at their smirking goddamn faces. But I did not do what they're saying I did—rub it around and stuff ..."

In any case, nobody looked at the incident as alarming enough, if true, to cause a pause in the prosecution of Betty Broderick.

And then, typical of Betty's often astounding personal control, despite the trauma she had just been through, she walked out of her isolation cell the next morning to appear before the nation on *20/20*—where she delivered one of her most articulate, focused, subdued interviews yet. Although she lapsed periodically into the minutiae of "the story," she mainly managed to present herself to a national news program as a symbol of universal issues confronting women. Later, she was proud of her performance.

"I said this country has to reevaluate its definition of a weapon. No woman can take on an angry man ... the law has to take into account the differences between men and women in terms of their respective power. Men have all the power. I said, 'Sure, his friends are now building all these shrines to him—but that only reinforces my case. You bet—Dan Broderick was a great lawyer. That's why he could do to me what he did. Joe Blow couldn't do half of that to his wife, because he wouldn't have the know-how or the clout. This whole case is a story of extremes—extremes of poor to rich, and all the rest. I said that I represent the extremes of what can happen to women in divorce courts."

In a predictable bid for higher respectability, *20/20* cloaked its subsequent program in rhetoric about the pioneering aspects of the Broderick case in the largely untapped field of emotional battery. At bottom, however, it was also so pro-Betty that, as one of Dan's friends remarked bitterly, "It was barely a notch above *Hard Copy*. I expected more from Barbara Walters."

Then it was trial time again. Jury selection would begin on Friday, September 20.

Meanwhile, Earley, Pasas, and Bowman were all out of town for part of the week. Sitting alone in jail the prior weekend, Betty was semi-hysterical, as visibly unwell as she had ever been. She literally screamed over the phone, "Where is Jack's outrage? Where is my legal representation here? I should have a press conference!"

Dian Black, on a weekend visit, meantime, listened to her rave about how Patti Monahan had once borrowed an expensive white leather jacket from her and never returned it, "and she wanted it back," said Black. "She spent ten minutes telling me how she was going to write Patti a letter, demanding that jacket back." She also wanted Kim to return the $10,000 watch Betty had given her. What's more, she also wanted Black to return a copying machine Betty had loaned her. On the eve of her second Judgment Day, Betty was, in short, not reflective. Instead, she had escaped entirely into an obsession with "things."

That same night, she was also served with the deputy's lawsuit.

"How pathethic can you get ... they're suing me for $25,000?" Betty hooted. "You never ask for less than $2 million!" Dan had taught her that.

But, on the bright side, *People* magazine was coming to interview her next. She was looking forward to it, despite the fact that Earley was advising against it. Something about the reporter had alerted him to bad news ahead. Well, screw Jack. She was doing it anyway, she declared. And later, of course, Jack would be glad, she added sarcastically. "He'd be happy to see his name in a Dell comic book."

(Earley's instincts turned out to be right: *People* became one of the few national publications to take a decidedly sour note in the Broderick matter, openly hoping, in its eventual story, entitled "Rage of a Woman Scorned," that the second Broderick jury might be nicer than the first.)

That weekend, too, Betty somehow found a pair of scissors and cropped her hair as short as it had ever been. "It's a Geraldine Ferraro wedge cut," she said over the phone, sounding as giddy as someone on a drug trip. No more Danielles. She had also lost all interest in her wardrobe for Trial Two. She would wear the same two or three pants suits the whole time (Escadas, of course). "Why not?" she asked. "Look at all the shit the 'La Jolla socialite' took last time for just trying to look like me! Maybe I'll just wear my jail sweats the whole time, make that bitch Wells have a cow. After all, that's who I am now. Right?"

It was the only evidence in nearly two years since the killings that she was tiring, or changing, in even the smallest ways.

Chapter 40

Trial Two: Hitmen, Hotel Rooms, and Other Ugly Things

The second Broderick trial was, in most ways, a repeat of the first. Most of the same witnesses returned, and the essential trial themes were unchanged—was this an evil, hate-filled narcissist, or an emotionally abused housewife driven to kill?

But there were a few significant differences—nearly all of them to Jack Earley's disadvantage.

First, Kerry Wells was in better command of both her own emotions and the facts this time around. Now she knew the chronology and minutiae of the Broderick divorce inside out. Never again would Betty be able to make a fool of her over what fine occurred when, which incident involved dogs versus puppies.

And no more one-woman show. This time, Wells brought a partner to court, deputy district attorney Paul Burakoff. Thirty-something and prematurely gray, Burakoff was there strictly as window dressing, to convey to the jury—just as Larry Broderick had urged—that the State of California placed top priority on putting this dangerous killer away for life.

In a third major difference, adding up to more bad news for Earley, Judge Thomas Whelan was clearly determined from the outset that this trial would be more strictly focused than the first on the killings than on the domestic disputes that led to them. In a pretrial hearing, Whelan warned that he might exclude certain "expert" defense testimony as irrelevant. "What was relevant last time may be irrelevant this time, and what was irrelevant last time may be relevant this time."

Thus, this time, he ruled out any discussion of either Betty's abortions or Dan's drunk driving arrests, and he refused to admit into evidence Betty's Marriage Encounter letters, which had only recently been located. Dan's letters, however, were admitted again—over Wells's same objections.

Whelan also once again denied Earley's request that he should be allowed to argue that Betty was a battered woman who had killed in self-defense. "I'm asking the court to find new definitions for self-defense," Earley said. No, said Whelan. It was up to the legislature to change the laws, not him—and no existing law permitted a self-defense argument when the victims had been shot in their bed.

In another major difference, Betty Broderick now commanded such interest, coast-to-coast, that her second trial was televised live, all day, every day, by *Courtroom Television*, a relatively new national network, which divided its airtime between Betty and the rape trial of William Kennedy Smith. It was just one more ironic touch to this tale that Betty Broderick—who had spent years comparing the Broderick clan to the "drunken Irish, sexist Kennedys, who'll kill you if you cross them, just like Marilyn Monroe"—was now sharing their celebrated company before a potential six million viewers in forty-four states.

This saturation coverage was a mixed blessing for the defense. On the plus side, due to the exposure, Jack Earley received a few sensational new tips from strangers who had tuned in. Three of them were people who said they had heard Dan Broderick discuss ways either to kill his wife or drive her crazy through legal harassment years earlier. A fourth was a local hotel manager who said Linda once told him that she had been sending Betty anonymous fat and wrinkle ads. Someone else also tipped Earley that he might find it worthwhile to subpoena Linda Kolkena's Delta employment record.

On the downside, a few of the La Jolla ladies who had willingly testified for Betty in the first trial now backed out, after hearing with their own ears some of Betty's messages to her children—especially, her thirty-minute conversation with Danny.

But, perhaps worst of all for Earley, all this new publicity also sparked a new flood of fan mail to Betty, which in turn only rendered her more aggressively unrepentant—and less docile—than ever before. At the most critical hour, all the media exposure that Earley himself had so actively promoted was exploding in his face. His client had become almost impossible to work with. Now, instead of merely nodding sweetly to his requests, she was flatly telling him what she would and would not do, what he could and could not say. She was a star. She was going to walk. Her public said so.

And it only got worse. Before the trial was over, Betty would be sitting in the courtroom, oblivious to testimony, as she wrote angry letters of reproach to the producers of *Courtroom TV*, whose commentary was negative. In an equally bizarre, matching footnote, the program's reporters said that Larry Broderick, watching the trial from Denver this time, was calling their bosses in New York almost nightly to provide his own criticism of their commentary, which he found too favorable to "the murderess."

Just in time for trial, too, the *People* magazine interview was published. In the last paragraph, Betty once again exonerated herself, but with more bald sanctimony than usual. "I have regrets, not remorse. I regret my husband had no character, that my children lost their mother, home, and stability. I didn't do the legal bullying. I wasn't the one who had the affair. I won't accept the blame for what happened." Wells later read the passage to the jury.

Jury selection was the same grueling three-week process as before—the only difference being that the defense found the pool even more unfavorable than last year's. More minorities, more heavily blue-collar. Almost no educated, white, middle-aged divorcees for Kerry Wells to bounce.

Worse yet, the new, aggressive Betty was interfering this time. In one skirmish, for example, Earley wanted to accept a jury panel that included an elderly man Pasas was convinced was "our second Walter Polk." But Betty refused because she didn't like one particular woman—a forty-year old divorced mother of two—who had also been seated.

"She said, 'I will not go to court with this jury. I hate this jury,'" said Pasas. And so, against their better judgment, Earley and Pasas had let her force them into getting rid of the woman—which gave Wells an opportunity to get rid of the man.

When jury selection was over, the sworn panel included seven men and five women, aged twenty to fifty-nine. Three were Hispanic, two were black, one was Italian born. Two were college students, two had graduated from college, two were retired Navy men, and four were currently employed by the U.S. Navy in capacities ranging from mechanic to supply officer. The panel also included a city surveyor, a pharmacy technician, and a sheet metal worker. Several of the jurors had either been divorced themselves or experienced divorces in their families, as well as alcoholism among friends and relatives. One juror had been acquitted on a burglary charge years before—thanks, he said, "to a good lawyer." He liked lawyers—a lot. Earley worried about him.

None expressed strong views on profanity, but a few were avid gun collectors. The two youngest jurors, both women, aged twenty and twenty-one, were students: one in pre-nursing, the other in theater arts.

All in all, it was a blue-jeans jury of lively personalities whose lives had not been picture-perfect. There were no prim preschool teachers like Eloise Duffield here—and, certainly, there were no courtly gentlemen in suits and ties, like Walter Polk, who had been married for forty years or more. Wells, a wiser woman now, had seen to that. In fact, in this jury selection, she was even keener on getting rid of elderly men than aggressively independent women.

But, in the end, only two of the jurors would really count. One was George McAlister, forty-one, a Seventh Day Adventist with a master's degree in library administration, then working as a medical center librarian. The father of two children, married to a speech pathologist, McAlister was easily the most articulate of all the jurors in voir dire. And he became jury foreman. "Oh God," muttered Pasas, when she learned of his selection. "If he's for us, we're in great shape. If he's not, we're sunk, because his personality is strong enough that he's going to take the others with him—and no way is he going to let them out of that room this time without a verdict." She was right, too.

The other was Vivian Lou Smith, fifty-nine. A Protestant Republican and a widow with several grandchildren, she was a high school graduate, recently retired after twenty-five years as a switchboard operator for Lockheed. She lived in a condominium thirty miles north of San Diego, and was obviously something of a free spirit. Trim, dark-haired, and attractive, she sometimes came to court dressed like a proper grandmother, but other days showed up in skintight jeans. Smith smiled constantly at everybody—reporters, court-watchers, the defense team, the prosecution, and Betty. "She's driving me nuts," muttered Earley one day. "She smiles at me, and I think, 'Great, I've got her.' Then I turn around and she's smiling at Kerry, too. Goddamn."

On her questionnaire, Smith said she liked walks on the beach, belonged to her neighborhood *Crime Watch*, visited her children often, and "hated unpleasant things." For that remark alone, Pasas wanted to bounce her off the panel, but then decided that maybe Smith was passive enough that she might not hurt the verdict either way. As it, turned out, Smith was the closest the defense would come to a victory.

"We have the worst jury in the world," Earley later moaned into the phone to a fellow attorney, berating himself for letting Betty interfere with his own better judgment. "Nobody on that jury is going to relate to her when she starts talking about Danny's 'cherished spot' at Bishops, and her $16,000 a month. They're going to laugh!" Oh well, he finished, gathering himself. "What the hell—it's her trial."

Like nearly everyone else in the country, Betty spent the weekend before her trial watching the Senate hearings on Anita Hill's charges that U.S. Supreme Court nominee Clarence Thomas had sexually harassed her.

Unlike most, Betty related the historic event to herself. She believed Anita Hill, of course, she said over the phone, because she knew Clarence Thomas. "He's just like Dan Broderick, with his attitude that 'I won't descend into this, it's beneath me'." She also related to Anita Hill, whose female critics "all called her a woman scorned, just like they try to say about me."

In other national news, the case of Milwaukee serial killer and cannibal Jeffrey Dahmer was also on her mind. His bail had been set at some impossible figure—but, still, bail had been set.

"I should've eaten them," she said with a manic giggle. "Then maybe they would've given me bail, too."

Opening arguments were pretty much the same as before, although both Wells and Earley had sharpened their rhetoric. Wells referred now to Betty as "the executioner," Earley spoke of Dan as "a gladiator."

Wells didn't focus any more on Linda than she had the year before. It was still, to her, a Betty and Dan story—and it was obvious from her opening remarks that she had decided to dive even deeper into the divorce trenches than before, rather than back off. She intended to expose every single lie Betty had ever told, large or small.

She spoke at length, again, of Betty's privileges, her narcissism, and her deceptiveness. "There's a lot more to this woman," she said, than meets the eye. Betty Broderick "wanted nothing less than to keep on being Mrs. Daniel T. Broderick III." Wells played some tapes and, in her own moment of theater, strode about the courtroom, at one point holding Betty's gun in a two-handed grip.

Earley was both more articulate and aggressive than he had been the year before. He spoke more specifically of Betty as a physically and emotionally battered woman. He stated flatly that she had been driven crazy by the time she drove over to Dan's house that night. The woman jurors saw sitting before them now, he said, was not the same woman she once was, either physically or mentally.

This year, too, Earley was far more specific about events in the bedroom that night. He stated unequivocally that the victims had been awake, that Betty had been panicked into shooting when Dan had lunged for the phone to call the police. This time there was no question left, either, that Linda had shouted "Call the police."

As for gimmicks, this year Earley opted for a family portrait, covered by Saran Wrap, which he dramatically shattered at one point in his argument, as he discussed how Dan had shattered the family itself with his philandering and lies. Later on, in his closing, he set up a metronome, which ticked loudly as he listed the escalating pressures that drove Betty to kill. ("I wish he would drop that drip drip drip shit," Betty later remarked.)

Wells's witnesses were more relaxed and more aggressive the second time around. The touching nervousness that accompanies most first-time witnesses to the stand in a murder trial was gone. Helen Pickard, for example, had lost weight, grown her hair out, and was dressed with stylish flair. She was also so much more self-possessed that, at times, she became almost antagonistic toward Earley.

For his own part, in what was perhaps his single worst verbal blunder of the entire trial, Jack Earley managed, during his cross-exam of Brian Forbes, to make it sound that it was he, Earley, and not Larry Broderick who had referred to the jurors as "lower-middle-class, less-than-average intelligence jurors." He didn't even notice his gaffe until it was pointed out to him later. "Oh, shit," was all he said.

That this was going to be a down and dirty trial was clear from the first day. Already, for example, Earley was trying to keep Kim Broderick out of the courtroom on grounds that she was influencing the jury by sitting in the back row and crying sporadically all day. He failed.

Among Wells's first witnesses was Dan Jaffe, who repeated his earlier testimony about the house sale and his advice to Betty. Earley barely challenged him. Instead, he used his cross-examination only to worm in the news that Dan's former attorney, Thomas Ashworth, now presiding judge of the San Diego domestic court, had not only just been arrested on his second drunk driving charge, but had also recently settled a lawsuit out of court for an alleged $1 million.

Wells yelped an objection, too late. The jury heard.

It only got more squalid. Once, for example, when Wells called housekeeper Robin Tu'ua back to the stand, Tu'ua, looking directly at a Hispanic juror seated nearest her, managed to blurt out that Betty had once told her she "was lower than a Mexican." Like Wells, Earley yelped, too late. The jury heard.

For his part, Earley managed to blame Kim, on national television, for introducing her sister, Lee, to drugs in the first place. He also suggested that Dan himself may have had a drug problem, beyond alcohol.

Wells, meantime, just kept punching the tape player, flooding the room with more and more nasty Betty tapes.

In another truly macabre twist of Trial Two, on the opening day of the defense case, Jack Earley actually set up the death bed in the courtroom, within five feet of the jury box—complete with the actual sheets and coverlets upon which Dan and Linda Broderick had last lain. The white sheets were no longer red with blood, of course. Now the large stains had turned a muddy brown: the droplets of blood spray looked more like mold or insect droppings.

It was astounding, watching Earley and an assistant rearranging the sheets just as they had been when the bodies were found. Then two life-sized mannequins were laid amid the sheets, pink, faceless things representing Dan and Linda.

For the next hour, Earley marched a forensics expert around the bed. His object was to establish that Dan and Linda had been awake and in motion, based on the various distributions of blood pools and blood spray. The grisly testimony of the expert was too complex to follow—and hardly worth the shock value of showing those sheets to twelve jurors.

Not least, Earley's tactic, which he obviously hadn't discussed with his client in advance, devastated Betty for the better part of the morning. The minute the bailiffs led her into the courtroom, before the jury arrived, she burst into hysterical sobs and had to be taken back to the holding tank. Trial was delayed for fifteen minutes until she had at least partially collected herself. She returned to court with swollen, streaming eyes, unable to look at anyone.

Not until recess was it fully clear why she had broken down so badly.

It wasn't the sight of the sheets, said Betty's sister-in-law Maggie—they were mostly out of her view anyway. It was the lovely, delicate blue-and white needlepoint coverlet at the foot of the bed that had so pierced her. It was a coverlet Betty had bought in Pennsylvania, in Amish country, during the earliest days of their marriage, said Maggie. Dan was still in school, and they really couldn't afford it. But Betty had thought it so beautiful that she had bought it for their bed anyway.

Apart from the Broderick children, none suffered more from these killings than the aging parents of Dan, Linda, and Betty. Shortly after her son's death, Dan's mother had a stroke, followed by a fall that left her with a broken shoulder, arm, and pelvis. Linda's parents, both already in fragile health, fought with shock and anguish. "Our nonappearance at the trials was not a matter of disinterest," Dan's father wrote to Judge Whelan prior to sentencing, "but rather due to health problems." Atop his wife's critical physical problems, he said, "We both suffer mental depression from which there seems no surcease ... We are in our seventies, and this crime has shattered any hopes we had for peace and contentment through our declining years."

Betty's parents were equally devastated. Not until her second trial did Frank and Marita Bisceglia collect themselves enough to come to San Diego to sit through a week of testimony. They were a touching sight as they arrived each morning at 8:30 to take their place on the narrow wooden bench outside Whelan's courtroom, where they waited for trial to begin. They walked slowly, these two upstanding old people who had led such exemplary lives, clinging to each other and usually holding hands. She was taller, a large-boned woman, in her late seventies, dressed now for comfort, not style, in baggy clothes and soft suede flats or tennis shoes; he was smaller, neatly dressed each day in a camel-hair jacket and tie, his blue eyes alert to the audience around him. She avoided eye contact with strangers. The shame was still very great for Marita Bisceglia.

In the beginning, she went into the courtroom with her husband. But, when the time came for her daughter to testify, she sat all day alone in the hallway outside, with a prayer book in her lap, a Neiman Marcus bag containing snacks and cough pills and Kleenex at her feet. Betty Anne didn't want her to go inside during her testimony, she explained, "because she doesn't want to hurt me. She said she would be uncomfortable if I was there. So I'll just sit out here. What matters is that she knows I'm here, just outside the door."

It is so easy to see Betty in her mother. Just like Betty, Mrs. Bisceglia tries to hide all unpleasant feelings for the sake of strangers. She was friendly, charming, and determined to maintain a bright, chatty facade, no matter what the interior cost. In March, she confided brightly, she and her husband would celebrate their golden wedding anniversary. She was planning a large celebration for at least one hundred family members at a club on Long Island Sound. "And we already have a court order saying that the boys [Rhett and Danny] can attend," she added.

But no aging lady, no matter how tough, could keep it up for long, not in circumstances like these.

"My beautiful, intelligent child ..." she said next, wistfully, fingers fluttering nervously in her lap, her worried eyes tearing over as her mind wandered. "Now, of course, she's lost all her looks, but ..."

She blinked hard, gathering herself as proper ladies must publicly do. "If only she had told us what was going on," Marita Bisceglia continued. "But she never did! I know she says now that we abandoned her, but we didn't. We just didn't know how bad it was. Betty Anne was always so upbeat when she called—'Oh, everything's fine, the weather's so beautiful.' I think she was so afraid she would disappoint us— her brothers and sisters all have such wonderful marriages, such beautiful families ...

"But we would have always been there for her, you know—if we had only known. There's nothing I wouldn't do for my child... Oh, I should have known," she went on, punishing herself. "Betty Anne always had so many nice boys chasing after her ... I should have warned her from the beginning ... I should have seen it ..." Her voice went cold with a protective mother's belated hate. Then her mind was lost in time, back to Betty's wedding day, and she talked again about Dan's ugly brown shoes, and his arrogance. "I should've told Betty Anne to call the wedding off right then ..."

It was painful, listening to Marita Bisceglia second-guess herself, watching her wonder aloud, as any parent in her place must do, where she had failed. Verging on tears, she fled from the naked emotion, just as her daughter does. Pardon me, she said graciously—she had to run to the ladies room.

Frank Bisceglia was the opposite. By the time of Betty's second trial, he wanted to express his anger publicly—at Kim, at Gail Forbes, at Helen Pickard, and anyone else who had turned on his child. Daily, before court, he strode back and forth in the corridor, glaring at the gathering of Broderick siblings and friends at the other end of the hall. When Gail Forbes once approached him, smiling timidly, only wanting to deliver a polite hello, he said, "I told her, 'How could you turn you back on Betty Anne this way? I hope the next time you go to confession, you take an oath—otherwise you'll lie."

Saddest of all, neither of the Bisceglias could bring themselves to show any warmth or understanding toward their granddaughter Kim. She was a traitor in their minds. Pure and simple.

And Kim was too timid to approach her grandparents.

"Since they've been here," she said one day, eyes welling with tears, "they've taken my sister to dinner, but they haven't even called me. The only conversation I've had with them, here in court, they told me I hadn't done anything with my life. Grandpa told me that by the time Mom was my age, she had graduated from college, gotten married, and had me ..." She laughed bitterly. "I wanted to say, 'Yeah, Grandpa, and look where it got her.'"

"Why should we call her?" demanded Frank Bisceglia. "She knows what hotel we're in. Why hasn't she called us?"

That afternoon, he took the stand in his daughter's defense. He didn't have much to say, but Jack Earley didn't care about that—his only real purpose was to present this sweet-faced, silvery-haired old man to the jury as evidence that Betty Broderick was the product of the sort of upstanding, courteous, meticulous family that makes America run.

His conversation with Betty Anne the morning of the killings had been brief, no more than a minute long, said Frank Bisceglia in a strong voice. Betty had said she felt suicidal, but she never told him that she had just shot two people, he said. He had no idea. Betty cried silently the whole time her father was on the stand, paying attention to her miseries at last.

The Bisceglias stayed in a first-class hotel across the street from the jail. That night they hosted a gracious dinner for some of Betty Anne's friends. The trial was never mentioned. The loveliness of San Diego was discussed in detail. Frank Bisceglia told charming stories about the good old days in plastering, before drywall took over, times when people still cared for elegant rosettes and scrolls. Marita Bisceglia was a model of social grace and small talk. When the entrées were served, she said, "I have picked up my fork, so you may all please begin."

Betty was on the witness stand for almost five days during the second trial. She cried as frequently as before, if not as spontaneously. For the most part, her testimony was no more than a prelude to the drama ahead: the morning of the killings. This time, everyone knew, the scenario would change drastically, given Earley's opening remarks. This time, Betty Broderick would have to testify that she had been provoked to a panic by two people who were not sleeping, as Wells maintained, but wide awake.

And she did. Her face reddened and collapsed as Earley led her into the final scene. She had driven over to Dan's house, she said, with a jumbled mind crowded with feelings of fear and powerlessness. "All these thoughts kept churning in my head, like my eyeballs were turned backwards. It felt like the whole world was inside my head ... It felt like hell, actually." After she got there, all of it was "like a slide show with a lot of slides missing," she said. It was dark. But it wasn't dark. She couldn't see them. But she could. She no longer remembered Dan sitting up and saying, "OK, you shot me, I'm dead." She no longer even remembered telling that to Lee or anyone else.

But she remembered the most crucial slide:

In contrast to her stark, one-line testimony a year earlier—that "They moved, I moved, and it was over"—she now said that she had barely stepped into the bedroom when Linda had yelled for Dan to call the police, She also remembered Dan lunging for the phone.

And "I screamed, 'No!'"

And she had fired the gun.

Or maybe she didn't scream.

She didn't really know.

"I grabbed the phone and ran out of there. I felt like I let out a huge scream. I don't know if I even made a noise ... it was all sensation ... this huge sensation ... I don't really know what happened in that room. It was all these flashes of things ..."

Then she began to weep again.

Before Earley concluded his direct examination, she also said, in a flat, steady voice, with her head down, that she regretted, after the killings, "that I wasn't able to tell anyone how sorry I was." That oblique statement was the most Earley would ever get from his client by way of remorse in Trial Two.

Wells wasted no time in her counterattack. If Betty was sorry now, then why hadn't she said so in any of the hundreds of letters, telephone calls, and interviews she had conducted over the past two years?

Betty had no good answer, beyond a vague explanation that her mail and calls were monitored by the jail.

Wells was cold and derisive as ever. And, as before, Betty instantly collected herself and concentrated. But, for all the many reasons of passing time, circumstance, and Betty Broderick's mysterious mind, she was no match for Wells this year. Kerry Wells would win this battle, if not the whole war, on cross-exam.

She called a jail deputy to testify that, during the first trial, Betty had gloated that "she had the jury eating out of my hands" with her tears. "Absolutely not," Betty said.

Wells then began a relentless march through Betty's entire story, again down to the most minute details.

But it was not the same game anymore. Wells was like a Doberman going for the throat—regardless of the rules of court. At one point, for example, in blatant violation of Whelan's pretrial instructions, she made passing reference to Betty's prior abortions. Earley howled in objection, and Whelan, visibly angry, instructed the jury to disregard Wells's remark as a violation of his order that Betty's pregnancies would not be discussed. Jurors should not assume that Betty had been purposely concealing information, said Whelan.

But, as always, it was too late. The jury had heard. And, in Trial Two, Jack Earley would never be allowed at least to place those abortions in the context of nine hard pregnancies, breach births, cesarean sections, and miscarriages.

He consequently grew increasingly temperamental over matters large and small. On one occasion, he erupted in anger after Wells tossed her pencil on a table in exaggerated disgust at Betty. Earley resented Wells glaring at his client, too, he said, almost shouting at both her and Whelan. Another time, when Wells was interrogating

Betty about a stack of bills Dan had paid, Earley angrily countered by holding up, in full sight of the jury, Betty's own thick stack of diaries. In so many words, he told jurors, in the form of a meandering objection, that this whole trial was dirty pool, from diary pages taken out of context to a few ugly phone messages culled from literally thousands over the years. They were getting a stacked story, not the true one.

"Knock it off, Mr. Earley," Whelan said quietly, but with menace in his tone. It was a line that would become an increasing refrain in the second trial, where, it seemed, nearly everybody's temper was ready to blow, except for Betty's. The more the attorneys yelled, the more serene she became. She enjoyed having people fight over her.

Wells continued to interrogate Betty about her failed marriage, the separation, and her behavior afterward. But, this year, Wells displayed a tactical genius to brag about. Methodically, she walked Betty through a dozen or more items of testimony provided by assorted witnesses. She did not preach, and, for once, she didn't divert attention by challenging Betty's every answer with domestic trivia. Instead, Wells simply asked her questions, then waited, arms folded, until Betty had answered, and went on to her next question.

And, one by one, Betty Broderick disputed the testimony not only of her former attorneys and judges but also of her friends, Brad, and even her daughter Lee.

Every discrepancy, Betty said—from whether she had called Gail Forbes from jail on the night of the Blackstone Ball or gone shopping with Lee on the Friday before the killings—was the fault of others who were either "lying through their teeth" (Forbes, Pickard) or "mistaken" (Lee, Brad). Virtually everybody's memory was faulty but hers.

Even hard evidence was in error. She repeated that her obscene phone messages were aimed strictly at Linda Kolkena's voice—despite so many tapes to the contrary.

She denied making any grisly remarks to Patti Monahan. It was only Monahan's boyfriend who remembered it—"eight months later," she added sarcastically.

Through systematic, controlled questioning, Wells led Betty to attack not only Judges Joseph and Howett as part of the conspiracy against her, but also three of her four lawyers: Jaffe, Smith, and Hargreaves. Once started, Betty couldn't stop talking. The only reason any of those attorneys had taken her case in the first place, she volunteered, was because it would be "a feather in the cap" of them all to be involved in her divorce. But, in the next breath, she contradicted herself by complaining that Dan Jaffe was "precisely the kind of lawyer I needed,"—which is why Dan wouldn't pay him. Yet she insisted Jaffe hadn't warned her about four-hour notices or bifurcation. Then, dismissing Smith, she complained again that no good local attorney would take her case.

Wells nodded, then went on to her next question. Earley buried his face. Betty's mind was going in irrational circles for all to see. She was no longer the glib, collected, furious defendant of last year, saying, 'Well, let me help you ... you've got it all wrong."

449

Now, time and again it was, "I can't remember, I'm confused ... I don't know ... they're lying ... they're mistaken ... that did not occur ..."

She again assailed the Forbes couple as "perverted" for criticizing her language when theirs was worse. She insisted that her support checks had been altered by Dan throughout 1987, well after his informal 'fines' had stopped, despite a stack of $16,000 deposits to the contrary.

Even Brad was mistaken when he testified that she had gone to bed around 9:30, instead of 6:30 on the night before the killings, she said. Nor could she have possibly told Lee about the legal mail on Friday because she hadn't gone shopping with Lee on Friday. Lee was mistaken. Nor had she invited Pickard to read the letters on Saturday. Pickard was a liar.

It was, in short, a devastating day for the defense. Only Betty could not see. Instead, she sat through it all, looking alternately complacent and confused, smug and sad, indignant and then intimidated. Only she could not see that she was asking the jury to believe that she was a woman who had, in effect, been sabotaged, in ways both large and small, not only by her husband but by almost everybody else in her life, too. Virtually everyone involved in her story had the facts wrong. Everyone but her. And only she, in this silent courtroom, could not see how far afield her make-believe world had run, how paranoid she had become. She could no longer separate Dan and her legal wars from the innocent elements of life. But, then, that had been the case for years.

"Jack should have asked for a halt to the trial right then and had her slapped into Patton [state mental hospital]," Pasas said later.

But that is not how modern American justice works. In a system that proclaims even Jeffrey Dahmer sane, Betty Broderick's mental condition added up to no more than ugly personality quirks: her memory lapses were lies, her world view was pure selfishness, her confusion was calculated cunning—all of it mere grist for Kerry Wells's inexorable grinder.

The Broderick trial had gone from bizarre, inept, and comic to cruel. And it got worse. Wells led Betty to reiterate that it had been the letter referring to her "mental disease" that helped push her over the edge on the morning of November 5, 1989.

But why would that be so, asked Wells politely. Hadn't Betty always been confident that it was Dan who was crazy, not her?

Betty's face hardened. Too late she saw the trap.

"Dan Broderick never had a mental disturbance," she snapped. "He was just evil, vicious, and mean."

Wells moved on to the main event. This time, she spent nearly an hour on the weekend leading up to the killings.

Among her first acts, she marched to the witness stand with photographs of the two dead people, which she placed directly under Betty's nose. Betty might have been looking at a housing blueprint, her expression was so blank.

Calmly, she repeated that she did not remember shooting them, or even seeing

450

them, or hearing Dan cry out that she had shot him.

"I was in a totally altered state of consciousness," she said. "I've already testified that I didn't remember driving there. I was scared to death at confronting Dan Broderick ... I walked into the room. I've testified that it was dark. It appeared that way to me. I moved, they moved, the gun went off ... I just tensed—like that!" She flushed, and grew more animated. "I don't remember pulling the trigger once, twice, three, four ... I just went AAAAARGGGH! And I don't know if a noise came out. I just had this screaming kind of sensation, and a tensing ..."

Wells tensed, too. Hands clenched into fists at her sides, she paced back and forth before the witness stand, speaking through gritted teeth. Her exemplary restraint was fast disappearing.

If Betty had taken the gun with her only to force a conversation, then why didn't she use it as such? "You didn't use the gun to say, 'Hold it, I want to talk to you,'" Wells yelled. "You shot!"

But Betty was back in charge. Yelling she could handle. She shrugged helplessly. "I'm telling you it all happened so fast. It wasn't a thought process. I moved, they moved, the gun went off. It was over that fast."

Why had she gone in the back door?

"I didn't want him to see me and call the police before I saw him." And why hadn't she mentioned that Linda had shouted "Call the police" during the first trial?

Betty almost smirked at her. "Did anyone ask me that?" she asked innocently.

"Yes!" yelled Wells.

"I don't remember you asking me anything about it," said Betty.

Wells fought for self-control. It had, of course, been Jack Earley, not Wells, who had asked Betty during the first trial if anyone spoke in the bedroom that night—and Betty had said no. A different attorney might have recited Betty's contradictory testimony to her own attorney—but Kerry Wells was either too sensitive or too proud. She dropped it.

If the shooting was just a reflex action, she demanded next, then how was it that Betty had managed to reflexively point her gun at two people and land her shots so well?

Betty didn't know. "I'm telling you, it was dark ... so I couldn't have pointed it at anybody's chest." Nor did she now recall pulling the trigger, as she had testified the year before. "I did not move the gun ... It probably bounced around a little, because that's what guns do."

And hadn't she hit Dan's hand, as she was ripping his telephone out of the wall?

Betty blinked at Wells, uncomprehending. She didn't recall that. "I don't remember seeing Dan at all." She hadn't seen anything, not even the furniture in the room, she repeated.

Wells stalked to her desk and flipped through her files to the report of defense psychologist Katherine DiFrancesca and then began to read aloud from the document—which had only recently been made available to the prosecution. Not only had Betty told DiFrancesca, prior to the first trial, that Dan had said, "OK, you got me," she had also told DiFrancesca that she had then "hit him on the hand, because I

451

didn't get him."

Betty listened attentively. No, she said, she didn't remember either doing or saying any of that.

Wells finally gave up, after accusing Betty of "embellishing" her story this year to save herself. Betty gazed at Wells with level eyes. "Maybe I'm just explaining it better this year," she said softly.

"Well, I didn't think it was that bad," said Earley later that night from his car phone. His voice was half whimper, half laughter.

Besides, why should Betty be faulted, he demanded defensively, just because she hadn't recited every horrid detail of the killing scene last year? Wells, after all, hadn't even asked her about it. "So, of course she has more details this year. She's had them all along ..."

Defense attorneys are a fascinating breed. Earley couldn't even be joked into letting go of that position. He cackled but he never cracked. Linda had screamed for the police from the start. He had always known it. He just hadn't chosen to fully reveal it until now.

Over the jail phone later that evening, Betty was doing her best to sound as perky as ever. She thought she had done just fine that day, she said. But she knew better. At one minute she was giggling, manic. But in the next, there was a powerful new wistfulness about her. Even her voice changed—softer, huskier. For once, it was easy to get a word in edgewise.

Well, what did it matter anyway? she finally asked. Her life was over anyway, even if she did get out of jail. And the truth was, she really didn't want out of jail, she said. She didn't want to face the life that awaited an aging double killer on the Outside. And, as always, she could conceive of no life at all, beyond being Mrs. Somebody.

"Who'd marry me? And I can't do anything. I'd rather be here than be a poor, toothless bag lady. If I met a man that I could really like, it would change my attitude completely. But I don't want to be another Patti Monahan."

She also talked about the pictures she had been shown in court that day, of the two broken bodies she had left behind. She denied seeing them.

"I've been steeling myself for two years for it, I knew it was coming, that sooner or later, Wells would try to make me look at those pictures. But I didn't look at them," she insisted. "I focused on a corner of the top picture instead." And, she added, almost gaily, it can be done. "Have you ever had a friend with a crossed eye or a hairy mole? You know how you learn not to stare at it? Well, that's what I did—I just concentrated on a tiny little corner of those pictures, and I was also focusing on her [Wells]. She scares me. Jack doesn't. So I just kept my mind busy, to be on guard for her next question."

And why couldn't she look at what she had done?

She was silent for a couple of seconds. Then, resentfully, impatiently: "Because I don't want to see anybody dead, especially my husband! What's the point of having nightmares for two years? And obviously I'm afraid that if I look, I'll see something I

452

will never be able to forget. Jack wanted me on redirect to say I'd seen the pictures so many times that they had no impact. Well, no! I'm never going to say I've seen bloody dead pictures of my husband, and that they don't matter to me. I'm just not."

My husband.

And what about this new testimony—that Linda had been awake? She stammered. Betty is a lousy liar when it comes to the big stuff. "Well, yes, she was awake. And she said that ... what Jack said she said ... and I'm only just now remembering some of these things. You know?"

And then, naturally, she had to go, end this conversation. The deputies, she said, as always, were "taking us in."

Kerry Wells came to court the next day again looking happy, smiling at reporters and pausing to make small talk with various well-wishers. A few congratulated her for her victory over Betty the day before. She accepted with a pretty blush.

Her good mood didn't last long.

Because, now it was Earley's turn again to question his client.

The scene was vintage Earley. It was midmorning, and he was droning along, asking a boring, routine series of questions, when suddenly, in the jumbled context of discussing the Broderick children, he asked Betty, almost casually, if Dan had ever talked with anyone "about having you killed."

It was a bombshell out of the blue. Courtroom spectators jerked to attention, wondering if they had heard right.

Betty gaped at Earley in shock, too. For reasons that remain a tactical mystery, Earley had obviously not prepped her for this one. No, she said, reddening, then bursting into real tears, she had never heard that Dan was thinking of having her killed—"Obviously not!"

Wells stiffened as sharply as if someone had just jabbed her with a cattle prod. But she didn't even have time to demand a bench conference—Whelan, frowning, was already rising, moving toward the corner of the courtroom out of hearing of the jury, where all private quarreling occurred. The rest of the morning passed in eerie silence with jurors and spectators watching the animated, hushed argument among lawyers and judge at the far end of the room. Betty sat on the witness stand and dabbed at her eyes with a Kleenex. She looked drained as the cameras focused tightly on her face. In the corridor, the Court TV reporter was sending urgent dispatches live to six million viewers about this delicious new development.

Jack Earley lost the argument.

After lunch, Whelan issued a stem admonishment to the jury, concerning Earley's remark:

"This morning, Mr. Earley asked if Dan Broderick had ever hired someone to kill Mrs. Broderick. There is no evidence before you that such a statement is true. And the defendant herself is not aware of such an assertion. It is a mere allegation, not relevant to these proceedings. So disregard that question. The question and the answer shall be stricken."

After that, despite Wells's earlier efforts either to keep him out or severely limit his testimony this year, Dr. David Lusterman returned to deliver his same, earnest lecture on the devastating effects of infidelity. But, this time, almost nobody was really listening. Too much new excitement was in the air.

After court Wells and Earley were swarmed by reporters wanting to know what Earley had been talking about. What plot to kill Betty? Wells marched off, stony-faced, without comment. Earley shrugged. He couldn't elaborate, he said, because the judge had ordered him not to.

But his docility would not last.

On Monday, the jury was excused for the day, and the courtroom was closed to the public and press for hours. Inside, Wells and her assistant, Burakoff, were now also trying to block most of the testimony of Earley's battered woman expert, Daniel Sonkin. When reporters were finally allowed back in for the remainder of the hearing, Jack Earley, looking as angry as he ever does, barely waited until everyone was seated before he promptly, publicly named his murder-for-hire informant.

He did it in the context of another chaotic sentence, protesting Wells's efforts to limit Sonkin's testimony: "Obviously, the court is taking a position at this time that, and still my position with Dr. Sonkin is, that we have the evidence of Paul Taylor, who Mr. Broderick solicited to murder ..."

Wells literally screamed her objection. Whelan was even angrier. No more gentle, sleepy-eyed "Knock it off, Mr. Earley" remarks. Red-faced, he accused Earley of posturing for the press and instantly cleared the courtroom again. Earley hung his head, wearing his most doleful face of remorse.

Reporters stampeded to the phones to locate this Paul Taylor.

Taylor was a cab driver—and he was not eager to talk to the press, beyond confirming that Earley wanted him to testify. Earley had learned about Taylor through a tip from one of Taylor's regular passengers, a woman who had been watching the Broderick trial on TV. She said that, after the killings, Taylor had told her about a conversation he once had with Dan about possibly having Betty killed.

Pasas wasted no time in finding Taylor for an interview. And she later reconstructed this version of their conversation:

Taylor had first met Dan sometime in the mid-eighties—he couldn't remember the exact year—when he went to Dan's office to deliver a deposition involving his daughter, who was then Dan's client. While he and Dan waited for a stenographer to arrive, he told Pasas, the conversation turned to the topic of wives. Taylor's own first marriage had ended on a sour note, and he, too, had won custody of his children. Taylor told Dan that he had gotten custody of his children by "getting rid of his wife temporarily," said Pasas. Namely, the wife had gone to jail over some undisclosed offense, apparently drug-related.

Dan had then told Taylor that sounded like something he also needed to do, except, "I need to get rid of Betty permanently," said Pasas, recounting her interview with Taylor.

Taylor told Dan he thought that could be arranged, said Pasas. From there, the two had a detailed discussion of what it might cost—Taylor thought maybe as much as $500,000. But Dan wanted assurances, Taylor told Pasas, that the murder could not be traced to him. Dan did not want to do anything illegal himself—"He wanted it to be risk free," Taylor said. When Taylor told Dan that nothing was ever entirely risk free, the conversation ended, according to Pasas, with Dan saying that "he would think about it." Taylor said he never heard from Dan again.

And that wasn't all. Thanks to the TV coverage, two more witnesses stepped forward to say that they, too, had heard a man they believed was Dan Broderick threatening to have his wife killed some years earlier—and at least one of them would be far more difficult for Wells to shrug off than Paul Taylor, because he was, like Wells herself, a deputy district attorney, from San Mateo County in central California.

Charles B. Smith, now thirty-two, entered this squalid drama because of a call made to Jack Earley by his onetime girlfriend, Teresa Naquishbendi. Now a suburban San Francisco housewife and mother of three, Naquishbendi, twenty-nine, had been folding clothes at home one day, she said, while she listened to the Broderick trial on TV. As she later told *San Diego Union* reporter Jeff Rose, she was only halfway paying attention, until she heard Betty mention taking ski trips with Dan to Lake Tahoe in the early eighties. Naquishbendi had also once taken a trip to Tahoe with Smith, then her fiancé. She was twenty at the time, and Smith was a twenty-three-year-old police officer about to enter law school.

Naquishbendi stopped folding her clothes and studied the overweight, weeping blond woman on the TV screen before her. And the memories began to return. She knew this woman. She remembered seeing Betty Broderick and her husband in 1983 at Harrah's casino. "She was dressed very nicely ... in a long gown, not a hair was out of place ... she carried herself like a queen. On TV, she certainly didn't look like that, but, as far as the eyes and nose being in the right place, yes, it sure was [the same woman]," she said.

Naquishbendi also vividly remembered being horrified at her boyfriend's account of a conversation he had in the bar one evening with a handsome, well-dressed young San Diego attorney, who had bluntly told Smith that he was either going to drive his wife crazy or kill her.

By now, the entire scenario recounted by Naquishbendi was beginning to strike both Pasas and Earley as almost too bizarre to be true. Pasas seized the phone.

Deputy DA Charles Smith immediately remembered the incident as clearly as his former girlfriend did. What's more, he spoke freely about it to both Pasas and to reporter Rose—and he was also willing to testify at the trial.

Here is what Smith and Naquishbendi told Pasas midway through the trial, and Rose in a long feature interview after the verdict:

Smith had been sitting alone in the bar, when he struck up a conversation with a stranger who said he was a San Diego attorney. When the discussion turned to Smith's engagement, the attorney—whose name Smith never got—had warned him against marriage and bitterly proceeded to describe his own miserable relationship. He then told Smith that he was either "going to drive [his wife] crazy" or, "if that didn't work, he was going to hire a hitman" to kill her, Smith said.

The whole conversation had struck Smith as far more than just another idle, angry barroom diatribe by a husband fighting with his wife that night, which is why he later told his girlfriend about it. "It just got completely surreal ... It was like something you saw in a movie where you overhear someone planning to kill somebody," Smith told Jeff Rose. "It was so horrifying that my eyes practically bugged out."

Naquishbendi recalled details that Smith had forgotten. According to her, Smith also said that the man had even detailed his plan, saying he intended to drive his wife crazy by taking her money and her children through legal channels. And if that didn't work, he spoke of having her killed "and making it look like an accident."

Naquishbendi had wanted to notify the police or hotel security immediately. But Smith wouldn't let her, on grounds that the man in the bar, for all his loose talk, hadn't actually done anything wrong. They would sound like fools.

"I said, [talking] is not a crime," Smith told Rose. Besides, he stressed, he wasn't even sure of the man's identity.

But Naquishbendi remembered that when she had later seen the couple going into a show, she had tried to approach the wife to tell her what her husband had said. But, she said, when the man saw her and Smith, he had turned abruptly away, pulling his wife with him.

Smith agreed that he had not wanted to cause trouble, to make a scene. But, he told Rose, he still remembers Naquishbendi's last words to him, after the couple had vanished into the Harrah's crowd that night: "She told me, 'You will regret this ... This is going to come back and haunt you'."

At the same time Taylor, Smith and Naquishbendi were surfacing with their memories, a local hotel manager named Steven Griffin also emerged, wanting to help the defense. Griffin wrote Betty a letter in the middle of her second trial apologizing for his inadvertent role in the destruction of her marriage and volunteering to testify.

He had been a friend of Linda's ever since she moved to San Diego in 1982 and was working as a receptionist at an office building near his hotel, he told Pasas—and, he said, he had been renting the same hotel room to Dan and Linda since early 1983. Furthermore, he said, sometime around 1987, he had heard Linda talk about sending anonymous things through the mail to Betty. In fact, Griffin told Pasas, Linda once asked him to mail a white envelope addressed to Betty with no return address, from El Cajon, a town near San Diego. He said he refused. And, at his final lunch with his friend in May, 1989, Griffin told Pasas, Linda had also told him that she and Dan intended to wear Betty down, sooner or later, through legal tactics.

Griffin's motivation in coming forward was never clear. He had apparently gone through a bad divorce himself and, it seemed, also experienced a religious conversion of some sort. Either his conscience was bothering him, or bitterness over his own divorce was.

Either way, here is part of what he had to say in the letter he wrote Betty in mid-November, 1991:

"Dear Mrs. Broderick . . . I've written to you for a couple of reasons: I want to apologize for allowing rooms at [his hotel] to be used for their meetings. I see that what I did was very wrong. Second, I wanted to let you know that I tried to tell the whole truth about what I was a party to from January, 1983-May, 1989 ...

"... I'm sorry for hurting you and your family ... I was told that the feelings were mutual in regards to both you and your husband being able to see other people; moreover, I was told you were aware of their relationship. Now I see that was a lie and how it hurt you and your children."

Griffin said he wanted to testify to all this but had not been allowed. "It is obvious to me they do not want your side of this story told. I had no reason to hold anything against them or you. I just wanted to tell the truth. I feel my testimony would certainly have tarnished the halo they seem to want held above their [Dan and Linda's] heads ..."

He ended by begging Betty again to accept his belated apology. "May the love of God be with you."

By then, too, thanks to another lead, Earley had also subpoenaed Linda Kolkena's Delta employment records. There is no overstating his glee when he discovered that Linda had been fired, not only for improper sexual conduct with a male passenger but also "for using bad language!" he reported, almost incredulous, as he sat in his office one evening. "And, in her own defense, she said she just didn't think anything about it! That she used (such language) all the time!" Earley's toothy python's smile was wide enough to gulp a full-grown goose.

A few blocks away, the atmosphere in the DA's office was apparently almost as comically incredulous. By then, Wells and investigator Green had also received defense copies of Linda's Delta files, which, according to Green, took the prosecution by complete surprise. "We didn't know whether to laugh or cry," he later recalled. "We just asked ourselves, 'How much worse can this get?'." Green had also interviewed both Paul Taylor and Steve Griffin with nearly as much haste as Pasas had—"and," he added dryly, "the worst part was that I didn't doubt the credibility of either one of them."

In their only comfort, the prosecution team knew that Judge Thomas Whelan would never admit any of it into evidence.

Earley knew it, too. He didn't even try to get Linda's Delta files admitted into trial. He knew Whelan would never let him go back that far in time to undermine her character. But he argued heatedly that Taylor, Smith, and Griffin should be allowed as witnesses to Dan's state of mind, and Linda's, throughout the years of the affair and the divorce.

Wells countered that all three were irrelevant—but, still, she was obliged to concede far more than she would have liked in making her case. She agreed, for example, that Dan had a conversation with Paul Taylor about hiring a hitman to kill his wife—but, according to Taylor in his interview with investigator Green, she pointed out, Dan had then said he would never do anything like that "because it's illegal."

Regarding deputy district attorney Smith, Wells dismissed his potential testimony as mere "hearsay" without "positive identification." And anything having to do with Linda Kolkena, including her alleged chats with Griffin about sending Betty fat and wrinkle ads, was "patent character assassination," Wells argued indignantly. The defense was trying to "produce by ambush."

Whelan agreed. Dan's state of mind wasn't at issue, nor was Linda's—only Betty's was. And, since Betty didn't know about any of these alleged plots and schemes, they could have had no bearing on her motivation in killing. Furthermore, since this wasn't a self-defense case, Dan's reputation for violence was also irrelevant, Whelan ruled. Thus, he banned all three witnesses from his courtroom.

After the hearing, Earley angrily vowed to reporters that he would appeal any negative verdict based on improper exclusion of evidence.

"The jury deserves to hear both sides, whether they believe it or not," he declared. "One of the problems is that the jurors are looking at Betty's testimony and saying, 'Hey, here's a woman who's a little bit on the crazy side', "he told the *San Diego Union*. "But, when you look at what she's been claiming all these years, when you look at the evidence, lo and behold, Dan was at least professing to other people— and so was Linda—that they were doing exactly what Betty said they were doing!" And was it logical, he demanded, to think that both Taylor and Smith—two men from entirely different walks of life—would fabricate the same tale?

Wells ignored all questions about Dan's alleged schemes to destroy Betty. "A lot of people don't realize how much information you get from crazy people out there," she snapped as she swept past.

Newspaper headlines the next day blared: "Broderick Target of Death Plot?" asked one. Just as San Diegans had begun to get bored with the Betty Broderick story, it became steamier than ever.

By Tuesday, Whelan had had it with all the gossip, innuendo, and media speculation. He was particularly tired of picking up the paper to see Jack Earley complaining about his rulings.

And so he slapped a gag order on both attorneys and their investigators, forbidding them from publicly discussing evidence or potential evidence, at the risk of going to jail. At the same time, contrary to his promise the year before that the Broderick trial would be wide open, he also imposed a ban on selected sidebar hearings, normally available in transcripts to the media, and ruled that certain hearings on witnesses would now be closed to the press, too.

It was all downhill for the defense from that point forward.

After hours of argument behind closed doors, Wells and Burakoff succeeded in so limiting the testimony of Daniel Sonkin that he finally walked out in a professional rage. In a press conference in the courthouse corridor, Sonkin reiterated his view that

Betty Broderick was a victim of not only psychological but also physical and sexual abuse. "But," he said angrily, by the time the prosecution and the judge were finished, he had been forbidden from even suggesting that Betty was either physically or sexually battered. Instead he would be permitted to testify only to his opinion "that Mrs. Broderick was emotionally abused ... but that is not the complete story, and it is not fair to trivialize the issue of battered women in that way."

Thus did the defense lose its only expert witness on emotional battery. Nor did Earley attempt to replace Sonkin at the last minute. What the defense had originally billed as a potentially pioneering case in emotional battery ended up with no mention of battered-woman syndrome at all—emotional, physical, or sexual.

Instead, aside from Dr. Lusterman's remarks on the effects of infidelity, Earley allowed Trial Two to limp to its lame ending with only the mental health testimony of psychologist Katherine DiFrancesca, who, for all practical purposes, might as well have been a prosecution witness, since she again testified that, regardless of Dan's role in Betty's emotional demise, Betty had a latent personality disorder from the outset. Betty remained stable only so long as her familiar anchors were in place, namely her identity as a wife and mother and respected member of the community, but once those supports were stripped away by the divorce and Dan's subsequent behavior toward her, said DiFrancesca, she had collapsed emotionally into a severely depressed, essentially defenseless victim of her own personality failings.

At the same time Earley's defense was fizzling to its finish, the prosecution was going all out for glamour to convict Betty. In place of Dr. Goldzband, Wells now produced Dr. Park Elliott Dietz, a $300 per hour forensic psychiatrist with a national reputation. Among his resume highlights, Dietz had testified for the prosecution in the case of John Hinkley, the would-be assassin of President Reagan, and for the defense in the case of Robert Bardo, the obsessive movie fan who shot television actress Rebecca Shaeffer to death. Never mind that Dietz had been on the losing side in both cases (he said Hinkley was sane and Bardo a schizophrenic). His credentials were enough to impress a San Diego jury. (After he finished with Betty, Dietz would go on to the sensational Jeffrey Dahmer serial murder/cannibalism case in Milwaukee—where he would testify that Dahmer was sane in part because he paused long enough to use condoms before sex.)

Dietz promptly declared Betty Broderick a flawed human being, an extreme narcissist with histrionic traits, suffering from a mixed personality disorder. But, he said, she was definitely sane and responsible for her acts.

"The person rules the condition, the condition doesn't rule the person," said Dietz. A middle-aged man with a bland, controlled manner, he was distinguished mainly by his devilish eyebrows, which shot like inverted V's nearly into his receding hairline. Also, he didn't blatantly curry favor with the jurors. He was too self-confident for that.

Dietz had, of course, not interviewed Betty. He hadn't even tried. He didn't need to. He could see all he needed to see, he said, based on many hours of reading through court transcripts, medical reports, and her own writings.

And what those materials had shown him, he testified, were the traits of a woman

459

who fit every single medical definition of a narcissist. While only five of the nine criteria defined by psychiatric manuals are necessary to qualify as narcissistic, Dietz found that Betty fit nine out of nine, ranging from grandiosity, swollen ego, and lack of empathy for others, to "a feeling of entitlement—that the world owes me respect, money, and fame." She was, in short, an extremely distorted human being, well before Dan left her for Linda, in the opinion of Park Dietz.

He supported his views by quoting extensively, but selectively, from both Betty's diaries and her Marriage Encounter letters—further enraging Earley, who had by now exhausted himself arguing the unfairness of these piecemeal excerpts from documents which he would never be permitted to enter into evidence in full.

Buttressing his assertion that Betty required undue, constant attention, Dietz read this passage from her Marriage Encounter letters: "I feel no one admires me and I need that," she had told Dan, at age twenty-eight. And, read Dietz, "The number one thing I loved about you was how much you loved me ..." Among other examples of her narcissistic grandiosity, he also quoted, in all seriousness, a flip remark Betty had once made to Kim that one day she would run away and marry a Saudi prince who would lavish her with riches.

And so on. Just about everything Betty Broderick had ever written or said, short of her grade school essays, was now being thrown in her face as evidence that she had always been a twisted personality.

That Betty was histrionic was obvious, Dietz said, as demonstrated by her constantly exaggerated emotions, temper tantrums, and colorful language—anything to keep attention on herself. "The emotional pitch is more important than facts to the histrionic ... it keeps them in the limelight." He also conceded that, if controlled, histrionics can be quite charming to others. Hollywood, he quipped in his only moment of attempted humor, was full of them. "They can be fun. They know how to work an audience."

But Dietz disagreed with DiFrancesca that Betty was a borderline personality, because, he said, borderlines normally can't get along with others, and obviously, for many years, Betty Broderick was very easy for everyone to get along with. Nor did Dietz think she was severely depressed after the divorce, since she had functioned so well. Dietz didn't believe Betty Broderick had ever been seriously suicidal either. Her one alleged effort, wherein she "had scratched her wrists," had been nothing more than an attention-getter, typical of her personality problems, he said, because "She's too narcissistic to harm herself, to harm such a perfect thing."

For the first time in Dietz's testimony, Betty glanced up from her legal pad with an expression other than benign. Who was this insulting asshole on the witness stand? She glared at him with purest contempt.

Earley's cross-examination of Dietz was interminable. It also got nowhere. Afterward, Wells dismissed Dietz quickly. It was four P.M. on the evening before a four-day Thanksgiving recess, and she had something more powerful than Park Dietz in mind for the jurors to take home with them for the holiday.

She marched again to her tape machine, which had begun to resemble nothing so much as a machine gun aimed straight at Betty Broderick's head.

Earley stiffened, called for a bench conference, lost, returned to his table, and listened to the tape with a stone face.

This was a tape Wells had apparently just discovered, since she had never played it before. It was a conversation between Betty and Rhett, just before Thanksgiving, 1987. Rhett was sobbing from the beginning. At issue was where he and Danny would spend Thanksgiving. Dan had said they couldn't go to Betty's, and Betty was demanding to know why not. Here is their exchange, in part:

Rhett: "I dunno. He just said no." [crying]

Betty: "What are you gonna do over there?"

Rhett: "I don't know." [crying]

Betty: "What's the matter?"

Rhett: "My stomach ..." [crying]

Betty: "Well, I'm going to make a wonderful, wonderful Thanksgiving dinner, with all my wonderful food, and the Forbeses are coming, and the Michaelsons are coming, and the Sarises are coming. [cheerful] We're all going to have a wonderful time ... and you guys need to be here. You don't belong in the slums with the cunt and your father and his drunken, divorced asshole friends like last year. Remember last year—the cunt said, 'Your father's an asshole'?"

Rhett: "Yeah." [sniffling]

Betty: "She was right. [laughing] But he's a rich asshole and she's too smart to walk out on him ..."

Then, from Betty:

Betty: "Poor little Muffy [Rhett's dog]. I put her out back to get some exercise and sunshine, and she's crying. She wants her babies back."

Was she giving the puppies away? Rhett cried, sounding heartbroken.

Betty: "We're giving three away! I can't keep them. There's nobody here to play with them."

Rhett: "NOOOOO! [crying] Can't we keep them?"

No, said Betty. She then told him whom she was giving the puppies to.

Rhett: "But I want a baby!"

Betty: "You had a baby. Muffy. But you missed her growing up ... because Daddy's such a fucker. Right?"

Rhett: "Right."

Betty: "So, why give you another baby and you'll miss it growing up again ...?" The boy was silent, except for his sniffling.

"Rhett, I hate to tell you this," his mother continued, in a tone of weary patience. "But you've got to learn to stick up for yourself. You've got to speak up to Daddy and the cunt. He's killing you all. He's ruining your lives and killing you, and you've got to speak up and fight back."

Rhett: "I'm not dead." [crying]

Betty: "Well, maybe you're not dead physically, but emotionally you're dead. You don't have anyone who loves you or cares about you over there, and he mistreats you ... treats you like a little piece of shit, and he's a coldhearted bastard fucking an office cunt ... what kind of a parent is that?"

Rhett: "A cold one?"

Betty: "A bad one. A very, very, very, very bad one. And you shouldn't put up with it anymore. You should tell him to fuck off. You and Lee Lee and Danny should say, 'Fuck off, asshole,' and come over here. Tell him to drop dead and go away. And then you'd be happy over here. Right?"

Rhett: "Right."

Betty: "You gotta stick up to him ... he's a maniac. He is a raving mental maniac."

Rhett: [muffled response]

Betty: "Just get away, just get over here. I'll get the police to beat the shit out of him."

She went on to tell Rhett that maybe she would even "come over and bring the TV cameras," too. It would be a rescue operation, she quipped, "like getting the hostages out of Lebanon ... the Iranian hostages, a sneak attack ... You're little prisoners of war. Poor babies."

Then, all lightness gone, annoyance in its place, she demanded: "Rhett, when are you gonna get over here?"

Rhett: "I don't know ..." [sad]

Betty: "When he tells you you can't come over here for Thanksgiving, don't you say anything back? Or do you just say, 'Oh?'."

Rhett: [no answer]

Betty: "Well, go fight. Beat up Daddy. Bye."

Rhett: "Oh, wait! Mom?"

The buzzing dial tone rang across the courtroom, intermingled with the little boy's shrill, pleading cries.

"Mom?"

"Mom ...?"

But Mom had hung up.

With that, Wells briskly wished the jurors a happy holiday. Earley looked like he might vomit.

Betty was as oblivious as ever on the phone that night. "What are we going to do here? Nothing is getting out!" she fumed. "Where is our expert on litigious assault? Where is our expert on codependency?"

It was the first time all year that she had expressed any real interest in witnesses to address those themes. Always before it had mostly been battered-woman's syndrome.

She didn't want to discuss the Rhett tape. But, like the Danny tape, she didn't think it was that bad—and everything she had said "was true."

Almost incidentally, she also mentioned that, after court that day, the bailiffs had allowed her parents to remain behind for a few minutes to talk to her. It was the first time they had been allowed past steel and glass to touch their daughter since the killings.

"And you know what the first thing my stupid-assed mother said to me was?" she asked, laughing, mimicking her. "'Oh, Betty Anne, if only you'd married Eddie Frye!' I didn't even remember who Eddie Frye was! I said, 'Mother, who the hell is Eddie Frye?'."

"'Oh, he was the nice boy whose father owned the flag factory'."

Meantime, she said, passing over it, her father had only hugged her and cried.

Then the moment was gone. In the next breath, Betty Anne was a prisoner again, giggling over the phone at one of her cell mates.

"They just love me here," she exclaimed. "The girl on the next phone was just telling her boyfriend that she's in jail with Betty Broderick, and she told him, 'If you don't say "I Do," I'll kill you!' Her laughter was wild.

And that was the end of Trial Two. Earley's only real defense, beyond Betty's own testimony, amounted mainly to the same parade of La Jolla women who had appeared in Betty's behalf the year before. With a couple of exceptions, they all returned, to say the same things. But this time, they better understood the rules of the game. If they wanted to take a swipe at Dan, they knew they would have to do it on their own, apropos of no question. Some were almost amusing in their determination.

Asked something innocuous about Betty's baby-sitting days, for example, Wilma Engel suddenly blurted out, "I always felt Betty was intimidated by Dan. Dan Broderick even intimidated me, and I'm not easily intimidated." Marilyn Olsen did the same thing. Out of the blue, she declared that "Betty was very dynamic, very intelligent. Dan just seemed like an overgrown fraternity boy."

Wells's jaw muscles were always the best monitor of her mood. Now, as these infernal women kept up their unsolicited remarks, she looked like she was grinding molars to hold her tongue.

But Wells scored a few points of her own.

Lucy Peredun, Betty's former roommate at Calle del Cielo, testified that Betty had told her, falsely, that all her attorneys had cruelly quit on her at the last minute, which was why she was representing herself in her divorce trial.

Besides Pickard and Forbes, Wells herself also called another member of Betty's former La Jolla set: Liz Armstrong, a friend from Betty's investment club, testified that Betty was a whiz when it came to the stock market—not a woman apt to be so financially helpless as the defense claimed.

That night Betty called, fuming as usual over all the wrong things. Her mind was mainly on Liz Armstrong. "She made it sound like I'm plugged into flicking Wall Street! I didn't even know how to work my computer! It was for the kids—little green frog games!"

From there, she went into a tirade over what she suspected Jack Earley intended to say in his closing argument. This time, Earley had hinted to her strongly that he was going to beg for a manslaughter conviction.

She was livid. "He better not! I will stand up and scream and make a scene if he asks for manslaughter! Sure, he would consider it a major victory if he got

463

manslaughter—but after I've gone this far, why should I accept that?" She was still expecting an acquittal.

Closing arguments were predictable. Wells was swift and to the point; Earley took half a day. In her most theatrical moment, Wells marched around the courtroom, brandishing Betty's gun; Earley hooked up his ticking metronome.

Wells again asked for two counts of first-degree murder. She pointed to the contradictions in Betty's testimony between the two trials. This year, Betty said she had been spooked into shooting by Linda's cry to call the police; but in the first trial Betty had said nothing about Linda speaking. Which version, Wells asked, did they believe?

Wells also played the feminist angle this year—but in reverse. Sure, she said, maybe Dan should have been more honest with Betty from 1983 on. But, she said, trying to blame Dan for his own death—as the defense was doing—was similar to accusing a rape victim of asking for it by virtue of her dress, her language, her walk.

She finished by saying, "If this isn't murder, I don't know what is!" Then, almost wearily, she begged the jury to return, this time, with a verdict—any verdict. "Make a call," she urged, and sat down.

When Earley rose, the entire audience rustled audibly, shifting back, settling in for the long haul.

With his metronome ticking, dramatically, he argued again that it was the accumulation of psychological abuse that had led Betty to snap. He paused, allowing the jury to listen to the tick-tock of his clock for a few seconds. "It goes on and on ... the sound is enough to drive you crazy after you hear it over and over again ..."

Betty's crime was committed in the heat of passion—it was not premeditated, he said. By the night of November 5, 1989, she was "so far gone" that she was incapable of premeditating anything. She was reacting only to the pressures. Then, coming as close to feminist oratory as he ever had—in fact, copying Betty's own language—Earley told the jury that Betty Broderick was being held to an age-old, sexist double standard. Any man who had been similarly stripped of his job, his children, his dreams, and his ambitions would probably have reacted even more strongly than Betty had, and sooner. But the legal system would have treated him with far more leniency. What man, for example, would have been jailed for dirty language alone?

Earley also argued that Dan had never been afraid of Betty, that the drama he made over her loose remarks and threats to kill him was strictly for show to protect his own image, to exonerate himself, just as Betty had always said. Otherwise, asked Earley, rising to his booming best, why was it that Dan Broderick, a multimillionaire, had made such a big show out of hiring security guards for his wedding, but failed to invest a few hundred dollars in an alarm system that would have instantly alerted him to any intruder creeping up his stairs on the morning of November 5?

Because, thundered Earley, answering himself, "He wanted to announce, 'World! I have a crazy wife!' And a security system doesn't stand on a corner and wear a badge. The world doesn't see that!"

In conclusion, he asked the jury for a verdict of voluntary manslaughter. This time, Jack Earley was unequivocal. Betty's crimes had been provoked in a heat of passion, after years of torment. "She was so far gone by then," he said quietly, in a tone of real pity. She deserved compassion, not condemnation. She deserved manslaughter—not a life condemned to prison without possibility of parole.

The hokey metronome aside, Earley was very good. Later, in the first and last compliment she would ever accord him—and despite her fulminations beforehand—even Betty agreed.

The jury went out on Thursday afternoon, December 5. Like the first jury, they were not sequestered, and they would also remain out for four days.

Earley was both morose and melancholy at lunch that first day.

"I'm gonna lose, huh?" he asked everyone at the table. Nobody answered. Pasas checked out her newly refurbished nails. Dian Black changed the subject. Earley sighed. He needed to go over to the jail to talk to Betty, he said. But he was afraid to. She was going to yell at him, he said, for asking the jury to convict her of anything.

So he didn't go until the next day. By which time, his mood was better. It was Friday. Once again, the jury hadn't humiliated him by returning with a verdict in two hours.

Chapter 41

Whelan's Bar

It was midafternoon on Tuesday when the jury returned. Some looked upset, but nobody was crying.

They found Elisabeth Anne Broderick guilty of two counts of murder in the second degree.

Wells listened grim-faced, jaw muscles working. Earley bowed his head; Marion Pasas put her arm around Betty.

But Betty needed no comforting—at least not then. Not publicly. Never in public. Instead, she patted Earley's hand and smiled at the jurors as they were individually polled. She might have just been told that she had lost a class election.

"When they said 'second,' she turned to me and whispered, 'How many years is that?'" Pasas recalled later.

In the back of the packed courtroom, Kim cried, and Larry Broderick hissed "Jesus Christ" loud enough to draw attention. Lee was not there. Whelan set sentencing for February 7.

Two years and two trials later, it was over.

Wells hid her disappointment well. Even if she hadn't won her first-degree convictions, she hadn't entirely lost either. At least she had crossed the line from manslaughter to murder. This time she didn't appear anywhere near tears.

"I believe that she did premeditate these murders," she calmly told the swarm of reporters in the corridor. "But jurors are obligated to give a defendant a reasonable doubt, and they did on that issue."

Best of all, she had at least gotten a verdict. The nightmare of another hung jury had evaporated. Relief set in fast. According to a *Tribune* reporter, as she strode out of the courthouse afterwards, she raised a clenched fist and, beaming, said, "Thank you, God. Thank you, God."

But, again, nobody was any happier on verdict day than Jack Earley. He emerged from the courtroom, solemn-faced but with a bounce to his step, a gleam in his eye. He promptly vowed again to appeal the verdict, based on evidence Whelan had excluded, but he also pronounced the second-degree verdict a victory for Betty. It was, in effect, another hung jury—a compromise. What's more, he said, if the defense hadn't been so fettered, he was certain the verdict would have been manslaughter.

When one reporter snidely asked why Betty had smiled when the verdict was read, in a rare display of impatience with the press, Earley snapped. Part of what this case was all about, he said sharply, was Betty Broderick's infinite capacity to put on a happy face, regardless of her interior misery. "Betty was a social people-pleaser.

Even in the worst of circumstances, she will smile. Her kids ask her about prison, and she tells them she will go to a happy little trailer, so they are not worried."

Twenty minutes later, out of sight of the TV cameras, Earley was, as in the year before, beside himself with delight. He had won. With all her advantages, Wells had once again failed to score her first-degree convictions. "I wanted to tell those cameras, 'I'm thrilled!'." But, it was more than professional satisfaction. Jack Earley also seemed genuinely relieved for Betty. From the beginning, his idea of victory had always been two second-degrees. Now, at least, Betty was saved from life in prison without possibility of parole. Not that the alternative was much better, he added. For a few seconds, sadness softened his matter-of-fact face. At minimum, second-degree murder meant a fifteen-year sentence, per count. In the best of all worlds, Whelan could sentence her to concurrent terms—meaning she would be eligible for parole in nine years. But Earley was under no illusions about Whelan's frame of mind. This judge would not be lenient: Whelan would instead slap Betty with the maximum—consecutive sentences, totaling thirty years. She would not be eligible for parole for nineteen years—or the year 2010. She would then be sixty-three.

"Poor Betty," he said quietly, glancing away. "Maybe she'll cry her heart out tonight. But she's really out in left field. I don't think she realizes yet what's really going on." That she was facing anywhere from nineteen years to life in prison. A long, long time.

Then, in the next breath, with a wry smile, Earley's moment of sorrow had flown. "Still, that's more than Dan and Linda got," he said. Criminal defense attorneys are a fascinating, inscrutable breed.

The Broderick camp convened at Reidy O'Neil's to mourn the verdict over Irish ales, in the melancholy gloom of the plush green room filled with photographs and drawings of Dan Broderick. Bittersweet Irish ballads played softly in the background.

Larry Broderick's frustration was total as he raged to reporters about "the monster" who had just escaped full justice for killing his brother. "I'm outraged that the jury did not convict this woman of the crimes that she committed," he said bitterly. "What's the matter with a system that allows this woman to threaten these people dozens of times, buy a gun, take shooting lessons, blow them away in their sleep—and that's not murder one in this goddamn country?"

From Portland, Linda's sister was more benign. The Kolkena family was just glad it was finally over, said Maggie Seats. Whether it was a verdict of first-degree or second-degree didn't really matter that much to them. It wouldn't bring Linda back.

Betty had no family members in court that day, but, from Nashville, her brother Frank told reporters that he had hoped for a manslaughter verdict, "but I'm not living in Never Never Land." For the moment, he was more worried about his parents than Betty. Their hopes dashed, the elderly Bisceglias had retreated behind closed doors to grapple with the latest reality to shatter their golden years: Their daughter was now a convicted murderess.

But the main attraction of the day was the jurors. Five had remained to speak with reporters. Foreman George McAlister did most of the talking.

It had been a painful emotional experience for them all, he said, and it was clear from the outset that another hung jury was very possible. Several jurors, himself included, had leaned toward first-degree murder, but at least two were in favor of voluntary manslaughter—and one of those had vowed that she would never vote for first-degree murder. She would hang the jury first.

And so, they had been obliged either to compromise or return no verdict at all. At times, said McAlister, discussions deteriorated into an emotional brawl.

As with the first jury, the debate had centered on the issues of malice and premeditation—or, Betty's state of mind. "And there was so much aberrant behavior on Betty Broderick's part, not acting as a reasonable person would act. Her perceptions of the world seemed somehow different than what a normal person would perceive ..." But since no insanity defense had been raised, McAlister said, jurors simply did the best they could with the legal instructions they were given.

Several jurors were convinced, based on Betty's testimony, he said, that she wasn't stable enough at that point to premeditate anything. Which ruled out first-degree. That left only second-degree as a viable compromise. McAlister had then gone around the table, he said, and asked everyone if they could live with "murder two." But, up until the last hour, "a couple of people" still wanted to think it over one last time during lunch hour. In the jury's final act before lunch, he said, they had listened one more time to Betty's conversation with Danny in 1987.

After lunch, he said, "We all held hands," and the holdouts had joined with the rest in agreeing to second-degree murders.

Other jurors who spoke to the media were shy, vague, and generally imprecise. "People were crying ... yelling," said one man, who thought it was first-degree. "It was quite a load for a simple person like me," said a middle-aged machinist, but "[McAlister] was great. Without him, we wouldn't have come to a decision ... he got us to agree."

So in the end, just as Earley and Pasas had feared, one strong juror had shepherded his flock to a definitive vote.

Ironically, McAlister's main roadblock to consensus was Vivian Smith, the heart-faced grandmother who, like Betty Broderick herself, always had a sunny courtroom smile for everyone. Albert Vargas, the thirty-seven year-old Naval security assistant who had once been charged with burglary, had initially sided with Smith, although without the same passion. In the end, it was Smith alone who threatened to hang the jury until an hour before the final vote.

But Smith, the oldest member of the jury, was no Walter Polk. She rolled over. If it was Vivian Smith who saved Betty from a first-degree murder conviction, it was also Smith who finally handed Wells her second-degree murders. It was Vivian Smith who spared Kerry Wells another crushing defeat, and denied Jack Earley another overwhelming victory.

Even her voice sounds remarkably like Betty's. Chipper, bright, suggestive of a woman who lets very little in life get her down. Nor was she later agonizing over her capitulation after the verdict. But her views on the case remained strong.

"Dan wanted her put away as crazy so he could run around with that little twig tail," she said, disgusted. "He threw her out like a piece of garbage. She didn't deserve that. She put him through school. If he'd have given her the children and the money, it wouldn't have happened. But he was so powerful. Nobody could come up against what he had ..."

Smith also disapproved of Kim's role in the trial. "I know Kim loves her mother. But she should have stayed out of it, like the other daughter did. I think Lee is the smartest one, staying out of the media and all of it ... My daughter told me just the other day, 'I could never testify against you, no matter what you did!' I think Kim is going to regret this, the way she hurt her mother. I feel sorry for her."

As for the attorneys: "Kerry Wells was cold as ice and very calculating. But she is a very smart, articulate woman ... she convinced jurors that she knew what she was talking about."

Earley, by contrast, "was pretty good ... but," Smith added delicately, "he rambled. Sometimes you didn't know what he was talking about." On the other hand, she added, determined to be fair, "He was also very limited. We could all see that. And when I found out later what we didn't get to know—that Dan was planning to do her in! And he would've gotten away with it!"

But what shocked her nearly as much as the hitman scheme itself was the fact that Earley hadn't prepared Betty to say she knew about it so that the evidence could be admitted. "I don't know why Betty didn't just lie about it!" she said, laughing nervously at her own lawless thoughts. Even sweet grandmothers like Vivian Smith obviously get savvy fast, sitting as jurors in first-degree murder trials.

Smith said she believed every word of Betty's testimony. "And I don't feel she's a menace to society. It's ridiculous. She's so sweet. I think she just temporarily lost it. He flipped her out. He killed her first, her spirit—that's how I feel. I began to see how Dan and Linda had victimized her. It's like teasing an animal until it runs after you."

But Smith finally decided to abandon her voluntary manslaughter stance because, she said, she could see jurors defecting to first-degree by the hour. "Several thought Betty was lying about the whole thing ... So I thought, 'My God, this is getting worse than I expected.' I felt I was doing Betty a favor by going for second." Although jurors are instructed to disregard the penalty phase of the trial, Smith also admitted that she couldn't take her mind off the fact that first-degree meant life without parole. "I wanted to save her from that. I would have just cried my eyes out to see her ever get first-degree!"

Smith thought the Danny tape had hurt Betty more than any other single piece of evidence in trial—it turned several jurors against her permanently. "It was very, very damaging—I think that if Betty could have just said she was sorry, it would have helped her out," said Smith. "I mean, I know how she felt. If I'd been badgered that way, I'd probably have killed him even sooner—but she needed to show more remorse."

Toward the end, Smith said she was taking terrible heat in the jury room. "For four days, they yelled their heads off at me. But I just didn't believe Betty went in with

469

malice. I thought she went to get their attention and maybe kill herself ... I mean, I've been around the corner a little bit. I know what pain feels like. As a woman, you have to bear a lot of things or you're lost from the beginning. But all those young women on the jury—they were just kids, they didn't have enough life experience to know anything." Then, when Vargas defected to second-degree, she finally stood all alone in that last hour. And so she folded.

But, to the later dismay of Jack Earley, who initially entertained hopes of a mistrial based on undue pressure on a juror, Smith insisted, firmly, that she wasn't browbeaten into changing her vote. "I don't want to imply that I was badgered—I think I did the best thing for Betty. If I could have been sure there wouldn't have been another trial, I think I would've just stayed [on manslaughter], but ..."

Besides, as Vivian Smith saw it during the weeks after the verdict—and prior to the sentencing—second-degree wasn't really all that bad. "She'll probably get maybe seven years, less three for time served. She should be out in four or five years, don't you think?"

Vivian Smith had no idea that the maximum sentence Betty Broderick could receive was thirty-two years to life. "No!" she gasped. "Oh God! I just can't believe Judge Whelan would do that! He seems so kind! I thought he was just wonderful ... I'm sure he'll be lenient. If I had thought she would get more than a few years," Smith added, "I would definitely have hung in. But, no—I just don't believe that Judge Whelan will make her serve more than five or six years."

Betty called that night, laughing happily. "Can you believe the scoop—they never even considered first-degree!"

She seemed not to grasp that nothing had been won, in terms of the rest of her life. It wasn't real to her, any more than it was to Vivian Smith. She reveled in the courtroom reaction to her conviction. Rosie, the clerk, "almost cried," she said. The bailiffs almost cried. "They all love me." And all the girls in jail cried for her. "They were sobbing! And I was saying, 'Guys, it's gonna be okay.'" Always, always, poor starved Betty clung to affection, wherever she thought she saw it, blinding herself to all else.

She only laughed at her own courtroom composure, like an actress on stage. "Oh, I knew I would do that all along. Betty Broderick doesn't break down in front of people," she said proudly. Not anymore, at least. Never again.

Then, as she so often does, she abruptly switched personalities. Within the space of five seconds, she was a different woman. This Betty was introspective, tentative, almost shy. Even her rat-a-tat-tat speech slowed to normal.

"You know I'm not brave," she said quietly. "But I've got this thing, I grew up with it. We all did in my family—you don't shame yourself by crying in public. You could cry for joy, but never for pain. I remember once when I was just a little kid, about eight years old, this aunt of mine died—Aunt Vi. I really loved Aunt Vi. And after the funeral, my mother had this wake at the house. It was supposed to be a celebration. No tears. No big shows of sadness. I remember crawling into this little closet we had under the kitchen stairs and crying by myself, because you couldn't cry in front of

470

anybody at my mother's party. It would have been too unpleasant. So I guess I'm still that way," she said, with another of her self-conscious, dismissive little laughs. "It's still me and Aunt Vi, hiding under the stairs. . . .

"Besides, I have to look at the bright side of this," she went on. "I was more scared of getting out than of staying in anyway. How does Betty Broderick build a life with nothing? I have no earning power. How was I going to get on my feet and have a life?" She paused, thought about what she had just said, then analyzed it herself. "I was so overprotected by my parents—I'm only just now realizing how sheltered I really was. I'm such a scaredy-cat. I always was. I never really got to spread my wings. So, yeah, I'm scared ... But, who knows?" she added hopefully, with determined cheer, "Maybe I can do something really cool up in prison. Women have no rights there. What I told myself today was that this was an act of God. If I could go up there [to prison] and do something worthwhile, it will all be okay."

Then, the quiet Betty was gone. Madcap, giggling, black-humored Crazy Betty was back: "Fuck, maybe I'll organize a Jewel Ball for the women in prison to raise money for more cosmetics and candy and stuff."

For the next month, as she awaited her sentencing, she acted more like a woman packing for an exciting new trip to an even bigger, better health spa than a convicted murderess bound for state prison for many, many years.

"Well, everything's relative," she once remarked cheerfully—and, having consulted with some of her old Colinas roommates who had gone on to state prison, she had learned, she said drolly, "that the service is supposed to be better there than in county jail. We get real coffee and there's dental. God, I have so much plaque!"

She made giddy jokes, too, about the importance of Brad keeping her credit cards up to date. "I want those credit cards. I can still shop from prison, you know. I can still order from catalogs." Then, in mocking parody of her own public image, "NO00Othing stops the La Jolla socialite from shopping! Hell, I still have $100,000 in credit lines I could blow in two days if I got the chance, no problem."

Meantime, she still had the media to keep her busy. Reporters continued to swarm about, now wanting her reaction to the verdict. "What's this town gonna do without Betty Broderick?" she quipped.

She had also heard that The Maury Povich Show was doing a program featuring Sharon Blanchet, Larry Broderick, Maggie Seats, and her daughter Kim. "Can you believe that little bitch?" she asked, not even angry. "I'm going to prison, and she's still trying to bury me!"

But Betty would have the last word. In the most exciting news of the new year, Oprah Winfrey wanted to do a full show on her case at the end of the month, just prior to sentencing. Earley would fly to Chicago for a live appearance, along with Dr. Lusterman, and Betty would be interviewed by remote hookup from the jail. "And Jack says they promised it would be just our side, none of the other stuff ..."

Upcoming, too, was the TV movie about her case. Although she was still indignant that she hadn't even been consulted, she was nevertheless excited. Good or bad, it was, after all, a movie about her.

Finally, she preoccupied herself worrying about where her two sons were going to wind up. Neither boy wanted to stay in Denver with Kathy Broderick and her three children. Betty wanted Danny to live with her brother Frank in Nashville, Rhett with her brother Girard in St. Louis. Both brothers were willing. Girard even hired a lawyer. Dan's eight surviving siblings, by contrast, were oddly silent about the fate of their brother's sons. Only one of his cousins eventually sought to legally replace Kathy Broderick as guardian. A custody hearing was set for two days before Betty's sentencing.

For all her singsong bravado, however, January was not a good month for Betty. Both of her sons came to San Diego for the New Year's weekend. They stayed with Mike Reidy's family. Helen Pickard had a party for them. But neither boy made the thirty-minute drive to Colinas to visit their mother. Betty was bitterly undaunted, blaming it all on pressures from Kim, Pickard, and the Broderick clan. "Given a choice, my boys will always want to see me," she insisted. "They're still hostages!" Of all the things Betty Broderick may never be able to face, even privately, the impact of her own actions on her children's subsequent reactions toward her probably is number one.

But, finally, she broke down. As usual, it was because of her parents. Her father had written her a letter, talking about "how hard all this has been on Mother" and saying that they were canceling their grand fiftieth wedding anniversary celebration because they were so devastated by the verdict.

Then she got a letter from her mother. She began reading from it over the jail phone one afternoon, her tone initially sardonic: "My doctors say I will never get well until I put this out of my mind," Marita Bisceglia wrote. "But I just can't accept what has happened to our wonderful family. None of us will ever get over this until the day we die. Please pray I don't get a stroke ... I don't want [your father] to have to take care of me."

Betty's voice cracked under the strain, thick with unshed tears.

"But not a word about me! I'm the one going to prison for who knows how long—thirty-two years maybe? And not a word that God will be with me, that they love me—nothing. Instead, she's worried about herself. At forty-four years old, I'd like to say it doesn't hurt, but it does." She fought to steady herself.

"Well, I have to hand it to her—Mother is consistent. She's been like this since I was a kid ... She's a control monster, just like Dan. I remember once in high school, she bought me a gray Belgian linen dress, embroidered. It was beautiful, but it wasn't me, so I never wore it. She got upset and tore it up! Literally tore it up!"

With that, Betty Broderick began to cry helplessly. "As long as I was properly married to the doctor-lawyer-Indian chief, I was the favorite daughter, but when I failed at that, I turned into nothing but a disgrace to her!"

And all the others, too. Old friends, relatives, Dan's family. After the divorce, "Everybody just abandoned me. They just took off. But why?" she asked shrilly through her tears. "What did I ever do to any of them?" Nobody was ever there for her except Brad. "And he never really understood what was going on with me. By the end, I was afraid of everything, I was afraid when it rained, I was afraid when the mailman came, I was afraid to go out socially. But everybody just said I was crazy!"

She was crying so hard that she couldn't stand it anymore. "I gotta go, they're taking us in now," she said politely. "Bye."

Two more unpleasantries finished out her month. First, the *Oprah* show turned out not to be the one-sided production Jack Earley had anticipated. Instead, it also included interviews with Larry Broderick, excerpts from the infamous Danny tape, and remarks from Kerry Wells. Earley barely got sixty seconds of airtime, and, worse, Winfrey herself seemed so concerned that her audience might think she was endorsing murder that she was almost hostile in her interview with Betty from jail. "She sounded like the DA!" Betty complained later, near tears. "Her whole approach was the same old shit—the woman scorned. She asked me at one point how I could be afraid of them when they were wearing bulletproof vests!" She had been so upset, she said, that she almost walked out at one point. "But I just couldn't. I can't be rude to anybody—much less on national TV."

Even so, it turned out to be the second-highest-rated show in the program's history. Which meant that Winfrey would not only come back for more eight months later, but her tone would be much, much nicer—and Betty, of course, would docilely play ball again.

At about the same time, the boys' custody hearing was also indefinitely delayed at the last minute, at the request of the Broderick attorneys—until well after Betty had been shipped to prison, far from San Diego. She was beside herself. Her hate surfaced as clearly as it had since the day she went to jail for murder.

"How can I still be divorcing this fucker who's been dead for two and a half years??!!!" she screamed over the phone. "It is never over! It's the same shit! I still can't even talk to my own kids! Dan Broderick got his balls shot off for that!"

And then the hour of sentencing was at hand. On February 7, 1992, Judge Thomas J. Whelan would at last do what two conflicted juries had been unable to do: He would crack down on Betty Broderick as harshly as the law allowed.

The little courtroom filled up fast, this time almost exclusively with family, close friends, and court staff. For the first time in two trials, members of Linda Kolkena's family—Maggie and a brother, Ray—were also in the courtroom.

For once, Betty did not turn and smile at her friends. She looked almost scruffy, in wrinkled blue pants with an orange blouse and plaid Escada jacket. Her hair was flat, she wore no makeup. She looked pale and tired. Even when Lee entered the courtroom, she couldn't smile. She only turned a wan face to her daughter and lifted the fingers of one hand, laying on the desk, in a small gesture of hello.

Earley entered his perfunctory motion for a new trial, which he knew would be denied, since no judge was likely to overrule himself. And he was right. At liberty at last to tell the world exactly what he had been thinking all this time from his bench, the benign Judge Thomas Whelan was no longer so benign.

No defense witnesses had been unfairly excluded, declared Whelan—and especially not Daniel Sonkin, since, in Whelan's view, there was no evidence whatsoever that Betty Broderick had been either physically or sexually abused by her former husband. But, for the record, Whelan was careful to stress that he had never ruled "against evidence of battered-women syndrome ... or emotional abuse." Instead, he had bent over backward in both trials, he said, to give Betty "wide latitude to speak ... she had a full and complete hearing."

Nevertheless, Whelan found that Betty Broderick really had no case at all. In his view, she was not a victim of legal abuse, any more than she had been a victim of sexual or physical abuse. "He [Dan] was not trying to drag her through the system." Instead, as Whelan saw it, Dan Broderick was "a man trying to bring this thing to a logical and speedy conclusion." In fact, Whelan thought Dan had been generous in his dealings with Betty. He cited two examples in support of his view:

First, Judge Joseph had once chastised Dan for changing his mind at the last minute and asking that the court not jail Betty after all. And, secondly, Dan had advanced Betty about $40,000 beyond her half of the proceeds on the sale of the Coral Reef house. Whelan was evidently unimpressed by the fact that, in lieu of jail, Betty had been fined thousands of dollars instead, and that every dollar of the house advance was ultimately subtracted from her share of their community property in the divorce trial years later.

In summary, it was the opinion of this San Diego Superior Court Judge that the San Diego judiciary had behaved in a consistently exemplary fashion, and so had the former president of the San Diego County Bar Association, Daniel T. Broderick III.

Jack Earley's motion was therefore denied.

Then came the sentencing.

Kerry Wells was, as ever, concise. If Betty Broderick wasn't punished for two murders, rather than one, she said, the message that would go out to all potential killers was that, "Hey, if you're going to kill one, you might as well take out a couple of others, too." She also argued that "beyond her clever self-promotion," Betty was "a very disturbed woman" who might kill again "if she felt wronged."

The saga of Betty Broderick had thus come full circle: from the crazy woman Dan Broderick had once defeated in divorce court so successfully that she had even been denied visitation rights with her own children, to the cold-blooded, premeditating killer of the district attorney's scenario who merely had a personality disorder and should go to prison for life. Betty Broderick was now, once more, a potential lunatic who might go on a murderous rampage again, if ever freed.

Wells saved her last angry salvo for the media, which had, in her mind, turned a merciless killer into an unwarranted star: "I think it's time for everyone—including the press," she said, staring idly into the press gallery, "to give [Betty Broderick] what she so richly deserves: Ignore her! ... She is not a martyr, she is a murderer!"

It was a good speech—despite the fact that it was rife with hypocrisy. Not only did Wells later grant press interviews with nearly as much enthusiasm as Jack Earley did, recounting how she had snatched victory from the jaws of defeat, but within weeks she even signed on as a paid consultant for a TV sequel to the upcoming TV movie of the week about the Broderick trial. Her fee was rumored to range anywhere from

$50,000 to $75,000.

It was then Earley's turn to speak. Jack Earley is not well suited to the role of beggar. But he tried. In a strained voice, he beseeched Tom Whelan to grant his client concurrent sentences, to show mercy "so that she will have some ability to die outside of prison ... Elisabeth Broderick will probably spend virtually all her life in state prison ... All I'm asking the court to remember is who she was before this ... that she is a victim, as well as Dan and Linda Broderick and the children, and the families ..."

He then went on to insult the judge. Earley was an angry man that day. He reminded Whelan, again, that if Betty had killed "a plumber, a banker, or a newspaper writer," her crime would never have attracted such attention. Next, he bluntly urged Whelan to "resist the temptation" to either look "like a hero" in the eyes of the San Diego legal community, or to worry over the potential disparagement he might face if he rendered a verdict of leniency.

"Jeez, was that stupid," investigator Bill Green whistled under his breath. But Jack Earley knew he had nothing to lose.

Whelan sentenced Elisabeth Anne Broderick to two fifteen-years-to-life terms, running consecutively. These were separate acts of violence, in his view. She had aimed her gun deliberately at both victims. Whelan was struck, especially, by the "high degree of callousness" displayed by her ripping the phone out of the wall and departing when at least one of her victims was still alive.

With 1,236 days of credit for time served, she would be eligible for parole in nineteen years.

Betty didn't bat an eye. But, this time, she didn't smile her Madonna smile either.

And so, at last it was over. Earley rose and, in the flat tone of a man asking for street directions, requested that Betty at least be assigned to the California Women's Institute at Frontera, about an hour north of San Diego, due to the superior psychological treatment available there. Whelan agreed. Court was in recess.

Afterward, Whelan walked over to Frank Bisceglia and wished him good luck. The old man flushed with pleasure and thanked His Honor profusely for his time and attention in the matter of Betty Anne.

* * *

Betty's father, brothers, and Lee were allowed to remain in the cleared courtroom for a few minutes after the sentencing for a final visit. Lee rushed into her mother's arms, sobbing. It was the first time since November 5, 1989, that the system had looked the other way while the two women touched.

Kim Broderick waited in the hallway outside. "I don't think I'd be welcome in there," she told a reporter, with a wan little smile.

Later, she and Lee, who was still crying, went off together.

The Broderick and Kolkena families and friends, meantime, departed to Reidy O'Neill's, where they were still celebrating hours later. Kerry Wells and Bill Green dropped by, to cheers and free drinks. Eventually, Kim came by too, without Lee.

Tom Whelan was the hero of the hour. "Everybody was so happy with him," said Helen Pickard later, "that everyone was joking that they should rename the place Whelan's Bar."

Chapter 42

Prisoner W42477

She was sent, not to Frontera, but to the Central California Women's Facility, a new prison with about two thousand inmates in the small central California town of Chowchilla—nearly an eight-hour drive from San Diego. Too far for Brad, Lee, or any of her La Jolla friends to visit on weekends.

She had hoped for a job either in the library or teaching illiterate prisoners to read, write, and speak English. Instead she was first assigned to the prison laundry, sorting and dispensing clothes. Then she was reassigned to the yard detail, "raking rocks," as she put it. She refused on grounds that, unlike "these black and Mexican girls, my skin won't take the sun, and they don't even give you visors or sun screen here." Prison officials threatened to "write her up" for insubordination. They told her it wouldn't look good at her parole hearing. "In the year 2011?" she hooted at them. "Who gives a fuck?"

And so she was assigned to janitorial duties instead, cleaning cells and toilets daily. "Now I'm a housewife again," she reported cheerily. "The other girls go to work, I get up and have my coffee and chocolate, and then I clean house all day. Just like before. It's perfect for me."

For the first few weeks, she seemed mainly intrigued "by all this serious prison shit. This is punitive," she remarked with surprise. "It's like a forced work camp in China. They don't want you to get well. I'm a political prisoner. I'm madder than hell." But she was still laughing, putting on her brightest face. "Because it's still fascinating. It's like someone sent me to the moon."

She soon learned the prison barter system—"You'd be amazed what a pack of cigarettes can buy—extra rations of clean underwear, a double dessert ..." She also quickly learned that, in prison, as elsewhere, there exists a social hierarchy. "There are a lot of rich bitches here. I heard that one woman has $3 million on her books [prison jargon for commissary credit]. I think she's in for killing her husband, too," she added lightly.

The harshest reality immediately to confront her concerned the telephone. Unlike county jail inmates, state prisoners are strictly limited to a handful of fifteen-minute phone calls a day. "And you have to sign up for the phone in advance and stand in line, and if you try to talk longer, they yell at you," she complained—or, worse, "the next girl in line gets really pissed." In this one instance, the panic in her voice broke through her usual efforts at gay good cheer. Now, not only did she actually have to go to work each day, Betty Broderick had also suddenly lost her most vital source of jailhouse recreation and self-therapy. "Send me a carton of cigarettes," she once asked, her giggle piercing in its false nonchalance, "because I can swap them for extra phone time." She sounded scared.

Still, in the beginning, she had ambitious plans. She promptly wrote to the other most famous female killer she knew, similar to herself —Jean Harris, the headmistress who shot her Scarsdale Diet lover to death after he jilted her. Betty's purpose was to inquire into a program at Harris's New York State prison that allows young female prisoners to keep their babies with them for the first couple of years. Betty thought she'd organize something similar at Chowchilla. She was thrilled when Harris (since paroled) replied, despite the fact that Harris told her, basically, to forget it: California doesn't have enough wealthy white Catholics to fund such a charitable effort.

She also immediately decided to run for president of the Women's Advisory Committee at the prison. "It's kind of like being class president, and of course I can win—piece of cake!" Already, she was a campus celebrity, she proudly reported. "It's like every day I have to go out to meet my public. Girls I don't even know come up to meet me," she said. "They call me the cruise director. They love me!" She was going to organize the place, just as she had once organized luncheons for La Jolla charities. Betty was going to become president of Las Patronas at last.

No epiphany occurred, in short, when the doors of the Big House clanged shut behind Prisoner W42477. Betty Broderick did not suddenly see the light, fall apart, and cry out, "Oh God, what have I done? What have I become?" No moment of clarity came to dilute her fury, soften her heart, and redirect her thinking. And no human help came her way, any more than it had at Colinas. So the same old reels still rolled through her head, a continuing, relentless slide show of all the injustices, real and imagined, she had suffered. The ruination continued, ignored, untreated, and unabated.

She grew more self-obsessed, more paranoid, harder by the day. Her mind turned ever inward, devouring what was left of its brilliance. Within six months of going to state prison, her personal world was filled only with enemies. The bubbly girl-at-camp persona vanished. Instead, her anger and self-vindication steadily spread over the next months, like a quick cancer, even killing out her bawdy black humor. Within weeks, Betty wasn't funny anymore.

First to change was her already graphic language. Now she added "butt-reamer" and "motherfucker" to her repertoire. And, increasingly, she made no distinctions in her audience. The old Betty, who could at least be canny and proper when it suited her purposes—as in her divorce trial, for example—disappeared. She spoke of butt-reamers not only with friends but even to her children's attorney. She wrote letters to her sons, which she knew were censored by their Denver therapist, Thomas Meehan, to "Dear Danny, Rhett, and Asshole Meehan."

And her remarks about Dan became ever more tasteless, flaunting, cruel. "Happy Saint Patrick's Day," she said in a postcard to a friend in March. "At least now I don't have to worry about Dan getting drunk and killing himself. [happy face] On another occasion, she remarked that she was glad to hear Danny was growing so tall. "I always wanted him to get big enough to beat up his Dad—but I took care of that for him. Ha Ha."

Eventually, nearly everyone involved in the ongoing custody debate over the Broderick boys agreed that it wasn't a good idea for them to visit her in prison that summer, and so they didn't.

In time, her anger even spread to Brad, the only friend to visit her in prison during the first year. Out of the blue, she suddenly decided that she wanted him to move out of the condominium she had given him two years earlier and sign it over to Lee, who was then working at a La Jolla restaurant. "It's the only fair thing to do," she said sourly. "He can get out as easy as he got in. He would've been paying rent somewhere else anyway." When he refused, she accused him of being like all the others, stealing from her, using her to advance himself.

And, as always, in her mind, her parents were failing her. When the Bisceglias, after fifty years in Eastchester, suddenly packed up their belongings and moved into a senior citizens' complex in Nashville to be near their oldest son, Betty could summon no compassion for them—instead, she saw it only as one more slap at her, one more rejection. "It's just their way of saying, 'See what you've done to us? Now we even have to leave our home because of you, because of the shame you've caused us.'"

Otherwise, her daily concerns were exactly the same as they had always been, since the first day she went to jail. She worried about her magazine subscriptions, and, within days of her arrival at Chowchilla, she sent a shopping list to Dian Black, asking for, among other items, "in order of importance": sunglasses; Estee Lauder makeup; bright 4 pc jog suits; tweezers and nail clippers (Revlon); Chanel #5 lotion, spray; Coppertone or Ban de Soleil tan lotion. Etc.. Plus, of course, the hair coloring. She also asked that the rest of the box be filled with food and stationery (4 Payday candy bars, 1 bag of mints, canned coconut, skinless boneless sardines, Triscuits). Brad, she told Dian, would pay for it all.

Then, there was her ongoing litigation. She refused to drop her appeal of the 1989 divorce settlement unless the Broderick estate reinstated Lee into Dan's inheritance—despite the fact that the Broderick attorneys were threatening to countersue for wrongful death, which would cost her children even more in legal fees. But Betty would not back off. Kim, who had enrolled briefly at the University of San Diego but then dropped out to work as a hostess at Reidy O'Neils, was still receiving support from her father's estate—reportedly around $3,000 a month. Kathy Broderick, meanwhile, was still receiving something on the order of $2,000 per month per Broderick boy, so long as she remained their legal guardian. Lee, meanwhile, got nothing. "It's just not fair," cried the Betty of old, whose lucidity still came and went. And when it came, it was, as ever, as sharply on target as a laser beam.

Compounding her aggravations, Danny, then sixteen, spent the summer living with, of all people, Helen Pickard, in heart of the enemy camp, where, according to Kathy Broderick's orders, he had to work—as a busboy at Reidy O'Neil's. According to Pickard, his designated allowance, as decreed by Kathy Broderick, was only $10 a week.

Betty's reaction was predictable. Not only was she outraged that her son had been ordered to bus dishes daily at his father's local shrine, in the company of "all his slobbering drunken friends," and in the shadow of loving photos of Dan and Linda, she was even more livid at the ongoing penny-pinching. A $10 allowance for her son, heir to a millionaire? While Kathy Broderick collected thousands each month for baby-sitting? "At the rate these bloodsuckers are going," she fumed, "by the time my boys are old enough for college, they're going to be broke. Why doesn't somebody stop it? It's grand theft!"

Inflaming her even further, Danny next decided that he didn't want to live with Betty's brother Frank in Nashville. He wanted instead to stay with Pickard and attend La Jolla High School. "I am his mother," she fumed, out of all touch with reality now, "but he will not obey me!"

Only little Rhett pleased her by agreeing to move to St. Louis to live with her brother Girard.

That fall, Kathy Broderick agreed to relinquish guardianship of both boys. Girard Bisceglia took Rhett, but legal custody of Danny remained at issue. None of the Broderick siblings asked for him; only a cousin living near Los Angeles apparently filed for guardianship. Eventually, after six months of living with Pickard, Danny was allowed by the courts to move in with his sister Kim—who was then sharing a La Jolla apartment with several other twenty-something young adults. "For God's sake," Betty hissed. "I'd rather have him boarding with that fat-assed cleaning woman [Pickard]. I hate her, but at least she makes her kids go to school and do homework! My son will never even finish high school, living with Kim! Would someone tell me, please, why the courts have abdicated all responsibility for my children now, when they were so fucking keen to run their lives while Dan Broderick was alive?" It was, of course, just another of Betty's many good questions, amid the madness.

But, before her first year in prison was over, she received what was probably her greatest legal satisfaction: bank attorneys for her sons filed a lawsuit against Larry Broderick for allegedly cheating them out of $295,000 in their inheritance by defaulting on their share of his unpaid $450,000 debt to Dan. The case is pending. For reasons of her own, Kim did not join in the legal action.

On the downside, a few weeks later, she learned that Danny, Rhett, and Kim had also sued her for "wrongful death," meaning that if she ever collected from her divorce appeal and the children prevailed on their claim, they might be able to collect monies from her. Most curious, according to the local legal newspaper, the suit had been filed under seal of secrecy two years earlier, in late 1990, although Betty wasn't officially served until March, 1993. Earley said he was taken by surprise, too.

Meanwhile, the media circus continued. The first TV movie about Betty Broderick aired early in 1992—with such high ratings that a quick sequel on her trials was instantly planned. Although the first movie was unsympathetic, and Betty never saw it, she still wrote Meredith Baxter a fawning fan letter.

"We have things in common. We're both forty-four. Our daughters Eva and Kim

480

are the same age ... You've always been one of my absolute favorites. You're beautiful, sweet, AND strong. You are shorter and thinner, but give me a chance to heal and then you'll only be shorter. I didn't gain weight till '87, two years AFTER Dan left. [happy face] ..." As for what she had heard of the movie, "... You totally overlooked what Dan and Linda were doing to me that made me react ... If you did not address the truth of what really went on with Dan and Linda, the aggressors, and me and the children, their victims, you missed the whole thing. [unhappy face]

She finished by inviting Baxter to visit her for the full story. Baxter never went. Instead, she invited Kerry Wells for tea to glean further insights into Betty Broderick's true personality—and, when the sirens of Hollywood sounded, Wells went running. She even had a cameo role in the second film, as a courtroom spectator.

Jack Earley, meantime, was as frustrated as he had ever been. Why was a TV movie being made, using his name and depicting his defense, when nobody had called either him or his client for their point of view? It was lousy, unfair journalism, in his view. He was of course correct—although, odds are, not a peep about integrity would have been heard from him had the tables been turned. Indeed, sacrificing the high road, Earley made at least one call to a Hollywood producer himself in the aftermath of the case, hoping to sell his competing side of the story. But nobody in TV-land was about to challenge a CBS production already under way. This time, Wells had definitely won.

The San Diego attorney assigned to handle Betty's appeal before a three-judge panel was thirty-nine-year-old Roberta Thyfault. The appeal, set to begin in April, will probably drag on through the summer. Meantime, Thyfault, who immediately set off a round of black-humored chuckles all over San Diego by gravely telling a *San Diego Union* reporter that she could not discuss the case and, furthermore, "had also instructed Mrs. Broderick not to speak with reporters."

"I wonder what rock she's been living under for the last two years?" cackled one journalist. At the same time, Thyfault also ordered Betty not to participate in a second *Oprah Winfrey* special, scheduled to coincide with the fall release of the second TV movie about her. Thyfault might as well have asked Betty Broderick to tear her tongue out—because, this time, in the flattery of all flatteries, the mountain was coming to Muhammad: Oprah was actually coming in person to Chowchilla to interview the woman who had made her ratings soar sky-high only a few months before. State prison authorities, evidently as star-struck as Thomas Whelan had once been in San Diego, immediately gave permission.

Betty did not acquit herself well on the Oprah show. Not that it really mattered. She was lent legitimacy merely by the fact that here was Oprah Winfrey, queen of American talk shows, strolling around the prison grounds in her leopard-print sweater, this time almost purring in chumminess at Betty Broderick. They might have been two sorority sisters discussing a broken engagement, as Oprah inquired, so hushed and grave, into Betty's motives for shooting two people to death.

Alas for Betty, she was unable to elevate the discussion beyond Oprah's fascination with the tawdry details of the shooting scene itself. Instead, clever, witty Betty lost her tongue in the presence of this icon of American values. She stuttered, stumbled, and in the end sounded mostly like just one more star-struck housewife, intimidated by celebrity, cameras, lights, and the prospect of around sixty million viewers watching her.

In her most glaring moment of failure, when Winfrey asked what lessons she thought her story bore for other middle-aged wives, Betty couldn't think fast enough, for once, to answer. After years of stating her case literally hundreds of times with furious eloquence, now she couldn't find the words, nor the memory to even mention Epsteins, bifurcation, no-fault, or ex parte hearings, much less the eternal imbalance of power between men and women in a white male-dominated legal system. Worse, she finished her performance by agreeing, for the first time ever in a public forum, that, of course she was sorry that she had killed two people—but, she added in the next breath, revealing more anger and hatred than she ever had, only because Dan and Linda weren't around now to see that "I survived ... a little pilot light in me wouldn't give up."

And that wasn't the end of it. Contrary to Betty's expectations, Winfrey devoted her next day's show to what she billed as a "dramatically different account" of the story, another version "of what really happened"—as told by the Broderick children themselves.

This time, not only did Kim appear, to say, among other things, that she thought her mother had premeditated the murders, but Daniel T. Broderick IV, sixteen, also appeared for the first time in public to discuss his mother. The boy was relaxed and cool, just as friends say his father always was. Tall and lanky, he also resembles Dan Broderick physically. In his main contribution to the show, he applauded his mother's performance on Oprah's show the day before, because she didn't go "over the edge like she normally does." He also told the world that he had heard his mother threaten to kill Dan and Linda—but mostly Linda—for years. "But I never thought she had the guts to do it." He thought her motive was jealousy. And he said that, yes, he and his brother had wanted to live with Betty, and at the time blamed their father for keeping them apart. But now, he said, he understood that it wasn't Dan's fault at all. It was the courts who wouldn't let them live with their mother.

Winfrey concluded the show with Maggie Seats, housekeeper Robin Tu'ua, and attorney Kathleen Cuffaro, all of whom portrayed Betty as nothing more than a totally loveless, dangerous liar.

Cuffaro's remarks were the most interesting—and distorted. According to her, the last letter she wrote to Betty's attorney, the one "that Betty says sent her over the edge," had been a letter flatly offering to return the boys to her if she would "stop leaving these nasty messages on the answering machine." According to Cuffaro, her letter had basically said, "If this [custody] is really what you want, then stop doing these things ... and we'll let you have the boys—we'll give it a try."

Oprah expressed shock. Betty knew she was going to get custody of the boys back? she asked, incredulous.

"Right," said Cuffaro. She did not mention the qualifications—the "trial period," the condition that Dan could unilaterally cancel the custody arrangement. She did not mention that child support was still unresolved. She did not mention the insulting reference to Betty's "pathological obsession" with Dan and Linda contained in her final letter. Cuffaro did not, in short, accurately convey the condescending, controlling contents of her last two letters, which might have sent even a woman far more stable than Betty Broderick into a rage.

In fact, Cuffaro continued, she thought the main reason Betty had killed Dan and Linda was because she finally knew she had it all—$16,000 per month, plus impending custody. The war was over. Betty had killed, Cuffaro said before sixty million viewers, simply because there was nothing else left to do. "... She knew she wasn't going to have anything else to fight about."

Not least, Cuffaro added that Betty had also received $40,000 more than her half of the monies from the Coral Reef house sale. But, typical of everyone in the Broderick camp, she made it sound like a gift.

Winfrey seemed to simply accept it all. "Betty, Betty, Betty," said Oprah, shaking her head sadly and peering mournfully into the cameras, burying Betty Broderick once and for all.

Betty, Betty, Betty, indeed.

She had, of course, asked for every bit of it. Still, it's hard to blame an irrational woman for her own self-destruction, particularly at the hands of the media, which contributed so hugely to her trusting, blind abandon and self-justification in the first place.

But Betty learned nothing from her latest media foray. Instead, typically, she only tried to blame someone else for the disaster—in this case, Helen Pickard and Kim, who, she insisted, had pressured Danny into appearing on the Oprah show. Nonsense, of course. But it didn't matter anymore. Betty was beyond the point of assimilating new information.

That same week, she also entertained a crew from *Hard Copy* in jail—wherein, more than ever, she blamed Linda Kolkena for undocumented cruelties. Even on the *Oprah* show, Betty still referred to Linda as "a cheap office girl" who never graduated from high school, although by then, Betty had been told dozens of times that, whatever else Linda was, she was not nineteen years old and in fact had graduated from high school.

But she was insulted to be told that her performance on *Oprah* was lacking—because, as ever, she had her fan mail to reassure her that she was both correct and completely charismatic. And, indeed, thanks to both the TV movie and the *Oprah* shows, yet another swamp of sympathy mail poured into Chowchilla from women who still found Betty a heroine. She received so much new mail, in fact, that she had to store some of it along the back edge of her prison bunk. Now she was literally sleeping with her fan letters. But, as always, she was most fascinated with letters from the smattering of her would-be male lovers. It is extraordinary, how many American males seem to have an abiding urge to die at the hands of one tough lady. Several were planning to visit her. One man, she reported giddily, was flying all the way from Pennsylvania.

Christmas came again—her fourth in jail. Her children did not visit. She sent out notes to friends bearing green and red tinsel decals in the shape of wreaths. "I shouldn't be in prison," she wrote to one. "I am not a murderer." From there, she then went on to blithely discuss an article she had just read in *Vanity Fair* on the death of Petra Kelly, founder of the Green Party in Germany. As ever, Betty still keeps abreast of the news.

Now, she sleeps each night in a room with five other women—mostly young, mostly minorities. She listens to them snore, moan in their sleep, grind their teeth, cry, and cough. She really doesn't know their stories, partly because they come and go so fast; not many are there for nineteen years at the minimum—and, too, she says, laughing, "it's prison etiquette, that you don't ask people why they're in." Besides, she doesn't care. None of them have been through what she has. None of them faced down Daniel T. Broderick III.

She reaches out at night and touches her mail. Never mind that she doesn't really even want out of prison, at least not now. How can they keep her here, when the whole world is on her side, when Oprah still features her on her show—even comes to the prison, for God's sake? When movies and books are being done about her? Her.

Her mind is wild. Her appeal will fail, she knows, because it's still in Dan's town. But maybe Governor Pete Wilson will pardon her. She danced with him once, at the Blackstone Ball.

And: "I want Barbara Bush to do a jacket blurb for your book," she said one day. "Because she and I are just alike. I love her! We have the same family values."

She isn't up and down all night anymore. She's too tired after a day of "being a housewife." She sleeps straight through, until the jailers bark, until her roommates begin to stir. At least now, the toilets are private. But before she drifts off to sleep she thinks of many, many disjointed things.

Danny. Growing up. Time for his first electric razor. She remembers when Kim had her first menstrual period. "Dan said it was the most depressing day of his life. He didn't want to be old enough to have a daughter with periods." Even from prison, she is still trying to be the perfect mother. Just that day, she wrote Danny a letter, advising him to buy a Norelco, just like his dad had. In fact, she wondered in her letter to him, where were Dan's things? Why couldn't Danny get Dan's razor? "Daddy always had the best of everything," she wrote.

From there her mind floats, always, every night, in so many directions. Her wedding china ... What did the cunt do with her china?

"I want to know where it is," she said one day over the phone. "Which one of her bimbo girlfriends is eating off my wedding china? I hope they get botulism and die. You find out where that wedding china is, because I want to know. I've always wanted to know. It was just to hurt me. I want to know who's got it. I want it back. It's got bad karma on it and they're going to die. Really. They are. They're going to choke on a chip and die."

She always prays at night, too, she says. "Me and God are old friends. He guided those bullets that night. He did. Do you seriously think I could have ever killed Dan Broderick by myself, without His help?" As usual, she didn't even mention Linda. Then, with an awed little pause, a hollow giggle: "You know, I still can't believe it— that just one little bullet could kill Dan Broderick."

Observations of General Mike Neil

Dan Broderick was, without question, the most civil, professional and friendly lawyer I have ever known. He was a paragon of virtue.

I had every reason to have some resentment towards him as I went up against him in court and he took me to the cleaners a couple of times. In fact, the last case we fought—the last case Dan ever tried—was the only case in which I beat him.

He was a wonderful father to his children and revered by his friends. Brian Monaghan, Dave Monahan, Ed Chapin, Leo Sullivan and I and others spent a lot of time with him. He was a prince among men.

I had a case with him one time where he had an issue with what his client was telling him. We were taking depositions and he said: "Mike, if when I take your client's deposition I believe him over my client, I will dismiss the case". True to his word, after taking my client's deposition, he told me he believed my client, and he dismissed the case.

Linda, Dan and I went regularly to Dobson's, where Dan proposed to Linda. We would have drinks and talk about Ireland (we were very interested in all things Irish), life in general and cases we were working on. A year after Dan and Linda died, I still had a reflex to go to Dobson's to have a drink with them after work. It was a hard habit to break.

Some people have suggested that Dan was 'cold' but I don't know what they are referring to. He was certainly businesslike, but never cold from my observations of him. Nor was he a heavy drinker. Dan never overindulged himself and he never drank more than moderately in my opinion.

Betty may once have been more loving and caring in their marriage but over time she seems to have deteriorated into a monster, a despicable human being. She did not just do terrible things to Dan and Linda, and to their respective families, but to his children too. I don't know too much about how Betty behaved during their marriage because the strange thing is that Dan never said anything against her as a mother or as a wife. Any other man would have done that, but Dan didn't say a word against her.

I took a group of people to Mexico for my fortieth birthday and my wife said to me the next day: 'What's wrong with her?' She was strange, very into herself, selfish, and very jealous of Dan and his friends. She seemed to live in a different world from the rest of us. Everything was all about her. And, no, I didn't stick my tongue in her ear on that trip. First of all, I don't ever do that kind of thing and, besides, it wasn't that sort of occasion anyway; we were a group of friends sitting in a restaurant having dinner. If anything, I ignored her that night.

Linda was absolutely the opposite to Betty. She was loving, sharing and warm—a real sweetheart. She never said a bad thing about anyone. She was always gracious and had an outgoing personality. She really complemented Dan. I doubt she had an enemy in the world, other than Betty. We were all so happy to see Dan so happy when he was with Linda.

I have no knowledge that Dan and Linda were conducting an affair before he left Betty. As far as I am aware, they didn't start dating until Dan and Betty were separated. Dan had one hell of a marriage to Betty and she drove him to leave her. If you ask me, Dan stayed with her far too long, but he was an Irish Catholic so he hung on as long as he could.

Those things Betty accused Linda of doing, sending photos of her and Dan with 'Eat your heart out' written on them, sending anti-wrinkle cream to her anonymously etc., that was not at all consistent with the way Linda behaved. She never engaged in profane or obscene behavior. She just wanted to keep out of Betty's way.

Dan didn't harass Betty in any way after they were separated. It was just the opposite. Betty dragged the divorce matter out over years, changing attorneys, making it a miserable, miserable process. Dan never used his legal skills to influence the courts. That was just not possible.

And the idea that Dan was looking for a contract killer, that is total nonsense. I spoke to Dan two weeks before he was murdered. I tried to persuade him to take Betty's threats seriously, to change the locks on his doors. I even told him to get a pistol and I would teach him how to use it at the range. He said he was not going to do anything of the sort. "She will never kill me," he insisted. Maybe that is why she did kill him: he never took her threats seriously, he wasn't afraid of her and she couldn't destroy his relationship with Linda, try as she might. He wouldn't let anything deter him from getting on with his life. How else could she get at him other than to kill him?

Observations of Robert Vaage

As background, let me tell you about my connection to Dan. I was a young lawyer working for Mike Neil, two years out from law school. Mike was a defense lawyer and Dan was a plaintiff lawyer. I wanted to do plaintiff work and Dan was apparently impressed by me, so Linda Kolkena, as she was then, approached me to ask if I wanted to work with them. I didn't want it to create problems so I talked to Mike and he gave me his blessing to go to join Dan, which I did for three years.

My father, who recently died, was my best friend and then I worked for Mike Neil, who was another great man, but aside from my father, Dan was the other major father figure in my life. He was the most honorable individual I have ever met, outstanding, remarkable.

Dan realized very quickly in their marriage that it wasn't going to work, but he was a Catholic and he had children, so that played its part. After he decided to leave her, he did everything he could to set her up—paying her nearly £20,000 a month, which was a fortune in those days. Dan bent over backwards to accommodate her. It would never have crossed his mind to have done anything unjust to Betty, or 'Bets' as he called her.

Dan was a game changer. He did Law at Harvard and Medical School at Cornell, he was handsome and had that ability only rare people have of when they walk into a room, making you feel the most important person there. He went way out his way for me. I still have a photograph of him on my desk. He was a great attorney and a great friend. A group of people—both lawyers and non-lawyers—still meet up regularly even now, twenty years later, and the only reason we know each other is because of Dan.

As a trial lawyer he had the remarkable ability of making highly complex issues simple for a jury. He was only forty-four when he died. The loss to the community of San Diego from his death is incalculable.

It is a tragedy that his reputation was besmirched after his death. The family made a mistake. We were asked not to talk to the press, so the only person who was heard out there was Betty because Dan was no longer around to defend himself.

And Linda, who tends to be forgotten in this story, was a wonderful woman too, always upbeat, always bright, always articulate.

If you have ever had a chance to listen to those tapes of Betty talking to her 9-10 year old son, you will know everything you need to know about her.

The idea that Dan would try to hire a contract killer for her is totally ridiculous, comical, absurd. She was the one who drove her car through his front door, who pulled a knife on him. Dan was a hell of a lot more understanding of Betty than any of us. He could have had her thrown in jail at any time. All the threats, all the diatribes were one way – from Betty. Nobody did anything to her.

Let's deal with those allegations that Linda harassed Betty … We were a very small, hard-working group of people in our law office—Dan, Linda, me and a couple of other people. We worked long hours together and socialized together afterward. Linda was chatty by nature and if she had been doing anything like that, I would have heard about it, we worked so close together. Besides, she would never have done it because Dan would have been most unhappy if she had. The chances of her doing that were nil. Linda didn't have a mean bone in her body. And Linda didn't need to tell everyone that Betty was crazy—everyone knew.

Nor am I aware that Dan and Linda were having any affair before Dan and Betty separated.

When Dan proposed to Linda at Dobson's, the event was covered in the local newspaper. The day the newspaper article came out, Betty called the office. I answered the phone. "This is Betty Broderick," she said. "Is my husband in?" I told her he wasn't. Could she leave a message, she asked. Sure, I said, knowing that it was likely to be something memorable. "You tell him," she said, "that he was down on one knee at Dobson's, but by the time I've finished with him, he'll be down on both knees."

She felt like she owned him. She wasn't going to let go of him. All her social status, her standing in the community, was tied up with being Mrs. Daniel Broderick III. She played every trick to hang on to him, including mis-signing her name on the divorce papers. She had a house in La Jolla, a substantial monthly allowance, but she wouldn't let him go.

Everyone knew Betty had a gun and was practicing on the range with it. One night Dan told me, "If she wants to kill me, it will be real easy for her. She only has to walk into my office and start shooting." He was resigned to that. He understood that the threat was real but he was just going to carry on. We went out to dinner together, and I dropped them off at home the night they were murdered.

I went to the parole hearing. There were three people on the board and they had a report from a psychiatrist basically saying that Betty didn't constitute any significant risk to the community. They started asking Betty questions to find out whether she had any remorse for what she had done, and she absolutely wouldn't go there. They asked her who she believed she had hurt. Every one of her children was there. Every one of Dan's family was there. She hesitated for a moment and then said, "My parents." Unbelievable. What does that tell you about her?

I was talking to the DA afterward, asking what would happen to her. There were various options—they could grant parole, or they could call for another hearing in 1, 2, 5, 10 or 15 years. The DA thought she should wait another fifteen years but expected five. The parole board only took twenty minutes to make up its mind and said she needed another fifteen years to think about what she had done. Watching her reaction to that, I think the remaining members of Dan Broderick family are far better off with her remaining in prison.

Betty Broderick's Handwriting

In 2013, samples of Betty Broderick's handwriting were given to a leading expert in graphology.

The samples were in the form of original extracts from letters which indicated that the author had experienced some difficulty with the law but did not disclose the nature of her offense or any other details about her beyond that she was an American woman in her sixties.

This was the analysis:

On the surface this person is capable of coming across as friendly, intelligent, organized, lively and logical (right slant; fluent writing; smooth ink trail; sensitive light pressure; fluent connections between letters; very connected writing; methodical irregularity in the height of the middle zones) with a willingness to be helpful (reasonable space between letters; some extended endings to words; right slant with loops) and to behave conventionally (copybook style; connected letters).She has mental enthusiasm (long and high 't' bars; some rising baselines – the baseline is the imaginary line beneath the middle zone letters such as 'm', 'n', etc.) and attempts to show determination to cope with her situation and personality (reasonably straight baselines; knotted letters; hooked letter endings; straight strokes going down into the lower zone).

Unfortunately, this mask covers a highly manipulative and invasive personality (angled 'u' structures; narrow margins); she is dissatisfied and easily annoyed. She can switch within moments from being friendly to being extremely egotistical, someone who completely overestimates her own importance (enrolled writing; some middle zone heights above 5mm).

She responds instinctively to people (up strokes have a strong right slant) and may find it difficult to check her emotional reactions.

She dramatizes everything she says because she believes others cannot understand the significance of her statements (excessive underlining and unnecessary exclamation marks; final strokes end in the upper zone).

She needs to justify her beliefs (squeezed writing with angles at top and bottom of letters) and because she is resentful, mistrustful, very sensitive to criticism (looped 't' and 'd' stems; narrow pen stroke), she feels taken advantage of and will be quick to contradict (straight brace strokes at the beginning of letters; 't' bars becoming thinner and ending in acute points).

She suffers tensions in her relationships and feels a need to humiliate others, run vendettas and take treacherous revenge (ovals with angles on the base line; parallel strokes; light pressure with angles).

She is evasive, tries to conceal things, blames others, and lies (excessive looping on ovals; curled in start to some oval structures). She will try to outsmart other people, strike at their weak points (spiky writing) and this may be particularly true in relation to her own family (shark tooth constructions of the 'n', i.e. the final stroke collapses into a 'c' structure).

So here is someone who tries to present herself as sociable (curved writing; dominant middle zone; close word spacing) but underneath there are strong feelings of resentment. When she is stressed her behavior will become increasingly unstable and infantile with a desperate need for attention. Pent up anger (forward 't' bars; downward 't' bars; arrow head 'i' dots; connected right slant writing) may burst out against those people she feels have shown her injustice.

For someone who attempts to put on a charming front, she can be nasty. She is capable of pathological jealousy and can show passionate and disturbing behavior.

Original acknowledgments

Now I understand why so many authors devote a couple of pages at the beginning of their books to those long lists of names that nobody reads, except for those named. The impulse is practically overpowering to thank all those who helped, in ways both large and small, to make the book possible—and, I have learned, they can number in the hundreds. How can I not, for example, thank court bailiff Rita Long, who always saved a seat for me throughout two trials, even on days when I was late? Or my friend, Los Angeles writer Paul Ciotti, who made house calls, sometimes almost daily, during my writing phase to help me understand and conquer the latest mysteries of my computer, without once yelling at me for being a technological nitwit?

And there were so many, many others, in San Diego and around the country, who helped in the reporting and writing of this story. You know who you are, and I am indebted to you all.

But a few names I must mention, since without them, this book either would not have been written at all or it would be an entirely different product:

*Marion Pasas and Dian Black, both of whom helped in so many different ways, from research to lessons in organization. Both also provided loving moral support, then and now. Thank you, ladies.

*Jack Earley, defense attorney, who allowed me as much access to defense thinking as discretion would allow. Also, assistant defense attorney Lisa Bowman.

*Prosecution investigator William Green, who, although restricted in his media contacts until after the trials, later did his best to help me double-check myself. He served as a sounding board for my conclusions and theories, helping protect me from falling into an unwitting defense bias or committing just plain stupid errors of fact.

*Many La Jolla women, past and present friends of Betty's, who spent hours helping me recreate a picture of her as she used to be. Among them: Helen Pickard, Ann Dick, Melanie Cohrs, Candy Westbrook, Wilma Engel, Vicki Currie, and Judy Courtemanche. Not least, my thanks to Maria Montez.

*Friends of Dan and Linda, who were willing to set aside their initial distrust of anyone in daily contact with the killer to help me understand two people who could no longer speak for themselves. I am especially grateful for the generosity of spirit provided by Sharon Blanchet, Ann Marie (Stormy) Wetther, Brian Monaghan, Mike Reidy, and Steve Kelley, five people who consistently tried to be fair, despite their feelings about Betty. I also owe thanks to Laurel Summers, Kathleen Cuffaro, Mike Neil, Sylvia Cavins, and Linda David for the time they spent with me.

Last but by no means least, my enduring gratitude and respect to Linda Kolkena's sister, Maggie Seats, who spent hours sharing the pain which any of us who have ever loved a sibling can understand. I am also thankful to three of Dan's sisters—Kathleen McCormack, Patti Cappelli, and Christy Emmanuel—for entrusting a stranger with some of their most personal thoughts about their oldest brother.

My gratitude, too, to Betty's parents, Marita and Frank Bisceglia, who finally were able to set aside their own suffering and shame to discuss their child during the second trial. I am also indebted to Betty's younger brother Mike, and her cousin Connie Lawler.

*San Diego journalists, who literally made all the difference. No reporter can overstate the debt owed to professional peers willing to help. Unfortunately, journalists, like dogs hoarding their bones, are often a selfish pack when it comes to sharing information. One San Diego reporter even asked me, early on, for a $10,000 consulting fee for her list of phone numbers, most of them easily available in the telephone directory.

But, for the most part, I was blessed in San Diego with some of the most supportive journalists I have ever met. The first person I called was Paul Krueger of the *San Diego Reader*, who, along with his colleague Jeanette DeWyze, had written the only story on the Broderick divorce before the homicides. I will never forget his immediate response, which was, in effect: "Here are all my contacts with phone numbers. Here are my opinions. . . . How else can I help you?" Next I met *San Diego Union* reporter John Gaines, now a columnist, whose reaction was exactly the same.

Later on, I met other equally generous reporters: Mike Granberry of the *Los Angeles Times*; Jeffrey Rose of the *Union*; Jeanette DeWyze of the *San Diego Reader*; Laurie Mosier, then with *United Press International*; Cynthia Queen of the *La Jolla Light*; and Claude Wolbert of the *San Diego Tribune.* Not least, Dave Nelson, then society writer for the *Los Angeles Times*, and his friend (coincidentally Betty's too), Melanie Cohrs, spent night after delightful night helping me to learn my way around La Jolla, explaining to me the pecking order, always with great wry humor. I also want to thank Karl and Barbara Zobell, Jeannie Lawrence, Henry Hester, and Phyllis Pfeiffer for further advancing my La Jolla education.

The writing phase is, of course, entirely different from the reporting stage. Reporting is fun; writing, at least in my view, is another version of hell on earth. When I returned to Los Angeles, tanned and serene, I had enough facts to satisfy myself. I had, in truth, too many facts. I had notebooks full of information on everything from La Jolla zoning issues to the Como Yei Indians, thought to be La Jolla's original inhabitants a few thousand years ago. I knew the details of Betty's dental work, where Dan got his hair cut, and how many balloons Linda floated at a birthday party she gave for a girlfriend. I had over-reported; I had no idea what to do with it all. Two people helped me.

First and foremost was my friend Noel Greenwood, then a senior editor at the *Los Angeles Times* and my former boss. There are not words enough to thank him for the time he put into discussing this story with me, helping me construct it, and then, line by line, editing at least three drafts from top to bottom. The fad that this book is merely long, rather than an encyclopedia on the destruction of one family, is due entirely to his editing skills—not to mention his black-hearted editor's pleasure in slashing a writer's priceless prose.

Second, but no less important, was the work done by my sister, Linda Goudge, in Denver. A computer whiz, she spent hours ferreting out the repetitions in my original manuscript, helping me recover quotes I had lost, advising me on content, and, not least, bickering with Noel over sections he wanted to cut and she wanted to save. They became at times almost a comedy team—here was one of the best editors the *Los Angeles Times* will ever see, sniping at my little sister, not a trained journalist but a well-read wife, mother, and scientist, who carped back, "He's cutting the wrong stuff!" Noel would growl, "She's given to excess, just like you."

When Linda and Noel had finished their work on the first drafts, a massively long manuscript still emerged. Editor Judith Regan was unsympathetic. "Cut it—a lot!" she commanded. Noel tried not to gloat, as he happily whacked out all the sections he wanted to cut in the first place. My sister persistently offered her own, alternative cuts. The bartering might still be going on, had it not been for two other friends who finally found themselves dragged into the process as arbiters: former *Los Angeles Times* writer Kathy Hendrix and Bret Israel, editor of the *Times Sunday Magazine*. Both spent countless hours poring over the manuscript, offering their own invaluable edits.

I also want to thank John Caldwell, Eric Furan, and Pat Olson for their support, and former *Times* writer Garry Abrams for daily black humor of the sort that perhaps only another book writer, sitting at home alone all day, facing the same subject week after week, can appreciate.

I will stop before these acknowledgments become truly tiresome. (But if you ever need the quickest, smartest transcriptionist around, call Paula Burns in Dallas.)

Made in the USA
Middletown, DE
16 July 2020